THE FOUNDATIONS OF AGRICULTURAL ECONOMICS

TOGETHER WITH AN ECONOMIC HISTORY OF BRITISH AGRICULTURE DURING AND AFTER THE GREAT WAR

Linches at Clothall, Hertfordshire

THE FOUNDATIONS OF AGRICULTURAL ECONOMICS

TOGETHER WITH

AN ECONOMIC HISTORY OF BRITISH AGRICULTURE DURING AND AFTER THE GREAT WAR

by

J. A. VENN, LITT.D.

PRESIDENT OF QUEENS' COLLEGE

Gilbey Lecturer in the History and Economics of Agriculture in the University of Cambridge; sometime Statistician to the Food Production Department

CAMBRIDGE

AT THE UNIVERSITY PRESS

1933

CAMBRIDGE
UNIVERSITY PRESS

University Printing House, Cambridge CB2 8BS, United Kingdom

Cambridge University Press is part of the University of Cambridge.

It furthers the University's mission by disseminating knowledge in the pursuit of education, learning and research at the highest international levels of excellence.

www.cambridge.org
Information on this title: www.cambridge.org/9781107475137

First edition 1923
Second edition 1933
First published 1933
First paperback edition 2014

A catalogue record for this publication is available from the British Library

ISBN 978-1-107-47513-7 Paperback

My young friend, as you have resolved on agriculture as the occupation of your future years, notwithstanding the very discouraging present, and "the shadows, clouds and darkness" which rest on the future, in the opinion of a large proportion of those engaged in the cultivation of the soil, I am anxious that you should start upon a sound foundation.

From "A letter on agricultural education addressed to a youth who had resolved on farming as his future occupation", by Charles Lawrence, Esq., 1851.

FROM THE PREFACE TO THE FIRST EDITION

This volume represents an attempt to bring within reasonable compass some account of the origin and incidence of the numerous economic problems which affect the agricultural community. The bulk of what it contains has been delivered in the form of lectures to third year and Diploma students, for whose benefit it was originally planned. Subsequently, I felt that, by the inclusion of certain additional matter, it could be made to form a connected narrative rather than a series of essays, and thus might also appeal to that wider class of landowners and farmers who are interested in knowing something of the evolution and history of their "burdens", of the past struggles of their predecessors and of the alternative methods of land-tenure and marketing practised in other countries.

It is inevitable in a work of this character that reference should frequently be made to bygone events, but I have purposely refrained from any excursion into agricultural history pure and simple, for, in Lord Ernle's *English Farming Past and Present,* there exists a monumental work which, so far as a descriptive account of the social life, the agricultural practices and the personalities of past centuries are concerned, must always hold the field. As regards the economic history of the subject, however, there does appear to be a gap in our literature. True, practically every branch dealt with in the following pages has its existing authorities, but it must be confessed that in almost every case there have been political axes to grind or particular theories to ventilate. Land-tenure, for example, has provided lists for the breaking of many lances; taxation has involved the historian, the economist and the politician in a maze of conflicting statements and counter-statements; the subject of marketing and co-operation has too frequently been reserved for the eulogies of avowed partisans; it has been left to foreign authors to treat unbiasedly such questions as those raised in the consideration of large and small holdings or the past and present economic situation of the farm worker; finally, the history of agriculture after

Press to reproduce the map of Lower Heyford, and I ought to state that the original of that of Rampton is in the possession of our own University Library. Acknowledgment of information derived from published sources has been made in the text, but I should add that the bulk of the figures and tables relating to British agriculture are taken from the official publications of the Ministry of Agriculture.

J. A. VENN

SCHOOL OF AGRICULTURE
CAMBRIDGE

June 12th, 1923

PREFACE TO THE SECOND EDITION

The opportunity, now presented, has been taken greatly to enlarge the work by the addition of seven new Chapters, of which the first, dealing with the interrelationship of economic theory and agricultural practice, makes good a serious omission in the previous edition; concurrently, much of the original matter has been re-written. Owing to the consequential increase in its bulk, it has been found convenient to divide the book into two Parts, the first being confined to the fundamental aspects of the industry, while the second contains an account of British agriculture during and after the Great War. A recent visit to the Far East, made under the aegis of the Ministry of Agriculture, has enabled me to draw upon the experiences and practices of the countries in question when dealing with certain features of rural economy.

I am indebted to the Editor of *The Economic Journal* for permission to reprint the bulk of two articles upon crop-estimating and forecasting, and I must also express my thanks to *The Times* for allowing me to make similar use of an account of the Buckden manor-court. One or two sections of the final Chapter have formed part of my Presidential Address to the Agricultural Economics Society in the current year.

My cordial thanks are due to Miss Ruth Cohen for much help accorded me in connection with the preparation of tables and diagrams. A friend, and former colleague at the Ministry of Agriculture, Mr E. L. Mitchell, has given me valuable information relating to the finances of the Land Settlement scheme, as has Mr D. A. E. Harkness, of the Belfast Ministry of Agriculture, in regard to rating and other matters in Northern Ireland; to Queen Anne's Bounty Office, to the Irish Free State Department of Industry and Commerce, to the Scotch Board of Agriculture, to the Irish Congested Districts Board, to the Representative Body of the Church of Ireland, to the National Association of Master Bakers, and, more especially, to the Ministry of Agriculture and Fisheries itself, I am severally indebted for statistical and other material. Dr A. S. Watt, Mr E. H. B. Boulton, Mr T. J. Hunt and Mr P. E. Graves, all of the Cambridge Department of Agriculture and Forestry, have also assisted me.

J. A. VENN

THE LODGE, QUEENS' COLLEGE
CAMBRIDGE
June 7th, 1933

CONTENTS

PART I

THE FOUNDATIONS OF AGRICULTURAL ECONOMICS

PART II

AN ECONOMIC HISTORY OF BRITISH AGRICULTURE DURING AND AFTER THE GREAT WAR

ILLUSTRATIONS

Plates

Maps and Diagrams

PART I

The Foundations of Agricultural Economics

Chapter I

INTRODUCTION

Definition of Agricultural Economics; the place of agriculture amongst man's activities; its natural and physical limitations; the agricultural complex; the many-sidedness of agriculture illustrated; economic divergences between primary and secondary industries; the Law of diminishing returns in its various aspects; demand and supply and their elasticity; prices and price-control; the meaning of money; fluctuations in the price-level; utilisation of labour, land and capital; factors in international trade; the position occupied by the agriculture of the British Isles.

If, in Marshall's words, "Economics is a study of man's actions in the ordinary business of life", then Agricultural Economics is clearly the study of man in his relation to the land. This involves an analysis of many factors, of which the more important are the distribution and utilisation of the soil, the nature of the resultant social life, the interrelationship of a preponderant primary industry with numerous secondary industries, the contributions—both financial and economic—made to their States by agricultural interests, the physical and financial handling of soil products, and, finally, the demand for, and consumption of, the latter. These, then, may be termed the foundations of a subject which, in both its theoretical and practical aspects, is being increasingly studied in most countries of the world; a description of them, accordingly, occupies the bulk of this volume, but, as their evolution cannot altogether be omitted, its pages necessarily contain also a certain amount of economic history.

Agriculture, which, in its widest aspects, must always be assumed to comprise every form of soil production, from forestry to glass-house culture, provides occupation for the vast majority of the world's population. To paraphrase the findings of a recent International Conference: the various products of agriculture represent in value the greater part of human labour, and their exchange against those of industry forms the basis of world trade; agricultural population remains for humanity a reservoir of energy, capable of preserving the nations from the rapid human wastage which may result from any excessive growth of industry; the quantity of foodstuffs and of raw materials produced by agriculture is one of the factors which determine the maximum limit of industrial development, and the interdependence existing between nations is no less close between the main classes of occupations—agriculture, industry and commerce—and it is vain to hope that one class can enjoy lasting prosperity independently of others.

This, then, is the nature and position of the industry, adhesion to which has, ever since man's first appearance on earth, formed his most vital duty. Indeed, it is no exaggeration to state that, for the millions of years in which he existed in a primitive state, the pursuit of food formed his sole activity and that, during all save a few hundred of the five or six thousand years in which he could be described as civilised, his entire energies have still been thus directed. Historically, it is only in quite recent times, and in a few countries, that any considerable proportion of the human race has been freed from this obligation, and, nowadays, out of a world population of just over two thousand millions, perhaps six or seven hundred millions are so situated. It has, however, come to be regarded as a sure indication of social progress when a growing proportion of any given race, released from labour on the soil, finds itself free to adopt other means of livelihood, yet, simultaneously, elsewhere a policy of "back to the land" may be in process of adoption—ultimately contingent, however, upon the willingness of those concerned to accept what they may perhaps stigmatise as retrograde conditions. A balance between primary and secondary industries is clearly desiderated, but, in the rapidly changing circumstances of the present day, it is hard to dogmatise for different countries. The pursuit of agriculture has also, upon occasion and in certain countries, come to be regarded as a method of life rather than as a means of livelihood, so that, again, social as well as economic influences obtrude themselves.

The intimate character of man's association with the land cannot be better illustrated than by saying that the "typical" human being is the peasant farmer. Large scale undertakings may be dominant in some countries, but in the world at large they are as nothing compared with the family holding, which is the real "modal" farm; in fact, Chinese rural life, portrayed so admirably in Pearl Buck's *Good Earth*, is more truly representative of world conditions than is any other mode of existence. Ultimately, too, four-fifths of the world's secondary—or manufactured—products depend for their consumption upon the purchasing power of the agriculturist.

Economists are agreed that agriculture is "characterised by a high

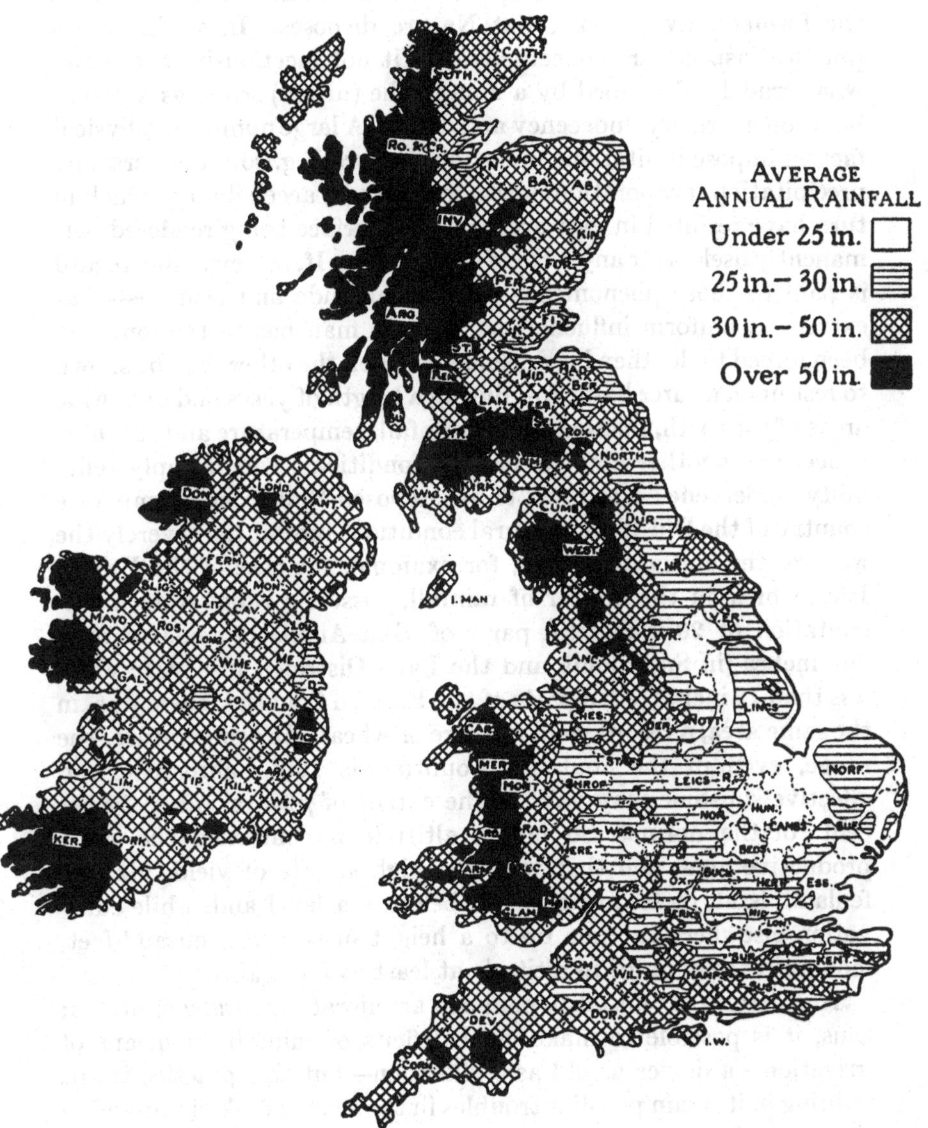

Rainfall of the British Isles

degree of economic uncertainty". In other words, unlike most forms of industry, it is a partnership between man and Nature, in which the former may propose, but Nature disposes. In so far as its practical aspects are concerned—was it not facetiously, but somewhat crudely, described by a man in the (urban) street as a "combination of cruelty, indecency and dirt"? A large number of physical factors impose limitations upon the venture, e.g. soil, temperature, precipitation, evaporation, latitude, altitude, accessibility, which in turn have resulted in vast areas of land surface being rendered permanently useless for any form of cultivation. If, however, due regard is paid to those phenomena—such as altitude and latitude—that exercise a uniform influence, as, indeed, man has in the long run been forced to do, then his dependence upon the others can be shown to rest upon a surer basis, for, during a length of years and over wide areas of the earth, fluctuations of rainfall, temperature and sunshine cancel one another and "average" conditions, which imply reliability, supervene. Nor must it be supposed that in any temperate country of the Old World natural conditions inhibit too severely the work of the cultivator. Take, for example, the case of the British Isles, which, in the matter of rainfall, possess a range from a precipitation of 20 inches (in parts of East Anglia) to one of over 200 inches (in Snowdonia and the Lake District); in a year when less than 12 inches fell in parts of the Eastern Counties, there was, in the same area, a record yield per acre of wheat. In temperature, the range, even in the Southern Counties, is 100° Fahrenheit, and effective sunshine may vary to the extent of *plus* or *minus* 30 per cent. of the normal. So far as altitude is concerned the most productive area, and that with the highest rate of yield, viz. the fenland, is at, or frequently even below, sea level and, while cultivation elsewhere extends up to a height of over a thousand feet, mountain sheep range in altitude at least as far again.

To a certain extent, also, man can ameliorate natural conditions; thus, it is possible to make good deficits of rainfall by means of irrigation—a device as old as civilisation—but this practice is apt to bring in its train peculiar troubles in the shape of alkali impregnation; glass-houses, too, are small scale, but expensive, methods of modifying ranges in temperature. Beyond these limited measures man cannot proceed.

Nature's living organisms also place in jeopardy the practice of agriculture. For examples of this, one need look no farther than the destruction of growing crops in Africa by locust swarms, the ravages of rinderpest and of tsetse fly and the losses occasioned to such diverse products as bananas, cotton, wheat and timber, by a whole range of living pests, whose attacks man is at present unable fully to counter, although there are successful examples—as in the case of the prickly pear infestation in Australia—of natural enemies being set to war upon one another. Again, in the life cycle of cattle, losses pursue the breeder from the onset of contagious abortion, which robs him of his unborn calves, to the ravages of the warble fly that depreciate the value of his mature beasts' hides. Indeed, the diseases that afflict domesticated livestock are more numerous and more potent than those common to man. In a brief space of time a poultry farm may lose its whole stock of birds from an outbreak of a particular infectious disease (bacillary white diarrhoea); the appearance of "big bud" on a fruit farm can necessitate the eradication of every black currant bush. Nor is man blameless in this respect, for, in numerous areas and during countless centuries, he has permitted his domestic animals not only to destroy the amenities, but completely to inhibit the pursuit of agriculture. In Classical times the shores of the Mediterranean were denuded of foliage by goats; the same thing is now happening over thousands of square miles in Africa, where excessive numbers of low grade native-owned cattle roam at will, and, in India, the sacred character attaching to the cow represents an annual loss of many millions of pounds.

It has become a habit to refer to the land as the "farmer's raw material", but a more accurate definition would be his "factory", and, while it would be an exaggeration to describe his activities as confined to two-dimensional space, yet few agricultural operations call for the use of more than a few inches of soil—the complexity of which, incidentally, none but the micro-biologist can appreciate. Raw material the land certainly is not, for, although necessarily reinvested by man with certain properties otherwise liable to attrition, it is not in the aggregate subject to removal or wastage. The fact that the cultivator utilises merely the surface of his land affords one of the many examples that differentiate this industry from others, in that such action imposes a limit to the extent of his operations, based upon sheer physical incapacity of supervision and of personal movement; the urban factory, susceptible of wide expansion in the third dimension, inflicts no such restraint upon its owner. This same factor, incidentally, puts an effective limit to the use of land, for, in many areas, no cultivator can increase his soil commitments without inflicting a corresponding loss upon others—land is limited, air is not.

The next feature of agriculture to be emphasised is its many-sidedness, and here it is not only justifiable but preferable to regard it, not as a single industry, but as many; this is, indeed, one of the causes of the popular misunderstandings that exist concerning its nature, its relations to other human activities and its peculiar economic disabilities. The interests of those severally engaged in primary production are often diametrically opposed, for the products of one branch are very frequently the first requisites of another; oats present a case in point. State or other forms of assistance intended to benefit one type of producer may positively handicap his neighbour. A survey of the range in types to be found practised in one country alone will bring conviction upon these points. In Great Britain, while crop and animal husbandry are frequently practised together, the latter, in its various forms, accounts for nearly three-quarters of the value of the total output, and the food of these livestock is produced, partly on the same farms, partly from other home sources, but also to a great extent from numerous countries situated in every continent—North and South American maize is fed to pigs; cotton-seed, linseed, palm-kernels, raised in Africa, are turned into cake for cattle, so, too, are the soya beans of the East. Many of the animals themselves have been born in one part of the country, reared in another, and "finished" in yet a third. Compare, in this connection, the movements of cattle from Scotland to Norfolk and thence to the Midlands, or backwards and forwards between the Eastern and Western areas of England. Are those concerned in these trades likely to see eye to eye with one another in regard to price movements? Larger issues of the same character emerge when the introduction of Irish and of Canadian cattle—once more to be subdivided up into stores, beasts intended for immediate slaughter or for breeding purposes—is under discussion. Certain areas are noted for their production of cereal and of other seeds, which are distributed throughout the country, but none would claim that the interests of those who raise them are identical with those of their (farming) purchasers. Poultry husbandry is a type which depends almost exclusively upon the produce of other farms, and its representatives are, therefore, the first to raise objections to any proposal aiming at an increase in the price of cereals.

Perhaps the most convincing exposition of the diversities in the agriculture of even this one small country can be obtained if a journey be made by air across the centre of England from, say, Yarmouth to Barmouth. One first traverses those coastal marshes, which, for two centuries, have fattened cattle as it is claimed no other district can do; then, after getting, to the North, a glimpse of the famous Broads area, devoted to the new industry of black currant and raspberry production, one sees, in the heart of Norfolk, arable land irrevocably associated with barley and sheep. The soil changes again, and we are over those sandy brecklands, which, while forming one of the greatest game preserves in the country, have otherwise up to recent times been popularly credited with an agricultural output confined to rabbits and rye, but are now the scene of great activities on the part of the Forestry Commission—in the production of yet another form of primary commodity. The next transition is a sudden one, for we quickly find ourselves over the most fertile and valuable agricultural land in these islands—the fens—and see in turn below us square miles of fruit (mainly of the "soft" varieties), of vegetables, and of flower bulbs reminiscent of Holland, while, as far as the eye can reach, the heaviest crops of cereals and of roots are also raised as well as vast quantities of potatoes and much sugar-beet. Crossing the river Nene we have, to our right, the Lincolnshire wolds with their flocks of grazing sheep, and below us the backbone of England, that outcrop of jurassic rock that, from Dorset to the Yorkshire coast, determines soil and, therefore, not only the distribution of crops and of livestock, but that of the lesser life, e.g. insects and, therefore, nightingales! For the next fifty miles we fly across the "Shires", which, oblivious of past times, when cereal prices were remunerative, nowadays provide pasture for countless thousands of beasts. Over Staffordshire we find ourselves surveying the activities of large numbers of relatively small milk-raising farms, whose produce is conveyed as far as London, and, if the day be clear, we see, far to the South, the Vale of Evesham, famous for its hard fruit, nor can we fail to observe the great number of poultry farms in this area. The lowlands of Wales, devoted to pasture, give place to its mountains, with their flocks of hill-sheep, and we finally sight the sea again above the arable fields of Cardigan Bay. Who would claim that those numerous and diverse forms of crop and of animal husbandry represent anything but separate industries? Multiply them again by taking a similar journey across Europe, and then, finally, picture the races of the world—white, brown, yellow and black—in temperate, subtropical and tropical countries, toiling to raise the thousand and one commodities that, under the generic term of "agricultural produce", minister to their own requirements and to those of the importing nations. Add an extraordinary measure of diversity in the actual practice of husbandry, in the very forms of crop and in the appearance of livestock; add, too, an almost infinite variety of social customs and habits and remember that systems of land-tenure are numerous. We have then a conspectus of agriculture, but it will convey an impression the reverse of that associated with a homogeneous industry.

The next outstanding difference to be noted as between this aggregate of primary industries and the secondary activities of the human species is what may perhaps best be termed the "immobility" of the former. Nearly all factory enterprises can adjust their organisation and their output in response to increased demands or in order to meet predilections that may change. In fact, the basis of many such undertakings is their ability quickly to follow—if not to anticipate—fluctuations in taste, fashions, and modes of life, taking immediate advantage, too, of altered economic and technical processes. To the farmer such actions are denied, for his partner, Nature, has placed such chronological restrictions upon their policy as to prohibit sudden change. The economic life of hard-woods may extend into centuries, that of even the conifers is equal to a human generation, while cattle mature at three years of age and the world's most imporant cereal crop takes up to eleven months to produce. The latter is often inextricably associated with some lengthy rotation, while a balance between field crops and livestock must, in many circumstances, be observed: the production of milk involves a policy built up during the passage of several years and all forms of horticulture rest upon a non-remunerative period which ranges, in the case of some soft varieties of fruit, from two years up to one, or even two, decades for the bulk of Pomona's gifts. Even the pig, that most prolific of domesticated animals, cannot be made to respond numerically to increased demands under six months. Here, then,

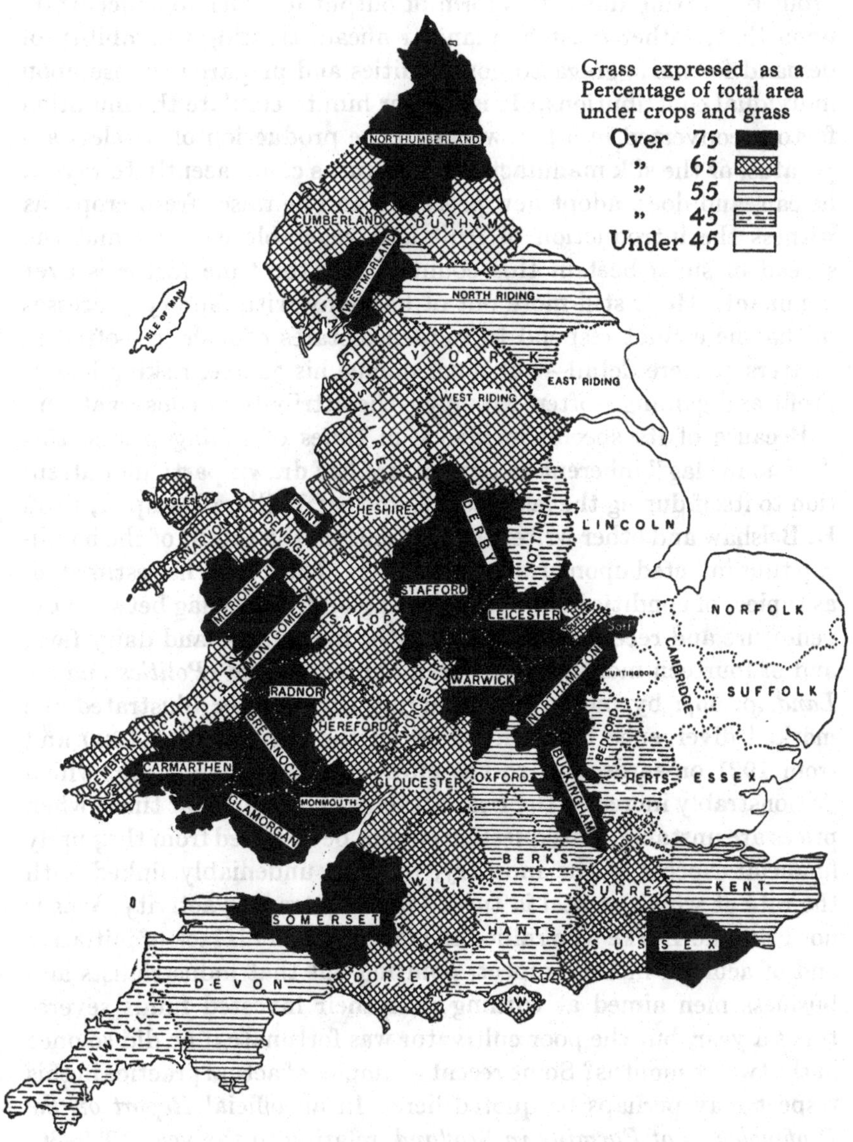

Distribution of arable land and permanent grass in England and Wales, 1932

are no opportunities for the primary producer to snatch a quick profit by cutting down this form of output in order to concentrate upon that; rather must he plan far ahead, trusting to stability of demand for his aggregated commodities and prepared to lose upon individual contributions. It is not for him to emulate the munition factory converted in a few weeks to the production of wireless apparatus, or the silk manufacturer who turns complacently to rayon; he can, and does, adopt new processes and he raises fresh crops, as witness the introduction of fruit and vegetable canning and the spread of sugar-beet in this country, but the time factor is ever dominant. He is still more out of harmony with factory processes in that he cannot respond to sudden dictates of fashion—often in matters of mere detail—but must pursue his course, risking loss of profit and gaining—often wrongly—the attribute of conservatism.

Because of its special incidence in times of falling prices, this "economic lag" inherent to agriculture has drawn particular attention to itself during the last decade, and Sir William Dampier, Prof. H. Belshaw and other writers have discussed the extent of the handicap thus inflicted upon primary producers. The former has estimated, as typical of conditions in Southern England, a time lag between expenditure and receipts of seven months for a grass-land dairy farm and of fourteen months for a sheep and corn farm (*Politics and the Land*, p. 65); by means of a diagram that author illustrated the marked divergence between profits in the periods 1914–1920 and from 1921 onwards, due to the effect of the economic lag, which demonstrably increases the risks attaching to farming at times when prices are unstable. This question cannot be divorced from the purely financial aspects of the industry, for it is undeniably linked with the rate at which capital is turned over by trading activity. Was it not Edmund Burke who rallied the farmer upon his lack of initiative and of acumen in this respect, pointing out that industrialists and business men aimed at turning over their invested funds several times a year, but the poor cultivator was fortunate if he did so once in the twelve months? Some recent examples of actual practice in this respect may perhaps be quoted here. In an official *Report on the Profitableness of Farming in Scotland*, relating to the year 1929–30, the wide diversity in rural economics is again revealed, for the rate of turnover applicable to circulating capital, therein referred to, ranged from once in 10 to 12 months (for sheep rearing and feeding farms) up to once in 3 to 5 months (for cheese and dairy holdings); if fixed and circulating capital were aggregated, the range was from once in 22 months to once in 8 months, while the overall average extended beyond the traditional annual turnover. In its *Economic Survey of Agriculture in the Eastern Counties of England, 1931*, the Cambridge University Department of Agriculture has demonstrated that profitableness is—at least in times of falling prices—directly related to the rate of capital turnover, for, in the case of over a thousand farms, those achieving an annual turnover of 50 per cent. (viz. once in 2 years) or less, registered a deficit of £380 per holding, those whose comparable figure was from 50 to 70 per cent. (say, 2 years to 18 months) lost on an average £230, while those—to the number of one-third—whose turnover exceeded 70 per cent. (viz. less than 18 months) found themselves in possession of a surplus of nearly £40. No commercial or industrial undertaking could indefinitely conduct its business upon a basis that saddled output with such heavy charges, for there was much economic truth in the old adage of "small returns and quick turnover", which, however, is an impossible ideal for any agriculturist unless he extends his activities into the field of retail selling.

The Law of diminishing returns, universally applicable to agriculture, next calls for consideration. In the majority of manufacturing and industrial undertakings it is rightly assumed that fresh application of capital, whether in the shape of giving employment to more hands by the erection of new buildings or otherwise by increasing output, will bring in a return at least comparable with that already accruing. Thus, a factory erected and equipped for the sum of £50,000, and engaged upon the production of certain articles for which there is a steady demand, may be making a net profit of 20 per cent., or £10,000, per annum. The accommodation for machinery and workers is then doubled, by the expenditure of another £50,000, and the output follows suit, still bringing in 20 per cent. on the whole capital invested. It is more likely, indeed, that there may be what is known as an "increasing return", for the capacity of the works may be doubled by an outlay of less than £50,000, as, for instance, if the accommodation for the management and clerical staff originally provided, suffices also for the additional buildings, when these and other overhead charges may not be increased proportionally. Thus, in ordinary business ventures the return secured by the promoter or shareholder from the advancement of fresh capital is usually subject to no retarding influences—always provided that stability of manufacturing costs is assured and that certainty of demand can be determined in advance.

If we turn to agriculture, however, a totally different proposition faces us, for we find that, in whatsoever form it is sought to apply more than a certain amount of capital to the preparation of the soil, or even to the feeding of livestock, there is a limit beyond which, not only does output per "dose" remain stationary, but rapidly declines. In theory there may be almost no limit to the yield of crops per acre;

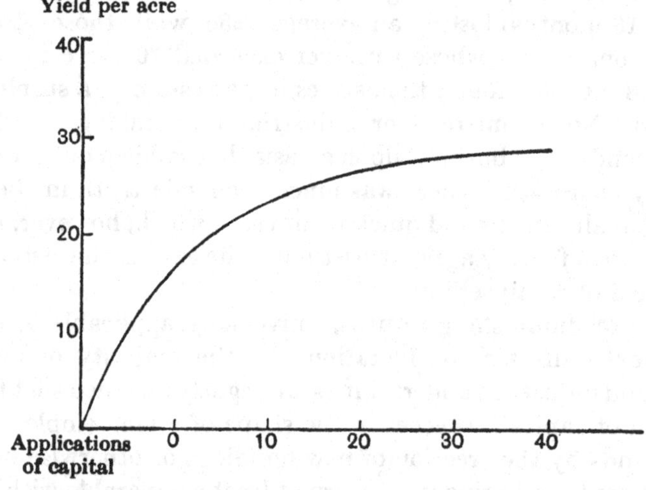

Diagram illustrative of the Law of diminishing returns

indeed, before the Royal Commission of 1893 one witness declared that, by an abnormal application of "capital" (in this case stable manure), he had secured a yield of wheat of 130 bushels to the acre. Sir J. B. Lawes, giving evidence subsequently, agreed that this might have been effected on a "few square feet" and with "the aid of pea-sticks", but emphasised the fact that the cultivation of land, if profit were the objective, could be very easily overdone; that, in other words, such yield achieved at enormous expense clearly could not "pay". Obviously, if a crop of twenty bushels per acre could be doubled and then trebled by the outlay of two and three times the capital required to produce the twenty bushels, all farmers would pursue such a policy and yields of forty and sixty bushels would be universal. Here, however, is a vital distinction drawn between manufacturing and agricultural processes—the intrusion of a factor that may be ever varying and uncertain in its incidence, but one that is never absent. The diagram on p. 14 illustrates in general the incidence of this Law, the figures on the base line of which may be taken as representing capital application in any one of several forms, e.g. weight of manure per acre, wages per acre on preparation of the land and so forth. The following Table also gives a concrete instance of its applicability to wheat production. These latter figures are taken from the *Book of the Rothamsted Experiments*, edited by the present director of that Institute, Sir John Russell, and display strikingly the diminishing returns, and, therefore, the increasing costs, resulting from the progressive applications of capital in the shape of nitrogen upon a world-famous field.

Experiments on Wheat, Broadbalk Field
(Averages, 1852–1864)

Plot	Manures per acre	Dressed grain		Straw	
		Produce per acre	Increase for each additional 43 lb. nitrogen in manure	Produce per acre	Increase for each additional 43 lb. nitrogen per acre
5	Minerals alone	18·3	—	16·6	—
6	Minerals and 43 lb. nitrogen as ammonium salts	28·6	10·3	27·1	10·5
7	Minerals and 86 lb. nitrogen as ammonium salts	37·1	8·5	38·1	11·0
8	Minerals and 129 lb. nitrogen as ammonium salts	39·0	1·9	42·7	4·6
16	Minerals and 172 lb. nitrogen as ammonium salts	39·5	0·5	46·6	3·9

The critical figures are of course those contained in the columns which record the increase due to each additional 43 lb. of nitrogen, for it is clear that the third and fourth "doses" were not resulting in gains that could be justified under commercial conditions. The figures of total produce per acre also harmonise well with the diagram, which, as stated above, is illustrative of the Law in general and represents no particular example. It will be observed that the curve becomes practically horizontal, and in fact might almost be described as cycloidal in shape. While there was in the past unanimity in regard to the prevalence of this Law, latterly certain economists have pinned their faith to the belief that "science", if it cannot already do so, will in the near future be able to surmount these difficulties, or, in other words, that the chemist or electrical engineer will evolve some process by which, at a relatively small outlay, the soil will be forced to give almost uniform returns. If such were ever accomplished, then indeed the Law would be a thing to ignore, but the last sixty years, although prolific in discovery, have given no indication of the birth of any revolution in agricultural practice. Such slight modifications as have taken place have had reference to agriculture as a whole; among these may be placed the greater use made of machinery, by which the expenses of labour have been reduced, and the introduction of subsidiary branches of cultivation, whereby a given tract of land has been made to yield a greater weight or value from the growth of intensively produced crops. The yield of the individual staple crops has, however, not been appreciably freed from the incidence of diminishing returns by any striking advance in science.

It must be emphasised that the critical point at which the cash return secured from the additional yield exactly counterbalances (and thereafter falls short of) the outlay on procuring it varies within wide limits (it is quite possible, too, that before this point is reached increasing returns may have been operative), and has reference to numerous factors, among which must be placed the nature of the land and its past history, the prices ruling for agricultural products and the cost of labour and of material. In this and other countries, where agriculture has been long established, the second and third of the factors just enumerated are more potent than the first, although this has always to be reckoned with in certain districts; in times of economic depression corroborative evidence is always present, for the cry that "high farming is no remedy for low prices" correctly directs attention to the Law, although the substitution of "higher" for "high" might be a more precise interpretation of the situation. In times of relatively high prices for wheat and other cereals, it "pays" to farm certain lands which would otherwise either go out of cultivation or remain under grass; the reason being the simple one that there is a larger margin available before the Law reminds the cultivator of its existence. Again, the advantages of climate and of soil in East Anglia have enabled wheat production to be carried on in that part of these Islands when low prices virtually forced its abandonment elsewhere. A distinction must be drawn between such a highly developed country as this and one situated in the newer parts of the world, for the settlers in Canada, Australia, the Argentine and other such territories, on commencing their operations, possess in their soil the stored fertility of past ages upon which to draw. At first no application of manure is called for, and their capital outlay is confined to the mere mechanical preparation of the richest tracts of land, even the rent of which is a negligible factor. As, in the course of years, this fertility is gradually absorbed, a relatively small application of manure, accompanied by a slightly augmented labour-bill, will bring the cultivator almost *pro rata* returns—he is still only to a slight degree assisting Nature. Within another generation or so, however, his land calls for as much "farming" as that situated in the older countries of the world, and the effect of diminishing returns, at first masked by the response of the virgin richness of the soil, makes itself felt when that wealth has been "stolen". Thereafter, as population increases, means of communication are established, and demand springs up for land when its products rise in value, the Law assumes its place in the agricultural economy of the country. Before this full development is attained, however, there is another direction in which its incidence seems to be obviated, and that is when the agriculture of a whole country or a province alone is taken into consideration. Then, the application of additional capital can take the form of adding fresh untilled soil to that already under the plough, when of course once more the latent resources are being drawn on and no unremunerative expenditure is being devoted to the assistance of Nature. Theoretically, such a position could be achieved in the case of individual farmers situated on the outskirts of land reclamation, whose properties were bordered by untouched tracts ready to be assimilated into the original holdings; thus, for the time being, even separate occupiers could, in a fresh direction, secure non-diminishing returns, but only precariously and at the expense of constant fresh commitments in real estate and of increasing costs of transport to markets. In general, farmers in the New World, where wages are high and other outgoings low, evade the onset of diminishing returns by maintaining a low standard of cultivation.

It will be appreciated that the dual aspects of the Law—viz. diminishing returns in profits and in yields—have been considered together in the preceding paragraphs, but it must be observed that the former is of paramount importance to the practising farmer, and, indeed, dominates all his actions and forms his financial horizon. Bearing in mind the cost of his labour and of other outgoings, and taking into consideration the present and possible future prices of his products, he must estimate with nicety the point at which he should check his total outlay. But for no product, for no area, indeed, for no farmer, is there a fixed or permanent indication of that optimum point; all the factors are in a constant state of flux and the cultivator who succeeds best is he who, by wise adjustments, secures the greatest return for a given outlay, or "dose", of expenditure.

There are several wider implications of the Law, e.g. its extension to the secular field of population in relation to food supplies, which would call for a long and detailed investigation of past movements and the forecasting of future economic and social tendencies, based upon most hazardous foundations. Again, much has been written during the last few years to demonstrate its universal emergence in natural phenomena. Thus, an American author, F. Lester Patton, in *Diminishing Returns in Agriculture*, brought within his purview such unorthodox examples as man's muscular output, the rate of growth of animals and the efficiency of machinery, all of which, together with numerous other marginal physical returns, he claimed must conform to the Law. The human being, too, was cited as amenable, in his managerial capacity, for, owing to his progressive inefficiency as the unit of size increases, this was held to be an important factor in e.g. the Westerly movement of the smaller farms in the United States. If, in the old days, the Law of diminishing returns was, by such a title, unknown to the farmer (but empirically and tacitly obeyed), is there not, at the present time, perhaps a danger of its becoming placed upon too high a pinnacle—and thereby acting as a deterrent to otherwise progressive farmers?

It now becomes possible to turn to consideration of the factors affecting the demand for, and the price of, the products of agriculture. The latter range from the rarest of luxuries to the most abundant of necessities, and include also the raw material destined for countless secondary processes. Every human want, we know, has a limit set to it and the utility, for the individual, of a given commodity diminishes as the supply increases. The popular illustrations of this Theory of Marginal Utility generally postulate a commodity costing *y* shillings per unit and a person whose predilection for it would lead him to absorb, say, twenty units if he could get it free of cost and one if the price were *5y* shillings; in practice he purchases twelve units per annum, the extra satisfaction derived from the twelfth as compared with that from the eleventh, in conjunction with the fact that he does not acquire a thirteenth is, therefore, regarded as indicative that *y* shillings measures for him the marginal utility of that commodity.

In these pages it is impossible to discuss the two other historic Theories of Value that approach the subject from the supply side—viz. that of Labour, which postulates that the value of anything is dependent upon "the quantity of labour expended during its production" (Adam Smith) and that based upon the Cost of Production which includes, in addition to labour, all other direct and indirect charges incurred prior to sale; the former has been rejected on the ground that other factors cannot be ignored; discussion of the latter is here omitted, but it may be said that it is in practice almost impossible to establish what is the cost of producing certain vital commodities or of performing particular services—and this is nowhere more difficult than in agriculture—while, even if ascertainable, the "per unit" figures vary with output. We must accept, therefore, as axiomatic that "value" is determined by supply and demand, and *vice versa*. If the price of a commodity is, for any reason, lowered, more of it will be sold; if demand flags, its price will fall. A certain quantity of a product will be offered for sale at a given price; if that price rises, more will be placed upon the market; if it falls, less will appear. Diagrammatic illustrations of typical demand and supply curves will be found in every text-book of economic theory.

In discussing demand it has, on the part of pure economists, been customary to differentiate between the various strata of human society, for what is to the rich person easily acquirable, will be utterly denied to the poor. Here, the subject must be treated of in relation to the individual commodities themselves—that subject, of course, being known as "the elasticity of demand", and defined by Marshall as follows: "The elasticity of demand in a market is great or small according as the amount demanded increases much or little for a given fall in price, and diminishes much or little for a given rise in price". It is, perhaps, significant that most of the tabular and diagrammatic representations of this rule adopted by classical writers relate to agricultural commodities; thus, Marshall himself first cites the case of green peas in relation to seasonal fluctuations (and to different classes of the community) and follows this up with a familiar example, relating to wheat consumption, derived from Gregory King's estimates. It is found, in practice, that, for a given class of the community, the demand for expensive commodities is, at first, slow to respond to reductions in price, but ultimately, with further falls, consumption is freely stimulated until at last a point is reached (that of "satiety", *pace* Marshall) when consumption is irresponsive. In other words, the demand, originally highly inelastic, becomes elastic and finally resumes its former state.

Broadly speaking, the demand for the staple articles of food is not elastic; human beings cannot cut down their consumption of bread, of rice or of mealies—as the case may be—below a certain point; nor, indeed, can they, due to obvious physical limitations, much increase its upward movement. Bread forms one of the most frequently cited examples of a commodity the demand for which is highly inelastic; in Great Britain, the price of the quartern loaf may range from 7*d.* to 11*d.*, but consumption will fluctuate scarcely at all. At the other end of the scale are found those purely luxurious products of the soil, the consumption of which increases progressively with a fall in price—evidence, according to the older school of economists, that, on the part of the *middle classes*, the demand for them is elastic. It is open to question, however, whether at the present time, when the spending power of many classes has been much increased and inequalities have been deliberately modified by means of taxation, such precise relegation into unchanging categories is possible, though, of course, all would agree that, at the extremes of the social scale, the demand of the very rich and that of the very poor for such products is still inelastic.

Between the extremes represented by the loaf and, for example, hothouse fruit, early imported potatoes or preserved tongues, are to be found ranged the majority of human foodstuffs. Of these, meat and dairy products (exclusive of milk itself) are, for people at large, in very elastic demand. In many countries the dietary of a large proportion of their peoples has, in fact, been altered by the partial substitution, for the standard varieties of food, of what a generation ago would have been regarded as luxuries. This does not necessarily imply an alteration in total demand, but merely the partial, or even complete, replacement of one article by some other; wheat and meat stand most frequently in this relation to one another; so, too, do butter and margarine. Since the war, English butchers have stated that there has been great difficulty in disposing of the cheaper and inferior joints of meat and that they have, as a result, been forced to maintain, or even to increase, the prices of the better varieties in order to secure normal profits from the whole carcase; such a tendency, however, is indicative, not of demand being elastic, but rather of increased purchasing power. Finally, where agriculture produces the raw material of other industries, demand, while less assured than in the case of human or animal foodstuffs, is generally more elastic. This is perhaps a suitable place at which to point out that many forms of agricultural output are "joint-products", text-book examples of which are most frequently selected from the live-stock branch of the industry in the shape of cattle (meat and hides), or sheep (meat and wool), but many tropical and sub-tropical types of plant growth might also be cited, e.g. the coco-nut (fibre, copra and oil), or cotton (fibre, cake and oil), while certain woods, soft and hard, produce both commercial timber and dyes, tans or resins.

Bearing in mind the analysis of primary production effected in the first part of this Chapter, it will not surprise any reader to hear that, where supply is concerned, elasticity is not great, for those familiar natural and physical factors hamper the producer in adjusting his output, and, in his comparative isolation, it may also take him some time to appreciate that demand has increased. Since, as was also demonstrated above, the bulk of the world's producers are peasant proprietors with comparatively small commercial incentive, the tendency to stabilisation of output, in disregard of price movements, is accentuated. As an illustration of this feature may be quoted a statement made in the House of Commons in 1933 by the Minister of Agriculture to the effect that, while the prices of agricultural products had, in three years, fallen by half, their output had declined by only 1 per cent. It must not be forgotten, too, that, as a class, farmers are retrograde in the use of accounting methods, and thereby handicap themselves when it comes to assessing their financial position or estimating their costs of production. If sufficient chronological latitude be granted, however, it will be found that, certainly where larger units are concerned, additional or alternative supplies are forthcoming in response to upward movements in price. Evidence for the first proposition need be sought no farther afield than in the increased wheat acreage of the world after the war, for the second, in the laying down to fruit of considerable tracts of English soil or in the additional production of vegetables for canning purposes.

The highly important repercussions of these demand and supply factors have been fully investigated, so far as one commodity subject to extreme fluctuations in price is concerned, by Ruth L. Cohen in *Factors affecting the Price of Potatoes* (Report No. 15, Farm Economics Branch, Department of Agriculture, Cambridge). From this very detailed study, it appears that growers would, in recent years, have received a greater aggregate sum had they produced less, while consumers, the elasticity of whose demand was small for increased quantities and markedly augmented for a below-average crop, paid the maximum aggregate sum for their supplies. It is shown, too, that variability of price is, in the main, due to fluctuations in supply, which in turn are occasioned by alterations in yield per acre rather than in area; the latter, with minor effects, follow changes in price with a time lag of from twelve to over twenty months. As always, therefore, the primary producer is at the mercy of Nature's vagaries, for it is, as yet, impossible for him to counterbalance anticipated variations in yield by acreage adjustment and, therefore, to stabilise outturn.

United States conditions bear out these conclusions, for J. F. Warren and F. A. Pearson in the Cornell monograph, entitled *Interrelationships of Supply and Price*, where "price" is regarded as synonymous with "purchasing power", found that, while consumers pay more for a heavy crop than for a light one, its producers receive a smaller sum; that fluctuations in the total food supply affect prices less than do fluctuations in that of a single commodity; and that it costs actually more to convey from producer to consumer an article when it sells cheaply than when it is highly priced.

Attempts hitherto made in the direction of controlling output have taken such crude forms as (*a*) destruction of surplus supplies (e.g. of coffee and of maize in South America—after, in the case of coffee, the failure of "valorisation", viz. the withholding of supplies); (*b*) reduction of output (e.g. of rubber under the Stevenson scheme and of sugar by conference agreement between Cuba, Java and other cane interests and European beet producers); (*c*) withholding, by the State, of supplies from the market (e.g. the United States Federal Farm Board's action); (*d*) imposition of financial or fiscal control (e.g. the famous Greek currant policy and the granting of large bounties by their State to Queensland sugar-growers in order to enable them to continue exportation when world prices were below their costs of production). All these methods, with the exception of the unique example quoted under (*d*), where a complete monopoly existed and where the crop represented the sole production of numerous cultivators, leave economic loopholes. Destruction or withdrawal of supplies, under present conditions of world trade, invariably gives opportunity to other producers of the commodity or to those who raise an alternative; controlled output is rarely effective over a sufficiently wide area—the rubber scheme failed because nationals, other than those bound by the undertakings, exploited the situation. Thus, in 1931, agreement to cut down exports could not be reached between Indian and Sinhalese tea-planters, with the result that in 1933 Ceylon interests independently petitioned for Government intervention and the introduction of a *quota* system for five years. On the other hand, a few agricultural products are virtually monopolistic; examples may be found in Philippine manilla, Bengal jute and Japanese camphor-wood, but, even here, full economic advantage of the situation has seldom been taken.

It is apposite to remember what has previously been put forward in regard to supply, to the elasticity of demand (and that of supply also) and to the Law of diminishing returns, as, for reasons then stated, agricultural producers find it difficult either to reduce their outturn with the object of raising values or, in response to new demands, to vary or to supplement their prospective endeavours. Such attempts as have been made to adjust output to demand have too often led to an amplification of the movements it was sought to check. Thus, a request to curtail the acreage of a crop is found to lead to excessive reduction in the first season, with a resultant increase in the value of its produce, which in turn causes an abnormal expansion a year or so later. It is obvious, too, in this connection that the advice to be given to one or two individual producers may be diametrically opposed to that properly tendered to all persons engaged in the same process; if a shortage is anticipated the few, benefiting by foreknowledge, will obtain higher per unit prices upon an increased outturn, while the whole body, acting upon similar advice, would probably receive a smaller gross sum for an inflated output. To such an extent is this phenomenon recognised that the English Ministry of Agriculture has set itself steadfastly against giving any direct indication of future trends in supply or demand. In the United States, where the opposite policy had at one time been pursued, it became necessary, in order to assess the net results upon outturn, to establish a separate bureau to study the probable reactions of the cultivators to the suggestions officially made to them. Quantitative control of imports may be a feasible practice in a particular country, but, apart from the case of a monopolistic commodity, there seems little reason to anticipate the emergence of a universal spirit of agreement, by which means alone the bounties of Nature could at first be regulated and subsequently directed throughout the world. Man must still defer to his dominant partner.

Some description having been given of the factors that determine price and of the difficulties associated with its regulation, it is now incumbent to discuss the monetary basis of exchange—for all purchases and sales are in effect merely the exchange, or barter, of one article for another. Money, in whatsoever form it is used—whether gold, silver, copper or notes—has its own "value", just like other commodities, and accordingly it is as legitimate to refer to gold in terms of wheat as to wheat in terms of gold. The larger the supply of either article, the "cheaper" it appears when measured by the other: when wheat is scarce its price rises, that is to say, more money must be given for it; when gold is scarce the price of wheat, other things being equal, falls—in other words, the same amount of the metal purchases more of the cereal. When a country is upon the "gold standard" or a "bimetallic" standard its currency will, in the former case, be linked with a given quantity of gold alone, in the latter, with a combination of, say, gold and silver. In this country, during the period between the Napoleonic and the Great War, the pound legally consisted of 123·27447 grains of gold of standard fineness; notes or other forms of money were convertible into gold;

silver and copper coins were merely "token" money (viz. utilisable for small payments only) and the banks held predetermined reserves of gold, upon which security they issued "credit" in its various forms up to several times the nominal equivalent of the gold. Clearly, therefore, the "value", or purchasing power, of money was determined by the "value" of gold (itself largely dependent on the monetary demand for it), which, although this was not always recognised by many of those who handled it, was in turn subject to fluctuation. If we study the trend of prices in the intervening years we observe slow upward and downward movements, affecting all commodities and payments. These were obviously in the aggregate not due to abundance or shortage of all forms of goods, but rather reflected variations in the value of gold itself and, therefore, of alterations in the supply or output of that metal in relation to demand; their causes, sequence and, in particular, their effects upon British agriculture will be found traced in Chapter XXII. Reference to what is known as the "velocity of circulation", i.e. the rate at which both currency and credit are turned over in a given time, and which, therefore, also affects the price-level, must, owing to lack of space, be foregone.

Consideration of the present and future position of this country in regard to the gold standard is deferred to the final Chapter, but it may be pointed out that the world output of gold has been increased by more than 12 per cent. in the last twenty years and that the latest developments in Africa point to an even greater supply shortly becoming available. The abandonment of the gold standard by a large number of countries, however, renders useless any discussion of the implications involved, nor is it yet *à propos* to canvass the adoption of either a "managed currency" or of bimetallism, which latter would involve an official ratio of exchange between silver and gold, the coining of both at the ratio in question and acceptance, as legal tender, of this currency.

The causes and nature of long-term movements in he general price-level have been briefly indicated above, and now something must be said in regard to those of shorter amplitude—the so-called trade cycle—whose life is perhaps a third or a quarter that of the generation-long swings which, during the last century, characterised the former type. Here, boom and depression alternate with almost rhythmical periodicity. Growth of confidence, a purely monetary reaction, some new technical process or invention, the obsolescence of machinery, change in requirements or an additional output from agriculture (attributable to natural causes) increases demand, credit expands and, consequently, prices rise; all forms of trade and of commerce are affected and prosperity flows—*crescit eundo*. Costs of production rise, cash is withdrawn into circulation, new goods appear upon the market, the central bank raises its discount rate, some firms go bankrupt, all business men become apprehensive, production, prices and employment alike decline; the boom has passed, then—*mole ruit suâ*—the trade cycle has run its course. In assessing the relative importance of the initiating causes, the more potent of which are referred to above, Prof. A. C. Pigou (*Industrial Fluctuations*, p. 50) holds that "large inventions may be significant, harvest variations are certainly so". In other words, evidence of a large forthcoming cereal crop in, say, North America is responsible for anticipatory reactions on the part of numerous intermediaries and others who will be eventually concerned in its handling. Full weight being given to this factor, it is generally held that nowadays monetary causes override all others.

In addition, of course, all individual commodities are subject to price movements peculiar to themselves, and, in the case of agriculture, some of these latter have, through their cyclical regularity, become notorious. Thus, both in Great Britain and elsewhere pigs and pig products conform to a recognised periodicity in this respect, for their prices move upwards and downwards over a four years' cycle which rests upon the response (after a brief time-lag) of breeders to the stimulus of higher values, followed by reduction after supplies have outrun effective demand. In this country these movements have a range as large as 40 per cent. from the normal, and are accentuated by the existence of a cycle in feeding-stuff prices which moves inversely to them.

There are, then, three distinctive price-trends which affect the primary producer, viz. the long-term, the short-term (or trade cycle) and that of the individual commodity; blended together, they form a ready indication of the economic ups and downs of his industry.

In the matter of wages, it is certain that two of the historic theories could not now be held applicable to the agriculture of this country, viz. (*a*) the "Subsistence Theory", resting upon the belief that labourers' earnings were just sufficient for their bare needs and that any increase thereof merely resulted in an augmented population, which, in turn, automatically reduced wages; or (*b*) the "Wages Fund Theory", which in effect regarded wages as dependent upon the relationship borne by population to capital. A third, the "Marginal Productivity Theory", may be said to hold the field; it declares that, as general wage rates are extraneously fixed, the farmer (or entrepreneur) will always seek to make the best possible use of his agents of production—land, capital and labour, and that, as the productivity of the last named—or the efficacy of its utilisation—is increased, the extra demand for it will cause a rise in wages. This, to agriculturists, general acceptable proposition raises the important question of the relationship of the three agents to one another. Throughout the different countries of the world are to be seen examples of almost every possible proportionate use of them. In Australia, where land is abundant and labour scarce, one finds the cheapest (land) extensively used and the most expensive (labour) husbanded and freely augmented by the third (capital) in the form of mechanical aids. In China or in India, where labour is superabundant and, therefore, very cheap, while land, relative to population, is scarce, the latter is, together with a minimum of capital, intensively used. The criterion is, in the first instance, the output per employee, in the second, that per unit of land. In every instance all three agents will be used to their best "productive" advantage, which, in the passage of time, may affect the *relative* degree of their utilisation, through, for example, the introduction of controlled wage rates acting as an incentive to the use of machinery or a rise in the value of land, when heavier outturn will be aimed at by means of additional application of capital and labour on, possibly, a reduced area.

Such matters as wages, both real and money, as well as the utilisation of labour upon the land, are treated of in their appropriate Chapters, but a fundamental aspect of the whole question must be mentioned here. It is this: ultimately, the proportion of any population engaged in raising food must depend upon the numbers of those prepared to adopt, or to remain in, such occupation, which in turn will be decided by the standard of living obtainable in this and in alternative methods of employment: finally, the relationship between land and population will determine that standard. This, then, brings us back to a familiar point, for the available supply of land is fixed and population, in the world at large, is steadily increasing. Accepting the statement of such a well-known authority as Sir Daniel Hall that we require two and a half acres each for our sustenance, comparison of the relative data will suggest that, secularly, the more distant future is likely to make greater demands upon both land and mechanical assistance. The extent to which individual countries may remain agricultural or succumb to a lopsided industrialism will, as in the past, be determined by many factors, of which the comparative cost of producing each alternative commodity will be paramount, so that there is small likelihood of the basic principles that have moulded the economic development of nations during the past century being modified. Country *A* will continue to manufacture and to export product *X*, while Country *B* concentrates upon commodity *Y*; in each instance natural and other circumstances have determined a policy which represents the most economic use of all instruments of production, and the aggregate output and trade of the two countries concerned will be at its optimum. Manchester cotton goods, South Wales coal and Yorkshire cloth pay for Brazilian coffee, Danish bacon and Dutch rubber, as well as for the manufactured goods we import. Great Britain will continue to produce these and countless other commodities so long as she can do so at a smaller expenditure than would be involved in making at home those articles she now obtains from abroad; that exports should pay for imports is an essential pre-requisite, but there is no valid reason why a preponderance of primary articles in the latter category should be stigmatised as evidence of retrogression. This country, and certain others, *could* grow more foodstuffs at home, but it does not follow that, if they did, their peoples would, by reason of the inevitable reduction in reciprocal foreign custom, have the purchasing power they now enjoy. It is dangerous to interfere with a highly complex organisation, which resulted from the untrammelled and efficient utilisation of numerous factors, and still rests upon "efficiency".

The principal economic theories in their application to agriculture in general have been sketched in the foregoing pages, as have also the attributes and limitations peculiar to the industry itself. It would perhaps, therefore, be well, by way of introduction and in supplement to the physical survey previously made from the air, briefly to say something concerning the position occupied by British agriculture in relation to other national activities.

Surprise is generally caused when the statement is made that agriculture is still unquestionably the largest employer of labour in these Islands; but such, indeed, is the case, for, in Great Britain and the component parts of Ireland, the total number of rural wage-earners is in excess of 1,100,000, while the next largest occupation is that of mining, with just under one million employees. Even in England and Wales, taken alone, there are approximately 700,000 workers, who, with the addition of their employers, make a total of fully one million persons engaged in raising food, with the result that, although they form only some 7 per cent. of the occupied population, here, too, the primary producers outnumber other separate types of workers; only if combined under such generic headings as "textile" or "metal" trades, do those aggregated industries approach agriculture in the number of their employees. On the other hand, within the area represented by the former United Kingdom there are at least 2,100,000 persons "engaged or employed" in agriculture. So much for the belief that our agriculture is, from the numerical standpoint, unimportant. The capital sunk in it by owners and tenants combined must, in the British Isles, exceed £1,400,000,000, of which the former class is responsible for two-thirds, while for purposes of comparison it may be stated that the equivalent commitment in our railways is about £1,100,000,000. The value of the output of the industry is, at present, not greatly below £250,000,000 per annum (£356,000,000 in 1925–6), and it still provides more than a third of the nation's food requirements from an acreage subject to an annual loss that may amount to as much as 100 square miles. In so far as technique is concerned, it has no reason to fear comparison with results achieved elsewhere; British farmers have led the world both in crop and in animal husbandry (the latter providing the only example of an export trade in our agricultural commodities, viz. that of pedigree livestock), and, if other countries have, in a few instances, caught them up or even slightly bettered their work, the industry as a whole is still second to none, and its followers have proved themselves highly adaptable, both to physical conditions and in the matter of keeping pace with the changes dictated by causes which are to them often obscure and sometimes inexplicable. They are apt to incur odium from a misunderstanding of their calling and of its potentialities and have too often been the shuttlecock of political parties. The tripartite partnership, peculiar to this country by reason of the extent to which it has been adopted, calls for skill, competence and endurance on the part of all three representatives, none of whose returns has for any length of time equalled what it would have been had secondary industry, trade or commerce proved the attractive force. This, then, is the industry whose economic foundations, resting upon the rock of history, are about to be discussed.

Chapter II

THE OCCUPATION OF LAND IN THE PAST

Man's first efforts at cultivation; examples found in this country; questions involved in the origin of the manor; early maps; the manor of Rampton; division of arable and grass land; modern survivals; Castor and Ailsworth; the Isle of Axholme; Laxton; Braunton Great Field; Rundale in Ireland; Scotch Runrig; the universal character of "strip" husbandry; allocation of grazing facilities; the Ings at Brotherton; rights of common; services and duties of manorial tenants; Courts Leet and Baron; Buckden's last Manor-court.

Any full description of land tenure calls for a series of digressions into legal and constitutional history, involving thereby the traversing of much debatable ground and the introduction of political colour. In such a work as this it is incumbent to avoid excursions of that character and to discuss each phase from the standpoint of the cultivator of the soil; thus, the present Chapter deals with the facilities for access to land (differentiating between arable and grass), that have existed under certain systems of tenure, while its successors investigate the more recent practices still to be found in this and other countries.

The earliest forms of intensive cultivation, as opposed to extensive —which implied a constant moving on of nomadic or other tribes— were, and still are, practised on the alluvial banks of such rivers as the Nile and the Tigris, while in more temperate countries, signs of occupation can still be traced on the lighter soils of hill-sides. That agriculture in such countries as Egypt has changed little in character will be appreciated by anyone who is familiar with the wooden models of granaries and livestock that have been discovered in tombs. In Europe man at first sought the light and sandy soils, shunning the heavy types with their dense forests, and that here widespread and long continued operations were carried out on the slopes of chalk hills will meet with general acceptance after a survey of our own Southern and Western counties, whose downs are scarred with terraces formed by generations of bygone ploughmen. Anyone familiar with the illustration of the "Linches" at Clothall in Hertfordshire, given in Seebohm's *English Village Community*, will be interested in comparing that woodcut with the photograph forming the frontispiece to this volume, which was taken from a similar angle in 1922. Whilst it is not claimed that these seven well-defined terraces represent a direct survival of prehistoric cultivation, they afford an excellent example of the appearance of hill-sides that have been under the plough for countless centuries. Facing North-West, and of an extreme length of some 260 yards, they rise in a series of steps some 5 to 8 feet in height, the largest having a width of 30 yards, the rest of some 5 to 8 yards. Modern farming operations have not permitted of their economic use, so that all save the widest remain overgrown with rank herbage, and the divisions between them harbour thorn bushes.

In practically all countries of the world, as soon as intensive cultivation succeeded to cattle raising and its accompaniment of extensive cropping, there came into existence those village communities that were, in Western Europe, to become the foundation of the manorial system, and that, elsewhere in the world, are still found in a less advanced state. Historians and lawyers have differed over many questions regarding their evolution, the most important point at issue being in regard to the original position occupied by the cultivators of the soil in relationship to the chief who was eventually to become the lord of the manor. Had all members of village communities at first equal rights, which were gradually dominated by the more powerful individuals, or did the manor derive from some former system in which groups of unfree cultivators had laboured for a master? Despite the brilliant advocacy of followers of the latter theory, it must be confessed that the probabilities are in favour of the former, for in all ages and among all groups of human beings, the power of those endowed with marked character or even with physical attributes is bound to make itself felt, and in communities such as those in question this would tend to the gradual establishment in some shape of over-lordship of the soil.

Throughout the greater part of England, communal husbandry in some form or other survived not only Roman influence but also, in common with those "minor monuments", lying a yard beneath it, outlived the "drums and tramplings of three conquests". In the extreme South-Western peninsula, however, in Wales, and, generally, in Scotland and Ireland, where grazing was the predominant industry, and where the advances of conquering races were rendered

PLATE I

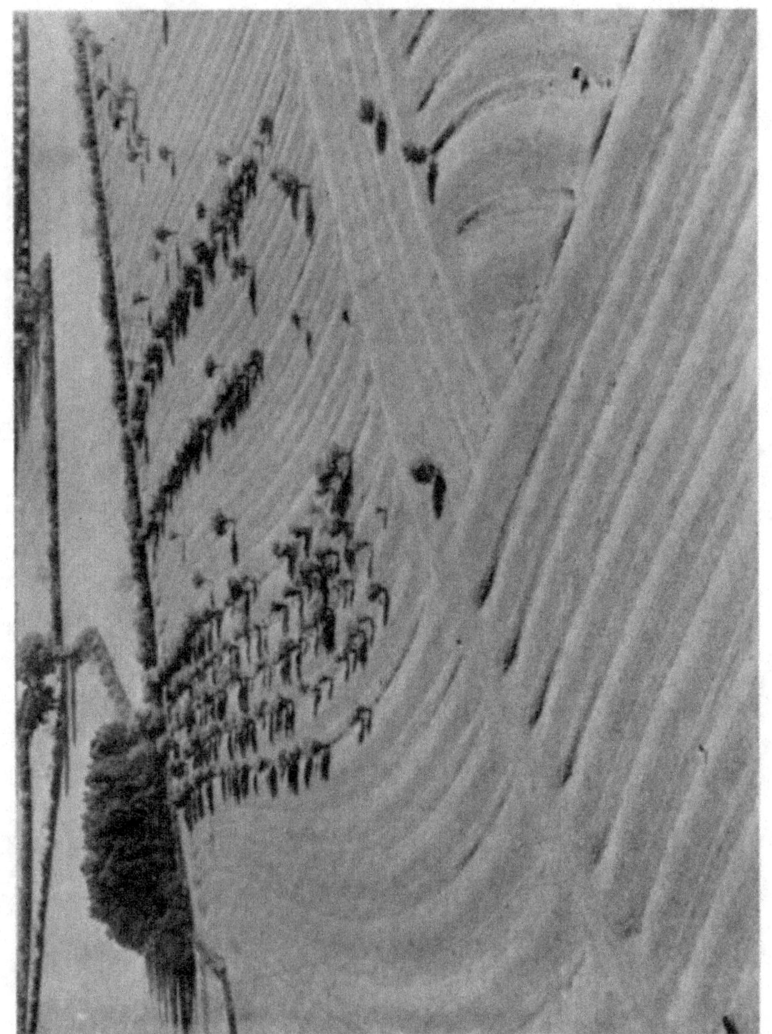

Grazing fields, showing pre-enclosure strips, balks and S-bends

difficult, conditions remained more primitive, and agriculture provided an individual and scattered occupation in which the maintenance of livestock played a major part. If feudalism came late into England, it was well established before the Norman conquest, and eventually reached, under the influence of the foreign invader versed in its principles, almost as high a state of development as it attained on the Continent.

Hereafter it is proposed to give some account of the systems of land tenure that existed from Norman times onward, and in this connection it must be borne in mind that, whatever modifications took place in the methods of holding land, the actual field operations remained for many centuries uninfluenced thereby; nor did economic upheavals, such as the Black Death, result in changes of practice—they merely caused a contraction or an expansion in the area of land devoted to the plough. It is scarcely an exaggeration to say that, until the tardy introduction of root-crops, followed by the enclosures of the eighteenth century, the methods of arable farmers had remained substantially unchanged from Anglo-Saxon times; the foundation of their practice was the three-course rotation, consisting of autumn corn (wheat or rye), spring corn (barley, oats, peas or beans) and bare fallow, although an earlier two-course rotation also survived in parts of the country. The efforts of livestock breeders have always been more appreciated by the bulk of the farming community than have those directed towards securing higher returns from land under the plough. Jethro Tull and Lord Leicester might, each in his own sphere, demonstrate the advantages accruing from the adoption of mechanical principles or from a study of soil conditions coupled with an adequate rotation, but for each convert that they made Bakewell or the Colling brothers, in their time, could secure ten. The reasons are not far to seek. Improved breeds of cattle and sheep were the achievement of "working" farmers, called for no application of fresh capital, and were free to spread throughout the countryside; new arable practices, at first almost the prerogative of "gentlemen" farmers, were accordingly assumed to be intended for landowners with money to waste; they depended upon a visit of inspection to obtain notoriety and even then did not at once bring conviction. The charge of conservatism so often in the past levelled against British farmers should properly have been confined to the arable side of their undertakings; thus, if, soon after the Restoration, they had adopted the new crops that were to hand, the face of the country would have been transformed more than a century earlier and the system of its tenure might have followed a different course.

This is perhaps a convenient point at which very briefly to expand, for the benefit of readers unfamiliar with it, the term "enclosure". The open fields, forming an integral part of the manorial system of cultivation and always undergoing some piecemeal amalgamation, were, at two widely sundered periods in our history, subjected to wholesale consolidation. The first movement, initiated by the shortage of labour after the Black Death, aimed at an expansion of grass at the expense of arable in order to reduce the costs of maintenance. After the factor in question had ceased to operate, the throwing together of strips continued upon a considerable scale throughout Tudor times, as it had become apparent that a larger output was possible upon enclosed land and that "Severalty" possessed numerous other advantages over "Champion" husbandry, but, even so, between the middle of the fifteenth century and the Civil War it has been estimated that only three-quarters of a million acres were enclosed; this land was confined mainly to the Eastern and South-Eastern counties.

The second, and by far the larger, movement (then already under way), was accelerated during the Napoleonic War by the demand for wheat and it accordingly abolished open arable fields by the million acres and at the same time led to the breaking up of the manorial commons and wastes, whereby severe hardship was admittedly inflicted upon many classes of small tenants. As much controversy has raged over the exact allocation of land ("allotments") subsequent upon this period of enclosure, the following extracts (taken from the 1877 *Report* of the Enclosure Commissioners) are now produced as evidence that compensation was wide-flung:

Since the Act (relating to enclosure) of 1845 was passed, nearly 600,000 acres of common and commonable lands have been dealt with. This has been divided amongst about 26,000 separate owners, in an average proportion of 44½ acres to each Lord of the Manor, 24 acres to each common-right owner and 10 acres to each purchaser of the lands sold to defray part of the expenses. Lords of Manors, to the number of 620, received, on an average, as compensation for their rights in the soil, about one-fifteenth of the acreage of wastes. As this is the largest and most general distribution of land into small properties that has taken

PLATE II

The Manor of Lower Heyford, Oxfordshire, in 1606

place in the country in recent times, it is of interest to know the quality and occupation of the persons into whose hands these lands have passed.

They were as follows: yeomen and farmers, 4736; shopkeepers and tradesmen, 3456; labourers and miners, 3168; esquires, 2624; widows, 2016; gentlemen, 1984; clergymen, 1280; artisans, 1067; spinsters, 800; charity trustees, 704; peers, baronets and sons of peers, 576; professional men, 512; various (including every possible type of person from the Crown to the domestic servant), 3000.

The Commissioners claimed that the influence of their work during a generation would be widely marked, for, by placing at the disposal of "individuals of intelligence" hitherto unproductive or waste land, they had appreciably added to the number of Small Holders; they had constructed over 2000 miles of roads and had redeemed at no cost to the public purse a total area of land equal to a county in extent; the value of this land they estimated at over £6,000,000, of which one-eighth had been devoted to purposes of public utility or convenience. Finally, they stated that 2,000,000 acres of "common land" (viz. almost entirely commons and wastes, as opposed to open-fields) still existed in England and Wales. For information relating to the actual procedure—legal and otherwise—followed when enclosure took place, readers are recommended to consult Lord Ernle's *English Farming Past and Present.*

Text-books, relating to both agricultural history and to general economics, have also devoted many pages to descriptions of the manor and of the gradual changes that it underwent, but, apart from sketches showing the holdings of an individual tenant, few have furnished photographic illustrations of the whole layout of an actual example, accompanied by an account of the different fields.

Maps alone have been occasionally published; a notable and little-known undertaking by J. L. G. Mowat, prepared and issued by the Oxford University Press in 1888, affords a striking example of the value in this respect of the contents of College muniment rooms, but as the work in question was confined to an edition of fifty copies its present rarity is not remarkable. The maps themselves number sixteen and illustrate seven different manors, the properties of Corpus Christi, Merton, Oriel and Trinity Colleges, Oxford. One of the oldest, that representing Lower Heyford, Oxfordshire, in the year 1606, appears facing page 34, the remainder illustrate the following manors in the same county, their dates being recorded in brackets—Whitehill, near Tackley (1605), Cowley (1605), Dean (1743), Chalford (1743), Cuxham (1767) and Wroxton (1768). Lower Heyford affords a good example of a typical manor and its surroundings, but as the bulk of the land had by the date in question fallen into the hands of two occupants, and the delimitations of furlongs and fields are not precisely recorded, its value is more antiquarian than economic.

Between pp. 38–39 will be found an illustration that calls for detailed description. The subject is the Manor of Rampton, Cambridgeshire, in the year 1754, the original map being now in the University Library at Cambridge. Rampton is a small village lying on the borders of the fen country, some eight miles due North of the University town, and would possess interest, if for no other reason than because of its adjacency to Cottenham, whose *Common Rights*, together with those of Stretham, were so fully described by the late Archdeacon Cunningham in a monograph published by the Royal Historical Society. The exact date of its subsequent enclosure is not recorded, but in the middle of the eighteenth century it provided an excellent example of all the features associated with the open field system of agriculture. Four arable fields existed, divided up, as the table on page 37 shows, into 46 furlongs (viz. "furrow long", or the length of land—generally *circa* 200 yards—normally ploughed without pause by a team of oxen) which were in their turn split up into over 900 strips. If comparison is effected between this map and the present day Ordnance Survey, it is still possible to trace the limits of these four fields, and the names also survive, Bellses having been corrected into Belsar's, while such designations as "The Snout" persist. Save in some four or five instances, however, enclosure has obliterated the boundaries of furlongs. The latter were disposed exactly in accordance with traditional requirements, and exhibit some quaint nomenclature, as for example "The Taughts", the derivation of which is obscure. There is even provided a gore, designated Huntington; this will be found occupying an awkwardly shaped site in Brook Field just above Britch Furlong.

The individual strips exhibit that universally met with feature—an S or double bend—that tradition associates with the outward movement conveyed to the plough as the leader of a long team of oxen was turned on reaching the head-land. So far as tenancy of the strips is concerned photographic reduction, from an original size of some 5 feet by 4 feet to that of an octavo page, has rendered the key provided almost illegible, so that a few words of explanation are called for. Fifteen tenants occupied the arable land, whose individual holdings (separately coloured on the map itself) ranged from 112 strips down to a single strip. In addition, the manor retained certain lands, and also let other manorial strips to tenants, whilst the church was provided for in the plough-land as well as more liberally by facilities for grazing. In connection with these ecclesiastical holdings there is an unusual feature to record, for in Fenn Furlong, in Brook Field, there is a single strip divided vertically into two equal parts,

(*a*) ***Bellses Field***

Furlongs	Strips
The Furlong below Portway .	31
The droves	13
Burney's dole Furlong . .	30
The Furlong above Portway .	24
Little Burney's dole Furlong .	6
Rush Furlong lower shot .	34
Little Portway Furlong . .	11
Rush Furlong upper shot .	29
Millers Close Furlong . .	10
Mear Furlong . . .	34
	222

(*b*) ***Little Field***

Furlongs	Strips
Portway Furlong . . .	12
Pages Way Furlong . .	15
The Taughts	22
Lane Leys	7
Town End Furlong . .	23
Upper Portway Furlong .	13
Lower Lambcoat Furlong .	25
Upper Lambcoat Furlong .	18
Cooper's Furlong . . .	12
Northland Furlong . .	31
Great Handstaff Furlong .	12
Bird Furlong . . .	7
Long Furlong . . .	17
Bush Furlong . . .	21
	235

(*c*) ***Mill Field***

Furlongs	Strips
Town End Piece . . .	10
Dole Furlong . . .	8
Redland Furlong . . .	54
Sand Pits . . .	11
Little Handstaff Furlong .	33
Pages Furlong . . .	15
Hoe Furlong	23
Waterland Furlong . .	12
Moor Furlong . . .	33
Farther Furlong . . .	18
Blackpitts Furlong . .	8
	225

(*d*) ***Brook Field***

Furlongs	Strips
Turn Furlong . . .	21
Fenn Furlong . . .	17
Clay Furlong . . .	23
Sand Furlong . . .	10
Black Mill Furlong . .	44
Little Moor Furlong . .	16
Huntington Gore . . .	16
Britch Furlong . . .	40
Nether Home Furlong . .	14
Middle Home Furlong . .	23
Over Home Furlong . .	25
	249

Total Furlongs 46. Grand Total of Strips 931.

Meadows and Grass Fields

Brook Closes	**Long Furlong Piece**
Brook Piece	**Millers Close**
Paddock Dole Piece	**"Brickiln" Piece**
Over Home Piece	**Cole's Piece**
Pierces Close	**Northland Piece**
Moor Closes	**Hardwell Close**
Town Leys	**Crab's Close**
Moor Furlong Piece	**Champion Close**
Waterland Piece	**The New Meadow**
Mill Piece	**Great Homehill Close**
Hare Park	**Little Homehill Close**
Page's Close	**Hardwell Close**
Bush Close	**Ware Roods**
Great Handstaff Piece	**The Pitts**
Little Handstaff Piece	**Twelve Acre Park**
Dacer's Ditch Piece	**Twenty Acre Park**
The Lockspit	**Seven Acre Park**
Wildfire Roods	**Four Acre Park**

Common Lands

The Hempsal	**The Old Meadow**
The Farther Iram	**Rampton North Fen**
The Hither Iram	**The New Ground**
Hollyman's Ground	**Cow Common**
The Snout (and various detached greens in the village)	

one-half bearing the cross emblematic of church-land, the other being clearly labelled "Whore's Broad". The writer has nowhere else come across any subdivision, other than longitudinal, of a single strip in the middle of a furlong, and the juxtaposition of church property with that bearing such a title raises curiosity as to the possible explanation.

The allocation of the grass-land in Rampton also closely followed traditional lines, for numerous "closes" and "pieces" abounded on the one side of the village bordering the furlongs, whilst, on the other, larger "meadows" and portions of reclaimed fen-land afforded the equivalent of commons in an upland manor. The majority of the closes and pieces were reserved for the manor farm itself and for the use of its principal tenants, but the six "cottagers", apart from the considerable areas of land round their homes, also possessed exclusive rights over several enclosures of grass. Two charities—Luke Norfolk's and Langham's—were also represented; the church claimed nine grazing sites, the Glebe one; in addition, common rights appear to have extended over some twelve fields and fens. Among the latter will be noticed such unusual appellations as "The

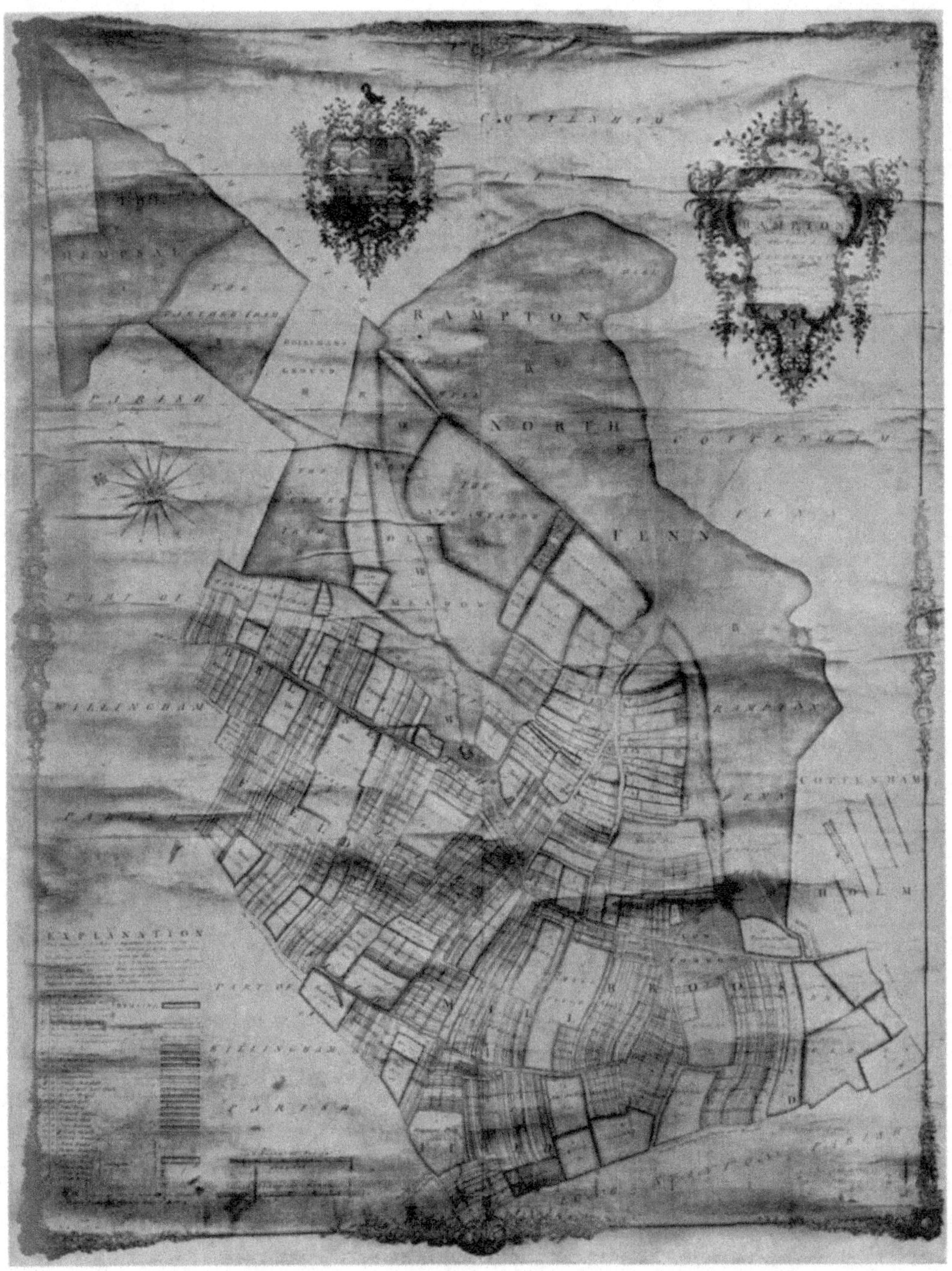

The Manor of Rampton, Cambridgeshire, in 1754

Hempsal" and "The Hither Iram" and "Farther Iram". It will be observed that the village itself displays those features that custom demands, for the manor farm and the church are found at one end of the street and a common, flanked by the dwellings of the cottagers, is evidenced near to the centre of gravity. The majority of the roads were obviously "green", for the lettering on the map apportions the grazing rights over them, but they are all still traceable at the present time, in most cases having been metalled.

Familiarity with the economy of the farming involved is necessary before any judgment can be formed of the systems under which it was practised. Enclosure had, by 1860, swept away, together with Rampton, all save a few of the open-fields in this country, but, before describing the present appearance of the three principal survivals, it may be of interest to quote the following description of another that has disappeared in quite recent times.

The open-fields of Castor and Ailsworth lay a few miles West of Peterborough, and were thus referred to by an Assistant Commissioner of the Board of Agriculture in his *Report on Northamptonshire* to the Royal Commission of 1893.

The 4865 acres arable and pasture are divided into about 5000 different plots, but they are all in the occupation of fourteen farmers. There is a map of the "fields" but no guide to it. The farmers trust entirely to memory, instinct, and the knowledge possessed by the labourers reared on the spot. The labourers recognise the plots by the variety of crop growing, the character and style of the cultivation, occasionally the distance from some untilled spot or landmark. It has happened before now that, on the death of some well-informed labourer, certain plots were completely lost, at any rate they could not be identified by the rightful owner, and no doubt accidentally went to swell up the acreage of a neighbour. At Castor we have fourteen farms occupying an average of 347 acres apiece, each farm broken up into an average of 350 particles. There are four arable fields: (*a*) for corn after clover; (*b*) for turnips, potatoes, or fallow; (*c*) for corn after roots or fallow; (*d*) for clover after corn. After the harvest the whole of the corn stubbles and young seeds are "open", and the stock roams at large. Every occupier of a cottage having a common right attached has the power to put two cows, one calf, and ten sheep on the "open" land during the autumn and early winter months, free of charge. A common right may be hired for one year, price ten shillings. In consequence of this extraordinary system, the fourteen farmers are forced to farm on the same rotation; should any of them sow a catch crop in autumn on the stubbles, the stock of the commoners have full liberty of access unless the plot is specially fenced off for the time being. During the "open" time there can be no such thing as "trespass" on the corn or seed fields. A badly farmed plot damages those near to it by seeding it with weeds, and one careless or failing farmer may, by his misdeeds, defeat the plans and destroy the prospects of the rest of the fraternity.

After perusing the above account, it will be agreed that Castor open-fields, with their five thousand strips, presented a far larger problem to those entrusted with their enclosure than had such villages as Rampton; the operation was, as a matter of fact, carried out in 1898, when the largest example of "Champion" husbandry in these Islands was swept away. Whilst the Commissioner was perfectly correct in making the above strictures upon the methods of farming involved by such a form of tenure in modern times, yet it is apt to be overlooked that under mediaeval conditions there were present certain countervailing influences. For instance, security of tenure was assured, and the very contiguity of the strips facilitated that co-operative labour and use of implements and beasts so essential if seasonal operations were to be carried out expeditiously. Large holdings, made up of these intermingled strips, held under leases would represent grave anachronisms at the present day but, as will shortly be shown, the same disabilities do not necessarily apply in the case of the peasant proprietors found elsewhere.

The Isle of Axholme in Lincolnshire, bordered on the East by the river Trent and on its remaining sides by the Thorne, Idle and Don, extends to some thousands of acres and includes within its boundaries the villages of Epworth, Haxey, Owston and Belton, in each of which are found hundreds of acres of land, hedgeless, and divided into the accustomed strips. But the analogy with Castor ceases at this point, for these "selions", to give them their old name, are in the ownership or the occupation of numerous small farmers, and no fixed course of rotation is called for, since enclosure technically took place many years ago, so that, as a consequence, the appearance of the land is totally different from that which is seen when open-field tenure survives in the hands of large tenants. As the photographs facing pp. 44 and 46, taken in 1922, clearly show, the diversity of crops conveys the impression of urban allotments or of fields in Northern France seen from an aeroplane rather than of English agriculture. One strip will be growing barley, the next potatoes or oats, then perhaps wheat or roots will appear, flanked by some vegetable crop, followed again by more cereals. They invariably exhibit the S bend, but, owing to the absence of balks, have in the course of time deviated from what must have been their original width of 5½ yards. Constant sale, and the resultant throwing together of adjacent plots, has also doubtless been effective, for measurements nowadays reveal widths varying from less than 5 yards to over 30.

In this connection it may not be widely known that a reasoned explanation of the length of the cricket pitch has been put forward by antiquarians, based upon that familiar agricultural unit, the acre, or a day's ploughing, varying with soil conditions but generally measuring 220 yards by 22 yards—the latter, of course, representing four divisions, each a pole (derived from the ox-goad and measuring 5½ yards) in width. It is suggested that the evolution was, briefly, as follows. Village lads were in the habit of setting up clods of earth on one balk and throwing stones at them from the next; in the course of time sticks took the place of the former and were defended in turn by the use of a larger block of wood. Then, on some particular occasion, an irate farmer descended on the participants in this game, and ejected them from his land. They, adjourning to the village green, continued their game, naturally setting up their stumps at the distance apart to which they were accustomed. Be this as it may, no book dealing with the history of cricket has attempted to account for the length of the pitch and, until another explanation is forthcoming, agriculture may legitimately claim to have had its influence in moulding the national game concurrently with determining the length of our unit of measurement—the "chain". The ubiquity of the acre of 220 × 22 yards is apparent by reference to almost any country in Europe. Thus, in a United States Department of Agriculture *Bulletin* (No. 1234 of 1924) Louis J. Michael describes and illustrates an Austrian common field in the possession of 34 tenants, which comprised 693 strips, "of an acre each", whose average length was actually 667 feet and average width 67 feet!

Many varieties of soil are to be found in the Isle, from the richest warp-land to strong clay, but the small farmers have naturally tended to congregate upon the best and most easily worked examples. Whilst the average size of a holding is very small, certain owners farm up to fifty acres or so, divided up into plots averaging perhaps a fraction of an acre each, thus disguising the fact that numerous scattered strips still present their economic problems. The exigencies [illegible] exhibit this trend, but, owing to the absence of [illegible] ... in the course of time deviated from what [illegible] have been their original width of [illegible] yards. [illegible] sale, and the gradual throwing together of adjacent plots, have also doubtless been effective. Recent measurements [illegible] reveal that the varying width [illegible] yards to over [illegible].

In this connexion it may not be without interest that [illegible] explanation of the length of the acre, which has been put forward by [illegible], based upon that [illegible] ... of a day's ploughing, [illegible] ... conditions being generally ... 220 yards by 22 yards [illegible] of course, represents four divisions, each pole ... upon the ox-goad ... (5½ yards) in width. It is suggested that the evolution [illegible] as follows. Villages [illegible] the [illegible] according to their ... one-half and three-quarters [illegible] ... the next ... of those ... took the place of the former and the addition of the use of a larger block of [illegible] ... conditions, a unit ... developed on the ... extended ... The village green, continued ... naturally ... the distance ... was ... with the ... of ... [illegible] the length of the ... [illegible] ... unit ... (No. 1284 of 1935) ... and the ... of ... which ... strips ... average length was ... and average width ...

Many varieties of ... are to be found in the ... from the ... were laid to ... but ... small farmers ... tended to congregate ... the best and most easily worked ... While the average size of a ... is ... small ... to fifty acres or so, divided up into ... the fraction of an acre each, thus ... the ... scattered strips still ... economic problem. The exigencies

PLATE IV

Portion of the Rampton Map, showing furlongs

respects. The owner or occupier of numerous detached strips certainly represents the *liber homo*, or the villein, of the manor; but the patchwork of crops gives an appearance to the landscape in no way resembling that which greeted the eye of the mediaeval traveller.

Laxton, in Nottinghamshire, lying some three miles West of the North Road, provides the only example still existing of the open-field system complete with its attendant rights of grazing and common. Here, at any season of the year, a casual glance at the landscape would fail to inform the visitor that anything abnormal surrounded him, for he would see large fields being prepared for, or bearing, cereal crops. Fundamentally, however, one is back in the Middle Ages. There are the three fields, Mill, South and West, under the traditional rotation of winter wheat, spring corn, and bare fallow; these are in the occupation, under the sole owner, Lord Manvers, of some twenty-five tenants, whose holdings vary from two to eighty acres. The soil is a strong marl, pre-eminently suitable for wheat growing, but offering few alternative possibilities when economic conditions are adverse. Here, then, is one of the practical distinctions to be drawn between Laxton and Axholme, and hence the absence of numerous Small Holders on the former, for there could be no refuge for them in vegetable production or in the raising of market-garden crops.

The explanation of the persistence of these open-fields at Laxton can be ascribed to the once dual ownership of the land in question between the Saviles of Rufford and the Pierrepont family, neither party being able to agree to the exchanges essential to enclosure; finally, at the beginning of the seventeenth century the Pierreponts secured complete ownership, and for generations have proved model landlords of this unique property, from their generous expenditure upon which they can have received but a very small pecuniary return. Within living memory certain consolidation of strips has, at great expense, been effected, and limits have been placed upon the access of sheep to individual fields, but substantially the grazing rights over both the stubble and the commons exist in their original form. Juries were annually appointed at the Court Leet, whose duties, *inter alia*, comprised the imposition of fines upon tenants who broke the rules in regard to stocking or omitted such duties as the cleaning of dykes. The pindar, by ringing the church bell, notified the village when, on the conclusion of harvest, the two fields were open for the admission of livestock. No less than 312 "gait rights"—the privilege of running sheep and cattle—exist, and in addition there are 104 common rights; the bulk of both belong to the landlord, but the former, of course, originally appertained to the occupation of land and the latter still go with the occupancy of particular cottages. In addition, certain small pieces of grass exist in the three arable fields, of which the rights of cutting are put up to auction each July, the sum received being divided among the owners. For a fuller account of these, and similar customs in the neighbouring village of Eakring, readers are referred to G. Slater's *English Peasantry and the enclosure of the common fields*. About the year 1850 the inhabitants of Laxton were described as "very rude and ignorant", the aim of the more thrifty freeholders being to sell their lands and to become tenants, thus obviating the otherwise inevitable subdivision of their properties. At the present time they are of course indistinguishable from any other agricultural community, and there appears to be no valid reason why their historical practices should not continue to exist, since they have survived all the vicissitudes which elsewhere have proved fatal to their counterparts.

Laxton, whilst fulfilling most of the requirements of the mediaeval manor, yet lacks the numerous balks that would have obtruded themselves between the furlongs in the arable fields of, say, Rampton, and the very homogeneity of the crops fails to convey the impression of scattered holdings left on the mind by a visit to Axholme. But it is too much to expect to find in one and the same area examples of every bygone feature, and anyone desiring to see balks in abundance need only traverse the Southern parts of Cambridgeshire or the North-Eastern quarter of Hertfordshire where, although enclosure has technically and legally overrun the country, yet physically it is non-existent, and the place of hedgerows, as boundaries between individual fields, is still supplied by these earthen ridges. The illustration facing p. 64 shows a typical example near Royston, where the whole countryside is devoid of any other form of division, and even the pedestrian on the road is only separated from the growing crops by a bank that a single stride will surmount.

Although enclosure had run its much smaller course at an early date in the West of England, there is yet one place in Devonshire where a remarkable survival of a common-field can be found. At

PLATE V

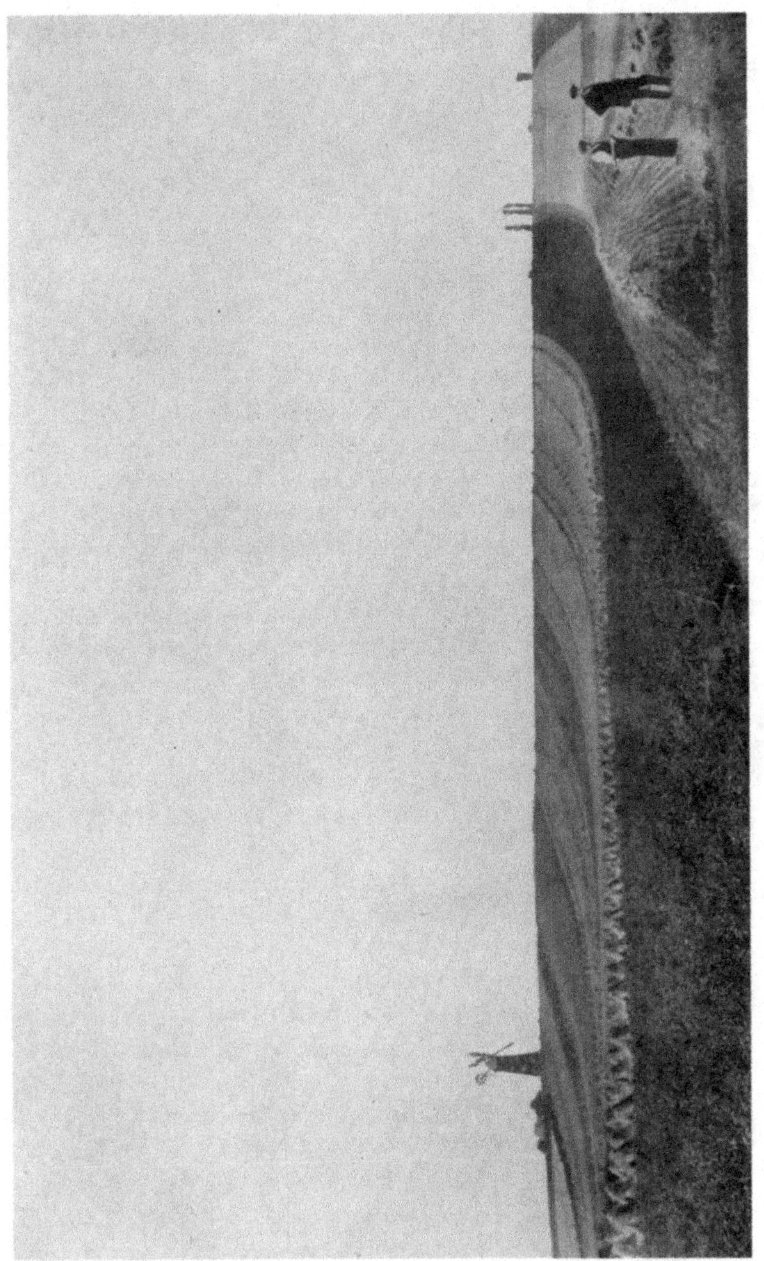

Epworth, Isle of Axholme

Braunton, a few miles from Barnstaple, the "Great Field" still provides approximately 300 separate plots, each of which is called a "land". The small area of some of these can be adjudged from the following announcement of a sale appearing in a local paper in 1923: "Lands in Braunton Great Field: Nos. 530, 987, Lower Croftnor 1 a. 2 r. 34 p., no. 759, Gallowell, 1 r. 14 p., no. 942, Pitland 2 r. 1 p., no. 669 Venn-pit, 3 r. 29 p." The Great Field itself is bordered by certain smaller fields which bear indications of having once formed part of it. This is borne out by a statement recently made by a very old Braunton inhabitant that within his memory adjacent hedges had been pulled down so as to bring once more former enclosures within the confines of the Great Field, thus affording striking evidence of the disadvantages attendant on small tillage-fields. It is noteworthy that the "lands" are generally divided by balks, known in Devonshire as "landsherds", and that the 16 furlongs are delimited by stones sunk in the ground. In the illustration facing page 58 will be seen several of these "landsherds", running at different angles. Common rights of grazing are now non-existent, and the appearance of livestock in the field is, therefore, limited to a few sheep hurdled on separate plots; cropping is no longer subject to the dictates of any universal rotation, and, as the soil is fertile, satisfactory returns are secured from widely diverse crops. Tradition, however, correctly refers to a not far distant period when a three-course rotation was practised, the sequence being wheat, barley, potatoes—the latter taking the place of the more normal bare fallow. At the time in question it is said that the field was used as grazing ground for a month or so after that great local event, Barnstaple Fair. Readers interested in this particular survival will find an excellent description of it, accompanied by a plan, in the *Transactions of the Devonshire Association* for July, 1889. There the area of the field was stated to be 354 acres, comprising 491 "lands" in the hands of 56 owners.

The above solitary example of a common-field in the South-Western peninsula raises the question how far the size of certain of the existing fields in Devonshire was determined when they were enclosed. W. Marshall suggested that the enormous dividing hedgerows were multiplied for the purpose of securing timber; other explanations have been that the land was so valuable that subdivision was carried to great lengths, or that shelter for cattle, combined with barricades against human aggression, was the object in view. Whatever the causes may have been, the average field is some four or five acres in extent, instead of the ten to twenty found elsewhere in England, and there is no doubt but that such parcels of land form a serious obstacle to efficient arable farming. Calculations have frequently been made to show that the direct loss of space from the excessively wide banks and hedges alone amounts to some 6 per cent. of the farming area, and, if the further loss caused by shade is included, this figure may be increased to anything from 10 to 20 per cent. Added to this is the handicap entailed by the use in these fields of abnormally small implements, and the sheer inability to introduce certain types of machinery into them. Whether it will ever prove a paying venture to throw two or three together must depend upon the particular circumstances of each case, but the relatively small amount of enclosure in this part of the country was perhaps carried out too severely, even when every allowance is made for the value of shelter on hill-sides swept by ocean storms.

In Ireland, "Rundale", and, in Scotland, "Runrig", were the terms applied to open-field farming, and examples of both survived in certain localities until recent times. Thus, Mackenzie of Gairloch within the last few years terminated the practice whereby grass-land was subject to annual division by string measurement, and in Torridon a chauffeur (of all anachronisms!) possessed a holding of thirty-six strips of land, none of which was contiguous. Although since abolished, it was held by competent authorities that, up to its end, Runrig resulted in heavier crops being produced than crofters in separate occupation could accomplish.

Of Rundale, the Rev. Caesar Otway, writing in 1841, thus describes the incidence in Achill and Erris:

> The farms under the landlord are held in common, as respects both tillage and pasture. In the land appropriated to tillage, each head of a family casts lots every year for the number of "ridges" (the local name for the strips) he is entitled to, and he is restrained from tilling those ridges in any other way, or under any other rotation than that of his neighbour. Moreover, the ridges change ownership every third year, a new division taking place. The head of the village, entitled "the king", originally the "Caunfiney", makes the division as equal as possible, requiring each man to cast lots for his ridge, one in a good field, another in an inferior, and another in a worse.

Two views of Haxey, Isle of Axholme

This latter custom represents a survival of practices that, in the case of arable land, had nowhere else persisted into modern times in these Islands. Achill, Otway declared, provided an unexampled instance of "that system which, before the English Conquest, prevailed all over Ireland; indeed, I consider that anyone who had the curiosity to become acquainted with the habits, the manners, the superstitions, the vices, the virtues, and the rural economy of the Ancient Irish, would find it still the best place for his enquiry; for I am convinced the people five years ago were in the very same state that they were one thousand years ago". It was with the reorganisation of such practices that some of the principal work of the Congested Districts Board was concerned, for in Achill and elsewhere Rundale existed until recent years. Facing p. 54 will be seen an illustration of one of these estates prior to being successfully "restripped". In another example, referred to in one of its *Reports*, the Board discovered that twelve tenants were paying a total rental of £14. 6*s*. 8*d*. for the occupation of 276 detached strips; these were consolidated into forty-six plots, but, as is always the case, the expenses incurred were heavy and not fully susceptible of translation into rent.

Historically, it is interesting to record that the early settlers in North America introduced this system of minute subdivision in order that all cultivators should have equal opportunities of access to the richer, or more easily worked soils, to water and to grazing. The system has, indeed, been universal amongst all races and in all climates. In pre-war Russia the open fields, lying apart from the villages (see illustration facing p. 96), were tilled by the community, while the non-application of manures made inevitable an uneconomic bare fallow. So it is, too, in the Far East and, in fact, in all countries wherein cultivation of arable land has been based upon equality of access, generally supplemented by co-operative labour. The difficulties inherent to the system have been frequently aggravated by customs in regard to succession, which in the course of a few generations have perforce brought about outside intervention for the purposes of restripping and consolidation. This situation has, in recent decades, come to a head in such widely sundered countries as France and Japan, Switzerland, Austria and certain South American Republics, where, in each case, the State has been compelled to rearrange and enlarge the dwindling and scattered units of production. Thus, the modern counterpart of "enclosure" runs its economic course, to the betterment of both agricultural and social conditions, but it is by heavy outlay upon the part of the community at large that "morcellement" and strips are diminished. Yet, the allocation of arable land, held in common, still persists in many parts of the world. In Japan, for example, may be seen a feudal survival of this practice, for, in the "township" of Namori, three villages divide up seventy-four acres every eight or ten years. Heads of houses, who pay taxes, are qualified to participate on one of three different bases: (*a*) by ensuring, irrespective of area, that each holding shall have the same productive outturn; (*b*) by equal division of the land; (*c*) by regard to shape and accessibility of the plots. (Iku Okuda, *The land allotment system of Japan.*)

Survivals of systems of land tenure, in so far as arable cultivation is concerned, have been briefly examined, but it must be remembered that, when stripped of their historical associations and deprived of their rights and their obligations, such examples can afford no criterion as to the economics or the amenities of their prototypes. The study of land tenure, however, calls for familiarity with the appearance and layout of the latter, and actual examples provide the best object lesson. Something can be gleaned from each type; indeed, it is necessary mentally to place the Hertfordshire balks between every group of Axholme strips, and then to add the three-course rotation of Laxton, together with the latter's rights of grazing and common, in order to complete the picture of the farmer's rights, duties and customs in bygone ages. Even then the all-important question of his former relationship to the owner of the land evades analysis. But, before dealing with that side of the problem, there remains for consideration the question of access to non-arable land.

Grass-land was divided up into three classes—first, the meadows in the particular occupation of individuals; second, those "Ings", or fields yearly subject to division from a certain date in February or March until Midsummer (but sometimes going with corresponding arable holdings) and, lastly, the commons. The first present no features of particular interest, but the second and third provide grounds for considerable research on the part of the local historian. For the former of these two a hitherto unpublished account of the exact allocation of the annual rights in a Yorkshire parish can throw light on what was frequently a very complicated procedure. The

PLATE VII

Laxton in March, 1923—the winter corn field

Rev. Charles Daubuz, vicar of Brotherton, in the year 1701, drew up the following exact description of the methods then employed to apportion the Ings in his parish; the original manuscript was copied by a successor in 1773, to which year the names of the holders recorded below refer.

BROTHERTON INGS

I. The By Law men and others are to meet on Vicar's Hill to draw lots after this manner. Three small sticks marked with one, two and three nicks are put into a Bunn. The stick marked with one nick is for the Lord; with two nicks for the Bishop; and with three for Peter Liberty. The Bunns are laid upon a long stick, and the first stranger that passeth by may be stopt to take them up. According to the order they are taken up, so they begin to measure that year, viz. if the stick with three nicks be taken the first, then Peter Liberty begins at the Tythe Piece, and so the rest go on as they be taken up.

II. The shorter rod is just sixteen feet long, and the long rod is two inches more.

III. The placing of the rods in measuring from the Tythe piece is as followeth.

1. The short rod at the upper end, or river side, from the Tythe Piece to Curty's Acre.
2. The long rod at the upper end in measuring long of the upper Lowance and short of the upper Lowance.
3. The short rod at the upper end in Bradmire's, short and long of the Ings' end.
4. The long rod is next the hedge in the short Lowance, and they begin from Bradmire's backwards.

IV. At the far and long Doles allow on measuring each rod only half a foot breadth.

At the long of the upper Lowance to the end of the Ings allow a foot breadth every rod.

At the short Lowance, at the end of each rod allow a whole foot length.

V. In the end of each Doal allow as followeth. Three foot at the end of Peter Dole, one foot and a half at the end of Bishop Hold, and only the common allowance at the end of the Lord's Dole.

Note, that lest the lower end of the Ings should be overrun by those who might get their hay very forward at the upper end and Tythe Piece, they begin to measure at first from the Long acres to the Ings end, and sometime after they measure out the far Doals and long Doals.

Quantity of Land in Brotherton Ings

	a.	r.	p.
Tithe Piece contains 24 rods	6	0	0
Far Doles ,, 23½ rods	5	3	20
Long Doles ,, 47 rods	11	3	0
Great Acres ,, 20 rods	5	0	0
Long Doles of Upper Lowance contains 23½ rods	5	3	20
Short Doles of Upper Lowance ,, 23½ rods	5	3	20
Bradmire's contains 47 rods	11	3	0
Long Doles of the Ings end contains 23½ rods	5	3	20
Short Doles of the Ings end ,, 23½ rods	5	3	20
Nether Lowance or Short Lowance contains 40 rods	10	0	0
Total	73	3	20

Besides these acres there is also the Bull piece and St Marie's Pieces, one of which lies at the end of the Ings and the other at the end of the Nether or Short Lowance belonging to the Bylaw men for their care and trouble.

Each person's quantity of land in the Ings and the number of their pasture gates

		a.	r.	p.	Pasture gates
The Lord	hath	21	0	20	18
Francis Crowder	,,	8	1	0	12
John Dickinson	,,	6	3	20	11
William Webster	,,	2	3	0	2
The Vicar	,,	3	3	20	6
Richard Green Esq.	,,	1	1	20	4
Sherburne School	,,	3	1	20	—
John Trickley	,,	1	2	0	2
William Sampson	,,	1	0	0	—
Mr Thompson	,,	4	1	20	6
Thomas Wilkes	,,	4	0	0	7
William Making	,,	1	1	20	2
Thomas Catton	,,	0	1	0	—
Dan. Gilson's heirs	,,	1	1	20	1
Samuel Scot	,,	0	2	20	1
Mr Haxby	,,	4	2	0	6
George Wilkes	,,	1	1	20	1½
John Longstaff	,,	1	0	0	2
Thomas Gilson	,,	1	2	20	3½
William Sharpe	,,	1	0	0	2
Michael Hallilay	,,	2	0	0	3
	Total	73	2	20	90 gates
M. Hallilay, T. Wilkes and T. Gilson have among them		0	1	0	6 overgates to repair the pasture dykes
	Total	73	3	20	96 in all

PLATE VIII

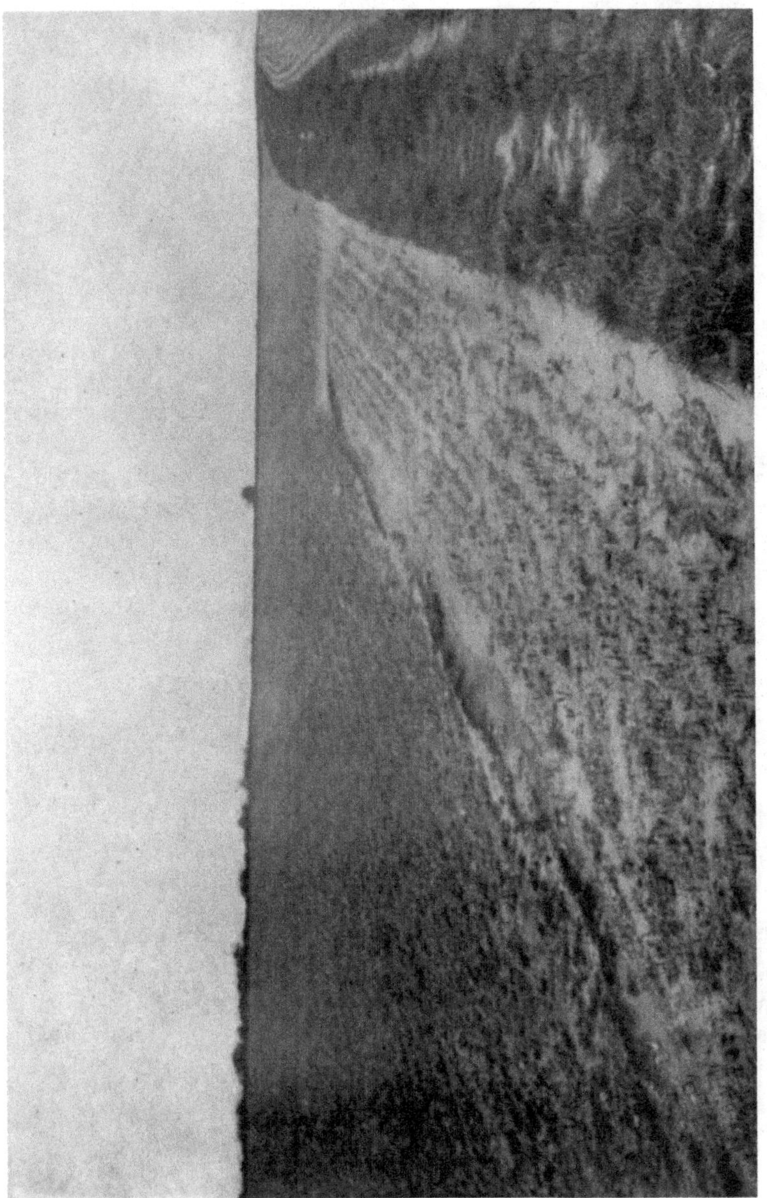

Laxton in March, 1923—the spring corn field

Lack of space precludes any reproduction of the complete distribution of these rights, but the arrangement of one Ing (see overleaf) will serve as an example of the rest, being extracted from "A true and perfect copy of the Terrier of the meadow Land within the Townships of Brotherton, called Brotherton Ings, divided by lots and possessed in the year of our Lord, 1773".

A few words of explanation are required in regard to certain terms and expressions in the foregoing transcripts. By Law men, more commonly spelt Byrlaw, were the chosen representatives of the parish, whose duties comprised this annual distribution and measurement of the Ings, their reward, as was shown, consisting of certain special plots of the land in question. A "bunn" was the bag formed by the folding of a cloth or napkin. "Gates" have already been referred to as existing at Laxton. Whilst the purpose served by the three sticks is plain, the exact origin of the nomenclature of two of them is not apparent. Peter Liberty and The Bishop invariably formed the two larger divisions to be split up between the ordinary gate holders, The Lord's reserves never admitting other occupants. Peter Liberty practically always represented twice as much accommodation as did The Bishop. Each year, of course, the relative sequence of the three divisions was maintained in every Ing, the purpose of the annual selection by lot being to ensure that the better portions of the meadows did not remain constantly in the same hands. A contemporaneous note adds the information that "5½ rods of meadow go to an oxgang in the Ings", and also "5½ yards of fencing to an oxgang".

Such an elaborate undertaking, which, in its final stages, involved the erection of temporary fences, is in these days of "several" husbandry wholly unnecessary for the purpose of securing an equitable division of hay, but throughout the Middle Ages access to grass in any shape had been a most cherished right, and one not lightly to be let fall into abeyance, as this record of only 160 years ago clearly demonstrates.

A very similar custom, still followed in the Oxfordshire village of Yarnton, was described by R. H. Gretton in *The Economic Journal* (1910, p. 39, and 1912, p. 53). There the meadow in question, some seventy acres in extent, is likewise subject to annual division. The strips, except those peculiar to tithe-owners, which are indicated by stones "almost as big as tombstones", are marked by rows of wooden

The Far Doles, 23½ rods	Peter Liberty, 12 rods	1 rod belonging to Forster Thompson
		2 ,, ,, ,, Mr John Haxby
		1 ,, ,, ,, Mr Webster
		1½ ,, ,, ,, the Vicar
		1½ ,, ,, ,, Richard Gilson
		½ ,, ,, ,, Sam Scot
		½ ,, ,, ,, Mr Webster
		1½ ,, ,, ,, Mr Dickinson
		½ ,, ,, ,, Thos Gilson
		½ ,, ,, ,, Rich. Green Esq
		1½ ,, ,, ,, Mr Crowder
	Bishop, 7 rods	½ ,, ,, ,, Geo. Wilkes
		1 ,, ,, ,, Mr Dickinson
		4 ,, ,, ,, late Fothergill
		1½ ,, ,, ,, Sherburne School
	The Lord, 4½ rods	4½ ,, ,, ,, The Lord

PLATE IX

Laxton in March, 1923—the fallow field

posts. Lots are drawn from a canvas bag by means of thirteen small balls designated again by personal names—Water Jeoffrey, Water Molley, Perry, Harry, Dunn, Rothe, Gilbert, Boat, White, Green, Freeman, Boulton and William. We read that

each portion, or "shot", of the meadow contains thirteen strips, corresponding with the number of balls. Each ball represents a right to mow the grass of one lot, and a subsequent right of pasture, and is either owned by some farmer in virtue of his farm, or bought, whole, or in portions of a right, from an owner of rights. Consequently, when the meadsman with the canvas bag, standing by the first post, holds it out to one of the company—if a lady be there as a spectator she will be courteously asked to draw—and the ball is drawn, the name on the ball is called out, and the question asked, "Whose is that?" The owner speaks up, and the other meadsman, who has a notebook in his hand, writes down the name.

Thus, each of the headlands in this T-shaped meadow is disposed of and every owner has three strips scattered in different portions of it. As the distribution takes place in July, the individual ownership is, for a brief period of time, revealed to the eye by the subsequent mowing operations.

Inhabitants of many old towns in this country have to walk but a short distance to find an example of the third type of grass-land—viz. the commons. In Cambridge, for example, there are no less than nine of these, not only surviving as open spaces, but carrying with them their ancient and exclusive rights. Typical entries in an official enumeration are as follows:

Coldham's Common (98 acres). For geldings, mares and cows from Old May Day to Old Candlemas Day.

Sheep's Green (22 acres). For sheep of freemen all the year; for cows of St Botolph and St Mary the Less all the year on Sundays, Wednesdays and Fridays, from sunrise to sunset.

In addition, the same town possesses no less than six separate areas of Lammas or "half-year" land, commonable in two cases from July 6th to April 6th, and, as to the rest, from August 12th to the same day in April. These very dates themselves show the antiquity of the rights they safeguard, and the tenacity of the latter was strikingly demonstrated in 1922 when a special Act of Parliament was required to terminate the rights over a portion of the Lammas land required, not for purposes of private development, but as a public recreation ground.

The more ubiquitous commons and the much rarer traces of open-field cultivation thus afford present-day evidence of what was once the universal system of combined husbandry and land-tenure. Close observers of the countryside, however, will find signs of the work of other ages confronting them in every village of the land, and, if they will ascend by aeroplane over the Southern Counties, they will see below them, in a clear chequer-board, the prehistoric cultivations of the Village Communities—generally referred to as "Celtic and Saxon fields"—which, in recent years, Mr O. G. S. Crawford, Archaeology Officer to the Ordnance Survey, in particular, has demonstrated thus to reveal their boundaries through the superimposed operations of centuries. Ridged strips exist by the hundred thousand in almost all grass districts—on heavy land sometimes rising to a height of two feet between the furrows—whilst venerable trees growing athwart them show the period of time that must have elapsed since the plough was last active there. Small and irregular fields often demonstrate the enclosure of a handful of selions or of some odd gore. Rights of grazing cause additional value to attach to certain dwellings. Indeed, most English villages, by the wide diversity of soil types found within their boundaries, afford present-day evidence of that far-off time in their history when it was essential that all their inhabitants should have equal access to water, to woods, to grass and a similar share in the light and heavy soils. The honorary freedom of some ancient borough conferred upon a distinguished statesman or soldier mainly connotes the right to depasture cattle at certain seasons and on particular lands. The copyhold tenant, whose very appellation forms a reminder of the cataclysm of 1348, is a direct descendant of the villein. Inexorably, however, these reminders of the past disappear. So, in the winter of 1932, there were felled, to make way for new University laboratories, the famous "Maitland" thorns which grew on what had been a balk of St Thomas Leys, once an open field on the outskirts of Cambridge. These old trees were originally recognised by that legal historian, Prof. F. W. Maitland, as occupying this site and were, at his suggestion, accorded iron supports in their old age; but, alas, they could not indefinitely withstand the spread of modern developments. Their existence will be recorded by a plaque in the floor of the new building. Our French neighbours, more careful in these matters than ourselves, provide, in their *Usages Locaux*,

PLATE X

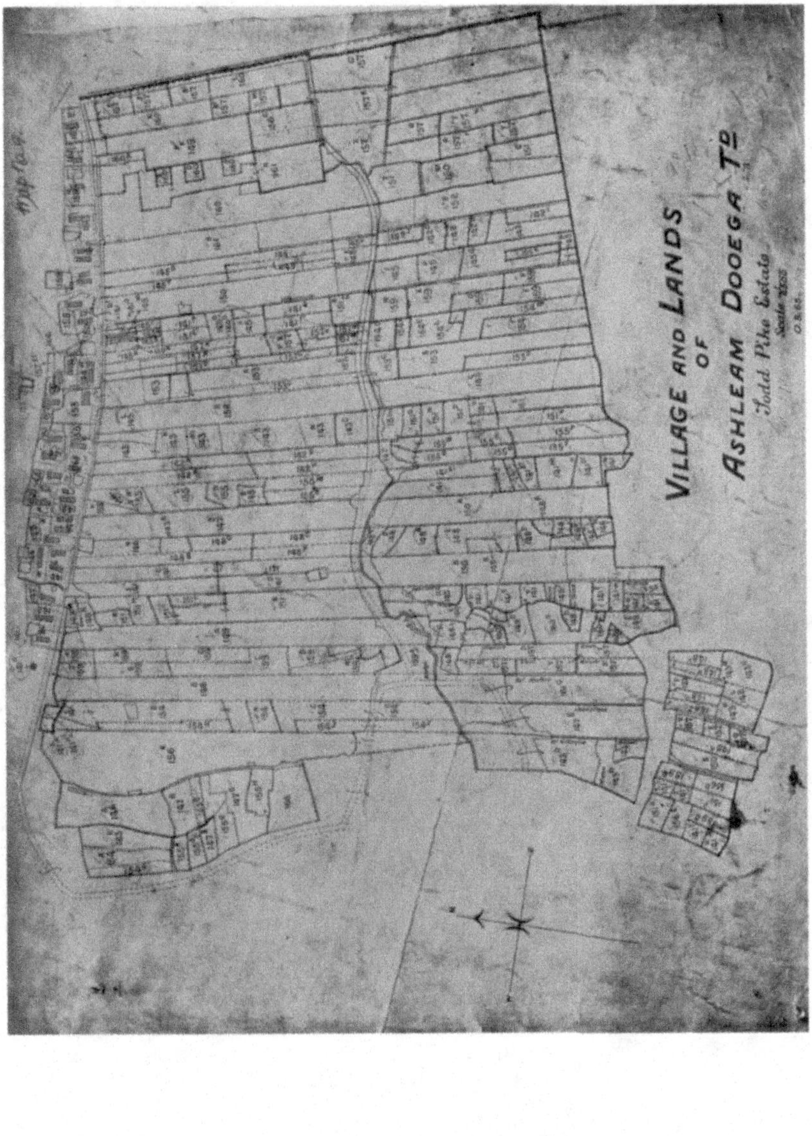

An example of Irish rundale

printed information relating to the former common-rights of nearly every village in Northern and Central France, where, too, the linches easily outnumber those to be seen anywhere in this country.

The personal, as opposed to the agricultural aspect of past forms of tenure calls for brief consideration. Numerous complete manor-rolls have been published, so that two or three extracts illustrative of the duties imposed on tenants will in these pages suffice. About the year 1375 in the parish of Westbourne, Sussex, a contemporaneous record (published in 1913 by J. H. Mee) ran as follows:

The Earl Marshall holds the manor of Stoghton by homage and rendering one soar hawk or half a mark. Also he holds land called Hurst by rendering one pound of pepper. Thomas Hokat for 4 virgates renders one pair of spurs or 6*d.* The same for a virgate of land called Aldwyne renders 12*s.* and 4 *li.* by way of relief [succession dues]. The tenant of the manor of Aldesworth renders one boarspear or 6*d.* The tenant of Whiteway renders 3*s.* and two pounds of pepper. The lord of the manor of Notborne renders 12*d.*

It is impossible to record in full the payments due from inferior tenants, but the following affords a typical example:

Richard Tanner for a messuage and five acres rendered 3/6, a hen, five eggs and two boonworks; he was bound to harvest oats for half a day, to weed for half a day, to do one day's carrying on foot, to make a hurdle out of withies provided by the Lord, to reap two and a half acres of wheat and barley and to move the hurdles of the lord's sheepfold.

Blount's *Tenures* will supply another example. Thus, the Knights of St John of Jerusalem had, at Newbiggin in Yorkshire, thirteen oxgangs of land, held as follows:

Baldwin held an oxgang for 2/0 and a half, and 2 hens, and 20 eggs and 4 days' work in autumn with one man, to plough twice, to harrow twice, to mow once, to make hay once and when there should be occasion, to repair the mill-dam, and draw and carry the millstones, and to wash sheep one day and another day to shear them. Bertram and Osbert, for 1 oxgang of land, paid 30*d.* and the aforesaid services, etc. And it is to be known that all the cottagers ought to spread and cock hay once, and to wash and shear the sheep and repair the mill-dam, as those which held an oxgang of land.

Whilst picturesque payments made by intermediate holders to their superiors are still occasionally leviable, kindred services by the humbler tenants of the manor were long ago commuted, perhaps the latest survival being provided by cottages held in part by "service" as late as the middle of the eighteenth century.

Before turning to the consideration of other forms of tenure, the functions of Manor Courts deserve some notice. The Courts themselves fell into two categories—Courts Baron and Courts Leet. The former were, in practice, associated with the social and cultivational relationship between Lord and tenant, the latter were, to all intents and purposes, Courts of Petty Session.

The Manor and Manorial Records by J. Hone will illustrate the intimate character of the relationship that existed between the Lord and his tenants, exercised in these courts through his representative, the steward. Thus, at Winterbourne in Berkshire, the suitors in the year 1493 presented that:

> William Barcoll, freeholder, hath closed his last day, who held of the lord certain lands by knight service. And they say that Alice and Sibell are daughters and next heirs of the said William. And that Alice is 5 years of age and not more. And that the aforesaid Sibell is 3 years of age and over. Upon this comes William Webbe and gives to the Lord a fine for the minority of the heirs, 3*s*. 4*d*.
>
> Also they present that the said William Barcoll held of the Lord, according to the custom of the manor the 3 messuages with their appurtenances, after whose death there falls to the lord by way of heriot a horse of a roan colour value 10*s*. And upon this comes the aforesaid William Webbe and takes of the lord the aforesaid 3 messuages with all their appurtenances. To have and to hold to him and Thomas and John sons of the said William for the term of their lives or of the one of them longest living, according to the custom of the manor there, by rent and other services therefrom aforetime due and of right accustomed.

Whilst it is doubtless true that the major portion of the duties of these Courts comprised the admission of tenants and the exaction of their dues, it is probable that the agricultural disputes coming under their jurisdiction excited more interest amongst the tenants themselves. Thus, a perusal of the findings of a Court in the fourteenth or fifteenth century will expose case after case of complaints that *A* has overburdened the common pasture with his sheep, that *B* has ploughed up a balk, or that *C* has appropriated two or three furrows of his neighbour's land. In later times the presentments assumed a more formal character, and references to individual delinquencies tended to disappear, but, right through the eighteenth century, such findings as these, culled from the records of the Dorsetshire village of Grimstone and printed in *The Marches of Wessex* (F. J. Harvey Darton), cropped up. "We present that Margaret Slowe hath a right to drive sheep and cattle to and from Grimstone Common to a close of meadow called Smithams over the currant (*sic*) called Muckleford Lake...and that Robert Wood and other the inhabitants of Muckleford have deprived the said Margaret Slowe of the way by enlarging the said currant about two foot wider than it antiently was" (1728).

Again, in 1753, the "tenants of this manor shall go out on the 6th day of March next and shall dig and drain the meadows for carrying off the water, under a penalty of 6/8 for everyone neglecting". And lastly, in 1781, "no pigs shall run about the streets or other commonable places of the said Liberty and Manor under penalty of 5/0".

As the manors slowly disappeared, their disciplinary and administrative work may be said to have devolved upon their modern substitutes, viz. the Parish Councils and the Courts of Petty Session, which can nowadays be considered as responsible for safeguarding those of the countryman's rights and privileges that have come down to him from remote periods of history. Copyhold having now been abolished, it may be of interest to record in more detail the method of holding a Court Baron in recent times.

In the winter of 1925, the following notice might have been seen prominently displayed in the Huntingdonshire village of Buckden.

Manor of Buckden Brittens.

Notice is hereby given, That the General Court Baron and Customary Court of Robert Holmes Edleston, Lord of the said Manor, will be held for the Manor aforesaid at the Palace Gatehouse, Buckden in the Parish of Buckden in the County of Huntingdon on Wednesday the thirtieth day of December at 5.30 of the clock in the afternoon, at which Court the Copyhold Tenants of the said Manor are required to attend to do and perform all such Suits and Services as to them shall severally appertain. And all manner of Persons claiming Title, and having to be admitted Tenants to any Copyhold Messuages, Lands or Tenements held of the Lord of the said Manor, are also required to attend the said Court to be admitted thereto.

Dated this 23rd day of December 1925.

(signed) GEORGE RICHARD GENT (Steward).

A few days later the present writer had the privilege of attending the Court, one of the last (owing to the then imminent abolition of copyhold tenure) to be held with such full ceremony. The following description from his pen subsequently appeared in *The Times*.

> Oyez, Oyez, Oyez! All manner of persons who owe suit and service to general Court Baron and Customary Court of Robert Holmes Edleston, now holden, who have been summoned to appear at this time and place, draw near and give your attendance, every man answering to his name as he shall be called, thereby saving his amercement. God save the King and the Lord of this Manor.

These words, spoken by the manor bailiff, inaugurated, for the last time, a ceremonial which had been observed for countless centuries in an East Anglian village. The occasion was the last day but one of the old year, the time evening, and the setting extremely picturesque, for, by the light of a full moon, we had assembled in the second-floor room of a red brick tower which once formed the gate-house of the adjacent, and now ruined, episcopal palace, where also Katharine of Aragon had lived for a time after her divorce.

Fourteen of us were present, the Lord himself, a most stately figure, the bailiff (who, in the absence of that official, acted as steward), and seven copyholders, the remainder comprising visitors privileged to witness the demise of a striking ceremony inextricably bound up with the legal and economic history of England. The Lord was seated at a table, with a Bible and various documents, including the Court Rolls, in front of him; the bailiff, gowned in black, stood at his right hand; the copyholders sat on one side of the candle-lit room, the spectators on the other; portraits looked down on the scene. The list of tenants was first called over by the bailiff, staff in hand; after each man present had answered to his name, they proceeded to elect a foreman, who was at once sworn in by the Lord in the following words:

> You, as foreman of this jury, with the rest of your fellows, shall diligently enquire and true presentment make of all such matters and things as shall be given you in charge or shall come to your knowledge presentable to this Court. The King's Counsel and your own you shall well and truly keep. You shall present nothing out of malice, nor leave anything unpresented out of love, fear, favour, reward, or affection, but in all things you shall well and truly present the same as it shall come to your knowledge. So help you God.

After a similar oath-taking by the jury, the actual business of the Court began, the niece of a deceased copyholder first being admitted

Two views of Braunton Great Field

to her holding. She was represented by "attorney", in the person of a male relative, who held one end of a magnificently carved staff while the Lord grasped the other.

Next, reference was made to the continued non-appearance of heirs to a certain acre plot of land, held under a fine of twopence, for whom proclamation had unsuccessfully been made as far back as 1884. The bailiff was ordered to descend to ground level and announce to the world at large the opportunity that still awaited it, but no claimants answered his, to us, faintly heard invitation. Some difficulty was experienced by the jury in recognising the piece of land in question, and, after the display of much local knowledge affecting ownerships and boundaries, the Lord undertook to circulate extracts from the Manor Rolls and himself to head a peripatetic inquiry.

The jury was then instructed to report any encroachments upon the Lord's property or upon the manorial waste, which resulted in reference being made to stones placed upon a certain green by the local parish council. Whereupon the Lord reminded the Court that it was competent to remonstrate even with such august bodies as this, and he emphasised the importance of safeguarding vigilantly the rights of the old against the new. As the manor lacked a Constable, the Lord requested the jury to elect one of themselves to this office, which, although a sinecure, gave to its holder, he assured the Court, powers of arrest stronger than those possessed by the village policeman. The mildest-looking of the jurymen was, after due deliberation carried on in undertones, chosen by his fellows and sworn into office.

There followed a most dignified address by the Lord, who explained, without recrimination, the provisions of the Law of Property Act, which in the space of thirty hours would sweep into the limbo of the past that Court, its officers, its ceremonies, and, finally, himself. He clearly set forth the procedure to be followed in each legal period of the coming years in the enfranchisement of copyhold land (even making kindly reference by name to Lord Birkenhead!), but he openly lamented that the future would permit only the holding of Courts Leet—mere empty shells of the past—bereft of ceremonial and impotent even as disciplinary bodies; he proposed, however, to convene these Courts so long as he was permitted so to do.

The final act was the formal closing of the Court by the bailiff, who utilised the same quaint phraseology as that in which he had opened it, his concluding words being a prayer for the preservation of the King and the Lord.

The lasting impression made upon the visitors was of the intense earnestness of the proceedings. The jury was, to a man, intelligent, and obviously took pride and interest in seeing that the Court was conducted in an orderly manner and according to precedent; the Lord himself was deeply steeped in the history of the past; it is hoped that the visitors, by their presence, did not detract from the setting. As we passed out once more into the modern world, represented by the Great North Road with its telegraph poles and brightly lit cars, leaving the tenants partaking of tea provided by the Lord on the ground floor of the tower, we felt sad to think that no such Courts would in future be held, and, pondering on the long line of bygone Lords, Stewards, Bailiffs, Jurymen, and Constables of which we had seen the last, and most worthy, representatives, we found ourselves repeating these words:

Oyez, Oyez, Oyez, God save the King and the Lords of all Manors.

Chapter III

MODERN LAND TENURE

Copyhold tenure; examples from the eighteenth and nineteenth centuries; the comparative values of lives; compulsory enfranchisement; the Acts of 1922 and 1924; preservation of manor records; leasehold in the past; the nature of rent; conditions brought about by agricultural depression; Tenant Right and Agricultural Holdings Acts; landlord's and tenant's capital; the value of agricultural land in England; suggested alternatives to leasehold; corn rents and profit-sharing; the Congested Districts Board in Ireland and the Crofters' Commission in Scotland; Land Courts; expropriation proposals; the scheme of Messrs Orwin and Peel.

Examples of former systems of tenure, as they affected the practice of agriculture and the amenities of the land, having been adduced in the previous Chapter, the more serious task of appraising their economic value and comparing them with alternative methods presents itself, but at the same time it is necessary, within the confines of such a work as this, to pass over the Constitutional and legal side of the problem, thus ignoring the restrictions imposed by, e.g., the Statute of Mortmain (1279), that of De Donis Conditionalibus (1285) and Quia Emptores (1290) upon the ownership of land and the repercussions of the fourteenth century legislation on the labourer's attachment and access thereto, together with the economic and social effects of primogeniture, of Borough English (succession of the youngest son) or of Gavelkind (equal inheritance of all children alike).

Copyhold and leasehold have, in the past, represented alternative forms for the occupation of land in this country. The former, evolved *via* the customary tenant, from the villeinage of the manor has, at its latter end, been declared to form the worst type of tenure that the laziness of man could invent. The latter, in its varying shapes, has, from its inception, presented the never ending problem as to what proportion of the capital required for the conduct of farming operations should be directly or indirectly provided by the landlord, and what time limits should be assigned to the occupation it granted. As copyhold, under the two recent Property Acts, has ceased to exist, pride of place must be accorded to it, with perhaps a word of explanation of the principles upon which it rested.

In this system of tenure comparatively large sums of money, the original "fines" of the manor, were rendered at uncertain intervals of time, being substituted for annual payments of rent. At first these fines were due, in various forms, from the successive heirs of customary tenants; in the passage of time, however, there occurred a cleavage into two distinct types—copyhold of inheritance and copyhold for lives or for years. The former of course represented the survival of the original conception, whilst the first of the latter implied the granting of tenure for a period covered, most frequently, by the lives of three persons. These might be members of the copyholder's own family or any named persons; Royalties and other well-known people were often thus selected. On the decease of one of the "lives" a fine was paid for the privilege of inserting a fresh name. The alternative, and rarer, form of "copyhold for years" simply represented a tenancy, granted generally for twenty-one years and renewable by fine every seventh year. "Leaseholds for lives" were almost exactly similar in principle, save that the rights of the tenant against the lord of the manor were better safeguarded in the former.

Whatever may have been the freedom afforded by it for a period of time, normal copyhold brought in its train considerable uncertainty as to the incidence of the prospective fines, and no certainty at all of ultimate renewal. The landlord received sums of money at irregular intervals, which in the aggregate might, or might not, amount to an economic rent, and concurrently he lost control over the upkeep of his property. The result was too often apparent when, after the failure to renew a life, estates fell into grave disrepair. Even during the last period the condition of the relatively few copyhold properties would have compared ill with similar leasehold or freehold estates.

The eighteenth century provided a time when this tenure had resolved itself into a series of calculations into the respective values of potential lives, which crystallised into tables published for the benefit of those concerned. Thus, in 1730, Edward Laurence, describing himself as a land surveyor, wrote "A dissertation on Estates upon lives and years whether in lay or church hands", wherein he emphasised the rather obvious fact that it was best either to keep copyholds full or else to let them run out completely. Further, in advocating the changing of copyholds for lives into leaseholds for lives, he remarked that such action would destroy the absurd custom of the "Widow's

Free bench" then existing in the West of England, and would bring tenants under proper covenants for keeping farms in a good state of husbandry. "Free bench", it should be explained, implied the continuation to his widow of the whole or part of the deceased's interest in the property.

Data were at that time available, which showed to a nicety the cost of adding lives, and the ages that presented the best expectations. A pamphlet entitled "The value of Church and College leases considered", which saw the light in 1729, whilst deprecating any sympathy with the methods that had led to the South Sea bubble, urged that the clergy, in times of general prosperity, should not be looked upon with contempt by other persons, but should be permitted a moderate increase in the fines they levied on tenants. For how many of the ten thousand clergy, the writer asked, had, in the last half century, left great estates, whilst lawyers, physicians and merchants were rising in wealth and standing, whose sons, also, "sparkled in their coaches and six"? Academic opinion naturally favoured this view, for the senior fellow of a College, the name of which is not recorded, upon "improvements" for the good of posterity being mentioned, burst out "We are always talking of doing for posterity; I would fain see posterity do something for us". The easier conditions generally enforced by clerical (and therefore by collegiate) landlords can be gauged when the comparative values published in one of the above-mentioned tables are investigated. For the privilege of adding one life in a church estate, where two existed, one and a half years' purchase was reckoned a fair demand; similarly, for changing a life a year's purchase should suffice, whilst five years was the figure suggested for adding two to one existing, and sixteen for granting a lease of three lives. The following warning was appended: "Note, age and infirmities of a third life ought greatly to be regarded"! On the other hand, lay owners were advised to demand two and a half years for adding one life to two, six years for augmenting one by another two, but sixteen was again the figure for issuing a lease for three lives. When the latter occasion arose, landlords were urged to include in the agreement stipulations against paring and burning the soil, ploughing up, sub-letting or selling off hay and straw that ought to be consumed on the holding; conclusive evidence of the powers that might be exercised by copyholders.

The openings for bargaining were, of course, unlimited, and, although owners held an overwhelmingly strong position, they were frequently cajoled into depriving themselves of large sums, as an actual example recorded some two hundred years ago shows. A clergyman let certain property on a copyhold tenancy for three lives. Almost immediately one life failed, and the tenant refused an offer to renew at one year's rent (£600). A second life then went equally unexpectedly, and, after much argument, the owner was persuaded to accept £1000 for renewal of the two, and at the same time to suffer a fresh life to be substituted for the third, which was obviously looked upon as of doubtful validity. Even further, permission to change a life at any time on payment of £50 was extracted. It was demonstrated that, in all, the owner thus lost some £2450, reckoning only five years' rent for the two lives renewed and £500 for the value of the change.

Various abuses, more often adversely affecting the tenant, were bound to occur when modern conditions were approaching, and, after a bill to compel enfranchisement had come to nothing in 1835, a Select Committee was appointed to enquire into the whole position of copyhold. Three years later its *Report* was circulated, the position being thus summarised: "This tenure is ill adapted to the wants of the present day and is a blot on the judicial system of the country. The peculiarities and incidents of copyholds (which have their origin in the villeinage of the feudal system) are at once highly inconvenient to the owners of the land and prejudicial to the general interests of the State". The Committee added that valuable products of the soil were not freely available, for the lord could not fell timber or secure minerals without the consent of his tenant, nor, conversely, could the latter do so without licence of the lord; a check was placed both on building and on agricultural improvements, and a tax levied on the capital of tenants. Finally, in advocating compulsory enfranchisement, it was stated that the Tithe Commissioners would agree to add this duty to their other obligations.

In 1841 an Act to facilitate the commutation of manorial rights and the enfranchisement of copyhold resulted from the recommendations of this body, and minor amending Acts subsequently passed the legislature, but voluntary methods were still employed. Some years later greater powers were invoked, for, by two Acts,

PLATE XII

Hertfordshire fields, showing a dividing balk

passed in 1852 and 1858 respectively, either landlord or tenant was permitted to apply for compulsory enfranchisement. The financial terms upon which this was to be carried out were subject to the decision of two valuers, except in the case of properties below £20 in annual value when this duty devolved on the local Justices of the Peace. Although, as a result of this legislation, copyhold tenures were for many years abolished at the rate of several hundred per annum, yet, so great was the number of manors and so numerous their individual properties, that even in recent times copyholders represented a considerable body of persons. In 1894 a fresh Act consolidated the laws relating to copyhold, and placed upon the Board of Agriculture the duty of sanctioning and supervising enfranchisements.

Finally, in 1922, under the auspices of Lord Birkenhead, a Bill was framed and passed through both Houses which gave effect to compulsory enfranchisement of all copyhold land after 1925. The delay in its coming into operation was due to a desire to allow time for the legal machinery involved in such a far-reaching change to be overhauled, and to permit of certain complementary adjustments being made in other measures. This Property Act might almost be described as an omnibus one, for, not only did it grant powers to convert all copyhold tenure, but, in conjunction with a second Property Act (1924), it also dealt with such questions as trusteeship, mortgage and settlements as they severally affected landed interests, and greatly facilitated the passing of real estate (thereby causing the final disappearance of the notorious "heir-at-law", in company with, as types of inheritance, Borough English and Gavelkind), which it was its aim to place in this connection upon a footing similar to that occupied by other forms of property. All manorial incidents possessing pecuniary value can, by agreement, be extinguished up to January 1st, 1936. Before January 1931, the tenant could legally require this to be effected. Subsequent to the latter date, the landlord can insist upon a settlement being reached by the end of 1935, by which time, if no steps have hitherto been taken, payments cease. For yet another period of five years, the Ministry of Agriculture will be invited to assess the compensation due to lords and other persons.

The main clauses affecting copyhold provided for compensation both to lords of the manor and their stewards—the latter of course for loss of office—payable either by a lump sum or by annual instalments; leases for lives were to be converted into leases running for ninety years, whereby the absence of legal expenses at each renewal will alone have represented a considerable saving.

Thus, concurrently with the disappearances of a system of tenure, have passed the ceremonies and customs inextricably associated with its existence for more than a thousand years. The interests of the historian and of the antiquary have fortunately been considered, for the Property Act provided that the Master of the Rolls should assume responsibility for safeguarding the records of manors. Within two or three years of 1926 information had been forthcoming in regard to over eight thousand obsolete manors, details of which had been registered at the Public Record Office. Due to the personal interest shown by the then Master of the Rolls, accommodation was shortly afterwards reported to have been found in every County of England for their relevant records. Accordingly, these invaluable documents now rest permanently in safe and accessible repositories where facilities for their study by all accredited persons interested in economic or local history are provided.

As it was claimed on behalf of the above two Acts that almost every advantage securable by registration of title would, in future, be conferred upon unregistered land, a few words must be devoted to that subject. Historically, such registration has hitherto been represented in this country in two forms—viz. registration of documents of title and registration of actual title. Under an Act of the time of Queen Anne registration of the first character was applied to the Ridings of Yorkshire and to the County of Middlesex, Deeds Registries being set up at Wakefield, at Beverley and, during the reign of George II, at Northallerton. All leasehold and freehold land within the appropriate Registrar's area is amenable to the conditions of the Act, the provisions of which are controlled by the County Councils, but the Registrar's own appointment has to be confirmed by the Lord Chancellor. Under an Act of Parliament, known as Lord Westbury's Transfer of Land Act (1862), a voluntary system of registration of title was extended to the rest of England and Wales, a Central Land Registry Office being set up in London. So far as the Metropolitan area was concerned, compulsory powers were added in 1889 and the whole system placed under the jurisdiction of the London County Council. Under the Land Registration Act of 1925 it is now open to any County Council, by means of a two-thirds majority, to request the Lord Chancellor to introduce registration within its particular area. Thus, Orders in Council, at the instance of the towns concerned, extended the system to Eastbourne and to Hastings, but no local Registries were established, the work being administered from the London Register Office. In 1930 there appeared a Report (Cd. 3564, 1930) by the Committee appointed to investigate the whole subject. Briefly summarised, the recommendations of that body were to the following effect: that eventually some form of decentralisation would be necessary, but that, for the time being, all fresh areas coming under the provisions of the Land Registration Acts should be administered from London. There, this large and very important matter now rests; it remains to be seen if the existing permissive regulations will be increasingly adopted, or whether, within another decade or two, public opinion will force the compulsory adoption of measures that elsewhere have proved highly beneficial. Only, however, in the latter event will the subject become one of practical interest to the owners of agricultural land, for whom at present it has but an academic appeal.

Leasehold tenure involves consideration of such questions as access to land and the relationship of the State to the individual; questions that in modern times are inextricably entangled with political considerations. But, as the legislation dealing with the provision of Small Holdings in this country will be found discussed at length in Chapter VI, the general principles involved in leasehold and the customs existing in other countries need alone be reviewed here. In general, it is fair to sum up the history of agricultural leases by saying that the more stable social conditions and—once a money basis had been introduced—the more stable prices remained, the longer were the periods for which tenants were admitted. Each upheaval, whether economic, constitutional or climatic, can thus be seen reflected throughout the length and breadth of the land.

At the present time approximately two-thirds (viz. 200,000) of all English and Welsh farmers are tenants, but the number of landowners is not now, and never has been, known, for this country has no system of *cadastre*, and, in the absence of the corresponding maps, can issue no official information relative to ownership. In 1873, however, at the instigation of the House of Lords, in order to allay hostility and to disprove a widely spread statement to the effect that there were only 30,000 landowners in England and Wales, a return was collected which purported to show their numbers in every parish. As *all* land outside the metropolis was included, the results have little bearing upon the problem of rural tenancy, but it may be recorded that some 270,000 persons were returned as owning land of one acre and upwards, and some 700,000 as possessing plots below an acre in extent. Statistically, this material is very suspect, as both contemporary critics and subsequent investigators have demonstrated. Indeed, the Hon. J. C. Brodrick (in a contribution to J. W. Probyn's *Systems of Land Tenure in Various Countries*) alone tore to shreds the exaggerated conclusions arrived at by the authors of this so-called "Domesday" book, for he made it clear that, excluding duplicates, there could not be more than 150,000 owners of land above one acre in England and Wales, that 15,000,000 acres out of 33,000,000 were in the hands of 2250 individuals, viz. half the then enclosed land was held by 1½ per cent. of all landowners. It is not surprising, therefore, that those responsible for the inquiry let matters rest where they were, and no further attempt on similar lines has ever been made. Prejudice is nowadays rarely invoked against rural landowners as such, and any political or other attacks are apt to take the more insidious form of proposals for additional taxation upon their possessions. The burdens and charges for maintenance of agricultural properties are sufficient evidence, even if none other was available, that their owners are not battening upon a class of helpless tenants.

An example of an early fifteenth century lease, taken from the *History of Hawsted*, by Sir J. Cullum, Bart., illustrates the principal safeguards that landlords in the Middle Ages thought fit to insert in such documents. Here, in 1410, the owner, when reserving to himself the customary rights that went with the property, specifically included the mill-house, stables and gardens contiguous to the manor house, together with all the ponds. The tenant agreed to maintain the houses in "covering and daubing" (in other words he was responsible for outside repairs), not to lop trees, and to receive a certain head of cattle at a valuation, the latter to be returned or their value refunded at the landlord's option when the lease expired. In addition, a proviso was inserted, whereby the tenant was compelled to leave "as many acres well ploughed, sown and manured as he received at first". Finally, and here comes the main distinction between such a lease and one granted in later times, if the rent was a fortnight in arrear the landlord might distrain; and if no payment was forthcoming after a month, he could re-enter and take possession. Each party signified his approval of these arrangements by agreeing to forfeit £100 in case of failure, this sum being actually equivalent to five years' rent. The reference to livestock is indicative of that form of lease known as "Stock and Land", by which an abnormal proportion of the capital obligations was assumed by the landlord, in that he provided a head of livestock numerically to be made good at the expiration of the lease. This had already become a popular system by the fifteenth century; it crops up, too, in modern times in many parts of the world and is indicative of the search for a method whereby tenants' commitments may be reduced to a minimum.

Technical improvements registered in the practice of agriculture were apt to be reflected slowly in leases, for the archives of the Manor of Hawsted contain their first reference to rye-grass, clover and turnips in a lease of 1753, and, although the landlord allowed two shillings for every load of manure or cinder ashes put on the land, Sir J. Cullum quotes the case of a tenant who, in twenty-one years' occupancy, had enriched his property by but a single load. Another, specifically compelled by his lease to lay thirty loads annually on a large farm, did so "very reluctantly". It has been declared that the devil always makes the landlords, but it looks as if his Satanic Majesty occasionally, in the past at least, experimented in the fabrication of a tenant.

In this country, with its predominant system of private landlord and tenant, the latter started with certain initial disadvantages which the passage of time has abrogated. For, just as the first half of the nineteenth century, through the Reform Act, brought social emancipation to the tenant farmer, so did the second half, with its numerous minor Acts of an agricultural nature, confer upon him economic freedom. Yet, writing between these two periods, Caird expressed his belief that landlords would in future reap additional benefits, and that the lot of tenants would become harder and harder. He based the first of these conclusions upon the strictly limited extent of the land available for agriculture and the certainty of its future diminution, and the second, he held, necessarily arose from the competition which tenants would have to meet from all directions, and the demands likely to be made upon them from their labourers. In regard to the first assumption, viz. that agricultural land must increase in value, it has since been cynically observed that the best course for the purchaser of real property to have pursued at the time in question would have been to acquire the ownership of the then valueless sandy areas bordering our coasts and of the similar inland heather wastes which were destined to become the sea-side resorts and golf courses of later generations.

In circumstances very different from those envisaged by Caird a quarter of a century earlier—viz. extreme depression—the landowners in the 70's and 80's assumed a very reasonable attitude towards their farming tenants, and later, in times of comparative prosperity, the very existence of leases of some duration frustrated any attempts that might possibly have been made by them to share in the extra profits won from the land. For example, the aggregate increases secured by landlords after 1914 were small, for only if the conditions prevailing from 1915 to 1917 had been perpetuated on a sound basis would rents in general slowly have moved upwards as leases fell in. As matters were, subsequent to a rise that, over the country in general, may by 1920 have averaged 20 per cent., reductions were soon being sought and landlords as a class received a very small proportion of the additional wealth gained during the few years when agriculture prospered. In general, the larger the owner's commitments have been in the past the smaller have been his proportionate net returns; proof of this can be seen by those who will read the evidence brought before any of the numerous Commissions appointed during the past half century. When agricultural land lies derelict by the hundred thousand acres, as has happened on at least two occasions in the last hundred years, the prevailing system of leasehold tenure is apt to be unfairly attacked, but the alternative, that of State expropriation, could not preclude such conditions, and would, when faced with them, merely shift the losses entailed upon the taxpayer. Under all normal conditions, agriculture practised under leasehold has returned to landlord and tenant as much as either had originally been led to expect, and the State has constantly effected minor easements to the advantage of the latter. Tenant-right is now a very different matter from what was implied by that expression in the middle of the nineteenth century, for numerous Agricultural Holdings Acts have since then been passed; the damage done by ground game is under the control of the farmer himself; he is no longer called upon to meet the demands of the tithe-collector—or, to all intents—of the rate-collector; he cannot be evicted except for the gravest dereliction of the basic principles of husbandry; he is assured of compensation upon the highest scale for any improvements he himself has effected; and, finally, if absolute security of tenure has not been granted him, freedom of cultivation and liberty of action—both of these are his for as long or as short a time as he cares to stipulate. It is not without significance that, during the last few years of falling prices, the majority of arable farmers have preferred a year to year occupation, with the opportunities for cutting losses thus provided, to any tenancy secured in advance for a period of years.

This situation has been built up, step by step, on legislation commencing with an Act of 1851, which attempted to improve the tenant's position in regard to fixtures. In 1875 the Agricultural Holdings Act granted compensation for certain improvements, but, although landlords were able to contract out of its terms, this represented a theoretical improvement upon the hitherto existing practice of give and take between the outgoing and the incoming tenants, whereby the former could return to the farm to recover certain crops and the latter could anticipate his occupation by entering upon the arable land in advance. A far-reaching Act was passed in 1883, which strengthened greatly the tenant's position in regard to notices to quit and again dealt with compensation, but this time stopped up the loopholes for evasion. Special compensation, over and above the normal, was granted to market-gardeners in 1895. The pre-war agriculturist attained his greatest step forward in 1908 when the Act of that year—complementary to the Small Holdings measure—granted compensation for unexhausted improvements, gave freedom of cropping and disposal of produce, permitted sale off the farm of hay and of straw and recognised in terms of money both "unreasonable disturbance" and the damage occasioned by ground game. Finally, the Corn Production Act and the Agriculture Act were designed to consolidate this situation, which the Agricultural Holdings Act of 1932 endorsed by granting the post-war farmer compensation up to the equivalent of two years' rent if given notice, except for bad farming (this was applicable if even one field was taken by the landlord) and permitted such greater freedom of cropping as virtually to rescind the immemorial obligation to return everything to the land, although, on the other hand, compensation is payable for "high" farming. The tenant can demand arbitration in regard to the amount of rent and, if dissatisfied with the result, can, on quitting, claim for disturbance. Allotment holders and the occupants of cottage gardens were, for the first time, included in the compensatory clauses, but their special case will be dealt with in the section devoted to Small Holdings.

There exists, in that well-known fruit-growing district, the Vale of Evesham, a peculiar example of tenant-right which the Tribunal of Investigation and private individuals have alike urged should be legally adopted elsewhere. By the custom in question the tenant's fruit trees are his own property and he has the privilege of selecting a successor who will take them over at a price agreed upon by the two parties. The landowner, provided he accepts the incomer, has no financial or other responsibility to bear; should he, however, refuse to endorse the outgoer's selection, then payment of compensation devolves upon himself. Whether this method would be applicable to all types of farms in the rest of the country is open to argument in detail, but the question deserves full investigation.

This being the position of the normal English tenant-farmer, what alterations, short of land nationalisation, thereby effecting a change in his landlord, have been suggested in regard to the only other factor susceptible of modification—his rent? There is no occasion to introduce into these pages a full discussion of the economic theory of rent or to refer to such matters as site value and unearned increment, for the occupation of agricultural land in this country affords insufficient data for a review of the principles involved, nor is the nation ever likely to reframe its whole conception of land-tenure. It may, however, be premised that rent is defined as that excess which the produce of a given area of land affords over and above the expenses of cultivation, and after a certain profit has accrued to the occupant; normal conditions of soil and skill on the part of the farmer are, however, connoted, together with uniformity in surrounding undertakings. It will be seen that, if this definition is pursued sufficiently far back, land, which from its inferiority can afford to pay no rent while producing a crop that just allows a profit, sets the standard for the better classes existing in the same neighbourhood, and that an infinity of factors arises as population increases, means of communication are provided, and especially as improvements in technical practices occur. The additional returns secured from better soil, or from such causes as those just enumerated, represent roughly the amount of "rent" that might be paid for the privilege of farming the land affected thereby.

Ricardo's familiar statement that "Corn is not high because a rent is paid, but a rent is paid because corn is high" is the counterpart of the dictum that "Rent forms no part of the price of agricultural produce", but represents a payment for differential advantages. In this and other developed countries it is, however, obvious that present day rents are to a decreasing extent remuneration for the use of natural advantages of land, whether arising from quality of soil or from position, but must be regarded as (the meagre) interest upon capital sunk during numerous past centuries in reclamation, improvement and maintenance, after deduction of which there may be, in such times as the present, a minus quantity left, as will later on be recorded. Marshall once wrote: "I admit that the soil of old countries is often as much an artificial product as those pieces of earth which have been arranged into brick walls, and that a great deal of it has yielded but a poor return to the vast capital sunk into it, even in recent times". Contrary, too, to the views, frequently expressed by those unfamiliar with English agriculture, the "amenity" value attaching to the majority of farms is negligible. Even if sporting rights are added under this head to the expression "social prestige", it is rare to find, outside the "Shires", parts of East Anglia and some scattered areas, any homogeneous district where the combined value of both would exceed a small percentage of the total rent. In many districts, e.g. the fens, there is not now, and never has been, a pennyworth of amenity attaching to the possession of the soil, for hunting, shooting, squires and "County society" are, alike, non-existent. From a strictly agricultural standpoint it is immaterial that there exist large tracts of land in Scotland whose principal value is derived from their sporting amenities. Nor, fortunately, is there in these Islands but seldom any opportunity for the agricultural community to indulge in "farming land values" —a practice which inevitably occurs in rapidly developing countries of the New World.

But, while the returns secured by an English landlord for market-garden properties in the outskirts of a town and by the owner of a grouse moor in Scotland or of prairie land in Canada may be fundamentally dependent upon similar factors, the cash expression in each case is widely dissimilar. Even in this country, agricultural—as opposed to urban—land varies widely, both in capital value and in rentability; for instance, in one and the same County two freehold properties, equidistant from rail and town, changed hands at public sales shortly after the war, at 15*s.* the acre and £172 the acre respectively. The first comprised some hundreds of acres of heavy clay land that had been allowed to go derelict, the second consisted of a few acres of rich grazing meadows in a fen district where arable predominated and where drought was at the time very serious. In 1907, a very competent authority, Mr R. J. Thompson (subsequently Assistant-Secretary to the Ministry of Agriculture) in a paper read to the Royal Statistical Society, estimated the unimproved value of land at £8 the acre and the permanent improvements and equipment at another £12 the acre, which gave the familiar total figure of £20. Sir William Dampier, many years later, pointed out in his presidential address to the Agricultural Economics Society, that, if interest were taken at 3½ per cent. on the £12 (equal to 8*s.* 5*d.*) and, on the assumption that from a gross rent of £1 repairs and other outgoings at 7*s.* were deducted, there would have been left a "true" rent of 4*s.* 7*d.* per acre. By substituting post-war values in 1930, relating to several estates covering a total area of over 40,000 acres, Sir William was able to demonstrate that the then equivalent Ricardian rent was a minus quantity to the extent of 9*s.* 6*d.* per acre.

More recent, and official, statistics are now available in this connection, for, as a result of the Census of Production in 1925, the Ministry of Agriculture issued the following data, which have been amalgamated by the writer.

The over-all average figures of 31*s.* and £31 (representing in effect a valuation based upon twenty years' purchase) would now, of course, be too high, for in 1931 a very comprehensive investigation into the farm economy of East Anglia, conducted by the Department of Agriculture at Cambridge, for this depressed area gave an average rent of 19*s.* 6*d.* per acre. The total value of all farm land (including, of course, farm buildings) in England and Wales was in 1925 calculated by the Ministry to have been £795,000,000, to which sum had to be added another £21,000,000 to represent the capital value of the rough grazings. Corresponding figures for the component parts of these Islands would raise the total to at least £1,200,000,000.

Average rent and capital value per acre (exclusive of rough grazings) of holdings of different sizes in England and Wales, 1925

Size groups	Mainly arable holdings		Mainly pasture holdings		Mixed holdings		All kinds	
	Capital value (per acre)	Rent (per acre)	Capital value (per acre)	Rent (per acre)	Capital value (per acre)	Rent (per acre)	Capital value (per acre)	Rent (per acre)
acres	£	s.	£	s.	£	s.	£	s.
1–5	46	51	62	64	54	56	60	62
5–20	42	46	52	53	46	47	50	51
20–50	36	39	44	44	39	39	41	42
50–100	30	33	37	37	33	33	34	35
100–150	26	29	33	33	30	30	30	31
150–300	23	25	29	30	26	27	26	28
300–500	20	21	25	26	22	24	22	24
Over 500	17	18	23	23	19	21	19	20
Overall Average	24	26	35	36	28	29	31	31

Tenants' capital (live and dead stock, included) might be taken at some £15 per acre, with a range from £10, in the case of large light-land farms, up to over £80 where poultry and fruit are raised: the proportions thus borne respectively by the landowner's and the tenant's shares—almost exactly two-thirds and one-third—emphasise the heavy commitments of the owners.

The relations between a tenant-farmer and his landlord were many years ago described as existing in an atmosphere of faith, credulity and chance, a state of affairs which, until the severe depression of the 'eighties and 'nineties came about, could perhaps be defended, but thereafter it was urged something more substantial than short-dated tenancies was called for. This claim was nothing novel, for Caird and others had repeatedly urged, some thirty years previously, that all tenant-farmers could reasonably ask for was certainty of tenure. Coke's example was still fresh in men's memories, and it was freely said that, if he could prosper when according leases for twenty years, smaller landlords, even in abnormal times, could surely follow some way in his footsteps. One particular feature in these Holkham agreements appealed to farmers, and this was that for sixteen years complete freedom of action was accorded both in regard to rotation, management of the land and sale of the produce;

only in the last four years had the Norfolk four-course rotation to be restored. Moreover, after this lapse of sixteen years, renewal for another twenty, on fresh terms for the last sixteen, would always be granted. Numerous witnesses before the Royal Commission of 1893 evidently hankered after something of this sort, for, while they gave instance after instance of the observance of good faith by landlords in the then difficult circumstances, they also naturally urged that sitting tenants should not be placed in the position either of offering an impossible rent or else of quitting their holdings. Others, whilst recognising the evil of short-dated tenancies, suggested steps that aimed further than any tinkering with tenure, by advocating the reorganisation of the terms of partnership; in other words, they implied that rent should bear a fixed relationship to farming profits.

Such schemes were generally based upon some modification of the principles contained in Elizabethan corn-rents, and were designed either to correlate exactly rent and the price of grain, or to defer the assessing of the landlord's return until the tenant's profits had been determined. An Assistant Commissioner of the Board of Agriculture quoted a case of the former method found in the Eastern Counties. Here, it had been agreed between the parties concerned, that rent should move proportionally as and when the price of wheat rose above 32*s*. 6*d*. per quarter or fell below 28*s*. 6*d*. The basic rent was £400, and on a wheat area of 70 acres, a hypothetical example showed that when the *Gazette* price fell to 25*s*., an average yield of 250 quarters (after the deduction of seed corn) would result in £43. 15*s*. being remitted in rent, i.e. 250 times 3*s*. 6*d*. If the price further declined to 21*s*. the rent would have been £306. 5*s*., a reduction of almost 25 per cent. Conversely, in times of really high values the landlord must have benefited very considerably, for had wheat fetched 60*s*. his receipts would have been almost doubled. Such an expedient, initiated in times of extreme depression, and practised in a wheat-raising area, when, moreover, prices of grain were not only exceptionally unremunerative but were also practically stationary, may have tided over a difficult situation, but for the country as a whole it would have represented an impossible proposition. To fix rent in relation to one agricultural commodity when diversity of output was increasing would have been grossly uneconomic, neither would it have been feasible to base it upon the principal crop found on each individual undertaking.

Historically, however, it may perhaps be of passing interest to quote from a pamphlet entitled *Corn-Rents and Money-Rents*, published in 1845 by the then Master of Corpus Christi College, Cambridge, in which it was sought to prove that leases granted on this basis had for many years been advantageous to both landlord and tenant. The College in question, after lowering rents in the 'twenties and 'thirties, had agreed with certain tenants, in lieu of further reductions, to accept payment on the current values of a fixed quantity of wheat—in one case 1350 bushels and in another 1100 bushels—these values to be determined by the prices ruling in Cambridge corn-market on the Saturdays preceding Lady Day and Michaelmas. It was proved to the Master's satisfaction that the College, in the intervening time, had received considerably more money than would have been the case if it had granted a lease based on a cash-rent pure and simple; but this calculation was made on the assumption that, in the latter event, a very low basis would have been adopted in a time of unique depression, and the fact that one of the tenants sent a most appreciative letter to the College tends to show that perhaps a private landlord would not have accepted conditions that met the requirements of a corporate body. The pamphlet itself thus enumerated the advantages of a corn-rent:

> The landlord during a period of years, in which the price of corn fluctuates, receives a fair average rent, the tenant being relieved whenever prices are low, the landlord proportionally benefiting when prices are high. If corn continue at a fixed price, the rent remains high. If corn continue at a low price the rent is low, but the landlord receives as much as he would do under a money agreement. A corn-rent removes the chief objection of the landlord to granting a lease on his farm; and checks in the tenant the spirit of speculation.

Finally, technical objections that this system could only apply to arable land, or that, precisely on those occasions when the farmer had a deficient harvest, and consequently the smallest output of wheat, would he be called on to pay the highest rent, were brushed aside by the assurances that grazing-land could be rented on the prevailing values of beef and mutton (expressed in stones of meat) and that, quite truly (when home supplies were predominant), increases in the price of wheat were disproportionately greater than the deficiency itself represented. Despite this, and subsequent advocacy, later generations, as has been shown, have not progressed beyond the stage of tentative suggestions for the introduction of some sliding-scale system between landlord and tenant.

Division of profits on the basis of a fixed return on his capital to the tenant, the remainder going to the landlord, formed a scheme that was frequently advocated some forty years ago, and has been mooted occasionally since. Here the tenant is entitled to, say, 10 per cent. interest on his own capital, whatever may have been the result of the year's trading, is held liable for the rent of his dwelling-house, and, in extreme cases, foregoes any further share in the business, in others he takes a varying and small percentage of the net profits. In good years such an agreement results in the landlord getting a relatively high return, but in bad seasons, or in times of continued depression, not only does he secure no farming profits but, even after offsetting the rent of the house, may still have to meet, from his own pocket, part of the sum due to the tenant as interest. Strictures passed upon this method have generally taken the form of pointing out that its efficacy depended upon thorough annual valuations being undertaken of the tenant's live and dead stock, and that there was more than a chance that unscrupulous occupiers would neglect their holdings, in the certainty of receiving a fixed income. Nowadays, however, valuations are a commonplace event, and the mere fact that they take place would deter the lazy tenant from risking an undue reduction in his own capital, and therefore in his income. From the landlord's point of view this kind of profit-sharing makes the least demand upon his capital resources, representing in other respects merely a case of farming by proxy.

But, in an alternative plan, referred to by the official of the Board previously quoted, profit-sharing could result in equally heavy losses to a landlord. Attention was drawn to a case in Bedfordshire, where the owner was a Cambridge College which had agreed, after allowing priority to the tenant in respect of a fixed 3 per cent. on his capital, to divide the remaining book-profits in equal parts. Such an agreement greatly favoured the tenant, even when his return was only at the rate of 3 per cent., for in no circumstances could he record an actual loss while his landlord might, when facing a deficit, in addition be called upon to present the tenant with a cheque for the whole of the latter's interest.

The difficulties involved in any attempt to depart from the straightforward system, whereby the landowner automatically advances the bulk of the capital and the tenant has complete financial freedom, have been illustrated in the foregoing paragraphs, where suggestions put forward in times of abnormal distress were purposely selected, for such periods are the most prolific of revolutionary ideas. If the reward to the owner was at the best of times considerably greater than it is, there might be a possibility of persuading him to risk the definite loss of money on occasions when he now at worst receives none, but if his return over a series of years be examined little surprise will be expressed that he clings to the existing arrangement. It is probable, too, that the bulk of tenant-farmers prefer something that pertains to a gamble, that is to say that, while a rent fixed in advance can almost always be met, it may enable a really large profit to be realised and, if conditions deteriorate, is generally susceptible of adjustment if not of complete remission, for has not the landowner been referred to in this connection as an "economic buffer"? Nowadays, indeed, it would appear as if the resiliency of the buffer's springs may have been permanently impaired, for reductions of rent are seldom restored in their entirety when prosperity returns. Again, if freedom of action is desired by tenants, freedom to select the latter has always represented a considerable asset to landlords. For these reasons any radical change in the prevailing custom of tenancy is a very unlikely event in relation to large and medium-sized holdings in this country, although it must be pointed out that the position of the agricultural landowner in relation to his outgoings has been an extremely difficult one during the last fourteen years, for all his costs of maintenance—such as building repairs—have been inordinately increased at just that time when his tenants expected the most from him in the way of relief.

The provision on lease of Small Holdings, however, presents a different proposition, and one which is discussed in Chapter v, but because the State itself has felt called upon to intervene in this particular case, and for the purpose of creating a fresh class of holding, it does not necessarily follow that the nation is the best landlord of farms in general. Whilst the setting up of Land Courts in this country has frequently been urged in previous decades, the progressive alterations legally effected in favour of tenants have resulted in less being heard of this form of official supervision. Even the advocates of these Courts have held that their main usefulness would be seen, not in the fixing of judicial rents, but rather in guaranteeing continuity of tenure, or the alternative of ample compensation for disturbance. Indeed, the feelings expressed by tenants themselves before the Royal Commission of 1893 were practically unanimous against any interference by the State in this matter, and remained so even in regard to a suggested Court of Arbitration. In both Scotland and Ireland legislation, now of some standing, has resulted in the State usurping the functions that are generally associated with these Courts, but it must be pointed out that in each case jurisdiction extends only to Small Holdings, where also in the case of England and Wales very similar powers have been created for, and are exercised by, those semi-official bodies—the County Councils.

In Ireland, the Congested Districts Board had, in the first instance, a unique task to meet, one in fact that comprised not only the re-establishment of other industries besides that of agriculture, but also the amelioration of social conditions over large areas. It will suffice to prove that this Board was not primarily a tribunal for the ordinary landlord and his tenant when it is stated that the total earnings of the families under its protection ranged down to £8 per annum (with an addition of £6 to represent the value of home produce), and that one of its main objects was to increase the size of holdings, almost everywhere blighted by the evil of minute subdivision, previously referred to in the case of Achill and elsewhere in the West.

That this trouble was of some standing, and that Irish landlords of the smaller sort had long needed a restraining hand, can be seen by the following extract from a letter written from that country by Lord Palmerston in 1808:

> Every farm swarms with its little holders who have each four or five, or, at the utmost, ten or twelve acres. They are too poor to improve their land, and yet it is impossible to turn them out, as they have no other means of subsistence. Their condition, however, will be improved as I gradually get rid of the middlemen and petty landlords. These people take a certain quantity of ground, reserve to themselves a small portion, and let out the rest to under-tenants. They make these unfortunate devils pay the rent of the landlords and an excess, which they keep for themselves and call a profit rent; while they live upon the part they reserve without paying any rent for it. In my last ride...the universal cry was "Give us roads and no petty landlords".

This appeal the Congested Districts Board, aided by Land Purchase, had a century later gone far to comply with, but its functions were

PLATE XIII

An East Anglian balk in process of being ploughed up

never those associated with the strict definition of a Land Court. Indeed, both the Free State and Ulster now provide eminently successful examples of State intervention by direct purchase, for, in each part of the country, are to be seen numerous small and medium-sized holdings that are in the assured possession of their occupiers, to whom it has always been immaterial whether or not the financial basis of their original contracts unduly favoured them at the expense of the (British) taxpayer and the majority of whom can equally ignore, in its national aspects, a most unexpected financial crux involved in the disposal of their land annuities. In fact, the only restraint legally exercisable against them would appear to be a wise provision of the Land Purchase Acts that forbids consolidation of their carefully apportioned farms without permission from the Land Commission or until the whole of the purchase money has been received.

The Crofters' Commission in Scotland was established under an Act of 1886 on analogous lines, its obligations including the fixing of fair rents and the supervision of such matters as compensation and succession; it also possessed the power to enlarge holdings where such action was considered necessary. Its area of operation was confined to the Outer Isles and to a few adjacent West Coast Counties. Here also, the expedient of granting considerable powers to a body primarily working on behalf of the really small tenant-farmer has met with undoubted success, and the eulogy of it contained in the *Report* of the Royal Commission on the Highlands and Islands was thoroughly deserved, but again no evidence has been forthcoming that a Court possessing similar powers over the larger farms of England would exert an all-round beneficial influence upon the conditions of their tenure. Subsequently, in 1897, a Congested Districts Board was set up, the functions of which closely resembled those of the English Development Commission or of its Irish counterpart. Just before the outbreak of war, a Small Landowners Act authorised the setting up of crofters' holdings, but its compulsory clauses were very limited. As was then the case south of the Border, post-war legislation rapidly facilitated the acquisition of land for all types of Small Holders, but the Board remained paramount within its own jurisdiction.

The *Report* of such a body as "The Land Enquiry Committee" shows clearly the lines upon which the advocates of State control had anticipated that progress would result. Generally, in the forefront of their proposals were placed claims that Land Courts would facilitate the acquisition of land for Small Holdings, but nowadays this duty is ably carried out by the County Councils, supervised by a Government Department. Next, it was urged that the obligation upon tenants to pay a "living wage" to their workers would be sympathetically considered, by forcing landlords to meet any additional payments thus given effect to, and the obvious deduction was drawn that the control of wages would form a corollary to the other duties of the Courts. Whilst the above examples demonstrated the ultimate aims of such thinkers, their actual arguments in favour of a Land Court were based upon the contention that the ownership of land represented a monopoly, and that, in "the so-called free bargaining" between owner and tenant, there was everything in favour of the former; "fair" rents by superseding "competitive" rents would therefore have adjusted satisfactorily this handicap. The difficulties attendant on fixing rents in face of economic and monetary changes were generally brushed aside by the statement that agreements would be confined to five or seven year periods, and that, to avoid the risk of stereotyping large farms, security of tenure would be conditional upon the non-requirement of the land for public purposes such as, for example, Small Holdings. Where improvements were not carried out by the owner, rent would be reduced accordingly; thus landlords would maintain their properties in a high state of efficiency.

Controversion of such of the above arguments as have not been subsequently met by legislation will be found in the *Report* of the Commissioners of 1893, whose opening words were as follows: "On the subject of land-tenure we have taken much evidence from the representatives of a section of agriculturists, who advocate drastic changes in the law in connection with that question. Indeed, we have taken from them upon this point more evidence than probably was warranted, either by their influence or numbers in agricultural circles". After summarising the arguments used by the principal exponents referred to, which were similar to those just enumerated, the Commissioners expressed the opinion that Land Courts would be exceedingly unpopular with the overwhelming majority of tenant-farmers, none of whom had called for their introduction. Finally, they declared that the tenants themselves

evidently entertain a wholesome dread of the unnecessary litigation which they would create, and are of opinion that they can make better bargains with their landlords for themselves than lawyers or Land Courts are likely to make for them. They believe that the adoption of the three "F's" (fair rent, fixity of tenure and free sale) in any shape or form would constitute an altogether uncalled for interference between landlord and tenant, and, so far from bettering their position, inevitably make it worse. We have no doubt these opinions are well-founded. So far as the landlords are concerned, the creation of any such tribunal could not fail to diminish the interest which they now take in their properties, and we are strongly of opinion that it would greatly decrease, if it did not entirely arrest, expenditure on permanent improvements. It is manifestly of the greatest importance to agriculture that every reasonable encouragement should be given to this expenditure; and that landowners should in every way be encouraged to take an active and personal interest in their estates, and by judicious expenditure of capital assist their tenants to compete with the producers of agricultural produce in other countries. We have therefore without hesitation arrived at the conclusion that the creation of any court or tribunal for the purpose of establishing, wholly or partially, the policy of the three "F's" would be a grave and serious injury to the agricultural community and to the industry which has been committed to our enquiry.

These being the views of a representative body in the early 'nineties, it may be asked if the passage of forty years may not have effected modifications in the situation. To this the answer is that, thanks to creative and protective legislation, the statutory Small Holder has, in his greatly increased numbers, received the three "F's" substantially intact, whilst other tenant-farmers have secured numerous concessions that have benefited them more than would any system of arbitration by the State. The upshot may even be that the position of tenants holding land under County Councils might, in times of deep depression, be slightly inferior to that occupied by others whose landlords could give practical expression to their personal feelings in the matter of adjustment of rent. Nevertheless, on behalf of both the Small Holder and the larger farmer, there have recently been put forward—by two political parties and by certain private individuals—elaborate proposals for State ownership. In these pages it is sufficient to describe the former schemes as based, in the one case, upon the assumption that State ownership is wholly desirable and, in the other, upon the supposed failure of private landowners to function adequately in times of extreme depression. The first party would expropriate, with compensation and upon a business footing; the second would attempt to transfer all the duties and obligations, hitherto performed by the private owner, to the care of Official Committees. Neither is likely to be implemented.

The private proposals, referred to above, however, deserve further comment, as they emanated from two such well-known authorities as Mr C. S. Orwin and Mr W. R. Peel. In this scheme, compulsory acquisition of all "agricultural" land in England and Wales (only) was advocated. The exclusion of Scotland enabled the special problems associated with the ownership of land north of the Border to be avoided. By the compulsory acquisition only of "agricultural lands and other forms of property falling *outside* all administrative urban areas", the undertaking would, it was claimed, have been immensely simplified and its cost reduced. Although an Act of Parliament may have defined an agricultural village, there exist innumerable areas which are to all intents and purposes urban in character, although still classified as rural by the Local Government authorities. The extension of modern means of transport has raised the value of large tracts of such land above an agricultural level, and, as lands "supposed to possess a prospective building value" would have received a ten years' moratorium, to permit of development, it is certain that a very large proportion of all property earmarked would have evaded acquisition. Conversely, it is probable that urban areas contain more land devoted to farming than was anticipated by the authors. Thus, Geary in *Land Tenure and Unemployment*, p. 184 (quoting H. of C. Paper 119 of 1913), refers to Rhondda, where 19,888 acres out of a total of 23,885 within the Urban District boundary are rated as agricultural, to Bradford with 14,534 similarly classified out of 22,843, and even to Birmingham with 20,000 out of 43,000. The State was only to acquire the surface rights, leaving minerals in private hands; such a policy would have involved complicated negotiations in many parts of the country. No acreage limit was mentioned, and, as the only exemptions comprised lands associated with public utility services, commons, churchyards, and vicarage houses (a specific reminder being inserted to the effect that properties of the Crown, County Councils, Charity and Church lands were scheduled for purchase), it must have been intended to expropriate the holders of quite small plots; thus, many cottagers, the occupiers of residential properties and the owners of semi-urban gardens would alike have swollen the enormous total of individuals with whom negotiations were to be initiated. As the avowed object was to acquire control over all farm properties, a more reasonable and expeditious method would surely have been to purchase only that land which figured in the annual returns of the Ministry of Agriculture. Owner-occupiers were to be offered the option of a tenancy for the term of their lives, of the lives of their wives, or of the survivors of them, or, alternatively, for a period of years. The interest of leaseholders would have been bought out side by side with that of their ground landlords, since in the case of buildings the existing value of the reversion was to be assigned to the latter and the remainder to the former. When the question of finance was reached, it was seen that the immense problem involved in the valuation of the property to be acquired was treated as "a mere matter of arithmetic", Schedule A assessments forming the basis for what, "at the present moment", would have represented twenty-two-and-a-half years' purchase. The figures mentioned were £1,125,000,000 as the capital sum, and £50,000,000 for annual value, but the majority of readers could not endorse the statement that "the financial side of the problem is not one which should present difficulty", nor were they ready to designate it "a relatively small transaction which should cause no embarrassment". It should be stated that the stock created, redeemable by a deferred sinking-fund, was to have borne interest "comparable with the yield of long-dated Government stocks". No further information was accorded, nor was any attempt directed towards drawing up a composite balance sheet or gauging the effects of this vast loan. The ability of the State to maintain its newly acquired property indefinitely at the high standard postulated, whilst at the same time conforming to its financial obligations to the holders of land bonds, was tacitly assumed. The possibility of rural land values falling was ignored, but it must be observed that, until the State had become absolute owner, it would have been dependent upon the future price-levels of agricultural commodities to maintain its rents. The necessity for providing additional money to make good the remission of death duties and the extinction of the Land-tax was apparently not admitted. Considerable attention was devoted to a precise description of the administrative measures proposed and of the personnel to be created. A new branch of the Ministry of Agriculture would have been established, to act as intermediary between the Board of Inland Revenue and the County Councils, for these latter bodies were to be dominant in their own areas. County, and, under them, District Land Agents, each with an area of 30,000 acres, were to be appointed, and County Foresters would supersede the Forestry Commission.

Such was the plan. It avoided certain fatal objections, which, from an agricultural standpoint, attached to previous schemes. It did not, for example, seek to impose a standardised control over actual farming methods, nor did it aim at the creation of a universal system of small occupying-owners, but tenant-farmers, the bulk of rural dwellers and the majority of landowners will trust that the necessity for putting this, or any similar proposal, into force will not in the near future arise.

Chapter IV

MODERN LAND TENURE (CONTINUED)

***Métayage* in France and in Italy; "share-cropping" and "share-renting" in the United States and Australia; Russian land systems before and after the war; expropriation in Europe and the "Green Revolution"; Denmark; the Near East; Spain; problems of land-tenure amongst native races in Africa and elsewhere.**

As the atmosphere engendered neither by the war itself nor by the social upheaval that succeeded it led to any alteration in the prevalent system of land-tenure in this country, it is extremely unlikely that economic depression alone will effect such steps, especially when the object lesson afforded by the way in which that system overcame the difficulties associated with the period from 1879 to 1895 is recalled. One has but to turn, however, to almost any other part of the world to find long-established principles flung to the winds, and every conceivable form of land expropriation and of benevolent State ownership introduced. But before taking a survey of what amounted, in some cases, to economic wreckage, it is advisable rapidly to summarise the alternative forms that tenure has assumed abroad.

Pride of place belongs to that most ancient of all, *métayage*, for, five or six thousand years ago, Babylonian cultivators recompensed the proprietors of their land by handing over to them annually a certain proportion of the grain they had raised. Modern *métayage* of course implies a reduced capital outlay on the part of the tenant and a correspondingly heavier demand upon his landlord, met by the latter receiving an augmented share of the farming profits, generally consisting of half of the output of crops and livestock. Although it is found still existing in other European countries and also further afield, as for instance in Egypt and in parts of India, it is to France or Italy that the enquirer must turn if he wishes to study examples in their fullest development. He will find to aid him in his researches, in the case of the former country, a very full account of the whole matter in the shape of the official *Rapport de la Commission d'enquête sur la situation du métayage en France*, instituted by the French Farmers' Society in 1912, and published in the following year. The description of *métayage* there given (and quoted in the *Bulletin* of the International Agricultural Institute) shows that in pre-war France, although less than one-tenth of the land was thus held, yet the system, embracing approximately one-third of a million holdings, possessed undoubted advantages, its extreme elasticity permitting a very fine gradation in the liabilities of the landowner.

The *Rapport* defined *métayage* as the result of "an agreement or a contract by which the lessor, the land-holder, the usufructuary or tenant-farmer of a farm gives the *métayer* or partial *métayer* (who gives his labour) the temporary enjoyment, under his own direction and supervision, of the land, buildings and all or part of the livestock and farm requisites, and shares with him the eventual produce in kind and money, whether equally or in some other proportion". Although this and other legal definitions and enactments relating to *métayage* exist, its advocates constantly harp on the freedom it confers on both parties, at the same time pointing out that such an intimate partnership rests on community of interests. The *métayer* is subject to supervisory visits from his landlord, who may determine the course of action for the ensuing months and merely leave the direction of field operations to the former, but it is on him that the amenities of the undertaking depend, for the landlord "trusts to the good sense, prudence and experience of his partner who has a more intimate acquaintance with the farm he works and the livestock he tends. He will consult him familiarly without too brusquely enforcing his own will; he will insinuate his ideas little by little; without bargaining he will advance the sums necessary, relying on the honesty and industry of the other, and will attempt to take the steps required and make the necessary changes in advance without waiting to be asked".

Statistics collected prior to the war indicated that, if *métayage* in France as a whole was at best stationary, there were some eighteen Departments in which this form of tenure outnumbered ordinary leases, and French opinion held that where it was still predominant, as in Dordogne, Gironde and the Basses-Pyrénées, it had resulted in improved agricultural practice. More machinery had been introduced, the use of fertilisers had increased, and noticeable improvements had been effected in livestock. The most frequent form of tenancy granted to the *métayer* was for a single year, terminable upon six months' notice, but a tendency to lengthen the span up to six or ten years was already noticeable, and, in certain arable districts, a four-course rotation was the determining factor. Obviously there could be no hard and fast rule as to the size of undertaking best suited to this tenure, but, if soil, situation, climate and type of product raised were taken into consideration, it appeared that the large undertakings were not well represented, that there was a reduction taking place in the average size of *métairies*, and that they tended to be concentrated on the better classes of land.

The details calling for discussion and agreement between the partners would strike the British farmer as being far too numerous and often annoyingly petty, but, doubtless, generations of *métayers* have come to regard their settlement as part of the routine work of the farm. Take the most important aspect first—the apportionment of the annual products. Whilst grain is usually divided equally, in some places the lessor takes a third of the wheat and rye and a quarter of the oats and barley; in the latter event the *métayer* would be expected to provide seed corn and two-thirds or three-quarters of the manure. Potatoes almost invariably go to the tenant, but in Périgord anything up to a third is the lessor's perquisite. According to the *Rapport*, even manure-heaps, old ricks, fodder and standing-grass in temporary meadows, if they escape an annual division, are yet subject to valuation on the termination of a lease, and any increase in their value is divisible. The allocation of the profits from the lesser livestock is reminiscent of the niceties once associated in this country with the apportioning of vicarial tithes, for the *métayer's* wife is entitled to the profits from the fowls, ducks, guinea-fowls, and pigeons, those from geese and turkeys being shared equally, but, again, the feathers of the latter belong to the wife. Whilst fruit is the *métayer's*, nuts and cider apples are apportioned. Generally, the profits from the sale of livestock are equally divided, but, where pigs are concerned, special consideration is shown to the tenant in the shape of allowances of food and the allocation to him of certain young stock. It is not uncommon to find the tenant paying small "*métairie* taxes" to his landlord, which are looked upon as "an indirect equivalent" of the land-tax paid in full by the latter, as well as an acknowledgement for the use of house, garden and wood, or of some special privilege abandoned exclusively to himself. On the other hand, it has become a custom in those corn-growing districts of Champagne and Berry, where large *métairie* farms exist, for the landlord to supplement the tenant's customary share by granting him a sum of money based on the area under corn. It is claimed that these particular undertakings, which may range up to four or five hundred acres in extent, have, as a result of this assured increment, achieved progressively improving yields from a naturally poor soil, and that the *métayer* is freed from anxiety as to the effects of weather upon his crops.

The equipment of the *métairie* farm is of course essentially the prerogative of the landlord, but in certain instances modern practice has altered custom, and it is now not unusual to find part or the whole of the livestock being supplied by the tenant. In its original conception, therefore, *métayage* was exactly akin to the English "stock and land" tenure, as any diminution in the numbers of animals evidenced at the expiry of a lease had to be made up by the tenant, or, alternatively, any excess belonged to him.

The division of responsibility is even extended to the cultivation of the land itself, for, in the case of the larger and more expensive types of machinery, such as steam ploughs or threshing plant, the landlord bears the overhead charges and the tenant provides for the attendant mechanics' requirements; field drainage, irrigation and other permanent improvements imply the provision of the material by the owner and of the necessary labour by the tenant. Crops, such as sugar-beet, that entail extra work, are encouraged by the landlord making a grant based upon the acreage concerned or the weight of the outturn secured. In general, what would in this country be described as tenant's improvements are, on the *métairie* farm, the subject of provision, in so far as the bulk of the capital is concerned, by the owner, but the labour and attention are provided by the tenant; liming, marling and the application of fertilisers, the influence of all of which is felt over a length of time, if borne equally, become the subject of compensation from a tenant who quits before the expiration of his lease. Although the *métayer* is generally held responsible for repairs, the landlord is frequently the person who pays for them. There is some weight of evidence to the effect that the landowner gets a slightly better rent under this system than would be the case were another basis adopted, and there is certainly proof that the *métayer* is financially better off than if he were engaged as a wage-earner in his industry—which would be his alternative mode of life were he unable to become such a tenant. Both members of this close partnership are, therefore, satisfied with its results, but each party devotes the maximum of time and labour to meet its demands.

Sufficient description of this interesting form of land-tenure has perhaps been given to endorse the words of a French body of agriculturists, which declared that "where *métayage* has always existed and still exists, if it is well organised on the two fundamental bases of division of all the produce, and the chief management in the hands of the proprietor, on land of average fertility where livestock and cereal crops have almost equal importance, it is indisputably the mode of farming which assures the best revenue from the land. It must be added that *métayage* cannot be improvised in regions where it does not exist or never has existed; nor can it be imported. Trials made in this direction have had only an ephemeral success". The qualifications contained in the above statement will undoubtedly reinforce the views of English readers that, whatever advantages it has conferred in France, *métayage* could never have flourished in England; it calls for too domestic a partnership between landlord and tenant—a partnership that would be as uncongenial to the type of landowner found in this country as to his more independent tenant. Nor, in fact, are there many recorded instances of its occurrence here. In *Knole and the Sackvilles* (V. Sackville-West), however, the following reference is made to a mid-seventeenth century application of its principles on the Kentish estate of that family. We are told that the fifth Earl of Dorset accorded four farmers "the liberty to plough anywhere in the Park except in the plain set out by my Lord and the ground in front of the house, and to take their crops, and it is agreed that one third of each crop after it is severed from the ground shall be taken and carried away by my Lord for his own use. The third year the farmers to sow the ground with grass seed if my Lord desires it, and they are to be at the charge of the seed, the tillage and the harvest". Admittedly, this was nothing but a temporary leasing of grass-land for tillage purposes, but the basis of payment was essentially that followed in modern Continental *métayage*, and the provision of seed and the supply of labour also correctly devolved upon the tenant.

At the end of the eighteenth, and, indeed, up to the middle of the nineteenth century, *métayage*, as practised in France, was the subject of severe criticism from all English authorities including Adam Smith and Arthur Young, the latter, in particular, having nothing but caustic comment to make both upon the practice itself and those engaged in it. On the other hand the Italian *métayer* was always favourably reported on and his successful methods were the subject of special commendation by J. S. Mill, as well as by more recent writers. In modern Italy *mezzadria*, as it is normally designated (or *terzieria*, when the landlord takes two-thirds of the crops), forms one type of the widely spread "share tenancy", which covers more than one-third of all agricultural land in that country. In one form, popularly termed *tirare avanti*, the owner goes into partnership with a *contadino*, who provides his labour. After reserving 25 per cent. of the produce to himself as "rent", the proprietor halves the remainder with his partner and becomes responsible for the provision of machinery, drainage and the advancing of all money (without interest) needed for the year's working. This system merges into orthodox *métayage* as soon as the tenant supplies any of the capital required in the combined undertaking.

While referring to Italy, it may be appropriate to mention that *emphyteusis*, or the granting of leases in perpetuity, or for very lengthy periods, is still practised. This is really copyhold, for, the land so handed over, being generally of poor quality, or even, at the time, uncultivated, the tenant agrees to pay a very small fixed rent and in return is under obligation to improve the holding and, every twenty-nine years, formally to make a "recognition" payment to the owner. Post-war Italy has provided other, and larger, examples of land redemption, for she has succeeded in reclaiming and bringing under the plough many thousands of acres of malaria infested, or otherwise unproductive, soil which has been handed over, in some cases, to groups of peasants, working co-operatively, and in others, to independent tenants. Thus, "Bonifica", to give it the appropriate name, has won back from the Pontine marshes the new Province "Littoria" and claims in ten years to have brought into productive use no less than 17,000,000 acres of derelict land at a cost of only £45,000,000. The large landowners, too, have assisted this movement by establishing, in conjunction with local Fascist syndicates, co-partnership schemes for their labourers.

In certain of the individual American States, what in older countries would be referred to as *métayage* is found extensively practised under such titles as "share-cropping" and "share-renting", or even "bushel-renting". Any reader of such a compilation as E. G. Nourse's *Agricultural Economics* will there find a description of these systems, together with comparative analyses of the returns that may be anticipated from them.

In the case of share-cropping the same elasticity that characterises orthodox *métayage* is in evidence, and the significant fact emerges that this tenure is frequently most represented where the soil is poor and conditions generally unfavourable. Exact division of profits is the usual custom, and, although the bulk of all capital advances comes from the owner, the tenant is held responsible for providing half of the livestock. Share-renting is a modification of this method in that, for advancing a larger proportion of the farming capital, the tenant secures for himself a commensurately increased portion of the proceeds. Division takes the form of partial monetary payments—generally in the case of pasture-land—and of the handing over to the landlord of from one-fourth to one-half of the produce raised, customs varying in accordance with locality and the predominant crops.

Bushel-renting, when practised as in Iowa, implies an obligation upon the tenant to sell all the "corn" (i.e. maize) to his landlord at a pre-arranged price, this sum, apart from ordinary market considerations, again being dependent upon the proportion of the total capital advanced by himself; other cereals, when not comprising the main outturn of farms thus rented, are shared in kind on some fixed basis. It should be noted that here the explanation of the landlord's desire to secure considerable quantities of maize at a fixed price is due to the fact that he is himself generally engaged upon large-scale cattle raising in the neighbourhood, and is thus in effect sub-letting portions of his own undertaking.

While the first two of the above systems can be found in widespread operation in many States, modifications of them, too numerous to mention, also exist, being particularly favoured in the South. American opinion inclines to the view that, in a given area, the return to the landlord is somewhat higher when he enters upon one of these partnerships than is the case when he merely leases his farm to a tenant; indeed, figures relating to some hundreds of undertakings in a district of the Mississippi delta (quoted by Nourse from an official *Bulletin* of the United States Department of Agriculture) evidenced an average profit of 13·6 per cent. when the land was in the hands of a share-cropper, of 11·8 per cent. when occupied by a share-renter and of 6·6 per cent. when let on normal terms. Share-cropping, whilst obviously holding out the greatest possibilities, could, however, reduce the landlord's returns almost to nothing for, on occasions when his tenant lost money, it was conceivable that he would find himself in receipt of a 1 per cent. dividend, but, on the other hand, in good seasons the increased prosperity of the latter might be reflected in a return of upwards of 25 per cent. Here there is nothing novel or unexpected, but merely an expression of the fluctuations inevitable in farming profits; the question then arises as to whether the increased return to the owner recorded in these American examples can be expected in all circumstances and for long periods of time, also if it is accompanied by any altered standard of farming practice. In the absence of a full and impartial enquiry we are left in the dark in this respect, with a feeling that possibly in the passage of time, and with growth of population, that nation may tend to shed practices which elsewhere have been found in purely agrarian countries, and, incidentally, those not remarkable for their rate of production per unit of land. Thus in Australia, among other new countries, share-farming is found upon a considerable scale, being generally established upon the basis that the owner, in addition to land and buildings, provides half the manure and half the seed; in return for the labour of himself and his family, the share-tenant draws annually 40 per cent. of the ascertained profits.

Turning to the other extreme, from the New World to the Old, from a country which has always claimed to possess the freest institutions to one that, until recently, provided the only example of feudalism still extant, we find in Russia, not the opportunity to examine two-party profit-sharing schemes, but of surveying the transition from agricultural practices that we associate with Rampton and Brotherton, and of following the indifferent success that ensued from a too sudden sweeping away alike of tenure and of tradition. The bulk of the land in Russia was already in the hands of the peasants before either the war or the revolution occurred, but that it was economically farmed or was producing more than a fraction of what it might have done, cannot be substantiated. Personal emancipation of the serfs, dating from 1861, had been gradually followed by the appropriation to them of land previously subject to irksome service. But, by this very process, the individual peasant became in the majority of cases dependent upon the "Mir", or communal body; hereditary possession, or the freedom to purchase his holding, could, in neither case, agriculturally speaking, compensate for the grave disadvantages that common-field husbandry forced upon him—especially when it was still subject to arbitrary and annual redistribution between himself and his fellows. Certainly, the rate of production, especially of cereals, was the lowest achieved in the world, and for this the open-fields, that more than a century ago were swept away in the rest of Europe, must be held responsible. A *Report*, compiled under the auspices of the League of Nations, contains the following remarkable statistics: "The average yield of cereal crops per desyatin from 1861 to 1870 on proprietors' land was 33 poods, on peasants' land 29 poods; forty years later, in 1901 to 1910 the former figure had been advanced to 54 poods and the latter to 43 poods; the percentage of increase was therefore considerably greater on the large owners' farms than on the peasants' holdings".

It may well be that the typical Russian peasant would, owing to lack of capital, have been incapable of benefiting from individual occupation, and that interspersed strips of arable and grass-land, often lying at considerable distances from his village, were still best suited to his character and ability. Unfortunately, independent reports constantly referred to the apathetic attitude of the Mir towards the technical side of agriculture, and it would seem that these bodies were weighed down with their duties of an economic and social character. Certainly, accounts of the practices to be observed on the arable land of any Russian village were reminiscent, not merely of eighteenth century pre-enclosure periods in England, but, rather, of some decadent fourteenth century manor. The scattered strips, numbering sometimes upwards of a hundred, in the possession of one man, and subject to redistribution, the primitive implements in use, the three-course rotation, the absence of manure, the combined labour during harvest and the immense distances to be travelled, placed a premium on inefficiency, and, in case of unfavourable conditions, reduced the margin of safety to a dangerous extent. On the other hand, those undertakings directed by the large landowners, even if their equipment was not up to the standard of the majority of European countries, were better farmed and were rendering a more normal return in the way of crops. It was plain that, in a country such as Russia, large-scale operations were essential, at least for corn raising, although this need not, *ipso facto*, have implied the extinction of the peasant proprietor, for, if he could have been placed in possession of the technical advantages enjoyed by the large landowner, the great open fields, with their strips thrown together, would, decades earlier, have provided the opportunity for a large experiment in communal husbandry.

Just before the war the State apparently grasped the dangers of the situation and was attempting to reorganise both tenure and cultivation by handing over Crown and other lands to the peasants, by enforcing the amalgamation and redistribution of existing holdings and by virtually dissolving the powers of the Mir. Vast numbers of small farmers were thus, from 1906 to 1914, in process of being established on their own holdings and the area of the land farmed by large proprietors was steadily diminishing. Dr Pavlovsky, in *Russia on the Eve of the Revolution*, states that 43,000,000 acres had been transferred between 1883 and 1912. Leasehold was also on the increase, and the type of small tenant-farmer familiar to other countries was beginning to spring up. The effect of all this is reflected in the statement that in 1914 no less than two-thirds of the crops raised came from peasant-owned properties and only one-third from those of the former land-owning classes. That the official recognition of individual ownership on the part of the peasantry did not at once result in the disappearance of open-field farming was due to the fact that, where a majority of the Mir preferred to continue this form of cultivation, they were permitted so to do. Two potentially adverse factors arose as a result of the redistribution of land into separate detached holdings, namely the economic danger, always present where small occupier-owners exist, that succession might eventually produce minute subdivision, and the practical difficulty caused by the awkward shape (generally a long rectangular plot) given to the new farms, from a desire to include, for each occupant, samples of all types of soil, together with access to water.

It was upon this period of transition that the events of 1914 intruded, the ultimate results of which, as they affected wheat production in particular, will be found dealt with in Chapter XIX, but a few words of a more general character must be added here. The Revolution that followed the breakdown of Russia as a military

PLATE XIV

Air view (below) of a Russian "collectivised" farm and (above) of peasants' strip holdings

power led to a complete reversal of the process described above, for the people, not content with the normal routine of revolutionaries—the seizure of land belonging to the nobility and of other large owners—actually restored communal cultivation, and even essayed the subdivision of the newly-won freeholds of the larger peasants. That the Government saw the dangers of the situation created by this retrograde movement is certain, for it attempted counter-measures by the establishment of Soviet farms, but its initial efforts in this direction met with little success, and the so-called "rulers" tended to become the passive spectators of the spoliation of land upon the largest scale ever recorded.

The landless townsman and the very smallest peasant thus secured what they desired, and the average size of a "Small Holding" was increased, but the most experienced of those formerly connected with the land had been dispossessed, and the newcomers had neither the initiative nor the desire to cultivate beyond providing for their own immediate needs. Meanwhile the cities approached starvation. The *Report* prepared by the League of Nations, and previously referred to, contained extracts from official Russian sources that clearly showed this tendency. Thus, whilst in 1916 5,644,000 farms in European Russia had a sown area equivalent to an average of 4·97 desyatins per farm, this figure successively declined to 3·0 desyatins per farm in 1917 and to 2·46 in 1919—in other words, there was a decline of some 50 per cent. The Soviet Government was ultimately driven to intervene, and, by a series of decrees, sought to make land available to all who would cultivate it, whether on co-operative farms or on separate holdings, but the landless citizen, rather than the experienced peasant, was, as usual, the object of this solicitude, with the result that the worst possible type of occupier was placed in possession of the bulk of Russian soil.

The original Soviet farms soon proved useless, so that the work of individual revolutionaries, aided by the subsequent constructive efforts of their Government, had reduced the agriculture of Russia to a thing of nought. Famine followed, and the rest of the world could but stand by and watch events run their predestined course. In the spring of 1922—extreme subdivision of holdings having in the meantime been forbidden—certain steps aiming at an improvement in agricultural conditions were at last taken. These comprised the conceding of freedom of cultivation to individuals and to communes, the forbidding of the partitioning of meadow-land, and, most striking of all, the acknowledgement of the right of competent individuals to lease farms. The exact words of the last enactment may well be quoted from the League of Nations' *Report* dealing with this subject—"Farms temporarily fallen into desuetude as a result of famine, fire, loss of labour, cattle or other reason may be let out on lease either in whole or in part, in return for money, produce or other remuneration."

Thereafter, for some years, the agrarian position was, to the outside observer, obscure. He heard, on the one hand, that the Central Government was, whilst restraining the avidity of occupiers of larger areas, successfully "collectivising" the smaller type of peasant; on the other hand, he read of growing discontent in both town and country, of inadequate food supplies and of the threatened breach between rural and urban interests. In the circumstances, such a conflicting situation was not a matter for surprise, for the vast territory of Russia, its wide diversity of race, climate and soil, must all preclude generalisation, whilst political suspicion then prevented any but *ex parte* statements from receiving adequate consideration. When the curtain was at last lifted, there was revealed to be already at work a policy that has been described as "de-kulakisation", or the elimination of the re-established larger (*kulak*) peasant and, in process of preparation, a gigantic scheme for the commercialisation of agriculture—the Five Year Plan. This was in 1927, and within two, or at the most three, years, the kulaks had had individually to make their choice between exile and conformity with the new régime. Reliable reports show that nearly two-thirds of these persons were, by 1932 (viz. the end of the five years) found to be working on the collective farms. Not only was their land taken from them, but the resultant loss of livestock handicapped them in the new position; stores of grain were also confiscated. Communal labour on communal farms accordingly represents a social and economic reverse; simultaneously the strictly controlled and assessed labour involved in piecework and teamwork is irksome. It is claimed, however, that this system, whereby all modern methods of cultivation are made available to its members, and under which they share in the profits, is proving successful from the standpoint both of the nation and of the individual.

In so far as the Five Year Plan itself is concerned, final judgment must be suspended, but it can be agreed that, although the original conceptions have not been fully implemented, yet, nevertheless, a remarkable achievement has been accomplished, although in agriculture the results fall behind those obtained in the secondary industries. Briefly, the aim of those responsible for the scheme was to make of Russia the agricultural factory of the world; they planned to set up a very large number of gigantic farms (extending, if necessary, into an area reckoned by the hundred thousand acres), equipped with machinery of the largest possible size, directed by unquestioned experts, linked with the secondary industries of the country and correlated with its urban economy. The principal function of these farms was to provide a growing surplus of cereals and of other food-stuffs for export. In the course of 1932, it was stated that 12,000,000 peasant holdings (covering four-fifths of the cultivated land) had been amalgamated into some 200,000 collective farms, of which about one hundred were those of the above-mentioned largest class. The air photograph facing page 96 affords an interesting view of the two types of farming in juxtaposition; the typical arrangement of strips should be noticed. It is unnecessary here to quote statistics relating either to the number of tractors built (or of the much smaller number in full use), or to the increased output of grain secured, for it will suffice, in this connection, to point out that Russia, in 1930, resumed, for the first time since 1914, and upon a considerable scale, her export of cereals, and that in the next two years these shipments, although still below the pre-war level, were exercising the minds of her competitors in every Continent. Difficulties of a technical, rather than of an administrative, character have made themselves felt during these years and the fulfilment of the Plan will be delayed, so that questions such as the possibility of a permanent expansion of commercial agriculture in the Northern territories will not have immediately to be answered, for, in the meantime, there is still a surplus of the better and even of some of the very best (or black-land) soil available in the South-East.

The total area under cultivation in Russia had, by the end of the critical period, reached a figure of 340,000,000 acres as compared with 290,000,000 acres before the war, and, in view of the previous decline, this is of far more significance than any meticulous estimate of the exact figures by which the year-to-year achievements failed to come up to expectation. If the cultivational side be analysed in detail the results exhibit marked irregularities, of which perhaps the two most significant are the comparative failure to augment the head of livestock and the poor response to demands for increased output of such crops as cotton and tobacco—certain evidence, in the first case, of the reduction in personal interest. Administratively, too, it is likely that, in the future, assuming as is promised a second Five Year period to be entered upon, there may be difficulty in expanding adequately the output of tractors and of fertilisers; should continued importation of these essential requisites have to be relied upon, the Plan will again be endangered, as it will also be should it not be found progressively easier to train peasants as mechanics. The international aspects of Russia's demonstration may, too, in the next few years, have such far-reaching effects as to react upon the policy itself before its fullest economic possibilities have been demonstrated. Finally, it was obvious in 1932 that the peasants were still chafing under control and, at the same time, the towns were often short of food; neither of these features, however, was novel to Russia at any period during previous generations. Perhaps more significant was the formation of a "rural political police force", whose duties were to prevent the leakage of grain, to detect idle workers and to check cohesion upon the part of the peasantry. Whatever happens, the Russian Five Year Plan will always represent the largest and the most important experiment in the tenure of agricultural land that the world has witnessed and it is solely from that angle that it is cited in these pages.

Land-tenure in the rest of Europe, and especially in the Central and Near Eastern States, has within the last two decades been placed in the melting-pot, first by legislative action on the part of responsible, but harassed Governments, and subsequently by either veiled or open revolutionary methods. Untrammelled access to the soil for the most humble citizen and the establishment for him of State Small Holdings on land taken from private or from Church ownership have everywhere, from Denmark to Roumania, and from Portugal to Greece, been the objectives of the land reformers. As the economic limitations affecting such undertakings are discussed separately, a brief review of the steps taken in typical instances to effect this transference of land will, for the moment, suffice.

Denmark, one of the few non-belligerent agricultural nations, and one already recognising generously the claims of small owners, did not on these grounds escape a post-war extension of her agrarian legislation. Church lands, "entailed feudal estates", and lands acquired in the open market, were divided up and made available for occupation. Compulsion attached to the acquisition of the two former types, limited in some instances to a third of the total acreage involved, but in the case of private owners there was also a contingent liability in regard to one-fifth of the capital resources of the sequestered estate. Church lands "fit for agriculture" could be taken possession of in certain circumstances, as for instance when a vacancy occurred in a benefice; they were then sold publicly in parcels of a size sufficient to support a single family, but the incumbent received "rent" in the form of a 4½ per cent. dividend on the selling price of the property. The State itself also assumed a heavy financial burden in regard to the erection of buildings and the provision of credit to impecunious purchasers. That misgivings were already being felt as to the effects of the Acts dealing with the provision of Small Holdings passed long before this legislation, will be realised by all who have read in Rider Haggard's *Rural Denmark* the views of the Danish officials concerned in their administration. It was not unusual to find a strong feeling in existence that the creation, on very easy terms, of a large body of small freeholders was going to prove a mistaken policy, and that some form of protective tenancy might have to be substituted; indeed, the old Danish tenure, known as *Faeste*, and akin to a copyhold of lives, had been definitely suggested in this connection. Denmark, virtually still a free-trade country, suffered badly during the acute depression ruling from 1927 onwards, but there was no evidence to show that her difficulties were rendered greater than those of this country or other of her European neighbours, by reason that a large proportion of her farmers were owner-occupiers, or were farming small units of land.

In Poland, Czecho-Slovakia, Roumania, and, in fact, in all the newly formed or reorganised States of Central Europe, expropriation pure and simple ran its course after 1918. In some instances it formed merely the climax to a gradual process of curtailing the private ownership of large estates, in others it resulted from a sudden and irresistible onslaught. Perhaps the best example of the movement proceeding upon perfectly unobjectionable lines was provided by Portugal, where, in 1920, public bodies were authorised to take over all uncultivated lands, to subdivide them, and then either to dispose of them by auction or by contracts of *emphyteusis* (perpetual lease) subject to redemption by purchase.

Poland provides an example of a more drastic method, for, in 1920, the Diet ordered the expropriation and subdivision of land, the property, successively, of the following classes of owner—the State, members of former reigning families, the former Prussian Colonisation Committee, bishops, parishes and convents, public institutions. This seemed to provide a sufficiently comprehensive list, but to it were added, in order, all private properties "badly managed", "divided into plots without authorisation", "acquired between August 1st, 1914, and September 14th, 1919, by persons whose usual occupation was not farming" or by persons "unable to pay the price except by means of profits resulting from speculation", and estates that within the previous five years had changed hands on more than two occasions. Lastly, "all other private property" came within the ban of this law, for, after each of the above classes had yielded up to the State all its resources, any land still remaining had to follow, commencing with such as had been devastated by the war but remained unrestored by its owners. Varying upward limits were assigned to the area of holdings permitted to individuals, ranging from 60 hectares in suburban districts to 400 hectares in the Eastern part of the country. Whilst the first five classes of owner enumerated above suffered complete spoliation of their properties, it was arranged that the remaining classes should receive, in return for this "compulsory purchase", sums equal to half the average value of land in their district.

Roumania suffered from a serious peasants' revolt in 1907 that compelled considerable reforms, which in turn were superseded by post-war legislation of a most drastic character. The reforms themselves had included the abolition of customs almost feudal in their character, the standardisation of wages, and adequate provision for grazing facilities (a much needed want) for the smaller peasants. Lastly, the private ownership of land exceeding 4000 hectares in area was forbidden, thus affording a commentary on the undue size that private estates had attained. But the other extreme was now followed, for the ideal aimed at was the universal setting up of Small Holdings of some 5 to 7 hectares in area. Then, after the war, came what can only be described as confiscation, for individual ownership of land above certain limits in area was made illegal; these limits were fixed at 100 hectares in mountain districts and 200 elsewhere. Properties exceeding such dimensions were taken over, but compensation in the ordinary acceptance of the word was not given, for all land acquired by the State was valued on a pre-war basis (thus currency depreciation was ignored), and bonds equivalent to these low values, and yielding a very meagre rate of interest, were presented to the former owners.

Examples similar to this abounded in other countries; it was, for instance, reported in 1922 that the Latvian Government had handed bonds of the face value of 267,000 roubles, and bearing only 4 per cent. interest, to the former owner of an expropriated property that had been valued in 1914 at a million roubles. Although this point is not germane to the argument in general, it may be added that, as the owner was an Englishman, he received the equivalent of £236 for property which had represented to him an investment of some £100,000; moreover, if the land in question had descended through inheritance instead of by purchase the new Latvian laws would have prohibited any form of compensation whatsoever. In Esthonia again, where all the properties of the great landowners had been seized, in those instances where compensation was granted at all, it was based on the values existing in 1914. Czecho-Slovakia took as its basis the average values recorded in the period 1913–15, but, in the case of the larger properties, these values were subject to progressive deductions, ranging up to 40 per cent. for estates above 50,000 hectares. Ultimately, about one-third of all the land in the country thus changed hands.

Of all the peasantry of Europe, the French had the least claim to any further extension of their privileges, and it would have been difficult to suggest any method by which their access to the land could, in those times, have been facilitated. France did her best for them in other ways, notably by intensifying her fiscal policy. In Germany, on the other hand, the post-war land hunger was appeased by means of the National Settlement Law of 1919. This provided, in the first instance, the right to purchase, through the Public Utility Corporations, certain types and quantities of land; additionally, compulsory powers were granted in the case of large estates or of properties inadequately farmed. By these means, which stopped a long way short of those adopted farther East, a large addition was made to the number of small owner-occupiers in Germany. Nor should it be overlooked that, for two generations, the peasantry had, with the partial exception of the Northern and Eastern parts of the country, monopolised the soil and that a succession of enactments, that, literally, consolidated their holdings and, metaphorically, consolidated their economic position, had formed an integral part of the Empire-building policy.

In all the above referred to instances of State intervention it should be recorded that preference was generally given, in the first instance, to soldiers returned from the war, and, next, to former agricultural labourers on the expropriated lands; everywhere, also, steps were taken to provide the new cultivators with sufficient capital. This "Green Revolution" reached its peak about 1920, and, thereafter, most of the countries which it had overswept suffered reaction and either rescinded their penal regulations against private ownership of land or else tacitly ceased to enforce them. On the other hand, in later years, there were one or two fresh converts to Republicanism, when the familiar policy in regard to land was again pursued. Thus, after the Spanish revolution in 1931, all the land was declared to be national property and was taken over by the new government which, with certain familiar exceptions, gave compensation, based upon taxation values, to the owners. Cash was to be paid on a scale progressively reduced in proportion to the size of estates, ranging from 20 per cent. down to 2 per cent. of the whole value; the balance was payable in bonds at 5 per cent. These Spanish peasants are the latest recruits to the rural democracy of Europe; they bring with them, so far as Catalonia and some other provinces are concerned, a bitter feeling of hostility against the last régime and little enthusiasm for their new governors; they start their fresh activities, too, in no spirit of emancipation from the horrors of war, such as all their brothers in Central Europe enjoyed twelve years earlier. For them, perhaps, the future will, therefore, be the more trying. That future is everywhere difficult to forecast, for so immense an agrarian reformation, often in places hastily effected, cannot be expected to be permanently stable. In the case of millions of small cultivators, land-tenure has recently been superseded by land ownership, and democracy may have congratulated itself on the apparent simplicity of the operation, but economic laws, if sometimes they seem slow in action, are always certain, and, in relation to the soil, inexorable, and possibly the next generation will see new types of occupiers cultivating fresh divisions of the ever-disturbed soil of Europe. It is comforting to reflect, however, that revolutions have little effect upon rotations and that while crowns fall, corn still springs up.

Outside Europe, the practice of agriculture among the native races of the world, whatever system of occupation is pursued by them, may be said to involve two questions of paramount importance. The first is insufficiency of capital and the second the dangers attendant upon subdivision; there is a third, and this, from the European administrator's standpoint, is perhaps the most important of all, viz. what form of tenure should be granted to these indigenous races? The first of the above problems carries in its train—from India to Japan and from Morocco to South America—under whatever system he may labour—the economic bondage of the cultivator to human elements the reverse of desirable; the second, too, often inhibits him from making full use of his land and reduces, generation by generation, its heritable value. These two matters more properly pertain to other sections of this work, where they will be found expounded at some length. The third question, in relation to their Dependencies in Africa, calls for the serious consideration of several European races. Briefly, it resolves itself into this—should the native cultivator be suffered to own his land absolutely, should he be permitted merely to rent it from the government, or must he and his fellows be relegated to "reserves" where, while having freedom of action in this and other matters, they will, nevertheless, be virtually prisoners in territories "owned" by their forebears? If native ownership be permitted, it is frequently the case that severity on the part of landlords, perhaps in the end amounting to extortion, will occur, simultaneously with loss of prospective revenue to the administration; if tenancy alone is permitted, lack of initiative may be found and insecurity will be put forward as a reason for non-expansion of cultivation. Reserves carry, in certain quarters, a natural stigma, but if they are of sufficient extent, provide an ample margin of good land, are linked by modern means of access to the rest of the territory and are not subject to retrograde regulations, their establishment does, perhaps, present the best course to adopt. For it must be remembered that the races involved have frequently highly developed tribal customs, both in regard to

store. But is the first part of this contention correct? The manorial tenants, if cottars, could not have supported themselves on their few acres without eking out their living by working as labourers on the lord's demesne, and, if villeins, they were not small farmers in the accepted sense of the word, for they occupied arable acreage up to three figures in extent, and could only carry out their own field-work by mutual co-operation in the use of man-power, teams and implements. As we advance through the centuries we find each age lamenting the disappearance of the "yeoman"; but the term yeoman did not necessarily imply the ownership of land, for it frequently connoted merely a tenant, and, not necessarily, a small tenant. Economic changes, such as enclosures and alterations in systems of farming, admittedly caused a reduction in the number of smaller farmers, but on these occasions, if the position a generation or so later be re-examined, it would generally be found that, as a class, they reappeared again. The apparent exception to this rule is seen after the French war, when large arable farms were looked upon as the most efficient unit and when the labourer had lost his rights of common. But these rights alone had not constituted the worker a Small Holder, and some, at least, of their possessors were the antithesis of the modern conception of such a person; they gave considerable collective advantages, and their very abolition brought about a movement for the introduction of allotments; while many small farmers incidentally took the opportunity offered them at that time to consolidate their scattered strips. Economically, at least as important was the concurrent disappearance of the numerous rural industries, or rather of industries carried on in rural areas—which brought about a serious reduction in the family earnings of the class of person in question. Thereafter, Acts of Parliament specifically provided for the artificial creation of Small Holders.

Before discussing the question of large *versus* small farms, it is advisable to enquire into the distribution of each type in this country and in others abroad. The most complete analysis made in the past on these lines took the form of a paper read before the Royal Statistical Society by Major P. G. Craigie in 1887, and related to conditions two years earlier. On that occasion the number of holdings from one quarter of an acre to an acre in extent had been officially enumerated—a procedure that has not subsequently been repeated. The United Kingdom then contained 1,121,168 holdings above this quarter acre limit, of which 414,950 were in England, 60,190 in Wales, 80,715 in Scotland and 565,313 in Ireland: if we exclude the smallest size-group, these figures become, for the United Kingdom, 1,047,912: for England, 393,881; for Wales, 59,107; for Scotland, 79,355; and for Ireland, 515,569. On this last basis comparison can be carried out with the subsequent annual returns. For that purpose the separate divisions of the Kingdom, for which their respective official bodies are responsible, make the best starting point. In England and Wales in 1885 all holdings above an acre in extent numbered 452,988; in 1895, 440,467; in 1913, 435,677; in 1921, 420,133; and in 1931, 391,941—a steady reduction. The combined administrative areas in Ireland returned approximately 450,000 farms (347,840 and 101,047 respectively) in 1930, while the latest available figures for Scotland give 76,161. Caird's million farms in the United Kingdom are now, therefore, represented by a little over 900,000—or an over all reduction of 10 per cent.

The reduction has been progressive, but as it has at the same time been accompanied by a decline in the area of farm-land, that statistical fiction, the "average farm", of England and Wales has been little affected, having merely increased in size during the last ten years from some 62 acres to 64·5 acres. As is pointed out in the chapter on Statistics, the result of dividing the total area of land farmed by the number of undertakings themselves merely results in achieving the arithmetical average, while what is really wanted in this case is perhaps the "mode"—viz. the most frequently met with size—but this, to the perennial surprise of the townsman, is only about two acres in area. In 1885, Major Craigie gave the size of the average farm in England as 60 acres, in Wales as 46·8 and in Scotland as 60·1; figures which, as is indicated above, have since tended slightly to increase. The same authority analysed the distribution of holdings in groups of Counties, and showed that the North-Eastern and the South-Eastern contained the largest (averaging 69·6 and 69·9 acres respectively), whilst the Welsh (46·8) and the Northern and North-Western contained the smallest (48·7) acres. This feature is still to be observed, as reference to the more detailed Table at the end of the book will indicate; the explanation of course is that the corn-growing districts favour larger holdings than are found in milk-producing and livestock-raising areas, although close analysis will demonstrate that such a generalisation is unsafe and the multiplication of market-gardens outside populous centres and in certain favoured localities, combined with the artificial creation of Small Holdings, has to a certain extent modified Craigie's conclusions, but the larger farms are still centred in the Eastern half of England and in the Midland "shires". So we find that Northumberland has the largest average farm in the country (124·5 acres) and Rutland (the smallest county!) follows with one of 123 acres —devoted, since the 'nineties, to large-scale grazing operations. Lancashire, with an average of 41 acres, comes at the other extremity of the scale, followed by Cheshire.

The comparative movements of the different size-groups after 1885 deserve a few words, which the following Table will supplement.

Numbers of holdings in England and Wales

Size group (acres)	1885	1895	1913	1921	1931
1–5	114,273	97,818	92,302	81,217	71,204
5–20	126,674	126,714	122,117	116,159	102,339
20–50	73,472	74,846	78,027	80,967	77,374
50–100	54,937	56,791	59,287	61,001	61,951
100–300	67,024	68,277	69,431	67,842	66,927
Above 300	16,608	16,021	14,513	12,947	12,146
Total	452,988	440,467	435,677	420,133	391,941

It will be observed that the decline has been continuous in the two smallest size-groups, and also in that containing the largest holdings; medium-sized farms have been increasing numerically during the whole period. It inevitably causes surprise to persons who are constantly hearing of the creation and growth in numbers of Small Holdings to find that it is precisely those groups in which the majority would be looked for (one to twenty acres) that have decreased by no less than 41,000 during the years intervening between 1913 and 1931. These same eighteen years covered the period when active steps were being taken to place some thousands of ex-Service applicants upon the land and also to make secure in their occupation of this type of farm numerous civilian Small Holders. The accepted explanation of this decline is as follows. It is held, firstly, that the conversion during the war into allotments of fields in the outskirts of towns, previously in separate ownership, resulted in the disappearance of numerous small farms—a development with which the provision elsewhere of other similar-sized holdings did not keep pace; this movement, then, did not cause a reduction in the area under cultivation but merely transferred to spade husbandry land previously less intensively worked. It had been pointed out as early as 1913 that, since the Small Holdings Act of 1908 had come into force, over 11,000 small farms had been statutorily established, but that nevertheless there had been in the intervening time a net loss in the number of holdings below fifty acres in extent; for in normal times the encroachment of towns and the provision of "lungs" for their inhabitants inevitably tends to the extinction of small farms on their boundaries. The second explanation is that there has been, more recently, and by means of amalgamation of the smallest class of holding, a movement towards a concentration upon a more popular, or perhaps more economic, sized holding, ranging from 50 to 100 acres in extent. Lastly, it is stated to be open to argument whether a considerable proportion of the "farms" below 20 acres are really entitled to that appellation, for they frequently represent parcels of land detached from some estate or forming part of a residential property and possibly in no way conforming to the economic requirements of an "agricultural holding".

The size-groups of farms have so far been dealt with; there remains the question of the comparative acreage covered by each type. In 1885 Major Craigie wrote on that point as follows, confining his remarks to England, and including holdings above a quarter of an acre in his review:

> The area cut up into small holdings under 50 acres, and the area devoted to farms of 500 acres and upwards, are curiously enough nearly equal, and roughly the surface of England may be thus mapped out. In 294,729 small holdings under 50 acres there are 3,559,000 acres; in 115,525 medium holdings between 50 and 500 acres there are no less than 17,899,000 acres; in 4696 large holdings over 500 acres there are 3,434,000 acres. The smaller, or "20 acres and under" holdings in the first of these divisions would themselves suffice to occupy a County nearly of the size of Devon, and, roughly speaking, we may best realise the proportion of our small farms to the whole by imagining on the map of England that the three South-Western counties of Cornwall, Devon and Somerset had their entire superficies represented by the small "under 50 acres" holdings.

The majority of subsequent enquiries adopting England and Wales as the statistical unit, comparison with Major Craigie's simile is not possible, but, for the latter area, the following Table can be compiled for a pre-war and the two latest available post-war years.

England and Wales

Size group (acres)	Total acreage, 1913	Total acreage, 1921	Total acreage, 1924
1–5	285,000	253,000	241,000
5–20	1,373,000	1,310,000	1,264,000
20–50	2,623,000	2,720,000	2,691,000
50–100	4,325,000	4,443,000	4,414,000
100–150	3,942,000	3,955,000	3,924,000
150–300	7,844,000	7,475,000	7,421,000
Over 300	6,737,000	5,988,000	5,921,000
Total	27,129,000	26,144,000	25,876,000

The same features are observable as in the former Table showing numbers of holdings; that is to say, the relative importance of the extreme size-groups has tended to decline. Farms between 150 and 300 acres easily cover the largest area of agricultural land, half of which is still devoted to holdings above 150 acres in extent.

Two types of farmer have always been associated with certain sized farms, for it is popularly held that 50 acres forms roughly the dividing line between the holdings farmed by those who use their hands and those who use their brains, and, again, that the former class represents the reward of the successful farm worker, whilst holdings between 50 and 100 acres, at one time believed to afford a refuge for farmers who had failed on a larger scale, are now sought after on account of their technical desirability. Statistical tables cannot advance or refute such theories; in this case it can merely be observed that holdings between 50 and 150 acres have tended to maintain their numbers (and their acreage), and only in the very largest and the very smallest sizes is there found any serious reduction.

The distribution between ownership and tenancy is a matter to which enquiries have been directed upon several occasions. "Ownership" in the published statistics relating to this country is defined as comprising land "owned or mainly owned", hence comparison with conditions ruling in other countries is a speculative enterprise;

An unusual crop (*Papaver somniferum*) grown in an Isle of Axholme strip

but, if enquiry be confined to England and Wales, matters are otherwise. Prior to the outbreak of war there was a tendency for the numbers of owners to decline, as figures published by the Board of Agriculture in 1913 showed, for in 1909 there were owned in England and Wales 55,920 farms of all sizes, or 12·98 of the total enumerated; in 1913 the number was 48,760 and the percentage 11·19. Again, the greatest decline was in the ownership of the really large and of the smallest holdings. The war itself caused little change in the total number owned, and the medium and large increased numerically, while the owners of the smallest class declined, but after the conclusion of hostilities it soon became apparent that tenants were rapidly purchasing their holdings. At first this movement did not extend to the really small man, but after 1919 he, too, was enabled (or compelled in many instances) to become his own landlord, as the next Table shows.

Holdings owned or mainly owned in England and Wales

Size of holding (acres)	1913	1919	1920	1921
1–5	12,606	10,453	10,952	12,028
5–20	14,814	13,786	15,780	18,635
20–50	8,093	8,346	10,188	13,069
50–100	5,399	6,380	8,154	10,769
100–150	2,767	3,463	4,485	5,844
150–300	3,265	4,216	5,323	7,170
Over 300	1,816	2,021	2,352	2,954
Total	48,760	48,665	57,234	70,469

In two years there was thus an increase of some 45 per cent. in the number of owner-occupiers; an increase that was, however, unevenly distributed between the different size-groups. It was largest in that comprising farms of 150 to 300 acres and steadily declined as the size-groups themselves diminished, until, for that of one to five acres, it represented some 15 per cent. In all, 17 per cent. of the farms were owned by their occupiers. Concurrently, whilst in 1913 only some 10·7 of the area of farm-land was owned by those residing on it, in 1921 this figure had become 20 per cent., and in 1927—the last occasion upon which the Ministry of Agriculture attempted to secure information relating to this particular question—it was actually over 36 per cent.; thus 9,225,000 acres were in the possession of their occupiers—whose numbers had been trebled during the preceding thirteen years and who now also represented more than one-third of all the farmers in England and Wales.

War had, as was the case a hundred years before, caused a large transference of land. Much of it was undoubtedly purchased at fictitious and transitory values, and it was remarkable to observe how large a proportion of its new owners weathered the economic difficulties that subsequently ensued. Up to the present, despite the exaggerated reports current, matters are fortunately a long way removed from the state of affairs prevailing after the Napoleonic war, when hundreds of thousands of acres of land were lying derelict or were being offered for nominal sums. Universal occupying-ownership is no doubt a legitimate ideal at which to aim, but unless it is achieved on an economic basis, and in times of stability, it may become an incubus which overwhelms a large proportion of its adopters. Landlords have the power, and have in bad times invariably exercised it, to ease the financial position of tenants; occupying owners have no such extraneous help to fall back on and are lucky, indeed, if it is their own and not borrowed capital that they see depreciating.

Ample evidence has been adduced to show that this country is not associated with one particular size or class of holding, but that numerous examples of all can be found in every part of it. Before examining the economy of the large and Small Holding it is best briefly to review the corresponding conditions in certain other countries. But here, for reasons that will be found explained in the chapter on Statistics, we are at once on extremely treacherous ground. In France, all enquirers from Arthur Young down to the latest American investigator have agreed that the number of separate "agricultural organisations" is immense, but none has found a reliable basis on which to make comparison with conditions in this country. Again, all agree that peasant proprietorship is almost universal and that really small undertakings are, actually and relatively, far more numerous than here, for the Revolution removed all feudal obligations on land and virtually exterminated the larger landowner, the small peasant thereby becoming firmly established as a proprietor.

Taxation rolls gave, a few years prior to the publication of Craigie's paper, a total of over fourteen million *cotes foncières*, but

French authorities themselves suggested eight million as the total number of owners, of whom three million were exempt from taxation owing to the microscopic size of their *cotes*. Yet, again, subdivision of holdings into minute portions of land resulted in individual tenants farming, as a unit, soil belonging to several owners —*morcellement* at its worst, with 125,000,000 separate parcels of farmed land! Craigie tentatively accepted the results of an official enquiry held in 1873, which gave a total of almost four million as representing the number of owners, tenants and *métayers* engaged in farming, the extent of whose holdings covered 84,000,000 acres, or an "average" of 21 acres per individual cultivator. This latter figure is probably an overestimate, and subsequent statistics of farm acreage recorded a smaller "average" size. Later enquiries gave 5,672,000 as the number of farms in 1882 and 5,703,000 in 1892, while, at that latter date, there were still stated to exist over 8,000,000 owners of French soil and only some 1,100,000 farmers were returned as leaseholders or *métairie* tenants. A naturally popular French table is often quoted in this country. Compiled by M. de Lavergne, it conveniently and roundly grouped the component parts of the 1882 total into 50,000 large farms, 500,000 medium-sized and 5,000,000 small. No further statistics have since become available, and, if allowance be made for the transference of Alsace-Lorraine, the position probably remains much the same at the present time.

After perusing, therefore, the above figures it will be agreed that small proprietors were, and still are, vastly more numerous in France than in this country; it remains, then, to enquire how they are distributed and what they produce. Roughly, the Northern divisions of the country contain the larger farms and the South the smaller, but the nature of the soil and the presence or absence of vineyards affect the question. Corn-growing districts, as is always the case, are associated with the largest holdings, and, apart from the influence exercised by special types of cultivation, Small Holders are most frequently met with in the outskirts of towns. It is an undoubted fact that the standard rate of yield of cereal crops in France is little better than half that secured in England and Wales, but the dangers of arguing that this is attributable to the smaller average size of French holdings are too obvious to require attention directed to them. The potent factor here is doubtless that the protection so long, and so generously, afforded the French producer of cereals has induced him to keep under the plough some millions of acres of poor land that would otherwise have received scanty attention and that gives very small outturns, thus reducing the average yield for the whole country.

It is probable that the same area in France under large farms would produce a better yield per acre owing to the greater use that could be made of capital, of machinery and of scientific achievements, or, conversely, that a smaller area could produce the present output; but a reduction in employment might result, and the policy of France has always been to be self-supporting and at the same time to keep the bulk of her people on the land—the latest census figures indicate that over 50 per cent. of the population dwell in rural areas. In no other country, indeed, could *la noblesse paysanne* dominate an official list of 750 families that had occupied the same land for at least three centuries—the doyen of which claimed that his first known ancestor had held the property in the year 772! The war accelerated a gradual increase in grass-land at the expense of arable and, within seven years of the cessation of hostilities, the livestock of France had returned to its normal numbers and the war zone had been restored to its agricultural uses. This peasant nation of Europe may be said to have carried out the precept of her own Statesman and resumed the cultivation of her garden.

Germany differs from France in regard to the distribution of her holdings and in her policy towards the farming industry. The former consist of very numerous small farms in the West and of relatively few large ones in the East and North. Figures relating to the year 1907 gave 5,736,082 as the grand total—a result closely corresponding to the similar French returns and one that, if allowance be made for the transferred territories, differs little from the present. Space forbids an account of the causes that have led to the distribution of holdings, but the influence of soil and of nationality have played important parts, and the once open-fields of the plains and the grazing-land of the valleys can still be clearly traced by the forms of husbandry now practised and by the size of the different undertakings. The land divided between junkers and Small Holders, if we include only that which is comparable to the area "under crops and grass" in this country, now affords an "average" of some thirteen or fourteen acres per holding. Craigie gave fifteen acres as the corresponding figure in 1885. Sir Thomas Middleton, in his *Recent Development of German Agriculture*, has gone at great length into the economy of the "average" German farm in comparison with the corresponding English one. It is impossible in these pages to follow his calculations into the number of persons each supports, beyond remarking that the essential difference between the two countries consists in the fact that the bulk of the German farm is under the plough, whilst grass preponderates in the British area; it is of interest to notice that he holds that this country contains four times as many farms "of a doubtful size" (125–250 acres) as does Germany.

As in the case of France, the "average" holding is about one-quarter the size of that found here, but German thoroughness, in the space of two generations, has altered the whole complexion of her agriculture, and State aid in numerous directions, combined with a growing tariff on imported farm produce, raised the yields of all her principal crops to the level attained in this country. Germany thus improved her agriculture whilst becoming an industrial nation of the first class; rural France remained stationary.

It would be idle to deny, however, that the German Statesmen and economists responsible for agrarianism were not fortunate in many ways; for example, when prices rose the tariff policy secured credit which should rightly have been attributed to a world-wide monetary movement, brought about by an increased supply of gold, and climatic influences more than once countered fluctuations that would otherwise have proved difficult of reconciliation. The German peasant proprietor did not numerically dominate the agricultural position to the same extent as did his French neighbour, but he was perhaps more receptive of new ideas, more amenable to instruction and certainly was better organised. German thoroughness could thus bring about an admirable balance between industry and agriculture, developing both to the uttermost whilst retaining all that was best in peasant economy.

With the exception of Holland and Belgium, where small farms are the rule, it is safe to generalise for the rest of Europe and to say that, despite the Green Revolution, most other countries—not excluding Denmark—contain numbers of small farms intermixed with large estates. As has been shown in the previous Chapter, the policy adopted almost universally since the upheaval of 1914 has resulted in the compulsory splitting up of the latter and a resultant large increase in the numbers of the former.

In Roumania, where this policy was carried to an extreme, the effects are seen in the shape of the subsequent reduced exports of wheat, and in all cases it would appear that peasants, when placed in the ownership of land, are content with producing sufficient of the staple crops for their own requirements, and will not exert themselves to resume the same degree of exportation that their former landlords accomplished. Unfortunately only one country in Europe has ever compiled statistics of the relative yields from large and small farms and, oddly enough, that country is Roumania. There, for many years, a distinction was drawn between holdings above and below 100 hectares (247 acres) in extent, and separate statistics in regard to each group were published. The outstanding fact recorded is that for all crops, and under all conditions, ranging from bad seasons to exceptionally good, the yield per acre was consistently higher on the larger farms. Before giving examples of this, it is well to forestall criticism by admitting the obvious statistical openings for error. In the first place, prior to expropriation, the number of smaller farms exceeded a million, whilst the large numbered only some three or four thousand, but the total acreage concerned in each case was large. The average size of the holdings in the lower group was really small, amounting to less than four hectares (under ten acres). Moreover, the area devoted to the principal crops in each of the two groups was, prior to 1915, sufficiently large to form a basis for comparison. The acreage under wheat was almost exactly the same; the small farmer, however, grew more barley, oats, potatoes and especially maize than the large landowner, but the latter devoted more ground to sugar-beet.

A glance at Table X in the Appendix will demonstrate the effects of the post-war Roumanian land policy, which are evidenced by the great decline in the area under all these crops on the large farms and by their only partial transference to the land of the smaller men.

A standard objection often legitimately raised against the comparison of yields from large and small farms is that the nature of the soil may be the determining factor in the distribution of the holdings themselves. This, however, almost always operates in favour of the Small Holder, and there certainly appears to be no valid reason for suspecting, in the case of pre-war Roumania, that the large landowners had secured an exclusive right to the richest soil. If we accept the statistical samples as sufficiently large, and find no evidence as to irregular distribution of soil conditions, we are forced to the conclusion, after studying the Table itself, that, in the only European country which is available for investigation, the yield per acre of all staple crops was potentially greater on farms above 250 acres in extent than on those below that limit.

Partial returns exist in the case of Germany which tend inexorably in the same direction. J. H. Clapham (*Economic Development of France and Germany, 1815–1914*) gave figures for the yield of six crops in the province of Mecklenburg-Schwerin and also in Bavaria. No statistics for different sizes of holding of course existed, but Mecklenburg had 60 per cent. of its farm land in holdings above 250 acres, and in Bavaria 70 per cent. was then devoted to holdings under 50 acres in size. The soil of the former was "not naturally fertile" and that of the latter "is partly high and infertile, but also contains some very favoured districts". The Table itself is self-explanatory.

Average yield in 100 *kilogrammes per hectare for the decade* 1902–11

	Rye	Wheat	Barley	Oats	Potatoes	Meadow hay
Mecklenburg	17·9	23·7	22·4	21·2	141·6	41·2
Bavaria	15·8	16·0	17·1	15·6	116·9	48·6

The author comments thus: "The figures, if not exact, are telling. Where agricultural knowledge is least needed, in the hay field, Bavaria leads. Everywhere else it is hopelessly outdistanced, worst of all in the best crop—wheat". This again, affords a partial example on a small scale of what there is little reason to doubt is the true state of affairs in most countries; figures for post-war Russia have already been quoted as providing similar material. The foreign peasant *can* produce crops equal to those of the large farmer, but unless he secures special advantages from soil conditions he cannot generally obtain similar returns from cereals and roots; his inability may be variously attributed to lack of knowledge and initiative or to actual shortage of the more material aids to higher agricultural practice.

Recent investigations carried out by the Cambridge Department of Agriculture (and published in its Farm Economics Branch *Report*

No. 19, *An Economic Survey of Agriculture in the Eastern Counties of England, 1931*) provide certain material very relevant to this subject. Here (p. 51) in the case of sugar-beet the comparative rates of yield by size-groups of holdings are recorded as follows: 20–50 acres, 6·4 tons per acre; 50–100 acres, 7·0; 100–150 acres, 7·5 tons; 150–300 acres, 7·8; over 300 acres, 8·0 tons. The rate of increase is progressive throughout the entire range of farms concerned and is free from any correlation with soil or other disturbing factors; the sample was a large one. Sugar-beet is precisely one of those crops where this disparity would be looked for at its maximum, for it makes exceptional demands upon both the personal, technical and financial resources of its growers; here the scales are accordingly weighted heavily in favour of the large unit of production.

Generally, one finds in countries in which he does not predominate numerically that the peasant's handicap in the case of field crops is diminished by his settling on the richer land; again, this process may be simply economic in its origin, or it can have been stimulated artificially. Instances of both abound in this country. The Isle of Axholme, already referred to, and the Isle of Ely accommodate some thousands of small occupiers and proprietors, who have at their disposal tracts of the richest soil in the United Kingdom; the majority of the former are the lineal descendants of past cultivators of their land; many of those around Ely have been placed on their holdings with State assistance, although for centuries this part of Cambridgeshire had been noted for its productivity. Lysons, for instance, describing the neighbourhood in 1808, wrote: "Many of the inhabitants are employed in the culture of gardens; great quantities of asparagus and various other vegetables being sent by the gardeners to Cambridge and London. The cherry gardens are extensive—the soil indeed seems to have been from a very early period favourable for the growth of fruit—three acres of vineyard are mentioned in the Survey of Domesday; in 1368 an anonymous writer of a chronicle on the monastery speaks of the vineyard as very productive". The market-gardening industry of Bedfordshire also sprang up in that County because, as a trade, it calls for an easily worked soil.

The relative financial success of Small Holders, especially abroad, is often affected by the fact that such undertakings do not form their sole means of livelihood. Thus, recent investigation has shown that a hundred and fifty years ago, in a typical Norfolk parish, practically every occupier of land below twenty acres in extent was in active pursuit of some calling additional to husbandry, for the carrier, innkeeper, wheelwright and cordwainer, together with a host of others, all figured in the list of small tenants, none of whom was without some other form of income. During another inquiry into East Anglian farming held by the staff of the Cambridge Department of Agriculture, similar conditions were found to persist, for a surprisingly large proportion of those who were officially scheduled as occupiers of land in the smallest size-groups were discovered to be garage-proprietors, publicans, local government employees, small shop-keepers and so forth; many, indeed, rejected any claim to the title of Small Holder, including the proprietor of a menagerie in its winter quarters! The bulk were, it was obvious, subsisting upon a successful combination of agriculture and industry. Craigie included a Table in his paper, showing that the smaller the holding in a typical German district the larger were its occupier's extraneous and supplementary sources of income. This feature is one to be looked for in those countries or districts in which smaller farms have existed for some time, rather than where they have just been established. It is, indeed, only by long experience, and possibly in the second or third generation, that the peasant learns the wisdom, whenever possible, of keeping his eggs in more than one basket; the newcomer too often trusts to his own skill, some luck and an initial grant from a benevolent State.

Intimately bound up with the question of the preponderance of small farms is that of density of population. Generally, the less numerous the population per unit of area the larger will be found the "average" holding. The corollary of this is that the more recent the development of a country the larger its holdings. The United States and Canada provide cases in point, and, moreover, show in process of evolution, the reduction in size of farms as population, rapidly increasing, moves Westward. The farms in their Eastern and Middle Eastern districts are gradually cut up and subdivided, whilst the newly broken land of the West and North is parcelled out into larger undertakings. As has been repeatedly pointed out, under certain conditions of land-tenure and inheritance excessive subdivision in older countries becomes a positive drawback.

In Switzerland the majority of holdings are owned by their occupiers, and the average size of all is really small, for anything over thirty hectares (seventy-four acres) is described as "large". The head of the Department of Land Improvement in Canton Vaud contributed, in 1913, an article to the *Bulletin* of the International Agricultural Institute, in which he described the disadvantages attendant on the scattered strips of land held by individual owners, and explained the process of consolidation. He held that the large proportion of Small Holdings in his country was a benefit, but "we must endeavour to attenuate the evil effects of a too minute subdivision in the interest of the Small Holdings themselves, and try to increase their rental capacity". The arguments he adduced against the tenure of numerous scattered parcels of land were those with which readers are already familiar. In Switzerland the average number of separate parcels going with each farm was over fourteen, the smaller holdings suffering the greatest hardship in this respect, although enclosure, in the accepted sense of the word, had been facilitated by process of legislation from the year 1591 onwards. In fairness to the Swiss cultivators one must differentiate between the size of holdings and the multiplicity of their pieces of land when commenting upon the economic difficulties that they were encountering, for there is no evidence that large holdings would have more smoothly surmounted the drawbacks of such land-tenure. But the Swiss were in agreement that the advantages that followed on redistribution were felt most by the owners of really Small Holdings. These men had been the great sufferers from inability to make use of machinery and from the relatively greater loss of time and money in supervising distant scraps of land, and it was they who were, as a result of consolidation, now placed more nearly on an equality in this respect with the large farmer. Here was no question of the pros or cons of large or Small Holdings *per se*, but merely an admission that the owners of the latter had less margin to spare when suffering under physical and economic disabilities.

In many parts of France a similar state of things exists, where not only *morcellement*, but the diminutive size of certain complete "farms" prevents full use being made of the land. Many, indeed, will be familiar with the apocryphal account of husbandry pursued in these conditions when there is not room to wield a full-sized spade, and with the reputed impossibility of growing fruit trees owing to the danger of their overspreading one's neighbour's land! Concurrently with the resettlement of the war-devastated regions the opportunity has been taken to readjust boundaries and to consolidate scattered parcels of land. Thus, in certain areas of France this evil of minute subdivision has been checked, but not, it is to be feared, eradicated permanently.

In parts of India an approach to such a state of affairs is also found, for, under both Hindu and Mohammedan law, subdivision of land into equal parts is a recognised course to pursue in cases of family dispute, and inheritance also operates in the same direction. Where a system of joint cultivation exists the family holding may in a few generations thus become split up into an innumerable quantity of scattered strips and parcels. Conditions in China are familiar to so many people, that perhaps the following Table, relating to Japan, will serve to emphasise the ubiquity of the problem in the Far East and, incidentally, to demonstrate the still rural character of that nation.

Japanese land-owning families (1928)

Holdings of agricultural land	Number of families	Percentage of the total number of families
Below 1·2 acres	2,504,000	49·6
1·2 acres and above	1,240,000	24·5
2·4 acres and above	909,000	18·1
7·2 acres and above	228,000	4·6
12 acres and above	112,000	2·2
24 acres and above	45,000	0·9
120 acres and above	4,000	0·1
Total	5,042,000	100·0

Even in South America the question crops up, for in a work by L. Portman on Bolivia, the author states that there the law of succession decrees that a man's land shall descend in equal parts to his sons. The difficulties encountered in Europe and Asia in these circumstances are circumvented in Bolivia by the formation of syndicates which work numerous plots as single undertakings, but it is curious to find such a state of affairs existing in a country where the large farm is admittedly the economic unit.

The question of the relationship between population and the size of holdings was touched upon above, and there is another relevant matter that deserves a moment's attention here. It has on occasion been shown that a connection exists between the density of population and the rate of production of certain crops. This is a feature distinct from the well-known correlation between the area under cereals and the rate of yield, for there is clear evidence that the yield

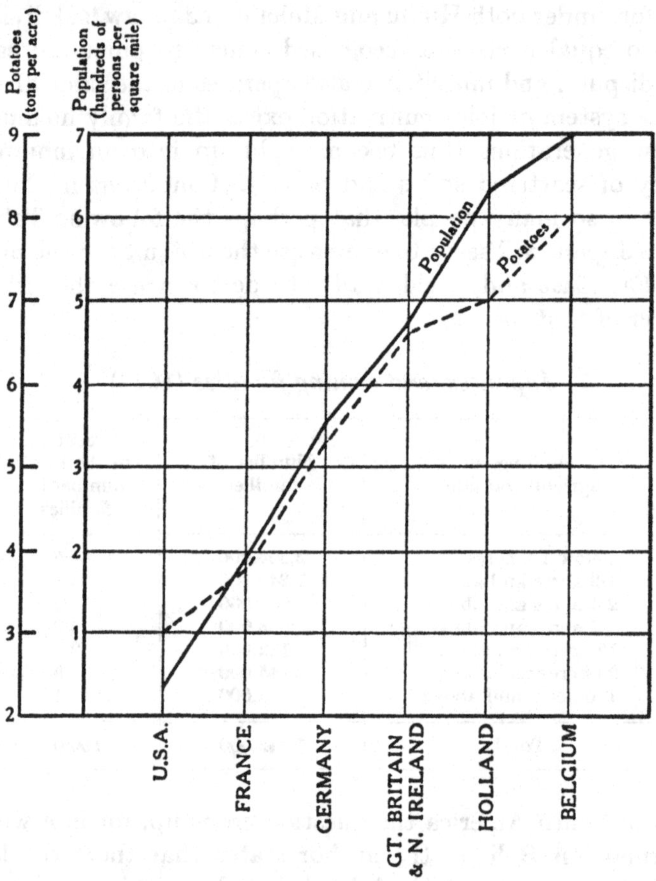

Density of population and yield per acre of potatoes

per acre of root crops, in particular of potatoes, increases as population becomes denser. A diagram illustrating this, by showing the rate of production per acre of potatoes in various countries, ranging from the United States to Belgium, is reproduced upon this page. In the States the yield averages approximately three tons per acre, and the population numbers a little under forty persons to the square mile, whilst the Belgian yield is actually as high as eight tons and the population approximately seven hundred persons to the mile. Intermediate populations and production fall more or less into line, but too close correlation must of course not be expected.

At first sight this is apt to be regarded as a direct result of the recognised preponderance of small farms in more densely inhabited countries, but the evidence for such an assumption is wanting. These increased yields apply markedly to root crops, and the greater use made of spade husbandry in the neighbourhood of towns, together with the greatly enhanced opportunities for securing plentiful supplies of fertilisers and of urban manure, are probably the basic causes. It would appear that the phenomenon is symptomatic of industrial, rather than of agricultural conditions, and that the size of unit employed is independent of it, unless the scale is descended sufficiently to include what, in this country, would be described as allotments. In that event a case might possibly be made out for the twofold proposition that, (*a*) the denser the population the smaller the size of the "average" farm, and (*b*) the smaller the farm the higher its rate of yield. As matters stand, however, whilst all evidence shows that (*a*) is certainly true, such as we possess is directly adverse to (*b*), provided of course that enquiry is confined to the yield of crops in general on farms of a commercial character; if, however, it is extended to include really small plots of land worked in the neighbourhood of centres of population, then, perhaps, there is justification for accepting the latter proposition as holding good in the case of some non-cereal crops. In other words, certain of what are field crops in newly developed countries, tend, with growth of population, to become the subject of more intensive cultivation or else to be grown on the best land.

Chapter VI

THE SIZE OF HOLDINGS (CONTINUED)

Development of small farms in the past; former discussions over their alleged advantages; provision of Small Holdings and allotments in the nineteenth century; effects of the period of depression; evidence adduced before the Commission; the Acts of 1892 and 1908; powers of local authorities; settlement of ex-Service men; financial aspects of the Land Settlement scheme; numbers of allotments; their distribution; the economics of large and small farms; output per man and output per acre; questions of livestock; summary.

Having traced the normal distribution of large and of small farms in this country and touched upon that abroad, some description must follow of the steps taken here to stimulate the development of the latter in the last hundred years. During the Napoleonic war, and for some decades afterwards, farming on a large scale was looked upon as the only possible method by which the industry could be made to render a sufficient return for the investment of capital. In consequence, the small man and the farm worker lost their direct and personal interest in the soil. "Allotments" of land, in lieu of their claims and rights of common, were made to them, and these formed the first definite examples, as has been explained above, of small plots suitable for individual occupation being recognised by Parliamentary intervention. Enclosure otherwise implied nothing but the multiplication of large holdings, and it naturally had the emphatic approval of almost all rural economists, even if a few of them, for reasons that were not always altruistic, regretted the disappearance of the small open-field farmer and the common-right owner. Sir John Sinclair, as president of the Board of Agriculture, was perfectly genuine in his advocacy of the better provision of allotments, and (in his latter days) Arthur Young and Lord Winchelsea also joined in the literary fight that raged over this question. It was then that Young gave vent to his famous, and often quoted, comment that, if one removed all that had made large farms what they were, one was left with the Small Holding. Some of the later appeals issued to the already urban majority of the nation on behalf of the dwindling rural population were pathetic, others were often abusive. A middle course was steered by such writers as J. H. Kent in his "Public letter" of 1844 to the then Duke of Grafton. This epistle represents one of the first studied attempts to place side by side the respective advantages and drawbacks of the Small Holding and of the large farm. If, nowadays, we cannot agree with much that Kent wrote, we can at least respect the sincerity of his arguments and follow with interest his account of "consolidation" as then practised in Suffolk. A generation later there appeared, in the person of J. S. Mill, one whose unbiased views on this subject then received a ready hearing, and, subsequently included in his *Principles*, they have naturally become to present-day economists a mine of sound argument.

During the troubles of the period 1816–34, two Acts of Parliament had been passed which aimed at facilitating access to the land. That of 1819 authorised Overseers of the Poor to acquire blocks of land up to twenty acres in area for the purpose of reletting them as allotments or small farms; that of 1831 recommended that portions of recently enclosed land should be similarly made available, and the limit was raised to fifty acres, whilst Crown lands, with the consent of the Chancellor of the Exchequer, might be similarly treated. Neither Act led to the establishment of many Small Holdings, and both were probably intended merely as window-dressing by a Government which, on the second occasion, was already occupied in repressing rural outbreaks. In 1832 another Act definitely instructed the Overseers to let land on similar conditions, thus anticipating the latter-day policy which, in the same field, also progressed from the merely permissive to the imperative. Farmers were emphatic in their opinion that allotments were unnecessary and represented a potential waste of time and labour which might otherwise be better employed; landlords, in the main, saw fit to agree with their tenants. Thus, the work of such bodies as the Labourers' Friend Society could achieve small results. On the other hand, unbiased persons agreed that, economically, allotments were sound—both from the standpoint of the labourer and of the owner of the land on which they were situated—but the proviso was generally entered that half an acre should be the limit to their size. If more was included a Small Holder was created, who had insufficient land from which to make a living, and so much on his hands that he ceased to be available as a farm labourer.

The years prior to the repeal of the Corn Laws were not propitious for the establishment of Small Holdings, and those that followed 1846 were also a time when large farms were considered to be the only economic unit for the industry. But allotments, in their present accepted sense of the word, did register a certain amount of progress, and, provided they were confined to the limit mentioned above, began to be tolerated by tenant-farmers. Thus, we find in 1843 a *Report on Allotments* which gave quite an encouraging account of their numbers and condition. They were to be found mostly in the Southern and Western Counties, and were almost unknown in the North, exhibiting therefore in certain respects a reversal of the present-day trend in distribution. Statistics were then given upon which was based the view that a quarter of an acre could feed an average family for three months in the year, and that the value to its owner was two shillings a week. Rents, which were on an economic basis, were seldom in arrear.

There for the moment we must leave the allotment movement and turn to the question of the provision of Small Holdings in the strictest sense of the word; allotments will be reverted to again and given separate consideration later. The development of large farms was, if anything, aided by the tendency apparent after the middle of the nineteenth century to return to grass. Whilst the raising of cereals had always admittedly been the prerogative of the large farmer, from then onwards he had opportunities of practising alternative methods of husbandry. The production of meat took its place naturally side by side with that of corn and "pasture farming came to be a necessary and lucrative supplement to the corn-growing of the large farm". Only a generation later did the smaller farm, at a distance from London or other great centres of population, arise to meet the increasing demands for milk and, even then, the present-day flourishing market-garden, vegetable, poultry and fruit-producing activities—now to be found in Kent, Cornwall, Bedfordshire, Cambridgeshire and numerous other Counties—were as yet unborn or in their very infancy. Such attempts as were made by benevolent landowners to encourage the formation of small farm units met with scanty success. All contemporaneous writers and official *Reports* commented on the tendency to consolidate smaller holdings and as opportunity arose to add to already large areas, for in times of depression fertility could be stolen from the ground by these means and the land worked to destruction.

Such was the state of affairs up to about 1880. Thereafter, in times of more acute depression, the voice of the reformer was better able to make itself heard, and advocates of State intervention, by the compulsory provision of Small Holdings, were numerous. The movement was partly political in its origin, for such men as Joseph Chamberlain and Jesse Collings played a prominent rôle in the work which resulted in the passing of the Allotments and Small Holdings Act of 1892. The period was a critical one for all sizes and types of farms, and the evidence regarding their comparative passage through it is apt to be conflicting. The *Report* of the 1893 Commissioners does not contain anywhere a considered or unanimous finding that any particular sized holding had suffered less than others, and one is forced to proceed by circuitous methods. There was, for instance, agreement that grazing districts had come through recent events with less difficulty than corn-growing ones, and witnesses had testified to the comparative immunity felt by those farmers who were producers of cheese, milk and vegetables. Now, the majority of these latter were to be found on smaller holdings than were favoured by the producers of cereals and meat, and, again, they were situated in the Western and Northern districts, whilst it was common knowledge that the Eastern half of the country had suffered worse than anywhere else. If, therefore, it is agreed that, as a whole, the smaller men had been less disturbed by economic conditions, it must not be assumed that this was attributable to the scale on which they conducted their operations, but credit must be given to the type of farming they mainly affected.

In regard to the provision of Small Holdings, or the success attained by the really small men, the Commission in question did not advance contemporary knowledge. The evidence of numerous witnesses was of a strictly non-committal or neutral character, but many individuals showed hostility towards the movement. The following are typical *dicta.* Witness *A* thought Small Holdings "excellent things where they existed or grew naturally"; he "did not oppose the artificial creation of Small Holdings, but had little faith in their development". Witness *B* "would give every facility for the extension of Small Holdings, but did not believe in bolstering them up with State funds". Witness *C* held that "the only way the Small Holder in the arable districts could possibly succeed was by doing the work of two agricultural labourers and living at the expense of one". No less an authority than Sir J. B. Lawes gave it as his opinion that Small Holdings were of benefit to labourers, but not nationally to such an extent as "to supersede farming". The most generous attempt at that time recorded to settle more workers on the land was one undertaken by Mr W. H. Hall of Six Mile Bottom, Cambridgeshire, who had started numerous Small Holders on his estate, finding, where necessary, half their capital out of his own pocket. Yet a Reporter of the Board of Agriculture could only say of this experiment that none "could have been undertaken with higher motives, or supported by more generous expenditure. It has largely failed as a practical experiment". Mr Hall himself stated that one-quarter of the holders were absolute failures, one-quarter were still struggling after a few years, and the remaining half had been moderately successful. The latter, significantly, were generally village tradesmen who had other irons in the fire. The professional views of representatives of the Board, acquired in their own districts, were even more pessimistic. The events of 1879 were still remembered and their effects felt by the small men in Lincolnshire. Many had reverted to the position of labourers, others, still struggling, worked "from daylight to dark, and so do their wives. It is a life of slavery, and they see at the same time what they have made slipping away from them. It is melancholy to think that these men have been the best labourers who have lost the savings of a lifetime". In Suffolk, Small Holdings of ten to fifty acres were "a complete failure", and "1893 had beaten men with small capital"; those who still kept their heads above water "worked from 5 a.m. to 9 p.m." These were, of course, exceptional times, but they showed that the small man had less reserves to draw on than the rest of the rural community.

It was in this same atmosphere that the Act of 1892 had first seen the light, and, such witnesses as recognised its existence, made it clear that they anticipated no future for it. This, the first Act of Parliament which aimed at the establishment of Small Holdings, as distinct from allotments, was correctly appraised by its critics, for it did not succeed. Its provisions were essentially permissive rather than obligatory, as the following instances show. County Councils were empowered to purchase land in response to a "demand" for Small Holdings; this land they had to acquire in the open market, but were prevented from paying any but really low prices by the knowledge that its future holders would, in their turn, be unable to meet such outgoings. The State provided the capital sums, but required the Councils' purchasers to put one-fifth of the price down, and the bulk of the remainder had to be paid off yearly, only a fraction of the cost being transferable into a rent-charge; individuals might, upon these terms, acquire up to fifty acres. Such tenancies as could be offered were also hedged in by restrictions, in that a limit of fifteen acres was decreed to them and their rent was not to exceed £15 per annum. It was the primary (and mistaken) object of this Act to encourage peasant proprietorship and not to multiply tenancies, but the inherent disinclination on the part of those concerned to sink their own capital in such ventures was too strong for it.

This lack of demand from purchasers in part accounted for the non-success of the Act, but other potent causes were also at work. The County Councils were not enamoured of their new duties, and, appreciating that the driving force of a Government department was not behind them, took no steps to bring them to public knowledge. Again, they lacked compulsory powers and had to acquire their small parcels of land in the open market and in competition with other and larger purchasers. Thus, while there was an acknowledged demand on all sides for the provision of Small Holdings on a tenancy basis, the only measure officially taken comprised the virtual obligation to purchase, or else, if tenancy were insisted on, only inferior land could be secured. In these circumstances it is not to be wondered at that only a handful of Counties put into force the main provisions of the Act, and that only 800 acres of land were acquired for Small Holdings.

Agitation by those interested, together with reports of public and private enquiries, led, after fifteen years, to a second attempt being made by the legislature in 1907, viz. the Small Holdings and Allotments Act, which came into force the following year. In the meantime an extension of the first Act had resulted in Parish Councils being empowered to acquire land for their inhabitants in plots up to four acres in extent, and it was in consequence widely held that labourers, at least, had then little cause to grumble, as they had secured the three "F's".

The essential difference between the Act of 1908 and that of 1892 lay in the fact that compulsory powers were now granted to the County Councils, and that the Board of Agriculture was associated in the movement, special Commissioners being appointed for different areas in the country, whose sole duty it was to investigate the requirements in their districts, and, if necessary, to use their own initiative in persuading the Councils to provide facilities. Compulsion might be applied in the acquisition of land for the purposes of hiring or selling to applicants, and the limits of fifteen acres and £15 under the former Act were now abolished. But compulsion was to be the last resort after the failure of other means of purchase, and was not employable save in the case of land that was already deemed to be agricultural in character.

Whatever may at first have been their personal feelings on the merits of the policy involved, members of County Councils loyally administered the provisions of the new Act. Evidence to this effect constantly occurs in accounts such as Sir D. Hall's *Pilgrimage of British Farming*, written when the Act was only some two years old. A full and critical appreciation of the situation created will be found in Levy's *Large and Small Holdings*, where the author impartially sums up as follows:

> The law of compulsory hiring expresses the fact that the form of landownership...now existing in England does not correspond to the needs of modern agriculture so far as the unit of holding is concerned; that is to say that large properties and Small Holdings cannot go hand-in-hand. The recent legislation endeavours to modify the harmful conflict of interests thus set up. It leaves to the landlord his property in the land, but it obliges him, when the need arises, to let it in accordance with the modern economic pressure for Small Holdings. The English landlord may in future still value his land for the sake of the sport it provides, the social consideration it ensures him, or the political opportunities it offers him, and may pay as high a price as he pleases for these qualities of land regarded as a luxury. But its value for these purposes can no longer prevent the increase of Small Holdings, for if the landlord refuses to meet an existing demand for them, the State will force him to use his land as is most desirable from the economic and socio-political points of view.

Up to the outbreak of the war, or rather by the end of December, 1914, some 12,600 Small Holdings had been set up, and another 1400 had been handed over to co-operative or similar associations. Here, then, was a totally different state of affairs from that found after a similar period in the life of the 1892 Act. But one must guard against crediting the provisions of the 1908 Act with the whole of these results. Certainly, the provision of Small Holdings had been facilitated, but, equally, the demand had from other causes increased.

The small man now had fresh possibilities before him in the shape of fruit, milk and poultry farms, which were proved to be paying ventures, and, moreover, there had been an upward movement in commodity prices. Once it was seen that a living could be made on a Council holding by one of these methods, the supply of prospective tenants was rapidly augmented. Almost 200,000 acres of land were acquired in the first seven years, roughly one-quarter of which had been leased and the remainder purchased. Of this, in turn, only some 20,000 acres had been compulsorily purchased and 15,000 similarly hired. These last figures falsified those prophets who had anticipated that the bulk of the land would not be obtained voluntarily. As was to be expected, where demand had free play, the distribution of these new holdings was irregular, for the reason that they predominated in just those districts where their chances of success were greatest. Cambridgeshire, Lincolnshire and Norfolk had established far more than Counties situated in parts of the country remote from access to centres of population or than those on heavy clay-land could have maintained. In other words, it was just in the particular Counties in which small farms were already automatically appearing and prospering that the Act of 1908 created additional examples. Lastly, there was nothing to cavil at in regard to the finances of the scheme; it was always solvent, and the losses sustained by individual County Councils were few in number and small in amount. From the standpoint of the Small Holder, the taxpayer, and the agriculturist, then, this Act proved an unqualified success, and it was the first that could claim that distinction.

During the course of the war various promises were made (both on behalf of the public and of the State) to serving members of the forces that their efforts would be rewarded by the greater provision of access to the land. When peace was restored there was naturally a demand that these promises should be redeemed, and special legislation was passed in consequence. Even now it is too near the time to essay an unbiased account of the proceedings that followed—history will be better able to judge a generation hence—but it is obvious that there was embarked upon a far too ambitious and hastily extemporised scheme. As early as 1916, warning voices had not been lacking, for in that year an article appeared in the *Edinburgh Review*, from the pen of Mr C. S. Orwin, entitled "The Small

Holdings' Craze", in which the author pointed out all the standard objections to a widespread scheme of Small Holdings, and also specifically advised those responsible for propaganda work not to promise an Arcadian existence on the land to all members of His Majesty's forces. Unfortunately, such warnings went unheeded. Upwards of 50,000 ex-Service applicants eventually materialised; in the end, a sum of £20,000,000 was set aside (of which only £15,250,000 was actually expended) and the County Councils were urged to proceed with purchases and hirings on a very large scale indeed. Fortunately, perhaps, such matters as the erection of buildings and the preparation of the land as it was acquired, delayed the rate of progress at which complete holdings were provided, and many prospective occupiers grew tired of waiting and withdrew. By this means the applicants were reduced in number by more than half, and those actually settled on the land numbered by the middle of 1922 some 17,000. From the nature of the case the class of men were—agriculturally speaking—extremely mixed, and no rigid tests as to their suitability or experience were applied. In these circumstances, the finances of the Land Settlement scheme would not bear close scrutiny; hasty purchases by harassed Councils effected at inflated prices involved a large prospective loss, and, by a piece of unavoidable procrastination, the financial day of reckoning was postponed until 1926, the Government having decided to transfer the obligations to the national Exchequer. Accordingly, the whole property was valued as on the first of April in that year, the ascertainment being extended to all the commitments of the County Councils in regard to their Small Holdings' programme, covering an area of more than 438,000 acres.

The results were as follows: The gross capital expenditure incurred in the acquisition and equipment of all the properties comprised in the valuation amounted, in round figures, to about £20,750,000, of which about £15,250,000 was attributable to the post-war Land Settlement Scheme. Approximately nine-tenths of this latter sum had been advanced by the Public Works Loan Commissioners—before the war out of the Local Loans Fund, and, after the war, out of the Land Settlement Fund. The rate of interest on nearly the whole of the pre-war loans was 3½ per cent., while on the post-war loans it varied from a maximum of 6½ per cent. to a minimum of 4¾ per cent., with an average rate of 6¼ per cent. The high rate of interest on post-war borrowings, coupled with the excessive cost of equipment of the Small Holdings provided after the war, were the two factors that accounted for the greater part of the excess of the Councils' annual expenditure over their net annual income. In considering the magnitude of the annual charge that will for many years to come fall on the State, it must be remembered that the Exchequer is receiving repayment of the whole of the capital monies advanced out of the Land Settlement Fund (which was provided by taxation) and out of the Local Loans Fund, together with interest at the rates current at the time the advances were made. Moreover, when the loan payments are completed, the Small Holdings estates purchased by the Councils will be entirely free of all capital charges. The contributions from the Ministry of Agriculture, which over the whole period will have aggregated about £40,000,000, may be regarded as attributable to the post-war properties, as it has been customary to assume that the pre-war schemes were self-supporting. The aggregate of the yearly payments to be made by Councils on account of Small Holdings charges in respect of their whole pre-war and post-war estates on the basis of the valuation is about £70,300,000. This figure includes loan charges, tithe redemption annuities, and other rent charges created on the acquisition of the land. It can be estimated that the Small Holdings charges in respect of pre-war borrowings outstanding on the 1st April, 1926, amounted in all to about £11,500,000. Assuming that the same figure would represent the total net income derivable from the estates during the period of the Ministry's contributions, the position is that the Small Holdings charges attributable to the Land Settlement properties will amount to almost £58,000,000, of which the Ministry of Agriculture will contribute the above-mentioned £40,000,000—a sum equal to the interest on post-war loans from the Public Works Loan Board. It should be noted, however, that, for the purpose of these figures, the cost of equipment provided by the Councils on their pre-war estates out of Land Settlement monies is included in the Land Settlement figures. This indicates that the Ministry is in effect paying the interest but not the sinking fund charges on the loans in respect of the post-war holdings. The net result, therefore, is that, although the whole of the capital advance will be repaid, the loans are in effect not bearing interest, inasmuch as the amount contributed by the Department approximates to the interest received by the Treasury through the Loan Board.

These extraordinarily complicated financial adjustments, therefore, make it possible to answer the question "What has the Land Settlement policy cost the State?" in either of two ways, viz. (*a*) that one-half (£7,600,000) of its contribution must be regarded as virtually irrecoverable, or (*b*) that the Exchequer will receive slightly under 3 per cent. return on its capital instead of the 6¼ per cent. which was the rate originally anticipated. The "normal" position is now as follows: An annual but diminishing deficiency contribution from the Ministry will run until the year 2002–3, the sum in question for the current year being approximately £826,000; in 1950 that figure will be £700,000, in 1970 £500,000, and in 1990 £240,000. The over-all average payment will be £565,000—approximately equal to £34 per holding. It may be observed that the average cost of the land acquired for the Land Settlement policy was £42. 10*s*. per acre, as compared with £32. 17*s*. 6*d*. in pre-war years—an increase of not more than 29 per cent.

Under the conditions prevailing in 1918 and subsequent years, and after the promises made, it is difficult to say what other course could have been pursued, for it is certain that the majority of the holders concerned could not, in the years that followed, have paid an economic rent upon the original cost of their farms, but the capital expenditure—in effect a "loss"—has been heavy. The inexperienced ex-Service Small Holder (often placed on totally unsuitable land) would inevitably have provided an undue proportion of the failures that were occurring upon all sides, but, as matters were, analysis indicates that, while some 18 per cent. gave up from one cause or another between 1918 and the end of 1922, only 6·5 per cent. of the newcomers, including a small number of civilians, actually went bankrupt. Indeed, the whole body of men thus settled came through the next decade with comparative ease; their landlords, the County Councils, were generous to them, remitted their moderate rents whenever necessary and gave them an abundance of technical assistance. As a corollary, it could not be claimed that, either from the standpoint of the ratepayer or of the taxpayer, the Land Settlement experiment was a paying proposition. Nor does it appear that the formation of Colonies—a most unfortunate word, reminiscent of centres for the treatment of those mentally or physically deficient—was financially more successful. By the Small Holdings Colonies Acts of 1916 and 1918 the Ministry of Agriculture was empowered to acquire up to 60,000 acres in England and Wales for the twofold purpose of establishing (*a*) large profit-sharing farms, and (*b*) groups of Small Holdings under a resident director. Several of these corporate farms were established in different localities, but in no instance could they be regarded as satisfactory, and as there was a heavy loss on practically all of them, they were, one by one, closed down until, in 1932, only six remained. Of these, five were suitably situated for the activities of individual Small Holders and were, in the then difficult circumstances, avoiding losses; the sixth, a large profit-sharing farm at Amesbury, Wiltshire, had, from its inception in 1919, annually failed, with two exceptions, to return a profit.

During the whole post-war period it was the policy of successive Governments to encourage, by every possible means, a yet further extension of the Small Holdings movement. Thus, in 1926 there appeared a fresh Small Holdings and Allotments Act which aimed specifically at providing "Cottage" holdings, viz. a house and "not more than three acres or less than forty perches of agricultural land". These properties could only be acquired from the Councils by purchase, and were not available for persons other than those possessing knowledge of, and aptitude for, rural life. Subsequent amendments, forming part of the comprehensive Agricultural Land (Utilisation) Act of 1931, modified these provisions by substituting "one" for "three" acres, by permitting tenancy, by defining more precisely the type of person to be considered eligible and by insisting upon permanent residence in the house provided. It had been intended that the Act of 1931 should extend the law relating to all forms of Small Holdings and allotments by (*a*) permitting the Minister of Agriculture to set up demonstration farms and (*b*) authorising him to create fresh Small Holdings wherever he considered that County Councils were failing in their obligations. Owing, however, to the financial situation that followed the passing of this Act, no steps have so far been taken to implement either of its main provisions, and County Councils were, indeed, instructed to confine their capital expenditure to the minimum possible, whilst continuing to administer the existing Acts.

Early in 1932, therefore, the position in general could be summed up as follows. Throughout the British Isles (for the other administrative divisions had carried out a campaign similar to that described above) there had been created a large body of Small Holders (in England and Wales, 27,000 tenants on 450,000 acres and 760 owner-occupiers on 6000 acres), who were, on the whole, solvent and doing better than the majority of large farmers. At the same time there were stated to be some two thousand approved applicants awaiting their holdings and over three thousand whose claims had yet to be heard—a total of 5600 persons; the movement could scarcely, therefore, be said to have spent itself. The provision of credit (dealt with in another Chapter) and of equipment loans has been facilitated for this type of farmer, and, in fact, everything possible has been done for him. Where he is placed on suitable land and has had previous experience, it is the belief of the County Councils that, as a class, he is doing as well as could be expected; as landlords they have, since 1926, lowered rents less than was anticipated would have been necessary and have had to write off a surprisingly small proportion as non-recoverable. The cost—at present nearly a million a year—to the State must, however, be borne in mind when any attempt is made to draw up a financial balance sheet for the whole undertaking.

Once inextricably bound up with the question of Small Holdings, allotments now call for separate treatment. Their development has already been traced up to the middle of the last century. Thereafter, in 1887, an Act of a permissive nature was passed, for, on a demand for allotments being manifested in any given area, the local authority was empowered, compulsorily if necessary, to lease or buy land and to let it out in parcels up to an acre in extent. But, owing to the enhanced prices that could be demanded by landowners for disturbance and severance, the resulting rents were often prohibitive, and little progress was, in consequence, made. Finally, the Small Holdings Act of 1908 also conferred powers on Councils in regard to the provision of allotments, and, thereafter, the administration of both these types of small cultivations went on side by side.

Prior to 1918 the latest enumeration of allotments in this country was represented by one taken as long ago as 1895. This gave their number in England and Wales as 483,000. Nine years earlier Major Craigie had published a comprehensive Table which included, under separate headings, "allotments detached from cottages"

(389,000), allotments of "one-eighth of an acre and upwards attached to cottages" (257,000), "potato plots" (93,000), and "cow runs" (9000), representing a grand total of 748,000 for England and Wales. Here, we have ample evidence of the difficulties attaching to the definition of an allotment, for, strictly speaking, the first class alone represents the ordinary acceptation of the word, and subsequent enquiries have been confined to those plots of land which were detached from the occupation of cottages. The distribution of allotments has always shown marked features, and these are evidenced in the returns for both 1886 and 1895. Briefly, the East Midland Counties and East Anglia provide an undue proportion, and the Northern areas are least represented. Major Craigie borrowed a Table prepared for the Commission of 1881, which placed side by side the density of allotments per thousand acres of farmland and the weekly wages of farm workers, showing that the former tended to increase as the latter fell. But as evidence is lacking to show if cottage gardens and cow-runs were included, these deductions may be subject to modification, as such Counties as Westmorland and Cumberland, which had only some four to six allotments to the thousand acres, might have favoured the former; at the other end of the scale Bedfordshire had a proportion of seventy per thousand acres.

But in any case it is probable that such figures represented mainly urban plots, as, despite the popular belief that allotments are the prerogative of the countryman, recent statistical enquiries have shown that the majority of them are located in towns. The East Midland and Eastern Counties enjoy the lowest rainfall in the United Kingdom, and the particular districts in which allotments are most numerous are also those in which there is an abundance of easily worked soil. In these conditions it is natural to find that the people of such towns as Bedford, Peterborough, Cambridge and Luton make much larger use of suburban fields for the cultivation of vegetables than do urban dwellers in the West and North of England; similarly, amongst the larger cities, Leicester and Coventry head the list with figures of 62 and 49 allotments respectively per thousand of population. Town allotments, again, are invariably what their name implies, and average in number some 15 to the acre, whilst the rural are frequently found to be synonymous with Small Holdings, and to cover plots of land up to some acres in extent. For that reason considerable care has to be exercised when instituting comparisons between town and country. The 1908 Act had provided 133,000 allotments up to 1918, but this figure afforded no criterion as to the immense increase in urban plots caused by the campaign to add to the home production of food-stuffs. Accordingly a census of all allotments in England and Wales was undertaken by the Board of Agriculture on three immediate post-war occasions.

The first, taken in April 1918, recorded a total of 1,350,000, covering 195,000 acres, the second, in December 1919, 1,250,000, and the third, a year later, 1,330,000. Comparison is rendered difficult by the fact that the 93,000 plots owned by Railway Companies were not included after the first enquiry, and certain adjustments of a statistical nature were necessitated by the failure to extend that census to centres of population below 300 persons, but the outstanding feature is that the pre-war total had been increased by more than 100 per cent. The greatest individual additions had, of course, taken place in the towns, and especially in those centres which had previously been interested in the movement. Many urban centres trebled and quadrupled their allotments, whilst the country districts added at most two-thirds to their previous total. The explanation doubtless is that the country suffered severely by the absence of farm labourers overseas, and that those remaining, together with substituted workers, were fully engaged in producing food on a large scale; the townsman, on the other hand, was encouraged by provisions of the Defence of the Realm Act (such as Daylight Saving) and the compulsory acquisition of land for the purpose (together with unreasonable demands from the retailers of vegetables), to turn to allotments as a useful hobby. Again, the countryman has a recognised disinclination to spend an undue proportion of his scanty leisure in raising food individually when his whole life is spent doing the same thing commercially. Fantastic claims were put forward on their behalf as sources of food supply during the war, but when every allowance is made for *ex parte* bias, there remains no doubt that certain essential commodities, particularly potatoes, were raised by allotment holders in very large quantities, and thereby helped to keep down prices.

The number of allotments (recorded as 965,000, covering 146,000 acres, in December 1930) will inevitably tend to decline further, since the emergency regulations affecting them have lapsed, but their popularity has been added to as a result of the war period, and in urban districts they will in future be afforded special encouragement by the recent legislation. In the country, any demand for them can, in common with that for Small Holdings, always be met under the powers possessed by County Councils. Thus, compulsion can now be exercised in acquiring land for allotments only; loans are provided by the Ministry of Health to local authorities to assist in their provision (£1,331,000 has so far been granted) and, under town planning regulations, they have precedence over many other interests; compensation, too, is payable to their holders for disturbance. Thus, spade-husbandry in England may now be said to have acquired its charter and formally to have taken its place in our agricultural complex. In 1931 and subsequent years considerable grants were made, partly by charitable bodies and partly by Parliament, towards the provision of allotment equipment for the unemployed. Some tens of thousands of additional holders were thus created from a class that was especially susceptible of benefiting from this form of activity.

Some account of the provision and distribution of holdings of all sizes having been given, there remains the more controversial question of the relative advantages or drawbacks that are attached to each type. Unfortunately, there is a tendency on the part of the rival schools of thought categorically to assert that only large, or Small, Holdings can succeed, or fail, in general. The truth is that, under different conditions, each possesses certain advantages and, accordingly, in most countries, there is room for both. It is also true, however, that the majority of the advantages belong to the larger undertaking, and that, even where other conditions are similar, the smaller holding is rarely placed on an economic level with the larger, although considerations of a social character, if introduced, may modify this conclusion.

It is best to subdivide into headings the various questions involved. Take labour first. Here, as will be shown further on, if the number of workers employed per acre is the one criterion, then the Small Holding is clearly the best from the standpoint of the nation, as it affords work for two or three times as many persons per acre. But, as Orwin has frequently shown, if we view the question from the altered standpoint of the value of the outturn per worker, then the large holding comes to the front. An illustration, culled from a survey of Welsh farms, of the working of this factor records an increase of almost 100 per cent. in this value (£317) on holdings over 250 acres in excess of those below 50 acres (£169). But, again, there is a reservation to make: the sales per acre of land were greater on the small farms in question, although both types were producing the same commodities. The above writer's own summing up was as follows:

Taking the results as they stand, the fact emerges that employment and production vary inversely with the size of the holding, but that the production per man employed varies directly with the size of the holding. Thus, on the one hand, the advocates of closer settlement and the intensive methods which must necessarily follow if men are to live by the cultivation of small areas of land would seem to be justified, in that the results shown by the survey indicate the highest amount of employment and the greatest product-value in the smaller groups. On the other hand, the advocates of more extensive methods of farming can point to their justification in that it is clear that the efficiency of management is greatest in the larger groups if the standard of measurement be that of product-value per man employed. However, it is clear that either party is drawing conclusions from incomplete data. The efficiency of any farming system can only be judged by an examination of the extent to which all the factors of production are utilised and balanced under it. Each of the assumptions made from the figures above ignores entirely the factor of capital. Land, labour and capital are all required for production, and the *optimum* system of farm management is that which utilises all three together so as to secure the maximum result from each. If information were available as to the capital utilised in each of the groups in the survey it might be found that in the smaller groups labour was being wastefully employed, and that an equal number of men working on a larger area of land with more capital in the form of machinery equipment, would produce an equal product-value per unit of land with a higher rate of output per man employed. Equally it might be found that in the larger groups the use of more labour, or a reduction in the area of land, might produce the same product-value per man with a higher rate of output per unit of land. Obviously there can be no absolute answer to the question of what constitutes the most economical unit of land for farm production.

Here, then, it is clear that no final decision can be reached—too many factors must be taken into consideration—for the old problem of the comparative value of different methods to the individual farmer, or to the nation at large, crops up, and is complicated by the need to decide whether production from a given area of land or from the employment of a specified amount of labour is the desideratum—in turn depending on the density of population, the value of land and the prevailing wage-level.

Some further relevant economic evidence on this and other aspects, culled from the previously referred to Cambridge *Report* upon the Eastern Counties, may be interpolated at this point. Upon the farms therein investigated (983 in number) it was shown that the per acre figures for capital and for gross output, as also that for gross output per £100 spent on manual labour, were linked progressively with the size of holding, as the following Table indicates.

Size group (acres)	Farm capital per acre (£)	Capital turnover (%)	Gross output per acre (£)	Manual workers per 100 acres (No)	Gross output per £100 manual labour (£)
20–50	13·4	76	10·1	5·6	187
50–100	10·8	69	7·4	4·2	183
100–150	10·3	68	7·0	3·6	203
150–300	9·3	64	5·9	2·8	212
300–500	8·3	58	4·9	2·3	215
Over 500	8·1	60	4·8	2·4	215

The next point—that of the rate of production per acre—has already been referred to. Here—with the exception of sugar-beet—the principal evidence available comes from abroad and tends to show that the large farmer raises heavier crops than the small man. On the other hand, it is clear that, in certain picked localities, the latter secures a better yield from fruit and vegetables than does his rival, who only treats such crops as side-issues in his system of farming. This is, of course, attributable to the constant individual attention bestowed on his property by the owner of the small undertaking, and evidence is not lacking that this personal factor is also becoming effective in the case even of the standard farm crops of this country. It is hardly necessary to point out the obvious distinction that must be drawn between the rate of yield per acre and the value of the produce per acre when comparing class with class. It is, however, often loosely asserted that the "produce per acre" of the Small Holding exceeds that of the large; this is true, but only because the former is mainly devoted to intensive forms of husbandry that result in a greater weight and value per acre than accrues from the raising of standard crops.

Lastly, there is the important aspect of the pecuniary returns to be looked for from each type of farm. And, as before, no hard and fast rule can be laid down. The real Small Holder, who is prepared himself to work full-time on his property, has the assistance of members of his family, is established on suitable land, has a ready market for his produce and, most important of all, is properly capitalised without too much recourse to loans, can generally make a living, but, as the statistics given above show, this does not necessarily imply a cash surplus of any magnitude. If, however, more than one of these advantages is wanting, then his position is precarious. Let us take each branch of farming and discuss his chances in it.

General arable farming (covering of course the production of cereals) is essentially the large farmer's prerogative, and represents the maximum disadvantage under which the Small Holder can struggle. The latter lacks sufficient capital to farm his land properly or to make use of essential machinery; he must often buy at retail prices feeding-stuffs that the larger farmer himself raises or can purchase in bulk at preferential rates; his financial position also frequently compels him to realise his produce the moment it is secured, regardless of the state of the markets. The small mixed farmer cannot conduct seasonal operations on any considerable scale without recourse to outside help. Finally, his rent will, rightly, be heavier, per acre of land utilised, than that of his larger neighbour. None of his protagonists has ever suggested that sheep farming is a possibility for the small man, and, in regard to meat production, the pig is his principal stand-by, although a few beasts can be reared on Small Holdings as a side-line. Milk, if seriously adopted, is apt to make heavy demands on the labour of his family. When statistically arranged, the different types of livestock found on each class of holding generally conform to a predetermined distribution that is not unexpected. The following figures have been extracted from the *Report of the Census of Production*, and, although they relate to Great Britain in 1908, scarcely any modifications have since occurred.

Numbers of Livestock per 1000 *acres of land under crops, grass and mountain and heathland used for grazing*

Size of holdings (acres)	Horses	Cattle	Sheep	Pigs
1–5	120	215	331	557
5–50	57	229	473	160
50–300	42	191	609	72
Over 300	32	135	817	42

The *Report* again classified these various groups of farms as arable, grass and mixed, when detailed examination brought to light the following not unexpected tendencies. Horses were more employed on arable holdings, where the main increase was in the larger examples, but the density of cattle was between two and three times as great on the grass farms of all sizes; the increase in the case of sheep on grass-land was some 50 per cent. on all holdings, and slightly more marked in the smallest size-group; pigs predominated on arable farms, where their density ranged from 690 per 1000 acres (on those from one to five acres) to 62 (over 300 acres), while on mixed farms the corresponding figures were 606 and 44. Over twenty years earlier Craigie had prepared a somewhat similar Table, which evidenced the same distribution, but to a more marked degree, and very similar characteristics are observable in the numerous Tables given in the *Agricultural Output of England and Wales, 1925*, where differentiation is effected between the distribution of crops and stock found on "mainly arable", "mainly grass" and mixed holdings in every size-group.

In the 1931 Cambridge enquiry the distribution in the case of cows and sows came out as follows:

Size group (acres)	Cows		Sows
	Per farm	Per 100 acres	Per farm
20–50	3·3	9·3	2·5
50–100	7·7	7·5	3·7
100–150	8·1	6·4	3·8
150–300	11·5	5·3	5·1
300–500	12·5	3·2	7·0
Over 500	22·5	2·9	15·1

All relevant data emphasise the handicap under which the smaller undertaking suffers in the use of horses, for the small man has to maintain relatively far more of these animals than does the one in a larger way of business, and at the same time he cannot make full use of them. Another Table (see overleaf) from the last-mentioned source well illustrates this point. Alternatively, if he turns to machinery it is again difficult to utilise most implements to their full extent, and co-operation, when called to aid, does not seem to meet his requirements in this respect. Figures have often been published showing, distributed on an acreage basis, the relative costs of utilising machines ranging from drills to chaff cutters. In all such examples the man operating on a larger scale has an overwhelming advantage.

Size group (acres)	Working horses per farm	Arable acres per working horse	Gross output per horse
20–50	1·93	11·9	£184
50–100	3·02	16·2	£182
100–150	4·23	18·7	£209
150–300	5·54	23·4	£233
300–500	8·20	29·4	£281
Over 500	13·27	35·3	£319

Impartial accounts of typical groups of mixed Small Holdings bear out these conclusions, and one, relating to those in Oxfordshire published by A. W. Ashby, may be taken as typical of others. Briefly, it was found there that too many horses were kept, scarcely any sheep and many pigs. Market-gardening and poultry keeping appeared to demand a minimum of 4 acres, milk-production one of 25, and sheep of at least 50. Mixed operations called for as much machinery and as many horses on 25 acres as could have been economically employed on 100. The writer held that, under the existing conditions, 300 acres of land were necessary to support six families, and he considered that the general farm equipment was poor. The conclusions therein reached, augmented by reading similar accounts elsewhere, compel agreement with his statement that "the position of the Small Holder is better than that of a labourer in housing and food, but not in respect of work or cash receipts". So far as the questions of amenity and the occupation of the farmer's own time are concerned the Cambridge statistics indicate a range throughout the usual size-groups from 43 weeks spent in manual labour and 5 in a managerial capacity (20–50 acres), through 38 and 11 respectively (100–150 acres), up to 7 and 34 (over 500 acres). The corresponding data relating to "cash receipts" are as follows. If allowance were made for interest at 5 per cent. on farm capital, £2 per week charged for the occupier's manual labour and £4 per week for managerial work, the average surplus ranged progressively from minus £103 on the 20–50 acre holdings up to minus £516 on those over 500 acres in extent. Prior to such allowances being made, the range was from an average "profit" of £28 down to an average loss of £60.

There remain the typical cases of fruit, vegetable and poultry farming as they affect the Small Holder. Here, when in the vicinity of markets and on easily worked soils, he finds his best chances of success, but, even so, he is placed in an inferior position to that occupied by any rival who goes in for similar forms of production on a larger scale. The latter at once secures advantages in the matter of purchasing his requirements, and gains concessions from railway and other transport agencies in return for forwarding larger consignments. The one asset that the small man has consists in the greater amount of personal supervision he can give to the various operations on his land.

One is accordingly drawn to the inevitable conclusion that in every type of farming the larger undertaking has great initial advantages, and only in two or three branches can the smaller unit compete on anything like equal grounds, and, even then, is still labouring under economic disadvantages. But the example afforded by Denmark is always quoted in refutation of this, and co-operation advocated as a corrective to lessen the handicap of the small undertaking. This latter question is dealt with separately, but it must be pointed out here that the case of a people entirely dependent on an export trade (and concentrating its activities upon certain standardised forms of livestock products) represents the antithesis of what is to be found in these islands.

It is often said that the formation of Small Holdings has suffered from fictitious objections raised by private landowners on the score that additional work is thus thrown on their agents, and also that the provision of farm buildings, roads and water supply entails a relatively high outlay which cannot be recouped, but such arguments are only of limited validity in these days when it is the statutory duty of public bodies, rather than of individual persons, to meet the demand for these properties. On the other hand, the views of those for whom this type of holding is intended are sometimes strangely perverted, as the reputed comment of a farm-labourer shows. "Small Holders", he said: "Why, first they starves the land, next they starves the cow, and then they goes and starves themselves"!

The fact remains that numerous Small Holdings, as distinct from small farms, were spontaneously arising under suitable conditions before the second, or 1908, Act was passed, that the latter encouraged and fostered their multiplication, and that, until the war with its aftermath of necessarily uneconomic schemes supervened, the movement as a whole was proving financially successful both to the individuals concerned and to the nation.

Writing of peasant proprietorship in France, Lord Ernle, in a well-known passage, declared that "the small proprietor is worse housed and worse fed than the English labourer. His cottage is a single room with a mud floor in which he and his family and live-stock live, eat, sleep and die. From morning to night his toil is excessive and prolonged; female labour is the rule; children are continuously employed, while his little property is often mortgaged. Arthur Young talks of the magic of property, but there is such a thing as the demon of property". If such a picture is not true of the corresponding conditions in England now, it must not be assumed that the Small Holder's lot here is an easy one. He is called upon to work at least as hard as any labourer, and neither he nor his family has much time to spare from the demands of their holding. For this reason it was a sound custom of the pre-war regulations affecting the choice of applicants for holdings whereby preference was given to those with previous agricultural experience, and it is proper that this proviso should have been reintroduced by the administering Councils.

Finally, it must be remembered that in creating small units of production in agriculture one is proceeding contrary to the long recognised principle followed in all other branches of industry. If the establishment of Small Holdings is allowed to proceed on its own lines, with the aid of permissive, rather than of creative, State support, then it should not outrun economic possibilities, but danger lies ahead in the event of widespread and artificial stimulus being applied. In this country, such a policy, therefore, if carried beyond a certain point, must rest not upon grounds that cannot be substantiated—such as a better technique—but upon the much safer and surer basis of national well-being and social progress that is associated with an evenly distributed balance between town and country life. That, on the other hand, the really large farm may have a greater future before it, is possible, for, in the present time of depression, authorities are not lacking who hold that, for both arable and mixed farming, the unit of one or two thousand acres can alone provide economic employment for highly-paid workers and that the future tendency will be to move away from the medium-sized holding to one which can give full scope to machinery, or in other words that the output per man will be the standpoint from which agriculture over the greater part of this country will have to be judged in the future.

Chapter VII

TITHE

Its origin amongst non-Christian peoples; introduction into this country; the objects that were tithable; law-suits relating to vicarial tithes; difficulties caused by the introduction of new crops; examples of tithe incidence in certain parishes; upon agricultural labourers' wages; in Ireland and in Scotland.

Up to quite recent times the principal "burdens" or constitutional charges—whichever appellation we prefer to give them—affecting the British agriculturist would have been correctly described as four in number—Local rates, Income tax, Tithe and Land tax. It must be premised that these are "direct", as opposed to "indirect", imposts, the latter type not calling for consideration in such a work as this. May it also be expressly stated that all taxation falls upon persons, and not upon property—whether in the form of land or otherwise? Farmers, however, have now been relieved, to all intents and purposes, from the whole of the first-named charge; they receive very special consideration in connection with the second, while the third and fourth, being levied upon the ownership of land, only affect those who occupy their own farms. Tithe is now not only pecuniarily the heaviest of the quartet, but is historically the most ancient impost known.

Among early civilisations it was of universal application. In Babylon, Egypt, Greece and China, a portion—not necessarily always a tenth—of movables was exacted by rulers from their subjects, or by victors from the vanquished. What more natural than that the custom should be extended to meet the needs of religion? The Old Testament abounds with references to tithes on corn and on flocks being handed over to Hebrew kings. Thus, we read, "And of all that thou shalt give me I will surely give the tenth unto thee" (Genesis xxviii. 22); "And all the tithe of the land, whether of the seed of the land, or of the fruit of the tree, is the Lord's" (Leviticus xxvii. 30); "And all the tithe of the herd or the flock, whatsoever passeth under the rod, the tenth shall be holy unto the Lord" (Leviticus xxvii. 32). The final stage was in that society reached when these payments became due to the priests for their own support and for the upkeep of the temple.

In Western Europe in general, tithes were paid to the Church in the first centuries of the Christian era—paid, it was subsequently sought to prove, by divine law. This view was refuted by Selden in his *History of Tithes*, who showed that custom had gradually come to the assistance of the Church. It is agreed by all authorities that the payment, theoretically at any rate, was voluntary, but the power of the Church over men's souls was a great weapon in her favour. Councils of the Church enjoined the amounts and methods of payment, but no trace of any legal authorisation, outside that of the Canon law, can be found for centuries. It was only at the end of the eighth century that a law of Charlemagne directed that this payment should be made towards the maintenance of the clergy, the upkeep of the Church itself and the assistance of the poor. It is probable that the decree of a Synod in 786 effected the same ends in Britain; certainly the payment of tithe was ordained by the edicts of later Anglo-Saxon rulers, notably that of Edgar in 960.

The rights of the Church to tithes being recognised, there followed a period of time in which the grounds of the age-long dispute between payer and receiver were shifted. It must be remembered that the early Church maintained no parochial institutions. Monasteries and itinerant clergy represented her activities, and, accordingly, it was to the monasteries that the tithe-payers were called upon (under pain of excommunication) to render tribute. In 994 the *capitula* of Theodulf directed as follows: "Let no mass priest wheedle to his own church a man that belongs to the district of another's church, nor instruct him to come to his church out of his shire...and to pay him the tithes and rights which belong to the other". It is an arguable point for what length of time the individual payer might select the monastic institution which should receive his contribution, but in 1180 the Council of Lateran settled the question on a local basis—a basis which caused the payer's parish, as we now know it, to be the proper recipient. The establishment of these parish churches by wealthy persons, who endowed them with lands, got rid of the overriding position which "minster" churches had borne to others (and especially to churches which possessed no burial grounds) in the matter of the division of tithes. Traces of this evolution can still be observed in the absence of tithe upon certain manorial properties or upon land that was once monastic, and by its payment on land in one parish to a church in another. For instance, the strips in one of the common-fields at Cambridge "tithed indiscriminately to the various churches (in Cambridge) without any regard to parish boundaries" (Goodman, *History of St Botolph's Church, Cambridge*). The rectors of Theberton, Suffolk, have, ever since the thirteenth century, received no tithe from certain land in their parish—land that once belonged to the Premonstratensian Abbey of Leiston; for the dissolution of the monasteries did not affect this freedom, as Henry VIII ordained that tithe-free land should remain so for ever.

The above affords a brief review of the growth of this payment from primitive times up to mediaeval. Its exact incidence and development have for centuries been a source of contention among historians; all that concerns the agriculturist nowadays, however, is the fact that custom legalised its payment centuries ago. On the other hand, it is important that he should appreciate the different ways in which he and his predecessors have been assessed, and that he should know something of the events occurring within historic times that have led to the alienation from the Church of a portion of the money he provides.

First of all, upon what were tithes originally payable? In theory they were due upon (*a*) all things arising from the ground and subject to annual increase—grain, hay, wood; (*b*) all things nourished by the ground—the young of cattle, sheep, horses and poultry, and (*c*) man's labour, or the net profits of his industry, and even his wages. The first were styled praedial, the second mixed, and the third personal tithes. Praedial tithes generally comprised corn, hay and wood, but, upon occasion, came to be extended to other field crops and even to fruit. Although the rector generally received these great, or praedial tithes, while the vicar took the mixed, or small, this custom was by no means universal. It should be noted that, save by custom, examples of which are given further on, tithe was never payable upon wild animals or upon minerals. Barren land was, subject to certain reservations, free for seven years after conversion to husbandry; Royal forests and monastic property were exempt; land in the city of London originally paid by custom, being assessed in proportion to the rent it commanded. This "custom" was confirmed by Act of Parliament in the reign of Henry VIII and has survived up to the present time.

One of the first enumerations of articles that mediaeval minds held to be tithable was issued in 1175 at the Council of Rouen and runs as follows: "All tithes of the earth whether of corn, of fruits of trees or other fruits are the Lord's...; but since many are now found unwilling to give tithes, we declare that, according to the order of the Pope, they be admonished three times to pay the tithe of grain, wine, fruits of trees, young of animals, wool, lamb, butter, cheese, flax, hemp and of whatever is yearly renewed, and be laid under *anathema* if they do not amend". In 1250 the *Constitutions* of the then Archbishop of York aimed at unifying the systems of payment in kind, but reminded the faithful that the following also were liable—"the gains of negotiations, handicrafts and merchants ...that is, let tithes be paid of their wages unless they be willing to make some certain (i.e. fixed) payment". This is of importance in the light of certain occurrences centuries later. In 1305 the *Constitutions* of Merton claimed, *inter alia*, as tithable—fisheries, rivers, ponds, trees, cattle, pigeons, seeds, fruits, warrens, fowling, gardens, turf (where dug), eggs of swans, hedgerows, bees, honey, wax, mills, huntings. As will be seen directly, the tithability of nearly all these was at some time or other disputed in the Law Courts.

This was the situation up to the time of the dissolution of the monasteries, an event which directly caused the transference of much tithe-ownership to lay hands, and raised opposition, which still finds expression, to payment in these circumstances. For, when Henry VIII handed over or sold the properties of the monasteries, there naturally accompanied them the rectorial tithes. These became the personal property of the new owners, whilst a vicar attended to the cure of souls and received usually the small tithes. Subsequently there has been no legal obstacle to the sale of this form of property, and at the time of commutation, in 1836, approximately one-quarter of all tithes were in lay hands.

So far as the history of tithing has been traced, it cannot justifiably be held that, irksome as it was, it had inflicted any direct deterrent on agriculture. Matters were to become altered, however, and by the seventeenth century its incidence had become a millstone round the neck of those who wished to improve their methods of farming. It was not the cost of the charge itself—whether paid in money or in kind—for that could be, and was, tacitly taken into consideration when rents were fixed or agreements for sales of property signed; it was rather the knowledge that there was always present a sleeping partner to share in the gains of husbandry but never to risk any capital—one who appeared and claimed a tenth of all the results accruing from improved methods and from the introduction of new crops. For nearly a hundred years this direct handicap has ceased to exist, but the antipathy to tithe paying has, nevertheless, been in evidence—not, as on the Continent during the eighteenth century, from anti-clerical causes, but simply on the grounds that payment represents a "burden" under which other industries do not suffer.

There is one important aspect of the matter which has received scarcely any attention from historians or from agricultural writers in the past, and that is the history of the collection of tithes in kind, particularly during the seventeenth and eighteenth centuries. All books on the history of agriculture compress this period into a short paragraph giving an account of the *modus* (a fixed annual payment, usually in money, in lieu of tithes in kind), and most ecclesiastical writers omit reference to any matter lying between the Reformation and 1836. Two points strike the historian who enters this almost virgin field. The first is astonishment that agriculture could be carried on under such incessant friction as took place between the clergy and the farmers, and the second is wonder at the pertinacity of the former in securing their dues, and, if frustrated, their litigious energies. To one who has consulted all the reports of legal cases concerning tithes from the fourteenth century up to the nineteenth, it is further a matter for wonder from whence the clergy found the money to embark on these suits. The overwhelming majority of the cases concerned small tithes, for there were few instigated by, or against, rectors. On the other hand, there were a certain number between vicars and rectors as to the ownership of particular tithes. The earliest cases, those in fact up to about 1500, mostly dealt with the principles of payment, the persons liable, and the courts appropriate for suits; from the sixteenth century up to the middle of the eighteenth century, as will shortly be seen, questions connected with agricultural practice and the complications caused by the introduction of new crops initiated the majority of suits, whilst, in the last decades prior to the Commutation Act, the law was generally invoked to decide upon the rights of individuals to tithes.

Let us glance at some reported cases. We find a vicar in 1595 instituting a suit for the payment of tithe on turkeys and tame partridges; he failed, as it was held, naturally, in the case of the latter, but surprisingly in that of the former, bird, that both were *ferae naturae.* Next year saffron, much grown in East Anglia, was adjudged a small tithe. An attempt to secure payment as early as 1314 on colts born at the King's stud farm at Woodstock was successful, as was another seventeen years later against the King's keeper for underwood sold off a Royal estate. The question of timber was always a controversial one, but the law generally held that the body of the tree and its branches were privileged, and a test case went against the vicar who demanded tithe of the "germins", or shoots, growing from the roots of felled trees. A *confrère,* however, secured his tenth of acorns, as these were clearly yearly renewable, and, as early as 1640, a nursery gardener was held liable for payment on all young trees that he sold out of his orchard. One hundred and sixty years later the Rector of Elmsett, Suffolk, proved his right to payment on wood converted into charcoal. In 1716 the Rector of Hurstpierpoint, Sussex, went to law to secure the grain that fell to the ground from the bottom of the tithe cocks, and the Master of a Cambridge College, as late as 1808, actually enforced payment on the stubble of wheat and rye. The Law Courts had on another occasion to decree that tithe was not due on the scraps of hay produced on the balks and headlands of common fields. In the seventeenth century one vicar claimed successfully upon fallen apples; a few years earlier another had won his case for tithing wild cherries. It is almost inconceivable that persons could be found in the position of the clergy who would deign to set such an example to their parishioners as did these two incumbents; one-tenth of the value of a few wild cherries or of windfall apples brought both parties up to London for cases that lasted days, and must have cost hundreds of times the value of the objects concerned. But worse can be found, for in 1681 a vicar confidently claimed payment on the wild ducks taken in an East Anglian decoy, and, naturally losing, then had the *sangfroid* to enter a plea for his tenth of the eggs laid by the few tame ducks used for decoying purposes! Some incumbents suspected collusion against themselves; this was doubtless the cause of the suit which went in favour of the vicar when it was shown that an apple-grower had allowed someone else to pluck his fruit, payment being thus avoided; on the other hand, it was held that, if the fruit was taken by unknown persons, the vicar had no remedy.

Tithe on livestock led to curious actions. Keen incumbents saw great possibilities in sheepfolds and grazing meadows, and did not always rest content with their share at clipping time or with a *modus* on calves. They were, of course, entitled to the "whole of the meal of milk every tenth morning and evening" (Chigwell, Essex, 1678), but must the vicar fetch his pailful himself or should the cowkeeper deliver it? If the latter ruling was given, where should he take it to—the vicarage or the church-door? A majority of the bench decided that this, being a small tithe, the cowkeeper should deliver the milk at the church-porch. Great tithes, of course, devolved on the owner to fetch and garner. Cattle bred for "pail or plough" were exempted in cases tried early in the seventeenth century, but cattle depastured in a parish in which they did not work at plough were tithable for agistment there, though exempt in their own. Saddle horses escaped the legal net at Sudbury in 1716, when the vicar failed to secure tithe of agistment from owners who had depastured them on commons. But an innkeeper, half a century before, had had to pay for the herbage travellers' horses had consumed while their owners put up at his hostelry. Previously a similar decision had gone against a tithe-owner, but in his favour so far as the agistment of working horses was concerned. In the case of sheep there was constant friction as to the exact time at which the vicar could claim his share of the "increase", and whether his claims for wool were met fully at the annual shearing. In 1752 it was decided that tithe of wool was due at shearing-time and formed satisfaction for the past year's pasturage, but flocks fed upon the stubble for the sake of the manure were not tithable; lambs paid when they "could live without their dam".

If these cases seem to have involved difficult matters of principle at law, put money in the pockets of the lawyers, and caused endless annoyance in half the villages of the country, yet matters were even more complicated by the introduction of crops from abroad. Turnips afforded the most litigation, closely followed by hops. By 1630 "all those new things, tobacco, hops, saffron", were reckoned as small tithes, and in 1670 cole-seed had been adjudged to the vicar. In 1691 hemp and flax, being "exceedingly difficult to tithe, it is ordered that a sum not exceeding 4*s*. per acre be paid for all". Potatoes, although "grown in great quantities in common fields", were yet small tithes, and turnips in similar circumstances in Suffolk in 1718 had to be set out in heaps for the vicar to tithe, but, if grown on a small scale, he was entitled to each tenth individual root.

There was worse to come, however, for when turnips were fed to sheep the position became hopelessly involved. In 1777 the Rev. F. Paddey, vicar of Kellington, Yorkshire, gained a decree in the Court of Exchequer by which he was adjudged entitled to full tithe on all turnips "drawn and eaten by unprofitable stock—that is, the tenth they were let or sold for", and, further, "all sheep fed on turnips and sold to the butcher before clipping-time to pay the full value of the tithe of turnips eaten by them". The defendant parishioners had, as defence, urged that a *modus* of 1*d.* per head of the flocks met both these demands. This case cost in all £700 for law expenses, and the value of the living was some £200 per annum! An early instance of turnips grown on a considerable scale occurs in *The Manor of Theberton*, where we read of a rector in 1674 making arrangements with his parishioners for two eventualities—namely, turnips sold to feed fat stock, which were to be tithed, and those fed to milch cows, which were to be exempt. Cases from Kent went to show that the accepted method of tithing hops was by measure in the bins when they were picked, and not by the pole or hill on which they were grown.

If an interpolation may be pardoned at this point, it seems worthy of note that Coke's *Institutes* of 1628 contained rulings on nearly all the questions involved, and yet actions were even more frequently entered upon in later years. The following (*Inst.* II, 652) appears to cover most of the ground.

> Tithes shall not be paid of anything that is of the substance of the earth and not annual, as coals, turf, etc. nor of beasts that be *ferae naturae*, nor of agistment of such beasts as pay tithe, nor of cattle that manure the ground, but of barren beasts the parson shall have tithe on agistment of herbage, unless they be nourished for the plough and so employed. No tithe shall be paid for after-pasture, nor for rakings, nor for *sylva caedua* employed for hedging and repairing of plough, and two tithes shall not be paid of one land in one year.

Whilst fish were only tithable by custom, this did not prevent many sea-board clergy from instituting suits which they must have felt, from the lack of historical support, were, from the beginning, hopeless. An interesting example is the case of the vicar of Yarmouth, who sought to secure one-twentieth of the fish landed in his parish that had been caught off Iceland; Cornwall also provided many instances, e.g. the vicar of Mevagissey obtained his tenth of pilchards, but there fish taken for bait were held to be tithe-free. Oysters and oyster-spawn were not allowed to the tithe-owner at Brightlingsea in 1713. At the end of the twelfth century there is a recorded case of two whales being tithed in France (Rodney Gallop, *A Book of the Basques*, p. 269).

Market-gardening raised fresh difficulties; generally a composition called a "garden penny" was accepted by the tithe-owner, but one case led to a considered judgment from the Courts in the following terms: "Peas and beans sown in rows and banks and managed in a garden-like fashion which had usually been paid to the vicar when hoed and managed by hand shall be paid to him [and not the rector] when the ground has been turned with a plough which does the work of a plough *and* a spade". Upon such small points did the disposal of tithe so often depend.

Tithe on minerals, except in rare cases where custom allowed, was not recognised, but this did not prevent an ingenious Derbyshire cleric from seeking to prove that veins of lead ore were subject to annual growth, and therefore came within the well-known definition of tithable objects.

Mills were tithable, as representing personal profits, and accordingly paid on that basis, and not, fortunately for the miller, on their output of flour. There was generally a distinction drawn between newly created and "ancient" mills, in favour of the former.

Having seen the efforts of the clergy to secure their rights, and often far more than their rights, some account of the small tithes actually paid in a particular parish may be of interest. Take Brotherton again, where the Rev. John Law, who was vicar in 1770 (at the time when the Ings were still annually divided) has left the following exact description of his dues.

According to an old *modus* with the parishioners of Brotherton a Pidgeon Chamber pays one shilling and threepence, a Dove Coat half a crown, a new milch cow two pence halfpenny, a strip't cow three-halfpence, a foal four pence, every house ninepence halfpenny, a swarm of bees two pence, the old stock a penny. Everyone above the age of sixteen pays two pence as a communicant. Turnips are paid for according to their value, or as they are let. Potatoes are paid in kind if not compounded for. The tythe of Orchards, Pigs and Geese are also paid in kind, if not compounded for. Rape and all new species of vicarial tythes are to be paid in kind unless compounded for, but Hemp and Flax must be paid according to Statute. The Marsh Mill pays an old *modus* of 2. 6 yearly, and tho' I have agreed to take the same for the Windmill, yet my successor is not obliged to do the same, but may demand the tenth part of the Moultre after all reasonable expenses are deducted. The new Shelling Mill built last year in the quarry Holes is also titheable, after it has been so long employed as may be fairly supposed to reimburse the proprietor the expense of the building.

N.B. If Clover and Saint Foin stand for seed the Tythe thereof belongs to the Vicar, but if it is cut or made use of for Hay, the Tythe belongs to the Appropriators, or Lessee of the Dean and Chapter.

It should be observed that one or two of the above payments are, strictly speaking, not tithes, but represent Easter offerings. In the year in question, Mr Law collected 347 separate sums (the vast majority being a few pence only) from 132 different persons, amounting to £28. These payments, it must be remembered, were additional to the great tithes, with which, being a vicar, he had no concern. He appears to have carried out his invidious job with patience, tact and kindness, as the following extracts from his tithe account-book show. He let a widow off ("poor and deserving"), a male parishioner ("lost a leg"), another also ("very poor"); but he could be firm when necessary ("by warrant of distress", and "distrained on"). He had occasional bad debts—("died insolvent", "ran away", "left the town", "worked in the garden"). He allowed J. Robinson, on payment of 2*s.* 6*d.*, to keep his tithe pig "as they sold dear", and gave half (nine sacks) of his tithe of potatoes to his curate. But another farmer paid after "much threatening and many altercations", whilst in 1772 he secured process against fifty-seven persons, but failed to get anything from a pigeon loft ("rats"). He was often dependent on the farmers' employees for important information relating to operations about which he was otherwise ignorant—"R. Kitchen sold certain turnips to Mr Simpson and eat others with his own sheep, for he was seen to bring some home in a cart". He could not always believe what he was told as to the prices that produce had fetched, and once noted that "Mr Furnish was either a bad farmer or a dishonest man". On one occasion tithe geese flew away, and he observed that "their wings must be clipped in future".

The above is, no doubt, typical of conditions in thousands of parishes scattered all over the country. Is it, therefore, to be wondered at that the position often became unbearable? Should we not rather express surprise that the system worked at all?

There remains one important feature to be illustrated; that is the incidence of tithe on wages. We have seen that theoretically it was leviable on all clear profits and salaries, but the writer only knows of two instances where the wages of agricultural labourers were held liable. From a quotation in Coke's *Institutes* from an Act of Edward VI it would appear doubtful if these payments were legally enforceable in the case of farm labourers. The section in question reads as follows: "That every person exercising merchandise, bargaining and selling...(other than such as be common day labourers) shall yearly...pay for his personal tithes".

The first case occurs in that interesting work, the *Rector's Book of Clayworth, Notts*. Here, after giving instances of the usual trouble with recalcitrant payers and others who even professed their ignorance of the existence of tithe, the rector in the year 1683 wrote as follows: "When I was about to enter on this living I heard Dr Mapletoft, my predecessour, say that there was one thing in ye Parish which he would not lose of all things that belonged to it, and that was a farthing in the shilling of all Servants' Wages". After securing details of this payment in his predecessor's time, the rector then sought to collect it himself, but met with violent opposition, and was finally informed that "it would much gratify ye neighbourhood if I would foregoe it. But I answered, that if it was so long since it was paid, there was the more need to look speedily after it, least it be lost for ever. I presently took out a citation in the Spiritual court against Ralph Mears, Thomas Searcey and Richard Hallifax, who thereupon submitted and paid, and others paid by their example. Thus was I now in peaceable possession and ye servants willingly paid for some years, till some of their masters, loath to pay their own tithes...thought it plausible to take their servants part and not to pay me as of late they had done. They told them that all I could do at them was to excommunicate them, which was only their not going to church". After threatened law-suits and an abortive arbitration, the rector reluctantly let the matter drop, and no more is heard of this interesting survival, but if the practice had ever been universal one hesitates to conjure up a vision of village life in the circumstances. What, for example, would the National

PLATE XVI

The Vicar receiving his tithes

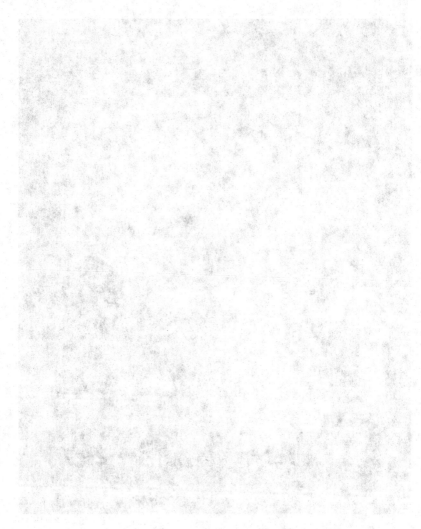

Union of Agricultural Workers have had to say to this levy on their members' earnings?

The second example of this exaction—for it can be described in no milder terms—occurred as late as 1832, and resulted in the imprisonment of the defendant, an agricultural labourer named Jeremiah Dodsworth, at the instigation of the Rev. Francis Lundy, Rector of Lockington in the East Riding of Yorkshire. Thirteen "servants in husbandry" owed arrears of payments of 4*d.* in the pound on their wages, "being tithes, offerings, oblations or obventions" as the writ described them. Twelve owed £2. 18*s.*, of which Dodsworth's share, being for two years, amounted to the princely sum of 9*s.* 4*d.* Distraint upon his goods yielding nothing to the rector's pocket, the constable was ordered, by a brother clergyman on the bench, to take the said "Jeremiah Dodsworth into your custody and keep him safe (at the House of Correction at Beverley) for the space of three calendar months". Comment is impossible. One can only note that the basis of demand was slightly lower than at Clayworth, where it was equivalent to 5*d.* in the pound.

While upon this particular subject, it is very interesting to find that, from the foundation of their house in 1347, the Fellows of Pembroke College, Cambridge, paid personal tithes to the Church of St Mary the Less—their opposite neighbour—whose parishioners they were. (T. A. Walker, *Peterhouse Biographical Register*.) Name after name occurs of members of the Society who paid these dues, or who were stated to owe them: thus, Thomas Toft paid tithe in 1385 on the "collections", viz. lecture fees, he had earned in the University Arts School. Matthew Wren (*op. cit.* p. 38) subsequently recorded, as did numerous successors whose names are preserved, that personal tithe was paid to Peterhouse (the patrons of St Mary's), *jure ecclesiae B. Mariae*, by the Master and Fellows of Pembroke, by the Principal of St Thomas's Hostel and by Masters of Arts who resided within the parish boundaries, in respect of the University offices of Vice-Chancellor, Scrutator, Taxor, Proctor, Orator, Bedell; and that Praelectors in Theology and in other subjects were also liable. Thus, for more than two centuries, the personal earnings and professional fees due to such University officials as came within this particular parochial jurisdiction were successfully tithed.

The above examples have all related to the incidence and collection of small tithes. Great tithes were, from their nature, less liable to lead to disputes in principle, but cases were frequent in the Courts affecting the method of their collection. All are familiar with the standard objections to the collection of cereals in kind—viz. the acrimonious disputes as to the exact time at which it was least inconvenient to set out the tithe, the expense of the provision of tithe barns and the conversion of the impropriator into a dealer in grain. The procedure involved could account for anything up to a quarter of the gross value of the tithe. The Law Courts furnished additional objections. The same rector of Clayworth on one occasion records that a farmer had led corn from a certain field before his servants had "viewed" it. As a result the rector had to take his share from the stacks themselves. A few years earlier he had obtained a cash payment in similar circumstances—no doubt in the nature of a fine. The rector of Reigate secured his great tithe on peas and beans gathered green, but he had to institute proceedings in 1715 in order to do so. An action proved the right of the rector's waggon, already loaded with sheaves from the land of one farmer, to enter the land of another tithe-payer. What possible objection there could be on the part of the second person to this procedure one cannot conjecture, but it was sufficiently powerful to involve him in a law-suit. The clergy almost necessarily won when the Law Courts were avoided, as witness the thirteenth-century story quoted by Coulton (*Social Life in Britain*) when the husbandman found the bad coin he had tendered the priest for tithe placed in his own mouth at the Communion table.

Let us now turn to Ireland, where, if we expect to find the business of tithe collection carried on with fervour and opposed by violence, we shall not be disappointed, for was not this the country in which even the fish had religious susceptibilities, as witness the case of the Protestant clergyman who, it was alleged, had caused the shoals to leave their usual grounds off a Catholic coast by attempting to levy tithe on them when caught? William Cobbett, in his pamphlet entitled *The Doom of Tithes*, especially singled out conditions in Ireland as calling for remedial measures. He strongly upheld the tithe-payers, and declared that it was iniquitous to mulct the peasantry in order to secure contributions for a non-representative church. But when he attacked the principle of commutation, on the ground that it would convert tithe-owners into landlords and lead to their becoming active partners in agriculture, he overstepped the bounds of wisdom, and his comments on the *Report* issued by a committee of the House of Lords were exaggerated in the extreme, as when he declared that "this document, will, a hundred years hence, be considered of as much importance as the declaration of the Dutch King when he first landed in England".

In 1833 Lord Westmeath's representative called for military aid in collecting tithes on his lordship's estates, and declared that violent language was being used in chapel by a certain priest—language "declaratory of his determination not to pay"; he added to his appeal the assurance that "had I not been armed on a former occasion I would have considered myself in imminent danger". This, and similar, incidents led to a ruling by Dublin Castle that the military would only be available for the collection of *arrears* of tithe. That there were then, as now, always two sides to any question concerning Ireland, we can deduce from another communication from the Castle to a certain incumbent in 1833. This gentleman was told that his parishioners had reported that, "in enforcing payment of your tithe in that parish their houses were broken into and some of their inmates beaten, and that the clothes of others were taken away, although they had actually paid your dues". In these circumstances, it was added, further assistance could not be accorded him. Small wonder was it that posters appeared couched thus:

> Citizens of Waterford! Those enemies of the people, of peace, of Christianity, and even of their own church, the collectors of incumbent money, are abroad. They have positive orders from their pampered and unfeeling employers to enforce payment of this hateful impost with an unsparing hand. Numbers of your poor fellow citizens have been already distrained. Citizens of Waterford! Refuse to become participators in the evil acts of these harpies and do not afford to them a market for the fruits of their peculation. Refuse, to a man, to purchase any article distrained for a tax so odious and unjust; and let not your houses be polluted by the reception of goods dragged from your neighbours.

No wonder, again, that we read complaints from prisoners condemned to nine months' imprisonment in Cork gaol for opposition —active no doubt—to tithes, or that, in 1832, a Select Committee commented on the "organised and systematic opposition to payment"—payment which could only be secured by the "protection of military and police given the clergy of the Established Church in their endeavour to secure their legal rights". But in many cases the clergy, "unwilling to risk the effusion of blood...have abstained from taking active steps". Whilst certain witnesses gave utterance to exactly the same complaints that have again been heard just now, namely that it was impossible under the existing difficulties for farmers to pay tithe, the majority held that it was unfair to tax Roman Catholics for the benefit of the Protestant minority. That argument, of course, was almost peculiar to Ireland.

In 1838 an Act was passed, which transferred the payment of tithe from the occupiers of land to its owners, thus antedating similar action in England and Wales by some fifty-three years. This was merely a gesture, and it was not until 1870 that disestablishment, under Gladstone, wholly freed the Irish nation from one of its very few legitimate grievances. Then, the tithe rent-charges were taken over by the State which, after liquidating therefrom certain small liabilities due to Church funds, diverted the remainder to such secular purposes as education—the principal beneficiaries being the Universities and Teachers' Pension Funds—and the administration of Agriculture (including the Congested Districts Board). These duties the Land Commission has subsequently administered.

In Scotland, tithe, under the name of "teinds", had pursued a course historically similar to its evolution in England, from which country, indeed, it was introduced, the greater teinds being originally payable in kind to the "parson" and the lesser to the "vicar". An Act of 1633 ordained the commutation of teinds, thus anticipating similar English legislation by two centuries, although the process itself proved to be a long drawn one. Thereafter, these payments became a charge upon the landowners, in the collection of which the beneficiaries had little active interest. The monetary basis adopted by the Act was that of "the fifth of the rental" and compulsory sale by teind owners to landlords was decreed upon the basis of nine years' purchase. Scottish historians point out that "vicarage" teinds could be lost by their non-exaction over a certain period of time, while this was not the case with those of the "parsonage", which were always legally recoverable before the special Teind Court. In the 'seventies of last century, Nenion Elliot, a solicitor of the Supreme Courts, Edinburgh, illustrated the absurdity and inconvenience of a system whereby the mode of assessing awards was based upon "such a quantity of victual, half meal, half barley, in Imperial weight and measure, as shall be equal to 18 chalders of the late standard weight and measure of Scotland, payable in money according to the highest fiars prices of the county annually". This advocate put forward proposals for a uniform basis of calculation, for the transference, from the Teind Commissioners to the Court of Session, of all duties associated with the matter and for the stabilisation of the value of teinds regardless of fluctuations in the prices of barley and of meal. It is, therefore, interesting to record that, in 1925, a Church of Scotland Act put into effect this latter proposal, whereby teinds were "standardised" in terms of money regardless of fiars prices, but a clause proposing compulsory redemption was, after strenuous opposition in the House of Lords, rejected and this procedure remains, as in England, optional. For a very full historical description of teinds, readers are recommended to consult A. A. Cormack's *Teinds and Agriculture*, from the pages of which it will be gathered that Scots payers and receivers have always held much the same views on this subject as those of their colleagues in England.

Chapter VIII

TITHE (CONTINUED)

Arthur Young's views on tithe abroad; clerical answers; rates on tithe; Commutation and the Act of 1836; Extraordinary tithe rent-charge; views of agriculturists on tithe; fluctuations in value; effect of the war; redemption in the past and at the present; the Acts of 1918 and 1925; the present incidence of tithe.

By the commencement of the nineteenth century the time was obviously fast approaching when something drastic would have to be done in the matter of modifying the incidence of tithe. Arthur Young felt strongly on the subject, and, as was usual with him in such circumstances, did not hesitate to give forcible expression to his feelings. He wrote, on one of his foreign tours, as follows:

In regard to the oppressions of the clergy as to tithes, I must do that body a justice to which a claim cannot be laid in England. Tho' the ecclesiastical tenth is levied more severely than usual in Italy, yet it never was exacted with *that horrid greediness* as is at present the disgrace of England. When taken in kind no such thing was ever known in any part of France where I made enquiries as a 1/10; it was always 1/12th, 1/18th or even a 1/20th. No new article of culture paid anything. Thus turnips, cabbages, clover, potatoes paid nothing. In many parts meadows were exempt. Cows nothing, wool nothing. Lambs from 1/12th to 1/21st. Such mildness in the levying this odious tax is absolutely unknown in England.

He made much of the fact that in France the Revolution had swept both tithes and the established Church aside, and warned England of the imminence of a like fate. France, America and certain Italian states, he said, had set us a noble example, and we alone, in company with retrograde Spain, adhered to this imposition; Holland and Switzerland, in common with France, had seized Church property.

Young soon found an opponent in the form of the Rev. John Howlett, vicar of Great Dunmow, who, in a small book published in 1801, attacked him vigorously. Had, he said, the previous mildness of the French clergy saved them from sequestration? Was not English agriculture, despite the much abused tithes, more flourishing than it had been for generations? He admitted inequalities in their incidence, quoting an example from Kent, where the tithe on an acre of hops, amounting to £3 or £4, was accompanied by a rent of only 40*s*. or 50*s*. He agreed that fresh outlay, which was unlikely to return more than 10 per cent., was not generally undertaken by farmers in consequence of the existence of the invisible partner. But he pointed out that the clergy paid many charges on this form of property, e.g. land-tax, rates and the expenses of collection, and he even carried the war into his opponent's camp by suggesting that, as farmers had not raised wages sufficiently, the poor-rates were unduly high and the value of the tithe thereby reduced to the recipient. He gave an alleged instance in which an incumbent, by threatening to revert to tithing in kind, in lieu of a moderate *modus*, had secured a rise of 1*s*. 6*d*. in the wages paid to labourers on a particular farm. This was an involved piece of agricultural economics, the possible value of which to the incumbent depended on the relative importance of the various ratepayers concerned. Howlett also referred to the case of a clergyman paying £900 in rates on £600 worth of tithe—a perfectly possible case at the time in question. He pointed out that in his own County of Essex hundreds of acres of woods, which paid no tithes, were being felled, and wheat, which was subject to the highest form of the tax, planted. Where, then, was the cause for complaint by farmers who were never so opulent before? He had the wisdom to urge the claims of commutation, but he feared that confiscation would be encouraged by its operation, and that "a set of atheistical, conceited, profligate men" might take possession, not only of Church lands, but of tithes also, and thus "strip thirty or forty thousand men of their property". Finally, he referred to the case of the vicar of Battersea, which had caused Young much mirth. This good man had taken to drawing his tithes of vegetables in kind and hawking them, by proxy, through the London streets. Howlett held that, so long as the vicar did not himself cry "Come buy my asparagus! O rare cauliflowers!", there was nothing *infra dignitatem* in the proceeding.

Charles Vancouver, at the same period, drew attention to the handicap under which fen farmers suffered. Tithe became due on the reclamation of their land, and the owners of rectorial tithes drew great sums from the produce of this rich soil—produce which they had in no way assisted to secure. This argument was, however, some hundred years out of date, as the bulk of the fens had been drained before the Restoration, and subsequent rents would have taken this factor into consideration. But the principle was correct, and the Law Courts had rendered it more stringent by ruling that fen-land so improved was liable at once to tithe, the only exception (seven years' relief) being made in the case of barren lands which required extraordinary efforts to render them fertile.

Impartial readers will agree that the evidence from the Law Courts, from Ireland and from the writings of controversialists all pointed but one way—and that way lay commutation of tithe. Whilst it is true that the bulk of payments were in 1836 already made by *modus* or other such composition, it must be remembered that the primary object of commutation was not so much the legalisation of this form of payment, but rather its stabilisation in relation to the general price-level.

From 1833 until 1836 four attempts were made by Ministers to effect legislation on these lines. The final success was accorded to Lord John Russell's bill, introduced in February 1836. The main difficulty encountered by all who had attempted to frame commutation Acts was in differentiating between tithe and rent; it was obviously highly desirable to make these two quite independent of one another, otherwise tithe became a tax on the capital invested in land, and not a charge depending on the value of the output of the soil. Adam Smith had pointed out that "taxes upon the produce of land are in reality taxes upon the rent, and though they may be originally advanced by the farmer, are finally paid by the landlord", for prospective tenants had always mentally deducted tithe and other charges when coming to terms with landlords.

The machinery set up to give effect to the Act of 1836 provided for the appointment of Commissioners and Assistant Commissioners, armed with considerable authority. Compulsory powers were accorded them as from October 1838, prior to that date opportunity being given for voluntary agreement. Their principal task was to assess the existing value of all tithes, on the basis of the average receipts by owners during the previous seven years. In view of a subsequent controversy it is perhaps well to record the exact instructions delivered to the Commissioners in regard to the treatment of charges on tithe. They were as follows:

Provided also, that in estimating the value of the said tithes, the Commissioners or Assistant Commissioner shall estimate the same without making any deduction therefrom on account of any Parliamentary, Parochial, County and other Rates, Charges and Assessments to which the said tithes are liable; and whenever the said tithes shall have been demised or compounded for on the principle of the rent or composition being paid free from all such Rates, Charges and Assessments, or any part thereof the said Commissioners or Assistant Commissioner shall have regard to that circumstance and shall make such an addition on account thereof as shall be an equivalent.

We may here note that as early as 1718 a vicar had been adjudged liable to poor-rate on his small tithes. It has unsuccessfully been held that the "Poor Rate Exemption Act" of 1840 was intended to afford relief to clerical tithe-owners in respect to their assessment on tithe *qua* salary. The Act in question abrogated rates on the profits of "stock-in-trade or other property", and specifically excluded from within its scope "tithes impropriate and propriations of tithes". The grounds for the unsuccessful appeal were that the above definition did not correctly apply to the tithe rent-charge attached to a benefice. This question of rates on tithe always cropped up when rates themselves were rising, and the post-war discussion centred around whether the 1836 Commissioners did, or did not, take into consideration the previous incidence of local rates. It was even suggested that a sum of about a quarter of a million pounds was "given" the owners at the time of commutation. Anyone who reads through the instructions handed to the Commissioners cannot, however, fail to agree that this sum—if it be a correct figure—represents the amount previously paid direct by the tithe-payer to the rate-collector on behalf of the tithe-owner, in cases where this procedure had been agreed upon between the parties. It must be remembered that, prior to 1836, thousands of individual bargains had been struck and rate-free compositions accepted by the clergy: in fact, the Commissioners discovered that in numerous such cases the clergy had secured considerably less money than if they had paid rates themselves on the gross sums concerned. The Commissioners' duty was perfectly plain; it was to discover the gross value of the annual payments, and, in cases where deductions had been made, to effect the necessary addition when fixing the commuted value. In answer to a question from the Land Agents' Society upon this controversial subject, the then Minister of Agriculture issued a statement which was accompanied by extracts from some of the original documentary agreements, showing in detail the sums thus proportionately determined. Thenceforward, the tithe-owner was legally responsible for paying his own rates on this form of property. The evidence of witnesses from the Board of Agriculture before the Commission of 1893 was unequivocal on this point. Nor was it agreed at that time that there were the germs of a grievance, in that by averaging the value of the rates paid prior to 1836 over seven years, a period was included which covered abnormal demands from the rate-collector —demands swollen by excessive distress and unemployment. As one witness said, the object of commutation was not to anticipate the future but to give expression to the past, and the reduction in rates that followed commutation benefited all payers and not exclusively those who were rated on the possession of tithe. In specific cases quoted wherein payers had, on composition, agreed to pay rates up to 19*s.* in the pound, the answer was that either they made bad bargains, or else that the bare composition did not represent the value of the tithe; it had been open to them to pay a composition only and to leave the owner to settle with the rate-collector. The object of the Act itself was "to stereotype the condition of affairs existing in the seven years prior to 1836". By the Tithe Act of 1899 clerical owners were placed on an equality with agriculturists in regard to rates on their tithes "attached to a benefice", being thenceforward liable for only half the usual payment, the other portion, until the State finally resolved the whole position in 1925, being met by the Inland Revenue authorities. The precise basis for assessment of tithe to local rates was frequently a source of friction and even of legal uncertainty, for, although the great majority of local authorities levied upon the full value, cases occurred, e.g. that of the Dunmow Guardians, where 20 or 25 per cent. was first deducted from the gross rental. Such an authority as Mr (afterwards Sir) Montague Barlow went further (*Economic Journal*, 1900, pp. 33 *et seq.*) and held that this form of property had been wrongly assessed ever since the Poor Law Act of 1601.

Having digressed upon the subject of the rateability of tithes, one must revert to the question of commutation. The Commissioners' labours resulted in a rent-charge of slightly over £4,000,000 being leviable in England and Wales, of which almost one-quarter was found to be in lay hands. This sum was subsequently reduced by redemption and other means to about £3,400,000 at the end of 1927, that is, prior to the coming into force of the legislation which will ultimately cause its disappearance, and in 1931 it was £3,176,000.

There was one class of land which presented difficulties to the Commissioners—namely that given over to market-gardens, hop-fields and fruit-farms. It was agreed that it would not be equitable to fix a high and permanent rent-charge on property of this description which might at any time revert to ordinary agricultural uses. Hence the creation of what was known as Extraordinary tithe rent-charge—a separate and additional payment over and above the ordinary charge, calculated on an acreage basis. A subsequent Act (1886) limited its operation to existing cases, and encouraged its capitalisation. Interest at 4 per cent. was to be paid on the ascertained capital value, and henceforward its incidence was fixed at that charge with power of redemption. Criticism was not lacking in the early 'nineties that hardships existed in the case of land once under hops, but since grubbed and still liable to the charge.

The average value of tithe in the past having been secured, there remained the task of making its purchasing power correspond in the future to the price of commodities and to the economic conditions of agriculture. This was achieved by correlating its value to that of the three principal cereals averaged over a period of seven years. In the basic year the sum of £100 of tithe was split up into three equal parts, and the number of bushels of wheat, barley and oats purchasable by each was evolved. The septennial average price of each cereal was then (and until 1918 subsequently) multiplied by these figures as "weights", and the total sum thus obtained represented the tithe rent-charge for the current year. Strictly speaking, these were "corn-rents", which were nothing new, as they had existed in numerous cases for many years, and represented commutations in particular parishes under the provisions of local Acts of Parliament made on the basis of the value of cereals—generally of wheat alone. They were subject to revision at stated intervals of years in order that they might keep in contact with current prices. Examples are still to be found side by side with the ordinary charge and are convertible into tithe rent-charge on special terms, and some, made in lieu of ordinary tithes, represent payments arising out of enclosures.

Two minor objections were at times raised to the principle involved; firstly, that the "weights" (in round figures, 95 for wheat,

168 for barley and 242 for oats) gave undue scope for fluctuations in the price of oats to affect the charge, and, secondly, that the *Gazette* average represented the enhanced price of the cereals when they reached the dealer's hands and not their value when they left the farm. The answer to the first point was that in normal times the prices of the cereals moved so closely together that the cost of oats never got out of harmony with that of the other two (moreover, it represented generally only half the price of wheat).

The second contention was borne out by evidence contained in the *Report* of the Royal Commission on Agriculture of 1893. It was urged that the official price took no cognisance of inferior grain retained on the farm, but did include several commissions and railway charges, resulting in an increase of 15 to 30 per cent. in its value. Instances were given of four sales being registered of the same barley, the first at 24*s*. and the last at 32*s*.—the official average price in this case being recorded as 27*s*. Farmers further held that only one-quarter of the sales of corn in the country came within the purview of the corn inspectors. The only answer that could be given was that the Act had always been administered as it was originally interpreted, and that the average prices quoted annually (to form the basis of the septennial figure) were collected in numerous corn markets throughout the country. There is no evidence that the 1836 Commissioners intended any other method of collection to be used.

A more general ground of complaint against the commuted charges made its appearance half a century later. It was then urged on behalf of Essex and other once prosperous East Anglian corn-growing Counties that, whatever the position might have been in 1836, it was no longer right in the 'nineties that these tithes should be equivalent to over 5*s*. an acre, whilst in the grass Counties of the North they should vary from 3*d*. to 1*s*. 2*d*. It was shown also that in a period of depression tithe was frequently larger than rent. It was certainly true that such Counties were unduly hit by the conditions then prevailing—bad seasons, intense foreign competition and extremely low commodity prices—and that their parishes with the heaviest soils, and therefore at that time with the largest derelict areas, were often called upon to pay the highest tithes; one has, however, to take long views in studying the economic history of agriculture, and the other side to the argument was that these were precisely the areas which, in pre-commutation days, could best afford to pay, that commutation had been carried out at a time when cereals had fallen heavily in price, and that, in such abnormal circumstances as then prevailed, even the complete remission of the charge would not have ameliorated the position to any considerable extent. Essex claimed both revaluation and nationalisation of tithe, but received neither, and yet within little more than a decade, thanks to an increase in the world's supply of gold, again produced wheat at a profit, and was able to meet the tithe-owners' demands.

On the same lines, but forty years earlier, we find Sir James Caird pointing out that Wiltshire tenant farmers, after the events of 1836 had freed them from fear of the tithe-owners' increased demands, actually broke up large areas of downland for tillage purposes. The freedom thus secured them was checked again at the time Caird wrote, but it was probable that farming had benefited in the long run. In periods of depression, whilst rents were lowered by landlords, tithe, however, was subject to no sudden downward fluctuations—its weight could be foreseen with certainty for lengthy periods. In such times it was usual to find the suggestion put forward that corn-lands should no longer be tithed in relation to the price of cereals, but, if total remission was not agreed to, some other basis should be chosen.

Commutation having thus been effected and the value of tithe rent-charge in 1836 fixed as parity, it remains to trace its subsequent movements, which the diagram on p. 181 will facilitate. Briefly, it may be stated that up to 1883 it maintained its level with fluctuations not greatly exceeding 10 per cent. above or below parity; the highest point attained, £112. 15*s*. 6¾*d*., was in 1875, and the lowest in 1855, when £89. 15*s*. 8¾*d*. was indicated. For the greater part of the half century it stood above £100. The effect of the repeal of the Corn Laws in 1846 was not felt by British agriculturists until the late 'seventies, owing to reasons which are dealt with elsewhere, but the policy embodied in that action has been held to afford special grounds of complaint on the part of tithe-owners. What exactly happened? From 1883 (the septennial average having exerted a delaying action) the value of tithe rent-charge declined annually, until, in 1901, it was worth £66. 10*s*. 9¼*d*.; for thirty-four years it remained below parity, and, despite participating in the admitted recovery that was taking place prior to the outbreak of the Great War, it was only the rapidly rising prices caused by the latter upheaval that propelled it above £100 in 1918.

The official reply to the complaints of owners during this long period was that the whole conception of the sliding scale was to bring the value of tithe into relationship with the cost of living, and that £66 in 1901 was the equivalent of £100 in 1836, commodity prices in general having fallen correspondingly. This was a perfectly legitimate answer, but one to be pondered over seriously when the policy involved in the official action taken in 1918 is considered. The value of the charge, to the nearest pound, was, in 1915, £77; in 1916, £83; in 1917, £92; and in 1918 exactly £109. 3*s*. 11*d*. Payers of tithe, accustomed for a generation to a below-parity value, became vociferous at what they considered the unfair share of the increased profits of farming being taken by the tithe-owner. Their outcry led to immediate legislative action, and the value of tithe was, by the Tithe Act of 1918, decreed to be fixed at its then level until January 1st, 1926. Thus £109. 3*s*. 11*d*. was the controlled value of this charge for some eight years. The Act fixing these terms also prescribed reversion to a fifteen-year average of the price of the three cereals after the expiration of the eight years in question.

The arguments used on both sides are familiar to all. The tithe-owner, especially the clerical owner, hit in common with the rest of the community by the increased cost of living, was denied the right successfully asserted by the vast majority of his fellows to a commensurate increase in income; it was immaterial that he might have received payment on a sliding scale when prices were low, there must be a limit fixed to the movement when they rose. The farmer-payer declared that payment at the rate of 9 per cent. above parity was far more than the owner of tithe had ever expected to attain, that the industry could not afford to pay any further share of its larger profits—if they were in all cases larger, which was disputed—to those who suffered none of the troubles connected with farming under war conditions.

What exactly did the owners lose by the Act of 1918? On a septennial basis the rent-charge value would have been £124 in 1919, £141 in 1920, £162 in 1921, £172 in 1922 and 1923, £166 in 1924 and £156 in 1925. High sums admittedly, but within the power to pay of occupying owners who had entered the industry on a pre-war capital valuation and had not invested all their profits of 1915–17 in land at current prices; certainly not within the power to pay of many of those who purchased land and farming stock in 1918 to 1920; probably not of landlords who lived on agricultural rents. The disadvantages attaching to the septennial average in such economic upheavals were thus illustrated, for it is certain that, whatever might have been the protests, it would have been easier to secure much higher payments on the basis of the actual values of corn annually recorded in these years than to have obtained the septennial average, whose delayed action would have drawn moderately high tithe-charges into a period of lower commodity prices. The actual yearly prices would have been as follows: 1919, £180; 1920, £202; 1921, £228; 1922, £149; 1923, £114; 1924, £101; 1925, £120.

There would have been another safeguard for the payer in the event of the annual price being substituted, for there is a clause in the Tithe Act of 1891 which provided that the tithe-owner should not be entitled to recover more than two-thirds of the gross value of the land (or the net annual value to the landlord). In the past there had not been general occasion to make use of this provision, and individual farmers had often been chary of claiming such relief, as it entailed making public their financial condition, but when the whole body of payers would have been similarly circumstanced (rents not having been raised seriously during the war) its application would have become widespread. It is probable, however, that the course adopted in 1918 was the best for both sides, but generosity towards the tithe-owner might have been carried a step farther than it was.

He was indeed, if a cleric, afforded further relief by clauses contained in the supplementary Act, passed in 1920, whereby rates on tithe belonging to an ecclesiastical corporation, as well as those attached to a benefice, received considerable remission. Such bodies, or persons, were relieved entirely of rates on this form of property if their total income from it did not exceed £300 per annum, and only became liable for half what they would otherwise have paid if the income lay between £300 and £500. The Inland Revenue authority still paid half the current rates under the Act of 1899, but any excess demand resulting from the clauses of the new Act had to be met by the general body of rate-payers. This concession, coming on the top of the 1899 Act, has been declared in certain cases to have resulted in an excessive charge being placed on the shoulders of non-clerical rate-payers. Instances must, however, be rare of areas where the major portion of rates is represented by the incumbent's tithe. On the other hand it was then advocated that all tithe should be freed from assessment to local rates.

Welsh tithe received special treatment under two Church Acts (1914 and 1919), whereby it was secularised and will eventually be transferred, through Church Commissioners, to the County Councils and the University of Wales to be expended upon higher education. It continues to be a legal obligation, but, to anticipate, unlike its English counterpart, has no connection with Queen Anne's Bounty, makes no contribution to a sinking fund and is, therefore, fixed at £105.

Before bringing up to date the history of tithe there remain two features to mention. One is the Tithe Act of 1891, which, apart from offering limited relief to payers of tithes which would otherwise have been excessive in amount, altered the legal position as between landlord and tenant. Prior to 1891 it had been permissible for tenants to deduct from their rents the payments they had made direct to the tithe-owner, but most leases did not encourage this custom, and a large proportion of all the payments was made wholly by tenants, although the Act of 1836 had evidently intended that the landlords should be responsible. The new Act enforced the payment by the landowner; it also effected alterations in the law relating to recovery and distraint.

Next comes the question of redemption. The advantages attaching to this procedure had for long been recognised, the *Reports* of most Royal Commissions and independent Committees containing recommendations to this effect. Sir James Caird himself had formulated a scheme in 1881, by which the Government would have taken over the charge, paid £75 for each £100 of value and allowed the remaining £25 to accumulate for forty-seven years at 3 per cent.; the capital sum thus raised would have guaranteed the perpetual payment of £75 to the owners. Wholesale redemption, as explained above, was effected in Ireland at the time of the disestablishment of the Irish Church, when the Government assumed its ownership. Piecemeal redemption in England was always possible after 1836, but it was so hedged in by restrictions and formalities that little recourse was had to it; indeed, up to 1918 only some £73,000 worth of tithe had been thus extinguished. Whatever might be the existing level of the charge, payment had to be at the rate of twenty-five times the *parity* value and redemption in the majority of cases called for the lay tithe-owner's consent, or of those spiritually concerned, in the case of clerical ownership. For the long periods of time during which the charge had been far below £100 it was manifestly absurd to pay twenty-five times the latter value; it is probable that, if at any time before the war parity had been reached, redemption would have automatically commenced.

With certain minor exceptions the legislature allowed redemption to proceed either on agreement between the tithe-owner and the landlord concerned, or on terms fixed by the Ministry of Agriculture as legal arbitrator. The principle involved was that by redemption the annual income of the owner, if invested in Government securities, should be equal to the net amount previously secured from the tithe itself. In assessing the net value of the tithe deductions were made for the cost of collection, rates and Land tax; these deductions were from a sum representing the fixed (i.e. unvarying) annual payment which the Ministry estimated to be equivalent in value to the varying tithe rent-charge. It will again be observed that the incubus of high rates disadvantageously affected the valuation, and in varying degrees in different localities, and that the terms were dependent on the class of owner—whether spiritual or lay—and the corresponding incidence of rates.

The result of this encouragement to redemption, in combination with the higher level of the charge, was to be seen in the number of transactions carried through after the Act of 1918 was passed, a single year effecting more than the whole period between 1836 and the latter year had done. There was, indeed, what might almost be described as a "rush" to redeem from 1918 to 1925, during which time tithe to the value of £382,000 was so treated. It had been suggested in evidence before the Commission of 1893 that, at the then rate of progress, 6000 years must elapse before all tithe would be redeemed; if the circumstances ruling after the war had continued for a decade or so, the problem of redemption would have settled itself in a very small fraction of that time. Apart from the encouragement then afforded by simplified legislation and the more advantageous financial terms secured, there was considerable inducement to both parties concerned to effect the change, for the landlord was saved the annoyance of making frequent small payments, and the tithe-owner was assured of a steady income from a source not open to criticism from any party or Church. In the light of the latest legislation—now to be discussed—the time is approaching when payment of tithe on the basis of the average value of three commodities will seem as crude as the incumbents' efforts two hundred years ago at Brotherton and Clayworth to safeguard their claims on bees, pigeons or labourers' wages appear to the present generation.

Long before the transitionary period enjoined by the Act of 1918 had expired, it was obvious that tithe-payers would strenuously oppose a reversion to any scheme that linked tithe with the price of cereals averaged over a period of years; thus, the fifteen year proposal was doomed in advance. There was also a recrudescence of agitation against tithe-owners and much frank criticism of the very principles involved—Tithe-payers' Associations sprang up and urged their members to oppose, by all and every means, any fixing of the charge above "an economic level". After much preliminary discussion with the parties concerned, the Government eventually introduced the most important and far-reaching piece of legislation affecting tithe ever discussed in Parliament. This became the Tithe Act of 1925, by which ecclesiastical tithe was fixed at £109. 10*s*., viz. £105 for every £100 of the originally commuted charge, with an additional £4. 10*s*. contribution to a sinking fund; the £5 was treated as a flat-rate payment (in lieu of the varying contributions to rates previously made) to be administered by the Exchequer, which makes up any deficit under this head to the local authorities. This form of tithe was, in effect, thus stabilised at £100—less, of course, taxation and certain small charges for collection—for a period of eighty-five years from March 1927. The administration of the scheme was placed in the hands of Queen Anne's Bounty, a very suitable quasi-legal quasi-ecclesiastical body, whose previous, and normal, work had been mainly concerned with the Church's first-fruits and tenths. Its obligations now comprise the collection annually of some £2,165,000 of ecclesiastical tithe and the handing over of it to about six thousand beneficed clergy—a minority of all owners having preferred to retain this duty themselves. Thus, unless the State intervenes again in the meantime, ecclesiastical tithe will disappear in the year 2012, and its then beneficiaries will be in possession of an equal money income from sources that none will be able to regard as suspect. There is, of course, one obvious criticism to level against this otherwise excellent and fair treatment of a most difficult and controversial problem, viz. the uncertainty that must necessarily attach to the future values of money; who can say, for example, what will be the purchasing power of £109. 10*s.* in 1940, let alone in 1960 or 1980? It should have been possible either to insert some clause in the Act giving Queen Anne's Bounty latitude to review the situation if, and when, marked fluctuations in the purchasing power of money occur, or else a sliding scale might, in the first instance, have been introduced.

Under the provisions of the 1925 Act lay tithe was also fixed, but fixed at £105, with no provision for a sinking fund and with no compensatory amelioration in rating contributions. The lay-owner, therefore, still pays in full under this latter head, and again, unless he redeems the charge, he and his successors will continue in its possession indefinitely. In the case of redemption, the limit, previously referred to, of twenty-five years' purchase has been rescinded and the Ministry of Agriculture determines a sum which will, when invested in Government securities, bring in the same net income; alternatively, redemption may proceed by means of annuity extending up to a sixty years' period.

Such was the revolutionary plan which, at first, seemed likely to satisfy, so far as that has ever been possible, the conflicting views of both owners and payers, for, through their respective organisations, each claimed that justice had failed! Within two or three years, however, it became apparent that the payers, faced with a continuous fall in commodity prices and rents, were determined to reopen the whole question. Discussion, and even public meetings, having failed to advance them, in many parts of the country there was commenced a campaign of refusal to pay. Forced sales and distraint generally followed in these cases and the Governors of Queen Anne's Bounty, together with private (lay) owners, found themselves, most undeservedly, the subject of considerable hostility. Their effective reply to the agitators, who frequently stated that tithe exceeded the value of the rent and even, on occasion, of the produce of the soil, was that their remedy lay in the previously mentioned provision of the Tithe Act of 1891, which ordained the remission of all tithe in excess of 13*s.* 4*d.* in the pound of the annual (Schedule "B") value of the land. They further pointed out that every reduction in rental value on account of agricultural depression lowered the margin above which a claim for remission of excess tithe could be made, and, in every such remission, the tithe-owner was already sharing in the loss. Nevertheless, despite this and a promise from the Bounty Governors that they would exercise clemency in all cases of real hardship, the agitation continued, and was especially marked in those parts of England where depression was most felt—e.g. in the heavy-land arable districts. Incidents occurred in connection with distraint which showed that organised opposition on the part of the recalcitrant payers' friends might have led to very serious results, but occasionally they revealed a humorous aspect. For example, the following description, relating to a parish in Kent, appeared in *The Times* during December, 1932.

> The second attempt to carry out the distraint was planned for this morning. It is stated that five lorries were brought to Canterbury from Essex for the transport of the goods, but the owner of four of the vehicles, when informed by telephone of the purpose for which they were required, ordered them to be returned. The fifth lorry, which had been hired separately, set off at an early hour with an escort of police in plain furniture vans, and arrived at the first of the farms to be visited shortly before 7 o'clock. In addition to the police in the vans others, including a number of officers in plain clothes, were observed near the farms. The constables had been brought secretly into the district from Ashford, Sittingbourne, and other places in East Kent. The first call of the solicitor was in respect of two Jersey heifers which, it was stated, had been seized and advertised, but the farmer declared that he had never had a Jersey heifer on the farm, and a search proved futile. No better results were obtained from other farms in the valley, and the only capture, during a round which lasted until midday, was a couple of hens taken from a small-holding. The fowls were running loose when the effort was made to seize them, and a crowd of farmers found amusement in the chase set up to secure the birds. When two hens were eventually placed in the lorry the farmers contended that distraint had been made on White Leghorns, whereas one of the birds taken was a cross-breed. The lorry and the police escort left for Canterbury about 1 o'clock.

How reminiscent is this of the eighteenth century tithe-owner's endeavours to secure his rights—the great preparations, the heavy expenditure, the striving after so much and the attainment of so little!

This is perhaps a suitable place at which again to recur to the question of the incidence of tithe as affected by recent legislation. On p. 174 it will be remembered were given the prices up to the year 1925 at which the charge would have stood had not the Act of 1918 been passed. In continuation of these figures, it may now be explained that, had the original septennial average been in force from 1926 until the present time, the course pursued by tithe would (expressed to the nearest pound) have been as follows: 1926, £147; 1927, £133; 1928, £117; 1929, £111; 1930, £109; 1931, £106. The corresponding gains to the payer, whether clerical or lay, have, it must be agreed, been very great. It must also be borne in mind that the Act of 1918 had provided for the adoption of a fifteen year

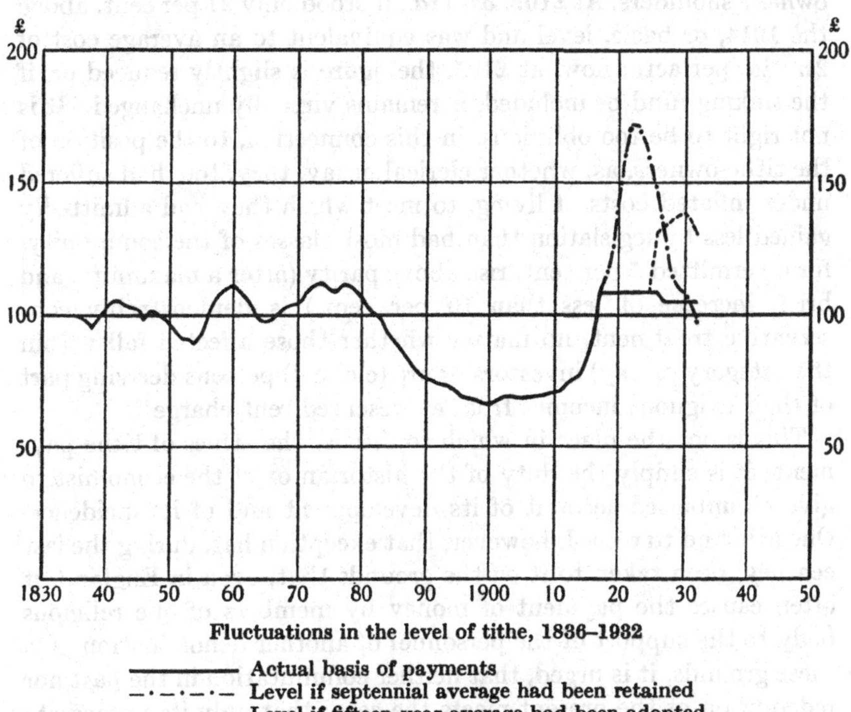

Fluctuations in the level of tithe, 1836–1932

average of cereal prices, to take effect in 1926. Had this been in operation, then the level of tithe from that year up to 1930 would have ranged from £131 up to £139; once again the difference between these figures and £109. 10*s*. (which includes the sinking fund contribution) constitutes a very great concession to the payer and a very great hardship to the owner of tithe, which the diagram above well illustrates. It has, indeed, been calculated that the combined results of the Acts of 1918 and 1925 have been to relieve landowners from the payment of a sum exceeding £14,000,000.

Reviewing the last twenty years' history of this payment, falling upon certain owners of agricultural land, one finds that in 1914 the then payment of £2,795,000 represented *an average* sum of only 1*s.* 9¾*d.* per acre of agricultural land, of £8 per "farm" or of £10. 17*s.* per "farmer"—not a crushing burden for the industry. On the other hand, instances would be found where it ranged up to some 10*s.* per acre, when it would be the heaviest charge on the landowner's shoulders. At £109. 3*s.* 11*d.*, it stood only 21 per cent. above the 1914, or basic, level and was equivalent to an average cost of 2*s.* 2½*d.* per acre; now, at £105, the figure is slightly reduced or, if the sinking fund be included, it remains virtually unchanged. It is not right to be too oblivious, in this connection, to the position of the tithe-owners, as, whether clerical or lay, they, too, had suffered under inflated costs of living, to meet which they had admittedly gained less by legislation than had most classes of the community, for a permitted 5 per cent. rise above parity (after a maximum, and brief, increase of less than 10 per cent.) is demonstrably conservative treatment, no matter whether those affected fall within the category of (lay) investors or are (clerical) persons deriving part of their exiguous incomes from a "reserved rent-charge".

This is not the place in which to discuss the ethics of tithe payment; it is simply the duty of the historian or of the economist to give an unbiased account of its development and of its incidence. One is bound to record, however, that exception has, during the last century, been taken to it on the grounds that, even in England, it often causes the payment of money by members of one religious body to the support of the personnel of another denomination. On these grounds, it is urged, that neither commutation in the past nor redemption at the present meets the case; that only its immediate and complete extinction or its forcible secularisation by the State to such purposes as education can assuage the claims of conscience. Surely the answer to this is that, for upwards of fifteen hundred years, custom has ordained its payment, not idly to any sectarian party, but to the partial support of the established and national Church—that Church which the vast majority of even its non-members call to their assistance on all the most important occasions in their passage through life?

Chapter IX

LAND TAX, RATES AND INCOME TAX

Origin of Land tax; its uneven incidence; Reports of Royal Commissions; its present weight; history of Local taxation and Poor-rates; rates in times of agricultural depression; suggestions for alleviation; who pays the rates?; railway property in rural areas; rates and other taxes in relation to farmers' outgoings; burden of rates in the Great War; the derating of agricultural properties; measure of the reliefs accorded; local rates in Scotland and Ireland.

As the only other charge peculiar to land, this tax naturally follows tithe, although it has nothing in common with it; for it is comparatively modern in origin, relatively unimportant in weight, and wholly arbitrary in its incidence. While some authorities have held that it was directly traceable to the feudal dues, such as tallage and scutage, the bulk of modern opinion inclines to the view that, historically, it must be treated as a separate charge, and that any continuity claimed for it must be based on the grounds that it took the place of the Tudor "subsidy", which was also a property tax, and a tax apportioned on a County basis.

The history of Land tax commences in 1692, when an Act of Parliament was passed to raise money for national purposes. This was, in effect, nothing but a property tax, and a widely flung one, for it contained provisions for taxing all three possible sources of income, viz. profits and salaries, interest on the value of goods, merchandise and other personal property, and, lastly, the annual value of all forms of real estate. In the light of subsequent controversy it is important that a right conception of the origin of this tax, and of the intentions of its framers, should be achieved. It has, for example, been repeatedly suggested during the last half century that it was always what its name implied, solely a tax on the value of land, and that it thereby set a precedent to modern legislators that they are urged to follow.

What, then, was the exact phraseology of the clause in the original Act dealing with personal property? It was as follows:

That every person, body politic and corporate, having any estate in ready monies, or in any debts owing to them, or having any estate in goods, wares, merchandise, or other chattels or personal estate whatsoever within this realm or without, shall yield and pay unto their Majesties four shillings in the pound according to the true yearly value thereof, that is to say for every hundred pounds of such ready money and debts and for every hundred pounds worth of such goods, wares, etc., or other personal estate, the sum of four and twenty shillings.

In other words, the rate of interest assumed from this form of property was 6 per cent., and the tax was imposed at the rate of four shillings in the pound. Salaries paid on the same scale as did real estate, the basis in the latter case being the full yearly value.

The total amount of Land tax raised by the Act in its first year of operation was £1,922,000. The next stage in its development comprised a slight modification by the reduction in 1697 of the rate on personal estate to three shillings in the pound: at the same time the amounts to be raised in each County or Borough were fixed proportionally to what they had produced in previous years. That it was, from the beginning, extremely unpopular, the following extract from a letter, written in 1693 by Sir James Shaen to Sir William Russell, demonstrates:

No man knows better than yourself how long and earnestly I have endeavoured to ease all ye real estates in England from ye insupportable burden of 4*s*. in ye pound, which must at last infallibly crush and ruin all ye landed men, but being without Doers [Doer = Agent or Steward], was deprived of ye means to bring ye same to its wished effect, tho' almost all ye members [of Parliament] severally desired ye same thing. (Legh MSS., *Lyme Letters*, 1660–1760, p. 201.)

Land tax was continued by aid of annual Bills for exactly one hundred years, always on the same lines and always covering the same forms of wealth, but the amount received under the headings of personal property steadily dwindled. This has been attributed to the lack of adequate machinery for its collection and to its unpopularity with both the payers and the officials concerned. In its incidence the tax as a whole was originally extremely unequal, and that inequality has, by law, persisted up to the present time. The Home Counties and East Anglia were, generally speaking, those areas which were most highly assessed, and the Northern and Western Counties escaped quite lightly. The explanation given by Walpole for this was that, in 1692, persons who had favoured the Revolution were more inclined to help the government by furnishing complete details concerning their estates than were those who had opposed the invitation to William and Mary. Again, Davenant held that the Welsh and Scotch border Counties had always been liable to disturbance, and had in consequence for centuries escaped their share of taxation.

In 1797 an Act was passed making the tax perpetual at a maximum rate of four shillings in the pound, but allowing the option of redemption; at the same time the quotas to be raised from each parish and County were irrevocably fixed on the then existing basis. Examples abound to illustrate the anomalous incidence thereby perpetuated. Lancashire paid half what Hertfordshire did, Cornwall raised £31,000 and Durham £10,000, Essex £89,000, and the whole of Yorkshire £91,000. The assessments of individual parishes contained even greater inconsistencies, contiguous areas being rated from the maximum of four shillings down to fractions of a penny in the pound. Despite the subsequent alterations in the relative wealth of different Counties, brought about by the industrial revolution, the decay of rural prosperity and the transference of population, this tax, originated in 1692, and perpetuated in 1797, is at the present time still based on these inequitable foundations. Its collection has always been in the hands of specially appointed Land Tax Commissioners, now acting under the general supervision of the Inland Revenue Department.

At the time of the Royal Commission of 1836 many questions were put to witnesses such as the Chairman of the Board of Stamps and Taxes (then the body responsible for administering the Land tax) with a view to discovering how it was that other forms of property had dropped out of assessment—it was, for example, admitted that the pension of the then Duke of Marlborough had paid up to the year 1835, that of the great Duke having been levied on from 1704; the Duke of Schomberg's personal annuity was also covered. In the case of personal property this witness thought that "difficulties arose, and the easier method of (taxing) land was taken". In answer to the specific question "Do you think that land then not only paid its own contributions, but also for the default of those who had personal property?" he replied that it was "very possible". Two generations later, before the Royal Commission of 1893, corresponding evidence was given. It was then elicited that in 1832, the last year before the repeal of the relevant section, that portion of the tax leviable on personalty actually brought in only £5200; this was theoretically collected from the whole personalty of Great Britain,

Ireland always having been outside the scope of the Land tax. The other clauses dealing with salaries and pensions were retained until the year 1876, but their efficacy in collecting money had become ludicrous long before the latter date.

The explanation of the official apathy towards this side of the Land tax during the first half of the nineteenth century probably lies in the fact that Pitt, after 1798, had a fresh weapon to hand in the shape of the Income tax—a weapon far more potent than any clauses of the old Land tax. The latter, however, was still a successful means of collecting money from those connected with the soil, so it was suffered to remain, thenceforward being in reality only what its name implied, even if, in theory, its provisions still applied to certain other forms of property.

Before discussing the incidence of Land tax on agriculture, there are one or two of its features which deserve attention. Exemptions are allowed to property owned by the Crown, by the Colleges of Oxford and Cambridge, by certain charities, and by two or three of the older public schools; further, it is not due from estates whose owner's income is below £160 per annum, and half of it is remitted where the income is above that limit but below £400. Redemption has always been possible since 1798, and has, indeed, been carried out on a much larger proportionate scale than in the case of tithe. Various rates of purchase were in vogue at different times, but, generally speaking, some thirty years' purchase was required—this was, in fact, the exact number of years provided for in the Finance Act of 1896; prior to that date a method, dependent upon the price of Consols, resulted in thirty-three years being the average. Despite the apparently high cost of effecting redemption, it has eliminated more than two-thirds of the tax, which in recent years has brought in barely £600,000 per annum. It has been the general practice of those about to improve the value of their land by the erection of buildings to redeem before commencing operations; thus, the majority of urban properties are now free from this tax, and the bulk of what remains is derived from purely agricultural property.

Complaints are heard in times of agricultural depression from those occupied in farming land in such Counties as Essex that Land tax constitutes an unfair burden upon their undertakings. In this connection reference may be made to a table drawn up to show the cost of the tax per acre of farm-land for different Counties, which was handed to the Royal Commissioners of 1893 by an Assistant Commissioner of the Board of Agriculture. This showed that Essex paid 11*d.* per acre, Northumberland 2½*d.* and Cumberland ½*d.* Whilst the answer to this, in general terms, was that normally the agriculture of Essex was far better able to pay a higher rate than that practised in the North, yet, in the circumstances then existing, the charge was a high one. Essex was in an exceptional position; in the first place it was one of the Counties above mentioned which had suffered for its adhesion to a political cause, and, secondly, being on the fringe of London, the redemption of a large amount of tax on land as it became ready for building purposes shifted an additional burden upon the rural payers. On these grounds it was urged by interested persons that the power of redemption should be terminated in order to check its operation in such instances as the following —certain fields in Kensington had been assessed at £62 per annum; this charge was redeemed and the land, worth £400,000, was entirely free in future. Essex farmers pointed to this as typical of what was happening on a smaller scale in their own County; they claimed re-assessment, and the reapportioning of the tax on a wider basis—a basis preferably covering all rated property. Again, the rate in the pound at which the Land tax was levied in Norfolk, Suffolk, Lincolnshire, and similar Counties especially dependent on their agricultural prosperity, became unduly high through the fall in the value of land at times of depression.

Remedies put forward then, and subsequently, have comprised suggestions that the tax should be amalgamated with local rates, entirely abrogated, or reassessed on a universal basis. Objection to its abolition has been raised on the ground that so much land having been already freed, it would be unfair towards those persons who have paid for redemption in the past if present-day payers were relieved from their still existing charges, but this scarcely altruistic argument cannot be considered sound from the point of view of agriculture as a whole. The amalgamation theory has been little heard of during the present generation, and any addition, however slight, to the burden of local rates would prove unpopular with the rest of the community, which has just witnessed agricultural interests securing complete freedom from that form of taxation.

In very recent times less complaint has been heard of its weight, as other forms of taxation have greatly increased, and attention has, in the main, been directed to these latter. Nevertheless, the findings of the Commission of 1893 on the subject are as true to-day as they were at the time they were published:

> It seems to us obvious that there is the greatest possible difference between a rent-charge voluntarily created by an owner for his own private purposes, and a compulsory tax originally imposed by Parliament for public purposes on all classes of property and incomes, and subsequently exacted for these purposes, solely from one class of property. The Chairman of the Inland Revenue Commissioners has informed us that in his opinion the Land Tax is not only a tax, but a tax which has of late years weighed very much more heavily on the land in agricultural districts than it ever did before.... In these opinions we entirely concur.

At its present-day level of a maximum of one shilling in the pound, to which it was reduced by the Finance Act of 1896, Land tax cannot generally be described as a "burden" upon the ownership of land, but, as explained above, its arbitrary incidence tends to make it very unpopular. It represents only a sum of 4½*d.* per acre on all the agricultural land in England and Wales, of £1. 9*s.* 3*d.* per "farm" and of very slightly more than £2 per "farmer". Most authorities hold that, when redeemed, this tax must still be regarded as a charge on the properties concerned; if this view is accepted, then the figures just given must be doubled. Even the method of its collection is open to considerable criticism, for an undue proportion of the yield is swallowed up in the process. This is attributable, partly to the large number of very small assessments, and partly to the actual cost of collection—the machinery employed being neither modern nor economical in working. Wherever, nowadays, this tax is found, the sale of land, it is alleged with a certain degree of truth, is disproportionately handicapped. Presumably it will continue to be collected from a dwindling number of property-owners, until the whole system of local and national taxation is overhauled. Meanwhile, from its name, but by an absolute misconception of its origin, it is adopted as the pattern for schemes by which "Single taxers" seek to recast all financial charges on to the soil.

In the case of the two remaining forms of taxation, agriculturists as compared with other payers have been accorded a preferential position. It is not proposed, as in the case of tithe and Land tax, to trace in detail the development of charges which closely concern, not only the farming community, but nearly all citizens, and the history of which has, times out of number, been published. Rather will the past connection of agriculture with these taxes be traced, and the attitude of the rest of the community towards this question, as it affects the farmer, be discussed.

LOCAL RATES

It is incontestable that local rates—and by that term is implied the Poor-rate—were at first levied on all forms of wealth. After centuries of charitable support of the poor, first by the monasteries, and, after their suppression, by the aid of the parish church and the parish officials, compulsion was gradually invoked, and Parliament forced those possessed of any form of wealth to part with a portion of it for the benefit of their poorer brethren. In the sixteenth and seventeenth centuries numerous Acts came into force, which ordained the bases of payment and left to local bodies the responsibility of their interpretation and the duty of raising the necessary funds thus legalised. The Poor Law Act of 1601 is often spoken of as if it originated the Poor-rate, but it merely consolidated the provisions of previous enactments. As was the case with Land tax, all forms of property were at first covered, and gradually all save land and buildings tacitly dropped out of assessment. Again, the explanation is the simple one that other forms of property were elusive, and also that the area of lands and the size of buildings, together with, in both cases, their recorded rents, formed an easier criterion by which to assess the wealth of individuals. Whatever aspect they may wear to-day, historically the rates levied on real property are merely a personal charge on the value of land.

Several cases were tried in the latter half of the eighteenth century in order to test the legality of assessing personalty to Poor-rate, in one of which the then Lord Chief Justice said "this is a question of great difficulty and of vast importance to the public". The legal upshot was that stock-in-trade was held liable by the courts, and other forms of personal property were acquitted. As late as 1840, Boards of Guardians were circularised to the effect that, by a recent legal decision, they were to assess the profits of stock-in-trade. This raised such a storm of protest that a Bill was at once introduced, which finally excluded this form of property from assessment. Once more the burdens of others were transferred to agriculturists—this time, however, not to them exclusively.

The question of the incidence of local rates as between tenant-farmer and landlord is thus raised, and must be treated of in the present tense in view of the fact that rates are still levied upon farm-land and buildings in certain of the component parts of the former United Kingdom. Text-books agree that, in theory, the landlord normally pays all such charges, although his tenant may sign the half-yearly cheques drawn in favour of the rate-collector. In so far as rates are concerned, it has become an accepted axiom that the tenant, when first leasing the property, mentally deducts such outgoings, and that, for example, if he thought it was just possible for him to make his living and get a minimum return on his farming capital by the annual expenditure of £300, the average demands of the rate-collector having been £50, he would offer the landlord £250 as rent. The remaining £50 would, if rates were non-existent, have doubtless been added to the rent offered. This conception holds good so long as rates are stationary, but the tenant who has embarked on a seven years' lease, and finds that his £50 creeps up to £60, and then to £70, is certainly himself for the remainder of his lease paying the balance. On its expiry a fresh bargain will be made between him, or his successor, and the landlord, based on the existing demands from the rating authorities.

That Poor-rate has on occasion in the past proved an excessive burden on agriculture those acquainted with the history of the period 1815 to 1834 will appreciate. In 1817 a Shropshire parish paid 33*s*. in the pound, and at Hindon, Wiltshire, the demand was for 50*s*. (*Report of Royal Commission*, 1894). Then, in many instances, Poor-rate collection had perforce to cease altogether, owing to the "landlords having given up their rents, the farmers their tenancies and the clergyman his glebe and tithes". Anyone who takes the trouble to read contemporary reports from the different Counties, will find therein lists of properties lying vacant, the rates on which amounted to more than the rents. Then rates and rent could change places, for in some Sussex parishes pre-war rents were eight shillings the acre and the Poor-rate was equivalent to four shillings the acre; in 1833 the rates were eight shillings and rent had been reduced to four. Yet as early as 1796 we find Kent writing "Poor rates, which no longer back than twenty years were so light that a farmer when he went to take a farm hardly thought it worth while to inquire the amount of them; but it is now become the first question he must ask". Yet so ingrained had the belief become that farmers have progressively suffered from increasing charges, that in 1924 a Norfolk audience, unwittingly, but enthusiastically, endorsed the exact words of a resolution protesting against the weight of taxation which had been adopted by their grandfathers, with far more cause, exactly a century earlier. The point to observe here is that the bulk of these inflated charges, raised during a time of acute depression, were extracted from that one industry which was most seriously affected by the economic situation. Agriculturists represented the bulk of the rate-paying community, and the very farmers who were upon occasion paying the equivalent of their rents to the rate-collectors were at the same time struggling against an unprecedented fall in the value of their products. In those days two remedies were put into force. Rents could be, and were, reduced; but such actions are slow in effect; wages ought not to have been, but were, reduced, with the result that the Poor-law officials paid the residue of the labourers' earnings from the rates, and farmed out the men to their own masters. Hence, those terrible years from 1817 until the Poor Law Act of 1834 mercifully placed the status of the agricultural labourer and his master once more on a business footing. No other steps were then taken to ameliorate the situation, which was thus guardedly referred to by the Select Committee on Agriculture, sitting in 1833:

> Your committee have endeavoured to trace the injurious effects of past legislation and to prove the caution necessary in future measures; it may be urged that they have stated many evils but have failed to suggest remedies; it should, however, be remembered that legislative measures once taken and long established can rarely be abandoned without danger, and that to retreat is occasionally more dangerous than to advance. In conclusion your committee avow their opinion, that hope of melioration of the Landed Interest rests rather on the cautious forbearance than on the active interposition of Parliament.

Agriculture thus passed through a crisis without relief from any constitutional charges, but the relationship between master and man was embittered for a generation.

Subsequent periods of depression were surmounted by direct action on the part of the State, for, in 1896, agricultural land was relieved of a large share of its burden. By the Agricultural Rates Act of that year the rate of payment on this class of property was reduced to half what it would otherwise have been; but unfortunately by the wording of the Bill the amount of relief thus accorded, in the shape of a direct grant from the Exchequer, was in future to be confined to a sum equal to one-half of the amount raised from agricultural land in 1895. Thus, local authorities received a fixed grant in lieu of the portion previously borne by agriculture, and not a sum annually increasing in order to keep pace with the constant fresh charges they were called upon to meet. This had, of course, the indirect effect of raising the amount of money to be collected from farmers themselves as well as from other rate-payers. Agriculture practised on the outskirts of towns received another small concession in the shape of assessment for the maintenance of purely urban amenities at one-quarter that applicable to other property.

The *Reports* of the Commissioners of 1893 afford abundant evidence of the actual decline in the weight of taxation before these statutory steps had been taken by Parliament, yet the statements made by witnesses before each Commission, from 1819 to 1919, are couched in almost identical terms. In fact, every generation of those associated with the land has considered itself exceptionally hard hit by what it designated as its "burdens". The Tribunal of Investigation was peculiar in this respect, for its *Report* contained no reference to the question. Were circumstances different in 1924, or did that body correctly and tacitly sum up the situation?

Between the years 1883 and 1894 the account-books of farms, scattered over England, reveal payments of rates ranging from 1·2 per cent. of outgoings up to 6·1 per cent., with an over-all average of under 3 per cent.—equivalent to a little more than 2*s*. an acre. Sir E. W. Hamilton, in evidence before the Commission, officially corroborated these figures, saying that the rates on agricultural land then averaged 2*s*. 2*d*. per acre. The total contributions to national and local taxation were, in the words of the Commissioners, "3*s*. per acre, of which between 2*s*. and 2*s*. 8*d*. may be taken to be rates". The following table, relating to a Suffolk farm of some six hundred acres, has been evolved from the *Report* in question, and exhibits the steady nature of the favourable movement which, it will be noted, extended to all the other "burdens" also:

Percentage of total farm outgoings

Years	Tithe	Rates and Taxes	All "burdens"
1839–43	6·1	3·9	10·0
1863–7	4·2	2·4	6·6
1871–5	3·4	1·3	4·7
1890–3	3·2	1·3	4·5

In the early 'nineties it could not be said with truth that the level of taxation was high, but the times were exceptionally difficult, and, as a result of the Commission's findings, the derating policy, since made familiar, was inaugurated by the passing of the 1896 Act.

Then, and on earlier occasions, it had been urged that Parliament should devise an equitable division of rates between the owner and the occupier; no such steps, in what would have proved an extremely difficult operation, were taken. But the Royal Commission on Local Taxation referred to "the baffling problems of the incidence of rates and taxes", and a well-known authority has said "there is no problem in the science of political economy which is more intricate, subtle or obscure, than the incidence of taxation. It is difficult enough to establish the primary incidence, or first blow, it is far more difficult, if indeed it is at all possible, to determine the ultimate incidence".

In view of what was tabulated on the previous page, it is not perhaps remarkable that local rates were not greatly complained of by farmers a generation ago; they were accepted as a "burden", but as they had not increased, and were, by present-day standards, absurdly low, their incidence was not made the foundation for a claim to revision. In 1894 it was shown that the produce of local rates in rural Unions had in the previous thirty years fallen by some 26 per cent. This was due to several causes, but mainly to reductions effected in farm rents. The unequal incidence, as between one County and another, and between one Union or parish and another was, however, a cause of grievance. The grounds for such complaint were frequently dependent on the quantity or extent of railway or mining property found in purely rural Unions. Evidence offered the Royal Commissioners showed that frequently such Unions contained railway property which represented up to 50 per cent. of their total assessable value. The passage of a trunk line through such a district as that comprised by Welwyn in Hertfordshire, Biggleswade in Bedfordshire, or Chippenham in Wiltshire, altered the whole incidence of local rates to the advantage of rural undertakings. On the other hand, some districts of Wales, the Cornish peninsula and parts of the South and East Coast benefited little. From 1870 up to 1894 this form of relief had been particularly apparent, as railway assessments were rapidly rising, whilst the value of other rural properties was shrinking. Between these two dates, for instance, the railway property in Newbury Union increased in rateable value from under £800 to over £6000, that situated in Newmarket Union from £1200 to £14,000, and that in Wolstanton, Staffordshire, from £1600 to £23,000. Forty years ago it was agreed that the majority of non-urban Unions had very appreciably benefited from the construction of new railways and from the improvement of old properties. This, in the areas in question, was a clear gain to the farming industry apart from commercial or economic advantages that might have followed the advent of improved means of communication.

At that time, too, the handicap inflicted by the rating of tenants' improvements was pointed out. This was of universal occurrence and was admittedly a check on enterprise, but its financial weight was not, from the nature of the case, especially serious in times of distress. It must be remembered that appeal existed, both against existing assessments, and against reassessments for improvements. If the same advantage was not taken of these facilities in rural, as compared with urban, districts the reason may possibly be that adduced by a witness before the Commission of 1893. He explained this hesitation as due to the fact that a successful appeal in a rural area resulted in one's neighbours being called on to make up the deficit; if they, in turn, appealed, and were equally fortunate, the adjacent areas were mulcted. It is hardly conceivable that this altruistic explanation could hold good in many cases, and it is probable that the vast majority of assessments were both opportunely made on the existing basis and equitable in their incidence as between one property and another. In normal times it is doubtful if the majority of tenants were deterred from making improvements because of the existence of the rate-collector, and the statement that any considerable body of them deliberately farmed badly in order to keep down its assessments is scarcely credible. Such a proposition entailed on the part of those who made it a belief that rates then bore as fixed a relationship to the value of output as did the incidence of tithe prior to 1836.

Up to the outbreak of the war, or, indeed, up to the end of 1918, the effective weight of local taxation bearing upon agricultural interests had, thanks to the 1896 Act, exceeded by little that of the 'nineties. Of this there is abundant evidence available in the fourth volume of the *Report* of the Royal Commission of 1919, where cost-accounts relating to 325 farms in England, Wales and Scotland are fully dissected and described in the evidence of Mr H. G. Howell. On the 146,000 acres of this really large sample, rates, including "possibly some Income tax and probably Insurance", averaged 2*s*. 11*d*. per acre, or still only 1·6 per cent. of all outgoings. Other witnesses agreed that the level of rates on agricultural land was about 3*s*. an acre. At that time wages accounted for some 24 per cent. and rent for 10 to 12 per cent. of expenditure, the heading "Purchases" (machinery, livestock, fertilisers, etc.), as usual, accounting for over half of the farmer's outgoings. Tithe was henceforward stabilised at £109. 3*s*. 11*d*., and, in regard to Income tax, the years of prosperity only witnessed a justifiable and brief altera-

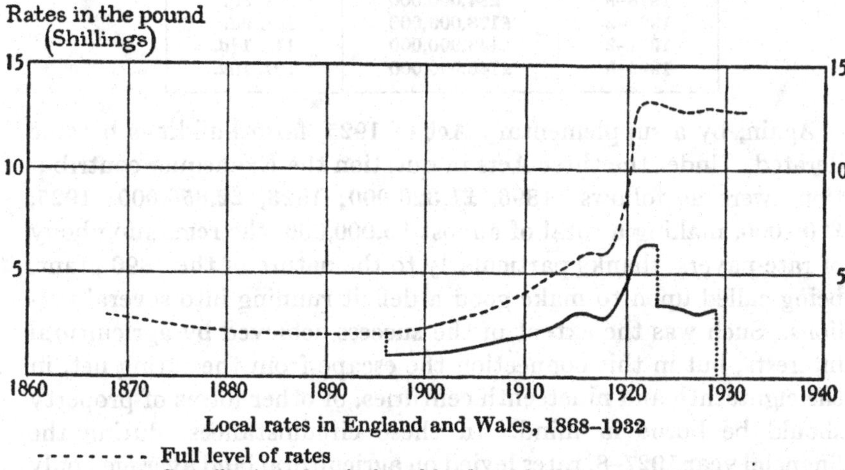

Local rates in England and Wales, 1868–1932

- - - - - - - - Full level of rates

———— Contribution of agricultural land and buildings from 1896 onwards

tion in the basis of Schedule "B" assessments. Prior to the post-war upheaval it is probable that landlords' burdens represented less than 2*s*. 6*d*. an acre, and those theoretically met by tenants a very similar sum.

During the next few years the customary steps were again taken, and the Agricultural Rates Act of 1923 once more halved the contribution of agricultural land, thus, in theory, almost exactly counter-balancing the increase of just under 100 per cent. in the average level of the rates themselves (6*s*. 8¾*d*. in 1913–14 and 13*s*. 5*d*. in 1927–8); as, however, rates in rural districts rose higher than those in urban areas, i.e. over 130 per cent., the effective increase, based on Ministry of Health official figures, lay somewhere between

35 and 40 per cent. Rather more than half of this was apparently due to assessments raised in conformity with the movement of rents.

The huge increase in the total sums raised by local rates in England and Wales at the end of the war can best be judged by glancing at this Table, which also exhibits the relatively small decline that occurred during the next decade.

Year	Total sum collected	In the £ (collected)
1903–4	£52,000,000	5*s*. 9*d*.
1908–9	£61,000,000	6*s*. 1*d*.
1913–4	£72,000,000	6*s*. 8*d*.
1918–9	£84,000,000	7*s*. 8*d*.
1921–2	£173,000,000	14*s*. 9*d*.
1931–2	£148,000,000	11*s*. 1¾*d*.
1932–3	£146,000,000	10*s*. 10*d*.

Again, by a supplementary Act of 1925, farm buildings became derated. Under the three Acts in question the Exchequer contributions were as follows: 1896, £1,320,000; 1923, £2,856,000; 1925, £700,000, making a total of almost £5,000,000, the remaining body of rate-payers, thanks particularly to the nature of the 1896 grant, being called upon to make good a deficit running into several millions. Such was the extent of the success achieved by agricultural interests, but in this connection the escape from the rating net, in the eighteenth and nineteenth centuries, of other forms of property should be borne in mind. In these circumstances, during the financial year 1927–8, rates levied on agricultural land averaged only 2*s*. 8¼*d*. per acre, or, if we exclude from our calculations the five million acres of "rough grazings", 3*s*. 2½*d*. Expressed alternatively, the contribution in question (£4,132,000) was approximately equal to £10 per "farm" in England and Wales, or £13. 13*s*. per "farmer". This was not a heavy burden, even if met in its entirety by tenants, for, on the majority of farms, rates still represented less than 2 per cent. of outgoings. In this connection, comparison should be effected with the major costs then entailed in the production of an acre of cereals—e.g. 35*s*. to 40*s*. for labour, and an average of 31*s*. for rent.

A subsequent White Paper affords the interesting information that the contribution to local rates by "agricultural land" in 1927–8 formed merely 2·4 per cent. of the total payments from all classes of property. Bearing in mind the capital sums represented, compare figures of 2·8 by gas and electricity undertakings, of 2·2 per cent. by warehouses, and of 2·6 by licensed houses. The Census of Production gave the value of the output of all such land (including rough grazings) in England and Wales in 1925 at £225,000,000, or £8. 10*s*. per acre. Once again, local taxation, even if wholly remaining with the tenant-farmer, represented only 1·58 per cent.—not an important element in the cost of production.

In 1929, under the provisions of the Agricultural Rates Act of that year and those of the Local Government Act (1929), the remaining rates, viz. the last quarter, on agricultural land (amounting in England and Wales to £4,132,000) disappeared as part of a comprehensive scheme for relieving "productive" industries, which involved the reorganisation of the system of Local Government prevailing in this country. Great expectations naturally attached to the undertaking, but it was difficult to endorse the findings of *The Times* leader-writer, who stated that—"If the farmer can only contrive to carry on for the next eighteen months, then there is a real hope that the large constructive policy set out in the Budget may bring back into cultivation land that has been left to run wild, bring tenants to farms that are now unoccupied—is this the process that is known as a 'dole to the landlord'?—and give British agriculture a new lease of life". To the historian or to the economist there inevitably recurred these words of the late Prof. J. H. Nicholson: "If we take the *Reports* of the last two Commissions on agricultural depression, we find that the main causes are, in the first period, bad seasons, and in the second, low prices. The precise influence of rates and taxes, even if considerable, would be overshadowed by these greater causes". This explanation, indeed, holds true with still greater force in the case of the third depression through which the industry is still passing. Incidentally, matters were not so bad as the leader-writer imagined (the conditions he described were those of a century ago); on the other hand, the reliefs to which he referred so hopefully were of far less magnitude than he postulated. A remission of two or three shillings an acre could not have brought about an agricultural millennium in the face of conditions that already prevailed. For diagrammatic representation of the process of relief from rates enjoyed by agricultural interests, readers are invited to look at the illustration upon p. 195.

Two or three factors call for brief comment. It is often stated that landlords will ultimately reap the benefit of this policy. Without entering into a discussion as to the prevalence of economic rents or the distribution of the two sets of profits concerned, it may be pointed out (*a*) that there is a little evidence that rents were raised shortly after 1896 or 1923, and (*b*) that lengthy tenancies, had they still been commonly in vogue, would certainly have secured to the occupier the clear reduction which in theory annual leases fail to accomplish. Again, it was inevitable that relief should be accorded without regard to comparative needs, and the successful market-gardener, the fruit-grower, and the fen farmer secured benefits greater than those granted the light-land farmer and the struggling producer of wheat on the heavy clays. It has been suggested that, in general, the grass-land farmer gained most, as, owing to his smaller wages bill, rates formed a larger proportion of his outgoings. Close investigation, however, indicates that there was little foundation for this belief.

The objection of the Departmental Committee on Local Taxation to the "unduly heavy burden" caused by the large amount of their rateable property in proportion to the "general ability" of farmers will henceforward have no force, and any suggestion for the remission of local rates on farm dwelling-houses will rightly meet with strong opposition; for such contributions, together with those on their cottages, now represent the only payments made by agriculturists for local purposes and, even here, in both cases, preferential treatment is accorded by assessment committees, for these bodies were officially instructed to deduct from 33⅓ up to 40 per cent. of the gross value when fixing assessments of farm houses and farm cottages of "persons primarily engaged in carrying on or directing agricultural operations...or employed in the service of the occupier thereof".

Farmers were thus progressively relieved of total payments equivalent to over 12*s*. per acre per annum (about £40 per "farm" and over £50 per "farmer"); more than half (£9,000,000) of the sum involved came from the pockets of the tax-payer, the remainder (about £7,000,000) from increased payments by non-agricultural ratepayers. If the last instalments of the reliefs were, to the farmer, relatively unimportant, the principle at stake had, on the grounds of equity, for over thirty years affected the whole community.

In the case of Scotland the position was already a complicated one and differed from that existing south of the Border, so that the legislative steps taken were necessarily peculiar to that country. Under a Rating Act of 1926, the owners were paying three-quarters of the rates on farms treated as a whole (i.e. land and buildings) and tenants were responsible for the remaining portion.

Under the provisions of the Local Government (Scotland) Act of 1929, the basis of assessment was reduced to one-eighth of the annual value—the estimated proportion borne by the dwelling-house to the assessment of the whole farm—the original proposal having been one-sixth, in opposition to which a figure of one-twelfth had been put forward by the Scottish National Farmers' Union. Under temporary arrangements, made to cover existing leases, the landlord was under obligation to pass on half of his relief to sitting tenants in the shape of a reduction in rent—such relief is equal to two and a half times the former's new rates under the Act. It is estimated that the total remissions are equivalent to £950,000 per annum, of which sum £800,000 nominally benefits landlords and £150,000 directly affects tenants. Where the tenant occupied the land on a year to year basis this arrangement—involving a considerable reduction in rent—was not to be extended beyond 1935, unless an express renewal of the lease were secured. Statutory Small Holders, within the meaning of the Small Landholders Acts, can claim return of rates from their landlord on the same basis as above until their fixed rent is altered upon application to the Land Court. Thus, Scottish farmers, as a body, benefited by derating to much the same extent as did their English brothers, but by a more involved method of application.

In Ireland, as a whole, a policy more similar to that of England had all along been pursued, for, under the Local Government (Ireland) Act of 1898, a sum equal to one-half of the combined Poor-rate and County "Cess" had been thereafter annually applied to the relief of rates upon agricultural land. No provision was, however, made to limit to one-half of the normal rate the future contributions from the occupiers of these properties. The total, and fixed, grant in aid from the British Exchequer was £727,655, which, at the partition of the country in 1923, was resolved into its components of £599,011 for the Free State and of £128,644 for Ulster. In the former country, the aid in question has, since 1925, been augmented by a similar amount annually voted, with the result that, according to a local *Report* upon rating, agricultural property in the South, instead of contributing £2,230,000, is now relieved of £1,198,022, or some 55 per cent. In the Spring of 1933 further concessions were granted, including total remission of rates upon the first £10 of agricultural assessments. In Ulster, a similar procedure was adopted in 1923 and was continued (with certain trifling exceptions) up to 1929, in which year complete derating of agricultural land and of buildings was effected. It should be observed that, as rates increased steadily prior to derating, the relief had been getting relatively smaller and in the last year or so occupiers were, it was estimated, contributing some 62 per cent. of the full rating charge.

What British farmers had, for many years, mistakenly described as their "raw material"—viz. the land—was thus freed from any contribution to local taxation; if correctly designated as a "factory", these forms of property would legitimately have qualified for such treatment, for, under the widely flung legislation affecting the rating system of the country, simultaneously put into operation, all factories, quarries, mines and transport systems were relieved of three-quarters of their rating contributions. It should be noted that relief to railways was conditional upon preferential rates being put into force for the conveyance of certain types of agricultural produce—this concession, it was then estimated, was equivalent to about £800,000 per annum.

Chapter X

LAND TAX, RATES AND INCOME TAX (CONTINUED)

Recent legislation affecting rates and local government; the position of agriculturists in relation to local administration; Income tax as a "burden" upon agricultural interests; the farmer's preferential treatment; Adam Smith's maxims; comparative weight of the existing rates and taxes; their combined effect upon agriculturists; taxation of land values; the 1909–10 Budget and Lord Snowden's proposals; Land taxes in Germany and in the New World; the British farmer's position summarised.

The opportunity at that time presented to reorganise and to re-adjust the financial relationship between the Central Government and Local Authorities was seized concurrently with the coming into force of the provisions of the Rating and Valuation Act of 1925, which aimed at effecting uniformity in the basis of assessment to rates. This latter question was one of great importance, for, while rents had risen during the previous ten years, they had not done so uniformly—either in regard to type of property or geographical distribution—and rates were generally out of harmony with them; reassessment implied, therefore, in effect, no reduction in total contribution, but a general lowering of "rates in the pound" and an increase in the contribution of many forms of property hitherto undervalued. The first-mentioned work involved, through the medium of the Local Government Act of 1929, a large increase in the amount of money given in the shape of "Block grants" to local authorities in connection with their obligations under the heads of education, roads and relief of the poor; it further necessitated the redistribution and enlargement of local assessment areas and the assumption by Councils of entirely new responsibilities. Thus, when the Poor Law system came under scrutiny, it was decided to hand over all duties in connection therewith to the County Councils and County Boroughs; this, in turn, meant the final disappearance of Boards of Guardians, of Overseers and of the "Unions" themselves —a severance that, historically, was little commented upon or apparently regretted—and the emergence of "Public Assistance Committees" of the County Councils. The Overseers of more than 13,000 parishes were, for rating purposes, superseded by some 1800 local Committees, and, instead of separate valuations for different rates in one and the same area, a single valuation was thenceforward made. By spreading these charges over the newly enlarged areas, a fairer distribution of the burdens was effected as between district and district, and, although it is yet early to express an opinion, efficiency and economy should both have been promoted. Thus, too, has history repeated itself, for, as a century ago the parishes, being found too small for the efficient administration of poor relief, were bound together in Unions, so now these Unions again proving insufficient in size have been amalgamated into larger units.

The system of Block grants previously in existence had grown steadily during the last quarter of the nineteenth century, until not even Treasury or other Government officials could either explain fully the origin of them all or account for their precise allocation. Concurrently, there had sprung up, on the part of County Councillors and other elected representatives, a belief that "grants in aid" of local rates were as manna falling from heaven and could accordingly be spent without thought. None seemed to appreciate that such contributions—frequently resting upon a pernicious "pound for pound" basis—obtained from "the tax-payer" were really being paid for by themselves. In the last year of this now superseded system, grants had represented more than a third of the total expenditure by local authorities, e.g. in 1926–7, while rates in England and Wales brought in £159,000,000, no less than £87,000,000 was derived from outside sources. Under the new method, the slate was wiped clean and a fresh start made, but simplicity could, even now, not be claimed as one of the resultant advantages, for the reformed Block grants were based upon the relative situation of each administrative County area in respect to its rateable value, to its population (weighted proportionately to its numbers of children under five years of age and of unemployed in excess of a certain standard), and to its density of population per mile of main road; they were not fixed for an indefinite period of time, but were to be subject to quinquennial revision. By these means any general increase in the sums to be raised locally was rendered unlikely, the extent of Government grants was known in advance and the total expenditure of grants *plus* rates had, by 1933, tended slightly to fall; the contribution of the State on account of loss of rates was stabilised at a little over £43,000,000 per annum, which sum included £5,000,000 for normal development. Perhaps the most serious aspect of local government finance was the enormous increase in the indebtedness of the authorities themselves. The loan debt in question rose from £560,000,000 in 1914 to £1,200,000,000 in 1931, and its service cost almost £90,000,000 per annum. This was a measure of the expenditure upon schemes for social amelioration, housing and so forth that the post-war atmosphere engendered; at least two more generations will be saddled with its payment.

In so far as County Councils are concerned, there is an element of danger in the present situation, for those persons—the farmers—who in the past have often been both numerically and influentially their most important members, have now little direct interest in their proceedings. This is especially the case in the Eastern Counties where, in the past, the relatively sparse population and predominant rural life caused agricultural interests to be accorded preferential treatment over urban and official views. Now, it is often stated, the farmer has little inducement to seek election to his Council and, if elected, has no incentive towards the pursuit of reduced expenditure or of efficient service. A generation ago, it was alleged against the agriculturist that, not only did he dominate the newly formed County Councils, but that he was obstructive to their work; it was even quoted against him that he opposed education, because the country child "was better without it", refused to vote money for the improvement of roads on the ground that they were good enough for his carts, and maintained that neither police nor asylums were called for in the country, since both malefactors and lunatics were products of the towns! Dismissing these statements as greatly exaggerated, it may, even so, be asked if the pendulum has perhaps not swung too far in the opposite direction, and if the Councils, in future, are to lack the restrained and informed criticism, together with the constructive ability, possessed by a body of men truly imbued with knowledge of, and love for, all that is best in the countryside?

As relevant to this subject, it may be observed that, under the Local Government Act of 1925, the authority and position of County Councils were further strengthened at the expense of non-County Boroughs and the other lesser units of local government, while the redistribution of boundaries frequently detracted from rural amenities. The traditional organisation, dating from the Local Government Act of 1888, was thus modified, and, although there still exists the sequence of (Urban) authorities, viz. County Boroughs now with 75,000 population as qualification, Boroughs and Urban District Councils and (Rural) County, Rural District, Parish (over 300 population) Councils and Parish meetings (over 100 population), the powers and duties of the smaller units are, relative to the larger, being progressively curtailed. Here again, rural and agricultural interests in the past coincided, as the three partners together did much for life in their villages by their presence upon Rural District and Parish Councils. Even if they were only concerned with the administration of charities, the supply of water, of libraries, or of allotments, or were engaged in preserving rights of way, these were duties that would lapse by default and were of the very essence of rural life. With the advent of quick transport and of easy communications, it is obvious that such work is being more and more concentrated in distant centres and placed in the hands of paid officials. Simultaneously, the level of rates in the counties is approaching that found in urban areas. The situation is not without danger, since, as shown above, one of the largest, and certainly the most important of, rural elements has now little inducement to take an active interest in the social or fiscal aspects of local government. Such tendencies are to be deplored when it is remembered that the area of practically every administrative County Council was framed to coincide with historical boundaries, and their functions are rooted in bygone country life. Must, for example, the Soke of Peterborough and the Isle of Ely lose every vestige of their past associations and merely represent synonyms for efficient bureaucracy? On the other hand, it is easy to argue that in modern conditions the division of, say, Sussex and Suffolk into two administrative areas is an expensive luxury.

INCOME TAX

Income tax may, historically, be said to date from 1798 when Pitt, for the purpose of financing the war with France, increased the existing "assessed Taxes"; the following year this took the form of a 10 per cent. levy on all incomes over £60 per annum. In 1803, after the peace of Amiens, Income tax again emerged, upon this occasion carrying with it the familiar Schedules A, B, C, D, and E. Repealed in 1815, its principles were once more adopted by the then Chancellor in 1842. In the nineteenth century its standard rate was as high as 1*s.* 4*d.* in the pound during the Crimean war (1855–7), and as low as 2*d.* in the pound from 1874 to 1876. For the space of four years before the Great War, it stood at 1*s.* 2*d.* and rose to its highest point (6*s.*) in 1918–19, thereafter resting at 4*s.* from 1925–6 to 1929–30 before being increased to 4*s.* 6*d.* for 1930–1 and 5*s.* for 1931–2. Before the war it produced about £40,000,000 per annum, and from 1923 to 1931 the corresponding sums ranged from £232,000,000 to £265,000,000—the latter being a third larger than the whole revenue raised in 1914. If Surtax be included, a further sum amounting, in recent years, to £70,000,000 or £80,000,000 has to be added. The receipts under the heads of Surtax and Income tax for the year 1931–2 amounted to the stupendous total of £364,000,000.

If carefully analysed during the past century, Income tax figures naturally reflect the economic history of the landed interest—the steady increase from 1850 up to 1880, and the subsequent decline, which left the total sum assessed upon the ownership of lands in 1918–19 almost exactly where it stood one hundred years before; in the meantime the contribution of other forms of property had increased many times over. We are not, at the moment, concerned, however, with the receiver of agricultural rents, but with commercial farmers. Thanks to his forebear's skilful action, entailing alleged illiteracy and complete ignorance of book-keeping principles, the present-day tenant has had conferred upon him the far-reaching and unique privilege of being assessed either upon his rent or upon his profits. Once conceded, neither the spread of education nor war-time prosperity led to the removal from agriculture of this relief. Naturally, the overwhelming majority of agriculturists have always elected to come under the former system, viz. schedule B, the number assessed under schedule D (profits) ranging between 200 and 2700 out of a total of 300,000. Prior to 1914, the actual assessment was made on the basis of one-third of the rent; this was slowly raised during the period of prosperity, until, from 1918 to 1921, the basis was double the annual value. In the post-war years of depression the yearly value was restored. Unfortunately, information is almost completely lacking in regard to the net payments rendered under the two schedules in question, but if it is appreciated that the average size of a farm is little over 60 acres in extent, that each "farmer" is only responsible for some 80 acres, and that the average rental of this land is now just over a pound per acre, then it is clear that, with the existing method of deductions and allowances, every married man farming land up to about 150 acres is totally exempt, and that possession of even a small family carries exemption up to 300 acres. As a matter of fact, less than one farm in eight exceeds 150 acres in area. The contributions, therefore, under schedule B, which, some twenty years ago (a period when figures were available), produced £203,000, must still be extremely meagre. During the war years, the 2000 persons electing to be assessed under schedule D revealed an average profit of a little over £300 per annum, or half what they would have been assessed upon under B. The only composite estimate of the contribution of farming profits is represented by an unofficial statement made to the Colwyn Committee, which placed the figure at £1,500,000 in 1922–3—this, in an admittedly bad year, was equivalent to less than £5 per "farmer". Practising agriculturists are too apt to claim that Income tax is an element in the cost of production, and when analysing financially their operations have been known to add 10*s*. an acre to each crop, on the ground that tax paid on other sources of income should be debited to these products as forming an essential part of their cost. Much can be urged against the retention of schedule B; thus, certain parts of the country have produced examples of heavy profits made on small areas of land (£5000 has been cleared on a farm of 200 acres producing carrots and onions), and the spread of education has made it possible for all tenants to complete the requirements of schedule D. They have, too, when assessed under schedule B the very important option of electing, if losses have been sustained, to transfer to schedule D. This approaches, from the standpoint of the non-agricultural Income tax payer, perilously close to running with the hare and hunting with the hounds! The time is over-ripe for the abolition of a concession no longer necessitated.

Whatever may be the position of the owner of large tracts of agricultural land, the tenant-farmer is not entitled to regard Income tax as a "burden". Examples abound, however, in the case of large estates where Income tax and Surtax absorb the whole of what their owners describe as "profits"; unfortunately, such properties cannot invariably be considered agricultural in the strictest sense of the word, as they frequently include amenities that are not essential to the practice of farming. Columns of *The Times* are often devoted to an analysis of the outgoings on properties ranging in extent up to many thousand acres; when represented as percentages of the gross income, typical figures for Income tax and Surtax may be as high as 30 or 40 per cent. Such figures are, of course, valueless to the rural economist who wishes to secure statistics of the expenses of that illusive thing—the "average" farm; they merely show, which is admitted on all sides, that large estates do not "pay", and at the same time afford an opportunity for their owners to complain of the assessment to Income tax of their gross incomes and not of their net profits. But the repayments that follow on this procedure are sometimes overlooked and fail to appear in the submitted tables.

These comments in no way detract from the truth of the statement, so often heard, that numerous large estates have to be broken up from the inability of their possessors to make both ends meet; they are merely intended as a reminder that, whilst agriculture embraces areas of land from less than one acre in extent up to many thousands, yet if it is to be dissected as a business concern, there must be excluded from scrutiny those undertakings in which the making of a profit is not the one and only end in view. Any increase in the growing practice of keeping analyses of costs among farmers is greatly to be encouraged, as it is by such means that knowledge of the respective weights of the various charges on commercial undertakings is acquired. Figures, collected from some hundreds of holdings of all sizes, to show the relationship borne by rates, tithe, Land tax and Income tax to gross or net profits have upon many recent occasions proved invaluable.

Before analysing the comparative incidence of the four charges falling upon the possessors or occupiers of land that have been discussed in the foregoing pages it may be well to repeat the postulates that Adam Smith laid down as axiomatic in regard to taxation in any form.

(*a*) The Subjects of every State ought to contribute towards the support of the Government as nearly as possible in proportion to their respective abilities; that is, in proportion to the revenue which they respectively enjoy under the protection of the State.

(*b*) The tax which each individual is bound to pay ought to be certain and not arbitrary.

(*c*) Every tax ought to be levied at the time or in the manner in which it is most likely to be convenient for the contributor to pay.

(*d*) Every tax ought to be so contrived as both to take out and keep out of the pockets of the people as little as possible over and above what it brings in to the public Treasury.

These maxims are as sound to-day as when they were first written, although the principle of equal payment has, in the case of Income tax, long been abandoned and preferential treatment progressively accorded those with small "revenues". Let us see to what extent the four charges on agriculture conform to them. Whilst justified historically and, doubtless, ethically as a charge on land, tithe does not come within the definition of a tax; it is now not of universal application, and its incidence bears no necessary relationship to present-day farming operations. As a charge on agriculture in general it is not of the first magnitude, but in certain individual cases it can still prove a handicap to occupying owners. On the other hand the bulk of it will be automatically redeemed, and the remainder can be so terminated by compounding for future payments.

Land tax comes in the same category. It is even less universal in its incidence; on the other hand, it is a national charge, and should therefore be historically above suspicion. It could not, however, claim an enquiry into its past with equanimity, and, if now relatively unimportant as a means of taxing agricultural land, it nevertheless stands in need of thorough revision or of abolition before private persons have had to complete the process by redemption. Although in a few cases it may represent a relatively heavy charge and complaints are heard against the methods employed in its collection, yet the industry as a whole is not clamant against it.

The remaining direct charges are generally placed by economists in two divisions—onerous and beneficial. Take rates first, although their incidence is agriculturally now negligible. These are local in their application and doubtless originally beneficial, but agriculture, up to its relief, claimed that the majority of the objects for the support of which it was rated were essentially urban, if not national, in their character. Rates, at one time, admittedly represented the heaviest extraneous charges on the land, and justice demanded that a full enquiry should be carried out into their incidence upon purely agricultural property. The verdict was hailed as vindicating the farmer's point of view, but its practical execution was eleemosynary, rather than economic, in character. Income tax is a national charge, but to what degree it is onerous—or, rather, non-beneficial—is nowadays a complicated question. Millions of pounds, raised by Income tax, are returned, in the shape of grants, to the districts from which they were taken.

It now becomes possible to compare the combined weight of taxation before the war and in the year (1927) when, prior to remission of rates on agricultural land, the gross weight of all charges upon the ownership or occupation of land may be said to have been at their maxima.

Acres of crops, grass and rough grazings	Per acre			Total	Total sum
	Rates	Tithe	Land tax		
1914 30,896,000	1*s*. 11¼*d*. (£3,000,000)	1*s*. 9¾*d*. (£2,795,000)	5*d*. (£640,000)	4*s*. 2*d*.	£6,435,000
1927 30,716,000	2*s*. 8¼*d*. (£4,132,000)	2*s*. 2½*d*. (£3,397,000)	4½*d*. (£600,000)	5*s*. 3¼*d*.	£8,129,000
Increase ...	38·7 %	21·8 %	– 10·0 %	26·5 %	26·3 %

Tithe and Land tax, redeemed subsequent to 1914, are excluded from this review, but their inclusion would not materially affect the figures. It must be generally agreed that a net increase of 26 per cent., at a time when every other industry and individual had been called upon to face far heavier increments, did not necessarily afford grounds for serious complaint.

There arises next the question of the allocation of the three outgoings in the above Table as between landlord and tenant. In 1914 the two charges falling upon the former were 2*s*. 2¾*d*.; they subsequently rose to 2*s*. 7*d*., an increase of 16 per cent., or considerably less than the (temporary) augmentation in tenant's contributions. It will be agreed that, no matter upon whom the first impact falls, the owner met (and now meets still more) the lion's share of these statutory charges, and the trend of legislation has been cumulatively to add to his load. While it is significant that the bulk of the agitation for the remission of rates emanated from tenants, and tithe increases were opposed by landlords, the latter have, in the upshot, secured smaller concessions, for, on the complete derating of land, when the total payments per acre were reduced by rather more than half, those remaining comprised owners' burdens. Although these charges then only amounted on the average to 8·3 per cent. of rentals, subsequent falls in the rents themselves added to their relative weight. The aggregate of the three principal charges is, however, now lower than it has been since the end of the eighteenth century. If no concessions had been granted to agriculturists during the last forty years, the incidence of rates and tithe would have been crushing, and, collectively, the charges would have made the position of the tenant difficult, that of the landlord almost impossible. As matters are, in 1933, the combined charges now remaining, viz. 2*s.* 7*d.* per acre, represent less than 3*s.* in the pound on the gross rents and are actually 38 per cent. below their pre-war level—of what other individuals, of what other industry can such a statement be made?

In both good times and bad, proposals for the adoption of a system of taxing land values, either in lieu of the then existing methods or supplementary thereof, have emanated from private individuals and from political associations. Whether deriving authority from the eighteenth-century French Physiocrats or, later, from Henry George's writings, these protagonists have relied upon the slogan "Land value is public value and should belong to the public". They have maintained that such a tax could not be shifted from one person to another, would not militate against capital or wages and would lead to uniform and ordered development of both town and country. To enforce their arguments, they have pointed to the profits made by land speculators, by suburban builders and by the possessors of sites in the centres of large cities. When conjoined with a policy aiming at amalgamation and enlargement of rating areas, these schemes, before the recent Local Government legislation rendered nugatory such combination, secured numerous advocates. The next stage generally entered upon by this school of thought has required the shifting of all taxes to real estate—and there, whatever he may have thought of the advisability of taxing urban property—the owner of agricultural land has parted company with this school. For, although the land-taxer may construct a plausible edifice for the taxation of land values in large and growing towns, when he comes to explain his proposals to the countryman he is forced to admit that the system would penalise the large landowner for the benefit of the Small Holder. Outhwaite gives examples in *Land Values Taxation* of the incidence of his suggested tax on agricultural land; here, his readers are assured that rents will fall, because the large landowner will be compelled to get rid of the bulk of his undeveloped property, that derelict holdings will be forced into cultivation, that the medium-sized farmer will be no worse off, whilst paying greatly enhanced wages, and that the really small man will contribute next to nothing, as the value of his land (given up by the aforesaid large owner) would be so low.

In these pages it is unnecessary to follow the different controversialists in their arguments, or to attempt to estimate the probable effects that would follow the introduction of a complete and exclusive Single tax; all that seems relevant is a brief description of the two minor proposals that have reached the Statute-book. In his Budget of 1909–10, Mr Lloyd George first introduced the principle of an "undeveloped land tax", which, it is most significant to state, was only to apply to urban land. Under this scheme there was to be paid a 20 per cent. duty on any increase over and above the basic (1909) value of these properties as revealed by sale, by transfer at death or when leased for periods exceeding twenty years; the land belonging to bodies corporate was to have been assessed as upon April 5th, 1914, and every fifteenth year subsequently. The "unimproved", or stripped site value, was the object of assessment, and the process was necessarily slow and complicated, resting, as it did, upon purely fictitious values. If the war had not intervened, it is possible that the intentions of its sponsors might have been achieved; but for this reason, and as a result of political changes, the whole undertaking failed to be implemented and there existed, when it was repealed twenty years later, merely a partial valuation of urban estates, which had cost £5,000,000 and brought in £1,300,000. It was claimed by opponents of the measure that a further result could be seen in the diminished number of houses erected, owing to the builders' fears of taxation; agriculture could, in any event, have regarded the whole matter with indifference.

Another Chancellor of the Exchequer, Mr (afterwards Lord) Snowden, essayed in 1931 a somewhat more ambitious undertaking, which it was intended should have come into force two years later. The basis of this so-called "Land tax" on unearned increment was to have been a payment of one penny per annum, commencing in the year 1933–4, upon every pound of capital value, revealed in the 12,000,000 hereditaments which the Chancellor believed could be satisfactorily valued within two years. He stated in the House of Commons, when introducing the Finance Act of 1931, that this tax would cheapen land and throw it open for use, and he gave many instances in which he alleged that excessive profits had been derived by private individuals through speculative land purchases or by reason of public development in which they had played no material part—in his own words, "the taxation of land values was a rent paid to the community". Once more, "stripped site" value was to form the basis of valuation, which was to be repeated at intervals of five years. Again, too, the value was to be that price which it was assumed a purchaser would pay if the site were vacant, but the surrounding buildings and all other amenities remained unaltered. Land which had no value higher than that described as "cultivational" was to be exempt, but, although this provision was expressly stated to apply to allotments and market-gardens, nevertheless, farmers situated in the vicinity of towns feared that they would be drawn into the net, for agricultural land was, despite urgent representations, to be included in the valuation, but with an assurance that only any excess over and above cultivational value would be taxed. It was the expressed hope of the party in power that one eventual result would be the transference from rating assessments of all houses and buildings to this site value basis. The proposal was not put to the test, for political vicissitudes shortly afterwards prevented the carrying into effect of the second attempt to tax in this country these elusive values.

In Germany, there came into existence in 1904, as an Imperial tax, incremental duties payable only upon the transference of urban land. Here a sliding scale was utilised, which ranged from 10 (where the increase did not exceed a similar amount) up to 30 per cent. The tax was gradually taken over from the State by the local authorities and, in 1911, more than six hundred of these bodies were collecting taxes upon this basis. The principal difficulties met with were in connection with the valuations.

In the New World, generally speaking, taxation of land values forms an important method of raising revenue, but always, it must be observed, is care taken to provide for preferential treatment in the case of agricultural properties. Throughout Canada, the system is widespread; in South Africa, too, it is found in most of the important centres of population; it has virtually ousted other systems in the Dominion of Australia and upwards of one hundred and fifty local authorities have adopted it in New Zealand; it is found in many parts of the United States and, often side by side with some form of local Income tax, has appeared in Central Europe. In practically all the above-quoted examples, however, it will be appreciated that the bulk of the charge inevitably, and of purpose, falls upon the owner of (urban) property in proportion to its development. It is, for the primary producer there situated, a method of raising revenue that is, at least, tolerable. In this country, when stripped of political colouring, discussion has generally centred round such academic aspects of the problem as the desirability of subsidising local rates from national taxation and the related question of the advantages likely to be reflected in the fuller development of urban amenities affected by the local retention of larger sums raised in taxation.

Curiously, it is a source of surprise to British agriculturists to find that taxation falling upon their opposite numbers in other countries may be higher than their own. Thus, in the Old World, the much-quoted Danish farmer contributes to taxation upon the lines just described and in accordance with the fertility of the soil he uses—the equivalent of 15*s.* per acre is reputed to be a common figure on medium-sized farms, and examples of £1 are not unknown. Income tax, too, is levied on a sliding scale, which extends sufficiently far down to touch the smallest proprietor.

In our own Dependencies, taking Canada as an example—whence comes the most serious competition with British farmers—charges may range from 10 cents per acre on prairie farms, up to 1 dollar 50 cents on suburban holdings; in such provinces as Ontario the average would appear to be in the neighbourhood of 70 cents—say 3*s.*—proportionately a far heavier burden than the very similar sum recently levied on English farm-land, where the outgoings and receipts per acre are approximately double those in Canada. Even the substitution of "fair values" for a flat rate system, which operates in favour of rural districts, has not in reality reduced taxation to the level which it is assumed by many persons on this side of the Atlantic to occupy.

Much light would be thrown on the whole question by a world survey of the incidence, or the effects, of taxation upon farmers.

This, surely, is a question for the International Agricultural Institute at Rome, whose functions are economic as well as statistical, for a remarkable opportunity is presented to investigate the comparative economic and fiscal position occupied by agriculturists in relation to their States and to other industries as well as the efficacy of different methods of taxing the owner of real property and the cultivator of the soil.

To sum up the present situation in this country. Neither the British tenant-farmer nor the occupying-owner of nine out of ten farms has, either now or for the last eighty years, suffered under heavy direct taxation—indirect taxation is, naturally, excluded as being dependent upon personal indulgences and predilections, not necessarily differing from those affected by other classes. Psychology, conservatism, ignorance of history and lack of knowledge concerning the contributions made by other groups of individuals were together responsible for a widespread belief that the agriculturist was subjected to excessive taxation. On the other hand, the contributions taken from the owners of considerable properties in the form, not only of annual contributions, but of Death duties, have progressively swallowed up a large proportion of the gross rents received by a numerically small body. The economic and socio-political tendency which leads to the shifting of burdens from the one class to the other has been encouraged by legislation. While there may be more equitable and more effective methods of taxing practising agriculturists, there is, certainly, little opportunity, or need, for further reduction in the existing forms, except possibly in one or two minor directions. Land tax might be abolished, and schedule B of the Income tax, as an option, should certainly be withdrawn; the incidence of Death duties on real estates might receive further sympathetic consideration.

After all, the passage of an extremely brief period in the life-history of British agriculture has resulted in remarkable changes. It has witnessed the disappearance of many anomalies, and it has revealed the land as possessing great recuperative powers; it has seen the defeat of the Physiocrats and of their successors; it has witnessed, not only the reversal of a tendency for taxation and rating to fall disproportionately on one particular class of property, but the progressive alleviation of charges deeply rooted in custom and tradition—it has even seen the roots themselves torn up;

despite the prophecies and fears expressed before numerous Commissions, the resulting transference of millions of pounds has been successfully accomplished. The final stages of the process, originally brought about by rural agitation, involved the reconstruction of the British system of local government, the wholesale reassessment of properties and the recasting of the relationship between the central Government and subordinate authorities. The dispassionate historian, looking back at the past century, sees the grandfather of the present farmer, in addition to meeting in their entirety the present-day emasculated "burdens" (e.g. rates at perhaps 20*s*. or 30*s*.; tithe, literally a tenth of the produce; Land tax at four shillings in the pound) taxed upon his riding horse, on his working horses, on his carts, on his gig, on the malt he produced, and on the windows of his house. But, in commenting on the extent of the grandson's victory, he cannot fail to express surprise at the calm attitude with which all the reliefs and grants have been accepted. Whilst struggling for reduction of taxation, three different generations of farmers have passed through periods of depression, surmounting on each occasion economic disabilities far greater than fiscal. If they have preferred to concentrate upon the task of securing remission here, rather than elsewhere, who shall criticise that policy? An age-long agitation, of minor economic import, but crossed by political, social and even religious issues, has drawn to a conclusion.

Chapter XI

AGRICULTURAL LABOUR

Labour in mediaeval times; the Napoleonic war and its influence on master and man; outbreaks and their suppression; origin of Trades Unionism; Joseph Arch and his work; the first strikes; progress of the National Union; disabilities under which Unions suffer; position of the employer of labour; agricultural "wages"; distribution of high and low rates; alleged superiority of North countrymen; numbers of persons engaged in agriculture; the war-time Agricultural Wages Board.

The above title is given to this and the following Chapter because they attempt to deal with the whole question of the application of man-power to the land, rather than to reproduce in detail once again the familiar story of the evolution of the agricultural labourer himself. Elsewhere can be read at length the history of this humbler member of the rural trinity—of his slavery under the Britons, his comparative freedom on the manor, his revolt and repression at the end of the fourteenth century, his "Golden Age" (if it really existed), and finally his loss of immemorial rights a hundred and thirty years ago. Here there is but one comment to make in regard to his history prior to 1800: viz. it is too often assumed, or even asserted, that, throughout the centuries, the agricultural labourer was little better than a beast of burden, that his environment was terrible, his social condition degraded, and his prospects hopeless. But any impartial historian is bound to observe that, whilst his efforts to improve his lot, whether in 1381 or at any intervening period up to 1830, were always justifiable, yet there has been a tendency to exaggerate the severity of the conditions he sought to alter, rather than to emphasise the ideals at which he aimed.

On the mediaeval manor we are, for example, led to believe that the lowest grades of employees or of tenants existed under conditions of inconceivable squalor and wretchedness; we are told of their hovels, their lack of clothes, warmth, light, and utensils, and the tacit assumption is encouraged that the lord meanwhile battened in luxurious surroundings. Surely it is more reasonable to assert that there was an almost total lack of what we now know as domestic furniture and also of conveniences in the dwellings of both the lord and of the labourer? It is questionable whether the latter's standard of living did not more nearly approximate to that of his master than does the corresponding manner of living of his successor to-day to that of his employer. Even as late as the sixteenth and seventeenth centuries inventories of the personal property of the well-to-do classes—clergy, squires and tradesmen—show an astonishing deficiency in those articles of domestic use which we have become accustomed to look upon as commonplace essentials in every cottage. Many of the peasants' risings were not really agrarian in their origin, for the objects of their leaders went far beyond correcting any abuses or disabilities under which manorial tenants may have suffered. No one will deny that, during the Georgian enclosure movement, great injustice was committed and individual hardships were frequent in that period, but the victims suffered from an economic upheaval in which the interests of the weakest were not safeguarded adequately or in time, rather than from legislation deliberately directed against one class of person.

Lastly, many writers hold that only at a few clearly defined periods in the history of this country was a ladder available, by the aid of whose rungs the agricultural labourer might possibly ascend to the proprietorship of a small farm, and thence indefinitely upwards. The truth, surely, is that, at all times up to the beginning of the nineteenth century, the agricultural labourer started with an initial, and often hereditary, advantage in that he had a direct claim to certain privileges attaching to the land; that after the second enclosure movement he lost this advantage and was placed in equality with those at the bottom of other industries. The majority of slaves were free by 1086, and subsequent manor records contain evidence of a constant upward social movement; whence, for example, came the dispossessed small farmers of the fifteenth and sixteenth centuries if not from the ranks of those who had once been partly cottars and partly day labourers? Anyone who has searched the College admission registers at Cambridge and Oxford will recollect that the sons of "yeomen" formed one of the most common types of student in the seventeenth and eighteenth centuries. Men who could afford such an education for their sons, and could, moreover, in days before education was compulsory, afford to lose their services on the land for some years, certainly came of a stock that was virile enough and independent enough to have attained its position by its own efforts; the sequel was generally apparent in the succeeding generations, which produced beneficed clergy, barristers and knights. Jesse Collings has enumerated a list of men, famous in every rank of life, whose parents were humble tillers of the soil. In agriculture, as in all other walks of life, there is room at the top, and at all periods of the last thousand years there has been in this and in other countries a steady upward movement of the best class of man. Character has always asserted itself, and in agriculture nothing is, or has been, easier than to rest quietly in a particular grade, but there have never been artificial restraints that prevented the advancement of the competent and of the hardworking. The true reading of history here is, surely, that for centuries the labourer in husbandry started with both feet on the lower rungs of the ladder, and that, during the last hundred years, the latter has remained, but he now stands on the ground facing it? On the other hand there is no doubt that a small stream of incompetent farmers was, and is, descending that same ladder, and reverting, within a generation or so, into labourers.

The history of the present-day hereditarily landless labourer dates from the war with France, when, in order that a large acreage of grass might be converted to wheat-raising, enclosure took away from him his privileges as a commoner and therewith, as we have just seen, his original advantage of being two or three rungs up the rural ladder. All are familiar with the exact benefits that these privileges conferred, and will observe that, as usual in economic history, the effects of their loss were not immediately brought to notice, being disguised to a certain extent by other factors that the years succeeding 1792 brought in their train. The sequel came when the peace of 1815 led to the usual deflation of money, unemployment, and a tardy reduction in the cost of food, but, thanks to the Industrial Revolution, the labourer and his family also lost those benefits associated with the ancillary industries of almost every district in the countryside.

In the meantime palliatives had been tried in the shape of the Settlement Acts and the Speenhamland policy, under which the industry suffered from an attempt to combine husbandry and out-relief. In consequence the twenty years lying between Waterloo and the Poor Law Act of 1834 represent the worst time in the history of the relationship between master and man on the land.

The following extract from *The Times* of 1822 will show that the system referred to was apt to be harshly administered.

> A paper of a strange description, regulating the allowance to the Southampton poor, makes its appearance in our columns. A certain number of magistrates met together at Winchester, and came to resolutions which we almost blush to transcribe. There are amongst them the names of rich men, who, never having felt what it is to be hungry, ought to decide with caution about the cravings of their destitute fellow-creatures. There are on the list five amply beneficed clergymen who ought to be liberal and humane. Yet we lament to say, a bench so constituted was capable of resolving that a labourer, with a wife and child to support, who refused to accept wages throughout the year, amounting in the average to 4*s.* 6*d.* per week, should forfeit all claim to relief from his parish. Gracious Heaven! are these unthinking or hard-hearted men aware to what torture they condemn a human being in this country, when they grant him for his individual maintenance but the sum of two shillings and threepence for seven days, of which six are to be consumed in labour? Less than 4*d.* for twenty-four hours, to find house and clothes, and food, and fire. Let these magistrates reconsider their resolutions, unless they mean to drive the wretched paupers within their district to utter despair, and to the infliction of all its tremendous consequences on themselves and on society.

The burning of ricks and destruction of machinery (undoubtedly the "tremendous consequences") went on for the greater part of the period, and, in the end, the burden of rates, rather than a sense of shame, caused the introduction of a new system and the disappearance of the Roundsmen. One reads accounts of the assizes held in the Southern Counties in 1830 and 1831, notes the severity of the judges, the transportations and the death sentences, but one often fails to recollect that some of the cases in question were the result of brutal attacks on unarmed individuals or of the terrorisation and robbery of defenceless persons by organised gangs, and that this was the culmination of a campaign that had lasted for many years. Nevertheless, a century ago the criminal law was administered on a widely different conception from present-day standards.

In 1823 when moving, in the House of Commons, for a revision of the criminal law, Sir James Macintosh had drawn attention to the fact that no less than "two hundred and twenty felonies polluted the Statute-Book", and that executions were taking place at the rate of over twelve hundred per annum. He held that, "when mankind beheld the life of a fellow creature sacrificed for a paltry theft, a trifling injury or fraud, their feelings at once revolted; they sympathised with the sufferer in his dying moments, and, ascribing his punishment to the effect of superior power alone, they often inwardly loaded both laws and judges with execrations". Death sentences being thus passed in normal times for petty larceny, the events of 1830 appeared to demand the maximum punishment that the law could administer. Equally hard cases are to be found in the years immediately succeeding the advent of peace when, too, agriculture was relatively prosperous. At the Lincoln Assizes in March 1818, for instance, several agricultural labourers were sentenced to death for alleged agrarian offences, among them being "William Kehos, aged 22, a private soldier in the 95th Regt. of Foot, charged with feloniously slaughtering and stealing from the close of Matthew White of Lincoln one wether hog". The 95th was one of Moore's famous regiments, afterwards to be known as the Rifle Brigade, and doubtless Private Kehos had been with it at Waterloo less than three years previously. Here was no case of organised destruction, but merely theft by doubtless an unemployed, and, possibly, hungry, "ex-service" man. Whilst such sentences as this were absolutely indefensible, it must be remembered, in visualising the events of the following twelve years, that any slackening of the severity of the law was clearly impossible in dealing with the outrages of armed mobs. If thieves were hung, determined rioters and gangs of fire-raisers must suffer similar penalties.

After a serious outbreak in 1816 at Littleport, in the Isle of Ely, when considerable damage had been done, although the disturbers had in the face of artillery retreated from a threatened attack upon the Cathedral city, the subsequent legal proceedings appear to have been conducted mainly with a view to the desired dramatic effect, and this equally applied to the character of the judgments recorded, as the following extract from E. Conybeare's *History of Cambridgeshire* indicates:

A Special Commission was held for the trial of these unhappy men. In spite of strong testimony to character, five were hanged, and five more transported for life, the rest undergoing various terms of imprisonment—all to the accompaniment of ecclesiastical rejoicings, the Bishop entering the cathedral in solemn procession, to the strains of the triumphal anthem, "Why do the heathen rage?", with his Sword of State borne before him (by his butler!), and escorted by fifty of the principal inhabitants, carrying white wands. No fewer than three hundred of these wand-bearers guarded the execution of the five rioters; yet the sympathy for them was so strong that the Bishop could not get a cart to carry them to the gallows under five guineas for the trip. Such was the last serious exercise of the Bishop's long-descended secular jurisdiction over the Isle. It died none too soon.

The revolts of 1381 and 1831 both failed, but in neither case can it be held that, as a direct result of their failure, the lot of the class responsible for them was made worse; economic happenings had at both times caused the outbreaks, and must bear the blame for the conditions existing after the suppression of the latter. No one will deny that the legislation passed to force the peasant back to work in the fourteenth century, and that extemporised to meet the demands for enhanced production in 1801, which removed from him his immediate access to the land, were utterly harsh and one-sided; but that admission must not cause us unreasonably to blame the executive that had, on each occasion, to restore order to the country in the light of the then existing moral and legal codes.

After 1834 emerged the labourer as we now know him; landless, and not for a full generation to be united or corporately represented. That same generation was to see the recovery of agriculture, the principle of Free Trade apparently harmlessly established, and the labourer obtaining at least a bare living. As these features are referred to elsewhere, it is proposed at once to trace the development of Trades Unionism as applied to agriculture.

All other methods having failed him throughout his history, the farm labourer was at length able to turn to a fresh tool—a tool, however, that has not been as useful in his hands as in those of other tradesmen. It may be legitimate to relate, as is frequently done, the formation of the first Union to those six Dorset labourers who, for banding together to assert their claims, were sentenced to seven years' transportation at the County assizes in 1832. Their claims had apparently been that wages should be advanced to ten shillings a week; instead, they suffered reductions until the sum of seven shillings was reached. Other methods of redress having failed them, a "Friendly Society" was thereupon formed. If this was Trades Unionism, then all those unfortunate men who appeared before the visiting Justices during these ten troubled years were also members in spirit, for "combination" for any such purpose was prohibited under the then existing laws. Trades Unionism in general was first recognised by that British panacea for all economic difficulties—a Royal Commission—and, as a result of its findings, two Acts of Parliament were passed to regularise the position—the first in 1869, the second in 1871. Prior to that time occupations other than agriculture had possessed Unions, but their activities had necessarily to be carried on unobtrusively. Spasmodic efforts to draw attention to their position by means of local strikes in Buckinghamshire and Hertfordshire were the first evidences of a corporate spirit manifesting itself on strictly legal lines among agriculturists. Two or three years later Canon Girdlestone took up the cudgels on behalf of the farm labourer—directly, by persuading numbers of them in the South-West of England to migrate to the better paid districts of the North, and, indirectly, by championing their cause in public.

Although East Anglia was, in future, destined to be the centre of the activities of the Unions, the original parent society was formed by the late Joseph Arch at Leamington in the spring of 1872. Arch was himself an agricultural labourer, but was also a talented Methodist preacher, and was thus afforded opportunities of reaching his members at times and in places where he was sure of an audience. The "National Agricultural Labourers' Union" quickly secured the adhesion of numerous small bodies of members in the Southern and Eastern counties, but it equally aroused the opposition of the farmers, and led to the formation of Farmers' Unions. At that time the principal objects of the Labourers' Union were represented by an agitation for advances in money wages, combined with shorter hours of labour. Only so far as persons such as Jesse Collings and Canon Girdlestone made such a course possible, was the work of these early societies directed towards a general improvement of their members' economic position. The provision of allotments and of cottage gardens, the abolition of child-labour, the better education of the young, the maintenance of the sick and the aged, the reform of local government—all these objects were to be found in the programme of those more enlightened reformers. Arch himself always emphasised the political side of the work, and incidentally made considerable efforts to foment antagonism between Nonconformity and the Established Church and between the squire and the rest of the village. Collings, one of his earliest supporters, brought with him his scheme for a new system of land tenure; this in turn led to the patronage of J. S. Mill and of other similar thinkers. The Union was well launched, and its membership rapidly increased, but, when it attempted to secure concrete benefits for its members by direct action, it was not successful.

Small strikes had been organised in the first few months, and Arch claimed that the rise (which varied between a few pence and some four shillings) in the cash earnings of labourers, noticeable in 1872, was entirely due to the work of the Union. But, as Hasbach has pointed out, even if the figures given are themselves reliable, these increases were proportionately much greater in the North (some 20 per cent.) than in the South (8 to 10 per cent.), and it was precisely in the North that the Union was not represented. It would appear, therefore, that any increases in cash earnings were due to causes other than the influence of Trades Unionism. A whole work (*The Agricultural Lock-out, 1874*, by Frederick Clifford) has been devoted to an account of the unsuccessful strikes in East Anglia that the Union in its prime attempted. Here one can only draw attention, in the briefest manner, to this interesting piece of rural history. Suffolk and Essex were the Counties affected, and the parish of Exning, within a few miles of Newmarket, was the scene of the principal struggle. In September, 1872, the local Union had demanded a rise of wages and a certain curtailment of hours of labour; the reply of the employers had taken the shape of actively forming a counter organisation. During 1873 a lock-out was conducted against the labourers, who were forced to retreat from their position. On February 28th, 1874, however, a fresh demand for an increase in wages from thirteen to fourteen shillings, together with a week of fifty-four hours, was put forward. This was a comparatively moderate request, for Arch's original manifesto had placed sixteen shillings as the minimum requirement. The masters again replied with a refusal, coupled with a lock-out. This time, although Newmarket and Exning formed the focus of the strife, subsidiary engagements took place throughout Cambridgeshire, Essex and Norfolk, the Unions claiming that some ten thousand of their members were locked out. The dispute lasted for no less a period than eighteen weeks; at the end of that time the men returned to work on their employers' terms. As a means of advertising their cause, and at the same time of raising funds, a pilgrimage had been organised by the Union officials which, consisting of some scores of their adherents, made its way to the Midlands on foot. Sheffield, Wolverhampton and other large towns were visited, and speeches were made; some £700 was collected as a result. The strike cost the Union upwards of £24,000, and, although in some districts it lasted throughout the harvest, yet, by defections from membership, and by the help of casual labour, no difficulty was experienced on that score, as the following extract from *The Agricultural Lock-out, 1874*, shows:

> Harvest began in some parts of the Eastern Counties in the third week of July, and the farmers at once found that they had as many hands as they required without employing Unionists, who therefore remained idle. The time had come when they were led to believe that their old masters would be forced to take them back; and they saw the harvest ripe and being gathered in by strangers. Only those who know the reliance placed by agricultural labourers upon the harvest-money can know how severe a blow this was to the Union hands. High wages seemed to bring plenty of people ready to earn them. Several hundreds of sturdy coprolite diggers were set free from the pits...a hundred or so of men were ready to come from Wiltshire, but were told they were not wanted. One farmer wrote that the labourers were leaving the neighbourhood wholesale "and if the Union leaders could hear the language used about them by the men they would learn for the first time how evanescent a thing popularity is". The struggle came to an end in July, as soon as it was found that the farmers could get the corn harvested without aid from their locked-out labourers.

Thus, the first and the largest strike (or lock-out) of agricultural labourers in this country ended disastrously for the Unions, and dealt Arch's movement a blow from which it took many years to recover. It was conducted by both parties concerned on perfectly correct lines, and was entirely free from outbreaks of personal violence or of intimidation on the part of either side. Although other strikes were organised in later years, this effort was the most ambitious undertaking of its kind, both in respect of the area covered, and its duration.

At this time the membership of the Labourers' Union was over seventy thousand, but within six years it fell to barely a quarter of that figure. This was attributable to two causes. In the first place a rival body had been formed in 1873, styled the Federal Union of Agricultural and General Labourers, which, as its name implies, embraced within its membership urban labourers; this and similar smaller organisations detracted from the numerical and moral force of Arch's adherents. Again, odd as it may seem, hundreds of members of the original society withdrew their membership, believing that the purposes for which they had enrolled were accomplished, or that the obligation no longer existed; incidentally, many members were in arrears with subscriptions. Then commenced the period of agricultural depression, which lasted from the late 'seventies for more than twenty years, the agricultural labourer suffering in common with the landlord and the tenant-farmer. Wage reductions were perforce effected, Arch himself counselling his members to acquiesce in this unfortunate necessity, and the Unions declined still further in membership. By 1890, so far as the labourers' organisation was concerned, a partial revival had set in and fresh societies were formed—notably in Norfolk and other of the Eastern Counties; but the climatic conditions of 1894 dealt a blow to the combination of labour. The explanation of the persistent vitality of the movement in East Anglia is due partly to the fact that labour per acre was "denser" in this arable area (and therefore more easily organised) and also because these Counties were always Liberal in their political tendencies and Nonconformist in their religious leanings.

Arch's Union, having previously lost the support of Collings, struggled on until the late 'eighties; other smaller bodies succumbed owing to the economic position. By 1906 only a very few independent societies remained. In that year, George Edwards (subsequently to be knighted) was requested by his Norfolk neighbours to expand his activities from the secretaryship of a small society to the formation of a more ambitious undertaking. Thus, the Eastern Counties Agricultural Labourers' and Small Holders' Union was founded, which lasted, under that title, until 1912, when it was reorganised as the National Agricultural Labourers' and Rural Workers' Union; finally, in 1920, this predominant Society adopted its now familiar title of the National Union of Agricultural Workers. The only other body, dating from the same period, that claims to cater for the rural worker, is the Workers' Union (now forming part of the Transport Workers' Union). That Society met with varying success in its efforts to attract agricultural workers and ultimately their numbers were negligible in its membership roll. Soon, the position of the labourer exhibited signs of improvement by participating in the recovery of the industry that set in just prior to the outbreak of the Great War. The National Union joined in this revival—its membership then being some eight to ten thousand—and was thus placed in a more advantageous position to represent its members in the claims which were soon to be entered on their behalf before the Agricultural Wages Board. The necessity for adequate representation in the presence of this important tribunal also caused a rapid expansion in the membership of the National Farmers' Union, and, at the termination of the war, both bodies were left in a condition, as to funds and membership, widely removed from their pre-war status. Accordingly, the activities of the Union were, if anything, increased and its officials were able to report extended activities in many fields, e.g. legislation covering wage regulations, insurance and housing, while they also claimed, in certain instances, to have safeguarded, or even to have enforced by legal means, the rights of individual members. It is, in effect, also an industrial Society, for, in return for a weekly subscription of 3*d.*, it affords its members a considerable measure of social insurance, while its publication, *The Land Worker*, disseminates its political views and coalesces its members. The numbers adhering to the National Union of Agricultural Workers, at that post-war period approached 150,000, but, by 1933, had fallen to approximately 40,000—less than one-tenth of the potential membership. Concurrently, the members of the National Farmers' Union had steadily increased from 21,000 in 1914 to 114,000, this being almost one-third of the maximum total obtainable from the occupiers of all holdings above an acre in extent, and fully representative of medium and large undertakings.

If the strike weapon has not been called into use during the last two decades to the extent that early agitators anticipated, it does not follow that other methods have been neglected. On the contrary, political and press propaganda have been effectively used. Arch himself lived to become the acknowledged representative of rural labour and to sit in Parliament for North-West Norfolk—a particularly appropriate seat, as it comprised one of the oldest of his strongholds.

The development of Trades Unionism in agriculture having been briefly traced, it remains to examine the reasons for its comparative inefficiency. In all other occupations one has become accustomed to regard it as an all-powerful machine, capable of paralysing—at any rate temporarily—any industry, and inconveniencing millions of neutral observers, if not at the same time being always successful in securing the bulk of its demands. In agriculture, however, one has seen nothing but spasmodic or local attempts resulting in failure; the Unions themselves have never enrolled more than a fraction of their potential members and defections have often been rife. What is the explanation?

In the first place, agriculture is, from its nature, a scattered occupation; to secure a hearing from some thousands of labourers, distributed over perhaps a hundred villages in every County, demands the multiplication of officials and a great outlay of time and money. The hours of labour are comparatively long, and there is no factory door at which to meet crowds of prospective members at a predetermined hour. Nor can members, once secured, be frequently collected to hear advice or to receive instructions from their local officials, and those in arrears with subscriptions cannot be constantly reminded of the penalties attaching to their position. Neither does abstention carry with it the disadvantages that exist in similar circumstances in other occupations. Non-members are not ostracised on the farm as they are in the factory, partly because only a small minority of the whole body of agricultural labour adheres to the Unions, and partly because field-work, in addition to being of an isolated character, is not exclusively confined to those of one sex or of any particular age group. Again, certainly in the past, subscriptions to their Union have represented a relatively greater demand on the pockets of the agricultural workers than do the corresponding payments by factory hands. In Scotland and the North of England, where "living-in" is the general custom, the normal attractions of a society, or its orders in emergency, are not likely to prevail with servants, who are, to all intents and purposes, members of their employers' households for a definite number of months.

The above represent the inherent difficulties against which the rural organiser of labour always finds himself ranged. The farmer at the same time is armed with equally potent advantages. His trade does not immediately suffer from a cessation of work as does a mine, a machine shop or a transport organisation. At most seasons of the year an arable farmer can watch his land remaining unattended with comparative equanimity for at least as long a period as his men can exist on little or no strike pay; in normal times livestock demands the minimum of man-power, and, on withdrawal of hired labour, the farmer, his family or some old employee can minister to its wants. If harvest or the period of some seasonal operation is selected for a strike, that is just the time when additional extraneous labour is most abundant. The prevention of non-unionist labour from participating at such times is singularly difficult in the case of agriculture—quite apart from the innate conservatism of the rural worker to methods of active opposition—spaces are great and workers are scattered. At times of pressure there are normally bodies of workers ready to go at once to any centre; prior to 1915 Irish harvesters always formed a nucleus of strike-breakers, and an appeal from farmers to townsfolk, in circumstances of stress, always results in numbers of unskilled labourers, school boys and well-meaning, but comparatively useless, individuals, hurrying to assist. During the greater part of the last seventy years the number of regular farm labourers was declining, and a reserve of older men had formed in the villages—men who were thoroughly familiar with every phase of work on the farm and who could, for a short time, resume their places thereon. Shortage of labour is seldom a difficulty that farmers have to contend with; in fact there has been for two generations a superabundant supply, always acting as a check on extremists in times of strike. Only during the last two years of the war was the farmer short of assistance, and then he was officially supplied with numerous substitutes. By 1920 matters had so far resumed their pre-war complexion that a labourer was heard to remark "farmers are getting independent again". This word is symptomatic of the position of the employer of rural labour; he *is* independent to a degree that is unknown in other industries. The National Farmers' Union and similar bodies have always been in a stronger position than the corresponding formations of other employers of labour. Indeed, such a thing as a complete national strike is an impossibility in the country owing to the widely different character of farming operations and to the divergent hiring systems in vogue in each area, which would preclude employees from united action and enable employers to make full use of substituted labour. Socially and economically, Trades Unionism on the land should have a future before it, but as a weapon for the sudden application of constraint to organised employers it is of little avail.

What are apt to be lightly described as "agricultural labourers' wages" afford one of the most difficult economic problems connected with the land. In all trades one is accustomed to the distinction to be drawn between money wages and real wages, but, in the case of agriculture, the position is complicated by the introduction of a third factor—the value to be attached to payments in kind and other benefits that are not immediately patent. Agriculture is peculiar in that the provisions of the Truck Acts have always been held inapplicable to it, and partial payment in goods is not illegal. Generally speaking, the further North one goes the more emoluments will be found to consist of payment in kind. In Scotland the system reaches its climax, and a labourer may receive in this form a really considerable proportion of his total wages, for, across the border again, the further North one travels the more one finds goods taking the place of cash, until, before the war, in Orkney and Shetland cash was represented by some 7*s.* and the value of allowances was 6*s.* 9*d.* A Scotch ploughman might receive 70 lb. of oatmeal monthly, half a gallon of milk daily and one and a half tons of potatoes each year, often together with a similar quantity of coal. The vexed question of the advantages attaching to the bothy system in Scotland cannot be discussed here, but it should be observed that the Scotch labourer differs from the Southern in that he lives on the farm whereon he works (if married, in a cottage, if single in a bothy), he is engaged by the half year or year, gets a larger proportion of his remuneration in kind, does scarcely any piece-work and receives no extra payment at times of harvest.

Allowances in England and Wales can still, despite the existence of Wages Boards, take many forms. Houses provided rent-free, or for a nominal payment, represent the largest addition to cash earnings; the supply of such products as potatoes, bacon, milk or vegetables is a weekly supplement in numerous cases; added to these are the smaller advantages frequently accruing from the possession of strips of potato land, the provision of beer or cider and of other gifts; lastly, in certain Counties, harvest money comes in once a year as a lump sum. As such allowances vary widely from County to County, it will be appreciated that it is a task of extreme difficulty to assess the average value of all benefits, but one of the most recent pre-war estimates—that of the Board of Trade in 1907—gave 1*s.* 1*d.* per week as their value in England and Wales. Here again a complication is introduced, for the different grades of employees received varying quantities of goods, and had varying claims on free quarters. The Board of Trade figure represented the average of all grades, the receipts of individuals being valued at 9*d.* in the case of ordinary labourers and 1*s.* 6*d.* in that of stockmen. The corresponding figure in 1918 showed a rise to 1*s.* 5*d.* for labourers and to 2*s.* 9½*d.* for stockmen. Specialists, wherever they are employed throughout the British Isles, always receive a larger proportion of their emoluments in kind than do ordinary labourers. The earnings of the latter class have generally been more dependent on piece-work, however, and in this instance allowance must be made for possible loss of time; again, local custom crops up, and the problem is complicated by the different systems that varying types of farm operations necessitate. In these circumstances, a statement issued by a Committee of the then Agricultural Wages Board in 1919 is apposite as showing the ramifications in the systems extant in England for rewarding agricultural labour:

> Farm workers are paid by many systems. Amongst ordinary labourers, some are paid almost entirely by time-rates, wholly or mainly in cash. Others, particularly in vegetable growing districts, are paid mainly by piece-rates, in cash. Between these extremes are men who are paid time-rates during the greater part of the year, with piece-rates, or bonuses, at special periods, such as hay-making and harvest. Generally speaking, the value of allowances in kind made to ordinary labourers is quite small. The skilled man, or, more properly, men who have responsibility with regard to stock, as shepherds, cattlemen and horsemen, are generally paid by time-rates. These rates may be paid wholly in cash, but more generally are paid partly in kind. These classes also sometimes work for piece-rates, or receive special rates for overtime, or bonuses for work in special periods. Further, some men amongst these classes are boarded and lodged, others are partly fed, by the employer. A few ordinary labourers are boarded and lodged, or partly fed by the employer, but the custom of boarding and lodging, or providing meals, is more or less confined to certain districts, and the number of men boarded and lodged, or fed, is comparatively small, especially amongst ordinary labourers.

Enough has been said to demonstrate the difficulties attaching to the compilation of any precise figure showing the "average" earnings of all agriculturists. Official figures are available which give the cash receipts for the different grades of worker, but these have necessarily to be subdivided into summer and winter rates, and accuracy requires that they be confined to County areas or weighted in proportion to the numbers of men employed in each class. Proceeding on these lines, we find that in 1907 the winter rates of labourers' cash earnings varied from 12*s.* 1*d.* in Dorset to 19*s.* 4*d.* in Lancashire, those for stockmen, horsekeepers and shepherds from 14*s.* in Wiltshire to 20*s.* 4*d.* in Durham. Summer rates were sometimes a penny or twopence higher, and sometimes a corresponding amount lower. To these sums must be added the value of allowances in kind, amounting, as we have just seen, to an *average* of 9*d.* for labourers and of 1*s.* 6*d.* for those engaged in the care of livestock. County rates again varied from 3*d.* per week in Middlesex to 2*s.* 2*d.* in Hereford, and stockmen in Bedfordshire received value to the extent of 11*d.*, whilst the benefits of those in Lincolnshire were assessed at 3*s.* 4*d.* the week. In the four East Anglian Counties harvest-money varied between £5 and £10, but it superseded ordinary weekly rates of pay so long as this work lasted. In the Kesteven division of Lincolnshire pre-war extras and allowances to waggoners might total over £17 per annum. In 1902 Wilson Fox's *Report* to the Board of Trade contained the following figures for the value of the total emoluments (weekly cash, allowances in kind and extra payments), for ordinary labourers, in England 17*s.* 5*d.*, in Wales 17*s.* 7*d.*, in Scotland 19*s.* 5*d.*, and in Ireland 10*s.* 9*d.*, for all forms of male labour 18*s.* 3*d.*, 17*s.* 3*d.*, 19*s.* 3*d.* and 10*s.* 11*d.* respectively. Actually, the lowest total earnings in the United Kingdom were found in County Mayo, where 8*s.* 9*d.* represented the weekly wages and value received by an adult labourer—his cash receipts being given as only 7*s.* By 1914 all investigators agree that a rise of at least a shilling had taken place in cash wages, and Bowley (*Prices and Wages in the United Kingdom, 1914–1920*) gives 17*s.* 10*d.* as their level in April 1915, or, say, 19*s.* as total receipts—these figures being for England and Wales alone. Stockmen and shepherds were of course earning at least two or three shillings beyond what the ordinary labourer commanded.

Cash wages, *plus* the value of allowances in kind and extra payments, represent the "total wages" earned by those employed on the land, but the figure thus secured is useless unless we correlate it with the cost of living, or, in other words, assess its purchasing power in commodities, thus obtaining a clue to "real" wages. Tables of cash earnings, and also of total wages, have been compiled at frequent intervals by contemporary investigators such as Young, Marshall and Caird, and we have evidence about corresponding payments centuries earlier in the researches of historians, but all of these findings require extreme care in handling when placed upon a comparative basis. It is for instance useless to know that in Essex in 1746 labourers' cash wages were 5*s.* a week, and thirty years later 6*s.* a week, nor can we appreciate their economic position when Young tells us that, fifty miles North of London, he found labourers earning 7*s.* 1*d.* in 1771. In all these instances, for the purpose of passing judgment on the position of those employed in agriculture, it would be essential to know the cost of the staple articles of food and of clothing that went to meet a typical labourer's household requirements. On many former occasions it has been sought to relate cash wages to the number of pecks of wheat that they would secure, and tables have been prepared on these lines. They carried, however, little conviction, for they ignored the fact that in times of high wheat prices alternative forms of food would be increasingly relied upon, and that in former periods the labourer's loaf contained other ingredients, while, fundamentally, they contradicted the recorded fact that wheat prices have rarely had any very close connection with the movements of the index-number representative of commodity prices in general. With these reservations in mind, it is interesting to note that Messrs C. S. Orwin and B. I. Felton have illustrated (*Journal of the Royal Agricultural Society of England*, 1931, p. 255) the steady increase, since 1866, of the purchasing power of agricultural wages, expressed both in fractions of a quarter of wheat and in pounds of beef. In both cases only minor setbacks are to be observed, and these occurred in the war years or during the life of the Conciliation Committees. At certain periods the figures themselves were as follows:

Year	Purchasing power of wages in quarters of wheat	Purchasing power of wages in pounds of English beef
1867–71	0·22	20·8
1892	0·44	33·6
1907	0·49	34·4
1919	0·52	33·6
1925	0·60	37·6
1930	0·88	41·6

The corresponding data for early in 1933 would have been actually 1·31 quarters of wheat and 47·2 pounds of beef. Man, however—even agricultural man—does not live by bread alone!

For all the above reasons it is not proposed to enumerate the fluctuations in the cash payments of the labourer in previous centuries, but rather to attempt some analysis of his economic situation during the last thirty years, to compare it with that prevailing during the former European war, and to comment on certain features affecting agricultural labour in general. Any comparison made even between total earnings nowadays and apparently comparable figures prior to the enclosure movement of 1790–1830 requires exceedingly careful treatment, for it must be borne in mind that, not only were the unenclosed commons a source of additional income to labourers, but that what we now attempt to resurrect under the title of "village industries" were then widespread actualities. Every household had the opportunity of creating some additional source of income over and above that earned by its head, whether it was glove-making, knitting, weaving, or a dozen other trades engaged in by the women and children. Then family earnings ought to have been the criterion for comparison, and there is still room to argue that this should be the basis even at the present time. For in few other occupations has it been so customary—or perhaps necessary—for women and children to add their labour to that of their men-folk. Even after the concentration —albeit in surprisingly small units (*pace* J. H. Clapham)—of industry in urban areas, one finds that the farm labourers' earnings were still augmented by the shillings and pence of his wife and children, not then gained by home-work but by field-work. The mechanic, the coal-miner and the railway employee, each with young families, are the only "bread-winners"; on the land, the larger the family the more it has always been capable of earning—despite the activities of the education authorities. Even at the present time the labour of children over the legal school-age, together with the assistance of those of all ages in times of holiday, considerably augments the total weekly earnings of a rural household. This is one of the unseen factors to be borne in mind when making comparison between agriculture and other industries, for, in official *Reports*, examples are recorded of North country families earning, in 1902, over £200 per annum on the land. It is also doubtless the explanation of the seemingly insoluble problem presented by the agricultural labourer of the mid-nineteenth century—the man whose cash earnings for sixty years of active labour never exceeded twelve shillings a week, and who, nevertheless, brought up a large family of children in health and decency. Medical officers and welfare supervisors of the present day declare that such things were impossible, but instances abound in which the generations raised under such conditions have subsequently advanced themselves in the world. Twelve shillings a week, *plus* a free cottage, *plus* allowances of food in kind, with, in addition, the shilling or two brought in each week by three or four children, formed a very different proposition from a bare twelve shillings. This is no defence of what were, even in Great Britain, inadequate cash wages, but it is merely intended to show that statements confined to the money handed over weekly to the farm labourer himself should not be seized upon as representing the total amount of his incomings. The Irish labourers, whose total emoluments averaged 10*s*. 9*d*. and ranged down to 8*s*. 9*d*. per week, fortunately represented conditions unknown in the rest of the kingdom; they are only explicable in the light of the popular belief that potatoes formed the staple dietary of these men.

The distribution of comparatively high or low wages affords an interesting side-light on economic history. Apart from the consideration of living-in arrangements or of the payments made to half-yearly farm servants, cash wages in the North of England have, for centuries, been higher than those in the South. The competition from mining and manufacturing centres must be held primarily responsible for this feature, which is also to be observed within a short radius of large towns. The demand for unskilled and semi-skilled labour on the outskirts of the latter in connection with horses, roads and railways is felt in addition to the direct call of the factory. As a frontispiece to Caird's *English Agriculture in 1850–1* will be found a map showing the range of farm wages in England. The line dividing high rates from low runs rather South of West from the Wash as far as Staffordshire and then turns North-West, reaching the coast on the borders of Cheshire and Flint. Thus, parts of Leicestershire and Shropshire were included in the high wages portion, and the whole of Northamptonshire, Warwickshire and Worcestershire were in the low. The *Report* of Wilson Fox relating to wages in 1902 contained a map of the United Kingdom on similar lines; here, the same features were observed, save that, additionally, Norfolk, Suffolk, Gloucester, Oxford, Berkshire, Wiltshire and Dorset were below the average for Southern England, and Surrey

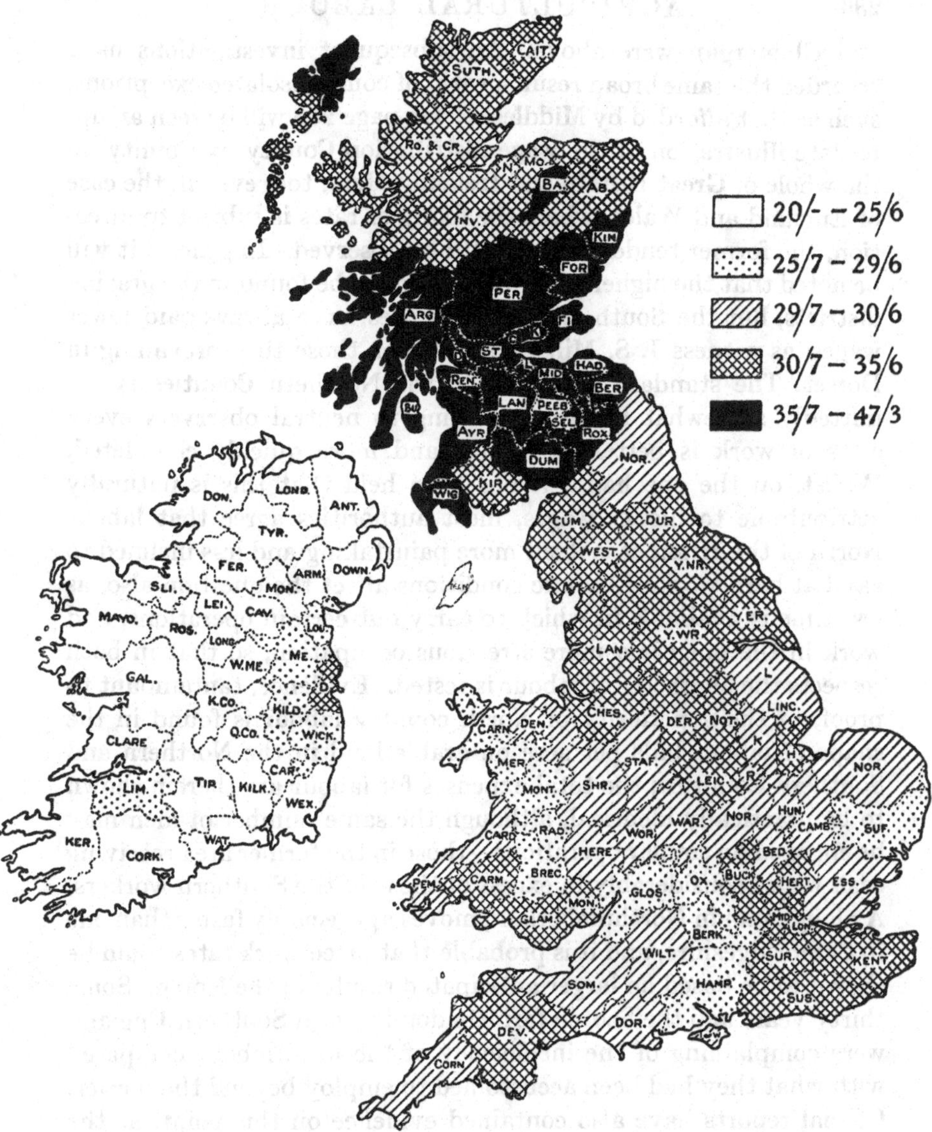

England and Wales. Minimum wages for ordinary labourers as established by the Agricultural Wages Boards, February, 1933.

Scotland. Estimated weekly remuneration for married ploughmen, Whitsunday, 1932.

Northern Ireland. Weekly cash wages of ordinary labourers, 1931.

Irish Free State. Average weekly earnings (in the month of July) in the five year period 1925 to 1929 of permanent male Agricultural labourers over 21 years of age, who were stated not to have had free house or allowance of any kind.

and Glamorgan were above. All subsequent investigations have recorded the same broad results, with, of course, isolated exceptions, such as that afforded by Middlesex. On page 235 will be seen an up-to-date illustration of the wage distribution County by County, in the whole of Great Britain and Ireland. Here, too, even in the case of England and Wales, where the fixing of rates is subject to direction, the former tendencies will still be observed. In general it will be noted that the higher paid workers are to be found in the grazing districts, but the South-Western Counties have always paid lower wages, as witness J. S. Mill's strictures on those then prevailing in Dorset. The standard of labour in the Northern Counties is admittedly somewhat higher; according to neutral observers every class of work is better performed and more quickly completed. Whilst, on the one hand, it has been held that this is naturally attributable to higher wages, most authorities agree that labour North of the Humber is itself more painstaking and less inclined to cavil at hard work. Climatic conditions affect the question also, as less time is available in which to carry out certain operations, and work in the open is a more strenuous occupation, so that in both respects the character of labour is tested. Evidence, tantamount to proof, of the superiority of North country labour is found in the shape of labour-bills per acre on arable land in the Northern and Southern Counties; the total expenses for labour are therein shown to be practically identical, although the same number of men may be engaged on similar operations—those in the former area receiving cash wages considerably in excess of those of the Southern workers. A ploughman in Northumberland moves appreciably faster than one in Cambridgeshire, and it is probable that piece-work rates could be shown to be based on larger anticipated results in the North. Some thirty years ago the Scotch farmers domiciled in Southern England were complaining of the inefficiency of the local labour compared with what they had been accustomed to employ beyond the border. Official reports have also contained evidence on this point, as the following example shows: "In reference to the slowness of the Southern labourer generally, a large Scotch farmer, of some forty years' experience in Surrey, used at one time regularly to import ploughmen from the South of Scotland. He paid them more than the average wage, and they usually stayed two years, when the many opportunities of better employment became too much for them. They used to plough an acre, sometimes a Scotch one (6000 yards) to the Surrey man's three-quarters of an acre in a day". Soil conditions must, however, be taken into consideration; thus, it was agreed by Scotch farmers in evidence before the Commission of 1893 that, in Essex, their best fellow countrymen could do little more work in a given time on the heavy clay than the natives could accomplish.

There are two outstanding periods in which it is well to examine the position of the English agricultural labourer; both are covered by a European war and both brought about an increase in the prosperity of the farmer, but the French war saw agriculture uncontrolled by the State, whilst the Great War supplied the first opportunity for a large experiment in Government control—a control that was extended to the determination of a minimum wage for farm workers. The first quarter of the nineteenth century represents one of the saddest periods in the history of agricultural labour. Commodity prices rose steadily for the first dozen years, while at the same time the hereditary benefits of the villager were swept from him, his subsidiary sources of income disappeared, and he became the *corpus vile* for experiments in Poor-law administration. Enough has previously been said to demonstrate the dangers attaching to any attempt to show the past relationship of earnings to expenses, but certain figures, compiled by Arthur Young, may be accepted as crude evidence of the seriousness of the position. That authority estimated the rise in bread prices by 1812 as 100 per cent., of meat 146 per cent., and of all provisions as approximately 135 per cent., cash wages on the other hand, he found, had only risen 100 per cent. Whilst these are obviously round figures, yet, making every allowance for possible inaccuracy it must be admitted that the incomings of a labourer's household were, by that date, quite incapable of meeting his barely essential outgoings. Space does not permit of any account of the slow fall in prices after 1815, or of the reduction in cash earnings effected by employers in an attempt to weather the inevitable after-war depression. It is only possible to summarise the history of the twenty years that succeeded Waterloo by throwing out the suggestion that, if war had inflicted hardships on the labourer, peace conditions joined the landlord and the tenant with him in common despair.

Between the two wars there intervened a recovery and another long period of depression—the latter, as has been shown, only beginning to pass away some few years prior to 1914. It had been accompanied by a decline in the numbers of those employed on the land, as the following Table, extracted from the *Census Returns* of 1911 shows, but the fall in the cost of living had undoubtedly increased the real wages of those workers who remained:

England and Wales

	(1) Numbers of male farm workers in England and Wales	(2) Numbers of males of ten years of age and upwards engaged in agriculture	(3) Percentage of (2) to all males ten years of age and upwards
1851	1,232,576	1,544,087	23·5
1861	1,206,280	1,539,965	21·2
1871	1,014,428	1,371,304	16·8
1881	924,871	1,288,173	13·8
1891	841,884	1,233,936	11·6
1901	715,138	1,153,185	9·5
1911	757,552	1,253,859	9·2

The above figures, in the case of workers, exclude men employed in trades ancillary to agriculture. They accordingly differ slightly from others given in similar Tables elsewhere. It will be deduced that the numbers of those engaged in farming as a business did not decline very seriously, but if we confine our examination to workers the results are very striking. Ten years later, that is in 1911, evidence of the recovery of agriculture could be seen reflected in the numbers of workers employed—representing the first increase in sixty years; it has, however, been suggested that the figures for 1901 were reduced by the absence of the Yeomanry Regiments in South Africa, and was thus not truly indicative of the number of workers normally employed upon the land. Despite a decrease of 38 per cent. from the year 1851, agriculture, in 1911, still gave employment to a larger body of male workers than any other industry save that of coal-mining and building. Moreover, if corresponding figures were taken for the United Kingdom, it would have headed the list, as it still does for England and Wales if employers are included. The relative decline in importance of agriculture as an occupation, however, is vividly shown by the percentage of males it provided employment for at the decennial intervals; in 1851 almost one in four made his living on the land, in 1901 less than one in ten did so. Nevertheless, it was an exceedingly important and peculiarly diverse and intricate occupation, the labour conditions in which an *ad hoc* body successfully attempted to regulate from 1917. Precedents for this action were not lacking, for, even if we exclude the efforts of the Justices of the Peace to correlate wages and food prices in the early nineteenth century, the Statute of Labourers of 1349 represents a direct, but mistaken, attempt at the fixing of cash wages.

When the Government claimed the right to compel agriculturists to farm their land in a particular way, and in consequence guaranteed them a certain monetary return, it was obviously bound to insist that they paid their employees a wage roughly commensurate with the enhanced profits then accruing, for, failing this, the experience of the French war would have been repeated, and wages would have been outstripped by prices. Part II of the Corn Production Act of 1917 accordingly contained provisions for giving expression to this form of war-time control. The niceties, in the first place of ascertaining the existing rates of pay and allowances in each County in Great Britain and Ireland, and, secondly, of assessing, for any given period of time, the purchasing power of constantly depreciating cash payments and the improving value of allowances in kind, will be understood by anyone who has glanced at the difficulties attendant on these operations even in times of economic stability.

When fixing remuneration the Agricultural Wages Board was directed by the Corn Production Act "so far as possible to secure for able-bodied men wages, which in the opinion of the Board are adequate to promote efficiency and to enable a man in an ordinary case to maintain himself and his family with such standards of comfort as may be reasonable, in relation to the nature of his occupation". The statutory fixing of wages had been a subject for academic discussion for many years prior to 1917. In 1796, when wheat was already fetching over 74*s*. the quarter, a definite request for the granting of a minimum wage to farm labourers was made to Pitt, who replied: "I will not do that; but I will do a better thing—I will take care that no one shall suffer from want: the poor people who cannot live on their wages shall be relieved out of the Parish Rates". The results of his methods afford a striking contrast to the success achieved by the alternative plan which was adopted one hundred and twenty years later. Such bodies as the Land Enquiry

Committee had, a few years before 1914, strongly advocated a minimum wage, and their arguments had been replied to by the Land Agents' Society. The objections generally put forward had been that casual labour would to a great extent take the place of permanent, that the old and relatively feeble labourer would be swept aside, and that arable land would revert to grass. Under war conditions there was of course no risk of the last disadvantage crystallising, and the first was negatived by the deliberate substitution of women, of German prisoners and of soldiers of a low category; that the services of the less physically fit were apt to be dispensed with there was slight evidence after the labour shortage was made good in 1919. As affording a demonstration of the practicability of enforcing a minimum wage in agriculture under war conditions the four years' life of the Wages Board was completely successful; whether, in the absence of a *quid pro quo* in the shape of guaranteed prices, it could have wielded sufficient authority to compel compliance with its regulations is quite another question.

The Corn Production Act set up a Central Wages Board for England and Wales, which in turn established District Boards; similar machinery was extemporised in Scotland and in Ireland. The Central Board was composed of sixteen representatives of farmers and sixteen of labour, with seven neutral representatives directly appointed by the Board of Agriculture. District Committees were similarly representative of all interests. Recommendations for alterations in the rate of wages were put forward by the District Committees, and were then adjudicated upon by the Central Board, whose published findings had the force of law. The Board was empowered to deal with the rates of remuneration for all forms of agricultural labour, that of women and boys included, and of persons employed in subsidiary rural occupations; it could fix scales both for piece-work, time-rates and overtime, as well as grant permission for payment at rates below the minimum; it had considerable powers of a quasi-judicial character and, as its deputy chairman, the late Sir Henry Rew, said, its work affected the lives of some five million persons. When it commenced its operations a minimum cash wage of 25*s.* a week was already enforceable under the provisions of the Corn Production Act—representing, by August 1917, a rise of almost 50 per cent. beyond the 1914 level. The successive minimum rates for ordinary labourers established by the Board were as follows: early in 1918 30*s*., a year later, 36*s*. 6*d*., in April 1920, 42*s*. and in August of that year, 46*s*. These of course were the rates applicable to those Counties or districts in which cash wages had always been low—those fixed for the Northern districts were naturally somewhat higher; as were the overall average rates for the whole country. Difficulties soon arose in the matter of payments to skilled men and to those in charge of livestock, whose remuneration had always been higher than that of the ordinary labourer. Certain Counties paid these workers the ordinary minimum wage *plus* such overtime as their special duties necessitated, others agreed to the raising of weekly cash wages to a level above that applicable to other employees. Even at the end no uniform system was in vogue, for the Central Board itself did not attempt to enforce one system for the whole country, but left the local Boards a free hand.

In 1920, fifty shillings, as a universal minimum, was the final aim of the men's representatives on the Board, who claimed that this was only in harmony with the cost of living index-number. If, however, the latter is plotted graphically side by side with the successive increases granted to agricultural labourers it will be noted (see page 246) that, prior to the advent of the Wages Board, the cost of living had outstripped the increase in cash wages, but, from the spring of 1919 until the middle of 1920, the latter were in advance of the index-number. Except for the brief "peak" period in the cost of living, this was the situation until the autumn of 1922, the lead in the subsequent decline being taken by that index-number. This is not the place in which to criticise at length the official index-number in its application to agriculture, but the nature of its composition must be borne in mind when comparing it with the cash earnings of an agricultural labourer. It is weighted by the inclusion of such items as railway fares, rent, rates, and general household expenses, several of which are not strictly applicable to the case of the farm labourer, and some are only so in part. Again, he still has the advantage of the free provision in kind of certain commodities that are of some importance in building up the index-number. If his economic position were, therefore, to be regulated by the movements of the general cost of living (which represents a predominantly urban budget) he would be thereby directly benefited, apart from participating in certain minor, but recognised, advantages which this method confers, e.g. the quality and type of commodities are assumed to be constant, and purchases to be maintained in quantity at the pre-war level. Economists are agreed that the lowest paid workers received relatively the greatest augmentations in wages during the period of rising prices; agriculturists certainly obtained marked increases in real wages. When the minimum level of 46*s*. was reached, the increases in total wages ranged from a rise of 245 per cent. in Oxfordshire down to one of 116 per cent. in Northumberland; in August 1920 the cash remuneration of ordinary farm workers in England and Wales represented an increase of 160 per cent. over July 1914; the cost of living index-number then stood at 155. Bowley shows that, in twelve principal trades, only bricklayers' and engineers' labourers and railwaymen had secured increases greater than this. Hours of labour had also been reduced, and, not only was overtime recognised, but enhanced hourly rates fixed for it, so that the opportunity of securing additional money was thus afforded; again, unemployment was absent, so that altogether labour was assured of a full week's work for remuneration at a higher level than that at which the cost of living index-number stood.

It is not essential in this Chapter to follow the course of events that led up to the repeal of the Corn Production Act; the majority of the nation was satisfied that the right course was pursued, and that the time had come when agriculture should again stand alone without direct and incalculable financial support. It is equally idle to enquire what would have been the movements in agricultural wages if the Board had not been formed. It is sufficient to suggest that during its lifetime it accomplished a vast amount of difficult, and often thankless, work with the minimum recourse to the Law Courts. Its last corporate action was to reduce the statutory wage from 46*s*. to 42*s*., leaving as a legacy to its successors the work of tiding over the even more difficult period of falling prices.

Chapter XII

AGRICULTURAL LABOUR (CONTINUED)

Conciliation Committees; subsequent reintroduction of Wages Boards; the cost of labour; migrant and casual workers; labour-gangs; emigration and movement to the towns; food and health of rural workers; amenities of country life; farm work a skilled trade; artificial steps for amelioration of rural conditions; statistics of labour employed on different types and sizes of holdings; cost of labour per acre and for different types of crop; labour's share in the profits of farming.

The Wages Board having ceased to exist as from October 1st, 1921, voluntary methods were given an opportunity of carrying on its work. Conciliation Committees, as they were designated, were therefore established on much the same lines as those of the former district Wages Boards; that is to say, they were composed of representatives of both masters and men, and comprised the same, or smaller, areas within their spheres of activity. Upon agreement as to hours and wages having been reached, two courses were open to these Committees; they could merely record this agreement and leave it to farmers within their district to pay, and labourers to agree to receive, such rates, or, if they so elected, they could formally submit their findings to the Ministry of Agriculture. Only in the latter event were the rates and conditions so fixed, after confirmation by the Ministry and local advertisement, considered as legally binding and enforceable in the Courts within a period of three months. As was to be expected, the majority of the new Committees preferred to look upon their proceedings as forming a voluntary basis for agreement rather than to feel that they were again committing themselves into the hands of the legislature; thus, in the first year only five reported their agreed rates. Naturally, also, under the prevailing conditions, Committees did not fix wages for any but very short periods of time. As was stated above, the Wages Board itself had left a cash wage of 42*s.* enforceable for the month of September 1921; this the Committees proceeded steadily to reduce, until the following spring, on the following lines: October, 40*s.*, November, 38*s.*, December, 37*s.*, January, 33*s.* 6*d.*, February, 33*s.*, March, 32*s.* 6*d.*, April, 32*s.*; from May, until after the harvest of 1922, 32*s.* was the prevailing level. Thereafter it became obvious that still further reductions were necessary, and agreements for payments in the region of 30*s*. became frequent. It will be observed that the above movements corresponded approximately to the cost of living index-number, only the later reductions after the autumn of 1922 failing to harmonise with it. In the light of what was said in regard to this question when the Wages Board rates were under discussion, it is clear that in spending power labourers' cash earnings were worth more in the summer of 1922 than they had been in that of 1914. The drawbacks to a hard and fast system of payment, which ignored individual ability and left mere age as the determining factor, were frequently tackled by the Committees. In some cases their regulations did not apply to workers over sixty-five or under twenty-one years of age; only in a very few areas were the rates for female labour settled, and, generally speaking, their findings were applicable to the "able-bodied". Hours of work were in many cases extended, and overtime was frequently left to individual arrangement, for the reduction in the number of hours worked each week as a result of the orders of the Wages Board had, it was claimed, seriously increased the labour bills on farms, instances adduced showing that where six men had been sufficient in 1912 seven were required in 1921. In the Northern Counties attempts were made to fix a value to allowances in kind and to other benefits (such as standardising the value of a free cottage), but elsewhere this side of the question was tacitly ignored. It is probable that Conciliation Committees eased the labour situation during a very difficult period of transition, by bringing together, for mutual discussion of their problems, those most intimately connected with the land.

The Conciliation Committees were, not unnaturally, never popular with the workers' representatives and tended to be ignored by employers of labour, so that, on the transformation of the political situation in 1923, it was not surprising to find the party then returned to power immediately setting about the re-establishment of Wages Boards upon a compulsory footing. In the meantime, the average weekly wages had fallen to 28*s*.; the smallest cash wage paid during the period between October 1922 and the end of 1924 being the 25*s*. of Norfolk and certain other Eastern Counties. Under the Agricultural Wages (Regulation) Act of 1924, County, or district, Boards were again formed, upon which sat equal numbers of representatives of the two parties concerned, together with certain independent members nominated by the Ministry of Agriculture and a similarly appointed chairman. These Boards were more autonomous than their predecessors, formed under war-time conditions, for they were empowered to put into operation their own recommendations—which were legally enforceable—without recourse to the Central Board in London, whose duties were now mainly of a supervisory character. Only if the County Boards failed to function, or to agree upon any important matter, would the overriding authority of the Board itself be put into action. By the early spring of 1925, orders determining rates of wages had been issued for every County in England and Wales. Agreements were generally in the neighbourhood of 30*s.* to 34*s.*, and the result was an average wage of 31*s.* 5*d.* for the country (viz. England and Wales) as a whole. It should, however, be noted that no longer was there any but voluntary determination of agricultural wages in either part of Ireland or in Scotland. After 1926 these controlled rates in England and Wales were destined to remain well above the corresponding position occupied by the cost of living index-number; hours of labour, too, became stereotyped in the region of 48–50 for winter months and 50–52 for those of summer—a considerable reduction upon the pre-war level. Additionally, the weekly half-holiday had been gained and overtime recognised by agreed rates of remuneration. For the following years, and up to the present time, the percentage increase above the basic, or pre-war level, fluctuated from 72–80 per cent., for wages have remained at an average of over 31*s.* since the Boards were formed in 1924; the actual range in County rates was, in the summer of 1932, from 28*s.* 6*d.* in Gloucestershire to 41*s.* in the Eastern Division of Lancashire. In the meantime, the cost of living fell—at first slowly, but subsequently, during 1930 and 1931, with some rapidity—and the result has been a very substantial rise in the real wages, or the spending power, of the ordinary agricultural workers concerned. Nor should the average of the County rates of remuneration be regarded as indicative of the *earnings* of the recipients in question, for special investigations, conducted by the Ministry of Agriculture, have shown that, in 1931, the total receipts for that class of employee were 33*s.* 8*d.*, or some 2*s.* in excess of the average Statutory minimum wage, while the total earnings of horsemen and of stockmen were about 37*s.* 6*d.* and 39*s.* respectively. The map on p. 235 illustrates the variations in normal wage-rates in the different Counties. It should, however, be observed that, in the case of the Irish Free State and Scotland, *earnings* have, in the absence of comparable data, been substituted for *wages*. By analogy with England, this would imply an addition of, perhaps, 1*s*. or 1*s*. 6*d*. for the former country and of 2*s*. for the latter: relatively few Counties are seriously affected but a certain number in South-eastern Scotland might, if substitution were possible, be degraded to the extent of one degree of shading.

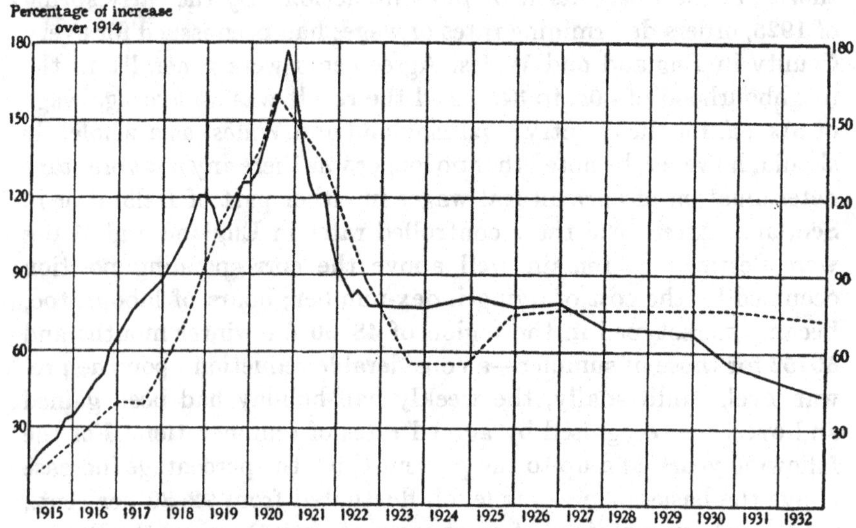

Wages (viz. cash and other emoluments) of agricultural labourers compared with the official cost of living index-number from 1915 to 1932

--------- Wages ——— Cost of living index-number

During the last two years, many appeals were made by employers to County Boards, urging a reduction in their fixed rates and, in a few cases, these representations were complied with to the extent of a shilling or eighteenpence, but the majority of the bodies expressed themselves bound to implement the clause of the 1924 Act, which charged them to provide for the agricultural labourer "such a standard of comfort as may be reasonable in relation to the nature of his occupation". It seemed impossible to convince such Committees that, if the standard of wages adopted by them in 1925 complied with these conditions—as presumably it did—then there had been during the next seven years a steady improvement in the standard itself. A simple calculation will demonstrate that if the cost of living index-number stood at 179 in 1925, when wages averaged a little over 31*s*., then, when it fell in 1932 to 142, the corresponding level of wages would have been 24*s*. 6*d*. It is always an extraordinarily difficult task to persuade an employee that his real wages increased in those years by a large percentage, but, when so many agreements in other industries have been based upon a sliding-scale adjustment, it seems very unfortunate that no such provision had been inserted in the Wages Act, or that no instructions to this effect were in the first instance given to the Boards themselves. As in the case of the agreements concerning tithe and certain other long-term financial obligations, it shocks the economist to see no means held in reserve, either to check fluctuations in the purchasing power of money or to correlate money wages with a standard of living. It is scarcely necessary in these pages to compare the present-day earnings of the agricultural worker with those ruling in other industries or occupations, but it may be stated in broad terms that the former has here little cause for complaint, for, according to statistics compiled by the Ministry of Health, the average increase in the rates of wages for adult workpeople in all trades in 1932, was no higher than some 72 per cent. above the pre-war level. If regarded, rightly, as a skilled worker, then the agriculturist is in a still better position than his opposite number in most trades, for in coal mining, engineering, building construction and most factory processes, the skilled employee finds himself only earning from 30 to 50 per cent. above the *datum*. It is the unskilled worker and the general, or manual, labourer who has succeeded in retaining increases that range from 80 to 100 per cent. All these figures, of course, exclude consideration of the prevailing standards of 1914, a point very relevant to the discussion, but one that is dealt with elsewhere in these Chapters.

The Wages Boards, in contradistinction to their predecessors thus firmly established, were enabled to tackle more fully the questions involved in the assessing of the more important benefits, with the result that the rent of a cottage became almost universally accepted as worth three shillings per week and full board and lodging as equivalent to fifteen shillings. The pre-war local variations in harvest rates and in customary payments were also perpetuated on scales conformable to ruling conditions, and the Boards found it possible, in all cases, to prescribe and enforce rates of remuneration for women, as well as for boys and girls of varying ages. Thus, the difficulties anticipated in these fields, when stable conditions were re-established, did not materialise.

In Scotland, where complete freedom in the matter of wage-fixing remained, rates have been maintained at a level quite commensurate with the increase in the cost of living, otherwise very closely retaining their original local variations. For adult male workers, cash ranged from 20*s.* per week in Banff and Aberdeen to 39*s.* in Renfrew, with, in addition, perquisites of 10*s.* to 14*s.* in most districts. In 1932, there were very few Counties in which a total wage of less than 30*s.* was being paid, and the comparatively high level of Scottish wages in general is illustrated by the map.

In Ireland, the average total remuneration for the Free State and Ulster (combined) declined from 26*s.* 3*d.* in 1925 to 23*s.* 6*d.* in 1932. Leinster (23*s.* 6*d.*) and Munster (24*s.* 3*d.*) were, in the latter named year, remunerating their workers better to the extent of a shilling or so than were Connaught or Ulster. None of these Irish figures is disproportionate to the pre-war rates found in that country, for they were, indeed, almost exactly double those ruling at the time of Wilson Fox's investigation thirty years earlier. It may, therefore, perhaps be argued that, although conditions in Ireland are ever a law unto themselves, British rates, if permanently decontrolled, would not have fallen below the comparable level represented by some 25*s.* to 28*s.*

Thus, in both Scotland and Ireland the restoration of free bargaining between master and man led to nothing worse than a reduction in money wages which left real wages slightly better than they were in 1914. The margin between that position and the 20 per cent. increase obtained by the English and the Welsh workers is the measure of the benefits derived by the latter from the statutory control of their wages. Ocular confirmation of the existence of this improvement can be obtained in every village of the country—better clothing for the members of the labourers' families, more, and better, food (butter has taken the place of margarine), more meat is consumed, indulgence in more amenities (motor cycles, wireless). None grudges this amelioration, but the employer, who generally failed to retain *his* improved status, points to his disproportionately inflated wages bill as presenting almost the only opening for reducing costs.

The National Farmers' Union estimated that the cost of agricultural labour had increased by 110 per cent. after the year 1929 and individual employers either endorsed that statement or held that it erred upon the conservative side. Independent investigators, in or about 1932, were prepared to agree that this item of expenditure, where conditions after the war remained unaltered, had, in the majority of cases, doubled. The explanation of the disparity between increase in wage rates (or in earnings) and in the cost of labour to the master lies, of course, principally in the reduced number of hours now normally worked and in the extra outlay involved in the payments for overtime. Whatever may have been the case just after the war, it is difficult, now, to subscribe to another explanatory statement, viz. that labour is not so efficient as it was: it is a cry that has echoed down the centuries. The seriousness of the situation to the employer can be appreciated when it is remembered that, in arable areas, the cost of manual labour now forms over one-third of all outgoings. Thus, in the latest enquiry carried out by the Cambridge Department of Agriculture (Farm Economics Branch, *Report* No. 19, 1932) covering, approximately, one thousand farms in the Eastern Counties, it was found that labour represented 37·7 per cent. of all costs. That this expenditure has formed a steadily increasing proportion of farm outgoings is evidenced by the following Table, which provides an interesting conspectus of the situation over a period of about fifty years.

Distribution of outgoings

	1884–93 5 farms	1919 325 farms	1926 13 farms	1931 984 farms
Labour	20·5	24·0	28·9	37·7
Livestock, feeding stuffs, machinery and manures	52·1	51·0	43·6	35·7
Rent	17·3	10·0	11·6	13·0
Rates	1·8	1·6	1·6	—
Other expenses	8·3	13·4	14·3	13·6

The two earliest examples are extracted from the *Reports* of the Commission previously referred to in the Chapters upon Taxation. The increase in labour costs was steady up to some six or seven years ago, this item having risen from some 20 per cent. of the total to almost 30 per cent.; but, after the effective reintroduction of State control, the rise was more rapid. It must be noted, however, that, as other sources of expenditure declined, e.g. purchases of requirements and local rates, the *relative* importance of the labour bill assumed larger proportions, but this does not detract from the seriousness of the position that faces employers of agricultural labour. It is scarcely to be wondered at that, as a result, they are, upon occasion, either demanding the repeal of Wages legislation or else dramatically threatening a wholesale reduction in employment. That neither policy will be implemented is certain; but what repercussions there may be in the future economy of arable farming is another question that time alone will solve.

Agriculture, as an occupation, is peculiar in that it affords seasonal work for casual helpers; most trades are susceptible to recognised fluctuations caused by climatic and other conditions, but there are few that, at times of increasing output, can absorb many unskilled workers. Farmers, however, the world over, are in the habit of accepting almost any type of assistance for some two months in the summer and for shorter periods at certain other times of the year. Abroad, much of this help comes from the immigration of workers from neighbouring States; in France the Spaniard comes North in June and July and the Swiss and Italian cross the Alps, in Germany Poles flock over the Eastern frontier, and, with others, penetrate even to Denmark, in Canada and the United States elements of the town population move Westward for the harvest season. In the British Isles, however, our operations are on a comparatively small scale and our distances much less, so that regular migrations have been the exception. True, before 1915 gangs of Irish labourers visited parts of England, and, to a lesser extent, Scotland for harvest work, but their services have since been dispensed with, although they have occasionally returned to the Eastern Counties in connection with field work upon sugar-beet. In the old days they earned considerable sums of money, working under their own foremen upon piece-work, and were generally well-conducted. Present times afford no such example of male labour migrating on any considerable scale, but fruit and hop picking cause annual movements of women from London and other centres to Kent, Cambridgeshire and certain West of England Counties. The definition of casual or of temporary workers in agriculture is difficult, and results in ambiguities in the statistical Tables of labour employed in different parts of the country or at different seasons. For, although not subject to wide movement, labour, within quite short distances, is often migratory. Potato setting or raising, and fruit or vegetable production may alter the relative density and type of labour employed in two neighbouring villages within a short period of time. A farmer may be recorded as having work for ten men one week, six of whom he has taken on by a weekly engagement, and the following week he appears as an employer of four—the others having moved to a holding the nature of whose soil caused a delay in commencing some similar operation. As a class, temporary labour has steadily diminished during the last decade and now embraces only 100,000 persons, as compared with over 180,000 in 1921: the diminution has been in each category of sex and of age, but is most marked in that comprising men under twenty-one years of age, where there are now found only one-third of those figuring in the 1921 returns. So far as different types of farm affect employment of casual or of temporary workers, there is abundant evidence to show that the larger the unit the less the proportionate demand for this form of assistance. Thus, the Cambridge rural economists have recorded in *An Economic Survey of Hertfordshire Agriculture* (p. 66), the following relative decreases in "man weeks" of casual employment—farms of 20–50 acres, 11; of 100–150 acres, 21; of 150–300 acres, 27; and of over 300 acres, 57 man weeks. One-half of all the farms studied needed casual labour in June and in August, and one-third of them in July, September and October.

If the present affords no example of migration on a large scale, we have only to look at East Anglia from 1840 onwards to see the movement of labour artificially encouraged under the worst possible conditions. In the fen districts of North Cambridgeshire, Lincolnshire and West Norfolk a system of supplying seasonal labour to the large farms peculiar to that region had by then come into existence. These "labour-gangs", as they were termed, mainly consisted of women and children (although men worked indiscriminately in them also) whose labour was directed and farmed out by an overseer or gang-master. The latter lived on the profits he could make by entering into contracts for piece-work, or, occasionally, by reserving for himself a halfpenny per head for each of those under him. The system obviously lay open to abuses of every sort, and complaints of the brutality of gang-masters and of the physical and moral condition of their employees were always rife. From the farmer's point of view the existence of these gangs had certain advantages. He knew exactly what a given operation would cost him, he had no responsibility for feeding or housing the members of the gang (who returned to their homes daily), and, in case of bad weather, he was not paying for labour that was unremunerative. From the nature of the case the work was well supervised and quickly performed. Because this system was found to be paying its promoters well, farmers themselves turned to it, and organised what came to be known as "private" gangs. Hence, by 1867, several thousands of persons of both sexes, and of all ages, were found to be thus employed under conditions calling for public attention. A Gangs Act was passed, which drastically altered the form of labour-contracting, provided for the licensing of gang-masters, for the exclusion of children below eight years of age, and for the division of the sexes into separate parties. These gangs had for some thirty years provided seasonal labour in a part of the country where special conditions applied; elsewhere they were not called into existence. They flourished best where distances were great, villages under-built and large farms the rule. After the passing of the Gangs Act attention was paid to the better provision of cottages and this, combined with the subsequent Education Acts, effectively put a stop to the organised and mobile labour of women and children, in, frequently, deplorable conditions.

Acting as a reservoir to give winter employment, forests form an asset that is lacking in the greater part of the United Kingdom. Compared with farm-land, a given acreage of woods or of forest can naturally afford little regular occupation, but on the Continent it often provides the means of earning money at seasons when work on the land is otherwise out of the question. In the Eastern Counties of England and in some other localities there are now, however, similar opportunities being provided upon a small scale, for, in the Forestry Commission's newly planted areas in Norfolk and Suffolk, some winter employment is available for farm workers and, where Forest Holdings have been set up, the intention is that part-time work under the Commission shall be available for their occupiers. Sugar-beet factories also provide, again mainly in the arable districts, sheltered work at seasons when outdoor occupation is difficult to secure and unpleasant to perform.

Migration within the country, in the shape of permanent transference, was an economic weapon which other leaders of labour besides Canon Girdlestone attempted to use, but it was two-edged, for Farmers' Unions could retaliate by invoking the help of other classes of workers from a distance. Emigration itself was utilised by the Canon and his colleagues, as a factor in their fight for higher wages, and they claimed that several hundred thousand agricultural labourers had gone overseas at the instigation of the Unions. The number of British emigrants after 1870 was upwards of 100,000 per annum, and a large percentage of the men concerned were land workers, but it is highly probable that they would have emigrated in any case, and equally certain that Union funds did not provide the bulk of their expenses. For the next thirty years agriculture in these Islands could only support a diminishing number of labourers, as was shown by the Table upon p. 238. Those who did not leave their country are popularly supposed to have migrated to the towns. This statement requires a certain amount of modification, for it is often erroneously assumed to connote deserted villages and labour-bereft farmers. The census returns, however, show that, whilst all urban areas were rapidly growing, most rural districts were not actually declining in numbers, but were at least maintaining a stationary population. This has been equally true during the last forty years for while in 1891 the rural population of England and Wales was 8,107,000, in 1901, 7,470,000, in 1911, 7,907,000, in 1921, 7,851,000, by 1931 it had risen to 7,999,765. The proportions borne to the total population by urban and rural dwellers were, in 1931, 80 per cent. and 20 per cent. respectively (1891, 72 and 28; 1901, 77 and 23; 1911, 78·1 and 21·9; 1921, 79·3 and 20·7). The phenomenon is widespread, as the following extract from a *Bulletin* of the International Institute of Agriculture shows:

> In every country which has available statistics it is found that the rural population increases less rapidly than that of the towns. The percentage of the rural population to the total number of inhabitants has perceptibly diminished, and almost everywhere the *relative* smallness of the rural population is apparent. It is only in some countries long cultivated that a depopulation of the country districts in the *absolute* significance of the word has been noted.

In so far as the actual numbers of male workers in regular agricultural employment during the last decade are concerned, the accompanying Table demonstrates that, even here, there has been but a small decline.

Regular male workers over 21 *years of age in England and Wales*

1921	1923	1925	1927	1929	1931
457,000	427,000	441,000	453,000	452,000	435,000

In Great Britain there was admittedly a transference of many rural workers to the towns after 1870, but if one could visualise the whole scene one would see the older folk staying on in the villages and the younger men, who were surplus to the lessening demands of the land, divided into two parties—one setting forth abroad to continue an agricultural career, the other moving to the towns to adopt some other profession. This incidentally gives rise to the criticism so often heard that the younger generation, when it does elect to remain on the land, is not as painstaking or conscientious as its forbears. Certain manual operations are nowadays admittedly distasteful to the younger men—thatching and mowing are given as instances of this—who naturally prefer to take charge of machinery. But exactly the same complaints have been made by farmer witnesses before all the Commissions that have sat since 1833, and, if in every instance they were true, the standard of labour to-day would be farcically low. Incidentally, it must be observed that the *laudator temporis acti* seems always to have been recruited from the ranks of agriculture!

There is one factor that must always be kept in mind when discussing the question of the alleged attraction exercised by the towns upon rural labourers. Whilst in many cases town life does genuinely appeal to those reared in the country, yet, on the other hand, there are countless townsfolk who leave highly paid employment to seek a healthier and quieter life on the land—incidentally often diminishing the supply of cottages in the villages or raising their rents; again, the last decade has witnessed a great expansion in the numbers of town workers who, while living in the country, find it possible to travel daily to places of employment. There are also countrymen who thankfully return to their villages after experiencing the nature of urban employment. Enhanced cash wages do not necessarily connote a higher standard of living, and factory life may well be more monotonous than field labour, and not as healthy. The census figures for 1931 do not bear out the "deserted village" theory, and it would seem as if modern improvements in the means of locomotion, combined with the winning of the weekly half-holiday, have brought the amenities of town life sufficiently near the villages to make the majority of young farm hands think twice before removing themselves and their families into the heart of large cities.

There is a curious feature of the acrimonious discussions that broke out at frequent intervals during the last century concerning the pros and cons of country life; the horrible conditions of existence to be found therein were expatiated upon and, almost in the same breath, followed the claim that the country produced the strongest and healthiest citizens. In 1842 the Poor Law Commissioners issued a *Report* on the condition of the labouring population, which evidenced a very serious state of affairs throughout rural England. Overcrowding was rife, sanitation was practically non-existent, and immorality rampant. During the next three decades similar investigations had led to similar verdicts. But when comparison was extended to the quantity and type of food obtained by urban and rural workers, the other side of the question was opened up, for medical enquiries elicited that the subsistence minimum for an able-bodied man, both in regard to carbonaceous and nitrogenous food, was, for agricultural labourers, exceeded by a considerably larger margin than existed in the case of the majority of industrial workers. Individual Counties varied greatly in this matter, but, as would be expected, conditions were generally best in the North and worst in the South-West. The reservations made at the time were that, whilst the men folk might be sufficiently nourished, in the case of those with large families the pinch was felt by the children. Matters have greatly improved in the last two generations, and, as a result of the powers conferred on County Councils, housing conditions in the country are now generally good. Life in the open air must cancel any disadvantages that accrue from any lower standard of life, for the records of all countries show that in time of war a higher proportion of what were, in England, designated A 1 men comes from rural than from urban districts; the same is true of peace conditions, for the majority of the recruits for the police force, where physique is the main requirement, are secured in the country. Again, when National Health Insurance was introduced, it soon became apparent that the country was contributing unduly towards the benefits derived by the townsman. The Registrar-General's returns show that the annual death-rate in rural districts is well below that found in urban; this is also true of the individual rates applicable to children under one year of age, of infantile mortality in general, and of deaths from infectious diseases, as well as from tuberculosis.

Any present-day discussion of the value of the labour of women on the land is apt to be complicated by the introduction of reference to their services in this capacity during the war. But the women who helped the farmer from 1915 to 1919 can no more be classified as trained agricultural workers than could those of their sisters, who temporarily took men's posts in numerous other occupations, claim to be tradesmen. In all such cases theirs was emergency work, and it would be unfair critically to assay its value in after years, but it may be noticed that when fifty years earlier the labour-gangs were at the height of their power it was claimed that young and active women were equally as efficient as men and equally capable of carrying out a full day's work. The labour of village women in agriculture has principally been of a seasonal character, save in the North, where greater advantage is taken of their regular services. In 1931 some 93,000 women and girls were recorded as working upon the land in England and Wales, of whom 64,000 were regularly employed, the remainder being classed as "casual". The employment of children upon the land was gradually and progressively discouraged as the School Boards gained strength. Complaints were frequently heard from farmers in the 'seventies of the last century, when restrictions were placed on the work of children below certain ages (unless a minimum number of attendances at school could be proved), that the former tidiness of their land was lacking. Child labour had been to a great extent utilised for weeding and stone-picking—operations that tended subsequently to be neglected; it was also objected that education caused boys with ambition to leave their homes and take up work in the towns.

The amenities of the labourer's life are often spoken of as if they lacked much that is to be found at the disposal of the town artisan. But, if one examines his present-day position one is bound to modify such views. It is certainly true that by 1932 the ratio of population to houses was lower in the country than in the towns, for the majority of villages had by then been supplied with officially erected dwellings, and the census of 1911 had already shown that overcrowding existed mainly in urban centres—and this state post-war conditions had aggravated. One of the minor advantages accruing from war control was the Rents Restriction Act and the consequent certainty of tenure for agricultural workers, which made it no longer possible for cases of eviction to be carried out on flimsy excuses; on the other hand, employers occasionally found themselves saddled with individuals as tenants, whom, as employees, they had discharged. There is, fortunately, no occasion in these pages to enter upon a defence of the "tied cottage", but it will suffice to point to history and expediency as together forming valid objections to any sudden revolt from conditions that are universal wherever livestock forms an important element in rural economy.

Allotments are really the countryman's overflow gardens (despite the circumstances attendant on their inception and despite their subsequent widespread adoption by urban dwellers), and in the country the supply has seldom fallen short of the demand; in fact, the great increase in their numbers from 1915 to 1920 was entirely due to the townsman's demand to be supplied with the countryman's facilities for growing his own vegetables. If the size of rural allotments is unduly increased they cannot be efficiently tended by their owners, who must accordingly choose between neglecting their plots or losing wages. This is a factor that is frequently overlooked when the provision of more numerous or larger allotments for farm labourers is urged.

The benefits of State unemployment assurance have hitherto not been applied to the agricultural labourer, but this is mainly because both his own representatives and his employers have in the past agreed that the extension to him of the existing scheme would be alike unpopular and unfair in regard to its financial obligations. Unemployment in agriculture is not in normal times one of the fears that haunt its regular and able-bodied workers; nevertheless, when the Unemployment Insurance Commission was sitting in the autumn of 1932, it specifically called for expert evidence upon this matter. Of two witnesses summoned before it, one—Mr C. S. Orwin, Director of the Agricultural Economics Research Institute at Oxford—stated that, in his opinion, it would be advantageous for the industry upon occasion to be able to stand off its employees in the knowledge that they would be provided for by insurance. Sir William Dampier, Secretary of the Agricultural Research Council, was the other witness and he, also, but somewhat doubtfully, endorsed this view.

He expressed the opinion that anything which would tend to retain the rigidity of wage rates should, in such times of falling values, be deprecated and he would, on those grounds, prefer to wait until the existing Insurance Acts were modified before adding rural workers to the ranks of their beneficiaries. He further gave it as his opinion that both the Farmers' Union and workers' organisations were wrong in their conclusions—the former believing that employers would lose by such a policy and the latter that its members had everything to gain thereby. Sir William believed that the masters would gain on economic grounds, viz. that, in the arable districts, they would be able to dispense with anything up to a quarter of their men in winter and that, financially, workers in regular employment would be in a worse position. A memorandum prepared by the Ministry of Labour stated that there was no reason to suppose that the administrative machinery could not be adapted to cope with the new entrants, but that, on the side of benefits, there might be difficulty in providing for claimants tests of inability to obtain alternative forms of work. There, for the present, the whole question rests, but it can only be a matter of time before these privileges, in some form or another, are extended to include rural workers, for the principles and the spirit of insurance are permeating more and more into every walk of life.

Provision for sickness and old age in these Islands had first been made privately, and afterwards, publicly. The village clubs and Friendly Societies deserved much credit for carrying on the business of insurance against sickness and for providing other minor benefits under financial and actuarial conditions that were often the reverse of sound. The National Health Insurance Act of 1910 made the continued existence of such bodies unnecessary, and the provision of old-age pensions transferred to the national exchequer the duty of providing for the rural labourer in old age.

The "ladder" is always available for the keen and industrious worker to ascend, since County Councils normally give preference to men of this type when selecting applicants for State-provided Small Holdings. Scholarships to secondary schools and to the Universities are available for his sons and his daughters. The evidence adduced before recent Commissions, and that contained in official *Reports*, all points to the frequency with which labourers become tenant-farmers or occupying owners.

Finally, his is a skilled trade. It seems absurd that this should have to be emphasised, but it is necessary to do so, for it has become the custom during the last century to speak of the "agricultural labourer" as synonymous with the lowest type of worker—this is doubtless attributable partly to ignorance of the nature of his duties and partly to subconscious association with his small cash-wages. In reality he is master of several trades; for the same "general" labourer is expected to undertake such diverse operations as ploughing, hedging and ditching, rick and stack building; he must be familiar with many different types of moving and of stationary machinery, and must be capable of caring for and managing horses and other livestock. That well-known authority, the late K. J. J. Mackenzie, once expressed the situation vividly, by citing four typical farm operations. Thus he said (of ploughing a ten-acre field):

> You give him two or more horses and a somewhat complicated implement. You ask him to cut off from the surface of mother earth 880 strips of soil. These 880 strips have to be of equal depth and width. He has to cut them off in a way that he can turn them one on to the other to form parallel lines across the field; he puts all that is found on the surface under ground, and he cuts off all weed roots springing from the earth beneath his work. Further, he has to lay these 880 strips together in such a way that the greatest possible area of surface is exposed to the action of the weather. Again—take a stack in which is stored the corn from the ten-acre field—do the scoffers realise there are over 40,000 bundles of corn—straw and grain—from six to eighteen pounds in weight, that have to be built up and fitted in to one another in such a way that the stack does not fall down, and the rain is not only shot off the roof, but is kept out from the sides for months after the stack is set up? On one acre of land you plant a strip about three and two-thirds of a mile long. In due course this strip becomes covered with a braid of small plants numbering some two hundred thousand, mixed with innumerable weeds. You give the labourer a hoe, and ask him to single out and leave standing, at equal distances from one another, some twenty thousand small turnip plants, and at the same time to kill all the weeds.

Lastly, in the case of the self-binder he sits "all day on a complicated machine actuating three levers, watching five distinct pieces of machinery in motion, and guiding two or three horses". Nowadays, too, the care of tractors and of other power machinery—even electrical in type—falls to his lot.

Each of the above pieces of work requires years of practice and of expert knowledge. Yet his "skilled" rival in workshop or factory in most cases performs year in and year out the same repetitive work. The mechanic in charge of a lathe is a mere attendant, the bricklayer always performs similar operations with the same tools, the shoemaker sticks to his last—but only the farm labourer is capable of turning his hand, at a moment's notice, to a dozen different branches of his profession. Moreover, his Union, if he belongs to one, does not forbid him freedom of action in this respect, whilst the urban Unionist is compelled to confine himself to one particular section of his trade.

On the part of certain sections of the public there is a growing tendency to intervene in village life. It is declared that a "brighter village" will transform and elevate the farm labourer, and that this essential object can be achieved by the lavish provision of village institutes, libraries, clubs and so forth. On similar lines are found references to some mysterious period in the history of the country when England was "merrie", and, apparently, all the villagers incessantly performed Morris dances on the green. Whilst the reasonable provision of such facilities is desirable, it is also possible to lay too much stress upon this side of rural life. The countryman appreciates certain elements of town life, but he generally prefers to have the opportunity of visiting them himself and of seeing new faces and fresh sights. The urbanisation of the country, for it is nothing more, is undesirable from every point of view and is not always appreciated by those whom it is intended to benefit. Far better than bringing the town into the country is the provision of quick means of transit between the two, so that the country can enjoy, upon occasion, the change to town life. Artificial encouragement of a closer *rapprochement* between labourer and farmer will not hasten the agricultural millennium, and history is perversely distorted when its aid is sought to prove that mediaeval villagers had more time on hand to spend in social enjoyment than have their present-day successors.

The history of the remuneration and social life of the land worker has been briefly reviewed. It remains to examine what use is made of his labour by employers, and to discuss its relative value in different places and in various branches of the trade. First take what is always described as the "density of labour". The following Table appeared in the *Report on the Agricultural Output of Great Britain*, in connection with the Census of Production, and related to conditions in 1908.

Workers per hundred acres of cultivated land (i.e. land under crops and grass) in Great Britain

Size group of holdings (acres)	Permanent			Temporary		
	Males	Females	Total	Males	Females	Total
1–5	8·0	5·4	13·4	2·0	0·6	2·6
5–50	4·3	2·2	6·5	0·8	0·3	1·1
50–300	2·5	0·8	3·3	0·3	0·1	0·4
Over 300	2·3	0·3	2·6	0·2	0·1	0·3

It should be noted that these figures relate to Great Britain, and not merely to England and Wales, and that farmers' families are included among the permanent workers, as this has an important bearing on the results given for the two smaller size-groups. The fact at once emerges that the larger the holding the smaller are its requirements per acre in the way of labour, but it is also apparent that the labour of the occupier and of his wife and family is responsible, to a large extent, for the preponderance of workers on holdings of the smallest class. The personal factor is introduced in the case of those holdings in which the labour is confined to one or two employees, for, in such cases, it is held that the constant presence and power of supervision exercised by the master makes for more efficient work. Employment on small farms is certainly not popular with labourers, but the output of work secured from individuals on different sizes of holdings is not expressible in statistical form. For a general review of the data concerned above one cannot do better than quote from the *Report* itself:

On the smallest holdings—1 to 5 acres—the number of persons permanently engaged (including members of the occupier's family, but excluding temporary labour) is 13·4 per 100 acres, the average size of a holding of this group being 3·2 acres. There are about 31 occupiers to every 100 acres. Including the occupier, therefore, it appears that 100 acres divided into holdings of this size would permanently employ 45 persons, and provide partial employment for between two and three more. Or, put in another way, it seems that holdings of this size will, on an average, provide continuous employment for one person to slightly more than two acres of "cultivated land" or, if the rough grazings attached to the holdings are taken into account, one person to about six acres. It is necessary to remember that, of the total land occupied in these small parcels (including the rough grazings), only about one-ninth is under arable cultivation. In the next size-group—5 to 50 acres—the "density" of labour is considerably less, being in fact about half. About five of these small holdings would occupy 100 acres of cultivated land so that the total number of persons engaged, including the occupiers themselves, would be 11·1 (including temporary labourers, 12·2) per 100 acres, being about one person for every nine acres. If the rough grazings attached to these holdings are reckoned, the ratio is about one person to 18 acres. The proportion of arable land in this class of small holding is about 17 per cent. of the total area, including the rough grazings. For all holdings classed as exceeding 50 acres the "density" of labour appears on the average to be much the same, being slightly less on farms above 300 acres than on those between 50 and 300 acres. Taking into account the rough grazings attached to holdings above 50 acres, it appears that they employ on an average one person to about 35 acres, the proportion of arable land being about 38 per cent. Incidentally, attention may be directed to the distribution of arable land as between the different size-groups. As a rough generalisation it may be said that the larger the holding the greater the proportion of arable, or, in other words, that small holdings are preponderatingly pasture. This fact tends to accentuate the greater density of labour on the small farms. If the proportion of arable were as great on the small as on the large farms, it is evident that the number of persons engaged upon them would be very largely increased.

The following is an adaptation from two tables contained in the Board of Agriculture's *Report on Wages and Conditions of Employment in Agriculture* (Cd. 24, 1919).

Area	Persons engaged per 100 acres of cultivated land	Persons employed per 100 acres of cultivated land	Persons engaged per holding
I A Bedford, Huntingdon, Cambridge, Isle of Ely, Suffolk, Essex, Hertford, Middlesex, London	6·2	4·6	4·7
I B Norfolk, Lincoln, Yorkshire East Riding	4·2	3·3	3·2
II A Kent, Surrey, Sussex, Berkshire, Hampshire, Isle of Wight	5·9	4·2	4·1
II B Nottingham, Leicester, Rutland, Northampton, Peterborough, Buckingham, Oxford, Warwick	3·9	2·8	2·9
III A Salop, Worcester, Gloucester, Wiltshire, Monmouth, Hereford	4·0	2·6	2·6
III B Somerset, Dorset, Devon, Cornwall ...	4·1	2·3	2·6
IV A Northumberland, Durham, Yorkshire North and West Ridings	3·5	1·9	2·1
IV B Cumberland, Westmorland, Lancashire, Cheshire, Derby, Stafford	4·9	2·7	2·4
England	4·5	3·2	2·9

The expression "persons engaged" included of course farmers themselves and the members of their families, while "persons employed" covered workers of both sexes. Here again it is obvious that the density of labour was mainly determined by the preponderance of arable land, and to a lesser extent by the nature of the soil. Such Counties as Bedfordshire and Kent for instance maintained additional labour on their market-gardens and hopfields respectively, and Middlesex supported 7·5 persons per holding while Westmorland had 2·2. Where milk production was extensively carried on it resulted in giving work to more persons per acre than did the business of sheep and cattle raising, as witness the comparison between divisions IIIB or IVB and IVA. In such districts, again, holdings were apt to be small, and therefore the labour per farm unit was further affected.

It will be observed that England, as a whole, provided work for 4·5 persons of all types per hundred acres of cultivated land. Comparative figures for foreign countries were issued by the "Land Enquiry Committee", but, as is pointed out in the Chapter on "Statistics", there are many pitfalls encountered in such a proceeding—e.g. what exactly comprises "agriculture", "cultivated land" and "persons employed" in other countries? The densities in question, however, were confidently recorded by that body as varying from eighteen persons per hundred acres in Austria down to seven in Denmark. They should be received with caution. One must also guard against generalisations on these grounds in favour of Small Holdings, for labour density is but one of many factors affecting the economy of large and small farms, all of which have been dealt with in Chapters V and VI.

More recent official statistics, viz. those contained in the report of the second Census of Production, in 1925, gave the density of all workers for England as unchanged at 3·2 per hundred acres. Here the complete range was from 19·37 in the case of fruit and vegetable holdings down to 2·31 for farms which were mainly under grass. Individual Counties varied from Middlesex, with 11·6 persons, down to Northumberland with 1·9.

Still later figures, in this case relating to the arable land of East Anglia, are available in *Report* 19 of the Cambridge University Farm Economics Branch where, on p. 21, will be found, for 1931, this

Table, with which has been amalgamated a statement showing the gross output per £100 spent on manual labour. Both sets of figures have been quoted in Chapter VI.

Size group (acres)	Manual workers per 100 acres	Gross output per £100 manual labour
20–50	5·6	£187
50–100	4·2	£183
100–150	3·6	£203
150–300	2·8	£212
300–500	2·3	£215
Over 500	2·4	£215

Next to the number of hands employed, the most important factor for their master is the question of the cost of their labour to him. Movements in the rates of weekly remuneration of farm workers have previously been examined, but there is another aspect of the question, and that is the labour bill per acre of farm-land. Various elaborate calculations have been made on these lines at different periods, and for separate types of farm—e.g. Caird in 1886 estimated wages at £1 per acre for arable land and 5*s.* for grass, Craigie in 1878 had given 30*s.* and 9*s.* 6*d.* respectively. Curtler in 1916 published, through the medium of the International Agricultural Institute, a most comprehensive enquiry of this nature, but in 1919 the Wages Board held that such findings were "not entirely reliable", owing to the impossibility of excluding from their scope certain non-relevant factors. With this proviso borne in mind, we may briefly glance at Curtler's figures, and perhaps accept them as providing an approximate indication of average conditions then pertaining. The term "wages" here implies total emoluments, and includes payments made both to women and children and to temporary and casual workers. The average wages per acre for 308 farms of a typical character were £1. 5*s.* 7*d.* in 1913–14, the lowest (found on stock-raising farms) being exactly £1 and the highest (on corn-producing farms) £1. 7*s.* 10*d.* The enquiry also extended to holdings specialising in potatoes, where the wages bill was £2. 15*s.* 6*d.*; in fruit growing it was £11. 4*s.*, and in hopfields no less than £24. 14*s.* 10*d.* In comparing his results with those secured by the earlier enquiries, Curtler came to the conclusion that the labour bill per acre had varied little in the course of thirty years; yet he calculated that machinery had, in that space of time, effected a reduction in manual labour to the extent of some 50 per cent.; but "the land is not so carefully tilled" and "is often labour starved", therefore, "the labourer does less work for more money than he did a generation ago".

Again, it was suggested by the same writer that higher wages were, in the long run, more economical than low; for, on twenty-one farms in Lincolnshire, where wages were £1. 0*s.* 11*d.*, the labour bill per acre was £1. 6*s.* 3*d.*, and on thirty-one Norfolk holdings, with wages at 17*s.* 7*d.*, the bill per acre was £1. 13*s.* 8*d.* These samples were really too small to afford safe grounds for such deductions, and also for the corollary statement that, because of their higher wages, Lincolnshire labourers produced better and heavier crops. The outturn per acre in Norfolk was in the case of almost all standard crops admittedly inferior to that achieved in the three divisions of the former County, but should not the credit rather be given to the soil? Curtler boldly said "of wheat and barley the highly paid labourers produce more than the low paid, although the latter are more favoured by climate. In the case of oats there is little to choose. In the production of potatoes the superiority clearly lies with the high wages, as it does in that of swedes and turnips...in the growing of hay, especially from rotation grasses, the well paid labourers easily beat their less fortunate rivals". Surely, a possible alternative explanation may have been that the comparative inferiority of the Norfolk land necessitated more continuous or prolonged operations than were required on the fen soil that predominated in Lincolnshire? Or perhaps the whole question was misjudged by the transposition of cause and effect: for, if Lincolnshire labourers were intrinsically better workers than those of Norfolk, this would have resulted in their receiving higher wages, and might have reduced the cost of labour per acre proportionally, as we have already seen could be the case in the North of England. This would partially, but not of course entirely, explain the phenomenon.

A few years later R. J. Thompson, in a paper read to the Royal Statistical Society (March, 1926), made an estimate of £2. 10*s.* per acre in the case of Great Britain and at the same time, figures prepared at Cambridge—and based upon actual costings but relating, however, to a period before the reintroduction of Wages Boards—indicated a sum of £2. 15*s.* as applicable to arable holdings. Considering the widely different circumstances, neither of these figures is greatly out of harmony with those referred to above, as admittedly wage rates had more than doubled in the intervening years. Thompson also effected comparison with similar expenditure in Denmark, and was able to show that, on the average, the cost per acre was there considerably in excess of ours, e.g. making allowance for the prevailing rate of exchange, it cost in 1922–23 some £3. 8*s*. per acre for the labour of hired workers. In England, the work of the Wages Board was reflected in this field, for Cambridge costings gave an average of £3. 14*s*. 4*d*. per acre for 1927–28 and of £3. 13*s*. 9*d*. in 1928–29, since when there has been little or no change to record. These figures afford corroboration from an independent angle of the farmer's statement that his outlay upon labour has been at least doubled as a result of the war. In the case of root-crops such "per acre" costs are high, amounting to £10 or £11 for potatoes or sugar-beet.

Expressed alternatively, in terms of "man hours per ten acres of crop", the various field products make the following divergent demands: sugar-beet, 2095; potatoes, 1802; mangolds, 1614; winter beans, 608; spring oats, 435; spring barley, 410; wheat, 342; winter oats, 309; hay-making, 194 (W. H. Kirkpatrick, *Report* 14, Farm Economics Branch, Cambridge University Department of Agriculture). Perhaps more than any other item of expenditure, these figures are affected by the predominant size of field. In the case of sugar-beet cultivation the variation has been shown by R. McG. Carslaw to range inversely, thus:

Size of field (acres)	Labour cost per acre
5 or less	£11. 13*s*.
6–10	£11. 8*s*.
11–15	£10. 2*s*.
Over 15	£9. 19*s*.

This is yet another argument in favour of large fields for arable operations, supplementary to the familiar appeal resting upon the more economic use that can, in these circumstances, be made of machinery and the smaller non-productive charges that follow upon a reduction in the total length of hedges and ditches.

The seasonal distribution of farm labour has received considerable attention during recent years, and the diagram given below (borrowed from W. H. Kirkpatrick's above referred to monograph) will illustrate the principal month to month fluctuations evidenced in typical East Anglian conditions at the present time.

Enough has probably been said to indicate the difficulties attendant on any examination into the comparative labour expenses relating to different types of holding even when cost-accounts are available. Subsequent investigations have tended to show that, of the three factors involved—the size of the farm, the percentage of the land under the plough and the type of farming practised—the last has most influence on the expenses per acre for labour.

What is known as labour's share in the business of agriculture remains for consideration. The pre-war Census of Production gave

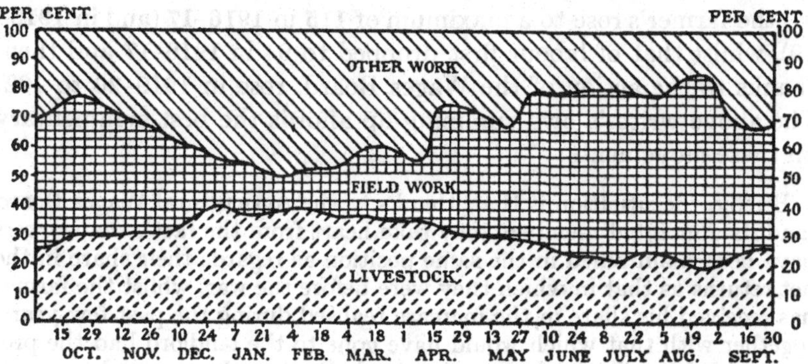

Seasonal distribution of manual labour

£129 as the gross value of the output per person permanently employed in agriculture. This figure was arrived at by dividing the value of everything produced on the farms of Great Britain (whether sold off or consumed thereon) by the number of employees who had assisted in its raising. If farmers themselves were included the corresponding sum was £90. By themselves these figures were meaningless except as an indication of the low values of agricultural, as compared with secondary, products, but it has since been possible to supplement them. Thus, in *Four Years' Farming in East Anglia* (previously referred to) there are Tables which give corresponding data relating to different types and sizes of farms in recent years. On heavy land, a typical figure in the period 1923–27 was £130, on relatively light-land holdings it was £160, which those undertakings below 120 acres in extent raised to £173. The average for all farms falling under scrutiny was £144—not very different from the 1908 value, recorded above.

Orwin (*Farming Costs*) and others have shown the approximate division between landlord, tenant and labourer of what is known as the net returns of the industry. Net, or social, output represents the amount accruing to the farm as a whole. On this basis Orwin showed that, in pre-war years, 40 per cent. went to the farmer, 20 per cent. to the landlord, and, again, 40 per cent. to the worker. In a later memorandum the same author traced the movements in the relative distribution of these percentages during the war and post-war period. In this case, assuming 1913–14 to be represented by 100, the landlord's share progressively declined, until in 1918–19 it stood at 87, the farmer's rose to a maximum of 115 in 1916–17 (and in 1918–19), whilst that of labour first dropped to 94 in 1916–17 and then, thanks to the action of the Wages Board, rose in 1919–20 to 102. The above writer's own summing-up affords the best commentary on these movements:

> Briefly, the situation is that, thanks to the Agricultural Wages Board (and its appointed members may take heart from the fact), the workers have been maintained in the same position as regards their share in the net returns as that in which they were before the war, whilst the farmer has received his share in the increase realised during the past few years, together with that which would have gone to the landlord had the pre-war scale of distribution been maintained. Rents and wages under normal conditions are slow to adjust themselves to changes in farming fortune, and, except in a time of violent economic upheaval, it is right that this should be so, for if the landlord may be regarded as a debenture holder, and labour as a preference shareholder, then the farmer, as the ordinary or deferred shareholder, has to bear the brunt, and if he must take the kicks, so also is he entitled to the halfpence.

If it be desired to bring these figures more up to date, certain material collected in the previously mentioned Cambridge *Survey of the Eastern Counties* may, with considerable reservation, be adduced. Those arable Counties, in the year 1931, revealed a net output of £360 per hundred acres of crops and grass, to which must be added another £36 representing the value of tenants' drawings in kind. Preliminarily, of this total sum (£396), 65 per cent. went to labour (including family labour, other than that of the occupier himself), 24 per cent., or £97, was handed to the landowner—out of which he had to meet taxes, tithe and maintenance charges—and 11 per cent.

was retained by the tenant. This equivalent sum (£43) was required to reimburse the latter for his own labour and to meet interest upon all forms of working capital. If the necessary adjustments are made, which involve a reduction of gross rents by three-fifths to cover the outgoings just mentioned, then both net output and the landlord's share of it are reduced by £60 per 100 acres and the respective partners' shares become: labour, 76 per cent.; landlord, 11 per cent.; tenant, 13 per cent. Finally, expressed as index numbers upon Orwin's (1913 = 100) base, the figures become 55 in the case of the landlord's share, 32·5 in that of the tenant and 190 for labour. The situation may be put into tabular form, thus:

	Landlord	Farmer	Worker
1913–14	100	100	100
1918–19	87	115	102*
1931	55	32·5	190

* 1919–20.

In 1922 the Labour party's election programme contained the promise that, if that body were returned to power, the landlord would "be required to sacrifice rents rather than to ask the farm workers to accept starvation wages". The whole history of agriculture in this and other countries negatived the feasibility of an economic burden being thus, for more than a very brief period, shirked by one partner in the industry. The return to those who advance the bulk of the capital employed has always been smaller than from other investments, and its complete cessation would have made the final plight of the other two partners still worse. Since then a decade of increasing losses to the tenant and of reduced rents for the landlord has been accompanied by a substantial increase, not only in money rates, but, disproportionately, in the spending power of the third partner. The qualities, naturally attributable to such a trinity of interests, have been severely strained, and it is earnestly to be hoped that the many steps taken by the State to alleviate the situation will be in the near future effective. British agriculture has in the past attracted landowners, despite the pecuniary return it offered; tenants, despite constant anxiety; and labour, despite low cash wages combined with heavy toil; and, if all its members will pull together, it should still be possible for it, once rehabilitated, to regain its attractive force.

Chapter XIII

MARKETS AND MARKETING

Origin of fairs and markets; Defoe's account of Sturbridge Fair; the Royal Commission on markets; Irish conditions; weights and measures; methods of selling grain in this country and in the United States; marketing of livestock and sales by weight; the Federal Farm Board and "orderly" marketing; Wheat Pools in Canada and the Dominions; questions involved in the marketing of livestock; sales "by eye" and by weight.

Among early civilisations, when religious or other gatherings were held, such opportunity was frequently taken to indulge in barter and trade, for scattered populations thus found one of their few means of exchanging commodities. On the introduction of Christianity into Western Europe the practice of combining church festivals with what are now known as fairs came into existence. Thus, in mediaeval times in this, and in other countries, fairs and markets were already of long standing; indeed, it has been asserted that certain French fairs were directly traceable to Roman origin. Gatherings of traders on recurrent days evolved into markets, whilst concourses at annual or other lengthy periods—generally on the day set aside to the memory of a particular saint—have come down to us in the shape of fairs. A famous definition of Coke's that a fair represented "a greater species of market recurring at more distant intervals" is, therefore, self-explanatory; a mart, he considered, was "a greater species of fair". As population grew and means of communication improved, both institutions increased in number and in prestige. Markets lay within the power of the Crown to set up by grant of franchise, and none was recognised without this authorisation; the early feudal lords could grant permission for the holding of fairs. As centres for trade, fairs and markets expanded when agriculture passed beyond the self-supporting stage and provided a surplus of goods for extraneous consumption; they reached their prime when, in addition, foreign trade developed in the fifteenth and sixteenth centuries. Thereafter, as successively roads, canals and railways detracted from their value, they declined in numbers and in popularity. Fairs have come down to us in a less reputable form, whilst markets survive practically unchanged. In the middle ages the former were of far greater importance, and, with certain exceptions, catered for all trades, whilst markets were generally confined to transactions in particular commodities. The social influence exerted by fairs must have been great, as they afforded the only opportunity for numbers of persons from different parts of the country to meet together. After the eighteenth century they had outlived their usefulness, and those that survived except in name became the excuse for annual outbreaks of horseplay and disorder. Markets, as will be shown later, had a different history.

Certain fairs have attained a fame that extended all over the civilised world. Such, at one time or another, have been Sturbridge, Leipzig, Nijni Novgorod and Hurdwar. The latter, situated on the Ganges, still attracts natives by the hundred thousand from all India, Persia and even from Tibet; during the nineteenth century Nijni Novgorod was annually credited with trade to the extent of many millions sterling. Sturbridge, as the only English representative among those of world repute, deserves a short account to itself, even if this entails a diversion from purely agricultural history. It was held in the outskirts of Cambridge, and the earliest reference to it consists of a Royal grant made, *circa* 1211, to the lepers of Sturbridge Hospital, to hold a fair in their close on the feast of the Holy Cross. From this sprang up that annual concourse of buyers and sellers which, in the middle ages, became famous throughout, not only this country, but Europe itself. The fact that Sturbridge was contiguous to the river Cam, whence small ships could navigate to the sea at Lynn or by devious channels to the Midlands, must be held responsible for its popularity, for, without access by water, heavy goods would have been debarred from entry. Owing to the presence of the University, jurisdiction over the fair was not absolutely vested in the town, but was shared between the two bodies; hence frequent disputes. The University authorities proclaimed the fair, and its officials provided on the opening day an oyster lunch and a stupendous dinner, but the town was generally the recipient of the Royal charters and licences. As showing the ramifications of the trade carried on, it may be mentioned that at various times the corporation was engaged in litigation with such towns as Lynn and Northampton in regard to the exaction of tolls, and in 1676 we find it opposing a fair as far distant as Maidstone on the ground that the latter was prejudicial to Sturbridge.

The following affords an interesting account of the conditions still ruling some two hundred years ago, being extracted from Defoe's *Tour Through Britain.*

Having been at Sturbridge-fair when it was in its Height, in the month of September, I must say, that I think it equals that kept at Leipsick in Saxony, or the Mart at Frankfort on the Main.

It is kept in a large Corn-field, near Chesterton, extending from the Side of the River Cam, towards the Road, for about half a Mile square.

If the Field be not cleared of the Corn before a certain day in August, the Fairkeepers may trample it underfoot, to build their Booths or Tents. On the other hand, to balance that Severity, if the Fairkeepers have not cleared the Field by another certain Day in September, the Ploughmen may re-enter with Plough and Cart, and overthrow all into the Dirt; and as for the Filth and Dung, Straw, etc., left behind by the Fairkeepers, which is very considerable, these become the Farmers Fees, and make them full Amends for the trampling, riding, carting upon, and hardening the Ground.

It is impossible to describe all the Parts and Circumstances of this Fair exactly; the Shops are placed in Rows like Streets, whereof one is called Cheapside; and here, as in several other Streets, are all Sorts of Traders, who sell by Retale, and come chiefly from London. Here may be seen Goldsmiths, Toymen, Brasiers, Turners, Milleners, Haberdashers, Hatters, Mercers, Drapers, Pewterers, China-warehouses, and, in a Word, all Trades, that can be found in London; with Coffee-houses, Taverns, and Eating-houses, in great Numbers; and all kept in Tents and Booths.

This great Street reaches from the Road, which goes from Cambridge to Newmarket, turning short out of it to the Left towards the River, and holds in a Line near half a Mile quite down to the Riverside. In another Street parallel with the Road are the like Rows of Booths, but somewhat larger, and more intermingled with Wholesale Dealers; and one Side, passing out of this last Street to the Right-hand, is a great Square, formed of the largest Booth, called the Duddery; but whence so called I could not learn. The Area of this Square is from 80 to 100 yards, where the Dealers have room before every Booth to take down and open their Packs, and to bring in Waggons to load and unload.

This Place being peculiar to the Wholesale Dealers in the Woollen Manufacture, the Booths or Tents are of a vast Extent, have different Apartments, and the Quantities of Goods they bring are so great that the Insides of them look like so many Blackwell-halls, and are vast Warehouses piled up with Goods to the Top. In this Duddery, as I have been informed, have been sold 100,000 Pounds-worth of Woollen Manufactures in less than a Week's time; besides the prodigious Trade carried on here by Wholesalemen from London, and all Parts of England, who transact their Business wholly in their Pocket-books; and, meeting their Chapmen from all Parts, make up their Accounts, receive Money chiefly in Bills, and take Orders. These, they say, exceed by far the Sale of Goods actually brought to the Fair, and delivered in Kind; it being frequent for the London Wholesalemen to carry back Orders from the Dealers, to 10,000 Pounds-worth of Goods a Man, and some much more. This especially respects those People who deal in heavy Goods, as Wholesale Grocers, Salters, Brasiers, Iron-merchants, Wine-merchants, and the like; but does not exclude the Dealers in Woollen Manufactures, and especially in Mercury-goods of all sorts, who generally manage their Business in this manner.

Here are Clothiers from Halifax, Leeds, Wakefield, and Huddersfield, in Yorkshire, and from Rochdale, Bury, etc., in Lancashire, with vast

A booth at Sturbridge Fair (from an old print)

Quantities of Yorkshire Cloths, Kerseys, Pennystones, Cottons, etc., with all sorts of Manchester ware, Fustians, and Things made of Cotton Wool; of which the Quantity is so great, that they told me there were near 1000 Horse-packs of such Goods from that Side of the Country, and these took up a Side and Half of the Duddery at least; also a Part of a Street of Booths was taken up with Upholsters Ware; such as Tickens, Sackens, Kidderminster Stuffs, Blankets, Rugs, Quilts, etc.

In the Duddery I saw one Warehouse, or Booth, consisting of six Apartments, all belonging to a Dealer in Norwich Stuffs only, who, they said, had there above 20,000*l.* Value in those Goods.

Western Goods had their Share here also, and several Booths were filled with Serges, Duroys, Druggets, Shalloons, Cantalloons, Devonshire

Kersies, etc., from Exeter, Taunton, Bristol, and other Parts West, and some from London also.

But all this is still outdone, at least in Appearance, by two Articles, which are the Peculiars of this Fair, and are not exhibited till the other Part of the Fair, for the Woollen Manufacture begins to close up; these are the Wool, and the Hops. There is scarce any Price fixed for Hops in England, till they know how they sell at Sturbridge-fair. The Quantity that appears in the Fair, is indeed prodigious, and they take up a large Part of the Field, on which the Fair is kept, to themselves: They are brought directly from Chelmsford in Essex, from Canterbury and Maidstone in Kent, and from Farnham in Surrey; besides what are brought from London, of the Growth of those and other Places.

The Article of Wool is of several Sorts; but principally Fleece Wool, out of Lincolnshire, where the longest Staple is found, the Sheep of those Parts being of the largest Breed.

The Buyers are chiefly the Manufacturers of Norfolk, Suffolk, and Essex; and it is a prodigious Quantity they buy.

Here I saw what I have not observed in any other County of England, a Pocket of Wool; which seems to have been at first called so in Mockery, this Pocket being so big, that it loads a whole Waggon, and reaches beyond the most extreme Parts of it, hanging over both before and behind; and these ordinarily weigh a Ton, or 2500 Pound Weight of Wool, all in one Bag.

The Quantity of Wool only, which has been sold at this Place, at one Fair, has been said to amount to 50 or 60,000*l.* in Value; same say, a great deal more.

By these Articles, a Stranger may make some Guess at the immense Trade which is carried on at this Place; what prodigious Quantities of Goods are bought and sold, and what a vast Concourse of People are seen here from all Parts of England.

I might proceed to speak of several other Sorts of English Manufactures, which are brought hither to be sold; as all Sorts of wrought Iron, and Brass-ware from Birmingham; edged Tools, Knives, etc., from Sheffield; Glass Wares, and Stockings, from Nottingham and Leicester; and unaccountable Quantities of other Things, of smaller Value, every Morning.

To attend this Fair, and the prodigious Crouds of People which resort to it, there are Hackney Coaches, which come from London, and ply all Day long, to carry the People to and from Cambridge; for there the major Part of them lodge.

It is not to be wondered at, if the Town of Cambridge cannot receive or entertain the Numbers of People that come to this Fair; for not Cambridge only, but all the Towns round are full; nay, the very Barns and Stables are turned into Inns, to lodge the meaner Sort of People: As for the Fair-people, they all eat, drink, and sleep, in their Booths, which are so intermingled with Taverns, Coffee-houses, Drinking-houses, Eating-houses, Cooks' Shops, etc., and so many Butchers and Higglers from all the neighbouring Counties come in every Morning with Beef, Mutton, Fowls, Butter, Bread, Cheese, Eggs, and such Things, and go with them from Tent to Tent, from Door to Door, that there is no Want of Provisions of any Kind, either dressed, or undressed.

In a Word, the Fair is like a well-governed City, and there is the least Disorder and Confusion (I believe) that can be seen anywhere, with so great a Concourse of People.

Towards the Middle of the Fair, and when the great Hurry of Wholesale Business begins to be over, the Gentry come in, from all Parts of the Country round; and though they come for their Diversion, yet it is not a little Money they lay out, which generally falls to the Share of the Retailers; such as the Toy-shops, Goldsmiths, Brasiers, Ironmongers, Turners, Milleners, Mercers, etc., and some loose coins they reserve for the Puppet-shews, Drolls, Rope-dancers, and such-like; of which there is no want. The middle Day of the Fair is the Horse-fair, which is concluded both with Horse and Foot-races. In less than a Week after the End of the Fair, scarce any Sign of it remains, except by the Heaps of Dung, Straw, and other Rubbish, which is left behind, trod into the Earth, and is as good as a Summer's Fallow for the Land; and, as I have said above, pays the Husbandman well by the Use of it.

I should have mentioned, that here is a Court of Justice always open, and held every Day in a Shed built on Purpose in the Fair: This is for keeping the Peace, and deciding Controversies in Matters arising from the Business of the Fair. The Magistrates of the University of Cambridge are Judges in this Court, as being in their Jurisdiction, by special Privilege. Here they determine Matters in a summary Way, as is practised in those we call Pye-powder Courts in other Places, or as a Court of Conscience; and they have a final Authority without Appeal.

Henry Gunning, an eighteenth century Esquire Bedell of the University, has also left an amusing description of the lighter side of the fair, including its theatrical performances, and of the inaugural dinner given by the University, at which the Vice-Chancellor took the head of the table, in front of a large dish of herrings, and the Senior Proctor the bottom. By the early nineteenth century Sturbridge had ceased to attract attention outside the precincts of the town, and its subsequent history comprises a degeneration into an annual pleasure fair; ultimately, a street called "Garlic Row", where mediaeval coins are still dug up, and an ephemeral collection of "merry-go-rounds" alone record the existence of that famous institution.

As fairs declined in importance, and were reduced in number by the action of local authorities under the Fairs Act of 1871, so markets tended to increase and to become specialised. At first consisting of gatherings held at the cross roads in town or village, they gradually developed into authorised centres for trading, and in course of time there was scarcely a town of any importance that did not possess at least one weekly market. The ultimate trend of events can be seen at Smithfield, Billingsgate and other great centres for the sale of special products, but, on certain days in the week, provincial towns still afford the best example of the general market as it has existed for centuries, providing, as it does, at one and the same time, an outlet for the agricultural produce of the neighbourhood and facilities for the purchase of farm requisites. Markets conferred an undeniable prestige upon towns, not the least because the right to hold them was granted by the Crown itself; incidentally, in early times it is very probable that only well-protected places and those with adequate facilities for approach were so favoured.

A Royal Commission, whose terms of reference extended to an enquiry into markets and tolls, investigated the state of affairs existing in the latter part of the nineteenth century; its findings were issued in 1890, and contain a full account of the history of this form of trading. Matters at the period in question courted investigation, and the Commission's labours were not in vain, as the bulk of its recommendations were adopted and introduced into subsequent legislation. The laxity of control, together with the abuses and irregularities then existing in English markets, have been quoted by several writers, so the strictures relating to Ireland, as affording a sidelight on perhaps the worst conditions in the whole United Kingdom, will be pursued here. Markets were held in 349 Irish towns and villages, for 125 of which no patents were found, and in 103 cases where patents existed the market days were other than those specified. Fairs were found to exist to the number of 1297, but again authority was in most cases lacking, for 485 had no patents and 324 occurred on unauthorised dates. The Commission expressed itself in the following general terms:

> When we consider the present state of most of our Irish markets, the filth, the confusion, nay, the actual danger, women and children thrown down, the passengers obstructed by horses and cows, sheep and pigs, all indiscriminately mixed up together, or by the stall of an apple-woman or the covered standing of some little vendor of calico and ribbands who has erected his temporary shelter in the thoroughfare, whilst at every outlet, toll-collectors armed with bludgeons are claiming and enforcing their obnoxious claims; compare this with the condition of Continental markets; the secure pens for cattle, the secluded abattoirs, etc.

Conditions of course were not as bad as this in other parts of the United Kingdom, but the necessity for the overhauling of a system that had remained untouched from mediaeval times was obvious.

Apart from the actual inconveniences and discomforts that awaited persons visiting such markets, there existed still greater abuses which insistently called for remedial measures. The first was connected with the system of tolls and dues extracted from those who sold goods, and the second was represented by the anomalous system of weights and measures currently in use. To a much smaller extent both disabilities were also found to exist on this side of St George's Channel, but as the historic instances of the tolls found at Newcastle-on-Tyne and certain other towns have been frequently described, and as the question of weights and measures will be dealt with as a whole, Ireland may again furnish exclusive evidence. Tolls, in one or in many forms, had been extorted from sellers, or prospective sellers, at practically all Irish markets from time immemorial, but, some twenty-five years before the Commission's enquiry, extensive rioting had caused their abolition in many towns of Leinster, Ulster and parts of Munster. Those that were met with were of many types. One, known as "toll thorough", and described as "the worst in Ireland", was collected at the entrances to towns upon all merchantable stuffs, whether sold or not, the proceeds being theoretically devoted to the repair of walls, streets and bridges. The "gateage toll", found in Cork, was exceedingly unpopular, being "in fact a tax levied upon agricultural produce of the surrounding country for the purpose of defraying expenses which should in justice be borne by local taxation; and no part of it is applied in affording any accommodation or equivalent to those who contribute almost exclusively to its production". The system by which such tolls were leased out was condemned, and instances quoted in which the collectors ranged from the above-mentioned individuals, armed with bludgeons, to illiterate old women. All vendors, including of course women, were liable to be closely searched by these custodians, who were respecters of nobody, and extended their demands to cover payment on small quantities of provisions, such as eggs, fish, apples and so forth, introduced by women and children. *À propos* of this, the *Report* contains the following passage: "For instance the stockings that girls carry to market are subject to tollage. At Gort a woman carrying a bundle of straw on her back, which she sold for fourpence, was charged a penny toll. In Skibbereen a woman bringing in three fish on a Sunday morning was stopped and one of the fish seized because she was unable to pay a penny, the toll demanded". In consequence of this obnoxious system the Commission found that evasion was very rife and that counter measures were in the habit of being taken, which led to yet further irregularities. For instance, an Act of the time of Queen Anne had ordained that cattle remaining unsold at a market might be removed free from payment of toll, but "we found the persons employed as collectors in many places endeavouring to meet the constant evasion of tolls by obliging all persons leaving the fair with cattle, and claiming to be exempt as unsold, to go through some form, such as touching a piece of paper posted on a board or a book fastened to a pole, and to pledge themselves thereby to the truth of their statements. This is called 'clearing the cattle' and, we regret, is very extensively practised". It will be agreed that perhaps the Englishman's ideas of Donnybrook Fair are, after all, not so exaggerated as the natives would have him believe.

The Commission recommended—and its recommendations were applicable to the whole Kingdom as well as to Ireland—that proper sites should be provided for markets, that responsible persons should be placed in authority over them, that facilities for the erection of stalls and for the provision of weighing scales should be available, and, lastly, that all deductions and allowances for "tret, beamage, porterage, brokerage" should be illegal. It is doubtful if tolls had exercised any direct influence upon the sale of agricultural produce or upon its cost to the public; rather were their drawbacks reflected in the general sense of interference with individual liberty and the inquisitory powers they conferred. The charges made for the use of stalls or for the right of selling at present-day markets, in some cases represent tolls once levied, but they are sums that can be ascertained in advance and the incidence of which does not generally bear any fixed proportion to the value of the goods disposed of or to the volume of business transacted. Whilst a few markets are still conducted on the principle of charging *pro rata* for the produce entering them, tolls in the nature of octroi at the entrance to towns are now non-existent in this country, although notices concerning them may still be seen affixed to walls.

British weights and measures have always been a source of wonder to other nations, and, again, Ireland furnishes the most striking examples of confusion. A report, made to the Lord Lieutenant by the Registrar-General in the year 1856, contained the following extraordinary catalogue of units then in use. In different Counties wheat was sold by the barrel of 22 stones, the cwt. of 112 lb. or the stone of 14 lb.; oats, by the barrel, which might contain 12, 14, 24 or 33 stones; barley, by the barrel of 16 and 24 stones. Potatoes were dealt in by the barrel also, but the number of stones contained was variously found to be 15, 20, 21, 24, 32, 40, 48, 64, 72, 80, 95 and 96; they were sold, too, by the stone of 14, 15, 16, 21 and 23 lb., as well as by the hundredweight. Even in towns in the same County different weights were in use; naturally, comparison between the crops in various localities was thereby made impossible, as, for instance, a yield of eight barrels of potatoes per acre in Roscommon would be equivalent to one of thirty-two per acre in County Dublin.

A Select Committee, appointed to enquire into the question of the weights and measures used for the sale of grain in the United Kingdom, issued its *Report* in 1893. This document afforded an extraordinary commentary on the existing situation, for it contained a summary showing the various measures in use in those markets that came within the province of the Corn Returns Act. From these 189 towns came reports of no less than forty-six different weighed measures for wheat, which ranged from 52 to 90 lb. a bushel; there were also twenty-six measures varying from 42 to 70 lb., for barley, and thirty-six for oats, ranging from 35 to 63 lb. Each part of the United Kingdom advocated, through expert witnesses, the standardising of its own selected unit. Thus, the Scots corn traders urged that sale by the hundredweight was the only proper method for all cereals; the Liverpool Corn Association naturally wished to see their cental of 100 lb. adopted elsewhere, and groups of Counties such as Gloucestershire and Wiltshire maintained that a departure from the quarter of 496 lb. would cause complaint; the East Anglian coomb was declared unheard of in the West of England. Complications caused by the indiscriminate use of such terms as "sale by weight", "sale by measure" and "sale by weighed measure" led the Committee to recommend that, in sales by the latter method, for purposes of conversion, standard weights should be adopted. "Natural" weight was of course the root trouble in all such operations, but unexpected difficulties cropped up when it was suggested that it might be ignored; for instance, sellers of barley grown for malting purposes declared that here values did not depend on the weight of the grain, which was merely a secondary consideration. The Committee concluded its labours by issuing, with two very minor recommendations, the far-reaching one that the hundredweight should become the universal basis for sales of all cereals in Great Britain, as, by the time in question, it already was in Ireland. Exactly thirty years passed before legislation to this effect was put into operation. In the meantime the complexities revealed in the methods in vogue a generation ago were not abated, and the "natural" weight of corn was annually the subject of official appraisement and explanation.

Even during more recent years the existence of local measures was a constant source of trouble, for in an official enquiry by a Government Department during the war local agricultural Reporters referred to "loads" of wheat and to "Carlisle" bushels of oats, whilst coombs, bags, sacks, quarters and bushels were used indiscriminately in the same districts. Our national custom of having two different quarters in the case of home-produced and imported cereals caused endless confusion, and did not simplify the difficulties attendant on the negotiations between the farmers and the Government when the question of relating the price of British wheat to that of imported was under consideration. Fortunately this evil has been remedied, for, since January 1st, 1923, under the Corn Sales Act of 1921, the hundredweight has become the only recognised unit of measurement for the sale, not only of cereals, but also of meal, beans, potatoes and agricultural seeds; although it is not unusual to see recorded, side by side with it, the equivalent expression in quarters. How it was that steps to this end had not been taken years before will always be a mystery. Not only was the system of measures in vogue indefensible, but frequently the enforcing of it was neglected, and such powers as the Weights and Measures Act conferred were not taken advantage of as they should have been. The evidence adduced on this point before the Commission of 1887 was overwhelming, the vast majority of the sufferers being small agriculturists. As an extraordinary anomaly, it may be mentioned that the University of Cambridge was long invested by Act of Parliament with the custody and use of the weights and measures (including a rod used to check that peculiar local unit, the yard of butter) used in the town, and had the appointment of the Inspectors. Gunning, in his account of Sturbridge Fair, says that after the proclamation, solemnly announcing that punishment would be meted out to any who sold beer in mugs other than those allowed by the University, it would be observed that the majority present were partaking of that refreshment from mugs shamefully under the standard measure. He added that the publicans appeared genuinely to believe that the money they paid for licences at the Commissary's court was for permission to sell short measure. If such things could happen under University jurisdiction, what irregularities must have existed in remote markets to the detriment of the agricultural trader?

It is henceforward necessary to differentiate between the methods of sale traditional to each of the commodities produced by the agriculturist. In mediaeval times the bulk of the wheat, in common with other cereals, did not travel beyond the confines of the manor or parish in which it had been grown, but certain minor movements between individual manors have been recorded, and small quantities of grain were of course conveyed to the towns, but in general wheat was consumed on the spot. The necessity for conserving supplies was always present, for, during the Roman occupation of this country, stone-built granaries had been freely erected, and the clerical tithe-owners referred to in Chapter VII were constantly exercised as to the best means of storing their corn. When a surplus was made available by improved methods of husbandry, and its transportation facilitated by new means of communication, repressive measures, aimed at the middleman, were instituted. Even recognised dealings at approved centres were hedged in by countless restrictions, as witness an extract from the *Liber Albus* of the time of Edward I, quoted in the *Report* of the Commission on markets:

> Also as to corn dealers who bring corn into the city [of London] for sale—that no one shall sell by show or sample. But they shall come to certain places in the city established with their carts laden, and with their horses having the loads upon them, without selling anything, and without getting rid of anything...and that no corn shall be sold until the hour of Prime rung at St Paul's, under the penalty of forfeiting the corn.

Eventually dealers came to be recognised as essential links in the commercial chain, and, for the export trade at least, were granted considerable rights. East Anglia always provided a surplus for movement, either to other parts of the country or to foreign states, and here intermediaries were in the strongest position. Under the later Corn Laws it became necessary to ascertain the average price of grain, and for this purpose certain zones were at first delimited, but eventually numerous markets scattered about the country became officially recognised as providing the data required for such purposes as the Tithe Commutation Act of 1836, and certain of them were again adopted as centres under the Corn Returns Act of 1882. The average values prepared from the reports of Inspectors under the above Act have already been referred to as furnishing grounds of contention to farmers and other payers of tithe, but, from the statistical standpoint, they are of some value as showing the fluctuations in the quantities of cereals sold at different markets over a long series of years, but, of course, only a fraction of all the grain dealt in comes within this official purview. The prohibition of sale by sample, contained in the *Liber Albus*, would strike present-day vendors as an intolerable restriction, but the contemporary legislators doubtless had good grounds for distrusting this form of transaction and for standardising what came to be known as "pitch sales". The general tendency evidenced during the last half century has been towards the aggrandisement of certain already important grain markets and the decay of many of the lesser; this is mainly attributable to the introduction of large commercial mills which attract the bulk of the grain from districts within a considerable radius, while, at the same time, catering for foreign supplies. Apart from the markets specially reserved for dealings in imported grain, such as Liverpool and, in London, the Baltic, the largest transactions take place in a handful of centres mainly situated within range of the corn-producing areas. Prominent among these are Norwich, Cambridge, Peterborough and Lincoln. The old-fashioned miller, who often bought direct from the farmer, has in large measure disappeared, even as his wind and water mills have given way to steam—his place being taken by dealers buying on behalf of large companies.

Whilst perhaps something can still be urged against the anachronisms involved in the British system of selling grain, no complaints have been put forward that the middleman is, in this particular trade, taking an undue share of the profits, whatever may be the delinquencies of subsequent functionaries. Dealers have not been accused of securing more than a very small fraction of the cost of the grain, and, when it reaches the miller, British wheat has been saddled with only a few additional pence per quarter. The processes it then passes through before reaching the consumer, and the persons involved in those processes, must bear the brunt of the charges so frequently levied. From the farmer's point of view the selling of his grain is one of the most straightforward transactions that are open to him, for he is sure of finding purchasers at current prices whenever he chooses to part with it, and can rely upon securing immediate payment. Grain keeps better than most of the articles he produces, requires no preparation for market and travels well; if the same could be said for other agricultural products, some of the principal difficulties and expenses attendant on their sale would be absent. Incidentally, grain is almost the prerogative of large farmers, which no doubt accounts for the absence of attempts to extend co-operative principles to its sale in this country, and to their comparative failure, except for export trade, abroad.

Compared with conditions in the United States and other large exporting centres, the internal marketing of British grain seems a parochial affair. This country has need for no such organisation as that represented by the three-stage transportation found in North America, and lack of space, therefore, forbids an account of the conveyance of wheat from the field to the local market, thence to the primary market and finally to the seaboard, but certain features deserve a few passing words. The United States Government plays a far more intimate part in the handling and safeguarding of grain than is the case in European countries. By an elaborate system of inspection, from the primary markets onwards, it secures a high standard and strict classification in the various grades; it also takes steps to check the tendency for combinations among warehouse and elevator interests to attain too much prominence. The value of these measures can best be appreciated when it is stated that, prior to the war, the costs added to a bushel of wheat, after travelling from the central States to the sea-coast, amounted to about sevenpence. The suggestion sometimes put forward that operations on the Chicago and other exchanges were apt to raise prices unduly has been shown to be without foundation. But, if neither transport, nor financial dealings have so far adversely affected the final purchaser, there remain possibilities that will continue to require watching in the future. In no other country in the world has the cleavage between the producer and the middleman become so marked, and many thousands of persons make a living by buying and selling grain that they never handle. Then, despite State regulations, there exists what virtually amounts to a monopoly in the shape of Associations of dealers; the railway companies also generally succeed in fending off competition from fresh elevator interests by refusing access to their lines. The whole trade differs so widely from that found in this country that criticism or appreciation are both difficult, but, from the American farmer's standpoint, the rapidity with which he has hitherto been able to secure the bulk of his money, and the small amount of trouble involved after he has threshed his crops, are noteworthy features. If the American system of mixing and grading wheat appears open to abuse, it must be remembered that the State authorises, and, indeed, superintends, all processes which it undergoes in transit and that the producer benefits by having additional outlets for inferior qualities provided him.

That Wheat Pools never, in the States, made the headway they have achieved north of the International frontier, is, nevertheless, remarkable, since this form of control had been widely applied to other producing organisations from the end of the nineteenth century. The post-war movement started in 1919 with a Pool in Oklahoma, quickly followed by one known as the North-West Pool, embracing the States of Idaho and Washington. By 1922, there was a total of fifteen Pools, scattered over the wheat-producing areas of the country, but their further numerical expansion was checked by amalgamation of the smaller bodies. The following year the Pools then in existence could only claim to have handled a little over 3 per cent. of the total crop. With falling prices these American associations of producers found themselves in difficulties, which were accentuated by reason of the fact that they had not, in most instances, bound their members for periods longer than a year. Financial considerations loomed larger as advance payments were found to be out of harmony with the prices subsequently secured, and those responsible for the ultimate direction of affairs found themselves hopelessly engaged in defending "orderly marketing". With the advent of the Federal Farm Board the position was improved, for that body encouraged the formation of the National Grain Corporation, which in turn assumed control over a growing proportion of American wheat. Ultimately, in 1931, the Federal Farm Board, which claimed to have been holding over two hundred millions of bushels off the market and claimed correspondingly to have maintained prices, announced, on financial grounds, a discontinuance of this policy, with results that are referred to in subsequent pages. Here it must suffice to state that the only concession that could be made to wheat-growers was an undertaking that this grain should not at once be jettisoned upon the markets, but, save in the case of sales to foreign Governments for relief purposes or by barter, would be disposed of in moderate quantities. With prices falling still further, world competition demonstrated that the United States producer, even when bolstered up by "revolving funds", the McNary Haugen legislation and a Grain Stabilisation Committee, could not dominate the chronological and the geographical marketing of wheat.

Apart from Canada, other exporting countries of the world have not attained to American levels either in the physical or the financial handling of grain, for one finds in the Argentine and elsewhere human power taking the place of mechanical, and dealings confined within more exact boundaries both of time and of space. That within less than a generation from now the United States will possess an internal trade only in wheat is certain, and the importing countries of Europe will be more dependent upon nations some of whose methods of marketing will require to be remodelled; but producers at home will reap little benefit until that more distant time when world conditions and the world standard of production tend to equalise. Indications are not lacking, however, that most of the other British Dependencies will soon be equipped for cereal export on the United States plan, for South Africa, New South Wales and Victoria have already installed elevators in order to deal with maize and wheat in bulk.

Canada deserves special mention in this connection, for she was the pioneer in the development of Pools designed for exportation of grain upon a really large scale. A Dominion Wheat Board having been successfully operated during the war, in 1920 its continuation was demanded by the farmers' representatives. Failing to secure acquiescence to their wishes, they next persuaded the official organisations in such Provinces as Alberta, Manitoba and Saskatchewan to appoint committees of investigation. The recommendations of these bodies were unanimously in favour of pooling principles and, by 1923, legislative sanction for the formation of several Provincial Pools had been secured. That of Alberta was actually the first to commence operations; this was for the season 1923–4, during which time, with a membership of 29,000, it handled upwards of 30,000,000 bushels of wheat and demonstrated its ability to increase the price secured for its members above that ruling on the open market by 5 cents per bushel. Manitoba and Saskatchewan followed quickly, the former securing a membership of 10,000 by 1925 and the latter, one of 45,000; their controlled area amounted to over 7,000,000 acres. Thus, with the addition of smaller organisations, the movement had, within barely two years, enrolled almost 100,000 persons, who directed the produce of more than 11,000,000 acres of grain. Wisely, the methods adopted since the start had been, firstly, to aim at obtaining as members some 50 per cent. of the growers in the area about to be organised and, secondly, to bind them by means of five year contracts to deliver to the Pool the whole of their saleable grain; concurrently, there was an undertaking, on behalf of the Pool, to advance, as initial payment, a very considerable proportion of the value of the wheat—in the case of the Alberta Pool, this was 75 cents on a price that was finally just over the dollar. The next stage comprised an incursion by the Pools into a heavy capital development, in order to compete with the facilities offered by railway and elevator interests. The Canadian farmer had by now completely outstripped the American in this field and expansion continued upon a very large scale, until, from 1925 up to 1931, the Canadian Wheat Pool, an amalgamation of the three Prairie organisations just described, could claim that it had handled more than half of the Country's wheat. With the catastrophic fall in world prices, accompanied by abnormally large crops, and, consequently, by large unsold surpluses, the Pool was, after 1929, faced with financial difficulties, to alleviate which it was eventually forced to seek financial assistance from the State. The primary cause of its troubles was an over-optimistic advance made to members upon their 1929 crop, to cover which commitments the Provincial Governments had to give mortgages on the Pool's further stocks. Eventually, certain reorganisation took place in the Central body, accompanied by the delegation of powers to the Provincial Pools. In circumstances such as those ruling in 1931 and 1932, this implies no stigma upon the particular method of handling wheat, which will quite probably, in the near future, revert to its former position of strength. Extravagant claims have, of course, been made upon its behalf, but when they are discounted, it is obvious that a large Wheat Pool can perform valuable functions for its members—provided the latter are numerically dominant and are legally tied to membership for a lengthy period of years—upon a relatively small capital, can increase the returns secured by its members, but not for indefinite periods, and can, in normal times, handle its members' output more economically than would be possible for other undertakings. This, however, is not tantamount to claiming for Pools complete prescience together with the ability to perform financial miracles, both of which attributes would have been necessary possessions to enable them to come unscathed through recent times.

In Australia, compulsory Wheat Pools came into existence during the war years and, when peace returned, were succeeded in each of the separate States by very similar voluntary bodies; in New Zealand, too, the same system is in vogue. In all cases customs and requirements approximate to those already described in Canada, and, in most districts, a quantity approaching half of the total outturn passes through the Pools, whose officials regard themselves purely as selling agents and not as controllers of future prices.

The inhabitants of this country are apt to look upon the problems of wheat production overseas exclusively from their bearing on prices at home, but it must be remembered that the producer abroad is interested in getting the maximum price for his wares, and does not as a rule mind what their ultimate destination may be. On the other hand, British farmers are dependent upon conditions ruling abroad, and the prices of intensively raised British grain will always bear a close relationship to those secured extensively by these competitors, so that once again the old problem of the divergent interests of the producer and consumer is raised. Both British and overseas farmers see considerable profits made in the cereals they have raised, but these are realised in the last, or manufactured, stage, and do not represent potential gains lost to themselves. This factor has been frequently commented on in the past, for the disparity between the price of wheat and that of the quartern loaf has received full treatment from such writers as the late Sir H. Rew. In a contribution to the *Journal of the Royal Agricultural Society* some forty years ago he drew attention to the fact that, when wheat had stood at 39*s*. the quarter, the loaf was retailed at 5½*d*. but only a halfpenny reduction was effected when a 10*s*. drop occurred in the cost of grain. Similar evidence has been forthcoming on many occasions during the last century, so that after the fall in prices of 1921, the failure of the loaf to return to a level commensurate with that of wheat was nothing novel, for there is an ample margin for profit in those two trades which prepare the grain for consumption. Thus at the present time the cost of the wheat in the quartern loaf (sold at 7*d.*) does not exceed 2*d.* The consumer can always be interested in attempts at reducing the price he is asked to pay, but the agricultural producer, when naturally attempting to secure a larger share in those prices, ceases to be an object of sympathy to the former. Fuller consideration of this problem of the relationship between the price of wheat and that of bread is deferred to Chapter XVIII.

The sale of livestock, which represents another, and most important, branch of the agricultural industry, has not attaching to it the halo formed by legal custom and enactments that were observed in the case of cereals. Works, such as the *Liber Albus*, confine themselves in this connection to quoting ordinances such as the following, which merely deals with recalcitrant buyers—"and whereas some butchers do buy beasts of country folks, and as soon as they have the beasts in their houses kill them and then at their own pleasures delay the peasants of their pay; or else tell them that they may take their beasts..."; to this a list of penalties was appended. That the system now in vogue for transporting all forms of livestock is quite recent in origin is sometimes overlooked, for, almost within living memory, the marsh-fed bullocks of Norfolk were driven to Smithfield, and the North Road itself was incessantly traversed by parties of drovers and their charges, the latter having been specially shod for the purpose; calves were occasionally conveyed in huge two-storied wagons; turkeys from Norfolk and geese from the Midlands walked, by easy stages and in large flocks, the hundred miles to market, losing apparently little weight on the journey. The spectacle of frenzied cattle being urged through the streets was familiar to Londoners until the middle of the last century, when the advent of the railways finally obviated the necessity to convey livestock by road, and the increasing proportion of our meat supplied from overseas was reflected in the altered appearance of Smithfield and other markets.

Consideration of the methods of selling livestock must be confined to the problems involved in transactions between the breeder, or rearer, and the butcher, reference to such questions as the local movements and sale of stock for fattening purposes being omitted. The outstanding feature, and one which has been adversely commented upon for upwards of a century, is that animals are still, to a great extent, sold "by eye", and the farmers thus lose, and others gain, what must annually amount to a large sum of money. Sir H. Rew, when investigating the past history of this custom, showed that attempts innumerable had been made to demonstrate to farmers that weight alone should be the guiding factor in sales, at least, of cattle. Tables of calculated weights based on measurements were repeatedly compiled, and actual demonstrations, arranged by such persons as Sir John Lawes, showed convincingly the bias that existed in favour of the expert purchaser; but the farmer, who was the one person to have compelled a change in custom, seemed genuinely to prefer that sales should proceed without reference to any consideration other than that of the appearance of the animals. All impartial authorities agreed that the butcher, by dint of constant practice, must inevitably be a better judge of the amount of meat he was purchasing than was the farmer, and test after test showed the truth of this. In 1891 the Markets and Fairs (Weighing of Cattle) Act required those in charge of markets to provide means of weighing animals. This represented a considerable advance, but, so great was their apathy, that it is doubtful if the Act would ever have been placed on the Statute-book if it had been left to the initiative of farmers alone. For years after the compulsory introduction of these facilities little advantage was taken of them, but during the last twenty years there has been a steady accession to the numbers of beasts sold by weight. The Table on p. 290, issued by the Ministry of Agriculture, records the progress made during the first decade. It should be observed that the statistics relate only to certain markets, and that the years when rigid control of sales existed have been excised.

It is noteworthy that the percentage of fat cattle weighed was much higher than that of stores, but the increase in this figure during the ten years in question had been greater in the case of the latter. Scotland led the way in this connection, for there the proportion of fat cattle weighed was some 80 per cent. of the total, but of the numbers of livestock of all kinds changing hands in the United Kingdom, it is obvious that only a fraction passed over the weigh-bridge, so

	Fat cattle			*Store cattle*		
Year	Number entering	Number weighed	Percentage of number weighed to number entering	Number entering	Number weighed	Percentage of number weighed to number entering
1911	605,187	175,255	29·0	298,993	37,702	12·6
1912	483,837	151,102	31·2	314,248	47,980	15·3
1913	505,848	159,464	31·5	442,715	66,059	14·9
1914	486,187	164,453	33·8	382,121	63,896	16·7
1915	494,567	180,319	36·5	411,075	74,821	18·2
1916	511,086	188,809	36·9	415,260	80,113	19·3
1917	512,509	207,292	40·4	408,188	81,813	20·0
1920	171,437*	68,490*	40·0*	446,565	89,453	20·0
1921	337,829	153,787	45·5	332,519	60,160	18·1

* Six months only.

that there was ample room for further efforts to be made at popularising this method of sale. The usual reasons adduced against it are that "farmers prefer the old ways", and that, naturally, butchers do not urge its merits upon them. It is also possible that market authorities may in the past have been partly to blame, for, in many recorded instances, they appeared to consider that their liabilities were met so long as a weigh-bridge was installed somewhere in the vicinity of their market. Such erections are not likely to be in great demand if their presence is not patent, or if access to them is difficult, especially if there is a feeling abroad that they are merely intended to comply with some unnecessary regulation. Sale by weight at once introduces the question of the relationship borne by dressed carcases to living animals—a point that cannot be pursued further than by saying that over sixty years ago experiments at Rothamsted gave a figure varying from 58 to 60 per cent., and special investigations made for the Commission on Markets and Tolls in 1887 recorded from 55 up to 62 per cent.; fat stock at Smithfield has been found to yield over 64 per cent., and the Army Cattle Committee during the war published figures varying between 51 and 63 per cent. These results show that, even when the weigh-bridge is utilised, there is still considerable discrepancy between the quantities of meat butchers secure from different classes of animals—a discrepancy that some farmers would perhaps claim the traditional methods of sale would recognise.

Once more the disparity between the price secured by the producer and that charged to the consumer is apparent, but again it is most marked in the last stage. Meat is retailed in butchers' shops at prices that seem frequently to court enquiry, the explanation tendered being invariably associated with indirect charges. Here, as with that other raw material, wheat, the farmer is practically powerless, for the processes necessary to prepare both articles for human consumption are entirely outside his capacity to undertake. The urban dweller protests vigorously at the cost of his loaf and of his joint, expresses surprise that the farmer receives so small a part of the sum he pays, but, naturally, is only interested in steps that may effect a reduction in retail prices, considering any reallocation of profits as a matter outside his concern. On those occasions when farmers, or associations of farmers, have attempted to short circuit the middlemen by slaughtering their own livestock they have succeeded in demonstrating these facts, but have lacked the trade organisation to carry on such a policy indefinitely. Until recently it seemed as if, in the case of wheat and livestock, the agriculturist must look upon himself as the producer of raw material, and leave to the State the responsibility of checking the rapacity of those who afterwards handled or prepared it for market.

Chapter XIV

MARKETS AND MARKETING (CONTINUED)

Methods of selling other forms of agricultural produce; difficulties confronting fruit-growers; preparation for markets; cost of carriage; Government action in the United States; the organisation of producers in British Dominions; State action in Great Britain; the Empire Marketing Board and other bodies; the Agricultural Marketing Acts of 1931 and 1933.

During the last decade successive British Governments have stirred themselves into making very searching enquiries into all cognate matters affecting rural markets. In 1924, a Departmental Committee of the Ministry of Agriculture, popularly referred to as the "Linlithgow Committee", after its chairman, the Marquess of Linlithgow, reported fully upon the prices and methods of distribution of all agricultural products. Then, the Empire Marketing Board came into existence, charged, in the first instance, with the support of the home producer; the urban consumers' interests were remembered when the Food Council was established—a consultative and inquisitory body without much power of initiative. Most of these organisations have published extremely full and unbiased *Reports* upon different commodities in relation to supply and demand. The Ministry of Agriculture, too, has ventured further into this field, for, during the last seven years or so, it has produced upwards of forty remarkably complete and interesting *Reports* in its ("Orange") Economic Series; these, some of which have been fostered by the Empire Marketing Board, range from an academic monograph upon "Price Stabilisation" to reviews upon "Fluid Milk" and the "Marketing of Skins and Hides". A wealth of material has, accordingly, been made available for all classes of the community and there is now no longer any excuse to plead ignorance upon any matter affecting the business side of British agriculture. The very far reaching legislation that has recently been placed upon the Statute-book, mainly as a result of the prominence given to the whole subject by these means, will be found dealt with at the end of this Chapter. In the meantime, certain historical features, together with some widespread tendencies, call for preliminary discussion.

Where the producer raises articles that reach the consumer in practically unchanged form, he should be in a position to secure better terms, but, actually, he is often at a worse disadvantage than was the case with the staple commodities dealt with in the previous Chapter. Fruit, vegetables, eggs and poultry are purchased retail exactly as they leave the farm, but the apparent profit taken by the shopkeeper is apt to be out of all proportion to the producer's share. Here matters are on a totally different footing from the sale of wheat or livestock, and numerous attempts have been made to eliminate altogether the middleman and the retailer, but have not met with unqualified success. It must, however, be stated here and now, that many allegations of undue profit-making in these particular branches of the industry have, by the above-mentioned official investigations, been shown to be groundless, or else to have been greatly exaggerated; nevertheless, the opportunities for extortion are here obvious, and have frequently been seized. It is probable that, as, with the exception of milk, these commodities are mainly the stand-by of small farmers, the industry as a whole has not felt compelled actively to collaborate—large farmers who possess the necessary influence and capital often treating products other than cereals, livestock and milk as mere side-lines. Joint action on the part of producers has, on more than one occasion, enabled dairy farmers to counter the proposals of milk retailers, but here the producers have a virtual monopoly in their hands. All other "small stuff" has to meet competition from abroad, but the margin for profits is none the less large. That the bearings of the problem, both in regard to foreign competition and to the multifarious commissions sometimes extracted, are not new, can be seen from such excerpts as the following, taken from *The Times* of May 20th, 1822.

A vessel with 40 tons of potatoes arrived here [Portsmouth] a few days since, from Jersey, for which the master had given in that island 20/- per ton; immediately on her anchoring she was visited by a speculator in the article who purchased the cargo at forty-five shillings per ton; on his way from Spithead to the Point he met a second speculator, who gave him fifty shillings per ton, which this third speculator retailed in a few hours after the arrival of the vessel at eighty shillings per ton. If they were sold retail at the then market price £7. 6. 8 was obtained for what a few days before cost twenty shillings.

On all sides are seen comparable present-day examples of growers receiving pence for articles that are paid for by the public in shillings, and that have reached the latter in untouched condition. Reference to co-operation—the favourite remedial measure put forward—is deferred to a separate Chapter, but other suggestions deserve brief notice. The traditional method of securing direct access to the final purchaser is by means of the public market. There is no doubt that, formerly, the bulk of butter, eggs, fruit and poultry was so disposed of, but the multiplication of large stores and the trend of shopkeepers themselves to appropriate positions in the markets has modified the situation. The actual cost of engaging a stall was almost insignificant, but the obligation of constant attendance that devolved upon either a member of the farmer's family or upon a hired representative tended to act as a deterrent. That this form of direct sale can affect retailers is obvious when the growing number of stalls occupied by them in provincial markets is observed. The real Small Holder has another outlet, for he can hawk his goods from door to door in neighbouring towns. Associations of smaller producers, again, occasionally trespass upon the retailer's own ground by setting up shops for what amounts to co-operative sale; but here the necessity to provide permanent supervision involves considerable outgoings, and has frequently led to disunion between the undertakers. Arguments used against the individual system of sale mainly attach to its apparent wastefulness; it is pointed out that the bi-weekly setting forth of three or four men, each with pony and cart, to convey a few pounds' weight of produce to a distant market is uneconomic, and that a motor lorry would collect the articles from scores of such farmers and deliver them at less cost and in shorter time. But it is answered that the human element is apt to be left out of consideration, and the absence of the small farmer from his holding for a day does not necessarily imply a loss of efficiency, while an individual selling on his own behalf claims that he is more likely to secure good terms than is a paid representative. It is also said that regular visits by the farmer to market are conducive to widening his business aptitude, and, at the same time, facilitate the purchase of his own requirements. Where direct sales are the rule nothing save the institution of some form of duty on imported commodities that are in rivalry with his own can of course enable the grower to obtain larger returns than he already gets. When indirect sales are in question steps can be taken to invade the retailer's province, but, in this event, prices must of course be reduced to a lower level or, alternatively, better value be offered.

Milk, cheese, wool and fruit each present special problems. Transport of the former has expanded from a local into a long distance undertaking, and individual farmers are seldom concerned with the retail sale or the actual delivery of their milk, but where they are equipped to undertake these operations the results have almost invariably been highly remunerative. In the case of certain East Anglian farms it has been the possession of a "milk round" that alone has brought their owners through the last few years. Acting together, too, they have shown that this commodity, from its very nature, places considerable power in their hands, and, so long as there was no danger of over-production occurring, dairy farmers have generally succeeded in securing a reasonable profit. Cheese is nowadays rarely the subject of individual sale, for the bulk of it goes through the hands of middlemen at special markets. Wool, again, provides examples of large annual sales conducted on peculiar principles, that, none the less, appear to satisfy all concerned; here, it must be remembered that British farmers have by no means a monopoly, and prices are subject to wide-flung influences. Fruit presents special difficulties, for it is more prone to fluctuations in supply (and, therefore, in price) than any other product of the soil, and at the same time it is never free from potential competition from abroad; there is also nowhere greater disparity found between first and last costs. All are familiar with accounts of tons of plums consigned to Covent Garden or other centres of distribution, which, after picking, carriage and commission have been paid, returned merely a few shillings to the grower; but such things are bound to occur with commodities in erratic supply, and the regular returns from smaller consignments on other occasions are apt to be overlooked. The same argument applies to the profits secured by retailers in this trade, for it is too often assumed that their annual receipts are closely linked with the exceptional turnover occurring in a few weeks of summer. Probably much of the feeling engendered against them would be dissipated if the results of their year's trading, which covered long periods when overhead charges predominated, were laid open for examination by producers. Sale of fruit by commission is open to attack, but when, as a result, all the difficulties attendant upon finding a regular outlet disappear, it is not easy to put forward counter proposals. Nothing short of a complete retail organisation, and one capable of extremely rapid expansion, could meet the situation, but for long periods of the year charges would be mounting up while trade was at a standstill. Again, only a limited number of towns in this country can absorb large quantities of fruit, and, as matters now are, the producing districts send practically the whole of their output either to London or the great cities of the North, and no alteration in the system of retailing could affect the demands from elsewhere. All indications lead to the supposition that the commercial grower in the long run secures commercial profits, for the acreage under fruit increases year by year, and fresh districts are being devoted to this form of husbandry. The modern developments in preserving and canning are now widely available, and in response to good demands absorb growing quantities of both soft fruit and vegetables.

The sale of all types of small agricultural produce within Great Britain suffers under one unexpected, but serious, disability, for there is no legal compulsion requiring a certain standard of quality or level of packing, although the "National Mark" scheme has, in certain instances, been quite widely adopted. Overseas competitors —especially, for example, the Danes—are forced to conform to fixed rules in this respect, and the result is seen in the uniformly high quality associated with all their produce. The reason is two-fold. Practically confined to an export trade, producers are bound to join an Association, which in turn must enforce a high standard from its individual members. The State itself is interested in seeing that Danish produce leaves the country in a condition to meet severe competition, and therefore initiates, or supplements, every step taken by the Associations. British producers are free to adopt any, or no, standard, so that when their articles meet those of the foreigner, packing, grading and guarantees are at best divergent, and often inferior. It may be urged that in the case of a purely internal trade such things matter little, but second thoughts will show that, so long as growers are dependent upon retailers, a uniform standard that can be relied upon is a considerable asset. The efforts of individuals frequently need directing, and fresh openings could often be secured if attention were paid to certain elementary details. Ireland should occupy in relation to this country the position that Denmark has secured for herself; her climate and soil are more suitable for the production of bacon, eggs and cheese than are those of the latter, and she is within easier access. Peculiarity of temperament and a lack of the sense of corporate responsibility must be held to blame, of which defects the several attempts made by a certain English family to deal with Southern Irish producers will afford an illustration. An answer to an advertisement offering fowls for sale resulted in a pair of birds arriving, which, upon examination, were found to be perforated by innumerable pellets. On expostulations and enquiry being made, the reply came from Ireland that the birds were very wild and had to be shot when roosting in the trees! On another occasion an order for a turkey resulted in a magnificent bird being delivered in a condition that showed it had been high before it left its native country. A third effort was made when sections of honey were being advertised. This time the English post office notified the consignees that some sticky brown paper, which could not be placed in contact with other parcels, awaited their orders. The honey had been merely wrapped up in string and paper. Finally—and lastly, for that particular family—a sackful of wood anemone plants arrived, the contents of which had been shaved off level with the ground, and the long roots, of course, severed. The minute attention paid to detail by the French and other Continental nations would never allow such happenings as the above, and it is to be feared that when preference is shown for imported articles, the Irish producer often has nobody but himself, or rather, his kind to blame. The creameries established in Ireland, and the resultant large quantities of Irish butter sold in Great Britain, show what can be accomplished by a disciplined body, even if individuals fail to perceive that (in the event of direct sale) the producer's part is not accomplished when he has raised his commodities, and that the art of retail salesmanship consists, not only in securing a market, but in retaining it by the aid of satisfied customers.

If marketing Associations can but improve the means by which articles are prepared and delivered for sale, a higher value is bound in the long run to accrue to the latter. The contention that the costs of carriage eat up an undue proportion of profits is difficult to generalise upon, but it is significant that it is most audible when a "slump" prevails and prices have fallen. If plums are flooding the market, or a million additional tons of potatoes are available, the railway companies are certain to be blamed for the pecuniary situation created. They themselves made a very effective answer to these allegations when, in 1927, they issued a statement showing their actual charges for carrying different food-stuffs from the provinces to London. For the sum of one penny, five pints of milk could thus be conveyed from Salisbury, one dozen eggs from Bristol, three pounds of butter from Somerset, four pounds of meat from Liverpool, twelve and a half pounds of potatoes from Spalding and eight pounds of jam from Histon. The companies further convincingly demonstrated that the proportion attributable to transport of the full price paid by the consumers was less than it had been in 1913—typical figures being, pre-war 4 to 5 per cent., post-war 3 to 4 per cent. This, at a time when practically all charges were some 50 per cent. above the 1913 level and the cost of railway labour had more than doubled, was unanswerable. Subsequently, it will be remembered, as a result of partial derating, the companies passed on their reliefs to the consignors of agricultural commodities, which meant an aggregate reduction of £800,000 per annum upon a class of goods that could not previously have been described as overcharged.

That a widespread system of delivery by motor lorries would be cheaper than rail transport, even for distances from fifty to one hundred miles, is doubtful; that it would be as certain and efficient in functioning under the rapidly changing conditions associated with the marketing of agricultural products is highly improbable. The alleged preference accorded consignments of imported fruit by British railways has also been shown to be baseless; the British producer has only to offer his wares in equal bulk to secure at least comparable rates. On the other hand, attempts made by the companies to help small producers—notably that of the former Great Eastern Railway, by which not only special rates were granted, but even boxes supplied—have not been favourably received. Two quite recent steps taken by the railways have, however, met with considerable success—the provision of large tank cars for the conveyance of milk and the extension, by means of rail-head centres, of their motor-lorry service into rural districts, often far distant from the lines themselves. Their organisation, too, of the concentrated but fluctuating traffic in connection with the sugar-beet factories has again demonstrated to farmers that they have not only friends upon the railway administration, but also an extremely efficient and adaptable service at their command. Foreign competition in all subsidiary branches of the industry has been intensified, and it behoves the home producer to see that he leaves no stone unturned to improve his means of countering it, for he cannot expect to rely entirely upon direct support from the State.

Indirectly he had secured a small measure of State assistance before the imposition of duties, for certain imported articles had to be marked with their country of origin; this, however, was not necessarily always a handicap to them, and indeed sometimes it has been in the nature of an advertisement. The provision of markets and their adequate maintenance represents the State assumption of duties afterwards delegated to local authorities. The collection of statistics relating, not only to prices current, but to the quantities of certain commodities exhibited for sale, is perhaps not the least useful function undertaken for agriculturists by the administration. A description of the former will be found in Chapter xx, and, in regard to the latter, it may be pointed out that only in the case of live-stock and cereals (and in certain markets) is there any statutory obligation on the Ministry of Agriculture to prepare data on these lines. That very comprehensive official descriptions of conditions ruling at numerous centres are available each week for producers is therefore due to voluntary action on the part of the Ministry in issuing its "Return of Market Prices". The value of these accounts is apparent to anyone who will take the trouble to glance through the so-called "market reports" of provincial papers—reports which would otherwise afford the farmer his only source of information. There, only inaccurate generalisations repeated week after week, exaggerated reports, or such extraordinary statistical expressions as that "prices have fallen 100 per cent." greet his eyes. Here, too, the previously mentioned "Orange" series of *Reports* have been of inestimable value, and mention must also be made of the Empire Marketing Board's publications dealing with supplies of primary goods, both from the producer's and the consumer's standpoint. Lastly, the material annually incorporated in the statistical returns of the Ministry of Agriculture completes a "documentation" which is not only unrivalled in other countries but ridiculously cheap to acquire.

In the United States the problem of affording some measure of help to agricultural producers had, until recently, been left in the hands of individual States, with the result that "Bureaux of markets" and "State Directors of Marketing" appeared, the activities of the latter officials covering such widespread duties as the dissemination of information relative to prices and statistics of supplies and to the movements of farm products; the promotion of co-operative associations; the encouraging of standardised packing, grading, inspection and methods of sale; the issuing of official marks for approved merchandise; the supplying of advice and assistance to individual producers; and generally the facilitating of the internal and external sale of their State's agricultural commodities. As the typically American cry of "Swat the middleman" was raised in regard to the marketing of such articles as fruit and vegetables, it was not surprising to find that Market Bureaux extended their operations to include direct intervention in certain methods of sale. For instance, James E. Boyle in *Agricultural Economics* declared that the New York Department of Foods and Markets "pursued a militant course from the start. The New York bakers were forced to restore the 5 cent loaf of bread, after raising it to 6 cents. The price of cold storage eggs was attacked. Jobbers and retailers were required to put signs on cold storage eggs. To help the milk production interests, an auction of dairy cows was held under the supervision of the Department. Farm shippers used the Department in investigating claims against transportation companies". The same writer held that under a law, passed in 1918, "the State of New York is equipped with the most complete administrative machinery in the field of marketing to be found in the United States. Aside from investigation, advice etc. provided for in all recent market laws, this New York law provides for the establishment of public markets in cities, towns and villages, and for State financial aid to those markets to the extent of 50 per cent. of the expense". With the exception of the attack on the New York price of bread described above, almost all these American plans had, as their primary object, the transference to the producer of the retailer's profit. That, except in the case of fruit, where it was some 30 to 40 per cent., or vegetables, the retailer's rate of profit was not then really excessive in America, was shown by an analysis, brought together in Boyle's work, of the distribution of the total cost of different products. For cattle, the relevant figures appeared to be in the neighbourhood of 25 per cent., for butter from 10 to 20 per cent., for eggs 16 per cent., for potatoes 15 to 30 per cent. All the above figures must be accepted as merely affording rough indications of the division of the ultimate cost between the retailer and the producer; they do not, of course, offer any criterion as to the rate of return on capital secured by each party, and the comparative expenses involved in raising and selling the different commodities are also left out of the calculation. When comparing marketing conditions in the United States with those in this country, it must not be forgotten that, not only do the distances involved call for the provision of storage and other facilities on almost an export level, but that the machinery of transport is on a vastly different scale, thirty to forty ton trucks being the unit.

The United States Tariff Act of 1922, representing a measure of universal, as opposed to local, assistance, imposed really high duties, on, among other commodities, practically all forms of agricultural products, ranging from livestock to fruit trees. Whilst this Act afforded unmistakable evidence of the States' solicitude for trade in general, it soon became apparent that, for the American farmer in particular, it would turn out to be a mixed blessing; before, however, discussing these wider aspects of the trans-Atlantic situation the circumstances that led up to it call for explanation.

A Commission that investigated the conditions of agriculture in America ten years ago made recommendations under the following ten heads:

(1) That co-operative combinations of farmers for the purpose of marketing, grading, sorting or distributing their products be legalised.
(2) That the banking system be adapted to allow farmers to obtain credits corresponding to their turnover with maturity of from six months to three years.
(3) That the warehousing system be made uniform in all the several States of the Union.
(4) That reductions of freight rates on agricultural produce are absolutely necessary.
(5) That the statistical divisions of the Department of Agriculture be extended, particularly to improve the livestock statistics.
(6) That agricultural *attachés* be provided in the principal foreign countries.
(7) That more accurate, uniform and practical grades of agricultural products and standards of measures be developed.

(8) That better book- and record-keeping of costs of production be promoted.
(9) That practical and scientific investigation directed towards reducing the hazards of climate and weather conditions and of plant and animal diseases and insect pests be provided.
(10) That facilities for distribution at large consuming centres be better organised and more adequate facilities be provided for handling produce.

The importance attached both to internal and external facilities for marketing is thus well illustrated, for only two of the sections failed to deal directly with this problem. Although, in the meantime, progress had been effected in all these fields, yet neither the control exercised by individual States nor expansion in co-operative activities could counter the financial difficulties which supervened nine and ten years later. It remained for the United States Government itself to take action, the results of which, so far as wheat alone was concerned, have already been briefly sketched.

The Agricultural Marketing Act, which was passed by Congress in June 1929, was the foundation of an edifice in which the Federal Farm Board formed one storey. The policy itself was, in the preamble to the Act, declared to be as follows:

To promote the effective merchandising of agricultural commodities in interstate and foreign commerce, so that the industry of agriculture will be placed on a basis of economic equality with other industries, and to that end to protect, control, and stabilise the currents of interstate and foreign commerce in the marketing of agricultural commodities and their food products:

(1) By minimising speculation.
(2) By preventing inefficient and wasteful methods of distribution.
(3) By encouraging the organisation of producers into effective associations or corporations under their own control for greater unity of effort in marketing and by promoting the establishment and financing of a farm marketing system of producer-owned and producer-controlled co-operative associations and other agencies.
(4) By aiding in preventing and controlling surpluses in any agricultural commodity, through orderly production and distribution, so as to maintain advantageous domestic markets and prevent such surpluses from causing undue and excessive fluctuations or depressions in prices for the commodity.

There shall be considered as a surplus for the purposes of this act any seasonal or year's total surplus, produced in the United States and either local or national in extent, that is in excess of the requirements for the orderly distribution of the agricultural commodity or is in excess of the domestic requirements for such commodity.

The Federal Farm Board shall execute the powers vested in it by this act only in such manner as will, in the judgment of the board, aid to the fullest practicable extent in carrying out the policy above declared.

Overriding powers were conferred upon the eight members of the Board itself, which was authorised to carry out investigations into every subject—even remotely affecting the marketing of primary commodities—to advance loans to co-operative undertakings for capital or other expenditure, to set up "Stabilisation Corporations" and Clearing House Associations and in every other way to attempt to dam the economic flood. The famous "Revolving Fund", of 500,000,000 dollars, was placed at its disposal and a feeling of renewed confidence was optimistically engendered among American farmers. Broadly speaking, the principal steps taken were those in connection with the expansion and amalgamation of existing co-operative associations. Thus, in the case of cotton, the American Cotton Co-operative Association was formed—in order to handle the bulk of that crop in 1930 and later years; the tobacco producers were similarly reorganised and much attention was devoted to the fruit and vegetable industries. To the livestock and dairy trades, where co-operation was already firmly established, the Board gave encouragement, financial and otherwise. After two years of falling prices, the depletion of the Revolving Fund was nearly complete, but the Board could claim that, either directly or indirectly, it still held off the world's market vast quantities of American farm products, which would otherwise have reduced prices still further. In the Board's own words at that time, "the first half of stabilisation—accumulating supplies—has taken place within the last two years; the second half—disposing of the accumulated supplies—is still to be completed". It appeared that many of the corporations concerned wished always to buy and never to sell! Attempts made to effect acreage reductions of certain crops failed to bring about any tangible results and suggestions were advanced simultaneously for the transference of certain less suitable lands to afforestation. Ultimately, as previously recorded, the Federal Farm Board was forced to curtail its financial support and in the case of certain commodities to withdraw from its holding position. It had maintained prices for a period of time; it had, for a shorter space of time, restored some degree of confidence to the producers and it had been responsible for a widespread and successful inculcation of co-operative principles. In the circumstances prevailing, nothing further could seriously have been expected from it. The selling—whether for external or internal consumption—of American primary products has thus not been revolutionised by means of an Agricultural Marketing Act; progress has, in certain cases, been expedited, and important lessons have been learned. Revolving Funds might dizzily revolve, but the laws effective of supply and demand remained immutable and, except so far as reduced purchasing power and unemployment were responsible for modifications, the normal elasticity of consumers' different demands remained unaffected. In a word, such a policy could not render economic forces impotent; it did, for a time, delay their onset; it would probably have been better in the long run if matters had been allowed to pursue their normal course, for acreages would have been reduced and marginal producers eliminated. However, such practices were, the whole world over, in those times debarred and "orderly marketing", "stabilisation" and "price control" expensively substituted.

Our own Dominions and Colonies have, as has been described previously, in several instances adopted "farmers' pools", or national marketing schemes, over which the State exercises considerable hold, and it is not surprising to find the Union of South Africa, New Zealand and the Australian States, not only making regulations in regard to packing and grading, but able fully to enforce them. The Marketing Boards themselves act as agents for disposal, but in many instances share with the executives the duty of compelling a high standard in their countries' products. The South African fruit trade, in particular, has been built up on a judicious combination of compulsion and co-operation. Producers' Societies organise their members, supply them with every facility for handling and packing their products and advertise the latter in this country. The Union Government, in collaboration with the steamship companies, exercises a rigid system of inspection and, by means of rejecting any package not up to grade, ensures the maintenance of a really high and uniform standard.

In all the constituent States of Australia, compulsion has been applied to the marketing of agricultural commodities intended for internal consumption as well as for export. Between 1924 and 1928, for example, dried fruit came under control in both Western Australia and in Queensland, marketing Boards (not, by any means, always in supersession of existing Co-operative Societies) having been accorded power to purchase and sell all such products and to raise levies for the financing of this work. In Queensland in particular, and also in New South Wales, the Boards were rapidly extended, until their activities covered every type of soil product, of which by 1930 they were handling more than one-half. Producers were well represented in their councils and, in some cases, compulsory voting had been introduced in order that their members in general should take an active interest in directing policy. As in the case of South Africa, where a purely export trade was concerned, the Australian Commodity Boards took steps to prevent any but approved consignments from leaving their shores; once again, the beneficial results of this policy are witnessed in every grocer's, fruiterer's and dairyman's shop in London.

In New Zealand, powers of coercion were accorded to a clear majority of producers, who might proceed to the formation of the usual type of fully representative Boards, the main activities of which centred upon the export trade, although provision was also made for the control of internal trade. Needless to add, compulsion extends to the packing and grading of all the products concerned.

The Irish Free State and Ulster have both passed legislation of a less drastic character than is implicit in the examples quoted above, but of a type that has gone far to ensure a greater uniformity in their respective products and has demonstrated the desire of both the Governments concerned to study the requirements of the great consuming centres so near at hand.

Overseas producers, starting with certain initial advantages, e.g. those of climate, soil and labour, have therefore had forced upon them the economic assistance provided by co-operation. By such means has their trade been fostered and expanded to its present dimensions. As abroad, so in Great Britain, has the whole question of the return secured by the farmer for his various products assumed more importance since the war and the position, to which the industry was previously becoming reconciled, has received fresh attention from the State and from the consumer. This is partly attributable to a feeling of restlessness engendered in the latter from the failure of retail prices to follow those of the wholesaler and the producer—a phenomenon that has been always observed in times of falling costs. During another period of depression the Royal Commission of 1893 secured the views of representative agriculturists upon this vexed question, when criticism of conditions existing at that time generally took the form of protests against the alleged masquerading as British of imported meat and other goods, whereby the home producer lost part of his market and the retailer secured fraudulent profits. More stringent regulations to compel the marking of all foreign articles exposed for sale were demanded. The existence of monopolistic markets was unfavourably commented on, and the unfettered provision of these facilities, at any time and in any place, was urged, one witness advocating the setting up in London of an equivalent to the Paris Halles, by which means produce might be safeguarded against the salesman. For the small producer it was suggested that the Post Office might come to his assistance through a lowering of parcel rates, thereby following precedents found abroad. The introduction, a few years ago, of the Cash on Delivery (C.O.D.) system has met this point and farmers are adopting it for the delivery by post of numerous light and perishable commodities. The position revealed some forty years ago differs little save in degree from that of recent years, but the tentative proposals of 1893, which the course of time has in the main seen effected, have been superseded by larger constructive efforts. The National Farmers' Union was as outspoken in its election address of 1922 as any individual representatives of the industry had been in 1893, for two of its demands were thus phrased: (*a*) "The way in which Government statistics of prices are presented to the public successfully prevents any proper comparison being made between the price *you* pay and that received by the producer. Farmers ask that full information shall be given to the public and that an enquiry shall be conducted into costs of distribution". (*b*) "Much imported produce is now palmed off on the public as home grown. Farmers ask that the Merchandise Marks Act shall be amended so that this fraud on the consumer may be stopped". The first demand was promptly met, on lines described a few pages back; the second statement, although probably an exaggeration due to the atmosphere prevailing at the time it was uttered, has now been rendered impossible of repetition by a combination of voluntary and compulsory marking regulations. The trend of public opinion having thus been illustrated with a brief epitome of the comparatively meagre legislative effects that had resulted, the time is ripe to discuss the drastic overhauling of the position that has, in very recent times, taken place. Certain premises concerning the divergent character of agricultural products themselves and of the types of farm from which they emanate must, however, first be postulated. British wheat is essentially the product of large-scale farming, and its price is not only governed by that of imported supplies, but its preparation into food accounts for the large charges added to its original cost; this preparation, moreover, is not within the power of the grower to undertake, for co-operative principles neither appeal to the large farmer nor are they generally efficacious when extended to manufacturing processes. Other cereals are consumed in the raw state, or, exceptionally, as in the case of malting barley, bring to the grower reasonably good returns in times that are normal. Cattle and sheep, in the main, represent the product of medium and of large farms, and there is considerable profit made by those who prepare them for sale in retail form. Again, however, these final stages cannot be undertaken by the farmer. Pigs intended for conversion into bacon stand in a class by themselves. They come preponderatingly from the small farm, and, if they have to undergo elaborate processes, the resultant food does not call for immediate retail sale. For these reasons co-operative, as well as individual, bacon factories have, even in recent times, been enabled to secure very good profits, and there appears to be every valid reason why, under the provisions of the Marketing Acts, their numbers should increase. Milk is produced upon farms of all sizes, and in both arable and grass districts, but calls for a most highly organised system of transportation and delivery. At first glance the disparity of prices here seems overwhelming, but this is one of the few articles which is delivered to individual purchasers, frequently after being conveyed very long distances. That the retailer makes large profits is not denied, but that the producer could everywhere satisfactorily usurp his multifarious duties is questionable. From its very nature, however, milk confers certain assets upon its original possessor, and combination for the purposes of withholding or diverting supplies has been shown to be a weapon of considerable utility.

One is now left with the "small" produce of agriculture. Fruit growing, whilst undoubtedly returning fair profits to favourably situated undertakings, satisfies neither producer nor consumer by reason of the unexampled disparity in values with which they come in contact, and the situation in regard to poultry and eggs is not dissimilar. In both cases, if large scale commercial undertakings be excluded, there appears to be considerable opening for some method by which the gap between producer and consumer could be bridged. District or village associations of producers, formed for the express purpose of retailing, either in shops, in public markets, or from door to door, those articles which are peculiar to Small Holders and small farmers, should have a future before them. Their only handicap is the inherent conservatism of their potential members, which perhaps certain aspects of the policy now to be described may, in course of time, dissipate.

For some ten years, under different Governments, attention was progressively paid to the selling, or marketing, side of the industry, in attempts to alleviate the position of British agriculture. This was inevitable when it became apparent that grandiose schemes, involving the application of direct subsidies, were receding from the realm of practical politics and when all reliefs that could reasonably be looked for under the heading of taxation had been granted, for, apart from fiscal innovations—only in the last resort to be adopted—there remained no other line of attack. The first move was made in 1922 by the appointment of the Linlithgow Committee. When its conclusions, which appeared two years later in a voluminous *Report*, came to be summarised, it must be remembered that the shadow of the war still overhung the country and affected the outlook of its members.

The Committee agreed that, in general, the spread between producers' and consumers' prices was too wide, although, here, they differentiated markedly between various branches of the industry; they further agreed that the preparation of food-stuffs for human consumption added greatly to their prime cost, but they held it possible to concentrate much of the intermediate processes into the hands of one functionary. The "position of the traders in agricultural produce during a period of acute depression in the producing industry" had, in their words, been "an enviable one". So, too, it was implied, was that still occupied by the workers engaged in the distribution and transportation of these same goods, for their real wages were considerably in excess of what they had been before the war. That upheaval, it was suggested, had left its mark, too, in the shape of an altered psychological outlook on the part of traders and of consumers: competition was reduced and energies concentrated upon methods of maintaining prices. Conversely, there were far too many small, or undersized, establishments engaged in retail business. The consumer, too, did not escape criticism, for he was blamed in that he required an extravagant degree of "service" in that most expensive stage—the retail. Finally, greater facilities for co-operation and for the provision of credit, the study of prices and the collection of statistics were demanded. More detailed findings were as follows: produce should be standardised; the producer himself should acquire a "marketing sense"; the railways ought to foster British agriculture; great importance attached to road transport and to the construction of new highways; the Post Office was, in effect, retrograde; market Bureaux should be established, whose province it would be to advise producers what to grow, when to sell and where to sell.

The Committee's views upon the different branches of the industry are also worthy of record. Cereals, they held, were less subject to competition than previously; there were too many mills which, with wages then doubled and with heavy overhead charges, could not make adequate profits unless they were working at full pressure. If distributive charges were recognised at their true weight, the loaf was not "unduly" expensive, but there was, admittedly, a serious time-lag when prices were falling. The all-British loaf (of "Yeoman" wheat) was recommended to the public. In the case of milk, London charges were said to be fair, but a tendency for them to be extended to outside areas was deprecated. Price agreements between groups of producers and of distributors were approved in principle, although concurrently some closer control over the actions of large combines was deemed necessary. The fruit trade presented "unique" methods of consignment and of distribution. Here, small producers should combine; Covent Garden was too small; wholesalers' profits were not excessive; commission agents required watching in such matters as averaging and re-consigning; non-returnable packets were better (and cheaper) than returnable; grading and packing were essential. In the meat trade there was evidence of the existence of "rings" at auction sales; the weights of fat stock should be exhibited before sale; little more than half the cattle markets had weighbridges within their confines; public abattoirs were desirable; retailers' profits had increased; the source—whether foreign or British—of all meat should be indicated upon it; bacon and pork could, with advantage, be handled co-operatively. As will be seen later, the majority of the actual recommendations were duly implemented.

Next, in order of chronological sequence, there followed a *Report* of the Imperial Economic Committee advocating a policy of "Empire produce for home consumption", which, it was explained, should imply first preference being given to home produce, the second to that of our Dominions and Colonies and relėgation to the last resort of foreign commodities. The clear identification of Empire goods was demanded and a vigorous educational policy for the consumer was coupled therewith. The urgency of endowing research in all branches of primary production, both at home and overseas, was stressed. These recommendations formally begat, in 1926, the Empire Marketing Board, whose tripartite functions—respectively the promotion of scientific investigation, the study of economic factors and the advocacy of Imperial unity—have been modelled upon them. Endowed at first with an annual grant of £1,000,000 (subsequently reduced to half that sum), this Board, thoroughly representative of all the interests concerned, quickly got to work, and, after certain initial difficulties had been overcome, succeeded admirably in harmonising the sometimes conflicting interests of its constituent members. It endowed Chairs in British and in Dominion Universities; it provided capital grants for the creation or enlargement of Research Institutions—ranging from those investigating problems of animal nutrition and of cold storage to the ocean transportation of fruit. By means of a press campaign and of a lavish display of posters, it popularised knowledge concerning the relative importance and the quality of British and Empire products. Its sub-Committees have studied, and reported upon, the economics of primary production in all its aspects and in every country of the world, while it has broken new ground with a statistical service intended to assist all persons engaged in the raising, handling and consumption of Nature's products. The E.M.B., to give it a familiar title, has been justified in most of its works, and can claim to have performed more than a minor part in preparation for the policy which culminated at Ottawa. It was, however, scheduled for extinction in the autumn of 1933, with the understanding that its work of supplying information relative to production and consumption of primary commodities would be taken over by other Departments.

Legislation, directed towards strengthening the position of the British producer in his dealings with the middleman, was the next phase to be observed, for, in 1926, the Horticultural Produce (Sales on Commission) Act provided safeguards against certain irregularities—to use no stronger phrase—which were rampant in the case of sales by commission. Hitherto growers often received, from those persons to whom they had consigned their goods, mere statements of the net sum alleged to be due to them, with no indication of the charges that had been previously deducted. "Averaging", too, was freely indulged in, whereby, when values had fluctuated, or individual quality had varied, a uniform rate of payment was adopted. The new Act required full details to be furnished to its sender, of all charges against every consignment, together with the actual prices realised by each separately. Whilst enforcing penalties for evasion and giving power of inspection over records, it is permissive, in the sense that its provisions can be contracted out of by mutual agreement between the consignor and his agent.

Next, what was popularly referred to as the "Rings" Act, but in reality the Auction (Bidding Agreements) Act, 1927, was placed upon the Statute-book. This attempted to cope with the long-standing abuses associated with local auctions, especially those at which fruit, poultry and similar produce changed hands under conditions which negatived the principles of fair sale. Rings, or associations, of buyers, after mutually eliminating competition and effecting, through one representative, their purchases, were—is it really safe, even now, to use the past tense?—in the habit of re-selling the goods amongst themselves. The Act declared such practices illegal at all public auctions, defining them as the "gift or offer to give any consideration...as an inducement or reward for abstaining from bidding"; significantly, perhaps, prosecutions under its provisions have been few and far between.

A year later there appeared the highly important Agricultural Produce (Grading and Marking) Act, the aims of which are clearly indicated by its title. It authorised the Minister of Agriculture, upon request made to him by approved producers, to permit the use of the official "National Mark". Amongst certain sections of wholesale and retail traders there was considerable opposition to this innovation, and, notably in the meat business, it was but slowly introduced. In most other branches of British agriculture however the Mark soon became familiar and, if not even now ubiquitous, it has succeeded in improving and making uniform standards. In the case of eggs and fruit, it met with special success, and the public have come to regard such commodities, when thus stamped and emanating from registered central packing or clearing houses, as of guaranteed standard and quality; in the long run, producers are bound to benefit financially by the adoption of this device. In 1931, the provisions of the Grading Act were extended to cover every form of primary product. Incidentally, it is still open to interested parties to proceed in specific cases, under the Merchandise Marks Act, by requesting that their origin should be indicated upon imported goods.

A new division of the Ministry of Agriculture was created concurrently with the coming into force of the above-mentioned Acts; indeed, this Markets Branch might claim to have been responsible for much of the preparatory legal work involved in their own passage into law. It soon proved itself to be one of the most active departments of the Ministry, and has worked in close contact with both the Empire Marketing Board and representatives of the farming community. Thus, a complementary link in the official machinery was forged. The Scotch and Irish Departments of Agriculture similarly bestirred themselves, becoming active in the promotion of schemes for the marketing of their farm produce and, in certain instances, for its marking.

After 1928, a pause might have been observed in these activities, partly attributable to political and economic exigencies, but mainly in preparation for the launching of a revolutionary scheme. Of this, the Agricultural Marketing Act of 1931 was the *pièce de résistance.* Concurrently, Import duties—both general and, in the case of Horticultural products, of a supplementary character—were put into force; by means of a quota system the price of wheat was artificially raised; and quantitative restriction of certain imported goods was agreed upon with the interests concerned. As the latter measures are dealt with in the Chapter covering post-war agriculture, they will here be ignored, while an attempt is made to describe the machinery and the aims of the Marketing Act itself.

First and foremost, this Act conferred powers upon a proved majority of growers to coerce the minority into a certain course of action. As was explained previously, this principle had been at the basis of the success attaching to overseas Pools, but it had only once before been attempted, or even permitted, in this country, viz. in the case of post-war hop-growers. The relevant section of the Act brought within its scope "any product of agriculture or horticulture and any article of food or drink, wholly or partly manufactured or derived from any such product, and fleeces and the skins of animals". Wherever, in Great Britain, producers of any of these commodities desire to control their sale or their marketing, they can, henceforward, submit to the Minister of Agriculture a detailed proposal to that effect; equally, the Minister himself can call upon a specially appointed "Reorganization Committee" to prepare a scheme, and he will then submit it to the producers concerned. It has been officially explained that these schemes may be of two types, (*a*) in which regulation would affect the marketing of a given product raised in the related area wherever it was sold, or (*b*) where regulation would be effective over the sale, within the particular area, of the product, wherever it had been raised. The first of these alternatives has, however, formed the basis of the schemes so far discussed and now in course of completion. Proposals for control may relate either to all forms of one commodity or merely to a given type of product.

After initiation, proposals must be approved by a two-thirds majority (in terms both of output and of numbers) of those competent to vote, and stringent safeguards are provided to ensure that opportunities should be provided for any subsequent representations to be made in connection with the polling. In due course, after public notice given, all schemes must be presented to Parliament for its approval and must finally pass through a "suspensory" period. The Act, then, is purely permissive and inflicts no form of extraneous compulsion upon British farmers, but it does enable them to apply coercion to their own brethren. Parliament will only intervene when, in effect, requested to do so by a majority of producers; it has, moreover, undertaken to make initial loans to the resultant Boards, up to a total sum of £625,000. It is intended that the Boards shall be of different forms, viz. trading, regulatory and also of a type combining these two functions. The first will be empowered to acquire, and to sell the whole of the commodity over which it has been given control; the second, whilst running less financial risk by reason of abstention from direct trading activities, may exercise considerable price determination and can affect widely conditions of sale. In both cases, it has been officially explained that really great powers will be possessed by the Boards, for it will be within their province to fix prices, both wholesale and retail—actual, maximum or minimum—to divert products to factory or other purposes, to deflect supplies into particular channels, to refuse recognition to certain qualities of goods, to select selling agencies, or to operate a pool; further, Boards may expend their funds—these funds, partly, if they so decide, to be derived by levies from registered members—upon investigations upon any scientific and economic problems that affect their interests. Primary producers should now surely possess almost every weapon to be found in the economic armoury!

Reference to the element of compulsion has been left to the last. Here, powers are conferred that enforce registration upon all producers of the commodity to be regulated—or, rather, deny to non-registered persons the right to sell that article—provision being made for the granting of exemptions in particular cases. Financial penalties will be enforceable for non-compliance with these conditions, and will also be applicable, in the form of a levy, to discourage increased output, e.g. the potato grower who, contrary to instructions, adds to his area may find that it costs him £5 an acre to do so. On the other hand, safeguards for the public will be provided in the shape of a Committee of Consumers, to be brought into existence when the first Board is formed. The Minister of Agriculture has also very great powers reserved to himself and, further, he is, by certain clauses of the Act, instructed to report to Parliament if he considers that any specific scheme is proving unsatisfactory.

Early in 1933, as a supplement to the above Act, another Agricultural Marketing Bill was introduced, which sought to bring under regulation supplies from extraneous sources. Here, the Board of Trade was empowered to restrict imports of any agricultural products already subject to the provisions of the 1931 Act, or, which, it was proposed, should be so controlled in the future. The Government then in power held that only by such methods could the (price-raising) intentions of the sponsors of the 1931 Act be adequately pursued. Further powers were also accorded to the Boards in process of formation in order to give them control over secondary products of the industry, e.g. bacon, ham and canned fruit, and a Market Supply Committee was set up to "review generally the circumstances affecting the supply of agricultural commodities". During the second reading of this Agricultural Marketing Act (1933) the Minister of Agriculture, Major Walter Elliot, claimed that, as a result of its past policy, "the Government had been able to secure a rise of 20 to 30 per cent. in wholesale prices, without raising the level of retail prices by more than 2 or 3 per cent."

In a general summary of the policy outlined in the preceding paragraphs the Minister also claimed that

> The Government had done their best to ensure that world trade was not strangled and restricted by a series of arbitrary decrees, and they would certainly ensure, in the discussions which took place in that House and with foreign countries, that the whole question of British trade, both export and import, was fully taken into account in making regulations under the Bill. They hoped to be able to do those things and preserve their friendship with foreign countries. Great Britain was the best market for agricultural produce, and for some commodities it was the only market, and the country had a responsibility as a great trading community which it certainly would not shirk. The Government proposed to deal with the problem by emphasizing the point that a remunerative level of prices was of advantage both to suppliers and consumers.

Such were the high principles attributed to a far-reaching experiment that, in some ways, resembled the overseas organisations previously described. What was officially termed "orderly" marketing had once again been put in the forefront of its objectives, but, significantly, perhaps, at first no provision was made for controlling output. Criticism was directed mainly against the alleged possible favouring of the less efficient producer at the expense of the more efficient and concerning the extent of the areas to be brought under control—admittedly a difficult matter. At the time of writing a Board has actually been adopted by the Hop industry, which had had previous experience (from 1925 to 1929) of voluntary regulation, under the aegis of Hop Growers Limited; the scheme was, in the winter of 1932–3, reported to be working satisfactorily. Certain Reorganisation Commissions have also reported, and the original Agricultural Marketing Act will probably next be extended to the potato, the milk, the pig and the fat-stock industries, but in the circumstances, it is obviously not possible to discuss any of these schemes in detail; they will, rightly, be applied to those farm commodities which exhibit, in a peculiar degree, features which it has been the aim of that Act to curb. The different branches of the milk trade present unique problems; pig prices fluctuate in a familiar short period cycle and are closely related to those of certain feeding stuffs; most forms of pig-meat are in keen competition with overseas products; co-operative methods are especially applicable to bacon factories. Potatoes form almost a monopoly of British producers, but are subject to severe seasonal competition from luxury varieties; they are principally produced in certain homogeneous areas; their output is subject to great variability; factory utilisation is possible. The fattening of stock has, in recent years, not been a remunerative branch of the industry; there is keen competition both from Imperial and from non-Imperial sources; consumers' predilections have altered since the war; the "spread" in prices is marked.

Here, then, are provided splendid opportunities to test the new machinery. British farmers, fortified by the Marketing Acts, wheat quota and tariff regulations, have had much done for them in regard to the economic and monetary side of their business—hitherto the least regarded aspect. Where conservative, they have been led; where recalcitrant, virtually driven. In turn, they will now be expected to study the consumers' wishes to, at least, the same extent as in the past have their overseas rivals, in order not to jeopardise their close connection with ten million (mainly urban) households whose members have, certainly at present, no such obvious reasons for welcoming the Agricultural Marketing Acts.

Chapter XV

AGRICULTURAL CO-OPERATION

Co-operation on the manor; its history and its advocates in the nineteenth century; agricultural co-operation abroad; Raiffeisen banks and alternative forms of co-operation in Germany; its development in France, Belgium and other European countries; in the New World; in India and Japan.

There is one method of organisation the advocates of which insistently claim could eliminate all the drawbacks referred to in the two previous Chapters. Co-operative principles, it is urged, if widely adopted, would, at one and the same time, bring the farmer a larger return for his produce, provide the consumer with better and cheaper food, and alleviate the whole agricultural situation by facilitating farm purchases, supplying credit and improving the standard of husbandry. *Ex parte* statements always require modification and, whilst certain of these contentions can be substantiated both here and abroad, many of them have yet to emerge satisfactorily from a prolonged practical test in these islands, and none of them is true for all countries.

The earliest example of co-operation applied to agriculture—and, indeed, to any industry—was the system of combined labour found on the mediaeval manor and in the still earlier Village Community. Co-operation was there literally typified, for each man, by furnishing oxen to the extent of his ability, assisted his neighbour at the plough; all helped in the general harvest-work and supported the common herdsman; ploughs and other implements were used by more than one cultivator. This was the form of husbandry extending over millions of acres in Western Europe for many hundreds of years. It was co-operative, so far as labour and the user of material were concerned, but, in the modern acceptance of the word, it lacked full development, in that an association of farmers was not the ultimate authority—the lord of the manor was always in the background, representing, in the eyes of modern critics, the capitalist. The lord possessed powers that no present-day body of tenants would tolerate, hence the analogy abruptly ceases, but, historically, one can point to this combination of tenants, for purposes of mutual benefit in actual field-operations, as of immemorial antiquity. The present-day societies of Small Holders, who band together to hire or purchase such machines as lie beyond their individual purses to acquire, are therefore but reverting to the customs of their Saxon forefathers. Both practices, however, represent co-operative agriculture, not agricultural co-operation—which is a very different matter. With the disappearance of the manor as an agricultural unit went this method of communal husbandry. It is a frequent form of accusation to make against present-day farmers that they are both backward in acknowledging the advantages of co-operation and antagonistic to its principles. Perhaps in the light of the above it is legitimate to answer that they were acquainted with these principles centuries before the birth of those industries which have now extensively put them into execution, and that, if they have not precipitately followed, it is because they have preferred to watch developments and to pick and choose those features that both tradition and reason suggested would stand them in best stead.

The next form in which mutual collaboration appeared in the rural districts of this country was represented by the village clubs and insurance societies which sprang up in the middle of the nineteenth century. A generation earlier co-operation had been tentatively applied to a few industrial undertakings, and at intervals throughout the century attempts were made on the part of individuals, by establishing groups of workers on a profit-sharing basis, to extend its principles to the tenancy of land. The former of course represented the beginnings of that vast and widely successful application of co-operation to all branches of urban distribution, initiated by the consumer; the latter experiments nowhere survived for more than a very few years.

It is, however, frequently assumed that there was an interregnum between the demise of the village insurance clubs and the inauguration of the modern societies at the commencement of the twentieth century. But, if actual associations were few in number, enthusiastic advocates were not lacking, and academic discussions at least afforded opportunities for familiarising rural districts with the principles at stake. Thus, in 1887, the position was placed very fully before the Essex Chamber of Commerce in a paper read by H. E. Moore, entitled "Agricultural Co-operation", in which the success achieved by such bodies as the "Western Counties Landowners' and

Farmers' Agricultural Co-operative Society" was referred to. Whilst it is impossible to follow the author's detailed account of the ideal society, acknowledgment must be made of the fact that he foresaw the lines development would follow, and correctly anticipated the difficulties that would be encountered. He summarised the aims of rural co-operators under the following nine heads:

1. To obtain for members foods, manures, seeds and implements direct from the wholesale manufacturer or merchant.
2. To obtain steam or other agricultural implements for the use of members.
3. To place the farmer in direct communication with the consumer by the establishment of depots and shops for the sale of agricultural produce.
4. To assist in the establishment of the factory system for dairy and other produce.
5. To provide free chemical analysis of manures and foods, and botanical examination of seeds purchased by members.
6. To offer prizes for every description of agricultural labour.
7. To make temporary loans to farmers.
8. To provide superannuation allowances for old servants.
9. To provide club accommodation for members, and to effect such union among them that they might be able to protect their interests.

This affords an extremely interesting commentary on the subsequent assumption of duties by the State and the farming community respectively, for almost all of these recommendations have since been adopted. The first four became essential elements in the programmes of co-operative societies, the fifth has been the subject of legislation, the sixth is still practised extensively, the seventh has been provided for—first by Societies and latterly by the State—responsibility for the eighth has also been definitely assumed by the State, and lastly the ninth has been carried out, as well by the Farmers' Union as by the formation of village clubs. Thus, even in agriculture the ideals of one generation become the accomplishments of the next.

The whole subject of co-operation received ventilation a few years later, when the Royal Commission afforded an opportunity for its disciples and its derogators alike to express their views. It is apparent, from reading through the evidence of witnesses, that many landowners assumed that co-operation implied some system of profit-sharing among employees, the success of which they did not anticipate. On the other hand, farmers, whilst almost invariably admitting that co-operation was not practised in their own neighbourhood, agreed that it should advantage them in the purchase of requirements and might do so in their sales. Fortunately, all were not so antagonistic as the Scots farmer who declared: "I think nothing of it all; everything is far better left to individual effort...; it [a Dairy Company] was to distribute milk cheaper and do everything to make things better, but the only thing it has done has been to lose a lot of money of the shareholders". The third class of witness, comprising the scientist and the economist, urged the claims of combination, especially in the realm of marketing, and advocated the setting up of creameries on the lines of the then already very successful ventures in Denmark. As a result of the Commission, no official steps were taken to aid the movement, and its history in Great Britain during the subsequent ten years contains little of moment.

From this point onward it is necessary to turn to other countries and to trace there the separate development of each branch, finally reverting to the United Kingdom for discussion of the modifications peculiar to it. Germany must be accorded pride of place, for with her are always associated the names of those two individuals who acted as pioneers in the first half of the nineteenth century—Friedrich Wilhelm Raiffeisen and Franz Hermann Schulze-Delitzsch. The organisation that derived its name from the former was in origin philanthropic and in scope rural, while Schulze-Delitzsch banks were grounded on a business foundation and practically confined to the towns. Raiffeisen, in his capacity of burgomaster, saw the peasants, whenever they desired to add to their capital resources, thrown irrevocably into the hands of money-lenders, and, in times of distress, permanently weighed down by their burdens. Accordingly he founded, in 1849, a "Loan-Bank", based on principles, which, despite subsequent modifications, still distinguish it and its successors from other banking concerns. In the first place none but persons of irreproachable character could become members, and secondly the activities of each individual bank were rigidly confined to some small area, such as a single parish or village. Strictly speaking, the liability of members is unlimited, and at first shareholders were non-existent, but ultimately, as a result of legislation, shares in very small denominations (upon which no interest was paid) were issued. The money to promote the objects of these banks is raised by members themselves, that is from the savings of the peasants, augmented by the help of their better-off neighbours. The aim of Raiffeisen was to enable the small agriculturist to borrow money for the furtherance of his business, hence the formation of members' committees to investigate applications for loans, which are only issued after close enquiry. Local Raiffeisen banks are grouped together into Unions, and these in turn draw upon a central bank. By these means money is borrowed at a low rate of interest and advanced on their corporate responsibility to individual members. This, briefly, is the principle upon which a system of rural credit-banks has successfully spread itself over Germany. There is little doubt that, by inculcating the advantages of thrift and of mutual help, they led to an improvement in rural conditions, but the claims put forward on their behalf, in this and in other countries, have frequently been very exaggerated, and many of their later advances into fresh economic fields have not been so successful.

Schulze was a man of different type from Raiffeisen. The object of this judge of Delitzsch, in Prussia, when setting up his first banks, was to encourage the town artisans and shopkeepers to improve their social position, by affording them facilities that they had hitherto lacked. These institutions were founded on ordinary business principles, paid dividends to their shareholders, advanced loans on reasonable security, without the rigorous personal enquiries common to Raiffeisen establishments, and extended their activities over wide urban areas. As agricultural interests were not specifically catered for by them, it is unnecessary to pursue their description further; they have merely been referred to in passing as evidence of the congenial soil that awaited any form of co-operative banking in Germany.

The predilection shown there for this form of co-operation was almost unique, for, in most other European countries, societies for the provision of credit to agriculturists have generally taken a secondary place to those having different objects. Statistics relating to all agricultural co-operative associations in Germany show that in 1918, out of a total of 29,600, no less than 18,200 were credit societies, the remainder being distributed between what might be described as wholesale purchase societies (3100), dairies (3600), and miscellaneous bodies (4700). The other distinction at once apparent is the predominant position agriculture had secured for itself in German co-operation in general, for out of 37,000 registered societies, the great bulk (consisting of the above-mentioned 29,600) were purely agricultural in character. Prior to the outbreak of war the accession of new societies averaged some thousand per annum, but in the four years that succeeded 1914 the net increase only amounted to thirteen hundred. An interesting analysis of what may be described as the density of these societies, both in relation to population and to agriculture, has been published by the International Institute of Agriculture. This shows that for the whole of Germany there was in 1918 one agricultural society for every 2192 persons and for every 1175 hectares of cultivated land. Individual districts of course varied widely in these respects, for purely rural States had provided one society to every 900 persons, and, on the left of the Rhine, there was a society for every 427 hectares, whilst East Prussia, where large estates were numerous, had only one for every 4264 hectares. Of this the *Bulletin* said: "During the last few years there has been little or no change in the situation as regards agricultural co-operative societies in the various districts. For the whole of Germany, as the number of societies is increasing, the average extent of cultivated land per society slowly tends to diminish; from 1238 hectares on June 1st 1914 the average area had fallen to 1175 hectares on June 1st 1918". This account of course fails to show the important fact that only a fraction of the potential rural membership had been secured. There were upwards of five million holdings under forty-five acres in extent, and it is apparent that not half of their owners adhered to the societies. Much remained—and still remains—to be done before agricultural co-operation can be described as universal in Germany—the home of the movement.

Before turning to other branches, it is important to note that even the credit banks have had their vicissitudes, for in 1913 a German *Report* was issued under the following title: "Causes and effects of the recent want of success in the department of co-operative agricultural credit in Germany, and the lessons to be learned from it". In one of the cases referred to, the village bank at Nieder Modau had invested its members' savings in such holdings as mortgages on building land. Inefficient management, combined with these and other insecure investments, resulted in members being faced with a very heavy deficit; this in turn caused a run on the central banks by other societies, which led to the Darmstadt bank suspending payment. In the end, co-operators in the Duchy of Hesse found themselves faced with a prospective loss of some eleven million marks. At about the same time the agricultural credit-bank of Frankfort-on-the-Main also failed for fourteen million marks—mainly owing to bad management. Judging from the recommendations that accompanied the *Report*, it would appear that these disasters were recognised as being due to the overgrowth and complex nature of the societies themselves. They had tended to become organisations for the transaction of every conceivable undertaking connected with land and with money, and their commitments were too wide-flung. With a view to guarding against further calamities, it was demanded that closer inspection and supervision should be extended to these bodies. In a word, it had begun to be seen that the splendid Raiffeisen scheme of the village Mutual Benefit Society was not only outrun but in danger of breaking up. Its very success had led to its extension into realms of trading and finance where safeguards were less easy to provide, and vigilance too often demanded.

The ramifications in question involved the classification of numerous types of society. A tabular statement of 1922 embraced those that had such divergent objects as the storage of grain, the sale of spirit, the provision of starch factories, the sale of honey, the acquisition in common of grazing land, the supplying of electricity, the desiccation of potatoes, the joint use of machinery, the provision of water, the milling of grain, and the combination of vine-growers. In addition, there were, of course, societies formed for the more usually accepted purposes, such as the marketing of fruit and vegetables, and the improvement of livestock. A further analysis of the financial results achieved by each of these divisions tends to bear out the strictures of certain German writers, for, so long as purely agricultural activities were indulged in, either profits were made, or losses kept within reasonable limits. But in 1914, when conditions were still normal, the majority of the electricity supplying bodies were showing losses, as were those providing water, utilising machinery in common, desiccating potatoes, and even those concerned with livestock. The impartial *Bulletin* says in regard to the milling, the distilling and the vine growers' societies that, although many made a profit, there were also in numerous cases considerable losses to record. Bearing in mind the post-war circumstances of

Germany it would be useless to compare the financial standing of the societies at that time with the position they occupied in 1914, but, during the first year after the war, and before the effects of defeat had made themselves felt internally, the *Bulletin* summed up thus:

> In 1919 there had been strong development of the credit-societies in regard to their very important function as centres for the collection of agricultural savings; increase of societies for purchase and sale, and side by side with a decrease in their business, a tendency, such as was noticeable before the war, to devote themselves more to purchasing than to selling; continued and aggravated crises in the business of the dairy societies; and finally brisk development of the miscellaneous societies.

This epitomised the tendencies that are always in evidence when agricultural co-operation in Germany is closely examined. The inborn thrift and frugality of the peasant needed but little stimulus to respond fully to every encouragement afforded him for the provision of banking facilities. As soon as the banks found themselves in a strong position, and suffered considerable freedom of action by the State, they launched out into diverse operations, the success of which depended on widely different factors. Of these operations, naturally the most favoured were those that appealed to the large farmer as well as to the small; hence the prosperity of the "purchase and sale", or supply, societies. Such organisations appear to be the only ones that can meet with success in all countries and among all types of agriculturists; the power to acquire small quantities of goods at wholesale prices is everywhere a great lodestone, and in Germany the "Supply Union" developed inevitably into one huge wholesale supply society. Corn-selling and granary societies, despite financial assistance to the latter from the State, had a much more difficult path to follow, appealing as they did only to certain types of farmer, and those not the smallest. Incursions into the fields of milling and baking, in attempts to eliminate the middleman, convinced those responsible for their guidance that here they lacked sufficient financial or moral backing to make any appreciable headway against strongly entrenched interests. Prior to the war, certain societies were embarking upon cattle-dealing operations, the success of which, judged alone, must, for reasons similar to those just recorded, have been very problematic. The orthodox societies, engaged upon the sale of the Small Holders' products, were in general flourishing, and certain of the miscellaneous ones, which would, in this and other countries, have lacked every incentive, were in Germany at least satisfying a demand, and remaining solvent, if they were not increasing in numbers.

During the decade after the treaty of peace, there was considerable expansion in the numbers of societies of each type—the grand total by 1928 exceeding 40,000—but credit associations (numerically some 21,000) were still predominant. There was then one society to every 716 hectares of farm-land, the comparative position ten years earlier being the previously stated one for every 1175 hectares. It is remarkable how well the banks and the credit institutions had weathered both the period of inflation and the still more difficult times that followed the rehabilitation of the German currency system. In many cases, of course, the nature and the sources of the credit itself had altered; it was, for example, a long time before the village banks were in a position to resume advances from their own accumulated resources and they leaned heavily for support upon the large banking institutions. Even the Raiffeisen Bank had to look to the State for financial assistance, and only subsequent amalgamations and a certain number of voluntary liquidations on the part of the large co-operative societies enabled the corner to be turned. Thereafter, a reorganised movement has been able to second the State in developing its agricultural policy, thus repeating a phase of history that had covered the emergence of the Empire.

The reasons why in the United Kingdom agricultural co-operation can never be expected to compare with the German organisation, will be adduced later, but it must be pointed out here that conditions in this country have never called for the provision of small credit-banks (that most successful of all co-operative ventures in Germany), and again that the German small farmer and peasant have always been, both in temperament and by environment, more likely subjects for the propagation of communal activities than are the natives of these Islands.

Among the Latin, as opposed to the Teutonic, peoples co-operation in rural districts has been distinguished by no marked predilection for any one branch, but has spread uniformly, and neither in France nor in Belgium has the provision of credit been the predominant issue. The French *Syndicats agricoles,* and later, the Belgian *ligues*, have undertaken multifarious duties and have met with considerable support. In Belgium, especially, during their process of evolution, they became the centre of religious and political strife, which ended in the Church authorities securing power in the agricultural centres and the Socialists having a determining voice in the town societies. Since their legalisation in the year 1884, French co-operative societies have annually increased in numbers and influence, and, after exactly thirty years, on the outbreak of war had a membership of a little less than a million. Now there are some 10,000 *syndicats*, with a million and a quarter members. Typical development has taken the form of decentralisation, which aimed at a reduction in the number of controlling societies and an increase in that of local bodies, the commune itself being regarded as the ideal unit. Every branch of agriculture is now catered for, from societies of vine growers to those connected with cheese factories, but insurance—mainly in connection with livestock—is predominant; their distribution geographically is of course uneven, but the bulk of the numerous dairying *syndicats* is found in the West of France. The total membership, compared with the rural population or with the very numerous Small Holders, is still meagre, and relatively falls far short of the German figures; the same remark applies to the Belgian *ligues*.

In Italy, Holland, Switzerland, and in fact in all European countries agricultural co-operation exists, the form in which it is most represented depending upon the predominant type of husbandry. For instance, in Holland and Switzerland dairy societies and those whose object is the insurance of livestock will be found in abundance, whilst in parts of Italy and Southern France societies for insurance against hail are much in demand.

In the Near East, Czechoslovakia and Roumania provide examples of reconstructed States with pre-eminently suitable material for the propagation of rural co-operation, for each has an abundance of peasants established *de novo* on expropriated land, and, therefore, free from economic or traditional handicaps. Their Governments have assumed the rôle of advocates and have given every form of encouragement to the extension of the movement, spending considerable sums on frequently non-productive enterprises. The results, without metamorphosing the country, have been very successful.

Enough has been said about the history of this movement on the Continent of Europe to show its ubiquity and, within certain limits, its popularity. After glancing at conditions in the newer countries and in one Eastern Dependency, there will remain for consideration the peculiar case of Denmark. In the United States, Canada and Australia, as was pointed out in the previous Chapters, are found large-scale combinations of farmers organised for the purpose of marketing grain or other staple products. This is a development that is naturally not met with in the European countries so far reviewed, but one that has thoroughly justified itself in cases where there is a large export trade. It is probable that the small Continental co-operator would look askance at this development, which in truth approximates to a ring or combine of sellers, and has little of the atmosphere of neighbourly help that is elsewhere associated with unions of agriculturists. During the war period, when Governments themselves bought and sold entire cereal crops, the obligation to present a united front led to the extension of these pools, such as the "United States Grain Growers Incorporated", and by the year 1920 there were in the Middle West alone upwards of five thousand co-operative storehouses of this description. There are two aspects of this type of undertaking which at once distinguish it from the older and more orthodox form. In the first place, the financial operations involved are on an extremely large scale; for instance, the capital required for the work of the above-mentioned association ran into hundreds of millions of dollars, the bulk of which must have been invested in buildings. Secondly, it is essential that membership should be placed on a quasi-permanent basis, for only by these means can a sufficient bulk of supplies be assured, and at the same time the less loyal or enthusiastic members be prevented from dispensing with the services of the organisation by withholding their crops or dealing direct with purchasers. The early British co-operators' ideal of "the strong helping the weak" is, therefore, little in evidence, and a stage still further removed from the village society is revealed if the corporate steps taken by the producers in a Colony or a Dependency are examined. When the fruit growers of Australia and of South Africa combine for the purposes of marketing their products in this country, they do so with the approbation and the encouragement of their respective Governments. The objects of each party are then as follows: on the part of the producers, that maximum prices should be secured and that they, as a body, shall be more formidable competitors in the British market than as individuals; on the part of their Government, the necessity—frequently overlooked by the producers—for a uniformly high standard, both of quality and packing, is the motive that causes State intervention, often sweetened by financial assistance. In every case combination for the purposes of securing admission to a distant market is preferable to individual effort, and, for newer countries attempting to obtain a footing for the first time in some established trade, it becomes imperative.

In America, co-operation for the purposes of both local and external marketing has already been referred to in the previous Chapters, where the elimination of the commission agent was shown to be the great desideratum. That much headway has yet to be made is apparent when it is ascertained that only a small percentage of American farmers is yet effecting sales through co-operative associations. Certain individual States, however, have had good records. Minnesota, for example, claimed as long ago as 1920 that co-operative societies had disposed of one-fifth of its potato crop, more than a third of its grain and almost two-thirds of all the butter produced within its boundaries; in addition, 65 per cent. of the livestock sent to market passed through the associations' hands. Every branch, from credit banks to hail insurance societies, is represented in America, and difficulties, not met with in Europe, are gradually being circumvented. Among these, American writers include the scattered nature of the farms, the long distances involved, and the heterogeneous character of the agriculturists themselves. The world-wide depression that set in after 1920 of course affected co-operating and non-co-operating nations indiscriminately. The American Commission of Enquiry into the state of agriculture, in common with similar bodies engaged upon like tasks elsewhere, regretted its inability to suggest any remedy, "legislative or economic, which will of itself reduce the difference between producers' and consumers' prices", but expressed the opinion that co-operative principles deserved encouragement, especially when they aimed at a higher standard of quality and better preparation for market. It held, however, that, until the grower, by these or other means, could assume responsibility for the final appearance of his products in the retail state, the middleman's share of the cost would remain at its existing level. From independent testimony it is apparent that the tendency to claim for the producer the whole of the extra profits obtained when the services of the middleman have been dispensed with is as general in America as in other countries. This disinclination to share with the ultimate purchaser any benefits accruing from more efficient methods of marketing is doubly unfortunate, for it militates against an increase in business and at the same time alienates sympathy from the one class upon which the producer is then dependent. If the co-operative spirit can succeed in checking this tendency in the Old World, or in the New, it will have deserved well of all consumers.

Amongst coloured and Eastern races co-operation has generally been fostered by the administrations concerned in attempts to counter the widespread activities of small money-lenders, who, all too often, have battened upon the peasantry. This evil has been particularly noticeable in India, with its half a million villages, where the activities of these parasites have ramified into all branches of the people's lives. The Government first seriously attacked the problem in 1904, when, as a result of close investigation into European—particularly the German—methods of State control, a wide-flung Co-operative Act was passed. As a result, typical development has followed Raiffeisen principles and there are now, scattered throughout British India and the Native States, upwards of 80,000 societies, the bulk of which are engaged in supplying small sums of credit to the humblest type of cultivator. These small organisations rest financially upon District Banks and, again copying German methods, appeal successfully to outside investors. Finally, the District Banks draw upon the resources of Central, or Provincial, Banks. The administration and control of these credit societies has become an increasing responsibility for the Civil Service and a complex piece of machinery has grown up, involving the employment of Registrars and Inspectors, with their deputies and their appropriate staffs. Societies both for the sale and purchase of agricultural goods also exist, and co-operation has, upon occasion, been extended into typical urban forms. Overwhelmingly, however, co-operation in India implies the substitution of mutual financial assistance for that hitherto provided by individual money-lenders. This was the subject of most emphatic recommendations by the 1928 Royal Commission on Indian agriculture. Its future lies with the people themselves, for, once they are set up, to them is left the responsibility of organising the societies. They have expert guidance and every form of technical advice at their service, but, rightly, are left in complete control of the societies. The principal handicap under which the movement has suffered can be summed up in the word "lethargy". All too frequently, societies have been allowed to wilt and perish from sheer lack of initiative or of willingness on the part of members to bestir themselves in their own obvious interests. Variations are, therefore, marked in the relative density of societies in apparently similar and homogeneous areas. These very important points may, perhaps, best be illustrated by reference to the case of Ceylon, where conditions are typical of India proper.

Briefly summarised, it may be stated that after some twenty years, while the number of individual societies still tends to increase, that of members reached its peak some five or six years ago. As both paid-up capital and reserve funds continue to grow, the true explanation is probably that one familiar to students of the movement in Europe, viz. the sub-division of areas and the successful attempts to limit the activities of each society to a single village. The Director himself holds that the cancellation of old societies incapable of reorganisation has now neared its conclusion; in the year 1930–31, there was a net increase of 150 societies. Statistically, the general progress since the inauguration of the movement by the State has been as follows:

Year	Number of societies	Number of members	Paid-up capital (Rupees)	Reserve fund (Rupees)
1913–14	37	1,820	8,200	23
1918–19	113	11,310	68,062	11,243
1923–24	222	26,757	238,607	44,603
1928–29	383	27,970	448,415	101,108
1930–31	600	24,068	505,108	136,212

It should perhaps be recorded that, after 1930, the supervisory organisation was detached from the Department of Agriculture, and became a separate entity. The island is divided into three areas, each in charge of an Assistant Registrar. The Director, in his last annual *Report*, classified the societies as "Model", "Good", "Poor" and "Those on the verge of liquidation". Inspection shows that, over a period of years, the second class had expanded fast, and that the proportion of societies in financial difficulties had remained small, but relatively constant. Comparative progress in the different provinces had been strikingly divergent, the explanation being, in each case, by no means obvious. Thus, a Registrar was constrained to write of one district as follows:

> Success always has a tendency to go to the head and there have occasionally been signs of a slight Co-operative intoxication in —— manifesting itself in attempts to undertake in a spirit of light-hearted optimism the most complicated and difficult operations, trusting to the improvisation later on of measures necessary to meet any difficulties which may arise. An embarrassing feature of this manifests itself in an idea that the Registrar is a sort of automatic machine, and you have only to press the right button and out comes a set of by-laws for a Boat Service, an Insurance Society, a Sale Society, etc.

In further instances he said:

> This Province retains its position as the mystery province of the Island. All the indications are favourable, but the big wave of progress, which these conditions ought to produce, for some reason never appears.
>
> I am sorry to have to admit the continuance of almost complete failure in this Province. The inhabitants do not seem to have the capacity or the desire for Co-operative organisation. They have had relatively more of the time of my staff devoted to them than any other Province, but the results have been most disappointing. Organisations laboriously built up crumble almost immediately, owing to the inertia of their members or the petty jealousies of adjoining villages or communities. Immense labour was expended on the formation of the —— Sale Society, which was intended to meet the constant complaint that they could not market their paddy. An order was obtained for it from Jaffna for a large quantity of paddy. The members did not pay the share capital they had promised and not even the Committee Members were loyal to the Society in bringing their paddy to it. The result has been that its turn-over was insufficient to carry the overhead charges, and a Society which ought to have been a great success, and the forerunner of many others in the district, ran at a loss.

In general it appears that the difficulties encountered in Ceylon are those always associated with the extension of co-operation among small native producers. Not the least of the complications is occasioned by the fact that in typical societies barely one-third of the loans advanced can strictly be regarded as falling under the head of agriculture—either cultivational or animal; money is being borrowed for paying examination fees, meeting the expenses of marriage, the purchase of a gun, the enlarging of a house, or for repayment of industrial debts or school fees. In numerous instances the local successes achieved are, obviously, in the main, due to the honorary native supervisors. Undoubtedly, however, the brunt of the work falls upon the European Registrars. While a certain amount of criticism is heard concerning the expenditure of State funds upon the maintenance and expansion of agricultural co-operation, it does not appear that, compared with countries of a similar character, an excessive proportion of the sum total devoted to the encouragement of agriculture is either in India or Ceylon being diverted into this particular channel.

Further East, Japan may illustrate what can be accomplished by energetic workers in this field when faced with Oriental conservatism. With the abolition, during the Meiji era, of feudalism and all that followed in its train, the rural economy of the country became available for social and financial reform. Limitations in regard to residence and restraints upon occupation were abolished, but still the peasant was in the hands of rapacious money-lenders, and, in the words of a native writer: "Many of them borrowed money at high interest from rich men of the cities by mortgaging their lands and houses, and in consequence they could not repay at the appointed time...and were obliged to offer their lands and houses inherited from their fore-fathers and become tenant farmers". Again, agricultural merchants and dealers were apt to squeeze the country-folk by compelling them to offer rice and other products at ruinous prices in return for deferred payments upon commodities they themselves had supplied. In the smaller towns, too, conditions were very similar and the working classes were in a parlous state. Then, just as had happened in Germany with Raiffeisen and Schulze-Delitzsch and in Ireland with Plunkett, there appeared Viscount Y. Shinagawa and Count T. Hirata to foster the co-operative movement. These two philanthropists had resided for some years in Germany, and had therefore seen for themselves the results of pioneer work in that country. Their opportunity came in 1891, when the Viscount was appointed a Minister. The first Bill to regularise the use of Co-operative Credit Societies—for this, naturally enough, was the initial development—did not pass into law, so the next stage was the political recognition of certain existing Friendly Societies, known as "Hotokusha" and "Ko". Actually, the first society so formed was the "Mitsuke" Society (1892), to be followed a year later by three others, sponsored, in one case, by Count Hirata himself. There was considerable opposition to the movement, and it was extremely difficult to secure the interest of persons competent to assume active responsibility for the management of the societies. Many Japanese, indeed, regarded such associations as akin to a dangerous form of Socialism: few possessed the knowledge to assist in drawing up the articles of association. Nevertheless, by the year 1898, there were known to be in existence over 140 societies, with a membership of nearly 22,000.

Prior to the existence of the above-mentioned credit societies there had been formed Silk Selling Associations, organised on a comparatively large scale, e.g. in Gumma Prefecture "The South Three Associations" dated from the year 1880. In the 'eighties, also, there came into existence the forerunners of purchasing societies—the object of which was almost universally the acquisition of manures for their members. By the late 'nineties purchasing societies had a membership of over 4000, and the selling societies, to the number of 80, possessed 11,000 subscribers. There were also known to exist a few associations providing tools and other forms of equipment.

A second attempt was made to legalise the whole movement in 1897, when, after discussion lasting for a month, by fifteen Commissioners, lack of agreement again resulted in failure to secure the passage of a Bill through the Diet. However, three years later the first Act was definitely passed; this recognised four kinds of agricultural co-operation, viz. Credit, Purchase, Sale and Miscellaneous activities. Shortly after its passage Viscount Shinagawa died, thus being denied the opportunity of seeing the full fruit of his labours. Prior to this legislation all the pioneer societies in the field had been compelled to rely solely upon the good-will of certain Government officials. Thereafter, not only were they legally untrammelled, but were free to promulgate actively their principles.

The Russo-Japanese War and its aftermath beneficially affected the co-operative movement, for economic and social reactions caused a steady increase in the number of members in every type of society. The Imperial Agricultural Association (Zeukokunojikai) assumed general control of the movement, and a certain number of officials in the Department of Agriculture and Commerce were engaged in the active formation of individual societies. In 1905, the Central Union of Co-operative Societies was set up as a result of the work of Count Hirata, in consultation with Viscount Kano and other influential persons. These two gentlemen became, respectively, President and Vice-president of the Association. Under the title *Sangyokumiai*, the first co-operative publication was then issued. Legal revision of the co-operative laws followed, and greater freedom was accorded individual societies in the conduct of their business; they were permitted an expansion in the matter of the supply of credit; representative meetings avoided the necessity for a system of federation; purchasing societies were permitted to undertake manufacturing processes; taxation of societies was modified; alterations were made in the methods of Government inspection.

So far the development of the movement in Japan had been rural in character, but immediately prior to the Great War there was in evidence a tendency to extend facilities, particularly in regard to the provision of credit by means of Savings Banks, to urban centres of population. The economic unheaval consequent upon the years 1914–19 caused marked expansion in this movement, and the combined Departments of Finance, Agriculture and Commerce took steps to secure the recognition, in cities, of the activities of the existing credit societies. Post-war conditions encouraged a still further growth, and the 38 urban credit societies of 1918 had, by 1925, become 224. Thus, again, was the history of co-operation in Western Europe repeated in the Far East.

War-time economic conditions led to the passing of the Agricultural Warehousing Business Law, which aimed simultaneously at regularising the price of rice and providing loans at moderate rates of interest to its producers. A recognised agricultural warehouse was also authorised to hold rice, cocoons and other products, and to undertake the business of their preparation, packing and transportation—both internal and external. It was claimed, at the time, that a complete marketing system for farmers had, by this means, been set up. The Government entered upon an ambitious scheme for the erection of no less than 4100 warehouses, viz. one warehouse to every three villages or towns throughout the country. In 1925, there were 1741 such buildings under the control of the co-operative societies themselves, while others were managed by public bodies.

The co-operative movement did not escape the post-bellum difficulties. Rice riots, brought about by the financial crisis, took place in many of the principal cities of the country. Class warfare raised its head. Tenant farmers and landowners were at loggerheads. Jealousy between town and country interests increased. Lastly, the terrible earthquake of 1923 caused moral and material damage to an unprecedented extent. The net result of all this was a remarkable increase in the number and activities of consumers' credit societies. Here, the towns took a prominent part, and the Co-operative Union was active in fostering the movement. The consumers' interests were further affected by the virtual collapse of the banking system in 1920. Numerous credit societies were involved in common ruin with the banks. It is interesting to record that certain consumers' societies were at that time organised by the "labouring classes" themselves and were reserved exclusively for such persons.

The fourth revision of the co-operative laws was effected in 1920. This was brought about by the high level of commodity prices, which in turn had expanded the work of the purchasing and processing societies. Further, by these and similar legal modifications, societies were authorised to extend their activities to the construction of dwelling-houses and the provision of hospitals, bathhouses, water supplies and other quasi-public amenities. Lastly, full federation of selling and purchasing societies was authorised. Two years later, having secured the necessary statutory sanction, the Union of Co-operative Societies established a Central Co-operative Bank. In 1924, with the approval of the Diet, this Bank began to function, almost simultaneously with the establishment, now on a national basis, of a single Co-operative Wholesale Society. This last organisation, known as the Zenkoku Kobaikumiai Rengokai, had actually begun its work on September 1st, 1923, the day of the great earthquake. These two organisations, it may be claimed, have consummated the co-operative movement, urban and rural, throughout Japan; as the Japanese themselves maintain, their foundation meant the realisation "of the control of national economic life based upon co-operative principles".

The penultimate stage had now been reached, in which it became imperative more thoroughly to supervise the formation of new societies and to eradicate those that were inefficient. As a result of the putting into force of such a policy, the number of societies was reduced by some hundreds between 1925 and 1927, in which latter year there were in the whole country 14,000. Concurrently, by a revision in the appropriate laws, non-members were allowed to make use of certain facilities hitherto reserved strictly for members; here the claim of public interest was to override co-operative control. This relaxation applied particularly to the user of factories and in the matter of access to water supply and to electric power. Reorganisation, upon a large scale, was also undertaken through the Agricultural Depository law, whereby an attempt was made to organise the marketing of the whole of the rice and silk-producing societies on a co-operative basis. Thus, the aim of those responsible for the movement was nothing less than a country-wide federation of all existing marketing societies. In 1927, there was a further collapse of banking institutions in Japan, and it became necessary to put into force a moratorium. In several prefectures the credit societies and their banks were severely hit, but, in the case of the majority, conservative policies had been the rule and they were enabled to meet all demands from their panic-stricken members. The direct effect of these occurrences was to divert a considerable stream of rural business from the smaller banks to the co-operative credit societies; thus, to quote again from a native writer, "the financial panic gave a most significant lesson for the Co-operative movement in Japan".

In general it may be said that co-operation in Japan has had a distinctly rural bias and that it has, as is everywhere the case, been fortunate in those who worked for it throughout good times and bad. The Emperor Meiji himself took a keen interest in the work, as did the Prince Regent and certain of the nobility, for financial assistance has been forthcoming from the Crown and honours have been presented to those in the forefront of the movement. Too much attention should not be paid to the merely statistical position of co-operation in Japan, where, as even in Germany and other peasant states of Europe, only a fraction of the potential membership has been obtained; rather should the pertinacity of its founders be admired and the difficulties envisaged that accompanied its establishment in a country so recently freed from feudalism, often disturbed by social and physical convulsions and always diverted by the imposition of Western influence.

If enquiry be pursued to the opposite point of the compass, the Horace Plunkett Foundation has reported upon the successful extension of co-operative principles to the native banana-growers in the British West Indies, whereby not only is that fruit made more remunerative to its producers, both by means of long-term contracts and the provision of modern facilities for its storage and handling, but land-tenure and the provision of financial assistance have both been ameliorated. Much prejudice, not only on the part of the native, but of the planter, has, nevertheless, had to be overcome, and if co-operation has not yet swept these Islands, its ubiquitous character is well illustrated by the considerable number of its coloured adherents in that part of the globe, whence return must be made to Europe in the next Chapter, although instances could be multiplied from every continent and race.

Chapter XVI

AGRICULTURAL CO-OPERATION (CONTINUED)

The special position occupied by Denmark; co-operation in England and Wales; the Agricultural Organisation Society; the movement in Scotland and in Ireland; the position in Great Britain summarised; future prospects. The provision of credit: Short-term and long-term loans; the Agricultural Credits Acts of 1923 and 1928; chattel mortgage; the work of the Agricultural Mortgage Corporation.

After passing in brief review examples of rural co-operation from widely divergent races of the world, the peculiar position occupied in this connection by Denmark now calls for attention. It has become the fashion categorically to claim that the placing of British agriculture upon a firm basis of prosperity could be achieved by sedulously copying the methods in vogue across the North Sea; that, in a word, every step taken in Denmark has but to be repeated here in order to effect a transformation similar to that witnessed there during the last half century. There are, however, certain fundamental differences between the economic and agricultural position of the two countries which are apt to be overlooked. In the first place, the vast bulk of the Danish farms are producing those commodities which are pre-eminently the most suitable for co-operative handling; in all countries of the world bacon, cheese, butter and eggs lend themselves readily to such methods. Secondly, and this is the most important factor in the success of Danish co-operation, virtually the whole trade is an export one, for there is only one large town, Copenhagen, which can absorb more than a small fraction of the agricultural output. This inevitably confers great strength upon the societies, for they can compel obedience to their regulations and insist upon the observance of a uniform standard. In other countries, where alternative outlets exist, there is, due to surreptitious sales, a constant leakage of the best type of article, which no rules can obviate. In Denmark, however, as in other exporting countries, it is a case of handing over to the societies the whole of one's output or of running the risk of losing the only existing market. This practice of selling picked samples behind, as it were, the back of the society, has unfortunately been much in evidence in Great Britain, and has tended to lower the reputation of the organisation, and simultaneously to cause individual members to look upon it as merely a channel for the disposal of their second-grade goods.

It is sometimes suggested that in Denmark Small Holdings are ubiquitous and have alone led to the formation of the co-operative societies. Statistics show that the "average" size of all Danish farms is in the neighbourhood of thirty acres, and that in 1916 small farms numbered 106,000, covering some eighteen acres each, while what were officially described as "large" numbered upwards of 78,000 with an average area of seventy-four acres. Subsequent enquiries have revealed a tendency towards a reduction in these average figures, and it may be pointed out that holdings now appear to average well under half the size of those found in England and Wales. That the larger are not mainly confined to the poorer and sandier soils, and therefore perhaps in reality "Small Holdings", is evidenced by the fact that the value per hectare of each class increases from the smallest to the largest size; again, even in Jutland, there are actually more small than large holdings. It is, therefore, very doubtful if the scale upon which agricultural operations have been conducted has had any direct bearing upon the course events pursued. Rather must the altered types of farming, forced upon the country two generations ago, be looked upon as giving a direct lead to the formation of combinations of producers. At that time Danish farmers suffered, in common with those in other European countries, from the exploitation of the cereal resources of North America, and they had also their own peculiar difficulties to contend with, caused by the recent loss of territory and of markets to Germany. They turned from the orthodox practices of cereal raising and cattle grazing to the intensive production of dairy products, retained a small area of corn on the best land, supported their cattle on the produce of their arable fields and, under Free Trade, fed their pigs upon imported maize. The large landowners shared equally with the small farmer in this metamorphosis, and, as co-operative societies came into being for the purpose of affording an outlet to the new products of Danish soil, they, equally with their smaller neighbours and tenants, enrolled themselves as members. At the present time the man who farms his two hundred, five hundred or even a thousand acres of land is, so far as membership goes, on an equality with the one who tends his five or ten acres. Very occasionally complaints are heard from the former that the principle of "one member one vote" in the councils of the societies presses hard on the large producer, but, in the long run, such absolute equality is recognised as the only possible basis upon which the whole structure can rest.

Co-operation in Denmark has been extended to every branch of purchase and sale, but the Raiffeisen system of credit-banks has not been taken up, their place being filled by the ample facilities afforded for the purchase of land on easy terms, and by the existence of a limited number of Credit-Union Banks of a private character, whose business is mainly the supplying of long-term credit. As might be anticipated, the strongest societies are those engaged in dairying, bacon-curing and egg collecting, but numerous others exist, whose activities extend to livestock insurance, the improvement of horse, cattle and pig breeding and all forms of wholesale purchasing. It is unnecessary to quote statistics to show the numerical and pecuniary growth of these societies; it is sufficient to acknowledge that practically the whole of the agricultural trade of the country is in their hands. But it is interesting to note, as evidence of the thoroughness with which those responsible for guiding the societies act, that organisations have been established in connection with the latter, whose functions are to collect economic and statistical data relating to both internal and external conditions. That this policy was adopted early in the movement is shown by reference to an account of Danish agriculture contained in the *Report* of our own Royal Commission of 1893. It is there stated that in 1880 the plan of delivering butter to local dealers, who in turn disposed of it through a broker to the exporters, was given up and direct intercourse between producers and exporters established. The next step was then taken, and the English agents' services dispensed with, direct business relations being entered into, first with the wholesale merchants, and later with the retail dealers in this country. The activities of Danish representatives became widely familiar to British traders when they were engaged in re-establishing their products in our markets after the return of peace, and it was due to their "intelligence branch", in conjunction with the undoubted superiority of the articles themselves, that such efforts were speedily successful. The Danes have learnt that it is necessary to study the foreigner's requirements, and even his peculiar fancies, on the spot, and they have effected numerous modifications in their methods of packing, expressly to meet conditions in Great Britain, which forms easily their principal market. Again, the fostering of farmers' clubs, the establishment of societies for scientific research and for the pursuit of economic problems, all come within the range of Danish co-operation. For an account of these multifarious activities it is advisable to read such a work as Rider Haggard's *Rural Denmark*, where, after giving a full description of all that he himself witnessed, the author sums up the principal lessons to be learned thus—

1. That in a free trade country of limited area and lacking virgin soil, co-operation is necessary to a full measure of agricultural success.
2. That only free-holders, or farmers holding under some form of perpetual lease, which in practice amounts to the same thing as free-hold, will co-operate to any wide extent.
3. That the accumulation of estates, which for the most part descend intact from one owner to another, and are hired out piecemeal to tenants, is not conducive to the multiplication of free-holders, nor therefore to the establishment of general co-operation.

It will be observed that this authority attributes the success achieved in Denmark principally to the system of land-tenure, rather than to the compelling influence of an export trade comprising precisely those articles that best lend themselves to co-operative handling. Nothing further will be said upon this question here, for the steps taken in Denmark to facilitate the establishment of occupying owners have been already discussed, and readers must form their own judgment as to the comparative influence of various contributory causes upon a movement, which, there is general agreement, has met with unqualified success while receiving the minimum of direct State assistance.

In Great Britain and Ireland the struggle to establish rural co-operation has been an uphill one, nor can impartial observers feel that its position is yet assured. In England and Wales the Agricultural Organisation Society, founded in 1900, had an independent life of over twenty years, and at its maximum development, some ten years ago, could claim that it had affiliated to it upwards of fourteen hundred societies with a membership of 145,000 persons. There were few societies that did not owe allegiance to that body, so that the above statistics of membership afford an indication of the maximum volume of support accorded to co-operation by the rural districts of this country. At first glance a membership of such proportions conveys the impression that, after the war, one in every three of the farmers in England and Wales adhered, at least indirectly, to the Society, but, if the figures relating to the different branches themselves are examined, it will be found that there were only some 227 Farmers' Societies, with a membership of 64,000, and that no less than 1054 affiliated bodies were solely concerned with allotments. These latter were a result of the war, and the bulk was centred in urban districts. Even if all the other miscellaneous societies are included as being representative of agriculture, there were then only 406 out of the total of 1460. It is therefore obvious that but a fraction of the farmers (approximately one in five) had been enrolled. If one turned to the financial position of the Society itself one found that it had been buttressed up with the aid of Government grants, received through the Development Commissioners. Immediately after the war these annual subventions were greatly increased to assist the Society in its attempts to extend its operations, and from the financial year 1919–20 to that of 1922–3 sums ranging from fifteen thousand to upwards of forty thousand pounds were allotted. After the latter year all forms of direct State assistance terminated and the Agricultural Organisation Society was left to its own resources. The financial standing of this body had been on a different basis from that of corresponding organisations abroad, where it is the exception to find State funds on a large scale placed at their disposal. The corollary of official grants in aid took the form of diminutive subscription lists, for during the year 1921–2, the independent income of the Society amounted to only £4500, of which £800 was derived from subscriptions, £3000 from farmers' societies and £700 from allotment societies.

The comparative popularity, at that time, of the different branches of the Agricultural Organisation Society can be gauged fairly accurately if their annual turnover is examined. Neglecting the allotment societies, it would appear that in the year 1921–2 feeding-stuffs, fertilisers, seeds and implements were purchased to the value of some six and a half million pounds, and agricultural produce disposed of for the sum of seven and a half million pounds. Feeding-stuffs accounted for over two-thirds of the former figure, and the latter was subdivided as follows—milk and dairy produce, £3,100,000; livestock, meat and bacon, £2,700,000; fruit and garden produce, £370,000; eggs and poultry, £540,000. In times of steady prices the fluctuations of these yearly turnovers might be accepted as affording an indication of the extent of the trade carried on by the societies concerned, but after 1914 such a method was obviously fallacious, yet writers were not lacking who adduced the figures of pre-war years as proof of the advance recorded. On the other hand, the war admittedly strengthened the economic position of the Society and of its branches, although it is unfortunate that its financial operations should have been selected as proof of this. Membership almost doubled between 1918 and 1920, whilst the value of the Society's transactions increased still more, but the bulk of the new members were allotment-holders and the peak of commodity values was only reached in the latter year; by 1922 members had seceded heavily, and the turnover of the Society reflected declining values. Two or three years later the financial position of the Agricultural Organisation Society, brought about partly by withdrawal of the Government grant and partly by this great reduction in numbers, forced those responsible for its management to approach the National Farmers' Union with a proposal that the latter body should take over the duties of its organisation. This step was eventually taken and the Union became the recognised head of the agricultural cooperative movement in England and Wales. This association of interests has, despite one or two abortive proposals for secession, been maintained up to the present time, and it would seem that the position has been consolidated. The latest statistics relating to trading societies upon the register of the Farmers' Union indicate a total of some 200 with a membership of 70,000. In even the most difficult of recent years the societies recording profits easily outnumbered those that had suffered losses, and their combined turnover was in the region of £8,000,000 to £10,000,000 per annum.

The principal activities of the parent Society have been indicated in the course of the last page or two, but there remain some comments to make on certain features that have been omitted. The Agricultural Wholesale Society represented an attempt to combine into one body the purchasing machinery of the dependent societies. Formed during the war, it traded at a profit at a time when it was virtually impossible to avoid prosperity; then fell on evil times and finally went into liquidation. Such an agency should, in ordinary circumstances, secure considerable support from the adhesion of numerous branches, for it is obviously to the advantage of the latter to effect their purchases through its medium. The difficulties this Society had to contend with, apart from the natural hostility of the dealers it sought to oust, took the shape of a tendency on the part of societies to refrain from placing the whole of their orders through it, or by their refusal to commit themselves to such a course of action for more than a short period of time. A strongly supported wholesale purchase society can confer great benefits upon agriculturists, not only by obtaining for them the highest class of goods at wholesale prices, but, by pursuing their interests back to the manufacturing stage, may cause competition for really extensive orders to result in further reductions.

The provision of credit had, up to the period of recent legislation, frequently been made the sole object of new societies, but almost invariably the latter failed to develop; in fact the number of affiliated branches devoted to this purpose shrank after the war, and at no time had their advances to members amounted to more than a few hundred pounds—in 1918 twenty-two societies, with a membership of 420, advanced £601. This failure was probably due to several causes. The Continental system appeals mainly to the peasant proprietor, and in many cases is contrived to benefit solely the small occupying owner—a type of farmer still represented by a small minority here. English farmers again have hitherto not appreciated the extension of co-operative principles to that intimate knowledge of one another's business affairs, called for by the typical Raiffeisen bank. It was always suggested, too, in this country that the provision of credit by dealers and merchants partly abrogated the necessity for borrowing by farmers. The combination of some, or all, of these factors had certainly resulted in little demand for fresh means of raising capital so long as times were reasonably prosperous. This was one of the matters specifically referred to enquiry by the Government in the winter of 1922–3, with a view to possible legislation. The deliberations of the Committee entrusted with this enquiry resulted in the passing of the Agricultural Credits Act of 1923, which made possible the provision of credit to two classes of agriculturists. In the first instance those farmers who had purchased their holdings between the passage of the Corn Production Act of 1917 and the repeal of its successor in 1921 were enabled to borrow, through recognised banks, up to 75 per cent. of the existing value of the land in question, such sums to be repayable within forty years upon an annuity basis. Secondly, short-term credit was made available to the general body of agriculturists by means of State aid.

Certain further schemes, by which the Government undertook to advance considerable sums of money to other forms of co-operative enterprise, were also approved at that time. Thus, £200,000 was set aside for loans to marketing associations, with a limit of £10,000 to any one organisation and of twenty years for the duration of the loan involved. Guarantees, too, were offered, under the Trade Facilities Act, to large undertakings, such as bacon and other factories, or to markets. In neither case, however, was there a wide response to the offers. Further discussion of this subject is deferred to the end of the Chapter, where it is dealt with in a separate Section.

In Scotland and Ireland are to be found examples of all the societies previously enumerated, but their comparative popularity, and, therefore, their development has been determined by local conditions. Thus, in Ireland the creameries have met with more success than all other types put together, and even credit societies were, prior to the war, more numerous than in England, whilst in Scotland purchase societies and those devoted to the sale of mixed products had the largest trade and membership. The growth of agricultural co-operation in Ireland has been credited to two causes—the individual efforts of the late Sir Horace Plunkett, dating from the early 'nineties, and the fact that the Land Purchase Acts of the British Government resulted, in less than a generation, in the bulk of the peasants becoming their own landlords. While it is invidious to attempt to differentiate between these two causes, the suggestion might perhaps be hazarded that the former, by precept and example, prepared the ground, and that subsequent land purchase caused numerous small proprietors to stand in need of organisation. The creameries are run on orthodox lines, and apparently leave little to be desired in the way of technical methods, but it is doubtful if the same thoroughness could in the past always have been claimed for their actual marketing operations. In this connection it must be remembered that they have been in active competition for the British butter trade with Denmark and New Zealand, and the admirable trading equipment of the former country has already been described. That co-operation could have been successfully applied to Irish agriculture in a much larger degree is widely acknowledged; that it might earlier have advanced results by raising the standard of production is also a subject of common agreement, but the Celtic temperament, especially when found in agricultural surroundings, requires patient methods, and cannot be hustled. In the Irish Agricultural Organisation Society is centred the controlling body—one that originated a few years earlier than the corresponding Society in England. It has achieved much, and the measure of the difficulties it has overcome can best be appreciated by those who have perused that excellent work, *Rural Reconstruction in Ireland*, by L. Smith Gordon and L. C. Staples. The authors themselves make the following reasonable claims on behalf of the movement in Ireland—

> As a business organisation the co-operative society has introduced its members to a field in which they had little practical knowledge. For the most part, the vision of the Irish farmer did not extend beyond the community in which he lived. If he sold his produce, it was to the gombeen man or to the buyer at the fair, who was his only connection with the outside economic world. Nowhere did farmers carry on their farming on a business basis. For them it was an occupation which in good years brought good living, and in lean years made it hard to get along. Cost-accounting systems, insurance, productive loans—these were matters beyond their ken. The co-operative society, which made necessary considerable business knowledge, developed capacities which were of advantage in individual business relations.... To-day Irish farmers conduct their co-operative societies for themselves. In their more individual relations they understand the nature of a productive loan; if necessary they are able to establish connections with buyers in England and Scotland. They have learned to demand a guarantee with their artificial manures, and are gradually understanding that the quality as well as the quantity of their products counts. They are undertaking, often on their own account, experiments in co-operative enterprise, are buying tractors and installing mills. In fact the farmer has come to realise that he is as much a business man as an agriculturist.

The absolute fairness of these writers, in contradistinction to the exaggerated statements only too frequently made on behalf of co-operation, is emphasised when one finds them pointing out that "the record of progress is indeed a great one in comparison with the records of most other agencies which have tried to do something for the betterment of Ireland; yet it is not particularly impressive from the point of view of the student of agricultural co-operation in general. Nor can the enquirers find, in visiting the country districts, more than a comparatively small number of societies which are in any way qualified to serve as patterns either of business methods or of co-operative faith". If Irish co-operation is as well served by its officials as by its historians it deserves to flourish in the future.

Its development in the Free State has brought into existence a large and prosperous Wholesale Society, and many of the first tentative essays in marketing have been expanded under State guidance into efficient organisations. Across the border, the corresponding duties are now performed by the Ulster Agricultural Organisation Society, the principal activities of which are centred upon its affiliated creameries, engaged, like their Southern counterparts, in an export trade to this country. In both territories co-operation has a congenial soil and is spreading its roots in all directions therein, but hitherto growth has not been so rapid as conditions might seem to have warranted.

In Scotland, the usual amalgamation of small associations led, early in the twentieth century, to the formation of a Scottish Organisation Society, which, aided financially by the Development Commission, successfully emerged from the war and post-war periods. In that country, the social problems relating to the Outer Islands and to the West Coast in general brought the movement into close touch with the Congested Districts Board, and Scottish co-operation still bears the impress of the peculiar physical and economic circumstances of the country. Numerical membership is now comparable with that of England, since about one-quarter of all Scots farmers adhere to one or other of the 150 affiliated societies, whose total turnover is proportionately larger than that of the English bodies. This is, doubtless, attributable to their concentration upon the marketing of animal products in general and of milk in particular.

A short description having been given of the past history of agricultural co-operation in this and other countries, it remains to discuss in general terms its future outlook here. For this purpose it is necessary to deal separately with each of the different forms the movement can assume. Take the purchase side first. Here it is impossible but that eventually the bulk of agriculturists will see the advantages attaching to corporate trading. This branch has the great asset of appealing with almost equal strength to the large as well as the small farmer, and, moreover, no manufacturing processes need obtrude themselves, as is the case where the majority of articles the farmer sells are concerned. There is also a more homogeneous trade in agricultural requisites than in products of the soil, for the requirements of all classes differ mainly in degree and but little in character, hence when dealing with manufacturers an additional lever is placed in their hands.

The provision of credit, for reasons already given, as well as owing to the fact that the State has now intervened, is never likely to be the subject of widespread organisation. In times of distress, schemes whereby insolvent agriculturists could defer the inevitable bankruptcy will naturally be well received, but in ordinary circumstances British farmers are sufficiently independent to negative the possibility of institutions of the Raiffeisen type meeting with success.

The communal ownership of machinery is a matter that has received scanty attention in this Chapter. Abroad it has secured a certain measure of support, but in the British Isles only spasmodic attempts have been made, and the majority of these have not achieved even local success. This is essentially an example of co-operative agriculture rather than of agricultural co-operation, and, as such, is of immemorial antiquity, but its extension to modern machinery on separate holdings introduces complications that were non-existent in "champion" husbandry. Thus, anyone who has followed the story of some local Association, formed for the purpose of acquiring by purchase an expensive piece of portable machinery, will agree that the human element frustrates the latter's equitable use. Many hundreds of pounds—doubtless borrowed from a bank—are expended by a group of small farmers on a steam-threshing plant. At once discussion arises over such questions as the following. What system of priority is to be adopted? Is the largest shareholder to have first claim on the machine, or is it to go to whichever calls for it first? When the machine is idle, how are such overhead charges as the attendants' wages to be allocated, and how are those due to varying lengths of journey from farm to farm to be equalised? How is the single-handed Small Holder to provide manual assistance when his farm is visited? Add to these human difficulties the economic factor that, unless such machinery can be kept fully employed, it is cheaper to hire from contractors, and there is sufficient explanation of why really expensive plant is not the subject of co-operative ownership. Opportunity for such use in the case of smaller implements has not arisen on any considerable scale between the final period of enclosure and the present time, except in isolated survivals such as the Isle of Axholme. Here one may see binders being worked by groups of adjacent strip-owners, and, in certain areas given up to Small Holdings, seasonal operations are facilitated by the common use of machinery, but these are exceptions to the existing custom whereby each farmer in the first instance provides himself with all the implements he will require. That a further extension of Small Holdings may result in co-operation stepping into the breach and providing some satisfactory method by which both machinery and implements are made available to their proprietors, is possible, but at present the signs are not very propitious.

Co-operative agriculture, pure and simple, has everywhere proved a failure, from the philanthropic efforts of individual landowners of the early nineteenth century down to the post-war Colonies provided for ex-service men by the State. In the former no doubt the human factor was again responsible, for no man will work as conscientiously or hard for a community as he will for himself alone, whilst in the Colonies, to these same influences must be added the wastefulness always associated with official control.

There remains, then, that large branch connected with co-operative sale, but here again subdivision is essential for the purpose of analysis. Corn, whatever may be the conditions ruling in the new countries of the world, has never lent itself to co-operative marketing in this country, and is progressively less likely so to do. Being essentially a minor product of large farms, and forming but a fraction of the total supply, it is entirely absorbed within the country and offers little scope for economies in handling, and none for collective bargaining. It also requires to undergo elaborate and expensive processes before it is fit for human consumption. Livestock, such as cattle and sheep, also present difficulties, for, despite all that has been urged against sales by auction or upon commission, these methods, in conjunction with direct dealings with butchers (on admittedly uneconomic principles), have become thoroughly standardised, and co-operative societies would have the active opposition of a powerful trade, as well as the lethargy of the farmer, to combat. Pigs present an easier problem, and already societies in all parts of the United Kingdom are doing considerable trade by buying these animals from their members, and, after completing the intermediate processes, marketing the bacon. Milk, in which the home producer has a virtual monopoly, has already shown the value of combination for the purposes of negotiating its sale, and Ireland has proved that, in grazing countries with an export trade, co-operation can be carried several stages further and made to include manufacturing processes. In all these fields the potentialities of the new Agricultural Marketing Acts will be appreciated, for some overriding form of co-operative endeavour will, it is quite clear, shortly be applied to several of them.

It is, however, when one approaches the typical Small Holder's and the market gardener's province that the latent possibilities of voluntary co-operation are opened out, and the fact that it has so far only touched the fringe of the problem becomes apparent. For here, in the collection and disposal of poultry, eggs, fruit and butter, there is a real opportunity afforded, at one and the same time, to reduce the cost to the consumer and, by eliminating the middleman, to secure additional profits for the producer. But the hasty and promiscuous establishment of societies in unsuitable localities, or staffed with officials dependent upon a distant headquarters, is certainly not the way to attain success. There are certain districts that, demonstrably, fulfil the necessary requirements; among these must be reckoned those containing small farms and commercial gardens to be found within a radius of all large towns, certain market-garden districts, such as parts of Bedfordshire, the Isle of Ely and the Cornish peninsula, and, lastly, the fruit-growing areas of Evesham, Cambridgeshire and Kent. In the first case an assured market is ready at hand for everything that the surrounding farms can produce, and in the other there is that homogeneity of interests, of soil, and of output that favours combination in every step taken to secure more distant outlets.

It is questionable whether the most efficient type of society for a group of Small Holders is not one, the complete responsibility for the running of which devolves upon the associates in common. If paid officials can be dispensed with, or their services confined to an occasional visit of an advisory nature, there is both a financial saving and a stimulus to work. The disposal of profits (after a fixed and small rate of interest has been paid on capital) can also be made to form a useful incentive by adhesion to the rule that members benefit in strict proportion to the volume of trade they have contributed. Absolute equality in regard to voting power, and the possession of shares limited to a very moderate amount are necessary features in any small society; liability must also be rigorously confined to the value of the shares subscribed. Further, it is not too much to insist that all the commodities produced by members should, for a fixed period, be handled by the society; this at once obviates the possibility of only inferior goods being tendered, or of extraneous demands being catered for, and leads to a higher standard being maintained in the society's output.

If the economic conditions postulated above are taken advantage of and the rules just quoted adhered to, there is no reason why agricultural co-operation in this country should not be extended without a reintroduction of artificial and deleterious State subventions—unless, indeed, the apathy of the small farmer is as great as is sometimes stated to be the case. Some twelve years ago Sir Daniel Hall wrote thus of the Small Holders in the Isle of Axholme: "We are told that the economic success of Small Holdings depends on welding them together into co-operative communities, but if the Isle of Axholme furnishes any indication of the future, the men who are going to teach the English farmers to co-operate have got an uphill task before them". The intervening years have shown a certain improvement in this respect, but, when one finds, even in France and Germany, only a fraction of the far more numerous small producers drawn within the co-operative net, is it to be wondered at that in this country progress is still very slow? The more sturdy and independent the individual—and therefore the more likely to succeed by his own efforts—the less does co-operation appeal to him, and no one familiar with the history of British agriculture will deny that in the past such men as these were the ones who came through bad times with least hurt. An appeal to them to throw in their lot with the average, and with the inefficient, farmer is not at first glance an attractive proposition, and the advantages of combination are not easy to place before them, yet this lies at the very root of the matter, for is not co-operation founded on the ideal of the strong helping the weak?

The reasons adduced in the foregoing pages for the comparative non-success of co-operation in this country—namely the fact that there is virtually no export trade, the absence of numerous Small Holders, and the inability of farmers, from temperamental causes, to pool their resources—are those universally accepted, but is it not possible that there may exist deeper rooted economic causes which might be additionally responsible? For instance, if it could be shown that British agriculture had never, in the course of the nineteenth century, touched the depths of depression that the majority of Continental nations experienced, or, expressed differently, that its followers had not been forced to work so desperately hard for such poor returns as their neighbours, might not this account for their failure to sink individualism while the German and the Dane eagerly clutched at the last straw—that of co-operation? Assume for a moment that the Royal Commission of 1893 had not resulted in the many minor aids to farming that owed their origin to its deliberations, and that the depression had continued in its severest form for another decade, is it not conceivable that, thrown entirely on their own resources, agriculturists would have responded more kindly to the overtures of co-operative leaders? Extreme distress led to the popularity of Raiffeisen in Germany, the Danes turned, incidentally, to co-operation when their whole outlook was changed by constitutional and economic losses, and no one would claim that Irish agriculturists were as prosperous as the English when their philanthropic countryman commenced his work. In this country agriculture has yielded better returns to those investing in it, or, conversely, has permitted a less strenuous life to be led, for the system of landlord and tenant, with its corollary of fair-sized holdings, has not made such demands upon the physical and financial resources of farmers as have systems in which small owners predominate. Margins have been correspondingly larger in this country, and depression has not resulted in such a body of acute suffering. Is it unreasonable to suggest, therefore, that the factor of compulsion has to a great extent been absent?

Throughout the world at large, however, co-operation, in one or another of its many forms, must clearly be the ultimate goal of hundreds of millions of white, brown, yellow and black peasants. In this connection, it is, indeed, fortunate that the memory of its great advocate, the late Sir Horace Plunkett, should be perpetuated by the activities of the Foundation, named after himself and endowed so generously from his own resources, for the existence of this body, provided with a skilled personnel and with all the material means to encourage and extend the movement, clearly points the way towards that "Better farming, better business, better living" which was his goal as well as his watchword.

The Provision of Credit

Prior to the passing of the 1923 Agricultural Credits Act, briefly referred to in a previous page, there had been—apart from the handful of Co-operative Credit Societies already existing—no machinery by which British cultivators could utilise their crops or stock as security for temporary loans. In most other countries of the world, notably in the newer territories of the Southern Hemisphere, it was customary to borrow for this purpose by means of "Chattel" mortgages. For a full description of these practices, and also for an admirable account of the theoretical aspects of the whole question, readers are referred to Prof. H. Belshaw's work, *The Provision of Credit, with special reference to Agriculture.* Here, three options, viz. (*a*) the banks, (*b*) professional money-lenders or (*c*) dealers and merchants, had presented themselves to a rural community that was traditionally reluctant to make known to outsiders its financial standing and, unlike all other types of business, regarded the act of borrowing as a stigma upon its character rather than as a necessary aid to better results. The banks, despite much ill-informed criticism, were generally willing to meet the requirements of their customers, so long as conditions were normal, but in bad times—when, therefore, there was apt to be the greatest demand—it was evident that the security offered was apt to be considered insufficient and the risk was often refused. Enquiries have shown that, while the great Joint Stock Banks of the country might have on loan to agriculturists, at any given time, an aggregate sum amounting to upwards of twenty million pounds, yet, compared with the value of the output of the farms concerned, such a figure was very small, amounting to perhaps 7 per cent. The second choice, that represented by money-lenders, if adopted, put the farmer in the same situation as that occupied by any other person foolish enough to respond to solicitations from Russian Jews, masquerading under the best Scots or English names, and couched in language designed to imply that business upon "note of hand alone" would be effected upon a 5 per cent. per annum basis. Such folk, whether urban or rural, have ever been fortunate if they ultimately escaped from the net in solvency and without recourse to the law. Advances from merchants and other tradesmen, with whom farmers normally come in contact, are of an indirect character, for they rest upon the deferment of debts, contracted in connection with the purchase of goods. In addition to a possibly reasonable rate of interest, they carry with them, however, the generally expressed obligation, either to continue dealing with the creditor or to transfer certain custom to him. These world-wide conditions have too often caused, even in this country, a virtual bondage from which escape was difficult. So, too, applications for the deferring of rent payments (or for remission thereof) have, in effect, also represented the transference of financial liabilities to another person, and, in this case, to one frequently in no position to accept them. True, one other possible course presented itself to the British farmer, viz. to proceed by means of a bill of sale, which implied full publicity and the consequential withdrawal of all business facilities.

These, then, were the circumstances in which the first Agricultural Credits Act was in 1923 placed upon the Statute-book. Its provisions concerning long-term credit, referred to above, were, so long as the peculiar circumstances attendant upon post-war land purchase lasted, taken full advantage of, but subsequently fell into desuetude. It is, therefore, only necessary to point out that this form had already been available, so far as landowners were concerned, since the middle of last century, for, through the Lands Improvement Company, it had been possible to borrow money at a very moderate rate of interest for purposes of permanent improvement over periods of time up to forty years. Upwards of £13,000,000 had been thus lent before the war and, although the Company's activities were paralysed from 1914 to 1920, in the latter year they were resumed. Both *de novo* purchasers of land and those who wished to improve their existing properties were, therefore, fully catered for—the first class by this Act of 1923 and the second by the means just indicated.

The real innovation was the provision of facilities for short-term credit which the Act embodied. It was declared that, in the event of Co-operative Credit Societies being formed, the Government would advance capital to them upon a pound for pound basis; since members would not be called upon to pay up more than five shillings in the pound, the State was in effect offering to accept responsibility for four-fifths of the share capital. Provision was made for subscribers other than those who would normally themselves be borrowers, and straightforward conditions were laid down in regard to the general financial arrangements of the numerous societies that were expected to result from the Act. Interest on the State advances was at first fixed at 5 per cent., which necessitated the societies charging their members 6 per cent. for their loans, but this handicap was mitigated when the rate was reduced to that of the Bank rate, with a minimum of 4 per cent. Not surprisingly, however, this scheme proved unattractive, few societies were formed and, once again, it was demonstrated that British farmers were not prepared to collaborate in furthering a typical Continental credit-supply movement. It had, indeed, for long been legally possible, under the provisions of the Industrial and Provident Societies' Acts (resting upon mutual guarantees) to form very similar societies, but, again, they would have none of them.

Five years went by, and then the most far-reaching scheme for providing farmers with both long-term and short-term credit facilities was launched. The resultant Agricultural Credits Act of 1928 was divided into two Parts, of which the first, appertaining to the former type, can be dealt with quickly. Here, an Agricultural Mortgage Corporation was set up, furnished with an initial loan of £650,000 and guaranteed an annual subvention of £10,000 for ten years. The function of that body is to advance loans through the banks for the purchase of farm land up to the usually accepted proportion of two-thirds of its (specially ascertained) value—these advances to run for a period not exceeding sixty years. The Corporation, when it commenced operations in 1929, found a warm welcome awaiting it, both in regard to the borrowing of money—some £5,000,000 was applied for in the first year—and when its own 5 per cent. debentures were placed upon the market, for the issue was promptly over-subscribed. A counterpart came into existence, four years later, in the shape of the Scottish Agricultural Securities Corporation, which functions upon analogous lines.

The second Part of the 1928 Act introduced the privilege of chattel mortgage to English farmers, for it provided that short-term credit, resting upon the security of growing crops, livestock or any "other agricultural assets" (as fully defined below)[1] should, through ap-

[1] The Act defined the property which might be made the subject of an agricultural charge as follows:

"'Farming stock' means crops or horticultural produce, whether growing or severed from the land, and after severance whether subjected to any treatment or process of manufacture or not; livestock, including poultry and bees, and the produce

proved banks, be made available to them. In accordance with existing practice in other countries, two options were permitted, viz. the creation of either a fixed or a floating charge upon farm assets —or, of course, a combination of the two could be arranged. These charges which, in turn, may be either specific sums or of fluctuating extent, legally rank second only to rent and taxes and are subject to compulsory notification at the Land Registry, but no list of them (or of the farmers concerned) may be published in any form. Money so borrowed may be used in any desired manner. Countervailing powers are, naturally, possessed by the banks, for they can, if necessary, seize and sell the property covered by fixed charges and can declare floating charges to have become fixed, with the resultant obvious implications.

Such is the scheme which has now been implemented and British farmers at last have at their disposal every recognised form of credit assistance. Loans under the first Part of the Act were, as was stated previously, quickly taken up, and at the annual meetings of the Mortgage Corporation, its chairman has subsequently been able to announce a growing volume of business. Thus, in his address in 1931, Sir H. Goschen reported that 500,000 acres of farm-land, valued at over £11,000,000, were under mortgage to the Corporation. The individual holdings were widely distributed, but Yorkshire, Kent, Lincolnshire and Somerset had provided a disproportionate number; in regard to size, the majority of advances had related to holdings not exceeding two hundred acres in extent. Repayments were, despite prevailing conditions, being well maintained and, in consequence, the Corporation itself was in a sound financial condition. The provisions of Part II of the 1928 Act did not come into effect until three years later, so that it is impossible, at this juncture, to assess the measure of success achieved in the more contentious and

and progeny thereof; any other agricultural or horticultural produce, whether subjected to any treatment or process of manufacture or not; seeds and manures; agricultural vehicles, machinery, and other plant; agricultural tenant's fixtures and other agricultural fixtures which a tenant is by law authorised to remove.

"'Other agricultural assets' means a tenant's right to compensation under the Agricultural Holdings Act, 1923, for improvements, damage by game, disturbance or otherwise, and any other tenant right.

"A fixed charge might include:

"(*a*) In the case of livestock, any progeny thereof which may be born after the date of the charge; and

"(*b*) In the case of agricultural plant, any plant which may whilst the charge is in force be substituted for the plant specified in the charge".

fickle field of short-term credit. It may be stated, however, without fear of contradiction that it will not be due to any lack of prevision on the part of those who drew up the conditions, if the terms of the latter, too, are not readily accepted.

The State has, indeed, now done all that can be expected of it in this, the only, branch of rural economy that could possibly hitherto have been termed "neglected". It rests in future with farmers themselves to demonstrate that they no longer regard the borrowing of money as tantamount to a confession of professional failure, but rather as giving expression to a normal business instinct the results derivable from which other participants in trade have likened to its "life-blood".

Chapter XVII

THE WHEAT SUPPLY OF THE BRITISH ISLES

Review of the present situation; the mediaeval loaf and its constituents; the value attached to wheat; growth of the Corn Laws; the Assize of Bread; conditions prior to, and during, the French War; the Corn Law Act of 1815; the situation prior to 1846; delayed results of the repeal; decline in wheat prices and, concurrently, of acreage; cycles; foreign competition; methods of production and rates of yield abroad; comparative supplies from different sources; effects of the Great War upon production abroad; conditions in Russia and elsewhere; the world's wheat exports.

An eminent authority once accurately summed up the immediate post-war position of this country in relation to its supply of breadstuffs by designating it "a nation of week-enders", for our requirements could then be met from the produce of our own fields as to one-fifth—or from a Saturday afternoon to a Monday morning; since then that exiguous proportion has still further diminished, being now represented by some 13 or 14 per cent. The whole history of farming in Great Britain is bound up with this question of the supply of the staple article of food, and it is not too strong a statement to make that, for centuries, the nation's only interest in the industry had been dictated by its varying dependence upon it for its daily bread. From time immemorial, until some hundred and thirty years ago, the matter of wheat production was purely a domestic one for this and other nations to settle, either by allowing free play to economic laws or by legislating to encourage growers or importers. Then began the transition stage when certain countries could, by no ordinary means, compass their own supplies, and attempts were made to create special privileges to meet their wants. Finally, appeared the beginning of what must be the ultimate stage in the development of a world wheat market—a stage in which the thickly-populated nations of the world concentrate on the production of other soil products, leaving to the new countries of both hemispheres the business of raising their cereals. At some future time, when that development is complete, there may still remain one source of anxiety to the wheat-consuming peoples of the world. A yield from the scores of millions of acres of prairie land of North and South America at the rate of perhaps thirty bushels to the acre, comparable rates of production upon perhaps two hundred thousand square miles in Russia and lesser tracts in Australia and other quarters of the globe, as yet untouched, will provide them with their food, but there will be ever present the haunting fear of what might happen if the rice-eating peoples of China, India and elsewhere changed their habits of diet, for the world could not indefinitely feed its total population (assuming a constant rate of increase) on wheat, even if the highest existing level of production became the universal standard. This, however, is an argument in the case of this country worn threadbare during the past century, as witness the unfulfilled prophecy of Sir W. Crookes, that we should be short of bread by 1930; its extension to the world at large will doubtless a century hence be the cause of alternating anxiety and satisfaction. In this and the following Chapter it is proposed, first to review the past position of the United Kingdom as a wheat producer and importer, then to describe the world's sources of supply, and finally to discuss the question of the artificial stimulation of production.

One is accustomed to read that in Anglo-Saxon and Norman times one of the common fields was annually sown with autumn wheat, and it has therefore been too frequently assumed that exactly one-third of the arable land of the country was devoted to the production of a white loaf, but recent investigations have tended to show that rye was frequently a larger crop than had been supposed by earlier writers, and there is distinct evidence of a diversion of the brown and the white loaf respectively to the manorial retainers and to the lord himself. That by the fourteenth century there was antipathy to rye, or other inferior types of bread, is plain from the well-known lines in *Piers Plowman*:

> Nor would beggars eat bread with beans in it,
> But stamped bread, fine bread, clear wheaten bread.

This aversion spread more rapidly here than on the Continent, and England was the first European country whose peasantry turned exclusively to the wheaten loaf. But even in Elizabethan times wheat was still not its universal constituent, for, in Holinshed's *Chronicles*, the following passage occurs:

> The bread throughout the land is made of such graine as the soile yieldeth, nevertheless the gentilitie commonlie provide themselves

sufficientlie of wheate for their own tables, whilst their houshold and poor neighbours in some shires are enforced to content themselves with rie or barleie, yea and in time of dearth manie with bread made either of beans peason or otes or of altogether and some acorns among, of which scourge the poorest doo soonest tast, sith they are least able to provide themselves of better.

The acreage under wheat and rye in mediaeval times has been a constant source of enquiry among economists, to whom Domesday has provided a foundation upon which edifices of conjecture have been reared as to the rate of yield obtained and the consumption per head of the population. More exact data are available in the records of prices current in certain districts for century after century, for there have been published, in such works as Thorold Rogers' *History of Prices in the United Kingdom*, annual tables, from which it is possible to trace, by the fluctuations in the price of cereals, the incidence of famine and of lesser failures caused by climatic conditions. Such records, indeed, form the oldest complete series of agricultural statistics that exist in this or in any country, and are of more use to the historian than categorical statements that so many hundred shiploads of grain were occasionally exported to the Continent, or conjectures that the rate of yield of wheat over a space of three centuries showed an improvement of so many bushels per acre. Prices give very clear indications of the existence of a shortage or of a surplus, and afford evidence of any tendency for supply to fall short of demand. The only proviso to make is that, in the middle ages, prices of grain were always extraordinarily susceptible to adverse influences. The slightest sign of an outturn below the normal had the immediate effect of advancing values out of all proportion to the anticipated deficit; this phenomenon has been frequently analysed, and it is no exaggeration to say that, while a possible decline in total yield of 5 per cent. might raise the price 10 per cent., a shortage of 10 per cent. would result in advancing it by 30 to 50 per cent. This was inevitable when alternative sources of supply were practically non-existent, and when the loaf represented a far larger element in the nation's total food supply than it does in modern times. The value attaching to wheat was indeed such that in the case of certain payments it was adopted as a standard of value in lieu of gold—e.g. in Elizabethan times and even later, as we have already seen, Colleges and other corporate bodies frequently prescribed that their rents should be rendered partly in the form of grain in order to obviate losses from fluctuations in the value of money.

Because of its paramount importance, the efforts of the State were incessantly directed towards the maintenance of adequate supplies of home-grown wheat, the provision of inducements to importers, the placing of severe restrictions upon those who dealt in corn, and lastly the actual control of the quality and size of the loaf itself. Space does not permit of a description of the individual Corn Laws, but the principle upon which they were conceived must be borne in mind. At first the whole system depended upon the virtual prohibition of export and the placing of no impediments in the way of importation. Gradually a measure of exportation was allowed, the deciding factor being the prices ruling at any given time. From the seventeenth century onwards a composite plan was in force, by which, in times of low values, export was actually encouraged by the granting of a small bounty, and imports subjected to a duty; as prices rose export was successively forbidden and imports finally rendered free. These measures carried the country to the time of the French War, but, after the first half of the eighteenth century, the position had become apt to be one of difficulty. Two points should be noticed before passing to the consideration of subsequent happenings. First, these regulations applied to all cereals, and not to wheat alone, the importance of which has subsequently tended to obscure this feature; similar encouragement was therefore afforded to the grower of other cereals. Secondly, whilst there is little doubt that the Corn Laws tended to maintain a steady, and probably enhanced, acreage under cereal crops, it is open to question whether, in the matter of prices, their effects were of great weight. It is probable that the weather had more influence than could be corrected by the action of artificial restraints. The whole of Western Europe was, and is, subject to very similar climatic conditions, and the mere fact that a bad harvest had occurred in England, causing a demand for foreign wheat, implied that Continental growers were suffering from similar disabilities. Also at times when export was permitted from our shores, the prospective supplies of those with whom we would trade were apt to be at their maxima.

The regulation of dealings in corn was a mediaeval method of coping with a difficulty which is still rife. The elimination, or rigid control of, the middleman, and especially of the speculator, seemed an obvious way of obtaining the maximum profit to the producer and at the same time of mollifying the purchaser. As the internal trade and commerce of the country grew, it became out of the question to maintain a form of restraint on one trade whilst permitting freedom to others, and gradually, from the seventeenth century onwards, liberty of action was allowed to corn dealers. The last link in the chain consisted of the Assize of Bread, and this persisted into the last century. Precedents can be found for almost all that is now looked upon as novel, and each step taken by the Ministry of Food had its counterpart in the history of agriculture. The war-time control of millers and of merchants was nothing but a reversion to the laws aimed at "engrossers", and the statutory ninepenny loaf, of a fixed weight and containing a legal percentage of admixture, represented merely a reintroduction of the powers possessed by those who sat in assize upon its mediaeval counterpart. Many are familiar with this excellent institution which placed in the hands of local Justices of the Peace the power to regulate the profits of bakers, and at the same time to ensure that consumers received loaves of a fixed weight and bread of a standard quality, but the fact that it persisted up to comparatively modern times is often overlooked. In the case of London, the Assize was abolished in 1822, but in the rest of the country it remained in force until 1836, and such notices as this appeared at frequent intervals in all local newspapers: "The Assize of Bread for this town was reduced ¾*d.* in the quartern loaf wheaten, the price of which is now 8¾*d.*" (*Cambridge Chronicle*, 1822). The nearest modern equivalent is the following: "The London millers announce that the current price of standard grade flour in the home Counties is now 23*s.* 6*d.* per 280 lb., 6*d.* to 1*s.* less delivered within the London district" (*The Times*, January, 1933). In the former case control was exercised by the appointed Justices, in the latter by combinations of traders.

Up to the middle of the eighteenth century this country had not only been self-supporting (except of course for individual years of shortage), but on balance had been an exporter of wheat. Additional land had annually come under the plough from the enclosure of wastes, augmented by such occurrences as the drainage of the fens (which provided the country with some hundreds of thousands of acres of the richest arable soil), whilst concurrently there had been a steady but unassessable improvement in the rate of yield per acre. Thus, an increasing population—and a population that was already beginning to show signs of becoming industrial—was still fed from its own resources. But the second half of the century saw increased demands made upon an industry that could only just maintain its position, and during a period when climatic conditions were on the whole distinctly unfavourable. The French War was the unlooked-for climax to a movement that was inevitably tending to bring the Corn Laws into conflict with a large section of the community. Coke himself, it was claimed, materially contributed to our victory by his own efforts and example in producing wheat, but the methods of all such "improvers in husbandry", if sedulously copied throughout the kingdom, could not have done more than postpone for a few years the civil strife between town and country that followed the French War. The prognostications of most economists, as well as of practical agriculturists, however, complacently showed that the country, thanks to the improved methods of crop-raising that, it was assumed, would soon be of universal application, could be self-supporting for indefinite periods; at the same time the physical impossibility of meeting from abroad more than a fraction of the nation's needs was convincingly put forward by others. In 1793, for instance, Thomas Baird held that Middlesex alone could meet the additional requirements of the nation by merely placing another 15,000 acres under wheat, "consequently it is an easy matter to prevent our being obliged to depend on foreign countries for bread. Encouragement to the husbandman, or rather the removal of discouragements, is all that is necessary for securing that valuable object". Then came Malthus and his disquieting doctrine, but as the latter was made public during the war, it, for the moment, received less attention than might have been expected.

This, then, was the position in 1792 on the outbreak of the war. If actual hostilities were not continuous up to 1815, certainly the whole intervening period was one of economic instability. The country emerged victorious, but possessed of legacies similar to those with which the present generation is again familiar. High prices had caused the widespread expansion of arable farming, which in turn led to the most rapid enclosure movement that the country has known. Upon this occasion it assumed a double form, by causing the disappearance of the open-fields and, unfortunately, also of the majority of the commons. As has been pointed out in the Chapters upon labour, the results in the first case were certainly beneficial, leading, as they did, to a higher level of cultivation, but the loss of the commons, for the avowed purpose of producing food in war time, was not made the subject of adequate recompense. The increased area under the plough, brought about entirely by the lure of high prices, would doubtless have carried the nation through the war period, but the Government, leaving nothing to chance, despatched purchasers to those foreign States with which our relations permitted trade to be conducted. Propaganda was also indulged in, for efforts were made to induce the consumption of bread made of flour of an altered extraction or diluted with oats and barley. A poster issued in 1795 by the Mayor of Chester pointed out that palatable bread could be made by the addition of one-third potatoes to two-thirds wheaten flour. In 1918 the State was setting up mills for the manufacture of potato flour, so even to the smallest detail does history repeat itself.

It is not proposed to record in this Chapter the fluctuations in the current prices of wheat at earlier periods, as information relative to the purchasing power of money in terms of present values would have to be added, and, after 1780, a glance at the diagram facing p. 386 will at once answer any questions; but, broadly speaking, the great rise in the price of all commodities, and of wheat in particular, brought wealth to farmers and increased rents to landlords in the last decade of the eighteenth and the first of the nineteenth centuries. The agricultural labourer alone suffered from high prices and wages that were insufficiently augmented to meet them. This, then, was the position in the last year of the war, and one for the perpetuating of which the agricultural industry, as represented by landlords and tenants, persuaded Parliament to legislate.

The Corn Law Act of 1815 was the result—an Act that deserves individual mention, as it formed the last serious attempt of an already declining section of the nation to secure for itself preferential treatment at the expense of the rest of the country. The Act in question, whilst permitting the importation of cereals, forbade their removal from bond for internal consumption until the price of British wheat stood at 80*s.* the quarter, rye, beans and peas at 53*s.* the quarter, barley 40*s.* the quarter and oats 26*s.* the quarter. When these price-levels were attained the grains in question might be withdrawn for consumption free of duty. Special treatment was accorded to Canada, for a clause permitted the introduction of her products when the following prices for British grain were touched: wheat, 67*s*.; rye, peas and beans, 44*s*.; barley, 33*s*.; oats, 22*s*. The principles upon which this Act was conceived were, therefore, two-fold; they comprised an attempt to maintain prices at a war level, and at the same time conferred a measure of preference on a British colony. The history of the previous year explains certain of these provisions, for the Act was substituted for an abortive Bill of 1814, which had ordained a sliding scale of duties, ranging from 24*s*. per quarter, when the home price stood at 64*s*., to 1*s*. when 86*s*. was reached; additionally, unrestricted importation was to have been permitted, and the bounty, previously granted, abrogated. Now, the last two clauses alone passed into law in company with the 1815 Act. Agricultural Committees and the landed interests had both held that sums varying from 120*s*. down to 80*s*. ought to be fixed as the limit at which the introduction of duty-free wheat should be sanctioned; on the other hand, in the words of M'Culloch, "manufacturers and every class not supported by agriculture, stigmatised it as unjustifiable artificially to keep up the price of food and to secure excessive rents and large profits to the landowners and farmers, at the expense of the consumers".

That, for the moment, the pendulum had swung in favour of the agriculturist, is by the passage of the 1815 Act obvious, but the times in which he might be granted exclusive privileges were fast drawing to a close. Moreover, the Act failed in its purpose, for, owing to good harvests, internal prices were not maintained at their expected heights, and only for a short period did its provisions come into effect. The country was still sufficiently self-supporting to meet its own needs in years of abundance, and in these circumstances no regulations could maintain prices artificially above their economic level. Just at first, in 1816 and 1817, it appeared as if the rural arguments were going to be borne out, for, as land reverted to grass, so the prices of cereals rose. But finally fresh areas were again sown to wheat, and favourable conditions brought about yields that, once and for all, demonstrated that low prices had come to stay. Economists, writing near the time, pointed out that the restrictions adopted occasioned the very evils they were supposed to remove and, in many cases, held that the bulk of the distress that followed was directly attributable to their influence. One writer, indeed, went so far as to say that Protection was an impossible policy, as not only did it fail to prevent the occurrence of low prices, but, as then contrived, made exportation impossible until values had sunk unnaturally low—in a word, he argued that the only sound proposition was to destroy a part of the grain produced at home in good seasons!

From 1821, after the setting up of a Committee of enquiry, the remaining Acts which led up to the repeal, successively reduced the disabilities under which foreign grain suffered, and standardised the principle of the sliding-scale duty. They were of course strenuously opposed by the bulk of the landowners, who still clung to the belief that their salvation rested upon Protection. The particular Acts passed in 1822 and 1828, apart from rousing the hostility of merchants, were not the subject of especial annoyance to the nation, for the reason that a series of good harvests supervened, and prices remained moderately low. Those engaged in the corn trade, however, held that, from the existence of the sliding-scale, the uncertainty attaching to the amount of import duty payable made their business a hazardous one. It should perhaps be explained that the necessity for ascertaining the "average price" of cereals had already led to the introduction of an elaborate system of checking supplies, which gave employment to numerous officials. In 1791 all the sea-board Counties of England had been grouped into twelve districts, and the inward and outward movements of grain were subject to the prices ruling within those divisions, these prices themselves being ascertained at four quarterly periods. Thirteen years later the official price was represented by the aggregate average of these areas, separate figures for Scotland being based upon the returns of four maritime districts. Finally, in 1805, Great Britain itself was taken as a single unit for the purposes of price assessment; the following year trade between the component parts of the United Kingdom was further facilitated by the extension to Ireland of freedom in the movement of grain.

The Acts of 1822 and 1828 proved merely the precursors to what was to become the greatest political and economic fight that has ever been waged round British agriculture. The second of these two has an academic interest, as it inaugurated the existing system by which returns of corn prices are rendered weekly by inspectors from numerous centres, to be incorporated into the official "*Gazette* average". Its main provisions, from causes that have already been indicated, proved innocuous until 1837, but, from that year onwards, prices rose very considerably and importation on a generous scale was necessitated. This led to the actual conflict upon which so much was then, and has subsequently, been written. An Act of 1842 once more toned down the duties on imported grain, and at the same time roused further opposition from farmers by making free the importation of live cattle and of other agricultural commodities. The slope that led to Free Trade was therefore fully embarked upon by the nation. It is not necessary to describe the steps taken by Peel that led to the introduction and passage of the famous Act of 1846. One must, however, point out that circumstances compelled legislation on these lines. The famine in Ireland in 1845 has been spoken of as an immediate contributory cause, but, famine or no famine, this country could not have maintained the principle of Protection for one branch of agriculture for more than a very short period. A population that could not be supported on the products of its own soil, even in years of bountiful harvests, was in a totally different position from that which it had occupied when a surplus of corn was a frequent occurrence and could be turned to advantage as a steadying influence on prices. Three years after the passage of the Act of 1846 Free Trade was nominally adopted, although for twenty years a small duty, amounting to a shilling a quarter, was in operation. Thereafter, but for one subsequent attempt to place an even smaller tax on foreign wheat, Free Trade was an actuality until 1932.

The position at the time of repeal can now be surveyed free from bias, and the only conclusion that can fairly be arrived at is that the attempt made on behalf of one section of the nation to secure for itself special consideration rightly failed. The interests of the country as a whole were paramount, and the Corn Laws had outlived their surroundings. Subsequent happenings confounded the prophets, both schools of thought being shown to be fallacious guides to the future. The farmers were not, to their surprise, immediately ruined, and the townsmen, equally to their disappointment, did not at once revel in supplies of cheap bread. Agriculture did not decay—even the acreage under the plough was, according to all contemporaneous accounts, well maintained; indeed, the conditions ruling from 1850 up to 1870 have sometimes been described as affording one of those rare periods when British agriculture was flourishing. The causes of the maintenance of cereal prices at a comparatively high level are familiar—unrest and actual hostilities in several parts of the world, the absence of large areas of newly won land abroad and of facilities for importing quantities of cheaply raised overseas grain, and, overwhelmingly, the abundant supply of gold in the world. It must be pointed out also that, despite an admittedly increased consumption of wheat (both individually and from the demands of a growing population), its cost, in a time of rising prices, remained stationary; there is no doubt that, but for the repeal, wheat would have risen very considerably during the next two or three decades. This feature is often overlooked when comment is made upon the apparently negative results of the action taken in 1846.

From the late 'seventies, however, the effects, thus postponed, were fully apparent, and the world price of wheat fell, naturally taking with it that of our native supplies. The causes are partly positive and partly negative in origin. On the one hand there was the absence of troubles abroad; peace reigned among the nations, which, on the Continent, had turned to hard work and industrialism, and, in the newer countries, to the development of their latent resources. The construction of tens of thousands of miles of railway, connecting the wheat-raising districts of the Middle and Western States of America with the sea-board, in conjunction with the progress made in ocean transport, had resulted in creating a form of competition with which later generations of farmers have perforce become familiar. Most important of all, the demand for gold exceeded its supply; many countries were clamouring for the metal, which the then existing mines were producing in reduced quantities. Prices of all commodities, expressed in terms of gold, necessarily fell.

Statistics of the acreage devoted to wheat from 1866, which was the year the official series commenced, will be found in Tables I and II of the Appendix, but the diagram facing p. 500 conveys, far more vividly than can bare columns of figures, the measure of the change forced upon English farmers; the term English is used advisedly, for those who were engaged in the cultivation of the soil in the other component parts of the Kingdom did not suffer to anything like the same extent. The area under oats in the United Kingdom remained almost constant from 1866 up to the outbreak of the Great War, and that under barley declined by only about half a million acres. The bulk of the loss fell upon the Midland Counties of England, and upon those particular districts of heavy land, which, wherever situated, are the first to suffer from a decline in the value of wheat. At some critical point in the scale of prices—indicated now (1933) by a level of 50*s.* the quarter—wheat ceases to be a paying proposition on this type of land, and the latter reverts (if circumstances are kind) to grass; failing that, it tumbles down. The diagram facing p. 386 will at once show the connection, after 1875, between prices and acreage, for, from an average of 56*s.* in 1871, the fall in the value of wheat was continuous, until, in the brief space of twenty years, it touched 30*s.* From 1890 there were few occasions when the price, if averaged over a series of five years, exceeded 28*s.* Only after 1907 could definite signs of improvement be seen, the cause of which was the augmented supply of gold from the South African mines. The acreage itself fell by a series of abrupt declines, superimposed on a regular annual loss; the incidence of such disastrous years as 1879, 1891, 1892, and especially of 1894, can easily be traced in the reduced areas sown in the following seasons. In the first few years during which official statistics were collected, the area under wheat in the United Kingdom had amounted to just under four million acres; in 1895 it was under one and a half million. At first, there is evidence that the wheat thus lost to the nation was replaced by barley, for, if the diagram be closely examined, it will appear that, up to 1880, heavy declines in wheat areas were partially made good by the sowing of the alternative cereal; after that year, however, the struggle to sustain arable farming on the accustomed scale was clearly surrendered.

Those readers who are interested in the theory of cycles, or of periodic movements, may perhaps wish to have their attention drawn to the fact that there was apparently some influence at work which led to an especially marked fall in wheat acreages every ninth year, commencing with 1877; for the years 1886, 1895, 1904 and, to a lesser extent, 1913, represent larger declines than any reached during intervening seasons. After the war continuously falling acreages masked this occurrence, but it may be seen again, after eighteen years, in the case of 1931. The cycle of nine years, if cycle it be, and not merely a coincidence, is not one that has been especially commented on by writers such as Sir W. Beveridge, who have detected numerous examples that might have a bearing on wheat prices; these range from those that appear at intervals of a little over two years to others that occur many years apart. They have been correlated to rainfall, temperature, barometric pressure and other natural phenomena, and include one that indicated in Greenwich temperatures a periodicity of nine and a half years. .Fluctuations in the acreage sown, rather than in the rate of production, have apparently not been considered as a possible circuitous expression of such causes. This connotes the carrying forward of climatic effects into the years succeeding bad harvests, a feature for the existence of which there is undoubtedly evidence.

On the other hand, attempts made to forecast coming seasons from past records have always met with failure, and recent instances are but the successors of those initiated more than a hundred years ago. For example, in 1817 Lieut. George Mackenzie confidently claimed to have discovered a method, based on the prevailing direction of the wind, whereby it was possible accurately to forecast the weather for several seasons ahead—indeed, he published forecasts for ten years in advance. He modestly expressed the belief that "the operation, however simple in itself, will not only distinguish Britain among nations, but it will also excite the admiration and gratitude of the rest of the world towards this forward country, through all succeeding ages". To the agriculturist, he held that his discovery was of the highest order, "inasmuch as the foreknowledge of the character of the seasons will ever after have the effect of preventing those sudden and calamitous elevations and depressions of prices of commodities which have occasioned hitherto the distress of whole nations and the speedy ruin of millions of individuals. The advantages derived extend to every inch of land in cultivation, the management of which will be varied according to the quantity of rain and temperature of the coming seasons". And yet neither Lieut. Mackenzie nor his present-day followers prepared the agriculturist for such seasons as 1879 and 1894! The more direct relationship between weather and crops provides a totally different field for research from that involved by forecasting climatic conditions in future years. And here such investigators as A. Wallén, in Sweden, and R. H. Hooker, in this country, have, by close examination of past records, shown a certain correlation between, for example, the quantity of autumn rainfall and the yield of wheat. This subject, then, opens up possibilities of real moment to agriculturists, by suggesting that short-dated estimates of yield may, in the course of time, be found feasible to make. This is, however, a digression from what is intended as an account of the plight of English wheat raisers in the second half of the nineteenth century; as a subject, too, it will be found more fully discussed in a later Chapter.

High farming, and all that it implied in the way of labour and purchases, was soon put aside as an impossible expedient in such times as those, and the conditions ruling in the early sixteenth century, after sheep farming had been turned to from causes widely different, seemed likely to reappear. Just in time, however, to save the bulk of the agricultural population came the opportunity, first to supply the townsman with part of his increasing supplies of meat, and afterwards, when competition from overseas appeared even here, almost entirely to meet his renewed demands for milk, fruit and vegetables. Arable farming did not cease to be practised; it merely dispensed with the services of a large proportion of its workers, reduced drastically its outgoings—whether in the form of rent or in the purchase of commodities—and turned to new methods. The days when wheat growing formed the staple branch of the industry had gone for ever, except in East Anglia, that highly favoured portion of the Kingdom where bread-stuffs have ever since been profitably raised in the face of the worst foreign competition.

This was the position in the United Kingdom after 1870; in the rest of Europe, however, protective tariffs still enabled other countries not only to raise wheat at a profit, but generally to be self-supporting, and in certain cases even to add considerably to their cereal acreage. Here, the nation as a whole had quite naturally decided that its needs were paramount, and that the growing millions of consumers in the North and Midlands must be its first consideration. A cheap loaf was secured for the latter, and the difficulties that faced the agriculturist were regarded as of secondary importance. The usual palliatives were tried, and the State eased certain minor burdens for the farmer, but it was left to him to raise corn or not exactly as he willed, and the reimposition of any special measures aiming at the encouragement of wheat production was not even mooted. Farmer witnesses before the Royal Commission of 1893 declared that in parts of Cornwall wheat was grown for thatching purposes, and others stated that the bulk of what they produced was ground and boiled, in lieu of cake, for stock; other witnesses confined their evidence to statements relating to the nature of the foreign competition, and gave forecasts of the ultimate possibilities of wheat production in India, the Argentine and North America that did not augur well for the British farmer in future decades. Indeed, only one dissentient voice—that of Sir W. Crookes—was raised at the end of the nineteenth century; he boldly prophesied, at a meeting of the British Association, that, within less than a human generation, this country would, in common with others similarly situated, be feeling the pinch of want. A very few years passed and it was obvious that he, too, must join that select group of experts to whom coming events were not revealed in advance. For, within twelve years, the wheat area in this country had taken an upward turn, and although the ends of the earth contributed to the supplies shipped to our ports, it was yet possible for us to produce a fifth of our supplies at a profit to growers.

The history of wheat production at home having been reviewed, our present sources of supply and the conditions in other countries deserve some notice before we pass to the consideration of the problems raised by the war. If we turn to figures relating to imported supplies of wheat some seventy years ago—by when Free Trade had been in force for over a decade—it is surprising to note the relative importance of the countries with which we then dealt. In 1860, for instance, both France and Prussia sent us over a million quarters, and there was not a State or dependency in Europe, from Turkey to Sweden, which did not add its contribution. Europe as a whole was more than self-supporting. India, Australia and the Argentine were still wanting as exporters, the only large quantities that came from

Percentage of total wheat imports (including flour expressed in terms of wheat) derived from different countries at certain periods

	1875–7	1881–3	1893–5	1904–13	1914–18	1924–27	1928–30
European Countries*	20·8	10·7	4·7	1·2	—	1·2	3·5
Russia	16·7	11·5	16·6	14·0	1·6	1·4	5·2
United States†	47·0	59·0	55·5	38·7	76·6	29·3	21·4
Canada						34·3	31·1
India	6·1	11·4	6·8	15·5	6·3	5·2	1·4
Argentina	—	—	11·0	17·6	8·3	14·7	24·3
Australia‡	—	—	—	9·6	6·1	12·5	11·4
Other Countries	9·4	7·4	5·4	3·4	1·1	1·4	1·7
Total Imports						100·0	100·0
British Countries						52·1	44·1

* Germany, France, Austria, Hungary, Bulgaria and Roumania.
† United States and Canada taken together up to 1914–18.
‡ Included in "Other Countries" until 1904–13.

non-European sources being the products of the quaintly described "British North America" and the "United States, including California". It is necessary to omit a detailed account of the development of what are now our main sources of supply; but the Table on p. 372 records this movement statistically, by giving the percentage of our total supplies derived from each source for periods averaged over a number of years in order to eliminate fortuitous causes.

It will be observed that in recent pre-war years our sources of supply emanated from five large exporting areas—in order of importance, North America (i.e. the United States and Canada), the Argentine, Russia, India and Australia. Only the first could be looked upon as really dependable, Australia and India in particular being subject to partial crop failure once or twice in each decade. For this reason, whilst, in the aggregate, the needs of the importing nations of the world were regularly met, the proportions of the total annually supplied by each exporting country fluctuated widely. Tables XIII and XIV in the Appendix contain records of the acreage and yield of the world's principal countries. Both acreage and yield are included, for it must be reiterated that acreage in no case affords any criterion as to outturn; it can, indeed, be shown that, as a rule, the greater the area under a cereal crop such as wheat, the lower the yield per acre. Again, those countries situated in parts of the world subjected to extremes of either heat or cold are not in the position to reap more than a varying percentage of the acreage sown. These circumstances, combined with the methods of farming practised in all the new countries, are responsible for the world's average yield of wheat being in the neighbourhood of barely fourteen bushels to the acre. The production achieved by dint of assiduous work and the expenditure of much capital on a few hundred thousand acres of selected land in such countries as Denmark and Belgium, affords merely isolated examples of what theoretically is possible elsewhere. Russia, on an area that formerly varied between seventy and ninety million acres, represented the other extremity of the scale, producing, as she did, only some nine or ten bushels to the acre; India and Australia on, respectively, a third and an eighth of that extent of crop, yield at the rate of eleven bushels, the Argentine, on fifteen million acres, at ten bushels. The methods of cultivation practised in Australia, the Argentine and Western North America have sometimes been compared with those in vogue on the mediaeval manor. This comparison has often been true so far as the non-application of any form of manure to the soil is concerned, and there is also similarity in the introduction of a bare fallow into the rotation, but the quantity of labour employed would be widely divergent. The rates of production attained eight hundred years ago in this country were doubtless equal to those which prevail now twelve thousand miles away, but whilst the actual treatment of the soil, by taking from it everything and returning nothing save the straw, may be comparable, the modern "land-robber" is enabled to make his profits by maintaining a paucity of highly-paid workers, or, even himself alone, with the aid of elaborate machinery, performing all the operations called for upon a square mile of wheat. The manor, on the other hand, provided "denser" employment for numerous workers and tenants.

After 1860 five exporting countries, three situated in the Northern Hemisphere and two in the Southern, gradually ousted other producers, and became responsible for meeting the ever-growing needs of Europe. For not only did France, Germany and the smaller States cease to be exporters, but the majority of them became, in varying degree, themselves dependent on extraneous sources. But in 1914 the world's supply of wheat was still abundantly able to meet the demands made upon it, and, as Sir H. Rew showed, between 1901 and 1911 the increase in the acreage under wheat in the producing countries more than counterbalanced the increase in the populations they were called upon to feed. Statistics relating to the world itself would be of course quite fallacious here, as the important consideration is the staple diet of the peoples concerned, but, so long as enquiry is confined, as in the case given above, to the wheat-producing and wheat-consuming races, one is on safe ground. If China or India, however, had turned to consumption of the wheaten loaf upon any large scale, the position would at once have become hopelessly straitened. Sir H. Rew's figures recorded an increase of 6·6 per cent. in the population of the British Empire and of 45·5 per cent. in its wheat-producing area, the corresponding figures for a selected group of countries being 13 per cent. and 22·9 per cent. It will be observed that the wheat figures related to acreage and not to the more vital question of total outturn, but nevertheless the position before the outbreak of war was clearly an improving one, and there seemed no reason to doubt that the next decade would continue to provide additional supplies of bread-stuffs, partly by an increase in acreage and partly by a gradual raising of the average yield. There was evidence that the latter was already taking place in the newer and larger countries, as in the case of the United States statistics showed that the gradual spreading Westwards of more intensive methods of cultivation was reflected in heavier yields per acre for the whole country. When it is stated that there was not a month in the year in which sowing and harvesting were not taking place in some of the wheat-growing countries, the ramifications of the commerce in grain will be appreciated, as also the small likelihood of weather conditions interfering with our supplies. It could, indeed, have been shown, on the assumption that a total failure in the outturn of each of the five principal sources occurs once in ten years—a quite abnormal frequency—that the odds against that event occurring in all five simultaneously were overwhelming. The partial failure of one exporting centre was a normal experience, made good from the surplus of alternative sources.

As growing interest is taken in this subject of the world's supply of wheat, and it is becoming customary for the inexperienced to forecast the position of the importing and exporting countries for some months ahead, it may perhaps be well to point out certain difficulties that are encountered in the procedure. It is, for instance, when reviewing the position of exporting countries, injudicious to calculate what is known as their "exportable surplus", merely by subtracting their estimated home consumption from their estimated outturn, for, in times of bounteous crops, and therefore of low prices, considerable quantities of wheat are diverted to such other uses as the feeding of livestock; in India and in China at such times, the native population turns to wheat as a change from rice. A "carry over" from one exporting season to another is, for similar reasons, an uncertain element in all such calculations. Equally, the demands likely to eventuate from European countries depend in varying degrees upon climatic conditions as well as upon the prices ruling for overseas grain, and all estimates may prove to be well under the mark if world prices fall substantially. That the operations in question are liable to be affected by numerous unexpected factors, anyone who has essayed this task in post-war years will appreciate, but elementary care in the handling of figures would obviate the publication of such extraordinary statements as the following: "Our farmers are wonderful growers of wheat, perhaps because of the almost terrifying fact that we need as much as two hundred million tons (*sic*) of imported wheat every year". The first words are scarcely accurate as representing the facts of the situation, our rate of production is not directly increased by our dependence on imported grain, and, lastly, the figure mentioned is more than twice the *production* of the whole world—tons and bushels being widely different units.

Before 1914 the demands of the importing countries were fairly steady and subject mainly to climatic influences of a similar character; during the first decade after the war, not only had their own resources diminished, but the majority of them, by reason of disorganised exchanges, could only afford to purchase within smaller limits. The United Kingdom was of course easily the largest importer of foreign wheat, our requirements representing approximately one-third of the world's export; we were followed, in order, by Germany, Holland, Belgium and Italy. The conditions created by the war are well illustrated by the following Table, which shows the quantities of wheat (and of flour converted into its equivalent of grain) imported into this country from each source at different periods.

British imports of wheat and wheat flour (in terms of wheat)

Thousands of cwts.

Imports from	Average 1910–14	Average 1915–19	1921	1924	1927	1930
Russia	13,691	198	—	753	2,462	18,718
United States	29,699	56,774	47,037	35,332	39,669	25,447
Canada	25,972	25,008	22,736	46,055	39,305	32,412
Argentina	14,133	8,965	4,240	24,446	20,578	16,004
Australia	12,830	7,577	21,911	13,133	17,305	15,087
India	18,603	4,610	2,669	9,819	5,020	3,370
Other Countries	4,120	689	3,655	3,224	1,320	10,026
Total	119,048	103,816	102,248	132,762	125,659	121,064

The defection of Russia is of course familiar to all, but the rapidity with which other countries added to their cereal acreage during the period of hostilities is often overlooked. Australia had, for example, some twelve and a half million acres under wheat in 1915, compared with nine and a half in 1914; the United States added seven million acres in the same time, and Canada almost five million. The wheat was in the world, only lack of transport prevented its carriage to

Europe. The Table appearing on p. 376 explains this fact clearly, for it shows that as soon as peace was restored the more distant sources of supply were again drawn upon, and what remained of their accumulated stocks imported. In the case of Australia the British Government had purchased the entire surplus of several seasons but was at the time compelled to divert ships to the shorter transatlantic routes. Facilities for storage were lacking, and a large proportion of this Australian grain was destroyed by weevils and mice, representing a heavy loss to the British tax-payer.

Russia presented a difficult problem, for, from being a large exporter before the war, she, upon one occasion, was reduced to the position of an importer. The drought and resultant famine would in any case have reduced her home crops, but there is little doubt that the social conditions arising out of the war had at least as much bearing on the position. The expropriation of land in all East European countries had similar effects in reducing the outturn of cereals; Roumania has already been cited as a case in point. Conditions agricultural in Russia had strong light thrown on them by the publication of C. R. Buxton's account (*In a Russian Village*) of a visit to that country in 1920. The author recorded examples of villages that then had under the plough some two thousand acres instead of the pre-war seven thousand, whilst, concurrently, the average peasant had increased his holding from eight to eighty acres. The normal system of land-tenure was still the "three field" with its inevitable bare fallow. The transference of the soil from its former owners to the peasants appeared to have taken place step by step, as, for example, when landlords fled, their tenants gradually appropriated to themselves further slices of the land so relinquished; thus "neither the landlord nor his manager ever returned. The peasants discussed the matter and came to the conclusion they had better divide up the whole estate. They had meant to take a part only and to leave the remainder to him. They now divided up, not only the land, but all the stock and the stores. Finally they pulled down the house and carried off the materials in every direction". Again, an owner of five hundred acres "argued and bargained, saying that he was prepared to give up a portion of it. The result was that he had to give up some of it at that time and more of it after the October Revolution. He now has forty-five acres". It was already evident that dissension was spreading between the different classes, and that "rich" and "poor" peasants were quarrelling over their respective rights to real property; meanwhile the land went out of cultivation, the tools and machinery lay broken and neglected, the horses and livestock disappeared and, as a climax, the towns demanded bread from the country. The charitably-minded, who, year after year, urged the duty of "feeding the starving Russians", did not grasp the fundamental difficulties that faced them. Russia herself had been wont to contribute liberally to the world's supply of wheat and of other cereals; it was therefore manifestly impossible for the remaining exporting countries (whose corn area was then reduced, in some instances, almost to a pre-war level), whilst making up this deficit, to feed in addition even a fraction of her teeming millions. Fortunately no other large exporter seriously failed in output during these critical years, otherwise the situation might have become serious. To exploit the drought and famine as not being accentuated by the economic conditions was misleading, since the landlord system had come through similar events on former occasions without reducing the country to a similar state of want. Had land-tenure not been interfered with, the acreage under wheat would doubtless have been sufficient to meet home requirements, and certainly seed corn would not have been consumed, nor earlier surpluses hidden in those "bursting bins" that proved such leaky structures.

For two seasons after the war, India was forced to prohibit export owing to partial crop failure, and this represented the only serious climatic interference with our supplies in the eight years that followed 1914. But subsequently, and for reasons partly economic, partly political and social, that country dropped out of the export trade and must now, indeed, be looked upon as normally an importer of wheat.

The position of this country in the wheat market was adversely affected during the war by the competition from allied nations. France, with a large part of her soil the scene of actual hostilities, and Italy both made heavy demands upon America and the Argentine, thereby tending, until co-ordinated purchasing was introduced, to raise even further the cost of provisioning ourselves and our allies. The total exports of wheat from the principal countries, before the war and after, were as follows. (*Wheat Studies of the Food Research Institute, Stanford, U.S.A.*)

Net exports of wheat and wheat flour.

Millions of bushels (60 lb.).

	1909–10—1913–14	1921–22	1925–26	1930–31
Russia	165*	0	27	111
United States	110	255	106	116
Canada	96	185	324	258
Argentina	85	118	94	123
Australia	55	115	77	152
India	50	—†	8	—‡
Danube Basin§	109*	21	45	45
Other Countries	8	7	14	23
Total	678	701	695	828

* For pre-war boundaries; not comparable with post-war figures.
† Net *imports* of 14 million bushels.
‡ Net *imports* of 5 million bushels.
§ Hungary, Jugo-Slavia, Roumania, and Bulgaria.

With the above figures in view, it is now possible to comment upon certain tendencies that have become noticeable during recent times. Broadly speaking, the principal differences between the average pre-war year and the latest example available (1930–31) lie in the assumption by Canada of the place of honour as predominantly the world's largest exporter; in the great increase of grain from the Argentine and Australia; and in the disappearance of India from the trade. While the total quantity of wheat exported will be seen to have increased, the importance of the Table lies in the redistribution that has been effected as between individual countries. So far as production is concerned, it can be stated that Europe as a whole has at last regained her pre-war level of output, that the four principal exporting countries of the world have increased theirs by about 50 per cent. and that Russia has succeeded in passing her maximum level of outturn prior to 1915. All recent investigators of the subject agree that, while the pre-war secular expansion has been resumed with almost exactly the former incremental speed, yet the effects of the war have not been made good, for, in no recent year, has the world's production of wheat attained to the level indicated by the trend constant before the Great War commenced. Judged purely upon an acreage basis, certain of the increases registered during the last twenty years by individual countries are striking; thus, Canada and the United States have each added more than twelve million acres, Australia over seven million and the Argentine five million. The net increase in Russia is already in excess of 30 per cent. The area under wheat in the world as a whole, including Russia, has been augmented by nearly 60,000,000 acres since the end of the first decade of the twentieth century, and there are now some 330,000,000 acres under the crop. The over-all rate of yield per acre has, however, been practically stationary, although individual areas and certain seasons afford indications that potential increases are evident.

So much in regard to total area and combined outturn. In so far as the British Empire itself is concerned, two statements of a statistical character may be made, which carry their own implications. Firstly, the Empire as a whole is, on balance, a net exporter of wheat; secondly, Canada has, in a season, exported wheat in excess of the annual average quantity imported into the British Isles. Individually, India may possibly be in a position to export small quantities again, but her home consumption has increased and the expansion of her agricultural resources in relation to her population is restricted, although fresh irrigation schemes may modify the position in this respect. In Canada, the progressive reduction in the economic life of the wheat plant (which has recently been brought down to some ninety days) has enabled production to be pushed farther and farther North, which in turn has brought about trade development in the Hudson Bay Territory. The pre-war price ideal of the Canadian (and of the United States) farmer was, however, "dollar wheat"; the present level is below 60 cents the bushel! Australian wheat has also benefited enormously by the work of the plant-breeder, and it is now grown in regions where rainfall had hitherto been regarded as totally inadequate.

Outside the British Empire, Russia, of course, presents the greatest problem. The wider agricultural aspects of her Five Year Plan having been commented upon in the third Chapter upon Land Tenure, it is here only necessary to point out that, after 1929, she had succeeded in re-entering the export trade upon a scale that could not fail to have an effect upon world prices, although the actual quantities of wheat thus handled have, even now, not attained to the average ruling in pre-war years. Their presence, however, upon a world market that was already digesting bountiful supplies from other countries, and in face of demands that were below normal, had effects of an economic and of a political character that were far reaching. Whether "dumping" was, from the purely economic standpoint, a correct definition of what took place is questionable, for precise evidence as to the cost of producing the grain in Russia has not been forthcoming, but nevertheless its presence in Western Europe was widely regarded as proving the existence of a scheme to oust other competitors regardless of any considerations affecting price. Russia's sheer necessity to secure some monetary return from extraneous sources, as well as her desire for reciprocal trade in certain directions, were both forgotten and the nations engaged themselves accordingly still more intently in raising barriers, fiscal and otherwise, against her alleged nefarious designs. The future is impossible to forecast, but another instalment of mechanisation, accompanying an increase in the number of "farm factories", might, within a few years, well place Russia far ahead of anything she has yet achieved and, if so, would make precarious the position of those other countries which are at present artificially supporting growers of wheat at the expense of their tax-payers and their consumers.

Our supplies of overseas wheat, in common with those of the other importing nations, have, then, been most amply restored, but the separate sources of supply have, relatively to one another, undergone great changes, and those not of a transitory character. See, again, in this connection the Tables printed upon pp. 372 and 376. Demand on the part of the importing nations as a whole has not been maintained upon quite the pre-war plane; the effects of the war—at first sheer inability on the part of certain countries to purchase their normal requirements, afterwards modified by altered tastes and habits, and subsequently nationalism, expressed by the virtual exclusion of outside supplies and (in some countries) a higher standard of living—have, individually or collectively, kept down the *per caput* consumption of wheat. On the other hand, there is evidence that, in the Orient, this cereal is being increasingly consumed and when in local abundance has, in many countries, even been fed to live-stock upon a large scale. Above all things, however, it must be remembered that the demand for wheat is most inelastic and, accordingly, neither the long drawn nor the precipitous falls in prices have had any observable effect upon its consumption amongst Western races. International Conferences have taken place, and appeals have been issued, both with the one end in view—to check the growth in outturn—but none has met with success, for, individually, each country has continued to bolster up by some means or other its own uneconomic or marginal producers. France, Germany, Italy have all progressively raised existing import duties upon wheat until their internal prices are now some two or three times the equivalent of those ruling here; nearly every country in Europe has adopted the *quota* system, whereby a certain proportion of home-produced wheat must be compulsorily milled; importation by licence or by State monopoly functions elsewhere and "import-export" licences, as in Germany, have played their part. Europe may still be predominantly rural in character, but she is asking much of her urban populations if she expects them indefinitely to meet the bill for these subsidies. If, for these reasons, acreages nearer home show no signs of reduction, as would always have been the result of such continuous low prices in the past, one must look farther afield, and it seems reasonable to anticipate that the great exporting areas such as the Argentine, Canada, Australia and, perhaps, the Danube Basin will be forced to conform to the realities of the situation. All authorities agree upon one thing—that wheat will continue to be abundant and, therefore, cheap for many years to come. Mechanisation of the industry, an extension of the wheat areas subject to extremes of climate, the accomplishments of the plant-breeder, large-scale farming—all these are factors which inevitably tend to cheapen production, and all are most susceptible of expansion in precisely those countries from which the importing nations draw the bulk of their supplies; for, odd as it may seem, Europe, with her peasant population and a high rate of yield per acre, looks for her requirements to the areas raising from ten to fifteen bushels to the acre. She may continue to look with complacency: no Malthus, no Crookes, prepared to risk eventual falsification, has in recent years been clamant.

Chapter XVIII

THE WHEAT SUPPLY OF THE BRITISH ISLES (CONTINUED)

Consumption in the United Kingdom during and after the Great War; price fixing; the Agriculture Act of 1920; Protection *versus* subsidies; cost of producing wheat; distribution of the different varieties; the price of the wheaten loaf; the 1932 Wheat Act; *quota* schemes at home and abroad.

A digression at some length has been necessitated into the question of our imported supplies of wheat and of the factors that have recently affected them. The measure of our dependence—some 17,000 tons of wheat daily to be imported—is however sufficient excuse, and it is now possible to turn to the purely domestic aspect of our wheat supply. The secular consumption of wheat and flour has been remarkably steady in this country, the Continental alternative of rye-bread having disappeared centuries ago. A calculation, recently made by the Stanford (U.S.A.) University Food Research Institute, gives 5·8 bushels as the present-day figure for this country, of which one bushel is utilised for industrial purposes or as food for livestock. Sixty years ago, the average consumption for all purposes, including seed, was approximately six and a half bushels per person per annum. Amongst the European nations, we fall behind France, Belgium and Italy as bread-eaters. During the last twenty years our total supplies of wheat and flour have been as set out in the Table on p. 384.

Cereal years, running from September 1st, are the measure of time, and the apparent discrepancy caused by the fact that the first and second columns, when added together, do not, in the war years, give exactly the totals recorded in the third, is explained by the stocks retained at the end of each year being taken into consideration. Until 1923–4 the data refer to the United Kingdom, including Ireland; subsequent to that year the Irish Free State is excluded therefrom. We now see in its true perspective the result of the food-production campaign, which, although it led to one-third instead of one-fifth of our wheat supplies being home produced, bulks small, statistically, when placed beside the figures representing imports. Even this increased supply was not fully utilised as human food—

for the records of the Ministry of Food show that instead of the anticipated, and theoretical, 15 to 20 per cent. being retained as "seed and tail" corn, 33 per cent. of the entire home crop in the years 1917–18 and 1918–19 failed to reach the millers.

Supplies of wheat (including flour expressed in terms of wheat) available for consumption.

Thousands of qrs.

	Home production	Net imports	Total
Average of 1909–10 to 1913–14	7,455	26,973	34,428
1914–15	7,804	25,078	33,329
1915–16	9,240	25,913	34,453
1916–17	7,472	28,597	32,744
1917–18	8,040	17,827	28,023
1918–19	11,643	22,213	35,817
1919–20	8,665	27,128	35,163
1920–21	7,104	25,287	32,391
1921–22	9,224	26,973	36,197
1922–23	8,156	26,914	35,070
1923–24	7,177	29,398	36,575
1924–25	6,470	27,692	34,162
1925–26	6,388	26,556	32,944
1926–27	6,176	28,550	34,726
1927–28	6,843	27,696	34,539
1928–29	5,963	27,142	33,105
1929–30	5,930	27,058	32,988
1930–31	5,197	30,403	35,600
1931–32	4,645	31,290	35,935

The saving effected in cargo space by the introduction of an increased proportion of our imported bread-stuffs in the form of flour does not of course appear in the Table; to the British farmer it implied a still further reduction in the amount of offals available. The diminution in total supplies for the worst year—that of 1917–18—compared with pre-war figures, was some 18 per cent., but, as previously stated, this deficit was made good by diluting the loaf and by altering the rate of extraction of flour from 70 per cent. to over 80.

Consideration of the methods employed by the State to secure supplies, when it had assumed responsibility for feeding the nation, can be omitted as not being of strictly agricultural interest, but it must be observed that the policy of subsidising the loaf, by fixing its legal price at ninepence, cost the tax-payer at least £160,000,000, and that, when the pound was at its lowest level in terms of dollars, the loss to us over the exchange alone on the purchase of a quarter of American wheat represented more than the pre-war value of the wheat itself. These are, however, merely the incidentals of State control in times when ordinary commercial transactions are impossible. Decontrol of the grain industry in 1921 was carried out gradually, but by the summer of that year private importers were again free to resume their business.

Wheat prices in this country have for more than two generations been dependent upon those ruling for imported grain; the latter in turn, up to recent years, being mainly affected by the American markets. Whatever may be said about the morality of gambling in wheat, there is no evidence to prove that dealings in the Chicago and other grain markets adversely affected prices; rather can a tendency in the other direction be traced, for records show a smaller margin of profit now accruing to the intermediaries than was the case some decades back, and these very dealings have resulted in smaller fractions of a cent becoming the basis for quotations. The principal attempt, apart from the historic case of Joseph in Egypt, made seriously to "corner" the market—that of Leiter in 1897–8—failed disastrously, and subsequently the power of Chicago to dictate world prices has been frustrated by the growth in the exportable surpluses of other countries, notably of Canada. A disproportionate increase in the cost of freight and insurance occurred during the height of the submarine blockade, which resulted in the pre-war cost of these two items for the New York to Liverpool voyage jumping from eight to ninety-nine shillings, and correspondingly for other routes. For two years after 1918 prices remained at an inflated level; in August, 1920, for instance, United States wheat was costing 140*s*. when landed in the United Kingdom. The impossibility of forecasting exactly when prices would commence to decline—for it was obviously only a question of time before more normal conditions of trade supervened—must partly bear the responsibility for the introduction of measures to guarantee certain rates of profit to the home producer.

Before discussing the question of the Government's policy from 1920 onwards, it is necessary to trace the course that in the matter of price-fixing it had already pursued. Untrammelled by legislation, the prices of cereals had, by December 1916, reached the following levels: wheat 73*s.*, barley 65*s.*, and oats 45*s.* Official steps were then taken to fix maximum prices for the crops of 1917 at, respectively, 73*s.* 6*d.*, 62*s.* 9*d.*, and 44*s.* 3*d.*, but in the meantime these maxima were temporarily exceeded. Under the Corn Production Act of 1917 minimum prices for the year in question (ranging, chronologically, in the case of wheat from 60*s.* down to 45*s.* in 1920) were theoretically in force, but were actually of course a dead letter. Subsequent developments took the form of guaranteeing that the prices for successive crops would not be reduced, and in 1919 fresh minima were fixed under that Act, but as the average price remained above the guaranteed level, these provisions did not come into force. Finally, in 1920 home producers were encouraged by the promise that they would receive prices up to a limit of 95*s.* per quarter based upon the cost of the imported wheat that had entered the country during the three preceding months. This system was in force up to the decontrol of the grain trade in August 1921. It is impossible critically to examine the above successive price-fixings, for the necessary data are now lacking, and also the perennial question of the respective claims of the producer and of the consumer obtrudes itself. It is, however, certain that cereals were not produced at a loss in any of the six years that succeeded 1913–14, but farmers grumbled bitterly when they saw foreign wheat being acquired at prices 50 per cent. in excess of those they were receiving. They forgot the inflated charges for carriage and insurance, and omitted to acknowledge the superior milling qualities of imported grain which automatically secures for itself a differential price.

After the summer of 1921 prices, on a free market, fell by 50 per cent., bringing about exactly the conditions ruling after the Napoleonic War. In the meantime the State had taken that far-reaching step of guaranteeing, in time of peace, certain rates of profit to the raisers of wheat and oats. History was repeating itself line for line, and the cry of the farmers had worked on the public's memories of the past and played on its fears for the future. Under the Agriculture Act of 1920 minimum prices for the wheat and oats of the 1921 and successive harvests were to be rigidly related to the costs of production, and were to bear the same proportion to 68*s.* and 46*s.* respectively (prices of the "standard year", 1919) as the costs of production in 1921 bore to the costs of production in 1919. After each harvest Commissioners were to ascertain the percentage

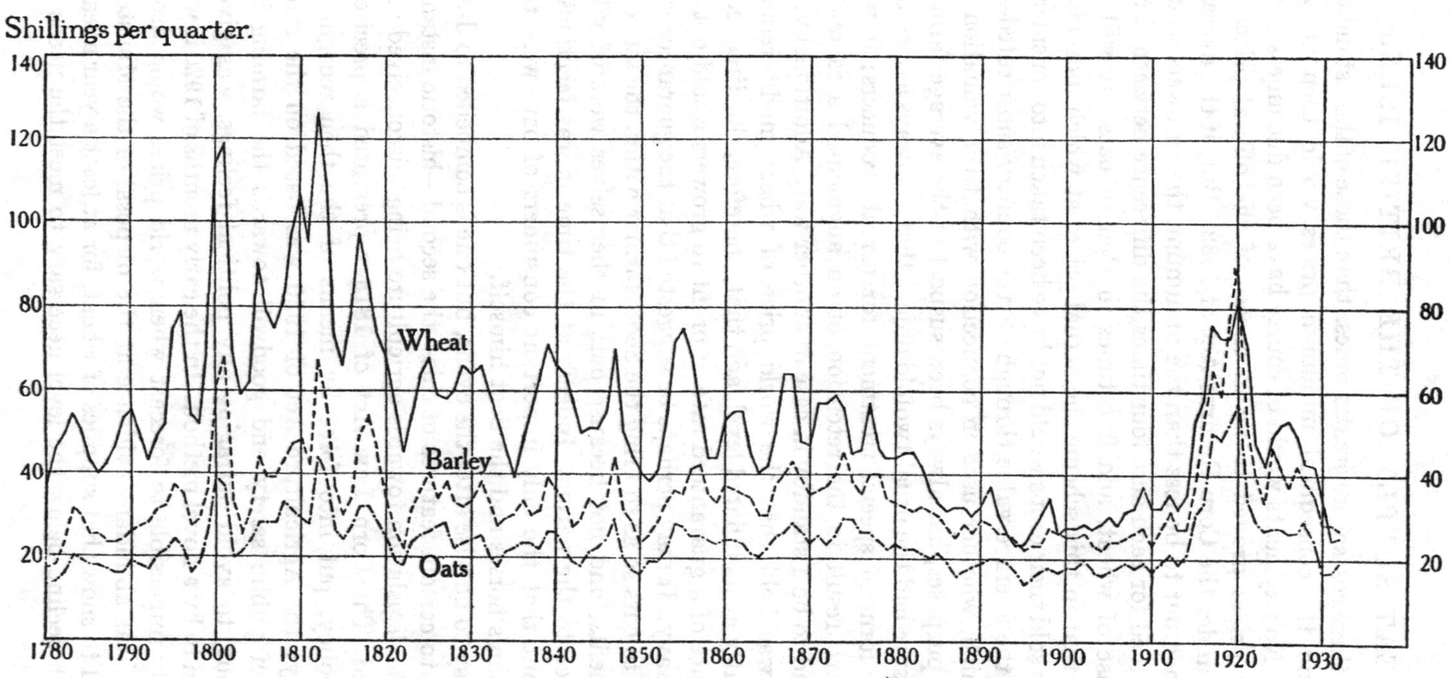

Average price of Wheat, Barley and Oats in England and Wales, 1780–1932.

25-2

by which these costs were greater or less than those of the "standard year", and the consequent minimum prices would then be announced. No payments would of course have been due unless these statutory prices proved to be in excess of the official prices as recorded under the Corn Returns Act of 1882. But, if the average price turned out to be less than the minimum, then growers would have received for each acre four times the difference between them in the case of wheat, and five times in that of oats. It will be observed that in this scheme the actual prices at which individual producers sold their crops would not have been taken into consideration, but the average value throughout the country substituted—a figure which, whether used in connection with tithe valuation or for other purposes, has always been suspect to the average farmer. This measure had the usual twofold object that is always associated with any form of special treatment for cereal producers; it was expected to result in the retention of an augmented area under cereals and to be a standby in case of another war. Additionally, in 1920, it was held that the world price of wheat might remain permanently at its inflated level, and that, therefore, the direct cost to the State of a guaranteed rate of profit to growers would not be unduly heavy. It may perhaps be suggested that the guarantee was extended to oats so as to bring the Scots farmer within the scope of these benefits, and not because oats in themselves were of vital importance to the nation. Indeed, at the time it was facetiously pointed out that the only important consumers of oats were the Englishman's horses and the Scot himself.

It is easy to be wise after the event, but one is compelled to draw attention to certain features of this—the second—historic instance of post-war legislation towards agriculture being misconceived and abandoned. The Corn Law Act of 1815 represented a precisely similar policy, put into force by means of the then recognised machinery; the Agriculture Act of 1920 was based on the same grounds of public safety and goodwill towards the farming industry, but, to avoid outraging any political feelings, was given expression to by a novel method. In the early months of 1920 it was admittedly impossible to forecast when world prices would drop, but there was abundant evidence at the disposal of the Ministers concerned to show that supplies of wheat, for at least a year ahead, would not decline below the level necessary to meet the needs of those nations that could afford to effect purchases. Russia and Roumania had certainly dropped out as exporters, but their loss had been more than made good by the increased deliveries of other countries. The fear of shortage in the immediate future was ill conceived, and everything pointed to an ultimate decline in prices. To what extent the Government was swayed by schemes, such as those to be referred to in Chapters XXIII and XXIV, did not appear, but no one who had the real interests of agriculture at heart, and could retain a sense of proportion in difficult social and economic circumstances, felt happy when the decision to subsidise British wheat and oats was made public. The annual sum that would have been payable was, of course, quite problematical, but it was anticipated that £20,000,000 would not be exceeded. It was, indeed, fortunate for those officials who would have been concerned in the administration of the Act that a reversion in policy spared them this duty, for an extraordinarily difficult task awaited them. The costs of producing wheat are in no parts of the country similar, and often vary considerably in the same County, or even in the same parish. A hard and fast ascertainment of these costs would have unduly benefited some growers and penalised others; farmers on certain types of land would have reaped undue profits, others, differently situated, would have struggled to make wheat production a paying business. Even when the "Standard cost" of production in any given year had been assessed, there would have remained the necessity to establish a complete organisation to remunerate individual farmers on the basis of the acreage they had grown.

In such cases the principle of equal treatment at once disappears, for the farmer who raises a crop of a few bushels to the acre on poor or unsuitable land receives remuneration at the same rate as the one who produces his forty bushels to the acre. Whilst, at first glance, this appears to place a premium on bad land and to confer a benefit on careless farmers, it must be remembered that the method usually suggested has been one whereby the grower would receive from the Government the difference between the price at which he sold his wheat in the market and a stated sum; for this reason the better farmers would not be so heavily handicapped, for they could obtain more cash per acre from buyers, and, for grain of exceptional quality, even prices up to the Government level, with the bonus as a subsequent addition. But, were acreage thus the sole basis, the feeling would inevitably get abroad that the State was not an advocate of good husbandry—a feeling that is certainly undesirable.

This particular attempt certainly adopted the acreage method of measuring the bulk of wheat raised (necessitating, indeed, upon the part of every claimant reference to the official number and situation of each field upon the twenty-five-inch ordnance map, together with its "ploughed area" under wheat and oats), but proposed to remunerate growers without any reference whatever to the prices that they, as individuals, had secured for their grain. This system of basing its value to the farmer on the official average, instead of enquiring into the nature of the hundreds of thousands of separate sales, was an obvious way of surmounting the difficulties opened up by certain tentative schemes referred to elsewhere. Whether a combination of estimated acreage, official costs of production and the never sacrosanct "*Gazette* average" as the basis for their remuneration would indefinitely have afforded satisfaction to agriculturists is very doubtful. Whilst the scheme might have proved capable of being put into execution, it is certain that its provisions would have led to great friction, and that, in any given year, the official cost of producing an acre of wheat would have conferred undue advantages on some growers and left others with very meagre profits. The obligation to check every acre claimed would alone have involved heavy expense.

Any such form of bonus also involved financial liabilities which could not be measured in advance, and might well have proved to be intolerable. Finally, it was very unlikely that any form of guaranteed price would have added to the existing areas under cereals; a check to the further spread of grass farming would at most have been effected, the actual extension of arable cultivation being an unlikely consequence. It must be remembered that the loss of ploughland after 1880 was not entirely due to the fall in prices of cereals, but that alternative forms of husbandry made independent claims upon farmers' attention. As a contingent guarantee that a spread of arable farming would ensue upon an arable bonus, it had sometimes been suggested that a proviso should be inserted by which payment would depend on a certain proportion of the recipient's land being under the plough, or that a minimum addition should have been effected within a given period. Such systems might be possible in times of war, but normally there are limits to the amount of interference that agriculturists will tolerate. The price obtainable for wheat will always decide the breadth maintained, and the nation would never agree to pay sums sufficiently high to create artificially large additional acres.

When prices fell in the Autumn of 1920 the Government saw the extent of its possible commitments, and fortunately had the strength of mind to repeal the misconceived Act. This repeal was accompanied by an undertaking to pay £3 per acre for wheat and £4 per acre for oats of the 1921 crop; again, the Scots farmer had scored at the expense of his Southern brother. The total sum thus expended was a little over eighteen million pounds; in addition, another million was granted towards agricultural education in its widest sense. Future generations will agree that, not only was a very wise course pursued, but that an exceptionally good bargain was made on behalf of the tax-payer by the expenditure of a single sum that was certainly smaller than the annual imposts would have turned out to be. Thus, in the course of only a few months a legislative attempt to direct the industry into particular lines failed. After 1815 it had taken successive steps extending over some thirty years to effect the same ends; this is the measure of the changed social and economic conditions of the times. On the former occasion the land-owning classes were determined to obtain for themselves special terms on the lines to which they and their ancestors had been accustomed, the bulk of the nation was agrarian in interests, and the majority of farmers were cereal raisers. In 1920 the landowner was not directly affected by the situation, and the remaining agricultural interests, representing but a fraction of the nation, were united neither in their methods of farming nor in their views on the suggested policy of the Government.

Two possible methods by which preferential treatment could be accorded to the producers of any particular crop had been tried and successively laid aside—the first after a long and honourable life, when it had become too effete to accommodate itself to the changing economic conditions of the time, the second, in its infancy, when it already displayed unhealthy signs. Other countries remained true to a system of Protective duties, but in each case their dependence on imported grain was normally much less than that of this country. France by these means had made herself almost self-supporting, but at the expense of an unduly poor rate of yield and, as many people think, of a devitalised population; Germany had judiciously combined Protection with other forms of State assistance. The continuation of the Corn Laws after 1846, or their reintroduction at any subsequent date, would have added a penny or so to the cost of the loaf, and possibly averted the bulk of the loss in our wheat acreage, but the small difference in the proportion of grain produced at home by these means would, on grounds of national security, in no way have made up for the increased cost of bread. The bulk of this urban nation argued thus: "The whole population consists of bread consumers, and any form of preference places a tax on them, whilst a bonus or guaranteed price, on the other hand, represents a burden on the tax-payer—and all bread eaters are not necessarily tax-payers". The question in its broadest aspect therefore tended to become political and social, for a large section of the people, forgetful of indirect taxation, erroneously assumed that a subsidised loaf was secured at the sole expense of the Income-tax payer, and was therefore prepared to acquiesce in the policy involved.

A bonus on wheat production was frequently mooted after Protection was taken away. In 1886, just when times were at their worst, such a scheme was put forward by an Essex agriculturist. After postulating the abolition of tithe, the halving of agricultural rates (an intelligent forecast of a coming event), and the drastic reduction of labour bills, rent and railway rates, the author asked if British farming would then be prosperous, and answered his own question by declaring that, even in such circumstances, fair competition with overseas producers would still have been impossible. He then elaborated a plan by which a bonus, ranging from 20*s.* the quarter down to 5*s.*, should be paid to producers—the annual amount due being dependent on prices ruling in the previous year. The money to meet this payment was to have been raised by taxes on foreign (as opposed to Colonial) wheat and on all imported flour, augmented by a duty on manufactured goods. Here was a very thinly disguised form of Protection, only the sliding-scale payment to the producer representing the modern conception of a subsidy. This and subsequent schemes were necessarily only of academic interest, but they exhibited, in common with the Act of 1920, the inherent difficulties attaching to the actual allocation of the bonus and the basis on which it should be paid.

Complete freedom having been conferred by the repeal of the

1920 Act, values of all cereals were again dependent upon the prices ruling for imported varieties, but the close connection formerly observed between home and foreign grain was not at once re-established. British corn was still unduly cheap compared with foreign, and this, combined with the exceptional disparity between the sums received by the producer and paid by the consumer, formed a particular grievance. Seasonal fluctuations in prices were expected, as there is a recognised tendency for the latter to decline immediately after harvest, owing to small farmers being compelled to market their grain. The causes in question were, however, deeper seated and owed their origin partly to a marked preference by the millers and the public for foreign wheat—hence the numerous suggestions put forward for the compulsory use in certain circumstances of British wheat, and the exclusion of foreign flour.

That the State was cognisant of similar tendencies, combined with the familiar "disparity" between the price of wheat and that of the loaf, many years ago is evident from the enquiries that were circulated to British Consuls in Continental towns during the year 1895. These representatives were requested to forward statements showing the local prices of wheat and those of bread, adding any comments that they might care to make. The fullest reply came from the consul at Rouen, who described the French system of fixing the cost of the loaf in relation to that of wheat. Powers were exercised by the mayors of some nine hundred towns and communes, in virtue of a law passed by the Constituent Assembly in 1791, infractions of it being punishable by fines. This official price, or "taxe officieuse", varied with the cost of flour on a scale commencing with 40 francs the sack, when bread had to be sold at a price not exceeding 26 centimes the kilogramme, and extending to 88 francs, at which point the loaf was given latitude up to 50 centimes. This scheme looked extremely promising in theory, but, in practice, flaws were found to exist, as the following comments of the Consul show.

This is the bread eaten by all the poor and in the kitchens of the richer classes, and it may be bought at that [official] price at any baker's shop in the town. Many other descriptions of bread are, however, sold in every shop and in every French town, and it is upon that "pain de luxe" that the baker chiefly makes his profit. These breads are eaten by all but the poorer classes, and as no limit is fixed by authority to the price at which they are to be sold, high prices are often charged for them....I think there can be no doubt that one effect of arbitrarily fixing the price of the bread eaten by the greater mass of the people at such a low price that the baker can barely cover the cost of production, is that the richer classes are made to pay higher than they otherwise would do for their bread. It is a popular measure, a species of protection of the "people", and though, unlike most protective measures, it lowers instead of heightens the price of the article, still it is paid for by other classes of the community than those protected.

The difficulties experienced forty years ago in France were easily surmountable, being in character social rather than economic, while the latter type would have been expected to predominate in any such scheme introduced here.

Turning our attention now to the last decade at home, a glance at the diagram upon p. 501 will indicate the decline in wheat acreage that supervened after it was apparent that the State had definitely retired from active participation in attempts to encourage production. From an area of 2,032,000 acres in 1922, nearly half a million acres were lost by 1925, in 1930 the wheat grown in Great Britain was exactly 1,400,000 acres and a year later it was 1,247,000 acres—the smallest total recorded since statistics were collected. The loss had been distributed much as would have been anticipated, for the typical wheat lands of the North-Eastern and Eastern areas registered proportionately the smallest declines and those Counties which either normally grew less of the crop, or which produced it upon heavy land, suffered most. In so far as the value of wheat was concerned, again reference should be made to the relevant diagram (p. 387) which shows that here the decline had been delayed until a final precipitate fall after 1926 had brought prices from over 53*s*. the quarter down to 34*s*. 3*d*. in 1930 and, disastrously, to an average of 24*s*. 8*d*. for 1931. Only once previously—in the notorious period of 1894–5—had British wheat fallen so low; it had then stood at 22*s*. 10*d*. in the former year and at 23*s*. 1*d*. in the latter. It will, of course, be noted that both the acreage and price of other cereals pursued similar courses, but, rightly or wrongly, the farming community has ever attached more significance to a loss of faith in wheat production, the national aspects of which are so easily susceptible to even minor repercussions. This, then, was what our American neighbours would refer to as "the statistical position"; it clearly called for some discussion by the State, but before describing the proposals and the final execution of relief measures, it is necessary

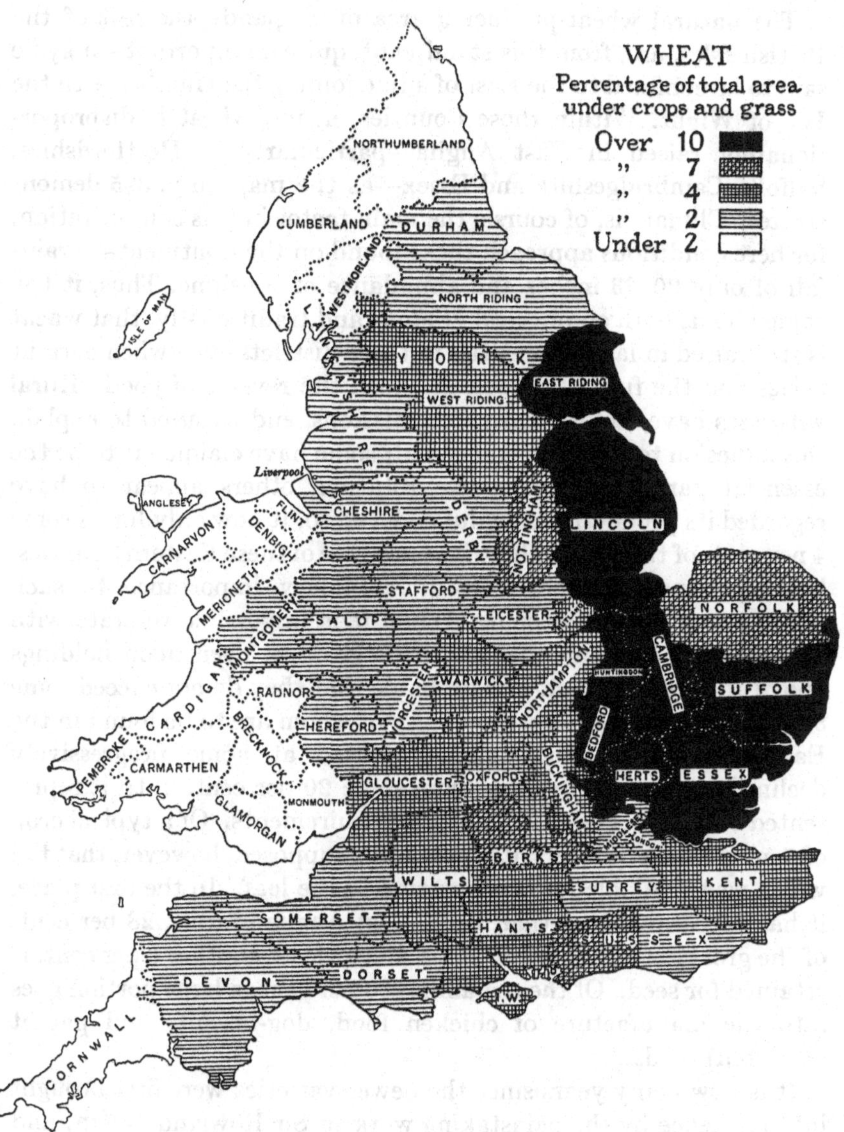

Distribution of Wheat in England and Wales, 1932

to review the economic position of the wheat grower at the time in question.

The natural wheat-producing area of England—the rest of the British Isles, are, from this standpoint, quite unimportant—may be said to be confined to the East of a line joining the Humber with the Isle of Wight. Within those Counties, again, wheat is disproportionately raised in East Anglia—particularly in Hertfordshire, Suffolk, Cambridgeshire and Essex—as the map on p. 395 demonstrates. Climate is, of course, the main factor in this concentration, for here conditions approach those found on the Continent—a rainfall of only 20–23 inches and abundance of sunshine. Thus, it has come about, both on physical grounds and traditionally, that wheat is still raised in large quantities in these districts even when current prices and the future outlook are both the reverse of good. Rural witnesses have, before many Commissions, endeavoured to explain this adhesion to the principal cereal; some have claimed it to be the essential part of a four-course rotation, others appear to have regarded its production as a duty. Even so, it now only forms some 4 per cent. of the total value of the produce of these Eastern Counties' holdings, and, nationally, is of secondary importance to such activities as poultry-keeping. While it is impossible to state with accuracy the total number of wheat growers, even upon holdings above an acre in extent, it is probable that they do not exceed some 80,000 or 90,000—the vast majority of whom are to be found in the Eastern Counties. The quantity raised at home progressively declined in post-war seasons from some 20 per cent. until it represented only 13 per cent. of our total requirements. Of a typical crop of 5 or 6 million quarters, it must not be supposed, however, that the whole was available for consumption in the loaf. In the first place, it has been calculated that, upon East Anglian farms, 28 per cent. of the gross outturn is fed to stock and at least another 6 per cent. is retained for seed. Of the remaining 66 per cent. a large portion goes into the manufacture of chicken food, dog-biscuits and patent (wheaten) foods.

It is now many years since the newer varieties were first brought into existence by the painstaking work of Sir Rowland Biffen, and ample demonstration has been afforded of the high milling and baking qualities of, e.g., his "Yeoman" and "Yeoman II"; indeed, the "all British" loaf, composed exclusively of these wheats, and sold under the National Mark, has been shown, times out of number, to equal any combination of Canadian or other "hard" wheats. It is, therefore, of interest to investigate the extent to which these newer varieties have, under commercial conditions, been adopted. Eight years ago, the Ministry of Agriculture, acceding to a request made from the Cambridge Department of Agriculture, added a questionnaire to its 4th of June schedules inviting occupiers (of all save the smallest holdings) in the wheat-producing areas, to state their acreage under certain named varieties. The results may be seen in a Table appearing in the Appendix. It will be observed that "Little Joss" and "Yeoman" (in its two forms) together accounted for almost half the total wheat area covered by the returns; the comparative popularity of these two types upon the different soils to be found in the administrative Counties also coincides with expectation, for "Yeoman" predominated upon the clays and "Little Joss" upon the lighter lands.

The cost of producing wheat in the East and South of England has in all recent investigations been shown to average slightly under £8 per acre, with a range, according to the nature of the soil and the size of the unit, from £4 up to £12. Typical figures, in this instance relating to 2600 acres of wheat for the years 1923–7 (Cambridge University Department of Agriculture's Economic *Report* No. 12, "Four years' farming in East Anglia"), were as follows:

Component costs per acre:	£	s.	d.	%
Seed		15	5	10·2
Farmyard manure	1	4	7	16·3
Artificial manures		7	8	5·1
Preliminary cultivations, drilling and after cultivations	2	2	0	27·8
Harvesting, stacking and threshing	1	6	9	17·7
Rent and rates	1	9	11	19·9
Overhead and sundry charges		4	6	3·0
	£7	10	10	100·0
Add residual values of manures, fallows and cultivation carried forward		14	8	
Subtract residual values of manures carried forward ...		14	1	
Yield per acre, 17·71 cwt.				
Net cost of wheat in stack	7	11	5	
Allowance for value of straw	1	1	11	
Net cost of grain in stack	6	9	9	
Net cost of grain per cwt.		7	3¼	
Threshing, marketing and granary charges		1	1	
Total net cost of grain per cwt.		8	4¼	
Total net cost of grain per qr.	1	17	10	

The last item possesses considerable significance, for it affords indication that the popular estimate of 40*s*. per quarter as a level below which it is at present unremunerative to produce wheat, is not without foundation in fact. Actually, at £8 per acre, and with a normal yield of just under 32 bushels to the acre, the cost per quarter is bound to approximate to that figure; it is obvious, however, that production upon the heavier and typical wheat lands must cost more; few Essex farmers, for instance, would agree that a sum below 50*s*. would leave them an adequate margin; doubtless Small Holders on light soils and above-normal producers on ordinary land avoid losses at levels down to 35*s*. and even lower. All, however, are in competition with Canadian and other overseas producers, whose costs per bushel are now perhaps half that of their English equivalents and, with a further substitution of machinery for man-power, may yet be reduced still more in the future.

As in the Chapters upon Marketing reference has already been made to methods of sale as they affect wheat, it is unnecessary to return to that subject at this point, but it must be reiterated that both the costs of milling and of baking have, since the war, remained unexpectedly high. Admittedly, the large mills—now predominant—are not working efficiently unless fully employed, and admittedly again, baking costs are lower in the largest and most modern bakeries, but, in both industries, large groups of employers have secured for themselves a very favourable economic situation and their employees are in receipt of most generous wages. The picturesque wind-mills have all but ceased to exist and their place, together with that of the water-mill, has been usurped by enormous erections at the ports of entry. Where scores of individual master-bakers once laboured, electric ovens now produce loaves by the hundred thousand. In effect the grain trade has become concentrated into the hands of relatively few and extremely powerful bodies. The majority of housewives still demand a door to door delivery of their bread and the roundsman, too, has retained a large part of his war-time augmentation of wages. For all these reasons, the cost of the daily loaf—whether made of British "Yeoman" or of Canadian "Marquis" flour—bears little relationship to that of the wheat itself. Compared with prices ruling in other countries, where fiscal and other expedients have raised its price, the loaf in England, taking into consideration the cost of its principal ingredient, is

An ancient mill

not unduly cheap. Expressed in tabular form, the price of flour and of the loaf have, in London, ranged as follows, during the last ten years:

Date	London Price of British Wheat, one month earlier (per cwt.)	London Price of No. 1 Manitoba Wheat, one month earlier (per cwt.)	Price of flour (per 280 lb.)	Price of quartern loaf
	s. d.	*s. d.*	*s. d.*	*d.*
Jan. 1924	10 3	11 1	38 0	8½
1925	12 10	15 6	54 6	10
1926	12 4	14 3	47 0	9½
1927	12 0	13 10	44 0	9
1928	10 4	13 7	43 6	9
1929	10 0	11 9	36 6	8½
1930	9 10	12 5	39 0	9
1931	6 6	6 7	22 0	6½
1932	6 9	7 7	24 0	7
1933	5 6	6 4	22 0*	7

* *Plus 2s. 9d. quota* charge.

The ground is now prepared for a description of the proposals that were, at first abortively, put forward for assisting the British wheat producer during the years that followed the repeal of the Agriculture Act. Early in 1923, the Agricultural Tribunal of Investigation had issued its *First Interim Report*, which contained the following statement: "We have considered with some care whether any direct financial assistance to wheat-growing should be given by the State. We have determined to make no recommendation". The minor question of wheat offals was, however, tackled, for it was proposed that importers should be required to link with their consignments of flour a corresponding proportion of offals. In order to benefit British farmers, the imposition of an *ad valorem* duty of 10 per cent. on exported offals was coupled with this proposal. No such steps were taken, and, within less than another year, the Tribunal (in a *Second Interim Report*) viewed with such grave concern the position of the industry that, after dallying with alternative forms of subsidy, it "definitely, but reluctantly" advocated a bonus of 10*s.* per acre on all arable land, with a similar additional sum upon each acre under wheat. It was estimated that the annual cost of the combined aids would, in the first instance, have been £6,075,000, which, if the wheat area had risen to a maximum of 2,000,000 acres, might ultimately have cost the nation £6,500,000. Again, this time owing to political causes, no steps were taken to implement these suggestions. It is, perhaps, not unfair at this juncture to point out the inevitable administrative and technical difficulties that would have faced those responsible for putting such a scheme into force. The Tribunal would, apparently, have been satisfied if the Minister of Agriculture had had power to reduce, or to withhold, the subsidy in cases where cultivation was demonstrably not up to the standards of good husbandry. The following matters, however, would inevitably have demanded attention.

In the first instance, rent restriction legislation would admittedly have had to be passed in order to prevent landlords from diverting to themselves a share of the bonus; in times of falling values, however, such as were certainly destined to occur during the following years, no such measures could have prevented owners from maintaining rents at existing levels, whereby they would (and rightly in the opinion of many persons) in effect have secured a portion of the Government's money. Secondly, even after agreement had been reached as to what was represented by the terms "agricultural holdings" and "arable land" in the different Counties of England, Wales and Scotland, it would have remained to secure unanimity in a general definition of "temporary leys", "bare fallow", and "catch crops", and to settle the status of fruit and market-gardens, as well as of hop-fields. Then it would have become necessary to decide whether payment to the (possibly three hundred thousand) farmers concerned should be made upon production of Ordnance maps (with marked references to each arable field), or whether their returns, furnished annually on June 4th, could be accepted as sole evidence. In the former event, a certain saving might have been effected if the areas actually under cultivation had been calculated, since headlands and the ground covered by hedges and ditches would have been eliminated; in the latter, incessant checking would have been called for on the spot in order to avoid false claims. In either case payments would have been inevitably delayed until the autumn of each year. That these were not unwarranted fears, perusal of the published material relating to the difficulties met with when, upon the repeal of the Agriculture Act, payment was effected upon wheat and oats acreages, carries conviction. On that occasion only some 186,000 claims were dealt with,

PLATE XVIII

A modern mill

relating merely to two crops. Yet, despite the apparent simplicity of the operation, it became necessary to compare the claims with the corresponding returns for June 4, when, to quote the official report: "this examination, whilst most effective in the direction both of verifying areas and discovering duplicate claims, involved a large amount of correspondence. In addition, the letters received on one subject or another connected with the claims were very numerous, and for some weeks during the autumn reached an average of about a thousand a day".

For a few years more, no official proposals in connection with assistance to the wheat crop were put forward, the State concentrating, rightly, upon that combination of minor aids which is described in several other portions of the book. Private individuals, however, were prominent in this field; their schemes generally aimed at a guaranteed price to the growers of wheat and also, in order to placate Norfolk and other East Coast interests, of barley. *Quota* schemes for the compulsory inclusion of a certain proportion of home-grown wheat in the loaf were also adopted from the Continent. Proposals, dealt with elsewhere, for subsidies on wages, in relation to the amount of artificial manures applied, or resting upon the nature of the soil utilised, were also canvassed. It was left to a fortunately situated National Government to carry through, in 1932, a far-reaching wheat *quota* scheme, and to add thereto a measure of protective, or, perhaps, of revenue-raising duty.

When introducing the necessary Bill into the House of Commons, the Minister of Agriculture stated that the Government had laid down four conditions precedent: firstly there must be an enhanced price for British wheat; secondly a secure market for home-grown wheat of millable quality; thirdly no subsidy must fall upon the Exchequer; and, fourthly, there must be no encouragement to the extension of wheat cultivation on land unsuited to the crop. Continental methods were, he explained, in many cases ruled out by one or other of these provisos, as was also any requirement that called for the physical admixture of grains from different sources, and transport of wheat from the producing areas to the great milling and consuming centres was also deprecated. It was intended, too, that millers in general should be given virtual freedom from inspection, and that the linked economy of the small country firm and the farmer should remain undisturbed. These objects were to be attained by imposing upon millers a payment "which in effect would commute the cost of an obligation to buy a *quota* of home-grown wheat at an enhanced price for its estimated equivalent in cash".

A "standard price" of 45*s.* per quarter, or of 10*s.* per hundredweight, was adopted—this being in excess of the 40*s.* which had formed the basis of preliminary discussions, and, as was stated previously, might be accepted as the "average" cost of producing wheat in England. The Wheat Act provided that every registered grower of wheat—and all farmers growing that cereal in 1932 had, as a preliminary step, to register themselves with the newly established Wheat Commission—should receive what was to be known as a "deficiency payment" in respect of all wheat of millable quality sold by him to a recognised miller. Deficiency payments were to be based upon the difference between the eventually ascertained average price of such home-grown wheat and the "standard price" of 45*s.* Here, then, it was wisely arranged that variations in the quality of individual consignments would receive recognition, for each producer markets his grain to the best advantage, and better parcels receive higher prices. Deficiency payments are, of course, fixed upon a uniform basis for all growers, so that the natural incentive still remains. It was clearly necessary for the Government to fix a limit to the total quantity of wheat which might, in any given year, rank for deficiency payments; this, in the first instance, was placed at 6,000,000 quarters. Thus, with an average price of 22*s.* to 23*s.*—which seems likely to be that ruling during the first year of the scheme—the total payment to growers will exceed £5,000,000.

Since it was implicit in the scheme that no additional cost was to fall upon persons other than consumers of bread, it was necessary to raise the money for the deficiency payments by means of a *quota* charged upon every sack of flour—whether imported or milled at home. It was at first anticipated that a sum of 2*s.* 6*d.* per sack would suffice, but, when the scheme was in working order, after a brief period during which 2*s.* 3*d.* was charged, 2*s.* 9*d.* became the statutory addition. The Minister had claimed that, at most, this was represented by a farthing upon the four pound loaf and, instancing the previous year, stated that had the *quota* been in force, there would, for eleven weeks, have been an increase of one farthing, while for the remaining forty-one weeks, there should have been no change in the price of the loaf. The cost per household, on the hypothesis that deficiency payments amount to £5,000,000 in the first year or so, and assuming (which, *pace* the above statement, should not be the case) that the whole charge is deflected to the consumer, may be placed at an average of ten shillings, or less, say, than twopence halfpenny per week. When comparing conditions in other countries, and in view of the prevailing low level of bread prices at home, it was impossible to cavil at these results, and the Wheat Act was accepted in its entirety. Certain discussions were engendered in regard to the definition of "millable quality" and in the matter of "drawbacks" upon exported wheat; the bakers, too, were at first hostile to the Act, alleging that the brunt of any unpopularity occasioned by increased prices would fall upon them.

During the first few months of its operation the Wheat Act worked smoothly in Great Britain and Northern Ireland, and in the middle of the winter of 1932 the Wheat Commission announced that an advance on account of deficiency payments would be made forthwith. A sum amounting to £1,250,000 was accordingly distributed to growers (who had submitted certificates showing that their grain had been sold and delivered to some one or other of the five thousand authorised millers or dealers) based upon a payment of 13*s.* 6*d.* per quarter (3*s.* per cwt.). It was obviously not only expedient to make this advance, but was financially safe, since there was clear evidence that the average price of British millable wheat for the year ending July 1933 could not be greatly in excess of 22*s.* per quarter. A second advance payment, at the same rate, was effected in the month of March 1933, which brought the total sum disbursed on account to £2,134,000. Over 70,000 growers had then received financial assistance in connection with 14,000,000 cwt. of wheat.

That these payments on account were not only considerable in the aggregate, but of great assistance to individual growers, is revealed by an investigation into the first distribution amongst East Anglian farmers. Here, in the case of some thousand holdings, studied by the Farm Economics Branch of the Cambridge University Department of Agriculture, it was shown that deficiency payments would be worth, on the average, £68 to each farmer. Correspondingly, their value per acre will, ultimately, be in the neighbourhood of £4. It is therefore obvious that, after the final payment has been effected, the position of wheat growers should have been greatly ameliorated. Thus, the Wheat Act of 1932 could certainly claim to have come through the initial stages of its career without friction and to have demonstrated that its theoretical conceptions could be effectively operated. The passage of time will doubtless demonstrate the existence of loopholes for evasion of its regulations, and familiarity with its working may cause a very small proportion of its beneficiaries to seek unfair personal advantages therefrom. If so—and there is already some evidence to that effect—either a tightening of the Wheat Commission's bye-laws or the provision of fresh legislation would doubtless be effective.

British wheat growers have thus secured preferential treatment upon most generous lines, and it is not surprising to find claims being put forward on behalf of barley producers and, from Scotland, for a *quota* system in the case of oats. For reasons already stated, it is not likely that the wheat acreage will be largely increased, but its return to perhaps 1,600,000 or, possibly, 1,700,000 acres would not be surprising. On grounds of national security the advantages of the plan are negligible; equally, few would claim that it had increased rural employment. Rather, must acknowledgement be made that its real function was to convince arable farmers, in the parts of the country most severely affected, that the State was cognisant of their position and intended to guarantee them, over a period of time, a remunerative price for what they and the nation, rightly or wrongly, still regard as their most important product. That this has been accomplished without recourse to taxation and with the acquiescence of the urban population, is in the nature of a social and economic triumph.

In conclusion, it may be of interest to compare these British methods with certain others adopted upon the Continent. In Germany, for example, under a milling *quota* law that came into force in 1929, a high and increasing proportion of all wheat milled within the country had to be of home produced origin. This proportion was at first fixed at 40 per cent., but was quickly raised to 50 per cent. and, ultimately, was subject to almost monthly variations ranging down to 15 per cent. and up to 80 per cent.; in 1930 55 per cent. was the general level, but a year later it stood at over 90 per cent. In that country, with nearly 30,000 mills, it is stated that only a few hundred of the largest type are subject to control by a semi-official body, the rest being left entirely free. This policy has been associated with extremely high duties on foreign grain; in fact, it is urged—on behalf of the agrarian party—that neither *quota* nor tariff could be operated satisfactorily without the other. Import-export bonds, too, have played their part, by encouraging the export of home-grown wheat against the equivalent value of imported grain or other commodities. In passing, it may be remembered that, at certain times, the resultant consignment of German wheats to our own East Coast ports led to vigorous protests from British growers. The ramifications of the system were extreme, for, in order to secure quantities of "strong" foreign wheat, millers were exchanging, with cash adjustments, the relevant certificates for others authorising the exportation of soft East German grain. This whole German edifice raised the internal price of wheat until it stands at nearly three times the corresponding British level. So long as Germany is prepared to pay for this luxury, however, other nations will not be altruistic enough to urge her to desist.

Notably in France (where the proportion was, upon occasion, as high as 97 per cent.), but also in nearly every other European country, a *quota* system was in operation by 1931, frequently augmented by the import-export certificate method, which is elastic enough to be applied to almost any commodity *vis-à-vis* wheat. Accompanied by tariffs, openly protective rather than revenue-raising in character, this composite policy has, in most countries, been successful in masking the world situation brought about by the partial over-production and partial under-consumption of bread-stuffs. The European peasant has received what must at first have seemed princely remuneration for his products, but, as the cost of living continued to rise, he and his urban compatriots have been frequently engaged in explanations—or even in unneighbourly wrangles—as to the respective allocation of cause and effect.

After remaining for long one of the only two Free Trade countries in Europe—Denmark is now the sole survivor—Great Britain, as a result of the Ottawa Imperial Conference of 1932, unexpectedly added an import duty upon foreign wheat to the very long list of other commodities that had just previously become amenable to this method of raising revenue. The duty was fixed at two shillings per quarter of 480 lbs., and was, of course, additional to the corresponding 10 per cent. *ad valorem* duty upon foreign flour which formed part of the general revenue charges imposed a few months earlier.

Thus, in one year, the general Free Trade principles that had been zealously guarded since 1846 went by the board; "the people's food" was taxed, and special methods were adopted artificially to raise the price of home-produced wheat. *Tempora mutantur, nos et mutamur in illis!*

Chapter XIX

FORESTRY

History of British forestry; impediments to replanting; effects of the war; statistics of British woods and forests; supplies of timber and the world's requirements; the Forestry Commission and its first ten years' work; Forest Workers' holdings; output of British timber in 1924 and in 1930; future official plans; the economics of timber production and utilisation.

Any review of the rural economy of this country must contain at least some reference to past and present forest resources, for timber, if not a farm product, is at least an agricultural one in the widest sense of that word. Moreover, the history of British forestry has much in common with that relating to its farming. Roman influence can be traced as well among our trees as our livestock; the feudal conception of land-tenure universally embraced forests; such occurrences as the Restoration affected almost equally the practice of farming and the amenities and productivity of our woods; lastly, critics would not be wanting to suggest that both farm and forest have, from the industrial revolution until quite recently, shared in a common neglect. These similarities, however, cannot be stressed beyond a certain point, for, during the greater part of their history, the forests of this, and of other European countries, not only formed exclusive preserves of the Crown itself (and in lesser degree of other landowners) but also extended their influence far and wide over what was otherwise cultivatable land, and brought in their train those selfish and aggressive laws associated with the preservation of game, which in turn made any commercial value of secondary importance. There is no need to discuss in detail any of the above historic features, but, it may perhaps be pointed out that, in the middle ages, the preservation of game restricted severely the practice of farming in many parts of the country where "forests" technically existed—but existed only in the sense of that word now associated with deer forests in Scotland. The King's warrens occupied thousands of acres of completely treeless land which would otherwise have been under the plough—thus denying to the countryside both access and employment. Small wonder, then, that such persons as the high-spirited scholars of Cambridge in the middle of the thirteenth century not only confessed to entering one of the King's warrens with greyhounds, for the purpose of coursing hares, but subsequently sought in Court to justify their conduct. If their modern successors still hunt hares over precisely the same area—thus proving this to be the oldest academic sport—they do so not in the face of Royal opposition over land left purposely unproductive, but with the sanction of numerous individual cultivators.

After the feudal restrictions over forest land had been swept away at the Commonwealth, and, when on the Restoration, Evelyn had been commissioned to write his *Sylva*, there appeared a possibility that the potential value of this branch of agriculture might at last be recognised. Where they still survived, all the annoying but picturesque customs were thenceforward powerless to prevent access to this form of land; gone were the "Verderers" and the "Regarders", their courts, their powers, and even the bulk of the beasts under their protection; gone also were the disabilities attaching to properties bordering forest land. The need for timber was never greater, indeed, the powers that were still exercised aimed at the preservation of such material wealth as had survived the neglect and destruction caused by the Civil War, as also at the direct encouragement of "afforestation", in a sense widely different from that which it had formerly possessed. Yet, despite the success achieved by Evelyn, which led to the paramount requirements of the Navy being met so long as "wooden walls" were depended upon, none has claimed that during the last two and a half centuries British forestry has occupied a position commensurate with that found in other countries. A probable factor to be reckoned with is the inability of the State and of the private landowner to see eye to eye in the matter, complicated by the fact that the least accessible parts of the United Kingdom, and those under separate jurisdiction, have always been the most susceptible to forestal improvement or development.

If the appeal of *Sylva* had been made principally to the private landowner, the State was, within a short time, sufficiently impressed by its obligations to pass legislation aiming at the maintenance of the supply of timber from the Royal forests, for, in 1698, an Act relating to the New Forest was placed on the Statute-book. In the preamble to the Bill, it was stated that "the woods and timber not only in the said New Forest, but in this Kingdom in general, have of late years been much wasted and impaired, and that the said Forest, which might be of great use and conveniency for supply of His Majesty's royal navy, is in danger of being destroyed if some speedy course is not taken to restore and preserve the growth of timber there." As a corrective measure, it was directed that some two thousand acres of waste land within the Forest boundaries should be planted, and, after the expiration of twenty years, a further enclosure of two hundred acres must be effected annually. The apathy and slackness, however, always associated with the work of replanting in this country was evidenced when, a hundred years later, it was necessary to pass another Act of Parliament with the object of preserving the amenities of the forest as a timber-producing estate. If this was the fate of a Royal forest, it can be imagined that private landowners were not solicitous in regard to the existence of woods possessing an immediate commercial value, and local demands, whether for the purpose of smelting Sussex iron, ship-building, mining or other trades in the North, in a comparatively short space of time, caused their almost complete disappearance.

The last few decades have seen repeated (but too often half-hearted) attempts made to encourage afforestation by private persons; and here one is insistently reminded of the classical story of the orchard. Upon a friend proposing to a young man that he should plant apple trees, the latter, in refusing, answered that, by the time they came into bearing, he would be dead; a similar suggestion to the father of the young man met with the same answer. But when the septuagenarian grandfather was appealed to, he immediately planted an orchard and lived to break his neck by falling from a tree when gathering a heavy crop. Requests from the State to landowners not meeting with success, generally for reasons akin to those expressed by the two younger generations above, it is satisfactory to observe that the former has assumed the rôle of the grandfather; it will certainly avoid his fate in the financial sense for, as a certain writer has put it, "the State is the only landowner that never dies, is never called upon to pay succession and estate duties, and is never forced to look for something like immediate returns from the financial investments which it deems judicious to make for the national benefit". Ample sites suitable for the purpose have long been available, but too often placed in the hands of those least able to advance the capital necessary to transform waste lands into ultimate revenue earning properties. For this reason, apart from the work of the Forestry Commission, the bulk of recent planting has been undertaken on semi-public land, such as the catchment areas of large waterworks and estates in the possession of corporate bodies.

Until the Great War the activities of the State were principally evidenced in the setting up of Commissions of enquiry. Thus, in 1887, a Parliamentary Committee reported; in 1902, a Committee of the Board of Agriculture recommended the provision of better means of instruction in Forestry; in 1906, a Royal Commission advocated the planting of nine million acres of land (of which six million were to be in Scotland). In 1910, however, more definite steps were taken, and the Development Commission allocated funds for the establishment of regional advisers in Forestry, and at the same time expressed its willingness to advance money to owners of land considered to be suitable for planting. Five pounds per acre was the maximum sum allowed, and a reasonable condition attaching to the grant was that land thus afforested should be available to the local Forestry officer for demonstration purposes. In both Scotland and Ireland, prior to the war, independent efforts were also being made to secure an additional reserve of timber.

This, then, was the position in 1914. Four years later a survey of the woods and forests of Great Britain would have shocked anyone familiar with their normal appearance, for the bulk of the coniferous trees had disappeared, having been felled for pit-props or otherwise converted to immediate commercial needs. The explanation was of course the simple one that timber, from its bulky nature, was soon removed from the list of imported articles to which preference could be accorded when cargo space was being allocated, and, as this declining space had perforce to be more and more reserved for human food, munitions of war and other essential commodities, so it ceased almost entirely to figure in bills of lading, and the alternative sources at home were drawn upon to a growing extent. The Government itself assumed responsibility for the felling operations that followed, although private owners were generally not loth to reap an unexpected profit from their woods. Home supplies thus met the requirements of the nation, but at the end of the war the margin was extremely small and the reserves for future years had disappeared. Replanting was of course an obligation devolving upon the State, and, in consequence of a *Report* issued by the Reconstruction Committee, it was proposed to plant with conifers 1,180,000 acres in the course of forty years, of which total 200,000 acres were earmarked for the first decade. In addition, some 20,000 acres of land suitable for the propagation of hard woods were to be acquired, and private owners were to be reimbursed for undertaking similar obligations. If this programme was not followed out in its entirety, the reasons were those associated with all similar enterprises—inability of private individuals to undertake post-war operations with grants of money incompatible with the ruling costs of labour and of materials, and the stringent economies effected in the direct expenditure of State funds. Under the Forestry Act of 1919 a sum amounting to £3,500,000 was set aside for the purposes in question, and the determination of the Government to proceed with its scheme was proved by the fact that the annual sum voted towards the expenses of the Forestry Commissioners increased from £99,000 in the year 1919–20 to £379,000 in 1920–1. But, subsequently, although the policy itself was not annulled, the work of restoring our timber resources was thus referred to by the Geddes Committee—"We cannot recommend that this expenditure—which will always show a heavy loss and which cannot reach full fruition for something like eighty years—should be continued". Certain reductions in staff were consequentially effected and further expansion of programmes was curtailed; the first decade, however, witnessed considerable progress, which is subsequently referred to in detail.

Comprehensive views of the situation created by the war had been taken by the British Empire Forestry Commission, sitting in London in 1920, and the need for a full enquiry into the timber resources of the Colonies and Dependencies was emphasised, but, again, nothing definite resulted. The position that Great Britain then found herself in was not dissimilar from that which she occupied in the matter of her wheat requirements, for in both cases she was, and is, preponderatingly dependent upon extraneous sources of supply. In other periods of timber stringency, however, such as followed the Civil War or the Napoleonic conflict, the actual duration of the shortage was determined by the rate of growth of hard wood, latterly, by that of soft wood. The schemes now being undertaken in this country will, therefore, produce commercial returns in a length of time less than half that experienced after previous replanting operations.

It may be asked what was the statistical position of Great Britain in relation both to its own needs and supplies, and also in comparison with other countries. The answer evidences the inexact and irregular nature of the economic data relating to this industry, for, while the import trade is of course the subject of full statistics, the woods and forests of this and of many other countries are not regularly surveyed, and the output of British timber has only been officially estimated on two occasions. The Census of Production of 1908 was extended to the woods and forests of Great Britain, with the result that the following Table was published, which differentiated between coniferous and hard wood areas.

	England and Wales (acres)	Scotland (acres)	Great Britain (acres)
Coniferous Woods:			
Scots Pine	49,000	156,000	205,000
Larch	69,000	25,000	94,000
Spruce	1,000	8,000	9,000
Others and Mixed	135,000	293,000	428,000
Total ...	254,000	482,000	736,000
Broad Leaved Woods:			
Oak	130,000	9,000	139,000
Beech	25,000	1,000	26,000
Birch	1,000	10,000	11,000
Others and Mixed	476,000	75,000	551,000
Total ...	632,000	95,000	727,000
Mixed Coniferous and Broad Leaved Woods	1,021,000	298,000	1,319,000
Total Acreage of Woodland	1,907,000	875,000	2,782,000

Whilst it cannot be claimed that these figures covered all the timber of the country, for very small areas were excluded, and the vast numbers of hedgerow and detached trees so peculiar to the English countryside were, of course, omitted, yet an enumeration of all woods of any importance was effected. Furthermore, the owners of these woods were requested to state the quantities of trees felled in the preceding year, together with their values. The result showed that, in a year which there was no reason to consider abnormal, some million and a half trees of all sorts were brought into use, supplying approximately fifteen million cubic feet of timber, valued, with thinnings, faggots and other by-products, at £800,000. The insignificance of these figures compared with the foreign trade of the country will be appreciated when it is stated that, at the time in question, some ten million tons of timber were being annually imported, the value of which was upwards of £26,000,000. Indeed, the United Kingdom absorbed more than half (both in weight and value) of the world's export of timber, our nearest competitor being Germany. Whilst a considerable trade was arising between the component parts of the British Empire, the latter was not self-supporting, but, for soft woods, drew heavily upon Russia and Scandinavia. The future supplies from these latter sources provided the main cause for anxiety; for the drain upon them was immense, and whatever country was turned to exhibited the spectacle of continuous wasting, unaccompanied by any provision for replanting. The hard woods did not provide a similar problem because, apart from escaping the insatiable demands of the paper-maker and the colliery-owner, they were essentially tropical or sub-tropical in origin, and correspondingly difficult of access; moreover, they represented an area almost equal to that occupied by the soft woods. Again, the consumption of timber per head of the population was rapidly increasing, and, if it had not attained the dimensions found in the United States, was adding to a position that was already precarious.

During the war it was of course assumed by all authorities that, when peace was restored, Russia would immediately be able to meet the heavy demands made upon her, and calculations were effected which showed that, with the inclusion of Siberia, her potential resources were almost unlimited. Here, however, expectations were upset, for timber, in common with wheat, was not exported on any considerable scale until after the passage of some twelve years from the cessation of hostilities. Whilst Canada and Scandinavia were able to supply the requirements of the importing nations, there was no assurance that the former might not have found her forests depleted unexpectedly quickly if export into the United States had occurred upon a grand scale. This, then, was the uncertain position that faced the country, for, while supplies were forthcoming to meet immediate requirements, those of the future were rapidly dwindling. None of course suggested that Great Britain could be self-supporting in the matter of timber—indeed the previously mentioned Government scheme merely aimed at establishing a three years' reserve of soft wood—but it was agreed that certain advantages would accrue from a thorough investigation into the possibility of afforesting those parts of the country that, from altitude, situation or soil, were producing little or nothing. A glance at the statistics relating to the land surface showed that there existed a vast discrepancy between the total physical area and that "under crops and grass", which even the inclusion of some millions of acres of "rough grazings" only in part explained. An unofficial estimate of the existing "waste lands" suggested that England contained 4,000,000 acres, Scotland 4,000,000 acres, Wales 700,000 acres and Ireland 1,500,000 acres, or a grand total of 10,200,000 acres. Whatever value might be placed upon the definition of the word "waste", the fact that more than 30,000,000 acres were—and, to a great extent, still are—excluded from the agricultural returns of the United Kingdom demonstrates that the figure quoted allows ample margin for error. What proportion of either acreage in question could with advantage ultimately be planted is a matter for expert opinion, but a survey of the whole was necessary to inform the nation of the latent possibilities.

Advocates of afforestation too often based their arguments upon data relative to the proportionate acreage under woods and forests in this and other European countries, or quoted statistics of the area thus represented per head of the various populations. It is easy to demonstrate that, for example, in the first instance, the United Kingdom compares badly with Germany, and that Sweden has some nine acres per head whereas Great Britain has ·07, but the mountainous nature of large parts of both those countries, and the undeveloped state of the latter, afford an explanation widely divergent from what inference might suggest. Indeed, the preservation of forests of long standing affords a totally different economic problem from that involved in their establishment where none has existed for centuries. Again, the argument that much labour would be absorbed as a result of afforestation on any considerable scale, is misleading, for it has been shown that, if the whole of this country were covered with forests, permanent employment would be provided for but a few hundred thousand workers; even the initial work of clearing and planting does not call for labour on a large scale. It was rather upon general grounds that the arguments in favour of a liberal scheme of planting eventually met with success. These included the provision of a reserve of soft woods sufficient to enable the country to pass through an experience similar to the Great War; the curtailment within more restricted limits of our bill for imported timber; the development of land that at present contributes nothing, or next to nothing, in the way of agricultural produce; a limited additional opening for winter employment of agricultural labourers.

The newly formed Forestry Commission had, as was previously noted, been authorised in 1919, by the Forestry Act, to start upon a ten years' scheme of planting, and had been promised a total sum of £3,500,000. Although in the end this full financial assistance was secured, the Commissioners had upon several occasions been placed in considerable anxiety as to whether their grant would not be curtailed. In reviewing their work at the end of this, the first, decade, they could point to a distribution of expenditure which showed that more than three-quarters of the whole sum had been devoted to forestry operations proper. The original (or Acland) Sub-Committee's proposal of 1917 had postulated the acquisition in the first ten years of 402,000 acres of land and a State planting of some 150,000 acres of coniferous trees, with, in addition, 110,000 acres of State-aided plantings. There were actually acquired 310,000 acres of land, of which 138,000 acres were planted (130,768 with conifers and 7500 with hard woods) while, with State assistance, 76,000 acres were afforested. The failure to implement fully the programme originally drawn up was due to unexpected difficulties met with in securing suitable land. In their tenth annual *Report* the Commission stated that the average price paid for plantable land was £3 5*s.* 9*d.* per acre—a reasonable figure—but there had frequently been entailed the necessity to take over properties containing large houses and numerous farm buildings which were useless to the Commission; this was clearly one of the penalties attaching to the purchase of second or third grade agricultural land in a period of extreme depression. Compulsion had had in no case to be exercised, although the Commissioners have been placed in possession of such overruling powers. In all, by 1930, they had under their charge over 600,000 acres of land, of which 250,000 acres had been purchased, and 230,000 acres leased (at rents that averaged 2*s*. to 3*s*. per acre); the remainder had come under their jurisdiction by transference from the Commissioners of Crown Lands.

The individual properties, numbering upwards of 150, were widely dispersed throughout Great Britain, but were numerically densest in North-West Scotland, and in Mid and South Wales; the largest single area was, however, in Eastern England, namely Thetford, which, with an acreage of 22,000, already exceeded even the New Forest in size. Here it was, indeed, that the greatest transformation was effected during the ten years under review, for, upon the borders of Norfolk and Suffolk, a wide expanse of the sandy breck-land had been acquired and planted with Scots and Corsican pines. Previously there had been a few scattered plantations of conifers, which the war-time demand for pit-props had completely destroyed. A very sparse population and low agricultural land values were desirable assets, not to be outweighed by an exceptionally low rainfall and the existence of game preservation upon a large scale. Twenty years hence the question of transport may loom larger than it does at the moment, for Thetford and the other East Anglian forests are far from the consuming centres and rail communication westwards is not particularly well developed; it is, however, to be anticipated that much preparatory work will be performed in specially established local saw-mills. At present, the principal repercussions have been those affecting archaeologists, ornithologists and botanists, whose access to a very happy hunting-ground has been rigorously curtailed. In the official list of British forests will be noted the names of practically all those familiar to readers of English history—a guarantee that these traditionally valuable sites are now preserved for all time; side by side with them can be seen the nomenclature of modern areas, at present conveying no such message, but which, a few years hence, when the areas involved are in full production, may be widely familiar.

In so far as the work of private owners was concerned, the effects of the war were not made good by 1929; indeed, the Forestry Commissioners have had occasion seriously to deplore the lack of enterprise shown by that class of person, and have even discussed the adoption of measures calculated to enforce a modicum of replanting. Landowners have been paid up to the rate of £2 per acre for new plantings of soft wood and up to £4 in the case of hard wood. A

Breckland before and after afforestation

further activity of the Forestry Commission itself has been the establishment of what are known as Forest Workers' holdings—viz. small plots of land, ranging up to a maximum of ten acres of (wherever possible) good land, to be held in conjunction with employment under the Commission. Nearly 10 per cent. of recent expenditure has been devoted to this development which is, of course, a typical Continental device to combine part-time forestry work, mainly in winter-time, with that provided by the employee's own holding. Here a guarantee of not less than one hundred and fifty days' work per annum is given, but, in practice, it would seem that the workers spend a far larger proportion of the time in their official employment. Since this scheme was inaugurated, in 1925, over one thousand of these holdings have been set up, at an average cost of somewhat over £500, and the demand seems at least to keep pace with the supply. Employment in the service of the Commission has steadily increased from the 400 workers in the first summers of the decade up to 3600 in the winter months of the final year; broadly speaking, there have been 50 per cent. more persons at work in the winter than in the summer. It is unnecessary here to describe in detail the ancillary work of the Forestry Commission, and it must suffice to mention that it trains forestry officers (for service both at home and abroad), assists financially the Imperial Institute of Forestry at Oxford, and undertakes considerable research into problems of an economic as well as a technical character.

In 1924 it became possible again to review the statistical position of the forest areas, for the Census of Production was, with considerable care, extended to forest areas and to forest products. As a result, there were recorded 2,958,000 acres of woodland in Great Britain, of which 1,074,000 acres were in Scotland. If comparison be effected with the enquiry held in 1908, it emerges that, while the total area had increased by some 200,000 acres, the subsequent inclusion of "scrub" and of "felled or devastated" areas more than counterbalanced that figure, and, in reality, the comparable total was below that of sixteen years earlier. It was estimated that one-third of the total volume of timber standing in 1914 had been felled shortly after the war terminated. In 1924, according to the special *Report* of the Forestry Commission, over 90 per cent. of the woods in Great Britain were in the hands of private individuals and less than 7 per cent. belonged to the State; 5·3 per cent. of the total land surface was under woods or forests. In more detail the technical distribution was as follows:

High Forest	Acres
Conifers	671,841
Hard woods	443,354
Mixed	301,695
Total ...	1,416,890
Coppice with standards	428,880
Coppice	99,800
Scrub	330,703
Felled or devastated	478,106
Other woods not available for commercial production of timber ...	204,293
Grand Total ...	2,958,672

In so far as quantities of timber felled in 1924 and its value were concerned, the Census gave the following results, which were based upon sample enquiries widely distributed: total felled of all classes, 56,000,000 cubic feet, valued at £2,036,000; soft woods represented almost exactly one-third of the total value. Great as the figures of bulk at first appear, the home production of soft woods merely represented 3·3 per cent. of the country's consumption of that commodity, while hard woods formed a quarter of the total supply; the total percentage of both forms derived from home sources was 5·4. Finally, this Census indicated that 19,000 persons found permanent employment in our woods and forests, while temporary workers fluctuated in number between 4000 and 10,000, according to the season of the year.

Six years later, in 1930, the Forestry Commissioners themselves conducted another enquiry into the production of home-grown timber—again based upon the sampling method. Upon this occasion the somewhat reduced yield of 48,000,000 cubic feet (valued at £1,545,000) was indicated. The corresponding figure for imported supplies in the year in question was 1,052,100,000 cubic feet, so that the contribution of Great Britain then represented 4·4 per cent. of its total requirements, as compared with 5·4 per cent. in 1924.

The activities of the State Forestry Department during those initial ten years have now been traced and the statistical position occupied by the industry in recent times indicated, so that the proposed future policy can now be unfolded. Prior to the economic crisis of 1931–2 the Commissioners had prepared a second ten-year plan which envisaged the planting of a further 330,000 acres, together with the creation of 3000 Forest Workers' holdings. The Treasury had agreed to make grants up to a total of £9,000,000—a very considerable increase over the sums hitherto available—and, as by then the trading receipts of the Commission would, it was estimated, amount to another £2,000,000, there would have been available a grand total of eleven and a quarter million pounds. The annual plantings were to be upon an increasing scale, rising from 25,000 acres up to 44,000 acres in 1938. The Committee on National Expenditure closely examined this scheme and, after a diversity of opinion had been revealed upon the part of its constituent members as to the extent to which the work of the Commission should be reduced, discussions took place directly between the Forest Commissioners themselves and representatives of the Government.

The upshot was that agreement was reached upon the following lines—for five years from 1932 the State would provide an annual sum of £450,000, which the Commissioners would have an entirely free hand in spending; they, in their turn, were to reduce at once their expenditure for the current year, but were permitted to complete the purchase of certain properties to which they were virtually committed. In view of the findings of the Committee, this represented not only a financial gain, but, still more important, it restored liberty of action in the matter of policy. Thus modified, the programme envisaged an annual planting of 20,000 acres, the purchase of sufficient reserve lands, the establishment of a few workers' holdings and the maintenance of existing research and educational facilities. Despite the uncertainty attaching to the situation during the first two years of the second decade, some 83,000 acres of land were purchased and over 50,000 acres were planted; thus, in twelve years, 189,000 acres of woodlands had been established *de novo* in Great Britain. When the provisional five-year plan comes to an end, the position, while immeasurably better than it would have been if the State had not assumed these duties in 1919, will be none too advantageous, for the official activities will have been, to a great extent, neutralised by the lack of co-operation upon the part of private landowners. It remains, indeed, seriously open to question whether at some time in the near future the State will not be compelled, on national grounds, to take over certain neglected or badly administered estates, for, as in the seventeenth century, so now, no form of appeal, dissemination of technical assistance or financial consideration appears to be effective in retaining in a state of efficiency even existing forestal areas. To the Forestry Commission, on the other hand, the country owes its possession of an exceedingly well-managed property which, while rendering good commercial returns, will within less than a generation form a valuable safeguard in case of national danger.

Compared with what has been accomplished upon the Continent, the above-described activities seem parochial in scale, for during the latter half of the nineteenth century both France and Germany reafforested inferior, waste or mountainous land by the million acres; even Denmark, at the time when she was transforming her agricultural economy, planted thus nearly a quarter of a million acres of unproductive heath-land. Outside Europe, to meet the insatiable demands for pulp, the depletion of the soft wood reserves has proceeded apace, and, already in the case of the United States—where the bulk of the virgin forests has been swept away—supplies are inadequate; in Canada, too, it is obvious that, within a generation, artificial regeneration will have to be practised upon a generous scale. In the Far East, Japan has added, in the last five years, 15 per cent. to an area of forest land exceeding 67,000,000 acres, but even in that country there is, on balance, a large importation of soft woods. These statements apply to coniferous areas, for, in the case of the hard woods, the position is very different, supplies being ample, but the most valuable sources are frequently difficult of access.

In so far as the requirements of the British Isles are concerned, the position is as follows: we import annually from eight to ten million loads, and are at present producing about one million loads. The bulk of the post-war imports have, until recently, come from Canada and Scandinavia, where Sweden alone had 58,000,000 acres under well-managed forests, but, as in the case of wheat, Russia has now resumed exportation. It is idle to discuss here the conditions under which labour is performed in the forests of that country—whether, indeed, the timber in question should be termed "slave produced"; it must suffice to record that, by agreement with a large group of British timber-merchants, nearly half a million standards of Russian soft wood were imported in 1932 and that a very similar quantity, valued at £4,500,000, was to be introduced in 1933.

The British Empire still possesses over one thousand million acres of woods and forests, of which half are found in Canada, but here, as in the world at large, the demand for soft woods, brought about especially by the introduction of artificial silk and newsprint, greatly exceeds the potentialities of replacement. Two illustrations must suffice: in his *Economics of Forestry*, W. E. Hiley, quoting Krawany, gives the world consumption of timber for paper-making purposes as in excess of twelve million tons annually, while a single saw-mill can devour upwards of sixty acres of growing wood daily. The position was admirably described at a recent meeting of the British Association by Professor F. Story, who stated that a world stock-taking revealed serious deficiencies. In Europe, including Russia, the annual consumption of coniferous wood exceeded growth by 3,000,000,000 cubic feet. In the United States the conditions were "desperate", since consumption was eight times the growth. Even in Canada, where, incidentally, fires and other forms of destruction eliminate three times as much timber as goes into consumption, the virgin forests would not last more than another twenty-five years. The speaker summed up the situation by stating that, in his opinion, the soft woods of the world would not suffice at the present rate of usage for more than thirty-seven years, and he accordingly looked for a steady rise in future timber prices; the crisis might come quite suddenly, when Great Britain would be one of the first countries to suffer.

To the economist, timber presents certain anomalies. The demand for it is unmistakably elastic—that is to say, price variations quickly affect the quantities going into consumption. Supply is also elastic in so far as the ability to draw upon virgin areas is concerned, but where, as in these Islands, any increased output can only be derived from pre-arranged plantings, there is obviously a very long time-lag to be overcome. It is possible for certain Continental countries to augment their fellings by such means as expediting the provision of transport facilities, by reducing the proportions of timber rendered non-productive in milling or other processes or by temporarily utilising larger trees. Above all, timber is in so many trades an alternative to other materials that the degree of its user may depend upon their relative prices. For examples, one has to look no farther than railway sleepers, vehicle bodies, pit-props, window-frames and even furniture. While the factors of safety, durability, appearance and costs of maintenance all affect the decision to be arrived at, yet initial cost is not necessarily of paramount importance in connection with the second and fourth items, for, where strength in combination with long life is desired, timber is now frequently displaced by steel. This tendency will certainly be more marked in the future as timber prices enhance. The use of timber, too, varies as between different countries in proportion to the stage of development that they have individually attained; in a new country, with a rapidly growing population, extensive demands are made for wood in the matter of house-building and the provision of rail transport, whereas in older countries, or in those with stationary populations, its consumption for these purposes is abated, simultaneously with increased usage in the luxury and decorative trades, e.g. paper and artificial silk manufacture. From the economist's standpoint, a few types of soft wood and many of hard wood are clearly to be described as joint-products; a good example of the former is found in the Landes Department of France, whence the *Pinus pinaster*, planted, in the first instance, for protective purposes, after producing turpentine, is shipped in the form of pit-props to South Wales. Many of the indigenous trees of India, the Straits and other tropical or semi-tropical areas are representative of the latter class, for from them are derived such sought after products as copal varnish, gutta-percha, dyes and tans, while the timber itself possesses considerable commercial value. Specific examples are *Sophora japonica*, of which the foliage is taken medicinally, the flowers yield a dye and the timber is valuable; sandal-wood (medicinal oil and ornamental timber), and *Acacia catechu* (cutch, for tanning, and sleepers) and specimens of *Shorea* and *Hopea*, which produce a good varnish with timber which takes the place of the cheaper mahoganies. On the other hand, no such use can be made of *Hevea braziliensis* (the india-rubber tree) and it would be difficult to prove that the conifers converted into pulp or artificial silk have any dual use.

Finally, in no other industry—primary or secondary—is man faced by such powerful natural and physical phenomena. Hundreds of thousands of square miles of timbered areas are, for many months of the year, subject to conditions of an Arctic character, while the winning of timber in the Tropics also involves extreme physical hardship; in general, none but the fittest of human workers can labour for long at these extractive processes. Nature, too, has marshalled all her animate forces against man's efforts to preserve and extend her provision of this material, for pests—insect, bird and mammal—are all actively engaged in attacking it below ground, in its matured heart and in its expanding foliage. Fire, whether humanly engendered or not, takes a terrific toll of the product. Man himself, through his domestic animals, has, from the shores of the Mediterranean in classical times down to African territories at the present moment, rendered sterile vast tracts of once forested, or at least adequately covered, lands. He has, moreover, none but himself to blame where, after generations of indiscriminate felling, Nature, subsequently left to her own devices, has revolted and reproduced, not the original valuable woods, but worthless scrub. Lastly, for many generations man exhibited the grossest carelessness, not only in destroying immature woods, but also in preventing any possibility of their natural regeneration.

Set against these physical and human factors of destruction the mollifying influences that a well-ordered system of woods and forests can exert. On the one hand, climate may be ameliorated and rainfall altered, animal and crop husbandry protected and extended, soil erosion and denudation checked; on the other hand, employment is increased, both directly and indirectly, and the human race placed in cumulative possession of one of the most universally beneficial and—whether viewed before or after utilisation—even aesthetically desirable of the primary products.

Chapter XX

AGRICULTURAL STATISTICS

Domesday Book and Gregory King's estimates; description of the first modern attempts made to collect returns in the British Isles; controversy over the utility of agricultural statistics; the present official series; methods employed in securing and analysing the information contained in the returns; economic statistics; suggestions for additions and improvements in the British series; Japanese statistical enquiries; Cost of Production studies and the Survey method; the International Institute of Agriculture; the World Census of Agriculture; notes on the handling and use of agricultural statistics.

In his *Journal*, under date June 8th, 1830, Carlyle entered the following appeal for statistical information: "Our political economists should collect statistical facts, such as What is the lowest sum a man can live on in various countries? What is the highest he gets to live on? How many people work with their hands? How many with their heads? How many not at all? and innumerable such. What all want to know is the condition of our fellow men; and, strange to say, it is the thing least of all understood, or to be understood, as matters go. The present 'science' of political economy requires far less intellect than successful bellows-mending; and perhaps does less good, if we deduct all the evil it brings us. Though young it already carries marks of decrepitude—a speedy and soft death to it". So far as statistics relating to our rural economy are concerned, what improvement in this respect can be recorded during the intervening hundred years? Would Carlyle now be satisfied with the official information obtained in regard to what is still the largest industry in these Islands and the most vital in the world?

The history of the collection of statistics relating to agriculture affords a striking example of the apathy of the mid-nineteenth century British farmer and of his advisers, for, when at length Government was empowered, or compelled, to obtain annual returns, complete statistics had long been available covering other, and less important, trades in the kingdom. On the other hand, agriculture can claim to have afforded the earliest example of a statistical enquiry held in this country. This of course was enframed in Domesday Book, and represented the economic state of England as it was in 1066 and 1086. It is quite legitimate to refer to this enquiry of William the Conqueror as an agricultural one, since primary production at that time virtually afforded the sole occupation. Domesday set forth the value of the lands held in each manor, the numbers of the different grades of society in those communities, of their livestock, of their ploughs, of their mills. It was compulsory, whereas many modern returns are voluntary. It was the obvious and businesslike action of a victorious sovereign who desired to compare, after twenty years' reign, the condition of his new territory with that pertaining in the last year of his predecessor's rule. It had for its main object the acquisition of knowledge as to the taxability of the country; and, from that date down to 1860, the fear of resultant impositions upon the land was always at the root of the opposition to any economic or statistical census. Domesday was compiled through local enquirers, prototypes of our "Crop Reporters"; it was, in the light of modern research, extraordinarily complete and accurate. Had it been followed by a series of similar visitations, even at intervals of a century, we should have been furnished with an invaluable piece of economic evidence. Even as matters are, comparison, based upon the answers contained in Domesday, has been made between the nineteenth and eleventh century areas under the plough in particular Counties. Thus, for the area South of the Tees and East of the Severn, it is probable that the land in common-fields, as well as that directly retained by the lords of the manor, amounted to about six million acres. At the present time the corresponding arable acreage is somewhat less than double. Under the two and three course rotation the acreage of certain cereals might have been approximately the same, but the rate of yield was of course less than half. One author has shown that certain Counties in 1086 contained three and four times as large an arable acreage as they do now, e.g. Somerset had possibly upwards of 500,000 acres in this state at the former date and only 140,000 in 1932.

After Domesday the curtain falls for a period of exactly six hundred years, and we have absolutely no statistical information as to the fluctuations in the numbers of men, animals or acres under the plough until 1688, when Gregory King prepared a very complete series of tables. He claimed to have enumerated all living creatures connected with the land—including, in each case, their families—from "temporal lords" (6400), "through knights" (7800), "gentlemen" (96,000), "freeholders" of one category (280,000), "freeholders" of another category (700,000), "farmers" (750,000), "cottagers and paupers" (1,300,000) to "beeves, sterks and calves" (4,500,000), and even "hares and leverets" (24,000) and "rabbits and conies" (1,000,000). We must not allow these last items, so precisely recorded, to blind us to the fact that King gave what was probably as accurate an estimate of the different grades of society as was then possible. He also produced a tabular statement recording the acreage under the plough and under grass, together with the annual value of all land in England and Wales.

From 1688 until the second quarter of the last century we are again without figures, although McCullogh, Porter and Adam Smith had lamented their absence, but, in 1808, W. T. Comber and, in 1827, W. Couling had prepared estimates of, in the case of the former, land under various crops, and in that of the latter, of arable, grass and waste. Comber's figures saw the light as a private publication, Couling's were produced in evidence before a Select Committee on Emigration, and, as the latter was by profession a surveyor, his data received considerable support. A generation earlier Arthur Young had made estimates of the numbers of livestock in the country, but this side of the question was ignored by his successors, who confined their efforts to urging the need for estimates being secured of the produce of the three principal cereals.

Chronologically, an attempt by the magistrates of Norfolk to obtain returns relating to the agriculture of that County in 1831 comes next—one year after Carlyle's diatribe. Of the six hundred and eighty parishes circularised, four hundred and twenty-six responded, and the remaining two hundred and fifty-four declined to further the project. A discussion upon the partial results obtained was indulged in at the meeting of the British Association at Cambridge in 1845, when reference was made to the number of agricultural labourers evidenced on different types of farms, and apparently the hazardous project of "raising" the few returns secured, in order to obtain figures for the whole of England and Wales, was mooted.

The next move was made in May 1836, when the President of the Board of Trade sent out "simple but comprehensive" queries to all the incumbents in Bedfordshire. This is the first instance of a Government department taking any official interest in the collection of these statistics, and Bedfordshire appears to have been selected for no other reason than that it was alphabetically the first County. This was admittedly a test case, and, if it had been successful, it was hoped to extend the enquiry to the rest of the country. Unfortunately, however, out of the one hundred and twenty-six parish clergy who were invited to help, only twenty-seven took the trouble to reply. The schedules sent out were extremely complex and, in addition to the more usual ones dealing with numbers and acreage, required answers to such questions as "modes of letting land", "depth of soil", "state of drainage", "rates of wages paid", "quantities of cheese and butter produced", and so forth. The majority of the twenty-seven completed forms showed evidence of a real desire to further the enquiry, but even these were freely sprinkled with such remarks as "farmers decline to say" and "unknown".

In 1844 correspondence between the Board of Trade and the Poor Law Commissioners resulted in a simultaneous experiment being carried out the following year in England, Scotland and Ireland. In the last-named Country (Bailieborough Union) and Scotland (Midlothian) the effort was successful, but in England (two Unions in Hampshire) the result was a complete failure. In 1847 a Bill to enforce the collection of agricultural statistics was introduced into the House of Commons, but did not secure a second reading. This Bill provided for an annual enquiry on June 1st relating to all holdings over three acres in extent, for which the Guardians of the Poor were to have accepted responsibility. The same year, however, saw the successful inauguration of very complete machinery relating to Ireland. Doubtless the impending famine expedited matters, but the result has been that Ireland, from that year onwards, possessed annual returns, covering her 500,000 farms, obtained through the medium of the Royal Irish Constabulary.

In 1849, members of the East Berwickshire Farmers' Club carried out, at a very small cost, a comprehensive enquiry relating to all the parishes in its area. Again, in 1853, the Highland Society collected statistics for the Counties of Roxburgh, Haddington and Sutherland, and, next year, aided by a Treasury grant, for the whole of Scotland. But for an unfortunate disagreement between the Society's officials and the Government regarding the precise allocation of the funds provided, it is tolerably certain that this experiment would have been the precursor of an annual series of returns for Scotland. The year 1854 saw the first large-scale attempt made in England and Wales, by which the following eleven Counties were covered—Hampshire, Wiltshire, Leicester, Norfolk, Suffolk, Berkshire, Worcester, Brecknock, Shropshire, Denbigh and the West Riding of Yorkshire. The measure of improvement—due either to the methods of those employed, the Poor Law officials, or else to an enlightened sense of the importance of the returns to farmers themselves—can be judged when it is stated that, out of 118,000 schedules distributed (although 17,000 had to be completed by the enumerators), only 8000 were not returned.

The feasibility of collecting agricultural statistics had by now been demonstrated, and the next dozen years were noticeable for the setting up of a Select Committee to enquire into the whole question, and for the appearance of several pamphlets and controversial articles on the subject. The principal witnesses heard by the Committee were those persons who had been primarily concerned with the above-mentioned enquiries, certain Poor Law Inspectors, Sir James Caird and individual landowners. All agreed as to the necessity for an annual return, but differed as to the machinery to be employed, the scope of the enquiry and the date at which it should be held. The great majority favoured the employment of the Poor Law officers, but Caird urged, in his capacity of *Times* commissioner, "that confidential and expert enquirers", to the number of two hundred, should perambulate the country during the three summer months, visiting twelve farms a day each. He estimated the cost of this method at £20,000. Caird's strong advocacy was nothing new, for in December 1851 he had urged in one of his "letters" the vital importance of agricultural statistics, placing their collection, indeed, as one of five *desiderata* in the forefront of his agricultural programme. Mr Maxwell (Secretary of the Highland Society), Sir John Walsham, who had been mainly instrumental in organising the 1854 experiment in Norfolk, and Lord Ashburton all advocated the employment of more numerous, but unskilled, local officials. Incidentally, these witnesses gave some interesting sidelights on the feelings of the rural community in the matter, for we learn that "combined opposition of the occupants in certain parishes" had led to difficulties in Norfolk—difficulties smoothed away in some instances by the action and example of the Earl of Leicester. This Committee unanimously recommended that an accurate return of the acreage under each crop and of the numbers of livestock should be collected, and that approximate estimates of the harvest should be tabulated.

Officially, matters rested there for several years, another Bill introduced in 1856 meeting with no better fate than its predecessor. Meanwhile, however, private persons were urging upon the Government and upon the farmer the vital need for the setting up of a comprehensive scheme. Foremost among these were J. M. Buckland, who described himself as a "Statist of Gloucester", John Hannam, Secretary to the Yorkshire Agricultural Society, and C. Wren Hoskyns, who, in pamphlets and articles, lost no opportunity of putting forward their views. They all stressed the importance of statistics being made available to show the probable outturn of the staple crops rather than numbers of livestock and acreage figures. They held that farmers in this respect were unduly handicapped by lack of knowledge, and adduced instances of individuals selling wheat at 40*s.* the quarter, and later in the same season at 80*s.* Lord Ashburton even pointed out that corn-dealers, as long previously as 1833, had informed a Select Committee that it was their habit to employ agents to travel the corn-growing areas of the country in order to secure advance reports of the probable outturn; thus, they were enabled to operate before the bulk of sellers knew current prospects. Whatever real importance may have then attached to this question, as the bulk of our wheat came to be imported it tended in later years to be modified, but at that time, and for propaganda purposes, it was doubtless a useful cry. These same "Statists" also flirted with the already thorny problem of the possibility of the United Kingdom being again self-supporting in wheat. Hannam wrote: "How great will be the interest that will attach to such statistics, when experience shall have pointed out to us the proper questions to ask and the best modes of obtaining the answers. How useful for all the purposes of enquiry. And when in fifty years hence it shall fall to the lot of some person to address himself to an audience on the statistics of agriculture, the volume will be open to him from which he may draw at once the history of the past, the moral of the present and the prophecy of the future as regards agriculture".

Not so the farmer and his friends. Contemporary fears were raised that rents would be advanced if stocks were shown to be large or that distraint would be enforced if they were unduly small. A speaker was quoted thus: "I'll willingly give a return of my crops if the grocer is made to return the quantity of tea and sugar he sells and the draper of his broadcloth"; and, again, the representatives of Downham Union, Norfolk, held that "Government might as well ask a farmer what his bank balance was or how many bottles of wine he had in his cellar". The farmer objected to the local Overseer of the Poor being empowered to interrogate him about his business. But Hannam answered, "The farmer has visited the markets with no more idea of the supply he must compete with, or the price his commodity was really worth, than if he were vending his produce in the planet Jupiter". On the same lines wrote Hoskyns: "You can be told every bale of calico that leaves the country, every box of gloves or yard of lace that enters it; you can hear how much tea, coffee, sugar and tobacco is consumed in the United Kingdom; but what is the growth, and what is the consumption of corn? The nearest weather-cock might be appealed to, with about as much expectation of a steady answer as the sources which exist and are usually taken as the data for calculation. Guess what you please, between twelve and twenty-five million quarters per annum, and you will have some statistician or other on your side". The same writer compared the country to a ship setting out on a twelve months' voyage, whose captain "steered on his errand across the trackless waste without any knowledge of the quantity or kind of food on board—its proportion to the number to be supported, and the length of the voyage". The writings of Buckland were directed to making the public familiar with the Norfolk experiment, and to setting forth details of a scheme for a full scale statistical enquiry, for which purpose he prepared schedules and forms and divided up the country into areas; but he also emphasised the unpopularity of the Guardians as supervisors of any such enquiry. All these writers were, however, apt to be carried away in their advocacy, as witness Hannam's question that had statistics of food supplies been available would 15,000 men have died during the Crimean War from sickness, starvation and neglect?

The penultimate stage in the campaign was entered on in 1862, when a circular letter was addressed by the Government to Chairmen of Quarter Sessions, seeking their opinion on the feasibility of collecting annually, or at longer intervals, such statistics as had been in the past experimentally obtained, and suggesting that the local police should act as enumerators. The Chairmen agreed in principle to the scheme, but demurred to the use of the police in this unorthodox capacity. Finally, in 1864, Caird carried a resolution in the House of Commons, by which the Government was irrevocably committed to undertake the collection of agricultural statistics through one of its executive branches.

Thus ended the thirty years' fight, waged by a few enthusiasts against official apathy and rural opposition, for in 1866 the first annual statistics relating to acreage and numbers of livestock in England and Wales were collected by the Board of Trade. In the late 'eighties, when the Board of Agriculture was evolved from a branch of the Privy Council, among its other duties it assumed responsibility for this work.

What exactly are the data which are secured by these annual returns, and through what medium and by what persons are they supplied? The two hundred and twenty representatives of the Board who acted as enumerators from 1866 until 1918 were the local Customs and Excise officials; since that year these persons have been superseded by three hundred and thirty specially appointed officials acting directly on behalf of the Ministry of Agriculture. The latter also act as estimators of the yield of crops, and are part-time officials only, being generally occupied in business of their own as land valuers or in similar avocations. In addition, since 1904, other part-time officers, known as "market Reporters", have been appointed, whose duty it is to furnish each week information as to the current prices of agricultural commodities at representative markets. In former years publication of the statistics was effected in five reports, but post-war economy necessitated their compression into two. The first of these deals with the numbers of holdings exceeding one acre in size, and places them in seven different groups, the smallest containing those above one acre and not exceeding five acres, and the largest those above three hundred acres in extent. Upon occasion a separate Table is given, showing, for similar size-groups, whether the holdings are owned or mainly owned by their occupiers. It should perhaps be premised that all figures are given for the areas of administrative Counties, and that these sixty-two Counties are, when necessary, themselves grouped into ten divisions. Only that portion of the 37,000,000 acres of England and Wales that is technically under "crops and grass", or covered by "mountain and heathland used for grazing", comes under review, and it cannot be too strongly emphasised that all holdings, whether farms, market gardens or allotments of one acre only or less in extent, are excluded. It is interesting to record that, in some of the earlier enquiries previously referred to, holdings above five acres only were covered, whilst it will be remembered that in the abortive Bill of 1847 it was proposed to enumerate those over three acres in size.

Naturally, year by year with the growth of towns, the extension of recreation fields, the construction of roads, railways, aerodromes and other urban conveniences, agricultural land tends to diminish, and this phenomenon is shown clearly by the loss of some thousands of acres annually. Returns are called for from the *occupiers* of holdings, so that as a result there are recorded the total number of agricultural *undertakings* and not the number of *farmers* themselves, for those persons responsible for two or more farms fill in a separate schedule for each. Again, these returns relate to the state of land on a fixed day in each year, viz., June 4th. This date was selected after mature consideration of the circumstances affecting agriculture from Land's End to John O'Groats (for the Scotch returns are taken on the same day and those of the Irish Free State and Ulster on June 1st). At first sight it seems a simple matter to decide upon some date in the summer when the bulk of the crops will be in the ground, but closer investigation will show that there is scarcely any latitude permitted, for it is essential to select one early enough to ensure that the first potatoes in Cornwall shall still be in evidence and yet sufficiently advanced to obtain a record of the last sowings of spring corn and turnips in the bleak Northern Counties. June 4th is the best approximation to this ideal, although, even then, the forms still contain the following instruction: "Land under preparation for a crop shall be returned as under that crop". The early advocates, previously mentioned, had assumed that their enquiries would be held in July or August, as they attached extreme importance to estimates of harvest yields, whilst Sir J. Walsham thought Christmas the most suitable time.

The date chosen must be rigidly adhered to, in order to maintain the annual series of Tables upon a comparable basis. It is of even more importance in the case of livestock than of crops, as certain incidents during the war exemplified. In one case, for instance, with a view to securing estimates of the future supplies of meat, it was decided by the Army Council to take a census of cattle and sheep during the early spring months, and, had the results been published without explanation, the public would have been extremely perturbed thereby, as decreases of hundreds of thousands of heads of stock were evidenced, due to the fact that the majority of births take place in the period from January to April. The same anomaly is liable to occur in the case of crops, but for a different reason. Here, if the time of enquiry be antedated there is a liability of more extensive areas being recorded as under cereals than the following returns of June 4th corroborate. An instance of this also occurred during the Food Production campaign, when a preliminary enquiry in the month of March showed a much larger area under wheat than did the subsequent one, the explanation being attributable partly to a desire by Government-ridden farmers to anticipate possible commands, and partly to a genuine intention to sow an extra breadth of grain which an unduly wet spring afterwards frustrated. Both these examples indicate the need for extreme orthodoxy and conservatism in organising any statistical enquiry relating to agriculture.

The type and area of land covered by these statistics, and the persons affected by them, having been enumerated and the chosen date accounted for, it remains to state exactly what products of the soil are included. The schedules served on occupiers contain upwards of eighty questions and numerous explanatory notes and definitions calculated to facilitate the answering of them. Over forty relate to the acreage under various crops, and the bulk of the remainder to the numbers of livestock of different classes and ages. Further spaces are provided for details relating to the amount of labour employed and the condition as to ownership or tenancy. It is impossible here to attempt a detailed discussion of these schedules; it must suffice to say that they have been gradually developed during the past sixty years, contain all the essential points upon which information can be legitimately sought and, most important of all, have become familiar to those whose business it is to complete them. In this connection it should be noted that the returns, now compulsory, were—save for four years during the life of the Corn Production Acts (1918 to 1921), and also in 1917 when they were enforceable under the Defence of the Realm regulations—voluntary in character. Yet this was one of the points upon which pioneers of the movement had been practically unanimous, and even the Bill of 1847 had contained provisions for inflicting maximum fines of £1 for refusal and of £5 for making false statements. Corresponding penalties had also been included in the second Bill—that of 1856. The accuracy of the returns was unaffected by their voluntary nature, however, and that for two reasons. In the first place only some 2 per cent. of occupiers failed to supply answers, which, from a statistical standpoint, was quite an immaterial proportion; and, secondly, the enumerators had access to local rate-books, and, with the information contained therein as to acreage, aided by enquiries on the spot, and the use of their own eyes, were soon placed in a position themselves to fill up the *lacunae*.

It is tempting to compare the earlier returns secured by the Board with the results of the experiments referred to previously in this Chapter, but prudence forbids it. In any case comparison could only be effected in the case of certain Counties, and, even there, the necessary bases are lacking. One can at best generalise and say that all estimates and trial enumerations, from that of Gregory King down to the experiment carried out in the eleven Counties, bear evidence of a considerable degree of probability; but that it is impossible to assign exact limits thereto or to say that the errors are within a certain percentage. It is worthy of note that, during the first few years of their existence, the official returns frequently called for answers to economic questions—questions which have since been tacitly omitted or left for special occasions or to individual experts. Such matters as the types and amount of machinery used on the land, the prevalence of silos and the amount of drainage work undertaken furnish cases in point.

The accuracy of the figures for acreage and numbers contained in the Tables is unquestionable; they probably represent the most complete and reliable agricultural statistics in the world, with the possible exception of those relating to India, where an immense number of skilled British and native officials is concerned in the compilation and where taxation is based upon the resultant statements regarding outturn.

Part I now contains the data relevant to rates of yield, which, from their inception in 1884, were until recently included in the second publication. For almost fifty years the official estimates of yields and of total outturn, of crop conditions and of the duration of harvest have thus been available. They stand upon a different footing from the statements covering acreages and numbers of personnel and of livestock, for the individual occupier is not concerned or consulted in their preparation. This work devolves entirely on the Crop Reporters, who furnish estimates of the yields per acre in each of the thirteen thousand parishes of England and Wales—each Reporter being responsible for a really large territory, amounting to an average of 80,000 acres of farmed land, embracing over 1200 holdings scattered in 40 parishes. These estimates are based on their own observations and upon local enquiry before and after harvest, checked by actual test weighings during threshing. They are applied to the parish areas and then added together and weighted to give results for the Counties and the country in general. Thus the results are representative, not of the arithmetical average of the varying rates of yield occurring from Yarmouth to Barmouth and from Teignmouth to Tynemouth, but, in theory, give expression to the relative importance of all the productive units concerned. This weighting can, in practice, be proved to affect little the results for England as a whole, especially in recent years, but it is, of course, an essential process in the construction of any figure expressive of results in the United Kingdom or other composite area. Admittedly, these figures are nothing more than estimates, but the only possible alternative would be to ask farmers to supply their own figures of yield. All experts, however, are agreed that the result would not be so satisfactory as that attained by the present method, for there is a world-wide tendency—probably psychological—on the part of all those concerned with the raising of crops to underestimate their yield and to exaggerate the effects of unfavourable weather conditions, whilst ignoring all countervailing influences. Official estimators and Reporters are not immune from this tendency, which, in the case of private individuals, is doubtless also partly attributable to a desire to withhold information from landlords and creditors, but it is certainly a factor to be reckoned with, and one that would make its presence felt in any returns furnished exclusively by those interested in crop raising. In addition, many occupiers would not be so competent as the Reporters to estimate the yields, and there would also be a risk of undue delay accruing in the work if it were left to numerous individuals.

Part II of *Agricultural Statistics* contains information relating mainly to price movements, and, to the economist as opposed to the statistician, is the more interesting of the two publications, as it provides the only authoritative annual summary of market prices for all forms of farm produce, from wheat to poultry, and also for farm requisites, from sulphate of ammonia to maize. It embraces Tables of foreign statistics, gives the quantities of agricultural products imported from abroad, broadcasts the *Gazette* average for British cereals, and issues agricultural index-numbers. These latter, when representing the price of a single article over a series of years, are of course free from misunderstanding; if wheat was selling at 32*s*. per quarter in 1913, 96*s*. in 1920 and 64*s*. in 1921, then, taking 1913 as the basic year, it is perfectly legitimate to state that the cost in 1920 was represented by 300 (or an increase of 200 per cent.) and that of 1921 by 200 (or an increase over 1913 of 100 per cent.), and so on for all the commodities that the farmer sells. Difficulties, however, commence when a composite figure is evolved, which attempts to show the fluctuations in the cost of all articles sold. The cost of living index-number of the Ministry of Labour has called forth certain criticism, partly no doubt owing to ignorance of its nature; and this corresponding number in the case of agriculture is apt to be similarly misjudged if pains are not taken to apprehend its limitations. It is, of course, weighted on the basis of the relative value of each of the most important articles marketed by farmers, the "weights" assigned to each article being proportionate to the estimated total value of all such sold (wholesale) from the farms of the country. There are thus shown the annual variations in the sales on an imaginary, or "average", farm—one that produces all the articles taken into consideration and markets them, moreover, in proportions corresponding exactly with the total sales off all the farms in the country.

The Ministry does not attempt to issue a composite index-number for articles purchased by the farmer, but is content with compiling separate figures for wages, feeding-stuffs and fertilisers, all of which must be accepted merely as indications of the fluctuations recorded by individual items in the farmer's outgoings.

Mention should be made of the prefaces to the two annual Parts, as they are the work of experts, and, if they were better known to the agriculturist, would be of considerable use to him, since they take longer, and generally more restrained, views of the situation than he is accustomed to meet with in unofficial publications.

Other official statistical reports comprise a weekly review of current prices at home, entitled *The Agricultural Market Report*, which it was intended should be found in every farmer's house, and a *Monthly Report* on agricultural conditions. In addition to the above routine undertakings, the Ministry occasionally conducts special statistical enquiries; among post-war examples of which are to be found censuses of allotments and of pedigree livestock—both matters of interest to different classes of persons, and both opening up a fresh field, for the vast majority of allotments, being less than an acre in extent, fail to appear in the June 4th returns, which also ignore the distinction between pedigree and non-pedigree stock. Separate enquiries have also been conducted into the numbers of livestock found upon farms during the winter, e.g. of cattle, sheep and pigs in the month of January. The above exhausts the list of enquiries for the conduct of which the Ministry of Agriculture itself accepts responsibility, but one other closely concerns agriculture—that is the Census of Production, which it was intended to hold every five years as an enquiry into the output of certain important industries in Great Britain, of which agriculture was one. Initiated by the Board of Trade and carried out by the Department of Agriculture on two occasions (in 1908 and 1924), it embraced many features which are not within the normal purview of the Ministry, such as the value of the produce of certain branches of agriculture, the extent of the area under glass, an analysis of the labour employed, the amount of machinery used and (as previously stated) statistics of the woodlands of the country. Upon a quinquennial basis such a census has obvious possibilities. It is only fair to point out that the cost to the country of all the annual returns collected by the Ministry itself is very reasonable, as it amounts to barely eighteenpence per holding for the enumerators' salaries and expenses plus certain headquarters and overhead charges.

The official annual statistics of this country have now been reviewed, and it is a suitable occasion upon which to enquire if they are susceptible of improvement in any direction. Of course, finality is never reached, and it is easy to compile a list of *desiderata* —it would be advantageous to know annually, for example, the real value of everything sold and the quantities also, the rent paid for various types of land and the use made of machinery, glass, silos and other scientific aids to farming. But funds will not permit of such extensions. The reformer is, therefore, reduced to suggesting possible slight improvements in the present series of Tables. For instance, there is considerable ambiguity in the classification of permanent and temporary grass, as certain Counties have, by custom, different age-limits at which grass becomes permanent; thus, temporary grass by the ten thousand acres in the Western Counties would be deemed permanent in East Anglia. There is apparently an opening here for more exact statistical definition, but, if a precise age-limit were fixed at which temporary grass became permanent, there would always be the possibility that new permanent grass would be designated temporary until it reached that critical age. This affords an example of the need for proceeding warily in such matters. Again, the area under "mountain and heath-land used for grazing purposes" is a suspect figure, partly because, on the same holding, it varies year by year due to weather conditions, and partly because complications are sometimes introduced by different occupiers having rights of grazing over the same land. Here a suggested remedy might take the form of the separation, for statistical purposes, of this type of land from individual holdings, and its relegation to a category by itself, as is already the case with commonable land. During the "Ploughing Up" movement in 1918 it was apparent from the schedules that much permanent grass had been transferred to the "rough grazing" section by farmers who desired to evade the plough and thought that the latter title sounded less attractive to prospective breakers up on behalf of the Government. There is, too, a possible source of error in the Tables of "holdings owned or mainly owned" by their occupiers, as it requires great alertness on the part of the enumerator to satisfy himself that all lettings and sales are immediately evidenced in the annual returns. Instances have occurred in which fields, reverting to their owner on the expiration of tenancies, have either fallen between the two stools and missed enumeration, or else have still been accounted for by their previous occupiers. Statistics relating to the supply of home-produced meat are susceptible of improvement, but the practical difficulties in connection with estimating the numbers of births and deaths and in ascertaining the weight of carcases are great. The output of fruit and vegetable areas is, again, far from easy to assess, and, in consequence, is an uncertain element. Lastly, it is at least open to suggestion that the official estimates of actual crop yields and of forecasts of prospective yields tend to undue conservatism, but this matter is covered at some length in a later section.

Amongst other methods of investigating the productivity and condition of British agriculture must be mentioned the semi-official series of Cost of Production studies that have been undertaken during the past ten years by certain Universities and Research centres. By this means it has been possible to ascertain figures indicative of both the individual and average per acre and per hundredweight cost of raising different products, but it has necessitated, on the one hand, very frequent visits being paid to the farms concerned over periods of time extending into several years, and, on the other, it has called for the completion in much detail by the farmers themselves of weekly returns. Further, agreement had to be reached among the various workers in this field regarding accountancy and statistical problems which were not always amenable to hard and fast rules. The results achieved, therefore, rested upon certain conventions which were not necessarily acceptable to the traditionally minded cultivators. For example, it has been the general practice when working upon individual crops (and, preferably, upon individual fields) to charge home produce used upon the farm at its cost of production and not at current market rates; to value stock in hand at cost; to make use of a flat rate throughout the year for the cost of horse-labour; to differentiate between the occupant's own capital and any borrowed for farming purposes; to adopt certain proportions for the value throughout the rotation of both artificial and of farmyard manures; to reserve for separate treatment interest upon capital and remuneration of the farmer *qua* manager or manual worker; to distribute overhead charges, in some instances against labour accounts, in others at a flat rate per acre. It will be appreciated that when these and numerous other adjustments have been effected, the results may not always be freely recognised as valid by all types of agriculturist, e.g. to the working Small Holder and the large-scale "gentleman-farmer", but, nevertheless, they have been a source of great interest, not only to those most directly concerned, but also to Government Departments and representative bodies of farmers. In particular, material collected in the Eastern Counties relating to sugar-beet has formed the basis of agreements reached between producers and factories; so, too, was there an equal welcome for the cost of production figures for wheat and milk as well as for the data relating to fruit and poultry undertakings. Anyone interested in the subject will find ample material in, e.g., the numerous *Reports* of the Farm Economics Branch of the Cambridge Department of Agriculture or those emanating from Leeds, Wye or Reading. Abroad, notable work has been done on these lines—in Switzerland, by Dr Ernest Laur and, in Denmark, by Professor O. H. Larsen.

Latterly, the more direct American Survey method has tended to supersede that of Costings. Here, by means of a single visit paid to each farm, it has been demonstrated that sufficient accurate information can be derived to prepare a very complete economic, statistical and financial picture, which, when aggregated with hundreds of others, will enable reliable deductions to be drawn for wide areas, for different types of holding or for varying lengths of time. Thus, for three years in succession upwards of one thousand farms will, in the case of the Cambridge Department, have provided material for a review that embraces practically every factor relevant to the economic situation of such a very representative sample. The results of two of these—the largest hitherto undertaken in this country—have, under the title of *An Economic Survey of the Eastern Counties of England*, already been published by the Department. One great advantage attaching to this method is the saving of time, of expenditure and of labour both on the part of the enquirer and of the farmer; in passing, it may be observed that the alternative Costing plan demonstrated that, once a reasonable degree of stability in regard to prices and wages has been attained, costs tend to vary little from year to year. If for no other reason, therefore, the Survey procedure is likely to receive further support in the future, for it gives results that are available quickly enough to secure approval from the countryman and sufficiently up-to-date to appeal to the legislator.

There is not space here to discuss seriatim the various systems employed abroad for collecting returns relating to agriculture, but, as a general rule, it may be stated that the more civilised the country and the more densely populated it is, the more complete will be found to be its economic statistics. Most European countries had such services in operation by the mid 'sixties of the last century, and, by the beginning of the twentieth century, there was scarcely a nation in either hemisphere which did not make some attempt to collect annual information relating to its agricultural output.

In the United States, where more than 300,000 persons are concerned in the work of collection upon upwards of six million farms, the full census of agriculture is held only every tenth year, information relating to the intervening periods being based upon estimates. There, too, an interesting development is seen when the estimated areas under certain crops are checked by means of journeys effected by road or rail in order to count the telegraph poles or other fixed indications of distances traversed. The results are claimed to form the most complete and accurate series of statistics relating to the industry obtained in any country; decennially, this claim may perhaps be substantiated, but the necessity to rely upon subsequent estimates, annually declining in validity, is at best counterbalanced by the extraordinarily elaborate forecasts that are so frequently issued in respect of crop conditions and of probable yields. In Canada also, as well as in most of the new countries in both hemispheres, this latter aspect of the subject has received more attention than has been the case in the Old World.

In the Far East, Japan presents a suitable example of the adoption of modern methods in circumstances that are not always easy. Figures relating to the industry were first collected in 1896, when the combined Department of Agriculture, Industry and Commerce was responsible for their compilation. In 1925, the newly formed Ministry of Agriculture and Forestry took over this work, the machinery and personnel of which was still retained in the hands of the local authorities. This handicap was, however, removed as from 1927, and subsequently a national fund of 370,000 yen (£37,000 at parity) was made available for these statistical investigations. In addition to a complete headquarters personnel, each one of the Prefectures, to the number of 47, has a staff of its own employed upon this work. Crop Reporters—in comparison with this country, more densely employed—are stationed in each administrative division, and, every year, representative villagers tender their reports to the Ministry. So far as facts dealing with areas, acreage under crops and the number of livestock are concerned, it would seem that the system is thoroughly up-to-date and efficient. Certain problems peculiar to such countries have, however, been encountered and satisfactorily dealt with—e.g. a considerable area of arable land comes under more than one cropping in each season, and the Japanese claim that their statistical service meets with unique difficulties by reason of the widespread damage caused by floods and by landslides. Again, the statisticians of the Ministry state that they find it extremely difficult to comply with certain of the conventions of the International Agricultural Institute relating to the distribution of the cultivated area among the principal crops, and they cannot always agree with the definition of "crops harvested".

In a minor direction their Crop Reporters are faced with additional difficulties in the shape of the number of crops that do not reach maturity in a year, e.g. Water-lilies (used for food), *Edgeworthia papyrifera*, Waxberries and Osiers. It is pointed out that, in the first and second years of their growth, these plants cannot be entered as occupying "areas sown from which no crop was harvested owing to crop failure or other destructive causes", nor as occupying "fallow land". For such purposes as the World Agricultural Census they were, therefore, inserted in a special column added to the normal form. Mixed crops in Japan, too, represent a statistical difficulty, as a very common practice is to grow soya-beans and barley on interspaced ridges, where the technical treatment meted out is thus described in the *Report* of the Nineteenth Session de L'Institut International de Statistique (Tokio meeting, 1930):

On one acre planted with companion crops, when that with *A* crop is not affected by *B* crop at all, it will be returned as one acre for *A* crop and also one acre for *B* crop. In this case, while the area of arable land is one acre, the planted area for *A* and *B* is returned as a total of two acres. On the contrary, if the area under *A* crop is decreased 20 per cent. by *B* crop, and the area under *B* is decreased 30 per cent. by *A*, the actual returns will show $\frac{8}{10}$ acre for the area under *A* and $\frac{7}{10}$ acre for that under *B*. In this case, while the area of arable land remains one acre, the area under *A* and *B* combined is returned as $1\frac{1}{2}$ acres. Here, it is irrational to return $\frac{1}{2}$ acre for *A* and *B* respectively, because in Japan, where barley and soya-beans are companion crops, the planted area of each is not so much affected by the other, but usually their yields scarcely change, or rather, show output as good as in the case of single crop. This being the case, it is preferable to show in brackets the duplicated area, rather than to treat the question in the manner indicated in the standard form.

All results are achieved by personal inspection of the land on the part of the local officials, augmented by direct questioning of the cultivators. The universal fear that such enquiries may result in increased taxation is familiar to the Japanese authorities, but it is held that the spread of education is removing this obstacle.

A complete Land-register was made between the years 1875 and 1879, and this has been subsequently kept up-to-date with tolerable exactness; it would appear that details in regard to ownership are more precise than those relating to the actual use of the land itself. This tendency would, by European experience, be not unexpected. Mainly as a result of this, a special investigation, relating to the area and utilisation of arable land only, has been conducted since 1903, but, as the Ministry of Agriculture was not satisfied with the returns concerned in their original form, a special effort was made in 1929, for which purpose 800 staffs were collected together in central and local districts, and no less than 180,000 enumerators, concentrated in 12,000 local areas, were engaged, with results that were highly successful, the State being placed in possession of accurate information of a character not frequently attained even in Europe. So far as statistics relating to forestry are concerned, decentralisation is also adopted, and local investigators supply the Forestry Bureau with material, dealing not only with the areas of various types of woods and forests, but also with the economic value of forest products. Detailed investigations are carried out every three years when, in effect, cadastral data are also obtained.

There is one outstanding organisation, which must be briefly described, and that is the International Institute of Agriculture—a body on a small scale typical of the League of Nations. Founded in 1905 by the King of Italy, at the suggestion of an American (Mr Lubin), its headquarters are at Rome and its members are representative of upwards of sixty countries. It is, as its name implies, an international body, supported by funds voted by its constituent members, and inaugurated by a personal grant from the King of Italy. Its objects are to collect statistics and economic information relating to agriculture in its widest sense, to disseminate the knowledge thus acquired, and to emphasise by every means in its power the international character of modern farming and of food supply. Its personnel is also international and its threefold publications relating to statistics, economics and the scientific side of agriculture are issued in English, French, Spanish and Italian. Although a permanent committee is in constant session, meetings of representatives from all contributing countries are held at intervals.

In the year 1930–1, it conducted a World Agricultural Census, when an endeavour was made to secure statistics relating to the farming conditions of every country. Schedules were prepared in collaboration with each of the national Departments of Agriculture and were distributed by the hundred million to the world's cultivators. Naturally, the enquiry concentrated upon an attempt to secure simple information covering such straightforward matters as the acreage under crops, the numbers of livestock and of persons engaged in the industry and of its gross outturn. An American organiser, Mr L. M. Easterbrook, paid advance visits to all the principal countries in order to prepare the ground, while the actual enquiry extended over a calendar year, since seasonal conditions in the Northern and Southern hemispheres precluded a simultaneous investigation. It is impossible, as yet, to judge of the results achieved, but the immensity of the task must be stressed and the inherent difficulties of defining universally such expressions as "agriculture", "farmers" and "crops" emphasised. Indeed, certain preliminary meetings of experts, held in Rome, failed to do more than discuss the bare possibility of estimating, e.g., the world's production of meat, of wool and of fruit; these bodies failed to discover any satisfactory method of comparing the level of rural wages in different countries and hesitated to adopt a basic index-number applicable to agricultural products; they discussed sympathetically the feasibility of extending Cost of Production studies, but were appalled by their complicated technique. Yet the World Economic Conference, sitting at Geneva, held that it was "no less necessary to organise, nationally and internationally, the speedy transmission to agriculturists of information on harvests, stocks, consumption and the movements of different commodities, these being important factors in the formation of prices". That Conference further urged that "the monthly publication of indices of comparative prices of agricultural products and industrial products would prove of great value, as would indices of the principal elements of the cost of production of agricultural commodities"!

If the Institute at Rome has not yet obtained the authoritative position that it is clearly entitled to, yet the results of its work are already apparent. In particular the researches it has undertaken, and the mass of information it has published, relating to such divergent questions as co-operation, the provision of credit, the supplies of wheat and of other cereals, the production of different types of farm, and the economics of forestry are invaluable to the student who wishes to secure unbiased evidence from world-wide sources. If the producer, the importer and the merchant have not benefited by its work to the extent that its founders anticipated, the blame must not be attached to it, but rather to international jealousies and rivalry. It is, for example, asking much from a country with a large production of a certain commodity to lay bare to all the world (and to its immediate rivals) the latest estimates of its outturn. Thus, hesitation has sometimes been apparent on the part of members of the Institute to part with their newly collected statistics with the knowledge that the figures would be broadcast throughout the world. For this reason the Institute is often unable to publish comprehensive forecasts relative to one hemisphere, or even to all European countries, until some time after the individual States concerned have themselves digested and issued separate reports. There is another drawback from which the Institute has, upon occasion, suffered in the past, and that is the form in which its statistical, as opposed to its economic, information was published, for frequently bare columns of figures of acreage or yield of crops were issued, which were meaningless to any but experts. Latterly, however, steps have been taken to improve this state of affairs and now, side by side with such Tables, explanations of them are freely appended. The World War seriously interfered with work at Rome, and from 1914 until 1919 the continuity of its records was broken. Financial difficulties had also to be reckoned with, for, in common with other societies, a certain number of members are liable to be in arrears with their subscriptions, and, with a membership ranging from Paraguay, Ethiopia and Turkey to China and Austria, bad debts were certain to be encountered after such an upheaval. The nucleus of an ideal and universal system of economic statistics is certainly present at Rome, as is that of a greater international fraternity at Geneva, and the passage of time and a peaceful world may achieve much within the next decade or two; in the meantime the publications and researches of the Institute deserve a wider recognition.

All the sources of agricultural economic knowledge have been passed in review. How should that material be handled, and to what uses can it legitimately be put? Nowadays statistics of any description are looked upon by the bulk of mankind as either the useless plaything of a small section of the community or else as a necessary evil to be mishandled and misapplied by all and sundry. To the former category no doubt belonged the British Chancellor of the Exchequer who, on being presented with a table of figures worked out to decimal places, enquired what "the d——d dots" were for. The second category contains the type of person who whenever he discovers a corresponding phenomenon in two sets of figures at once argues on the lines *post hoc, ergo propter hoc.* This doctrine is most evidenced in the columns of the daily press, where, for example, a rising death-rate is convincingly "proved" to be due solely to deficient ground temperature, lack of sunshine, excess of house-flies or numerous other causes. Its ultimate limit was reached when a close connection could be shown to exist between the prevalence of sun spots and victory by one University in the boat race. All economic knowledge, however, depends on the securing of certain statistical information, together with its careful handling, and, if any judgment on the past state of agriculture is to be formed or deductions made from the present, it is absolutely essential that such data should be available.

All statistics are full of pitfalls for the inexperienced and the hasty, agricultural statistics being, if anything, more prone to mislead than those relating to other occupations. For, at first glance, nothing appears more simple than to obtain the numbers of farms and their "average" size in two areas and to compare these figures, or to enumerate the livestock in the United Kingdom and, say, France and then to draw conclusions as to the "density" found in each country. An actual example of the need for circumspection in this respect can be given. Someone, hearing that a friend was working in the statistical branch of the Ministry of Agriculture, said to him, "Then you can of course give me such information as the number of celery plants in Cambridgeshire?" This is seemingly a perfectly simple question, always provided that the numbers of individual plants were collected—which of course they are not—but in reality to answer this query it would be necessary to demand three exact definitions, viz. (*a*) At what period of age, or on attaining what dimensions or weight, does a celery seedling become a plant? (*b*) what do you mean by "Cambridgeshire"—the whole geographical County, which includes the Isle of Ely, and, therefore, thousands of acres of the most prolific market-garden soil, or merely the administrative County, containing little soil suitable for vegetable propagation? (*c*) what does "in" mean—does it include only plants still in the soil (and in how small units of land?) or all celery plants raised, or in transit, at a certain point of time? This story exemplifies the extreme need for a clear definition, even at the expense of verbosity; other *desiderata* in a series are continuity (for numbers collected on isolated occasions are valueless), and what can only be described as comparability. Comparability should automatically follow on the first-mentioned point—definition—but, unfortunately, when dealing with conditions in foreign countries it does not invariably do so; hence the need for close enquiry into the nature and similarity of the figures one seeks to place side by side.

There are certain specific warnings, which should be heeded by all who seek to use the published statistics relating to British and foreign agriculture. Beware of that deceptive thing the "average" holding, and its comparative size in different countries. It is simply an arithmetical conception and may not be represented by a single example in point of fact. Take the case of England and Wales; divide the 25,000,000 acres under crops and grass by the number of holdings, viz., 395,000, and the result gives as nearly as possible 64 acres. Does this mean that more holdings of 64 acres are found here than of any other size? Not at all; for if the size-groups were closely analysed by sub-division it would be discovered that more holdings existed in the region of two acres in extent than of any other size—in other words the "mode"—perhaps, better termed the "most common type"—is thus represented. The "median", so far as the size-groups permit of dissection, would appear to lie in the neighbourhood of 28 acres. Students of statistics will of course appreciate that here one is dealing with a curve, at one extremity arbitrarily cut short by the absence of holdings below an acre in extent and at the other theoretically capable of infinite extension.

It is necessary when comparing English farms with foreign to assure oneself that the latter do not include what would be here classified as allotments or "gardens". Again, one may be comparing "holdings" in the one country with "farmers" in the other, and "Small Holdings" of three hundred acres with those of three acres. Livestock statistics contain serious traps, even when one is satisfied that the dates of the enquiries concerned are approximately similar; e.g. the British returns cover only horses "on agricultural holdings", not those employed in urban districts, whilst foreign statistics generally include the latter. Tables are published showing the "holdings owned or mainly owned" in this country; here it should be recognised that ownership, in the generally accepted sense of the word, is not necessarily implied, for a holding of five acres, of which three are owned and two held on a lease, does not represent "peasant proprietorship" on a basis comparable with that found, say, in France. The conditions under which the agricultural employee works have been discussed in previous Chapters, but it must be reiterated that cash wages in no country afford a criterion as to the emoluments received by workers on the land, and no international or even internal definition of the term "casual labourer" has been evolved. Forestry abroad employs many agricultural labourers in part-time occupation. What are "rough grazings" in England may rank as farm-land in one country abroad and be excluded altogether from the statistical abstracts of another. A million acres of wheat in England represents a totally different potential supply of breadstuffs from the produce of a corresponding area in Russia or even in France. In many countries the breadth of land seeded bears no necessarily close relationship to the area that may be harvested. In effect, agricultural statistics should be handled with extreme care. They can "prove" nothing, but, used with circumspection, may render valuable service by suggesting lines of enquiry to the State and by affording data for the farmer and the trader upon which to base their future actions.

Chapter XXI

CROP ESTIMATING AND FORECASTING

The work of Lawes and Gilbert; early estimates of wheat yields; crop yields in Scotland and in Ireland; the range in deviations from the average at home and abroad; yields in different areas; *The Times* series of estimates compared with official figures; effects of "weighting"; Japanese methods of crop estimating.

The problem of crop forecasting; meteorological and other influences; English methods; forecasts compared with final estimates; the tendency to under-state probable yields; analysis of a twenty-seven years' series of forecasts.

Crop Estimating

Historically, apart from certain well-known, and isolated, instances of estimates made by private individuals (e.g. those of Caird in the early 'fifties of the last century), no *series* of figures purporting to represent British crop yields was available prior to 1868. In that year Sir J. B. Lawes and Sir J. H. Gilbert together issued the first of a sequence of three enquiries, entitled "Home Produce, Imports and Consumption of Wheat" (*Journal of the Royal Agricultural Society of England*, vol. VI, pt. 2, p. 359, and, again, in 1880 and in 1887; see also the *Journal of the Royal Statistical Society*). Dissatisfied with the statements appearing in some of "our best-conducted agricultural papers", which were generally premature, and invariably referred to yields in such vague terms as "average", "over average", or "under average", they broke new ground by proceeding upon more exact lines. Their method was to correlate data relating to actual wheat yields from certain of the already famous Rothamsted plots with those obtained in other parts of the country; the figures of gross yield thus secured were checked by reference to the quantities of grain imported and fortified by independent estimates of consumption. It is unnecessary here to describe in detail the elaborate precautions taken to satisfy requirements in regard to such factors as acreage, soil conditions, the natural weight of the grain, and the number of types of plots judged fit for inclusion; it will suffice to say that the figures prepared thus by Lawes and Gilbert have universally been accepted as authoritative. Their investigations were, of course, confined to the one cereal, commenced in the year 1852, and were carried two years past the time (1884) when official records started; further, they embraced the component parts of the United Kingdom.

Briefly, the story of these thirty-three years is revealed as follows. The average yield for the United Kingdom worked out at 27 bushels per acre, ranging from 15½ bushels in the disastrous year 1879, up to the exceptionally high level of 38¾ bushels in 1863. The authors pointed out that this figure of 27 bushels was unduly low, being occasioned by the run of bad seasons in the second half of the series, represented by Brückner's "cold and wet" period of 1871–85. They gave it as their considered opinion that, in 1887, the normal average was 28¼ bushels. In the light of what is to follow, separate figures relating to each part of the country possess great value, and we find that when the United Kingdom average was 28¼ (1852–67), the Scotch figure was 27¾, the Irish 23⅞, and that of England and Wales 28¾; this was a time of high farming, and these yields probably represented the maximum achievement possible pending further scientific assistance. Lawes' and Gilbert's estimates afford a reliable starting-point for an uninterrupted survey of eighty years of wheat production—a period of time unapproached in any other country. Attention must be drawn in passing to two features observable in the early years: first, the relative position occupied by each separate part of the United Kingdom, and, secondly, the extent of the secular deviations from the normal, which the diagram three pages hence well illustrates.

What do the official statistics suggest have, during their lifetime, been the variations in the rates of yield of the more important crops? As the two diagrams on p. 453 show, wheat improved in the United Kingdom from 29 bushels in the decade 1885–94 to just over 32 bushels at the outbreak of war, barley from 33·3 bushels to 34·3 bushels, and oats from 39 bushels to 42 bushels. The second decade (1895–1904) was climatically favourable, and the third was not abnormal. The next ten years witnessed a decline of about ¾ of a bushel in wheat, of 2¼ bushels in barley and of 1½ in oats, in part no doubt attributable to war conditions (for the local effects of the ploughing-up campaign upon productivity see the next Chapter). If the constituent parts of the whole country are separately analysed, the discovery is made that England, except in the case of wheat and beans, played little part in the upward movement, for the credit must, in the main, go to Scotland and to Ireland, where, also, the conditions which supervened after 1914 failed seriously to affect the situation.

The following are comparative figures for each of the seven crops in the four decades available.

		Wheat	Barley	Oats	Beans	Potatoes	Turnips	Man-golds
England:	(a)	29·3	33·1	40·6	25·8	5·9	12·4	17·5
	(b)	30·5	32·6	40·7	27·4	5·8	11·9	18·4
	(c)	32·1	33·3	40·8	30·3	6·2	13·0	19·5
	(d)	31·1	30·6	39·2	26·9	6·2	12·5	19·1
Wales:	(a)	23·3	28·0	32·6	26·7	5·6	14·1	16·3
	(b)	25·0	30·2	33·2	24·7	5·4	14·8	16·2
	(c)	27·6	31·1	35·3	27·3	5·3	15·2	18·0
	(d)	27·9	28·5	32·6	27·6	5·3	13·7	17·1
Scotland:	(a)	35·3	35·3	35·6	30·5	5·6	14·9	16·2
	(b)	37·7	35·8	36·4	33·1	5·9	15·1	17·2
	(c)	40·6	36·1	38·0	36·7	6·5	16·5	18·9
	(d)	38·6	35·1	39·3	35·4	6·5	16·7	18·5
Ireland:	(a)	29·1	36·4	41·0	34·3	3·5	13·1	14·0
	(b)	33·0	39·9	44·7	37·7	4·1	15·2	16·5
	(c)	36·9	43·0	49·5	45·3	5·2	17·2	19·4
	(d)	35·2	38·8	45·7	—	4·9	15·7	18·0

(a) 1885–94, (b) 1895–1904, (c) 1905–14, (d) 1915–24.

If we accept as accurate the statements supplied by the Scottish and Irish Departments, the question at once arises as to why English yields, which in the case of most crops must, from their preponderating acreage, have swayed the gross returns, retarded the United Kingdom figures. Except in the case of Wales, these separate countries did not occupy a low position in the first period (whatever may have been the circumstances when Lawes and Gilbert carried out their investigation twenty years earlier), so it cannot be maintained that they had leeway to overtake. The yield of three out of four cereals and of roots was, and still is, higher in Scotland than in England; the same is true to a more marked degree of Ireland, save in the case of potatoes. In England the area under wheat declined by some 50 per cent. during the first two periods, that of barley by about 20 per cent., while oats were a stationary crop; elsewhere movements were unimportant, as the principal losses had occurred, e.g., in Irish wheat-land, before 1885. Now, as far back as 1890 the preface to *Part II of Agricultural Statistics* contained the following prophecy: "It may be indicated that there is good reason to believe that, especially in districts where a continual shrinkage of the area devoted to one crop takes place, as has happened in the case of wheat-growing, the reduction of the crop upon inferior, and its limitation to the more productive classes of soil, must assuredly tend to raise the standard of normal yield per acre". If we endorse this premise, then it is obvious that anticipations were not borne out, for the only real increase, neglecting recovery from climatic influences, took place after stabilisation of the English wheat area had been achieved. In justice to the reputation of rural economists, however, it should be pointed out that, in the case of this particular cereal, a contraction of area almost invariably implies also the loss of heavy clay soils, which, *ceteris paribus*, are productive of the weightiest crops. On balance, these two opposing factors were probably operative thus: over England as a whole the effect of shrinkage was beneficial to yield, but in the case of individual Counties—e.g. Essex and the East Midlands, where heavy land predominates—the opposite held true, and local yields were reduced; in other words, the total light land area concerned exceeded that of the corresponding heavy soils.

Reverting to Scotland and Ireland, it must be observed that economic conditions were not dissimilar from those pertaining in England; the weather was, as always, over a series of years, normally effective, and yet the stubborn ten-year averages rose markedly and uniformly from already high levels. It will perhaps be suggested that in Scotland advanced methods of farming (whether represented by better application of labour or of capital) were being progressively adopted, but north of the Border this was already the case by the commencement of the basic period, and in the mid 'eighties Irish farmers were famous for their barley and oats, complete produce statistics of which had annually been collected from as far back as the year 1847 on a scale unapproached elsewhere in the British Isles. In effect, the Scotch and Irish Departments of Agriculture had recognised an increase of some 25 per cent. on cereal yields in excess of the figures given by Lawes and Gilbert a generation earlier. In justification of these divergences, it has been claimed that wheat and barley have, during the last forty years, been grown "only on select and particularly suitable districts in Scotland and Ireland". Taking everything into consideration, this seems an inadequate explanation, and we are forced to enquire if the figures of English yields may not themselves be retrograde. Additional force is lent to this suggestion if the records of individual

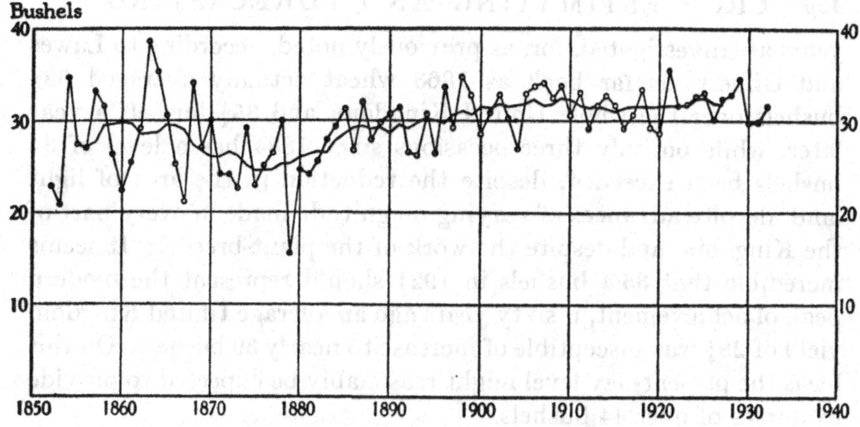

Ten year (moving) average and actual yields of wheat in the United Kingdom, 1852–1932
(Based upon the estimates of Lawes and Gilbert from 1852 to 1884, and thenceforward upon official statistics)

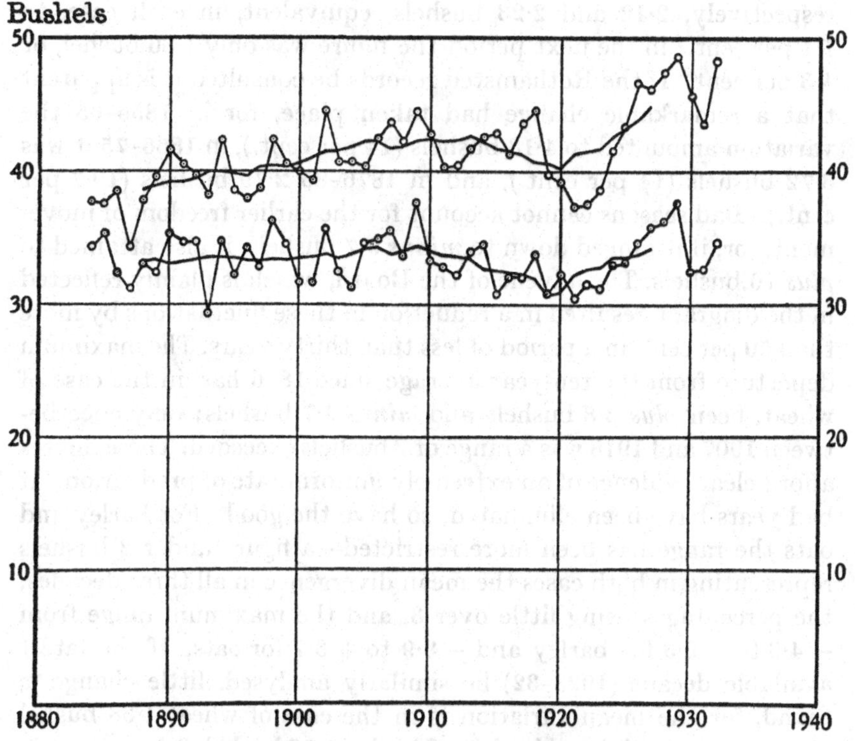

Ten year (moving) average and actual yields of oats (above) and of barley (below) in the United Kingdom, 1884–1932

years are investigated, for, as previously noted, according to Lawes and Gilbert, as far back as 1863 wheat actually averaged 38¾ bushels over the whole United Kingdom, and 35¼ bushels a year later, while on only three occasions since 1884 has a level of 34 bushels been exceeded, despite the reduction in the area of light land, despite advances of varying magnitude made in every part of the Kingdom, and despite the work of the plant-breeder. It seems incredible that 35·4 bushels in 1921 should represent the modern peak of achievement, if sixty years ago an average United Kingdom yield of 28¼ was susceptible of increase to nearly 39 bushels. On this basis the present-day level might reasonably be expected to provide examples of over 44 bushels.

In so far as actual fluctuations are concerned, the diagram may again be referred to, for it well illustrates this feature. In the two decades 1886–95 and 1896–1905, the mean deviations from the moving average in annual United Kingdom wheat yields were, respectively, 2·12 and 2·23 bushels, equivalent, in each case, to 7·1 per cent.; in the next period the figure was only 1·36 bushel, or 4·3 per cent. If the Rothamsted records be consulted it is apparent that a remarkable change had taken place, for in 1856–65 the variation amounted to 4·18 bushels (14 per cent.), in 1866–75 it was 3·72 bushels (14 per cent.), and in 1876–85 2·79 bushels (10·7 per cent.). Bad seasons cannot account for the earlier freedom of movement, for, if it ranged down to *minus* 9·7 bushels, it also attained to *plus* 10 bushels. The advent of the Board, which is plainly reflected in the diagram, resulted in a reduction in these fluctuations by more than 50 per cent. in a period of less than thirty years. The maximum departure from the ten-year average since 1886 has, in the case of wheat, been *plus* 3·8 bushels and *minus* 4·7 bushels; only once between 1907 and 1918 was a range of 2 bushels exceeded. These figures afford clear evidence of an extremely uniform rate of production. If bad years have been eliminated, so have the good. For barley and oats the range has been more restricted—a figure under 2 bushels representing in both cases the mean divergence in all three decades, the percentages being little over 3, and the maximum range from − 4·3 to + 3·3 for barley and − 3·9 to + 3·7 for oats. If the latest available decade (1923–32) be similarly analysed, little change is found, for the mean variation is in the case of wheat 1·38 bushel (4·3 per cent. again) and in that of barley 1·12 bushel (3·4 per cent.);

oats, at 2·16 bushels, show a slightly increased amplitude of 5·2 per cent.

It is opportune to ask what is the present-day range of deviation from the normal in other countries where production of wheat is on a level similar to that in these Islands. Enquiry on such lines gives the following results, which refer to a series of ten years from 1910 to 1919 inclusive: statistics of barley and oats have also been added, together with comparable figures for each separate part of these Islands.

Country	Wheat		Barley		Oats	
	Mean deviation	Maximum range	Mean deviation	Maximum range	Mean deviation	Maximum range
	(%)	(%)	(%)	(%)	(%)	(%)
Denmark	13·4	+ 21·8 – 29·9	7·3	+ 15·9 – 25·0	8·1	+ 10·4 – 20·7
Germany	10·4	+ 22·3 – 21·8	15·1	+ 24·1 – 28·6	18·2	+ 28·8 – 38·8
Holland	7·3	+ 18·6 – 14·5	9·8	+ 17·0 – 23·3	9·0	+ 14·5 – 23·7
New Zealand	13·0	+ 20·2 – 23·3	13·5	+ 20·0 – 22·7	11·1	+ 12·0 – 19·6
Sweden	10·6	+ 13·9 – 26·7	9·2	+ 20·0 – 19·5	15·3	+ 23·6 – 28·4
Switzerland	11·8	+ 43·6 – 18·8	5·3	+ 11·8 – 13·4	8·0	+ 30·0 – 19·6
United Kingdom	4·5	+ 7·1 – 6·4	3·2	+ 5·5 – 5·8	3·1	+ 5·7 – 5·2
England	4·7	+ 7·7 – 6·9	3·7	+ 5·1 – 7·7	4·2	+ 6·9 – 9·2
Scotland	4·5	+ 7·6 – 9·1	4·5	+ 8·3 – 13·1	3·3	+ 4·6 – 6·2
Ireland	2·4	+ 4·2 – 4·9	3·3	+ 6·4 – 7·6	3·5	+ 4·9 – 7·7

It will be agreed that the first six countries exhibit an elasticity in their rates of yield singularly at variance with those pertaining here, but neither natural conditions nor agricultural practices are widely different, while the figures themselves have been independently arrived at by the Agricultural Departments concerned. Two features must be noticed—in the case of New Zealand variations in wheat yields are admittedly related to the extent of the cropped area (see D. B. Copland, *Wheat Production in New Zealand*, and *New Zealand Official Year Book*, 1925, p. 411), and in Germany, although war privations reduced yields in certain years, such deficits were nevertheless equalled by corresponding excesses. Apart from these particular countries, there appear to have been no special influences at work, and, as an extension of this investigation to earlier periods or its prolongation chronologically invariably leads to the emergence of similar results, it seems legitimate to state that the normal deviation in yields of countries with small, or moderate, areas under wheat, and with a production of from 28 to 40 bushels per acre, is 10 per cent. to 12 per cent., with extremes of *plus* and *minus* 20 per cent. to 25 per cent.

It is now necessary to enquire if Crop Reporters under-valued yields *ab initio*, or whether they failed to record advances subsequently made in English crop husbandry. As a result of close examination of the later work of Lawes and Gilbert, there is considerable evidence for the latter contention. Thus, for 1884 these two writers estimated the United Kingdom yield as 29·4 bushels of wheat, the Board of Agriculture placed it at 29·9; in 1885 the Rothamsted figure was 30¼ bushels and the official estimate 31·24 bushels. These two years alone provide examples of double estimates, and they exhibit no serious divergence, but if there was no marked break at the junction, the previous analysis shows a conservative tendency to have been at once operative. Fresh light can be thrown on this matter from an unexpected quarter, for, from 1885 up to the year 1894, British Crop Reporters had been instructed to relate their annual statements to what was known as the "Estimated Ordinary Average" of their district—this figure having been originally evolved by themselves. From 1895 onwards the "ten-year average" of their own previous figures was substituted, and it is interesting to compare side by side these two standards. Now, the ten-year average was, for every crop except wheat, lower than the estimated figure, the difference in the case of cereals amounting to over a bushel.

	Wheat	Barley	Oats	Beans	Peas	Potatoes	Turnips	Mangolds
"Estimated ordinary average"	28·80	34·02	39·04	30·36	28·46	6·11	15·27	19·81
Ten-year average (1885–94)	29·32	33·02	38·21	26·04	25·20	5·82	13·09	17·45

In the case of individual crops and Counties these differences were often marked; thus, the standard for oats was in Cambridgeshire reduced from 65·11 bushels to 58·30 and proportionately throughout East Anglia. So the Reporters, who had in theory related their estimates to a figure of their own choice, were shown in practice to have remained upon a lower plane, for the weather of the period 1885–94 had been favourable. That the officials were acting entirely independently, and untrammelled by regulations, is shown by the fact that individuals among them recorded advances, but weight of numbers told against these persons, and "errors of judgment" did not "tend to compensate one another". The semi-official explanation of the discrepancies between the estimates of Lawes and Gilbert and the figures recorded by the Board of Agriculture is that the former were "untrustworthy" and cannot, therefore, now be accepted. If investigations are pursued either by means of maps shaded according to the weights of yields secured in each decade, as has been done by the writer (see end of volume) or by other diagrammatic methods, certain features at once obtrude themselves, for individual Counties exhibit wide divergences from the common level of their circumscribing neighbours. Most of these aberrations can be proved to be unrelated to any such causatives as geological formation or soil conditions, and they are particularly marked in certain small Counties where one, or at most two, Crop Reporters have been in charge.

In the shape of records published by *The Times* newspaper since the year 1863 there is available an alternative series of crop estimates; these represent the original Rothamsted figures, which were thus merged into annual statements, and now comprise data relative to harvest conditions in each County of Great Britain at monthly intervals from July to October, terminated by exact estimates of the weight of each crop. They deserve very close attention, for they form a sequence extending over a much longer period than that represented by the life of the official produce statistics, and they are based upon the statements of a body of agriculturists, numerically much stronger than the Crop Reporters, acting in an honorary capacity, and representative solely of landowners and farmers. Moreover, the figures supplied by these persons have been substantiated by actual weighings. As long ago as 1871 reference was made to "these statistics collected from as many as forty or fifty growers in each County, and those scattered through the different Poor Law Unions so as to embrace every district of each County under as many separate estimates". In 1910 no less than 750 persons assisted the enquiry; the normal number would, up to 1919, appear to have been half as large again as that of the Crop Reporters, viz. over 300. *The Times* itself has always maintained that its correspondents' estimates "if anything, err on the side of under, rather than over, estimating, as is shown by their marginal notes", while the correspondents themselves, as "experienced and eminent agriculturists...constantly bear in mind their previous estimates made in most cases over many years".

Of their methods it can be said that they closely resemble those pursued by the Ministry's Crop Reporters, but *The Times* has never anticipated any convergence in the results secured, even going so far as to warn readers in advance that its figures "will not coincide with the official estimates". Such warnings are quite uncalled for, as general unanimity of opinion could never be attained, and would, indeed, be looked at askance by statisticians, by whom either of two alternatives might be anticipated, viz. (*a*) that, despite wide variations in estimates relating to individual years, crops and areas, the rival figures over a large unit of time or space would tend to approximation, or (*b*) that, for reasons previously given, the unofficial Reporters would consistently record yields below those prepared by their opposite numbers. It is, accordingly, very surprising to find an overwhelming majority of the figures applicable to England, Wales and Scotland (*The Times* omits Ireland) in the case of all crops, cereal and root alike, year after year, reported by the newspaper as in excess of the official statements; wheat, in Scotland, providing the only exception to this rule. Confirmation that both authorities scrupulously recognise local conditions is shown by the fact that the yields of certain County areas differ proportionately, as do those relating to the separate crops; again, both agree in gauging the relative fluctuations between one year's outturn and that of the next. It resolves itself into this, that the one consistently remains upon a higher level than the other. Does the Ministry in any given year record the yield of oats in Hertfordshire as 38·18 bushels, then *The Times* gives it as 44·4 bushels; if Huntingdonshire officially produces 4·7 tons of potatoes, then *The Times* figure is 6·5 tons; of mangolds we have to choose, in Cheshire, between 34 tons and 23·3 tons, of turnips, in Kent, between 17 tons and 11 tons. Attention to local conditions is generally apparent, but the compilers agree regularly in differing as to the weight of crops.

The author has pursued the matter to considerable lengths by analysing the yields of four standard crops (wheat, barley, oats and potatoes) as recorded for each County of England in three widely separated years with varying climatic conditions—viz. 1906, 1912 and 1918. Briefly summarised, the results were as follows: in 1906, out of 123 instances *The Times* figures exceeded the official ones on 98 occasions, in 1912 on 87 occasions out of a similar total, and in 1918, 96 times out of 120 crop instances; the respective percentages were 79·6, 70·7 and 80·0. The differences in favour of *The Times* ranged up to over 25 per cent. in the case of cereals, and of more in that of roots, while in the minority of cases where the official figures exceeded the unofficial, they did so by much smaller margins. Of the three corn crops, wheat received more favour from the Ministry's officials, as out of the grand total of 82 occasions upon which its cereal figures were above those of *The Times*, 34 related to that crop, 25 to barley and 23 to oats.

If the ground is shifted, in order to illustrate the effect of such County records upon the separate countries concerned, the year 1922 may first be taken as typical. *The Times* figures are given in italics, those of the Ministry are in roman type.

	England	Margin in favour of *The Times*	Wales	Margin in favour of *The Times*	Scotland	Margin in favour of *The Times*	Great Britain	Margin in favour of *The Times*
Wheat	*33·1* 31·2	1·9 bus.	*29·0* 27·9	1·1 bus.	*35·3* 38·6	− 3·3 bus.	*33·1* 31·4	1·7 bus.
Barley	*30·9* 29·8	1·1 "	*32·3* 28·0	4·3 "	*40·5* 37·5	3·0 "	*32·9* 30·5	2·4 "
Oats	*37·8* 34·9	2·9 "	*36·5* 29·6	6·9 "	*46·7* 38·9	7·8 "	*39·8* 35·9	3·9 "
Beans	*26·6* 24·6	2·0 "	*21·0* 26·0	− 5·0 "	*38·7* 34·6	4·1 "	*27·3* 24·8	2·5 "
Potatoes	*7·8* 7·2	0·6 tons	*8·4* 6·6	1·8 tons	*7·9* 7·6	0·3 tons	*7·8* 7·2	0·6 tons
Mangolds	*25·1* 20·5	4·6 "	*17·1* 15·4	1·7 "	*20·4* 17·2	3·2 "	*24·3* 20·3	4·0 "
Turnips and Swedes	*18·3* 13·4	4·9 "	*13·2* 11·7	1·5 "	*24·3* 17·0	7·3 "	*18·5* 14·5	4·0 "

It will be observed that only in two cases—that of wheat in Scotland and of beans in Wales—were the official figures above those of *The Times*. Over a series of years, taken haphazard from 1906 to 1923, the margin in favour of *The Times* worked out as on p. 460.

There are unmistakable indications that these margins have widened during the last quarter of a century—and widened as the result of a uniform improvement in County figures given in *The*

Times' columns. If the earlier years are consulted, it can be seen that the standard adopted by *The Times* was slightly above that arrived at by Lawes and Gilbert, e.g. for wheat in the United Kingdom its normal "for a lengthy period prior to 1871" was 29½ bushels, corresponding values for England being 29·9 bushels, for Wales 27 bushels, for Scotland 29 bushels, and for Ireland 25 bushels —in other words, about 4 per cent. above the Rothamsted figure. A yearly comparison, extending from 1866 to 1879, shows Rothamsted to have been exactly one bushel below *The Times* (25·5 *versus* 26·5), due to the fact that the former series was more depressed by bad seasons—e.g. 1879, when it recorded 3 bushels below *The Times*. The separate countries of course occupied corresponding positions in each series, but oats, barley and, above all, potatoes were, according to *The Times*, notably heavier producers.

Margins in favour of The Times' *estimates as compared with the official series.*

	England	Wales	Scotland
Wheat	1·28 bus. + 3·9 %	2·42 bus. + 8·7 %	0·82 bus. − 2 %
Barley	1·49 bus. + 4·8 %	3·11 bus. + 10·4 %	2·27 bus. + 6·3 %
Oats	2·94 bus. + 7·6 %	4·79 bus. + 14·3 %	4·35 bus. + 11·4 %
Beans	2·01 bus. + 7·4 %	1·40 bus. + 5·3 %	0·30 bus. + 0·86 %
Potatoes	0·21 ton + 3·3 %	0·95 ton + 16·7 %	0·36 ton + 5·3 %
Mangolds	3·65 tons + 20·1 %	2·06 tons + 12·6 %	3·65 tons + 20·1 %
Turnips	3·53 tons + 31·3 %	2·70 tons + 20·5 %	4·19 tons + 24·8 %

Such are the broad results of a comparison between these two similarly collected sets of figures, the official and non-official. Before expressing an opinion upon their respective merits it must be enquired if there is any statistical disability inherent to *The Times* methods. The answer is that there is only one divergence in practice, which is as follows. *The Times* prepares County figures by taking the arithmetical average of its correspondents' statements, while, as already stated, the Ministry weights these areas; again, County figures are similarly treated by each authority in building up averages for the separate countries. Momentarily, this discrepancy might appear to be in part responsible for the difference in results, but it can be shown in reality to bring them closer together than would otherwise be the case. Thus, a test made upon the official figures for English Counties in 1886 gave these results:

	Wheat	Barley	Oats	Potatoes
Weighted average	26·87	32·23	39·98	5·81
Simple average	26·0	30·63	38·5	5·76

Here, then, there was a mean gain of 1·32 bushel, which could legitimately, and in proportion, be added to the corresponding *Times*' statements. In later years, due to the redistribution of the cereal-producing areas and the equalisation of "weights", the difference became less marked, amounting to 0·36 of a bushel by 1922, but in the case of potatoes it then represented half a ton an acre. Further, the smaller units are not adversely affected by this procedure, for an examination into the comparative values attributed to yields in such statutorily divided Counties as Lincolnshire, Suffolk and Sussex, with unequal areas under certain crops, reveals no variation from the standard difference, but possibly evidence of the difficulties attendant upon weighting. We are, therefore, left with the knowledge that any bias due to the composition of the statistics themselves has favoured the official series. It should be added that *The Times* figures for the United Kingdom *are* rightly weighted in proportion to the areas concerned in each separate country; failing this, such records would be valueless owing to the predominant position occupied by England among the small number of units concerned.

Effective remedial measures against the apparent tendency to under-estimate are not easy to propound, but certain safeguards might be instituted; thus, it would seem reasonable to insist upon the actual weighing, by the Crop Reporter, of a minimum number of samples per unit of area; this procedure would not supersede the existing peripatetic and inquisitory methods, but would provide an additional, and automatic, check upon human judgment. It is apt to be forgotten that the headquarters statistical staff is only concerned with the ultimate combination of the 330 area estimates, and is almost powerless to affect the results: everything depends upon the views of the local employee and upon his ability fairly to weight the numerous divisions of his territory. Better still would it be to put into force a proposal, officially mooted some time ago, viz. that "Standard" acre plots should be established in different parts of the country, under the supervision of Agricultural Research Stations, in order that their measured yields should be available as a basis of comparison, for a great authority has expressed the opinion that there is no more difficult undertaking than to assess the weight of grain, whether by eye when standing, or by hand when in sheaves—varieties of breeds alone can deceive even experts.

In connection with this "Standard" plot suggestion, it may be observed that such a method has been very fully developed in Japan, where test reapings of rice and of other cereal crops are of great antiquity, as for centuries they formed the foundation of the national system of taxation. The State Department of Agriculture now bases its estimates of yields upon personal inspection—utilising in this connection the services of over 11,000 representatives of agricultural societies—combined with numerous reapings of selected or "typical" areas (usually of 1 *tsubo*, or 3·3 square metres in extent). Meticulous care is taken in this work, for not only are conditions laid down in regard to altitude, soil and so forth, but it is ordained that the chosen area must be in the centre of a field, that reaping must take place at 2 p.m., that, before measuring the quantities of grain derived, all immature ears and waste material must be removed, that allowance should be made for damage by pests and due regard paid to the preceding crops. The fields to be investigated are first classified into irrigated or upland and then under various sub-heads, until thirty-six types are evolved. The actual number of plants in either a circular or rectangular *tsubo* are counted, and, of these, some fifty, deemed to be of uniform and typical development, are reaped and their yield weighed. This plan is applied, with apparently equal success, to fields sown in ridges, where ropes are utilised to measure the planted areas contained within rectangles of ten or twenty *tsubo*. It should be noted that, although the "average crop" used as a standard in the subsequent classification is the medium crop condition observed during the previous five years, yet this condition is not itself defined in precise terms; further, Japanese statisticians are anxious to make it clear that a "normal" crop in their country is to be distinguished from that represented by the corresponding term employed in the United States. The weighted results derived from actual reapings, and applicable to the country as a whole, are ranged in accordance with the following standards, where the normal is represented by 100: excellent 107·5, good 102·5, bad 97·5, very bad 92·5. The independent and preliminary estimates made by experts from the research stations are based upon inspection at the following customary times, viz. "the Great Heat, the periodical stormy day, the autumnal equinox, and the period of ripening and of full plant development". Here, any excess of 5 per cent. above the average is recorded as "excellent", a figure between 100 and 105 as "good", while 95–100 is "bad" and anything below 95 is "very bad".

In conclusion, no criticism of either the headquarters staff of the English Ministry or of the efficacy of its statistical methods, which have made our "agricultural returns" the envy of other countries, is implied by anything that has been written in the preceding pages; the suggestion is merely that its part-time employees may be unwittingly detracting from the accomplishments of English farmers. There is also the contingent possibility to be reckoned with that the practice of crop forecasting (discussed below), as carried out during the last twenty-seven years, has made its depressing influence felt upon the results ultimately recorded. It is only fair to state that a detailed defence of orthodox methods will be found in a paper read by H. D. Vigor to the Royal Statistical Society and published in its *Journal* (pt. I, 1928).

Crop Forecasting

In certain countries of the world, notably the United States, and, to a lesser extent, India, extreme attention is paid to estimating the future yield of crops; indeed, in the former country it is no exaggeration to say that millions of dollars change hands as a result of this work, concerning the preliminaries of which both the State and private agencies observe much secrecy. In the following pages description is confined to the purely statistical and economic aspects of the subject as reflected in the methods adopted in England.

The numerous factors affecting yields have been enumerated above, where reference was made to the difficulties inherent to estimation even of gathered crops, and the fallibility of the human machine, when engaged in combining varied rates of productivity, was stressed. Yet it would seem that the still more hazardous process represented by forecasting yields is, in certain quarters, regarded as merely dependent upon mathematical calculations. Thus, Professor L. W. Lyde, writing upon the subject of "Russian Wheat Supplies" (*The Times*, January 4, 1926), said:

For instance, in England the "Shaw" formula, even when not checked by the "Rothamsted" formula, is remarkably trustworthy. It computes the yield by subtracting from a *datum* of 39·5 bushels per acre a maximum of about 79 lbs. for each inch of rain that has fallen during the thirteen weeks of September, October and November, and the actual results show an astonishing agreement with the subsequent yield as given in the official returns. Why? Because we *know* that the "extra" rain prevents, or even postpones until spring, the proper preparation of the land, and it restricts root development. And we can put definite values on the various factors and make the necessary additions or subtractions. Indeed, one may say to-day with little fear of confusion that the yield of wheat in England next autumn will be certainly *circa* 33 (39·5 – 6·3) bushels. [Actually the recorded yield was 29·6 bushels! J.A.V.]

Here we find associated with the whole of England, a formula tentatively put forward by Sir Napier Shaw twenty-five years ago as mainly applicable to East Anglia. This method neglects variations in the local distribution and times of precipitation, ignores all reference to climatic happenings from January to July, and, moreover, assumes that effects upon clay, fen and breck-land soils are similar. It affords an interesting pursuit retrospectively to investigate on these lines the yields of past years, but although certain limited areas and some seasons may bear out anticipations, it is impossible thus to dogmatise upon results.

The writings of anyone versed both in meteorology and in agricultural statistics, such as those of R. H. Hooker, e.g. "Forecasting the Crops from the Weather" (Presidential Address, Royal Meteorological Society, 1921), afford a timely warning as to the limitations attaching to these enquiries. The best that can be said for them may be summed up in Hooker's own words:

I do not suggest that predictions should be based solely on statistical records of the past weather. But I do suggest that these records must not be ignored. It is abundantly clear that the weather plays a part, invisible to the eye, in the internal structure of a plant that can be measured by such statistics: something, we may say, goes on inside the plant which is not recognised by an observer in the field, and which only exhibits its matured effect in the ripe crop. It is quite obvious that these numerical records must be worked up and the results taken into serious consideration, and used in conjunction with other facts, such as those learned by actual observation in the fields, for foretelling the future harvest.

There we must leave these theoretical methods, putting beside them those much more venturesome long-term forecasts, based on apparent cycles in production, which, from time to time, cause no little stir, for we are here concerned with existing practices and possibilities.

The then Board of Agriculture inaugurated, in 1906, a system of forecasting probable yields of staple crops, based upon their condition at monthly intervals. Four statements are issued, which, up to 1922, recorded as percentages of 100 ("an average crop") their appearance on the first day of July, of August, of September, and of October (upon occasion, and for certain products); subsequently the basis was altered to actual yields in terms of bushels and of hundredweights. These figures are, in the first instance, prepared by the Crop Reporters, and then amalgamated in the usual manner by the headquarters staff so as to be applicable to the whole country. It is here not necessary to classify in advance the respective values of each monthly forecast, but it may be stated that for most crops each report tends to approach nearer to the "actual" yield ultimately recorded, although many aberrations are necessarily found, and, upon occasion, the trend is in the opposite direction, e.g. in 1916 barley figures ran thus: 95, 97, 99, while the yield was represented by 95. In the case of such a fickle crop as roots, forecasts made two or three months in advance possess little value, and only the last can generally be accepted as a serious contribution to the farming situation.

The following comments relate to an enquiry made into the accuracy of the last forecasts (i.e. September in the case of cereals, and October in that of roots) over the period 1906 to 1932 when compared with the yields subsequently reported. In general, they exhibit features common to such estimates whensoever made, and relating to whatsoever crops, viz. they tend seriously to underestimate yields. For example, H. L. Moore, in *Forecasting the Yield and the Price of Cotton*, devotes much space to this subject, and is satisfied that forecasts of the United States Department of Agriculture possess "inherent defects that lead to an under-estimate of the yield per acre. The official method of forecasting, if applied to the data referring to the condition of the crop during a period of twenty-five years, gives a predicted yield per acre, which is an under-estimate 19 times when based upon the May condition, 16 times when based upon the June condition, 15 times in July, 16 in August, 15 in September". We, in this country, are not concerned with divergences from that American entity—or fiction—"the normal crop", which is "*not* represented by an average condition, but a condition *above* the average, giving promise of *more* than an average crop", neither is it a perfect crop, for "the normal represents something less than this, and thus comes between the average and the possible maximum" (Official Instruction, U.S.A. Department of Agriculture).

Fortunately, the forecasts for England and Wales have taken as their basis the "ten-year average" crop, and are expressed as percentages of this figure. For the three principal cereals it will be seen (in the diagram opposite) that the last forecasts, made at a time when harvest is in full swing everywhere, and often actually completed in the Southern and Eastern Counties, tend seriously to understate the position. Thus, the very dry season of 1921 completely misled the Reporters, who did not recognise it as providing an abnormal crop of wheat (even perhaps under-stated at 116), but suggested as appropriate figures 100, 101, and, finally, 104, and at the same time forecasted the barley crop as 89, against results of 96. It is typical of their outlook that even the September forecasts failed to appreciate the situation, the majority of wheat reports recording "average", "slightly above average", or at best indicating a figure of 105 as applicable. All students of agriculture are familiar with such statements as the following, which emanate only too frequently from those connected with the land: "the worst harvest I have ever experienced", "results will be even worse than in 1879"; if these assertions are subsequently compared with the same speakers' reports, based on the yields of the threshing machine, their biased nature is apparent. Is it likely that local officials are entirely free from such tendencies? Deep-rooted motives, such as a desire to minimise a crop in order to enhance its financial value, can, of course, in this country, be put out of court. Psychology and conservatism alone appear responsible.

There is little to choose between the accuracy attained in forecasts of wheat and barley, save that the second, or August, forecasts of the latter have actually been inferior to those issued in July. Oats clearly afford the worst results, since only upon two occasions in twenty-seven years were September estimates above the final figures, whereas for wheat this occurred nine times, and for barley also on nine occasions. It would not appear that the comparative dates of commencement, or the subsequent duration, of harvest have influenced these results, for enquiry has failed to trace any connection therewith. There is no evidence to suggest that the margin of error in forecasting cereal crops has improved during the twenty-seven years they have been prepared, although the dates of

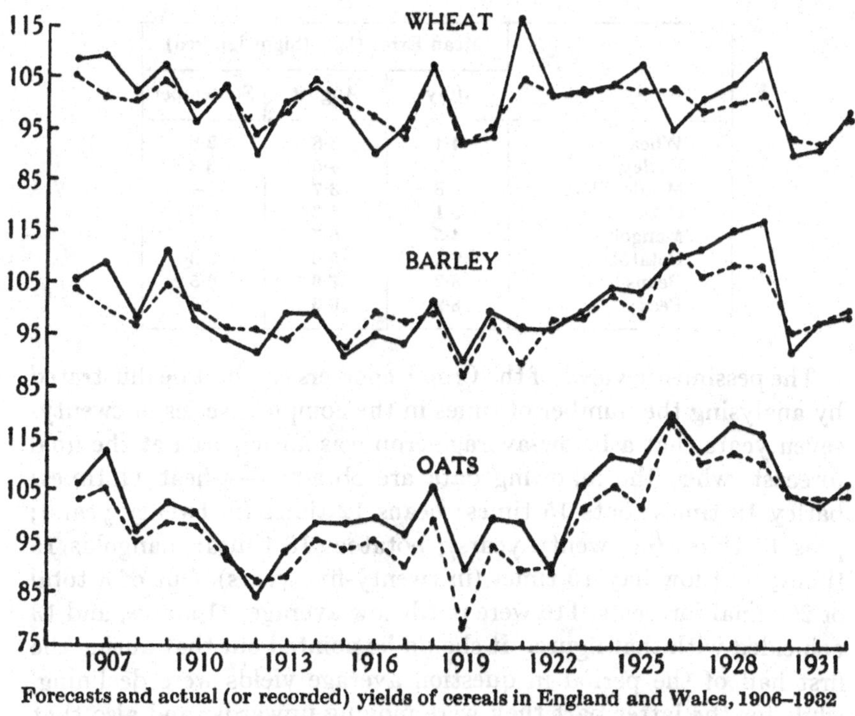

Forecasts and actual (or recorded) yields of cereals in England and Wales, 1906–1932

September forecasts - - - - - Recorded yields ———

issue have themselves been retarded; in any event September "forecasts" can generally be based on a proportion of actual weighings, and should be correspondingly facilitated. Since lack of space precludes any separate diagrammatic representation, the Table on p. 468 has been substituted, which well demonstrates the universal character of the tendencies referred to above, the principal crops subject to preliminary estimates being ranged in the order of their accuracy as revealed by the final forecasts during a period of twenty years (1906–1925).

It will be observed that the degree of accuracy secured in cereal estimates as between July and August is very similar, but in three cases (barley, oats and peas) the passage of a month results in wider errors appearing. The last forecasts for mangolds are worse than the first, the third for potatoes inferior to the second, but root crops are particularly subject to the onslaughts of pests and disease, so that such results are not unexpected.

	Mean Error (%). (Signs ignored)		
	July	August	September
Wheat	4·4	3·8	2·8
Barley	4·3	4·5	3·3
Meadow hay	4·8	3·7	—
Oats	5·1	5·3	4·9
Mangolds	4·5	5·7	5·6
Potatoes	7·1	5·6	6·3
Beans	8·2	7·6	6·5
Peas	8·2	9·3	7·6

The pessimistic views of the Crop Reporters can best be illustrated by analysing the number of times in the complete series of twenty-seven years that a below-average crop was anticipated at the final forecast, when the following data are obtained—wheat 11 times; barley 18 times; oats 15 times; beans 12 times (in twenty years); peas 14 times (in twenty years); potatoes 18 times; mangolds 15 times; meadow hay 13 times (in twenty-five years). Out of a total of 200 final forecasts, 116 were put below average, 71 above, and 13 coincided with that figure. It should be pointed out that during the first half of the period in question average yields were declining, while for the latter part they were moving upwards; and also that the margin by which estimates fell below the average considerably surpassed that by which they more rarely exceeded it.

It is unfortunate that strictly comparable forecasts are not issued by any independent body, so that it might be possible to place the official series side by side with extraneously prepared estimates, as was effected in the case of recorded yields. *The Times*, however, compiles preliminary statements early in the months of July, August and September, in which the condition of crops is recorded in percentages, where 100 equals "a healthy and average growth and development for the time of year". This figure, being somewhat akin to the United States "normal", its main function is to provide an indication as to whether improvement or deterioration is registered at each monthly interval, but a close examination of the final, or September series, extending over the twenty years from 1906 to 1925, provides evidence that they are at least free from any bias and, further, are in harmony with *The Times'* statements relating to final yields. Thus, for the six crops represented by wheat, barley, oats, beans, potatoes, roots ("turnips and mangolds"), the September statement of condition indicated returns above the average on 73 occasions, below it 45 times, and equal to it twice. For these same years, of the Ministry's (125) corresponding estimates no less than 101 were below average, 20 were above and 4 coincided with that figure. Incidentally, proof of the steadiness of *The Times'* final figures themselves is forthcoming when it is recorded that on 64 occasions these "actual" yields worked out as above the ten-year average of their precursors, and 56 times were they below it.

Grounds have previously been given for the belief that actual yields may not be quite as low as the official figures suggest, and it now transpires that the official forecasts too often fail to attain the modest level occupied by the latter. Admittedly, the task set the local officials is a difficult one, for, in this particular work, no methods of precision can avail, but, on the other hand, extreme conservatism—that inherent rural characteristic—should, by every possible means, be avoided.

PART II

An Economic History of British Agriculture during and after the Great War

Chapter XXII

BRITISH AGRICULTURE IN PEACE AND WAR

Agriculture prior to the war; monetary factors; rates of production of cereal crops in different decades; productivity of British agriculture as a whole; the extent to which the country was self-supporting in food-stuffs; their value; Government policy on the outbreak of war; steps taken to meet the situation; methods employed to secure additional land under the plough; yield from new and old arable land compared.

In 1914 such an event as a war that would directly affect him seemed a very remote possibility to the British farmer. The events of 1793 to 1815 were forgotten by that generation, however vividly they might have been remembered by its grandparents. The intervening period had been occupied by the fight over the Corn Laws, the ineffectual attempt to combine high farming with low prices, and, finally, the definite, but unjustifiable, relegation of the industry to a position of secondary importance. The State had considered its obligations fulfilled by the appointment of Commissions of Enquiry, and by the subsequent passage of minor Bills dealing with such questions as tithe, tenant-right, rating, and Small Holdings. Industries of a commercial character had become predominant, and the townsmen had increased in numbers and influence each decade.

Yet a few years before 1914 agriculture had turned the corner economically. By any test that might be applied this amelioration could be seen. The prices of almost everything the farmer produced had tended upwards from about 1906, the acreage under cereal crops reached its minimum in 1908, cash wages were already a shilling higher in 1914, and land itself was enhanced in value.

The causes were essentially monetary in character and rested upon the relationship between the supply of, and demand for, the world's gold. When that metal becomes more abundant, it also becomes, in everyday parlance, "cheaper", viz. a larger quantity of it has to be given in exchange for goods or services—prices accordingly rise. As all trade is, in reality, barter, it is open to anyone to express this proposition in the reverse way by stating that, e.g., a smaller quantity of wheat or of beef is then exchangeable against the same quantity of gold. Historically, the fluctuations in the economic position of agriculture and of all industries, not only in these Islands, but throughout those parts of the world where the gold standard had been adopted, can be shown to have been primarily dependent upon this factor.

Thus, during the first generation after the French war, a relative shortage of gold, due to business recovery and expansion, coupled with partial exhaustion of the South American mines, led to a fall in prices. Then, shortly before the middle of the century, new sources of supply were exploited in California and in Australia; gold became more abundant, and so remained for nearly thirty years, with the result that its purchasing power declined—prices rose. The third of these long-term waves set in during the 'seventies, when, owing to an increased demand for the metal from European and other countries which were in process of adopting the gold standard, demand outran supply and the price level fell in two decades by 40 per cent., with disastrous results to agriculture in particular.

That industry, from its very nature, suffered more than most, being plunged, indeed, into the abyss which culminated in such years as 1879 and 1894, when the weather appeared to have joined forces with the world's monetary system and the ends of the earth seized on new and cheap methods of transport to flood our markets. Bimetallism was very suitably put forward as a suggested remedial policy by certain banking and other financial witnesses before the Royal Commission of 1893, but that body avoided making any recommendations involving such highly technical and controversial considerations, although its attention was drawn to the favourable position occupied by two or three countries whose currency was upon a silver basis. The fall in general commodity prices was, as above stated, 40 per cent., which was exceeded by some agricultural products; thus, there was overwhelming evidence to prove the causes of "agricultural depression". To South Africa must be attributed the credit for a turn in the tide; here, gold had, by the beginning of the twentieth century, been won in sufficient quantities to raise prices, and eventually the discovery of the cyanide process of extraction and the utilisation of large numbers of native workers enabled the handicaps associated with Rand mining at immense depths (in some cases below the 7000 foot level) to be successfully countered. By 1914, the farmers of Great Britain were enjoying what almost amounted to prosperity, but few of them, indeed, could have explained the true reason why prices had risen by 20 to 30 per cent.

Not only was the industry as a whole better organised just before the war, but its activities were also more diverse. All it required was a continuance of peace at home and abroad and the minimum of interference; on these lines it is tolerably certain that it would have continued to enjoy fair prosperity. Technical progress was being registered; the yield of the staple crops, when examined over a period of some decades, exhibited evidence of improvement; the weight of carcases and the yield of milk were both moving upwards. Education was widening the outlook of all three partners in the industry, and research was adding weapons for the defence against nature's onslaughts. Lastly, the antagonism between town and country was almost forgotten.

It will be observed that the most real improvements officially recorded in the yields of cereals had been secured in the case of wheat and barley; this tends to show that the work of Prof. Sir R. Biffen, Dr E. S. Beaven and their fellow investigators was bearing fruit commercially, for their efforts had mainly been confined to these two, and oats had not received such full attention. A higher potential yield, without the loss of other desirable qualities, obviously appealed to the farmer's pocket, and if new varieties of wheat could be proved capable of returning an extra two or three bushels per acre, whilst retaining sufficient strength of stem to obviate the tendency to "lodge", and having the additional asset of meeting the millers' requirements, then it was only a question of time before such types should predominate. In the long run it is certain that improved weight of yields will be secured in this country, not from the universal adoption of high farming, but by the aid of science and the plant breeder. For high farming is a luxury rarely to be indulged in, while the use of improved seed is a permanent standby. Again, the selection of individual types of cereals in conformity with local soil conditions opens up considerable possibilities. Sir John Russell, in an article on increased crop production, after giving a summary of the soil and climatic requirements of different named varieties of wheat, barley and oats, concluded thus: "Much information of this sort is current among farmers, but it needs collecting and sifting. One of the great problems for the present is to make a careful study of the environmental requirements of the well-defined types of varieties, and one of the great hopes for the future is that new varieties may be found better suited to the various local conditions than those at present in common cultivation". In the Appendix will be found (Table XII) the results of a post-war enquiry—the first ever undertaken—into the distribution in the Eastern Counties of the more important types of wheat which implemented those hopes.

The series of maps recording the (official) decennial yields of each cereal demonstrate that wheat was an improving crop in the North and East of England. Whereas in 1885 to 1894 the majority of Counties were below the twenty-eight bushel level, by the next decade only Wales recorded yields of that weight. In 1905 to 1914 appeared a great advance in certain East Anglian Counties, coupled with fine yields in Lancashire and Northumberland, but it must be borne in mind that there were special reasons for this high rate of production in the latter Counties, and that the acreage concerned was small, but, as showing what could be achieved, the figures are of interest. From the national standpoint the increase in the yield of the Eastern Counties was the satisfactory feature, as an extra bushel or two on hundreds of thousands of acres was worth much more than a rise of 50 per cent. in the rate attained in the West of England. Barley affords almost a similar record of improvement distributed over much the same areas. Oats, with the exception of certain County fluctuations, were, in 1905 to 1914, in almost the same position they had occupied in the two previous periods.

As was previously pointed out, if the yield of each crop in every County is plotted separately, some remarkable anomalies are revealed, for cases occur in which two crops improved in the thirty years out of all semblance, and yet the third actually declined, and others in which all three first advanced, then one remained stationary and the others continued the movement. Such areas as the geographical County of Cambridge produced gross outputs by the thousand tons in excess of the normal, simply by reason of yields per acre which varied from 6 per cent. to 33 per cent. above the average. This was, in part, the reason why cereal growing was still a profitable business there, even in times of depression. It is also a factor to be reckoned with when accounting for the improved yield of wheat and barley over the whole country, as, when the acreage under these crops shrinks, the poorer land is always the first to be put under alternative crops, and in each individual district the best land is reserved for the most important cereals. The only reservation that should be made, is this—the heavy clay-lands of Essex and parts of the East Midlands (so expensive to cultivate), which in times of high farming produce above-average crops, are among the first to be discarded when prices fall, and, therefore, to a slight extent cancel out the gain in yield resulting from the above factors. But the acreage of the heavy land in question does not approach that of the other districts, and the net result in the past has been a slight but steady increase in yield for the country as a whole, which, for reasons previously given, there are grounds for thinking is understated.

The figures on which the maps have been based, together with a Table showing the yields of all three cereals in Great Britain during the last forty-eight years, have been printed for purpose of reference in the Appendix. Great Britain has been chosen as well as the United Kingdom for two reasons. In the first place, the United Kingdom no longer exists as a statistical unit, for Ireland has now two bodies charged with the collection of agricultural data, and, consequent upon the troubles of some years ago, there were at one time several *lacunae* in her figures; secondly, Scotland produces some of the highest yields of cereals, and the acreage under these crops is still extensive enough to warrant combination with the return for England and Wales. United Kingdom figures of cereal yields are, however, reproduced in the graphs upon p. 453.

The official average yield of the country as a whole had naturally not increased compatibly with the averages of the best Counties, for, generally speaking, those of the latter that had made the most progress retained the smallest acreage under cereals. The potentialities of the situation were, however, modified, and if a few years before 1914 a considerable extension of corn growing had been possible, the yield per acre might have shown some increase. If the improvement was slow, and was mainly confined to a levelling up of the poorer districts, it must not be forgotten that, when the statistics of yield were first collected, this country was far ahead of the rest of Europe in that respect, and that it took a generation for other countries to approach the British achievements of forty years ago. It is certain that had a period of high farming synchronised with the efforts of plant breeders a notable advance would have taken place; as matters were, there is no doubt that improvement was made—if not always adequately recorded—in the face of economic difficulties that might, if unresisted, have caused an actual reduction in the rates of yield after 1880. Competent authorities hold that the greatest effects of improved breeds are felt under adverse climatic conditions, and that nowadays yields are not reduced by excessive rain and cold to the extent that was the case in the 'seventies and the 'nineties. The weather factor cannot, of course, be eliminated, but by averaging over periods of ten years it is possible to minimise its effects, and it is unlikely that this influence has had any considerable bearing on the shading of the various maps. The main distinction to be drawn between the climatic conditions of each decade was the persistent lack of rain in the second period. Drought, however, is not always the precursor of low yields in the case of cereals, and autumn-sown wheat is rather favoured by hot, dry summers, as witness such a season as that of 1921. Finally, as has been stated before, it is open to argument that the methods of crop estimating employed may themselves have minimised improvements in the rate of yields applicable to English crops in particular.

The yields of all root crops, if similarly investigated, also exhibited a moderate rate of increase during the years in question. Thus, the rate of production per acre of farm crops was undoubtedly rising during a time when the gross output of the land was declining as a result of the contraction of the arable area. If, however, we take as our basis the gross value of the soil products, and, therefore, include the output of fruit and of vegetable farms, of hop gardens, of the acreage of crops under glass, and of pedigree livestock there is, in the absence of full statistics, room to question whether the total value of all the soil products did not increase between 1885 and 1914—neglecting, of course, any variations in money values. Nothing but a series of enquiries on the lines of the original (1908) Census of Production could, however, have answered this question satisfactorily. Nor do there exist any reliable statistics dealing with the production of meat in this country over a period of time. That same Census recorded the weight of dressed carcases, but in the absence of anything save individual estimates for former occasions—the earliest dating from the seventeenth and eighteenth centuries—we cannot register in number of pounds' weight the increased outturn of butchers' meat per animal slaughtered. Even the supplies of home-killed meat, have, with the exception of the war period, to be calculated (taking into review numerous factors) from the numbers of livestock annually registered on June 4th. Admittedly, the trend was to produce heavier animals, but the increased gross weight cannot be exactly computed.

The yield of milk per cow presents exactly the same problem. The Census of Production gave 550 gallons as the average yield per cow in milk, recorded the districts in which the highest rates were attained, and the percentage sold by farmers, but it provided no data for comparison with former periods. Estimates below 400 gallons had been made by separate investigators in the latter half of the nineteenth century, and met with corroboration from farmers themselves; the statistician must, therefore, fall back on the unsupported evidence of agriculturists in regard to the rate of progress achieved, always remembering that abnormal yields from a few selected herds are as nothing when balanced against the output of numerous ill-bred or neglected stock.

Apart from the valuable trade that had grown up in the exportation of pedigree livestock, the influence of the latter had begun to permeate throughout all branches of the industry, but, expressed as percentages of the total of each class of beast, the numbers of registered animals were shown, by a special enquiry held by the Ministry of Agriculture in 1919, to be relatively small. The *Report* that accompanied the published returns contained the following exhortation.

An examination of the returns shows that there is ample room for an expansion in the pedigree stock of the country, both for the home and export trade, and there can be no doubt that the use of a greater number of pedigree sires in non-pedigree herds will tend to grade up our stock and raise their productive capabilities, to increase the amount of meat and milk that can be produced per acre, and to increase the profits of the producer. The development of the pedigree industry, and the grading up of the stock of the country should prove not merely of advantage to stock breeders but of benefit to the nation, by the provision of larger supplies of meat and milk.

Each branch of farming surveyed has shown progress made in the generation before the war—progress that was not always capable of statistical expression, but which was nevertheless real, if it was not of the marked character that the latter half of the eighteenth century had recorded. In that period additional land had been secured for agriculture, and the output of crops and of livestock was also responsive to the slightest attention received from the most rudimentary "scientists" or experimental breeders. In the thirty years prior to the Great War agriculture was not only practised on an intensive, as opposed to an extensive, basis but its supply of land was actually decreasing, and the application of capital was only economic in directions other than those to which older farmers had grown accustomed. Influences were at work which rendered the industry a far more complex business upon which to embark, but one from which it was still possible for its followers to secure favourable returns.

The only steps taken to investigate our probable situation in the event of war breaking out had consisted in the appointment, in 1901, of a Royal Commission to enquire into the food supply of the country. As was seen in the Chapters on "Wheat", its findings led to no preparation for such an eventuality, but certain fresh data, relating to the consumption of cereals, were collected. It was so often erroneously asserted that we produced only "one-fifth of our food requirements", that it may be well briefly to enumerate the quantities that were actually raised prior to the war. On the average, there were produced the following proportions of our total needs: of wheat and flour, 21 per cent.; of barley, 58 per cent.; of oats, 79 per cent.; of beans, 72 per cent.; of peas, 56 per cent.; of beef and veal, 61 per cent.; of mutton and lamb, 54 per cent.; of pigmeat, 56 per cent.; of butter (and margarine), 40 per cent.; of cheese, 20 per cent.; of milk, 95 per cent.; of eggs, 65 per cent. Whilst the consumption *per caput* of cereals was very uniform, that of meat was increasing—figures were published showing it to have been some 103 lb. in 1877, and approximately 120 lb. in 1914. Concurrently, the quantity produced in the United Kingdom fell from 90 per cent. in 1870 to the figures recorded above. Our increased demands were being met from the ranches of the Southern hemisphere.

It will be observed that the origin of the belief that we only met one-fifth of our food requirements lay in the fact that this was the proportion of wheat raised in the United Kingdom. Of all the cereals together, we were producing almost exactly half—viz. 49·3—in 1913–14. In addition, we annually imported some two million tons of maize. The sources of origin of these commodities were, roughly, as follows. Half the imported wheat came from within the Empire, the other cereals principally from foreign countries, as also did the bulk of fruit and vegetables, while less than one-quarter of the imported meat was produced in our own Colonies. In addition, we required large quantities of imported feeding stuffs to raise our home-grown supplies of meat. The gross weight of food-stuffs imported or produced at home is, however, only one side of the question; another point that calls for consideration is their comparative value as nutriment. In regard to this a Committee, appointed by the Royal Society at the beginning of the war, calculated that in calorific value we produced 42 per cent. of our total needs, but this figure was subsequently slightly amended as a result of fuller investigation. The pre-war monetary value of our imported food-stuffs was in the neighbourhood of £200,000,000, of which two-thirds went to foreign countries; our home products were valued at slightly over £170,000,000. The proportionate values of imported and home produced commodities had changed greatly, even in the decades before the war, as can be seen from a Table published by Caird in 1878. Then the value of all imported cereals was about £52,000,000—in 1913 this figure had become £85,000,000; those of other important articles were as follows, the 1913 values being placed in brackets: wool £22,000,000 (£34,000,000), butchers' meat £22,000,000 (£56,000,000), cheese and butter £14,000,000 (£31,000,000). Corresponding statistics relative to the post-war situation will be found upon p. 528.

This, then, was the statistical position in a typical year before 1914. Whilst, however, our requirements were approximately known in advance and the sources of our supplies familiar to all, knowledge of the stocks of food in the country at any given time was generally lacking, this side of our economic statistics being eventually improved by State intervention during the war.

One is inevitably drawn into making comparisons between the Napoleonic war and the Great War in their effects upon agriculture. On both occasions we were technically blockaded, both times agriculture prospered during the period of hostilities, and both wars were succeeded by a period of extreme depression. There the analogy ceases, for one hundred and twenty years ago we could, if necessary, have been entirely self-supporting in bread-stuffs (without the campaign to reduce consumption of wheat and the purchases abroad by Government agents), the population was mainly rural, and the State made no attempt directly to control cultivation or to fix prices and regulate supplies. On the other hand, after 1914 agriculture became a matter of great interest to the nation and a source of anxiety to the Government, which sought by every possible means to direct, control and foster it.

As the effects of the war on all the several legal and administrative aspects of the industry have been covered under the appropriate headings in previous Chapters, it is proposed to confine the following pages to some account of the influence exercised by the Government upon the actual cultivation and management of the land and of its control of the economic machinery involved in price-fixing. For this reason it is necessary to omit any account of the effects of the war upon our own overseas Dependencies and upon hostile and neutral countries. It must, however, be pointed out that, except in the case of sugar, there was never any real lack of essential foodstuffs, but that distance and the time factor alone prevented adequately protected convoys from importing normal quantities. Luxury foods were of course drastically reduced in supply and many tropical and sub-tropical products, in common with such bulky materials as timber, ceased to arrive. The friendly and neutral nations in both hemispheres of the New World added largely, but not always altruistically, to their acreage under cereals, as did our own Colonies. Even in November 1918 the ports and warehouses of this country contained larger supplies of wheat than they had ever held before. The whole policy of the Government in connection with the increased home production of food was to use the latter as an insurance premium against the submarine blockade; for this purpose it was necessary to adopt every means, if necessary by frightening it, to persuade the nation at large to utilise each scrap of ground. This policy of State control falls naturally under three separate heads—viz. the actual steps taken to increase production, its effects upon farming practice, and the methods of price fixing. The first feature, as representing a purely constructive effort, will be considered first.

To find a previous instance of the State directly legislating in favour of a ploughing policy it is necessary to revert to the reign of Henry VIII, when similar steps were taken to redress a balance upset by the widespread introduction of sheep-farming. In the emergencies of subsequent centuries the free play of prices had always brought additional land under crops; this, of course, was the case in the previous European war when enclosure had run its course. For over forty years prior to 1910 the area under the plough had been steadily declining, the total loss in England and Wales amounting to upwards of 3,000,000 acres (see the accompanying illustration). The resultant diminution in staple crops had mainly fallen on wheat, as the larger diagram facing p. 500 shows. From an area of about 3,500,000 acres in England and Wales, it had declined to a pre-war average of little more than half that figure. The transference from arable to grass land had, of course, not been evenly distributed, and parts of East Anglia and the East Midlands still retained anything up to 80 per cent. of their cultivated area under the plough. In other words, cereal farming was mainly confined to that part of the British Isles in which climatic conditions afforded the best opportunity of

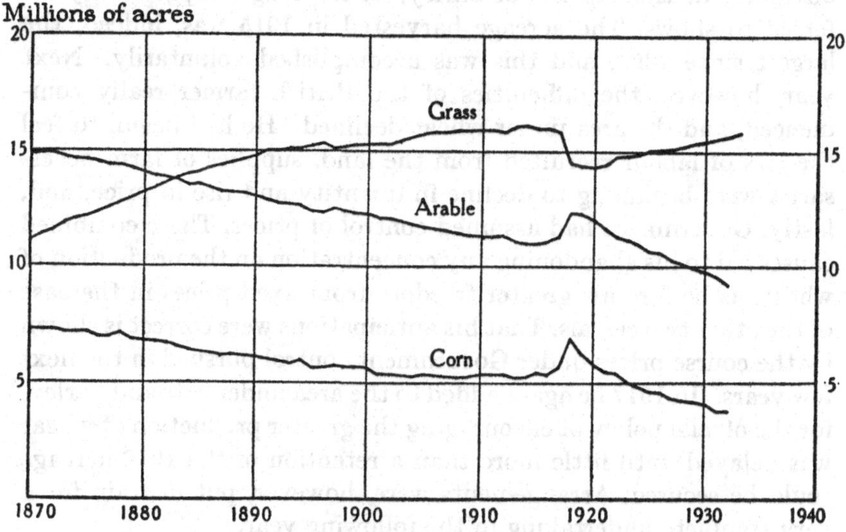

Extent of arable land, permanent grass and corn (wheat, barley, oats) in England and Wales, 1870 to 1932.

competing with the foreign producer. Those diagrams (to be found in this volume) illustrative of the annual rainfall, the acreage under the plough and under wheat respectively, at once afford evidence that our land was being divergently farmed from economic necessity and not from free choice. Two generations which produced successively legislative, economic and climatic handicaps to be circumvented had left their indelible impression on the face of the country. Thousands of grazing fields in the Western and Midland counties of England remained to show what once had been—fields that still retained the ridges and furrows caused by centuries of ploughing.

The war commenced, as it had always been anticipated would be the case, when the bulk of harvest operations in Europe were completed, and when, accordingly, we, in common with friend and foe, had our largest supplies of grain in hand. In our case this represented bread-stuffs for at most some five months' requirements, consisting of ten weeks' supply from our own resources and a similar quantity of imported wheat in warehouses and in millers' hands. In response to advice from the Board of Agriculture and also, doubtless, from an intelligent anticipation of the course that prices would pursue, a much larger breadth of autumn wheat was sown in 1914—obviously at the expense of barley, as the diagram previously referred to shows. The acreage harvested in 1915 was, indeed, the largest since 1892, and this was accomplished voluntarily. Next year, however, the difficulties of the British farmer really commenced, and the area under wheat declined. He had begun to feel the loss of labour recruited from the land, supplies of farm necessaries were beginning to decline in quantity and rise in price, and, lastly, Government had assumed control of prices. These combined causes led to his abandoning any concentration on the production of wheat, as he foresaw greater freedom from fixed prices in the case of the other two cereals. That his anticipations were correct is shown by the course prices under Government control pursued in the next few years. In 1917 he again added to the area under oats and barley, for the official policy of encouraging the greater production of wheat was delayed until little more than a retention of the 1916 acreage could be secured. Arrangements were, however, put in train for a very complete undertaking in the following year.

The submarine campaign reached its climax in the spring of 1917, and it was obvious that every additional acre under wheat would be of assistance, and that some hundreds of thousands might quite definitely turn the scale in our favour; accordingly, a free hand was given to the Departments concerned, and they were instructed to secure the greatest possible outturn of all cereals at the succeeding harvest.

Centrally, a special branch of the Board of Agriculture, entitled the Food Production Department, was set up. Locally, Agricultural Executive Committees carried out its enactments in each County, and the Irish and Scotch Boards of Agriculture were responsible for supervising a similar policy in their appropriate areas. The newly created Department was charged with the duty of advancing, by every means in its power (aided by the provisions of the Defence of the Realm Act), the increased output of all forms of home-produced food. This object might be achieved, in one direction, by the provision of fresh allotments, in another by the advocacy of the consumption of alternative forms of food, and, yet again, by the conversion of grass-land to tillage. The exact results of the latter scheme were known at the time to comparatively few persons, although the public at large appreciated that much additional land had been placed under the plough. As this is the first occasion upon which more than a cursory report relating to the results obtained from the new arable land has been published, no excuse is needed for treating its economic features at some length. The bulk of what follows was officially prepared at the time in question, and relates solely to conditions in England and Wales, as the Scotch and Irish Departments did not call for reports relating to the smaller areas of new land in their particular spheres of activity.

The original aim of those responsible for directing the scheme was to break up the bulk of the three and a half million acres lost after 1860, but this, from lack of personnel and of materials, was soon modified, and a figure of two and a half million acres was substituted, as representing a more feasible task. *Quotas* were then fixed, based in most instances on the proportions borne by arable and grass in each County in the year 1875, and Executive Committees were instructed to lay their plans accordingly. These *quotas* necessarily varied greatly; in general, the arable Counties had relatively much smaller tasks set them than had those in the West of England. The dotted line in the diagram on the next page represents the division between arable and grass in 1875, and therefore affords an indication of each County's aim. It will be noticed that Lancashire and Cheshire had, in 1917, already under the plough larger areas than in the earlier year; these two Counties thus afforded the only exceptions to the statement that the plough-land had decreased in the preceding forty years. In their case the presence of a dense population had led to the formation of numerous market-gardens, and they had also become great producers of potatoes.

It soon became apparent that both labour and machinery were insufficient to compass the ends in view, and, despite the driving force exerted from headquarters, County Committees could not always be made to see eye to eye with the officials whose business it

The ploughing-up campaign of 1917–18

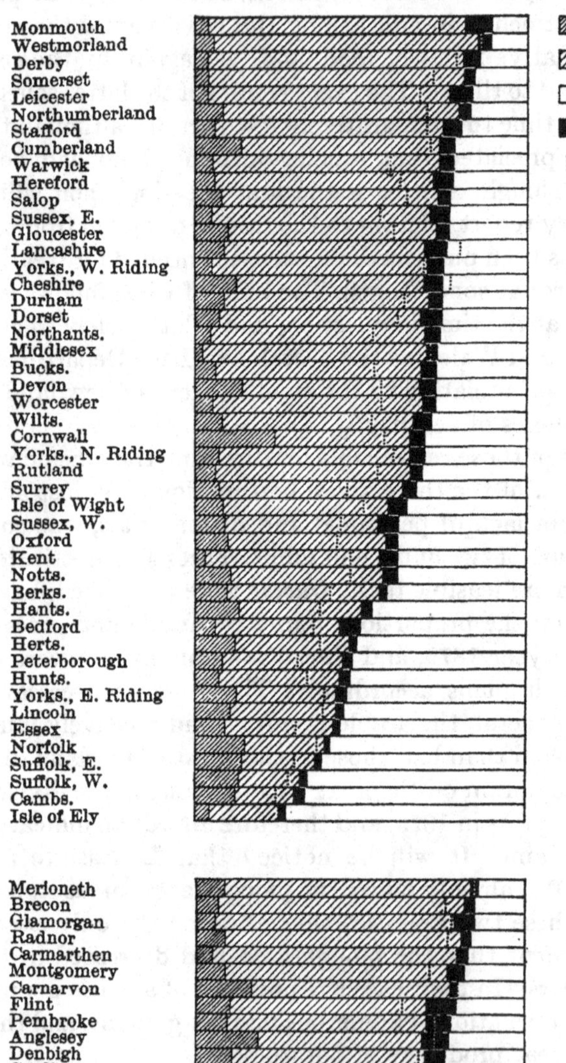

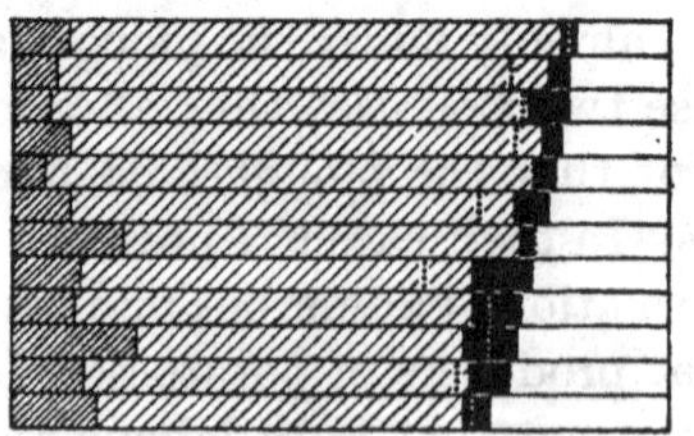

Proportion of Arable and Grass-land in the different Counties, June 4th, 1918

was to carry through the policy. In these circumstances it was no mean achievement to secure between June 4th, 1917, and the corresponding date in 1918, the breaking up of some 1,240,000 acres of grass in England and Wales. The new arable land thus secured is marked in black on the accompanying diagram, which shows that a few Counties, notably certain of the Welsh, did succeed in attaining the position they had occupied in 1875, others, especially those situated on heavy land in the South and in the Midlands, only secured a fraction of the new land it was intended they should have had under the plough. The means employed to attain even this limited accomplishment necessitated much improvisation. Neither ploughs, tractors, horses nor men were at first available in anything like sufficient quantities. The first two were imported by the thousand from the United States, horses and harness were bought by the Department (frequently in competition with the Army), and low category recruits, civilian substitutes, soldiers on lengthy furlough, prisoners of war, and, finally, women were engaged as workers. Nor could the organisation rest when it had secured the means of breaking up grass-land; it was essential that fertilisers, reapers and binders, and even binder-twine, should be available in quantities corresponding to the large acreage broken.

Executive Committees had to select land in their districts which they considered suitable for conversion, and, in the event of a refusal by any occupier to break a proportion of this grass, they then had the power themselves to enter the land, and, with their own implements, to carry out the operation. They could also terminate tenancies, or direct landlords to do so. It was inevitable, in the circumstances attending the whole campaign, that many thousands of acres of totally unsuitable grass were converted, and that owing to lack of skill on the part of the workers good fields were often rendered unfit for further cultivation. But it must also be remembered that an aggregate of at least a million acres of excellent arable land was obtained, and that mistakes were always commented upon, whereas successes were ignored by interested parties. All are familiar with instances of inexperienced persons being sent to break up fields of miserable grass with inefficient implements, of the advice of those with local knowledge being ignored, or of the operations being delayed until the late spring. But it is certain that, in the light of the economic situation then existing, everything done was justified. The expenses were enormous—both the horse-ploughing and the tractor-ploughing schemes were run at a heavy loss—and after November 1918 the horses and machinery were perforce sold for prices that compared ill with those at which they had been purchased. All this is now admitted, but he would have been a foolhardy person who, in the winter of 1917–18, had advised against the policy of State intervention with the cultivation of the land. The grass once broken, comparative freedom of cropping was permitted to individual farmers and no attempt was made to assign any exact proportions between the different cereal and root crops—all were vitally wanted. So long as the new land was sown and adequately tended, the regulations of the Department were adjudged to be met. Surprise was often expressed at the time by travellers that little in the way of additional plough-land was visible. Apart from the obvious fact that this new arable only represented an addition of some 10 per cent. to the old, there was another reason; the bulk of the former was situated, not in the valleys, where the majority of railway lines run, but on the lighter uplands away from the eyes of passengers by train. This was frequently attributable to the action of farmers who preferred voluntarily to sacrifice poorer land, as well as to inability on the part of Committees to tackle the work often involved by the heavier soils.

We have seen the quantity of land that was transferred to the plough; what, it may be asked, was produced from it? On this point very full information is now available in the shape of a report compiled at the time in question and based on complete data received from the Counties themselves. The sixty-one Agricultural Executive Committees were requested in August of 1918 to furnish the Board of Agriculture with particulars of the croppings and yields from the permanent grass-land broken up for the harvest of that year, based on a complete parish record for every 5000 acres converted. Reports were received from all but three geographical Counties—these being the areas selected for purposes of comparison. Some 78,000 acres out of a total of just 1,246,000 broken up came under review, of which 73,000 were in England and 5000 in Wales, whilst the yields from some 8795 fields, situated in more than 600 parishes, were analysed. This gives an average of thirteen selected parishes in every County and of fourteen fields to each parish throughout England and Wales. As in the majority of cases persons making the report were responsible for one, or at the most two, parishes, the completed summaries represented the combined judgment of a large body of men—a number sufficiently large in fact to nullify the effects of a few extravagant or pessimistic estimates. In the following pages the term "old arable", strictly speaking, represents "all" arable and should, statistically, be assumed to include the new in addition, but even if the Reporters of the Board in their ordinary annual investigations allowed for the presence of the new land, this would have had little bearing on the figures they produced.

Emphasis must be laid on the fact that these estimates of yields were made before harvest, and were based on what might reasonably be looked for on threshing out under normal weather conditions. The incessant rains and gales of September and October, however, played havoc with standing crops, and delayed harvesting to such an extent as to reduce the yields in certain Counties by as much as 20 per cent. when threshing eventually took place. This was the subject of emphatic interpolations by nearly every Committee. On the other hand, the yields of all crops in England and Wales in 1918 were well above the average, and due allowance must be made for this factor when appraising the value of that portion grown exclusively on one particular class of land.

Briefly to summarise the main results, it would appear that the yields of wheat and oats in England and Wales on new arable land, whilst equal to the ten-year average, were slightly below those obtained on old arable land, and that of barley was only mediocre. Potatoes and roots yielded returns above the average, and the other cereals showed tendencies to no wide divergence from it. The total area of wheat grown on new land was about 200,000 acres, of oats 850,000 acres and of barley 75,000 acres. The remaining area was probably divided up approximately as follows: potatoes, 32,000 acres, turnips and mangolds, 5000 acres, beans, 14,000 acres, peas, 15,000 acres, rye, 14,000 acres, dredge corn, 8000 acres. Other crops, such as mustard, market-garden produce and a small, but unavoidable, area of bare fallow accounted for the balance of the 1,246,000 acres.

Only in the case of the three major cereals were the "samples" reported on sufficiently large to justify raising the figures by County areas in order to obtain a weighted average for England and Wales as a whole; the yields from all other crops were confined to a simple average relating to the acreage actually reported on.

The normal proportions borne by the three principal cereal crops in England and Wales were, at that time, as follows: wheat, 32 per cent., oats, 40 per cent., barley, 28 per cent., and under stress of war conditions 37, 41, and 22 per cent. respectively, but, on the newly broken land only, they became: wheat, 19 per cent., oats, 74 per cent., barley, 7 per cent. With a few notable exceptions, this order held good throughout the Counties but in Cornwall, Gloucester, Huntingdon, Monmouth, Somerset and Worcester, the predominant position was accorded to wheat, oats occupying less than half the total area under cereals.

It is at once obvious, by a glance at the accompanying maps, that the yield of cereals was mainly determined by their position with reference to a line drawn from the Humber to the Bristol Channel. In other words, it follows that the arable areas did less well than those having a higher percentage of grass. Two possible causes suggest themselves, (*a*) that the area of grass available for breaking up was much larger, and therefore the selection of good land was facilitated, in such Counties as Warwick, Monmouth and Cornwall, as compared with Norfolk, Essex and Kent, or (*b*) that the rainfall during some critical period of the Spring was deficient over the East Midlands and the South-East coast. There was little evidence for the latter suggestion, however, as precipitation was almost normal, and the bulk of the wheat, at any rate, was autumn sown. It is, of course, a possible factor to be reckoned with in the case of spring sown oats, but in the majority of cases the first explanation is the true one, for tens of thousands of acres of rich grass were broken in the West of England, while smaller quantities of poor land, previously considered unfit for the plough, were so treated in the East. For all the cereals, taken together, the South-Eastern group (Surrey, Kent and Sussex) afforded a striking example of paucity of yield, and there was also another well-defined area, comprising the Counties of Leicester, Northampton, Bedford and Buckingham, where a return much below the average was obtained. Wales stands in a class by itself, many of the recorded yields being actually higher than those of the best English Counties. A perusal of the successive numbers of "Agricultural Statistics" shows that a far larger proportion of grass-land had been ploughed up in Wales prior to 1917 than had been the case in England, e.g., out of 64,000 acres broken for the season 1915–16 in England and Wales no less than 42,000 had to be credited to the

Map 1. Yield of wheat on new and old arable in 1918.

Counties shaded and unshaded represent respectively those which produced yields on new arable below or above those on the old land. Vertical lines indicate areas from which no reports were received.

latter country, and there was an additional 41,000 acres in the subsequent year. It is therefore possible that the experience gained in cropping such land previously had borne fruit by the season of 1918. In England, new arable land in the following Counties gave yields above those obtained from old arable for all three cereals—Lancashire, Monmouthshire, Worcestershire and the North and West Ridings of Yorkshire.

Over 14,000 acres of wheat were reported on as grown on converted grass-land in every County except Cumberland, Westmorland and Radnor. Whilst the tendencies above commented on are at once apparent on consulting Map 1, yet it is impossible to draw a fixed line of demarcation, as in the case of oats and barley, on either side of which success or comparative failure could be anticipated. There were only two districts in which the yield from several adjacent Counties was consistently good. The first comprised Lancashire and the two larger Ridings of Yorkshire, together with Derbyshire, and the second Hampshire, Dorset and Wiltshire. Suffolk and Essex provided the only instance of a yield of one of the three main cereals from new arable in the Eastern half of the country exceeding that obtained from the old land, and the South-Eastern group the most important example of failure to obtain even a moderate rate of yield. On the old land the highest yields in England were found in Kent (36·2 bushels), Durham (39·1 bushels), Stafford (36·4 bushels), Dorset (36·5 bushels); the lowest in Huntingdon (28·3 bushels), Warwick (29·6 bushels), Bedford (30·1 bushels) and Monmouth (30·2 bushels), whilst on the newly broken land the four best yields were secured in Cornwall (38·5 bushels), Dorset (43·2 bushels), Monmouth (37·9 bushels), and North Riding of Yorkshire (39·5 bushels); the lowest in Sussex (18·3 bushels), Buckingham (19·3 bushels), Surrey (22·5 bushels) and Huntingdon (23·8 bushels). Although the individual County areas reported on in Wales were small, yet in the aggregate it is obvious that the general conditions favoured a high yield there, as most Counties exceeded 32 bushels to the acre. The highest figure recorded in any one County was at the rate of 80 bushels on eight acres of land in Gloucestershire, the second highest instance being found in Northamptonshire, where sixteen acres were referred to as having produced at the rate of 70 bushels. The instances of complete failure were not numerous. Somerset and Cornwall would appear to have grown wheat on new arable land to the greatest extent.

Map 2. Yield of oats on new and old arable in 1918.

Counties shaded and unshaded represent respectively those which produced yields on new arable below or above those on the old land. Vertical lines indicate areas from which no reports were received.

Oats, easily the predominant crop on newly broken grass-land, were grown in every County in England and Wales, of which the yields from some forty-five thousand acres were analysed. As a crop they were, generally speaking, either very good or very bad, the ultimate yield appearing to depend too often upon the area of the fields which had produced no crops, or at the most 5–10 bushels per acre. Certain Counties attained yields on some hundreds of acres at the rate of 50 and 60 bushels, only to have their averages reduced to a little over 30 by the inclusion of a similar area giving 10 or 12 bushels. In all, it would appear that at least 12,000 acres of oats produced no return from the seed put into the ground. This is not a large figure compared with the total acreage sown on new land, but, in conjunction with a larger area of partial failures, it assumes considerable importance. Where causes were assigned by Crop Reporters for complete or partial failures the blame was most frequently attached to "wireworms" or "leather-jackets", occasional reference being made to "lack of cultivation", "bad farming", or "unsuitable soil". In this connection attention should be drawn to the case of Hertfordshire, where 226 acres, out of a total of 1222 acres reported upon, failed completely and were resown with barley. That the return for England as a whole was over 40 bushels per acre is explained by the fact that the heaviest yields were found in those Western Counties which grew the largest acreages, the lighter yields being obtained from the smaller areas of oats produced in the Eastern half of the country. On the old arable the highest yields were found in Pembroke (50·5 bushels), Lincoln (50·5 bushels), Norfolk (48·4 bushels), Cambridgeshire (48·8 bushels); the lowest in Yorkshire, West Riding (34·8 bushels), Gloucester (36·9 bushels), Oxfordshire (35·7 bushels), Warwick (36·0 bushels). On the new land the highest occurred in Pembroke (57·9 bushels), Cumberland (50·1 bushels), Dorset (49·7 bushels), and Stafford (48·5 bushels); the lowest in Surrey (27·4 bushels), Leicester (29·3 bushels), Huntingdon (29·6 bushels) and Hertford (30·0 bushels). Yields at the rate of 100 bushels per acre were referred to in the Holland Division of Lincolnshire (20 acres), of 96 bushels in the North Riding of Yorkshire (13 acres), 92 bushels in Suffolk, 90 bushels in Worcester and Cumberland, whilst individual instances of 70 bushels appeared in the reports of nearly every County.

Barley was a uniform crop, but, with the exception of the small

Map 3. Yield of barley on new and old arable in 1918.

Counties shaded and unshaded represent respectively those which produced yields on new arable below or above those on the old land. Vertical lines indicate areas from which no reports were received.

area in Wales and another in the North of England, a disappointing one with regard to weight of yield. The three Ridings of Yorkshire, Lancashire and Nottinghamshire produced crops well above the average, but the areas reported on were small. Norfolk, Wiltshire and Gloucester grew barley largely, but nowhere was the yield up to the average. Although the yields in Wales were high, yet again the areas reported on were very small and will not justify close comparison. The cumulative evidence, however, certainly points to the favourable conditions obtaining there. The uniformity of this crop is demonstrated when it is stated that no yield over a rate of 45 bushels was found, and no important case of failure was commented upon by any Reporter.

Yields of other crops were as follows, the figures in brackets referring to those obtained from the old arable land: beans 27·5 bushels (29·4 bushels), peas 26·9 bushels (27·5 bushels), dredge corn 36·5 bushels (35·7 bushels), rye 17·7 bushels (*not recorded*), linseed 18·5 bushels (*not recorded*), buckwheat 20·0 bushels (*not recorded*), potatoes 7·1 tons (6·6 tons), mangolds 28·3 tons (20·6 tons), turnips and swedes 19·0 tons (13·2 tons). The beans, peas and mustard were grown almost exclusively in Lincolnshire and Cambridgeshire, whilst the dredge corn was practically confined to the South-West of the country. More than half the area of rye was grown on light soil in Norfolk, where the yield was naturally very low—only a little over 11 bushels to the acre.

Chapter XXIII

BRITISH AGRICULTURE IN PEACE AND WAR
(CONTINUED)

Broad results of the ploughing-up policy; technical reports on new land; increased supplies of home-produced food; the war and livestock numbers; further schemes for securing more food from our own resources; prices of agricultural products during the war; consumers *versus* producers; price-fixing; comparison with conditions during the Napoleonic War; profits during the Great War; modifications in agricultural practice in times of depression; the cattle embargo.

These, then, viewed from the farmer's standpoint, were the broad results of the State policy. From that of the nation it has been calculated that some two to three million tons of cargo space were, by such means, made available for the transport of troops and munitions of war; but the potential value of this relief was not actually utilised in the case of wheat, as imports were maintained at a very high level throughout the whole period. The particular branch of the Board of Trade charged with allocating space for imports in the order of their importance, and with reference to their cubic contents, must, however, have been grateful for the increased home production of oats and barley. From the agriculturist's point of view the whole policy involved an unnecessary disturbance, but in the winter of 1917–18 neither the nation at large nor the farmer was in a position to judge of the dangers of the situation, and those to whom the duty of safeguarding the food supply of the kingdom was delegated were justified in all the steps they took. It was subsequently claimed that, if even half crops had been secured from the new arable land, such a return would have been advantageous to the morale of the people; as it was, the new land as a whole produced an average outturn. Even involved calculations to arrive at the net results of the food-production campaign gave evidence that, on balance, a gain was registered. For, as G. Udny Yule has pointed out, if the loss of meat and milk entailed by the conversion of plough-land be set against the gain in wheat and potatoes (confining the enquiry to the four commodities principally affected), on a common food-value basis, the operation can be shown to have added materially to the gross quantity of nutriment available for the people.

In the spring of 1918 a diagram illustrating what had been accomplished by the food-production campaign was issued, and led to considerable misunderstanding. It showed that in the year 1916–17 we had been self-supporting in bread-stuffs for a period equivalent to eleven weeks, that the following year this figure had been raised to thirteen weeks and that for the cereal year 1918–19 we should be able to meet our requirements for no less than forty weeks. The last figure was cavilled at, for, as was shown in the event, we succeeded in raising our normal figure of ten weeks' supply to barely eighteen. The explanation lay in the fact that the *per caput* consumption of bread in the last-mentioned year was assumed to have been reduced to its lowest possible limit, and that both considerable dilution of the loaf with barley, maize, rice and other substitutes had been carried to an extreme point, and the rate of extraction of flour to have been extended still further; the whole of the tail corn was also to be included as human food with a corollary that our livestock would have been sacrificed. Under such conditions we might have existed for four-fifths of the year on our own cereal supplies, but we could not have continued to wage the war almost indefinitely on these conditions, as the Germans would have been enabled to do by their policy of concentration on potatoes and pigs.

Percentage of home production of cereals to total supply in the United Kingdom from 1913–14 *to* 1922–23

	Wheat	Barley	Oats	Beans	Peas	All cereals
1913–14	21·2	58·1	78·9	72·0	55·7	49·3
1914–15	23·7	70·5	78·9	74·4	66·6	52·4
1915–16	26·2	54·1	82·4	77·0	59·6	51·6
1916–17	20·6	70·7	84·5	77·2	42·8	50·4
1917–18	30·5	75·4	87·5	83·7	39·6	62·8
1918–19	34·1	74·4	92·2	92·0	63·9	64·8
1919–20	24·5	67·1	89·9	*	*	*
1920–21	22·3	68·7	87·6	*	*	*
1921–22	26·3	64·9	87·2	*	*	*
1922–23	23·6	59·4	85·6	*	*	*

* No figures available for Ireland.

Although a proposed further continuation of the ploughing-up scheme was stopped the moment hostilities ceased, and arrangements were at once made to permit of the reconversion to grass (where necessary, compensation being paid for the loss entailed by the original operation), the decision was taken that it would be well, from the technical point of view, to secure a further report upon the yields of the new plough-land in 1919. Committees, therefore, furnished the Board with information relative to the second year's cropping on this land, for which period County summaries will be found in the Appendix, side by side with those relating to the previous year. Although, owing to weather conditions, the yield of all crops was abnormally low in 1919, yet those on the new arable gave relatively better results than in 1918, as the following figures for England and Wales demonstrate. Expressed as percentages of the yields on the old arable, those on the new had been in 1918, for wheat, 95·1, for barley, 88·8 and for oats, 98·5; but in 1919 the corresponding values were 98·9, 96·5 and 102·8. The yields per acre were, of course, slightly lower in the second year, but all were brought up practically to the standard level, and oats on new land actually produced heavier crops than on the old. The distribution of heavy and light returns was, in 1919, subject to no such strict definition as was witnessed in 1918, but the West Midlands continued to secure the best results, and the South-Eastern Counties had the lowest yields. But of wheat, better yields were obtained in the extreme South-West and in Norfolk, Lincolnshire and Cambridgeshire, whilst oats tended to transfer their worst outturns from East Anglia to the Cornish peninsula. Exact comparisons between the various Counties should be embarked upon with great care, as the acreages concerned in the reports were sometimes small, but the results as a whole afford an interesting sidelight on the improvements effected in unfavourable circumstances. The balance between the different crops on the new land had been considerably modified in 1919, the area under wheat being greatly added to, and that under oats reduced, until both stood at some half million acres. In 1919, root crops again proved very successful on the new arable.

In 1918 questions had been directed to the Executive Committees, asking for their views upon the different methods of ploughing and cultivating employed, the incidence of pests, and, in general, to what causes they attributed their successes or failures. The replies received were very conflicting, but it must be remembered that at least four factors were involved—the date at which the work was undertaken, the nature of the soil, the subsequent climatic conditions, and, lastly, the actual processes employed. Obviously, no hard and fast rule for securing uniform results from heavy clay or from light sandy soils could be evolved. It was very apparent that the former type of land benefited greatly from a previous summer fallow, and numerous instances of failure were recorded from districts which had been compelled to delay ploughing until seed-time, the turf not being thoroughly destroyed in consequence. On light land, also, the yield of spring corn was generally heavier when autumn ploughing and harrowing had been carried out, but much depended on the thorough consolidation of the soil—especially when wire-worm or leather-jackets were present. The importance of the land-presser and of the roller in this connection was very great, and striking instances of their effects were collected from all parts of the country. Steam ploughs, again, showed to great advantage on the heavy land, and, in fact, whenever circumstances permitted of their use, proved superior to tractors. This is doubtless mainly attributable to the fact that they were manned by experienced workers and, unlike the tractors, were not frequently set merely to skim the surface of the land. On the other hand, it must be borne in mind that the latter were always grossly overworked and frequently maltreated. The application of lime and of artificial manures, although not essential, was invariably shown to have been advantageous on both light and heavy land. The Committees themselves admitted that a large proportion of the complete failures emanated from land that, either from altitude or lack of drainage, ought never to have been tackled. The majority of the successes came from rich grass in heavy soil districts that had been broken up in good time, thoroughly worked, and that, consequently, tended to be immune from pests. The many failures on the light lands of the Eastern half of the country were most frequently due to failure to secure a proper tilth for spring sown corn. In 1919 the new arable tended to coalesce with the old, and the essential differences observable in its treatment were not so apparent. Thereafter, a general reversion to grass set in, and the only large attempt at a re-establishment of arable farming became a thing of the past. The actual increase of produce achieved by the ploughing policy (combined with the substitution of essential crops for those of less importance) can be seen on p. 502. This Table, of course, applies to England and Wales, and takes no account of the yields of war-time allotments or of any plots of land below one acre

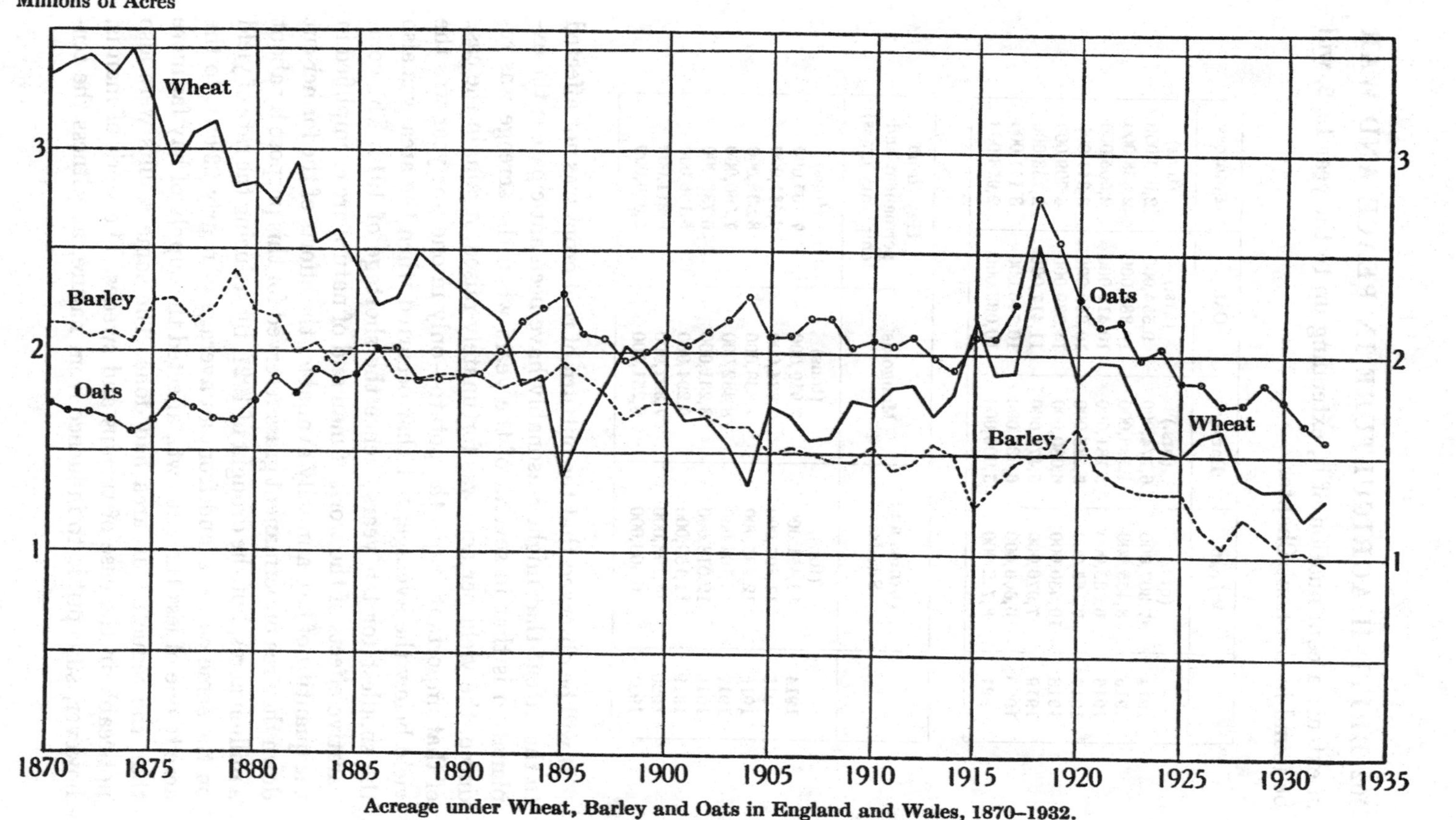

Acreage under Wheat, Barley and Oats in England and Wales, 1870–1932.

in extent; a continuation of it, extending up to the year 1932, will be found in the next Chapter.

	Wheat	Barley	Oats	Potatoes
	(qrs.)	(qrs.)	(qrs.)	(tons)
1914	7,307,000	6,174,000	9,554,000	2,953,000
1915	8,465,000	4,528,000	10,387,000	2,858,000
1916	6,835,000	5,181,000	10,411,000	2,505,000
1917	7,165,000	5,535,000	10,865,000	3,341,000
1918	10,530,000	6,080,000	14,339,000	4,209,000
1919	7,976,000	5,474,000	11,417,000	2,733,000
1920	6,669,000	6,335,000	10,746,000	3,151,000
1921	8,722,000	5,309,000	10,033,000	2,958,000

	Turnips and Swedes	Mangolds	Hay (from permanent and temporary grass)
	(tons)	(tons)	(tons)
1914	13,451,000	7,919,000	7,265,000
1915	11,807,000	7,834,000	6,587,000
1916	12,985,000	7,338,000	8,838,000
1917	12,164,000	8,482,000	7,560,000
1918	12,018,000	8,231,000	6,786,000
1919	11,159,000	6,294,000	5,186,000
1920	14,193,000	7,307,000	8,211,000
1921	6,608,000	6,251,000	5,339,000

It will be observed that the outturn of root crops was not affected to the extent that might reasonably have been anticipated; the explanation is that in several of the years when the acreage was reduced, the yield per acre was fortunately raised. Again, in the case of that important crop—the potato—only in one war year was the yield below the average, but that occurred when the area was also the smallest for ten years; hence the shortage of 1916. The comparative effects of the work of man and of nature are exemplified in the quantity of hay annually available; the efforts of the former cut down the area of permanent grass reserved for this purpose by about a million acres, but the drought of 1921, by reducing the rate of yield on the same class of land from an average of nearly 22 cwt. to the acre to one of less than 16 cwt., affected the supply of hay far more than the reduction in area had done. The same results were also noticeable in the case of turnips and swedes. The work of man is, however, susceptible to influence from nature, as witness the tendency to sow additional areas of any given crop following a shortage, or to reduce the acreage after an abundant harvest. An oscillatory movement is thus produced which has an unfavourable effect upon prices. These fluctuations were accentuated after the war, and a slight surplus of any crop has often resulted in a too drastic cutting down of its area in the following year, to be succeeded in turn by an increase in the third season.

For many years before the war this country had found it necessary to devote the bulk of its area, either directly or indirectly, to feeding livestock—a practice which, from a strictly economic standpoint, had much to commend it, but one that called for the minimum expenditure of capital and labour. Indeed, the gross weight of food raised exclusively for livestock in the United Kingdom exceeded many times over that devoted to human sustenance. How then did this branch of the industry come through the war? In the United Kingdom the numbers of livestock varied thus:

	Cattle	Sheep	Pigs
1914	12,145,000	27,886,000	3,940,000
1915	12,132,000	28,198,000	3,784,000
1916	12,413,000	28,771,000	3,605,000
1917	12,346,000	27,788,000	2,999,000
1918	12,274,000	26,981,000	2,799,000
1919	12,454,000	25,048,000	2,914,000
1920	11,732,000	23,332,000	3,103,000
1921	11,857,000	24,198,000	3,028,000

It will be seen that the head of cattle was well maintained, despite the reports current as to undue slaughtering of calves, and despite also the activities of the Army purchasing agents. But, after 1919, when control was abandoned, prices of veal rose rapidly, and large numbers of calves were killed, farmers being unwilling to rear them as steers under such conditions. Dairy cows were more numerous shortly after the war than before it, and, as larger supplies of feeding-stuffs again became available, the yield of milk was quickly restored to its former level. The reduction in the flocks of sheep was nothing new, as before the war it had become a recognised feature of the annual returns, when various explanations were being assigned to it, such as the increase in the numbers of Small Holdings, and the abnormally low prices ruling for wool and mutton. This movement was at first checked during the war period, but was then accelerated and, ultimately, the total loss compared with the ten years before 1914 amounted to almost 30 per cent. At all times the reduction had been more marked in the Midlands and in the Eastern Counties, and had least affected the mountain flocks of Wales and the North. It was therefore apparent that sheep on arable land were especially susceptible to the prevailing economic conditions. The high prices ruling for wool in 1920 caused a check in the fall, but the unique position occupied by this country in sheep-rearing, as compared with Continental nations, had for the time been modified.

Pigs decreased in number during the war by nearly 30 per cent., but release from controlled prices, combined with the acknowledged rapidity with which this form of livestock can be replaced, soon caused the losses to be made good. In general, the great decline in the quantities of imported feeding-stuffs, especially of maize and cake, was of far greater moment to owners of livestock than was the insignificant reduction in the outturn of hay and roots or the loss of access to a million and a quarter acres of grass. Of maize, the imports declined from about two and a half million tons a year to less than three-quarters of a million tons in 1918–19, oil cake suffered a similar reduction, and the altered rate of extraction adversely affected the supplies of millers' offals. The manufacture of cake was, after 1918, to a large extent transferred to this country from Germany and Holland as a by-product of the margarine trade, so that the quantities of cake imported before and after the war are likely to form a misleading basis for comparison unless the supplies of raw materials, such as copra, palm kernels, and seed, are also included. The world produced abundant yields of all feeding-stuffs during the war years; once again it was lack of transport that forced a reduction in home consumption.

What the agricultural industry of this country did during the war has been briefly related. In part voluntarily, and in part acting under dictation, it augmented the home-grown supply of wheat by putting an extra million acres under that crop, and simultaneously increased the area under other cereals. With a reduced personnel it maintained a larger area under the plough and kept up its herds and flocks, although compelled to forego the bulk of its former supplies of imported feeding-stuffs. Additionally, a large percentage of the urban population became self-supporting in the matter of vegetables. This was, in comparison with other belligerent countries, an accomplishment of which to be proud, but there are certain features resulting from it that call for further examination.

The success of the State's agricultural policy in war-time led to the appearance of numerous schemes, by the aid of which it was held that the United Kingdom might in future be made in whole, or in part, self-supporting in respect of its more vital food-stuffs. These suggestions ranged from level-headed appeals for the compulsory retention of a part of the newly won arable land, to those, uttered by enthusiasts, aiming at some eight or nine million acres under wheat alone. The latter class of person was, in theory, justified when he claimed that that area of wheat would (at normal rates of yield) feed the population, but he generally failed to appreciate some of the insuperable difficulties that stood in the way of his purpose. For example, the maintenance of an adequate system of rotation would have involved the conversion into arable of practically all the grass land in the country. Even if Scotland and Ireland were omitted, much of the land in the North and West of England is, from reasons of altitude and rainfall, unsuitable for the purposes in question, and the policy would have resulted in the formation of large farms—the very antithesis of State policy. It would also have compelled the British farmer to adopt a revolutionary system of rearing livestock. Lastly, it would have involved the permanent retention of State control, for nothing else could have forced the continuation of a policy repugnant to the industry.

Reasons adduced by the advocates of these schemes were diverse, but the danger of another war was generally put in the forefront. Such outbreaks as that witnessed from 1914 to 1918, however, occur at wide intervals (generally some hundred years apart), and, as an insurance against starvation at a remote period in the future, the annual premium demanded was excessive, especially when the possible developments that science may evolve in the meantime—either by making cheaper the raising of cereals or by bringing nearer in point of time our sources of supply—are taken into consideration. A second advantage claimed for increased production at home was that more persons would find employment on the land. Here the answer is that the bald statement is admitted, but the possible addition of many thousands of agricultural labourers to our rural population does not necessarily represent progress from a national standpoint. Better prospects would await these same men as practical farmers in our own Dependencies, where their presence would be far more desirable. Lastly, it was urged that our balance of trade was upset by the high values of our imported agricultural products. This argument, however, carried much greater weight in the closing years of the war and those that immediately succeeded it. Before 1914 our trade as a whole, and with the aid of its invisible exports, approximately balanced, and, with the rapid decline in the values of wheat, wool and meat that occurred after 1920 (combined with recovery in our exports of coal, steel and other commodities) this position was, in normal post-war years, restored and food imports were freed from the false stigma of being a heavy incubus upon trade. This point was also entirely lost sight of by those writers in the press and elsewhere who pointed to our staggering bill for overseas wheat and other soil products in 1918 and the two following years; they failed to consult the pre-war Board of Trade *Returns*, and assumed that values, inflated to the extent of two and three hundred per cent., represented normal conditions. The question of Protection *versus* a subsidy is discussed elsewhere, but it must be pointed out here that the policy of artificially maintaining a large area under cereals would have involved the application—and that upon a most generous scale—of one or other of these methods.

Some of the schemes propounded were highly ingenious, and had obviously been the subject of much thought. All seized on the recognised fact that both the weight and value of the produce from a given area under the plough greatly exceed those from a corresponding grass acreage, and that it is a wasteful process to rear livestock for meat-producing purposes on food that might be directly beneficial to human beings. But all perforce ignored the predilection of British farmers (forced on them by the events of the three previous generations) for an essentially "safe" system of agriculture, and also assumed that the economic conditions ruling in 1918 to 1920 would continue indefinitely, and that high farming would, therefore, be a permanent source of profit. The most popular suggestion was that we should be made absolutely free from the necessity of importing a single quarter of foreign wheat; but in this case the fallacious arguments advanced have already been exposed. Others recommended to the British farmer the example of Germany, by pointing out that the doubling of our arable area would place us on a level with the German people, provided that, at the same time, we copied that nation in technical practice. We must accordingly increase our application of artificial manures, adopt rural co-operation, organise widespread facilities for the provision of credit, and add greatly to our scientific and educational equipment. These steps, it was held, would, in conjunction with a measure of direct State assistance, greatly increase our outturn of soil products, but would not, of course, free us from the obligation to import a large percentage of our wheat requirements. This plan was a perfectly feasible one, but in practice it would have called for the frequent presence of Government officials on every farm to ensure that the area under the plough was maintained (for a State-assisted policy would not alone have guaranteed this), and that some predetermined standard of good husbandry was being observed.

When comparisons are effected between German and British farms it is too often forgotten that the soil and climatic conditions favour large areas of this country, and that the weight of manure applied per acre of land in each country is not necessarily a criterion as to the standard of farming, but rather of the requirements of the different soils; the same argument applies to comparisons between expenditure on rural education. To set side by side, on a comparative output basis, the whole farmed area of Germany and that of Great Britain is apt to prove misleading, for one is comparing an arable with a grass-land system. If, however, the Eastern Counties of England alone are compared with Germany on any basis—such as that of output or of labour employed, it will be found that this country has nothing to fear. Temperamentally, the German farmer was in the past prepared to submit to the dictates of his rulers in return for forms of assistance which his more independent British colleague preferred to go without, whilst at the same time pursuing his own course—a course less laborious and one which involved smaller risks.

Other plans involved the cropping of certain areas according to rule, the proposers of which, arguing from the acknowledged fact that a group of some half-dozen East Anglian Counties was producing its share (on an acreage basis) of the total food requirements of the United Kingdom, suggested a wide extension of arable farming on prescribed lines. The determining factors were "the quantities of starch-equivalent derived from wheat, potatoes, milk and meat". Certain North-Western districts, when analysed on these lines, could be shown to be producing almost their *quota* in the shape of milk and meat, and would therefore have been spared a drastic ploughing programme, but the greater part of the Midlands was to have been invited to return to this form of cultivation, and to produce beef and mutton from animals fed mainly on roots. That a greater supply of food-stuffs in general would have resulted is not questioned, but here the previous objections held equally good.

Finally, the nation itself was asked to co-operate with the farmer by adopting a fresh dietary, for, by concentrating on the raising of pigs and potatoes, the consumption of bread-stuffs, it was pointed out, could be drastically reduced. The creation of a permanently enlarged acreage under potatoes and their partial substitution, in a prepared form, for the wheaten loaf, together with the doubling or trebling of the numbers of pigs, would, it was urged, at one and the same time reduce our foreign indebtedness and lay the foundations for a reserve in case of war. Both pigs and potatoes are susceptible to rapid increase in emergency, and their rate of production per acre is high, but apart, once more, from the element of compulsion, this last suggestion contained the fatal claim that the State could dictate to the populace what it should eat in times of peace. Even if the prescribed diet were palatable to the bulk of the nation—which is extremely questionable—the mere fact that freedom of choice was absent would in normal times preclude such a scheme from being attempted. In times of emergency a Government can do what it likes, both with the cultivation of the land and in the matter of the people's dietary; but the possibility of war at some distant time would never persuade the nation to alter its habits in times of peace.

The plea on behalf of State granaries sometimes put forward before the war was, of course, not reiterated whilst hostilities lasted, but in 1922 it was again revived. The practical difficulties and expense involved in the purchase and storage of even a few months' supply of wheat had times out of number been shown to outweigh any possible advantages such a scheme might confer. It would have taken several years to effect the purchase of one year's supply, and the process might seriously have affected prices; the cost of erecting granaries would have been very great—nearly forty years ago it was estimated that seven and a half million pounds would be required—and their maintenance and staffing would have been an additional expense. Technical objections of a similar nature were present in the suggestion, made more than once, that a bounty of half-a-crown a sack should be paid to millers for storing flour up to a certain minimum quantity.

After 1920 direct appeals to the individual cultivator, coupled with explanatory tables of new cropping systems, ceased, and the Government itself took steps to perpetuate war practices in our system of agriculture. As the safeguarding of the wheat supply was avowedly the principal object of State intervention, consideration of the policy involved in the Corn Production and Agriculture Acts was discussed in the appropriate Chapter, but the view that a continuation of State aid and of State control in times of peace was a mistake must again be firmly expressed. Burke's words on this subject should not be forgotten, for he declared that "it is a perilous thing to try experiments on the farmer—on the farmer whose capital is far more feeble than commonly is imagined, whose trade is a very poor one, for it is subject to great risks and losses". After 1918 experiments *were* tried, and not only met with no success but caused disaffection and rancour.

Peculiar in being the only European belligerent to increase, during hostilities, her supplies of home-produced food, the United Kingdom, unlike other countries, also came through the war with moderate recourse to the rationing of food-stuffs; bread, in particular, if its quality was slightly lowered, was unlimited in quantity. But if quantities were subject to no restraint, prices were, and agriculture suffered from this form of supervision at least to the same extent as other industries. Being responsible for the supply of food-stuffs, the Government adopted a threefold scheme. In the first place, as has been related, it used every possible means to add to the home output; secondly, it assumed control of imports, admitting only those articles that it held to be essential, and then only in just sufficient quantities; and, lastly, it made possible the purchase of both home and foreign produce by fixing wholesale and retail prices.

In respect to this last feature, agriculture occupied a peculiar position. The Ministry of Food was charged with safeguarding the interests of the consumer, and was a more powerful body than the Board of Agriculture (not until 1919 also to become a Ministry), which was essentially the representative of producing interests. As a result, there was a certain amount of truth in the statement, so often heard, that the old rivalry between town and country was resulting in a distinctly favourable bias being manifested towards the former by the edicts of the Food Controller. Not only was the price of what the agriculturist sold determined by the Ministry of Food, but also of much that he bought, so that after 1916 little opportunity occurred of making profits on the scale that still obtained in many other industries. Again, not thoroughly organised, and being also far more numerous than other types of producers, the farmers were unable to combine effectively for the purpose of securing a hearing. Representatives of less important industries often succeeded in their dealings with Government departments where agriculturists failed. The value of this temporary co-operation can still be seen in certain trades—a co-operation between manufacturers, merchants and retailers that led to their mutual advantage and protection. The results, indeed, might have been observed for some years in the maintenance of prices which subsequent circumstances did not warrant.

As was pointed out in the Chapter on Statistics, it is extraordinarily difficult to compare the profits or losses of the industry as a whole, or even of any particular branch of it, by compiling two index-numbers, one to show the fluctuations in the price of the articles purchased, and the other corresponding movements in those sold. Speaking in very wide terms it is, however, certain that the cereal raiser made considerable profits in 1915 and 1916 while wages and outgoings on materials were still relatively low, and that in the latter years of the war there was greater scope for the milk and meat producer, with occasional openings to secure exceptional returns from such crops as potatoes. The accompanying Table (prepared from publications of the Ministry of Agriculture) shows the fluctuations in the prices of all the principal commodities sold by British farmers from 1914 to 1922; it is continued for the period 1923 to 1932 in the last Chapter of the book.

It must be remembered that all the commodities involved were subject to the price regulations of the Ministry of Food or of its dependent bodies, that a free market did not exist for the majority of them after the autumn of 1916, and that decontrol was only gradually carried out subsequently to 1919. It is useless attempting arbitrarily to account for the variations in the increases sanctioned, as so many factors existed to influence the decisions of those concerned. There was, for instance, the question of the possibility of obtaining alternative supplies from near at hand neutral countries, the comparative

Changes in the prices of agricultural produce in the years 1914–22 *as compared with the average of the years* 1911–13 (= 100)

	1914	1915	1916	1917	1918	1919	1920	1921	1922
Wheat	107	162	179	232	223	223	247	219	146
Barley	96	131	188	228	208	267	315	184	141
Oats	105	152	168	251	249	264	287	172	147
Cattle	106	136	158	205	211	232	263	227	163
Sheep	113	130	157	197	210	230	287	217	200
Pigs	106	129	167	226	266	276	330	228	187
Milk	103	117	157	191	251	300	303	263	179
Wool	109	159	146	162	174	308	353	84	114
Butter	101	117	136	177	209	215	299	215	161
Cheese	104	124	149	208	233	269	240	171	143
Poultry and eggs	98	117	144	183	284	259	265	219	192
Beans and peas	108	141	170	270	477	319	288	196	180
Hay	77	106	152	157	187	257	292	151	140
Potatoes	85	109	188	237	179	235	306	232	179
Fruit	84	95	138	154	411	318	379	283	188
Hops	46	68	81	91	193	213	205	211	123
Vegetables	108	124	154	238	257	257	219	246	196
General index-number	101	127	160	201	232	258	292	219	169

amount of the labour bills in raising different forms of food-stuffs, and the uncertain expenses of feeding livestock. No official, whether permanent or temporary, had had previous experience of the difficulties attendant on the process of price-fixing, and no figures were available for estimating costs of production. In the words of Lord Ernle,

> In normal times, varying rates, determined by the play of local markets, make the necessary adjustment between district and district. Now flat rates had to be fixed, and what was one man's meat was another man's poison. One man might get too much, another too little. Everyone knows, for example, that the cost of producing a quarter of wheat differs not only in each County, but on nearly every farm and on nearly every field. The outstanding question which persistently recurred was, how far prices should be regulated to stimulate production or in the interests of consumption.

It has been shown that, in the long run, the consumers' interests—when poised against those of the rural producer—were looked upon as paramount, as in fact they had been for many years. The diagrammatic representation of the prices of wheat, barley and oats for the last hundred and fifty years (see p. 387), when the periods covering the two European wars are compared, exhibits strikingly the varying effects of controlled prices and of a free market. In 1801 wheat reached an average of 119*s.* the quarter, and in 1812 actually 126*s.* (many sales, of course, being effected at prices well above these levels), but the corresponding figure during the Great War never exceeded 81*s.* The fact that the Government, from 1917 to 1920, was paying for foreign wheat landed in our ports sums above the prices current in the French war was one of the sources of irritation to the British farmer. The diagram demonstrates, however, that he received relatively higher prices for barley and oats than his ancestors had done. The demand in 1812 was mainly for wheat, and the other cereals, not being in such great demand, did not appreciate to the same extent. From 1915 onwards, by when all three were controlled, there was permitted to barley and oats a relatively much larger increase than to wheat.

If, in theory, farmers could obtain certain statutory prices, it did not always follow that in practice they were successful in so doing, or that they made commensurate profits, for the failure of seasonal crops, or a decline in output from causes beyond their control, frequently caused reductions in their outturn during the war years. Again, if the prices of home-grown agricultural products are placed side by side with those of other commodities, it will be seen that, as a rule, they did not rise to the same extent. Sir W. Layton (*Introduction to the Study of Prices*) places in three groups the percentage increases of the more frequently used commodities. The first group contains those articles which rose less than the general average—here are found four agricultural products—the second group embraces articles which rose to about the average, which again includes four food-stuffs (three almost entirely British in origin); the third group—commodities that rose above the average—contains only pork as a representative of agricultural produce. Consequently, the index-number of food-stuffs remained well below those relating to manufactured articles and to other raw materials; this was the penalty attaching to a trade of such vital importance. Neither did this index attain the height reached by corresponding figures in other countries, allied and hostile.

There was one peculiar feature in connection with maximum prices that deserves mention. It wassoon found that maximum prices tended to resolve themselves into fixed prices, below which no seller would reduce his wares. The term "Government price" became synonymous with a fixed minimum price, and no appeals, based upon falling costs of production, could persuade retailers to sell below what they held to be a statutory limit. This phenomenon was during the last few months of control especially rife in the fruit and vegetable trade, when it appeared that individual shop-keepers really believed that they were forbidden, for example, to sell their apples below the excessive price of 9*d.* the lb. The immediate result of decontrol was, in almost every instance, a sudden rise in price of the commodity involved, followed by an equally rapid fall, which brought it well below the former fixed level, and launched it on the steady slope that it was destined to descend for the next decade.

When the war ceased, agriculture at home was subject to immediate competition from the more distant centres of supply which, from 1914 to 1919, had been unable to transport their products to this country. Here again agriculture was at a material disadvantage, for, in the case of manufactured articles, a certain respite was afforded the home producer in the shape of the time occupied by his foreign rivals in collecting supplies of raw materials and carrying through the essential trade processes. The British farmer almost at once found his market flooded with Australian wool, wheat and frozen mutton that had accumulated overseas.

If we turn to the purchase side of the farmer's balance sheet during the war, we find that, here, the question was not merely one of prices, but frequently of the sheer absence of supplies. The Board of Trade had the power, and freely exercised it, to exclude altogether, or in part, such commodities as were in its judgment not essential to the national well-being, or those that, from their nature, made undue demands upon cargo space. Maize came in the first category, and agricultural machinery in the second. Not only were imported commodities, such as the above, reduced in available supply, but the production of millers' offals and brewers' grains was greatly cut down by the regulations affecting the supply and character of human food and drink. Therefore, although individual index-numbers relating to commodities normally purchasable by agriculturists were issued, their value as criteria of the actual outgoings on farms during the war years is insufficient to warrant reproduction. Their percentage increases were not out of harmony with the general price-level upon the sales side, but both basic slag and superphosphates (when procurable) had by 1920 risen above 200 per cent., and certain varieties of seeds were prohibitive in price. The difficulties of farming in the years 1920 and 1921 were added to by the fact that crops planted or sown at the peak of prices were frequently harvested when their value had fallen heavily—the familiar economic lag was making itself felt. The similarity existing between the state of agriculture in 1821 and 1921 did not extend to the matter of the purchase price of farm requirements, for a hundred years earlier farmers were sufficiently self-supporting to be almost independent of extraneous purchases; then no machinery, fertilisers, cake or maize figured in their annual expenditure. Wages, rent and rates formed their burden, none of which was dependent for its alleviation on the good-will or the business instincts of foreign peoples.

Yet conditions in the six or eight years that succeeded Waterloo and those that supervened on 1920 were, in certain directions, remarkably similar. Any one who has read an account of the social condition of the nation and of the state of agriculture in 1822, will agree that in the main it might have been written of 1922. *The Times* of June 6th, 1822, took up the question of the fall in prices of farm products, and, with less tolerance towards the countryman's point of view than it habitually exhibited a century later, attacked the landowners thus:

> The cry at present among the country gentry is "remunerating prices! remunerating prices!" We shall therefore in a few words explain what is meant by the expression. Remunerating prices simply mean such prices as shall enable the land-owners, at the expense of the country, to support all the extravagant grants which they themselves had made out of their estates to Ministers during the last thirty years.... There is also another cry, equally unjust and equally deserving notice and reproof. It is now said "Everything falls ultimately upon the land; the rates, taxes, tithe all fall at last upon the land". Why, gentlemen, we reply, you should have thought of this when year after year, you were burdening the land. It is too late to talk thus now, when the land simply stands, or staggers, under that load of taxes which you yourselves have put upon it. It is but three years ago, and long after the peace was concluded, that some of you voted an addition of ten thousand men to the regular army. Pauperism has regularly increased with taxation. You went on taxing; you even added three millions in one year after the peace was concluded. We pray, and firmly trust, that a benevolent Providence will frustrate your intentions, and that an abundant and well-gotten harvest will retain all the fruits of the earth at their present prices, beyond which they would never have risen but through your criminal subserviency.

It is symptomatic of the then changing outlook that prices were the nation's first consideration, and that the economic position of the agriculturist (whether landlord or tenant) was beginning to be of secondary importance. Alternative and supplementary sources of food supply were few, and the skirmishing that preceded the great fight between town and country was clearly commencing. A hundred years later *The Times* warmly supported agriculturists in their efforts to maintain prices and even exaggerated somewhat their hardships.

In this connection the value of accurate contemporaneous information concerning the state of the industry cannot be exaggerated; thus the accounts of past agricultural conditions, such as those prepared successively by Marshall, Young, Cobbett, Caird, Rider Haggard and Sir Daniel Hall is immense. Reports made by competent observers carry to many persons more weight than do bare statistics of acreage, yield and prices, besides giving to future generations a more human picture of the times. The study of agricultural history is an important subject for all connected with the land, and it is to be hoped that, in future, others will be found to follow in the footsteps of those illustrious "Reporters" who have given us such precise knowledge of the rural economy of their own times.

If a statistical expression to cover the financial standing of the industry during the immediate post-war years is lacking, evidence, culled from typical farms, is available both for isolated examples and for groups of holdings. A *Report*, made to the Agricultural Wages Board in 1919, contained balance sheets, extending over five years and secured from undertakings of all types and sizes. In the case of twenty-six farms, covering upwards of eight thousand acres (the percentage of which under the plough rose from forty-six to forty-nine during the period under review), the profit per acre in the years in question was given as follows: 1913–14, 5*s*. 10*d*.; 1914–15, 4*s*. 7*d*.; 1915–16, £1. 13*s*. 8*d*.; 1916–17, £1. 11*s*. 10*d*.; 1917–18, £1. 11*s*. 9*d*. On these farms there were no very material changes in the style of farming; for, apart from the slight turnover to arable, cattle remained stationary in numbers, sheep declined 10 per cent. and pigs rose 22 per cent. The balance of profits after the second year of the war tended slightly to decline, and, if similar figures had been available for the same undertakings in the following years, a further contraction would certainly have been revealed. As corroboration that profits per acre from corn-growing were high in the first years of the war, it is significant that the majority of individual farmers who made public their accounts compared the results in a pre-war year with those obtained after 1917. Other groups of farms selected in various districts showed very similar returns to those above, but, of course, in all these cases the pre-war capital invested is not recorded, and the return upon it in the basic year is, therefore, an unknown factor. Home farms exhibited those features which are naturally looked for in their case, and in the examples given in the *Report* an annual "loss" was turned into a small "profit" in 1916–17 and 1917–18. At the other end of the scale, co-operative farms revealed the uncertainty always attaching to this form of venture, for even after 1913–14 the figures relating to different societies generally exhibited losses alternating with profits. To what extent the above additional profits (or avoidance of losses) were due to a compulsory reduction in the use of fertilisers and of labour, leading to a consequential decline in the capital value of the holdings, is not discoverable, but it is generally acknowledged that the standard of farming was progressively lowered as the war continued.

Rents were certainly raised on the renewal of leases for perhaps three or four years after 1916, but, again, evidence is lacking as to the extent that landlords availed themselves of their powers in this direction; figures, provided by the Surveyors' Institution and the Farmers' Union, showed widely divergent results, dependent, of course, upon the character of the holdings concerned and upon their locality, but a figure of 20 per cent. might perhaps represent at most the average increase by 1919. Purchases, however, were increasingly frequent from that year onwards, and were effected at prices that represented higher rents than had formerly been paid.

If the period between August 1914 and the winter of 1923 could be financially reviewed as a whole, it would probably be found that the gains of the industry in the first six years had been almost entirely cancelled by the losses of the latter three and a half. The position of individual agriculturists at the end of that time depended upon when they had assumed their responsibilities, and, if they were in business in the earlier years of the war, what course they had pursued in the allocation of their profits. Farmers already established in 1914, who invested their gains in safe securities unconnected with their own enterprises, should have been in a position comparable with that which they occupied in the former year. Those persons who took up farming as a means of making a livelihood after the autumn of 1918 were, as a class, involved in the greatest difficulties; they were, indeed, fortunate if they had only risked their capital in purchasing farming stock at the inflated prices then current, and had not also purchased their land under similar conditions. Tenants adding to their holdings by purchase also saw a large part of their savings capitalised in vain. Such things always happen in times of high prices (and of apparent large profits), as the bulk of mankind assumes that stability will be maintained at the existing price level. A little knowledge of history would thus have been advantageous, but it is doubtful if its warning notes would have been heeded. A hundred years earlier farmers were reported to have said "What we want is another war". In 1922 and the following years their descendants would not have been inclined to re-echo this cry.

Only at these long intervals do human activities receive a crucial test—a test that tries at one and the same time their individual economic strength and their combined value to the nation at large. Agriculture enhanced its reputation by the way it added to the resources of the country from 1914 onwards, revealing thereby a latent power of expansion that was as unexpected by the urban population as it was valuable in the emergency. That, in the process, it was not permanently injured is certain; but, undoubtedly, the revival that was just beginning to be evidenced before the war received a serious set-back from the events that followed the restoration of peace. What permanent modifications in its practice this may have involved is not even yet certain, but any large extension of the arable land in the immediate future is unthinkable. An increase in the production of "luxury" crops, such as fruit, vegetables and the hundred and one commodities that the growth of urban population always calls for has, however, already been evidenced.

This tendency harmonises with the views of Caird in 1851, when he urged farmers to concentrate their attention on those articles that showed signs of improving in value. The produce of grass-land, he said, was increasingly taking its place in the household expenditure. As the national wealth was growing, so was the nation's consumption of meat, milk and wool—among the products of arable land only barley had increased in price, and that, again, was attributable to the greater demand for a "luxury" beverage. Caird quoted the instance of farms yielding, eighty years before the date at which he wrote, a £100 worth of meat, wool and butter, which in 1851 was worth £200, although neither the breed of stock nor the capabilities of the land had been improved, while corn-raising farms were still producing only an equivalent value of cereals at the end of the eighty years, and he held, further, that, here, the quantity each acre yielded had diminished. He advocated a reversion to grass, combined with the intensive cultivation of vegetables—in fact the pursuit of a policy calculated to secure to the home producer the maximum possible share of the population's growing expenditure. He stated that no anxiety need be felt for the people's bread, for, "if an emergency should ever arise, by which in consequence of war we should be driven back on our own resources, we would find that we had been laying up in our rich grass fields, and well-manured green-crop lands, a store of fertility which might be called into action in a single season, and which would yield ample crops of corn for consecutive years with little labour or expense". Sixty-three years later the emergency did arise, and Caird's prophecy was in fact borne out, but the labour and expense involved were not "little".

The war caused the extension of State control into every branch and detail of farming, and the first years that succeeded it saw the relaxation of control, accompanied by the efforts of those affected to expedite the process. The policy involved in the repeal of the Corn Production Act has been discussed at length elsewhere, but certain other features call for brief consideration. With the removal of the embargo on the importation of Canadian cattle the British farmer lost, for the moment, his last relic of Protection. The principles at stake were little understood by the nation at large, and for the townsman were also complicated by the inability of the industry to present, upon this subject, a united front. In previous discussions on the question of granting or of removing fiscal aids the farmers formed a homogeneous party, but on this occasion they gave vent to widely divergent views. The townsman was at first puzzled, and then apathetic. As soon as he was brought to see that there was little chance of his potential supply of meat being considerably augmented, or, therefore, of his pocket being affected, he decided that it was merely a domestic concern of the farmer. The main arguments round which the controversy revolved were, firstly the risk of the introduction of disease, and, secondly, the effects on the existing home supply of store cattle. The precautions to be adopted in Canada and *en route* were finally held to meet the first point. But, in the other case, agreement was not reached, the advocates of free admission pointing out that store cattle had been declining in numbers and increasing in value prior to the war, while breeders avowed their perfect ability to meet any future demands made upon them. In the end the breeders of cattle, as represented by the rest of England and Wales, lost their case, and the minority, consisting of the Norfolk and Southern Scotch fatteners had their way. The findings of the Commission appointed to enquire into the whole question were, briefly, that the introduction of store cattle might unfavourably affect certain classes of farmers, as, for instance, the Highland crofters and the Irish exporters, but that the industry as a whole, and the country itself, would benefit. This body expressed the opinion that the numbers of animals introduced would not exceed 200,000 annually, and that such a figure would be insufficient materially to affect the supply of meat, representing, as it did, only some 8 per cent. increase relative to the home supply. For similar reasons the milk supply would not be prejudiced. A reduction in the price of meat to a somewhat lower level was, however, looked for as a result of the measures to be taken; although, with the growing demands, it appeared unlikely that an additional supply on the scale anticipated by the Committee would have much influence on prices in future years. It was pointed out that, should matters turn out otherwise, revision of the policy could always be effected. The importance of the whole matter was, however, within ten years to be dwarfed by the effects of the policy pursued as a result of the Ottawa agreements and the quantitative control of imported meat—a subject dealt with in the succeeding Chapter.

If agriculture was relieved from the incubus of fixed prices, temporarily freed from paying a minimum wage (losing simultaneously in one branch its guaranteed profits), and left to compete in the open market with distant rivals, yet it was, in the winter of 1922–3, still subject to the direct as well as to the indirect effects of what had gone before. Quite apart from the then increased weight of the constitutional charges upon land, agriculturists were constantly reminded of their changed position by the retarded action of legislation effected during the war. The relationship of landlord and tenant was transformed, rent and the occupation of cottages were both subject to outside intervention, cherished units of measure were abolished, and what was regarded as the only possible standard of wages no longer bore a reasonable relationship to those of other industries, for Railway companies and employers of labour in rural districts had, voluntarily, or under compulsion, standardised the remuneration of certain workers at a level more than 100 per cent. in excess of the wages that the farmer could now afford to pay. This handicap also militated against the farmer's interests in the case of the distributing trades, for such classes of employees as milkmen's and bakers' roundsmen and shopkeepers' assistants were still being remunerated on scales that were exceptionally attractive. This was, in the majority of cases, attributable to the formation, during the war, of Trade Boards and it had the effect of enhancing the middleman's share of the total profits from the production and sale of agricultural commodities.

State assistance on the grand scale having been terminated, a period—devoted, on the part of successive Governments, to the study of the rural situation and by the agricultural community to quiet reorganisation—intervened before the more ambitious policies of a decade later, to be described in the next Chapter, were set in motion.

Chapter XXIV

BRITISH AGRICULTURE AFTER THE WAR

Falling prices followed by temporary stability; the *Reports* of the Tribunal of investigation; Sugar-beet in relation to British agriculture; analysis of the economic situation in 1925; Cost of Production and other methods of investigation; measures of relief accorded between 1921 and 1930; further proposals for subsidies considered; farm receipts and expenditure; an Eastern Counties' Survey; statistics of bankruptcies and failures among farmers; results of the Ottawa agreements; world aspects of depression and of monetary policies.

The decade comprising the years 1923 to 1932 in many ways represents the most remarkable through which the agriculture of these Islands has ever passed, for in it a policy of *laissez-faire*, when faced with growing difficulties, gave way to an intensive application of minor *ad hoc* remedies, to be in their turn succeeded by the unexpected introduction of drastic fiscal measures. In the following pages it is proposed to treat chronologically, rather than as subjects in water-tight compartments, the events that call for mention; such of them, however, as have, from the nature of the case, already been described in the foregoing Chapters, will merely be referred to in passing.

In the light of what was to follow later, it is now curious to read reports upon rural conditions written in 1922 or 1923, for many, even amongst independent observers, then considered that British farming was in a critical condition. Thus, we find *The Times* stating that "farmers of all classes, in all districts, are in serious financial straits. It will be hard to decide which was the more calamitous to agriculture—the unproductive summer of last year, or the low prices of the present [1922] year". A peripatetic investigation, undertaken by representatives of that same journal, disclosed "losses of £5 per acre" in Norfolk and of "£8000 upon 600 acres in Bedfordshire", led to farmers in the Southern Counties being described as "on the verge of bankruptcy" and the state of those in the North as "far worse than that of forty years ago". Other authorities concurred in this view of the situation. A glance at either the folding diagram between pages 540 and 541 or at the Table upon p. 511 will reveal the precipitate nature of the fall in values in 1921, for in twelve months the price of agricultural products had declined from 290 to 180. During that, and the subsequent, year farm wages remained well above the Cost of living index-number and other items of expenditure had not been readjusted, nor could it be foreseen that price stability would be virtually maintained until the end of 1925 or that those wages would, in the absence of control, shortly revert to a lower level.

On the grounds of urgency, therefore, an "Agricultural Tribunal of Investigation", consisting of three economists (with an agricultural assessor) was appointed, whose terms of reference were as follows: "To inquire into the methods which have been adopted in other countries during the last fifty years, to increase the prosperity of agriculture and to secure the fullest possible use of the land for the production of food and the employment of labour at a living wage, and to advise as to the methods by which these results can be achieved in this country". So impressed was this body with the critical nature of the situation that, in the course of 1923, it produced two *Interim Reports*. The first recommended the imposition of a duty of ten shillings per quarter upon imported malting barley and one of twenty shillings per hundredweight upon imported hops, with a preference of one-third in favour of the Dominions. It further proposed that importers of flour should be required to introduce a corresponding proportion of wheat offals (viz., 25 per cent. offals to 75 per cent. flour) and that the introduction of foreign potatoes should be permitted only under licence and for specified periods. None of these suggestions was adopted by the Government; all would have involved great administrative difficulties and some could not have been put into effect without breaking trade agreements with other countries. This *Report* also contained some proposals of a more general character, which included an extension of credit facilities, the reduction of railway rates upon all types of farm supplies and products, the reintroduction of Wages Boards and augmented expenditure upon agricultural education and research. These latter were in course of time, and by successive Governments, implemented. The Tribunal at that time (March 1923) expressly refrained from advocating any measure of financial assistance to wheat growers or to other arable farmers. Nevertheless, a very few months later, in a second *Interim Report*, a majority of its members expressed themselves convinced that more comprehensive measures were "immediately necessary", and that, in order to maintain the area of ploughed land, some form of guarantee or subsidy was required. After canvassing the respective merits of an acreage subsidy upon all arable land or upon wheat, of one upon agricultural wages or by means of relief from national taxation, they recommended (as was previously described in the second Chapter on wheat) one of ten shillings per acre upon all land under the plough in conjunction with an additional ten shillings on every acre under wheat. This, it was estimated, might cost £6,500,000, and would carry with it the corollary of wages control. One member, Professor D. H. Macgregor, did not sign this *Report* but expressed his agreement with the proposal in question, provided that the Government was satisfied that the maintenance of the existing arable area was necessary in the interests of national defence.

No official steps were taken in the matter and the Tribunal's final (majority) *Report*, which appeared in the summer of 1924, reiterated the belief that, if the nation wished to take steps that offered "a reasonable chance of staying the present decline", its own proposals afforded "the best means of preventing an immediate conversion of tillage to grass". The terms of reference imposed upon that body must be borne in mind when the divergent views of its members are discussed. Sir William Ashley, Professor W. G. S. Adams and Mr C. S. Orwin (the assessor) in effect endorsed the implications involved therein; Professor Macgregor clearly did not. The former trio accepted the lead offered them, and emphasised the lessons to be drawn from the methods employed and the output secured by British and Continental farmers respectively, evidently holding that increased home-production of wheat, and the corollary employment of more workers, was not only desirable but essential. They averred that, short of some form of "Protection", nothing but the extension of arable dairying and of stock-farming could maintain the tilled area of the country, and that, "if such experiments [i.e. arable dairying] are not carried out, or do not demonstrate the financial feasibility of the new methods, Great Britain must be content to see its agriculture dwindle greatly in all those respects which promote food production and employment on the land, or else it must resort to measures which will be essentially protective in character by whatever name they are called".

Professor Macgregor considered that there was little occasion for alarm in regard to the state of British agriculture, *per se*, and would appear to have agreed that, in its practices as well as in the amenities it provided, it could bear favourable comparison with that of other countries. Grounds of national defence were the only ones upon which he would discuss the advisability of increasing artificially its output, and, even here, he recommended deferring a decision by our military advisers until "the international future is more clear, national finance less strained and the post-war settlement is more complete". The possibility of a fresh decline in the arable area and in the number of farm workers he was prepared to weigh against an annual cost equivalent to that of a battleship, and it is clear that, personally, he thought the expenditure unnecessary. Perhaps the most striking commentary upon his *Report* is to quote in full one of its concluding paragraphs, which ran as follows: "The facts do not show that there is ground for depreciation of British agriculture as a whole. It pays wages that are high as compared with those in other European countries; the yield of the area which is under the chief crops compares favourably with that of the areas under the same crops abroad; while the actual decline of the agricultural population, as tested by male persons employed, has not over the whole length of our period of reference been so startling as is often supposed, or so rapid as that of other important European countries. Farmers are not responsible for the natural conditions or the national policies which have affected the form of cultivation that is most profitable; subject to the conditions, the cultivation of the land in Britain cannot be described as inefficient. Considered as a craft, British farming has in its time taught a great deal to other countries; considered as an industrial organisation, it may now learn something in turn". If the above review be placed beside the terms of reference, it becomes difficult to reconcile the two statements: certainly the words of Professor Macgregor do not suffer in the process.

The final *Report* forms a mine of valuable material, for all the members had contributed of their special knowledge; there is not a branch of agriculture that is not dealt with nor a foreign country that escapes a full investigation of its rural economy. On these grounds alone the work of the Tribunal would have been justified, but, as a method of enquiry, it also proved itself vastly more expeditious than its cumbrous predecessors in the form of Royal Commissions.

Lastly, if its major proposals were not implemented, many subsequent enactments were based upon its findings.

During 1924 and 1925 the prices of agricultural products, in common with those of industrial commodities, rose slightly, but, after the return to the gold standard in the latter year, the fall was resumed—if, upon a much lesser gradient, upon one destined to be uniform until the end of 1932. At that time it was estimated that the relief afforded to farmers by the 1923 Agricultural Rates Act—amounting to an average of three shillings per acre—had been far exceeded by the effects of this monetary policy which, by raising the value of the sovereign by 5 per cent., had reduced arable returns to the extent of some ten shillings an acre; further, the re-establishment of statutory Wages Boards had increased the farmers' outgoings by six or seven shillings an acre. As a net result of these alterations the economic situation deteriorated markedly and the already familiar discrepancies between the sheltered and unsheltered industries were exaggerated. British agriculture was now facing a situation to which its followers were destined to become inured. The comparative incidence of the depression in different parts of the country need not be assessed at this stage, but, in general terms, it may be stated that arable farms suffered more than grass-land and that, in the former class, those situated upon the heavier clays were in the worst case.

At this point State intervention is happily to be recorded in an entirely new direction, for, by the British Sugar (Subsidy) Act of 1925, the subsidising of sugar and of molasses derived from home-grown beet was, for a period of ten years, guaranteed. Payment to factories at the rate of 19*s.* 6*d.* per hundredweight for the first four years, followed by 13*s.* for the next three and, finally, 6*s.* 6*d.* for the period 1932–34 was conditional upon the manufacturers in their turn giving a minimum of 44*s.* per ton for beet of 15½ per cent. sugar-content during the initial four years. This crop, so familiar to travellers on the Continent, had, as a result of the British blockade, been introduced into France during the Napoleonic war. It had spread throughout Europe, notably in Germany, Austria and Hungary and, in conjunction with a widespread system of export bounties, had been the subject of many international agreements. Here, apart from a few isolated attempts to popularise it in the Eastern Counties prior to the war, it had been ignored and the country was in consequence entirely dependent upon imported supplies of cane- and beet-sugar. In 1920 one factory had been set up independently of any Government support and the area of beet was then some 8000 acres. Five years later the promised subvention had increased this figure to 55,000 acres. Thereafter progress was rapid and within three years no less than eighteen large factories were at work in Great Britain, and there was also one in the Irish Free State; the maximum area of 349,000 acres was reached in 1930, when over forty thousand farmers—mainly situated in the Eastern Counties—were raising this crop. Technically, also, progress had been well sustained, for in no year had the sugar-content fallen below 16 per cent. and it was frequently in excess of 17 per cent., while the yield of beet moved slowly upwards, and in 1930 stood at 8·8 tons per acre—not greatly below the Continental level. Simultaneously both gross and net costs of production declined, e.g. figures relating to "per acre" and "per ton" falling from some £19 to £14 and from £1. 17*s*. to £1. 10*s*. respectively. On these points British farmers were showing themselves as adaptable as their Continental brethren, whose level of attainment it is probable they will, in a few years, achieve. In many respects, too, advantage has been derived from the introduction of sugar-beet into the farming economy of this country: more labour has been employed, other crops have benefited, certain by-products (in the shape of tops and pulp) have been rendered available, no serious displacement of the root-break has occurred, nor has the keeping of stock been affected, while the standard of farming has necessarily been maintained in circumstances that would otherwise have witnessed its deterioration. Lastly, the financial returns which, incidentally, are kept at a higher level than elsewhere in Europe, have saved large numbers of arable farmers from experiencing the full effects of the depression in its later stages.

The cost, however, has been very great, for, up to the year 1930 inclusive, some £22,000,000 had been directly expended by means of the subsidy, while, if the duty preference be included as well, the sum total of State assistance had reached approximately £30,000,000, with another four years yet to run. It is unnecessary to describe in detail the basis of the annual agreements made between representatives of factory and of farm, but, in general terms, it may be said that the growers' price declined proportionately as the subsidy itself tapered, ranging (subject to sugar-content) from 54*s*. per ton of beet in 1925 down to 46*s*. in 1930, after which year individual contracts between different groups of interests tended to supersede wide-flung agreements. It is also impossible to answer in exact terms the frequently asked question "How much of the subsidy has reached the growers?" for there is no precise basis for calculating this figure, but it has been estimated (*Farm Economics Branch Report* No. 9 of the Cambridge University Department of Agriculture) that possibly two-thirds of the State's expenditure has remained with the factories. The most that can be said with complete assurance is that this crop has always been more profitable than any possible alternative.

There are already indications, that, at the expiration of the subsidy in 1934, agitation for its renewal will take place. On national grounds such a policy could not be defended, for at its maximum output home-produced sugar has formed but some 15 or 16 per cent. of the country's total consumption. The world position, moreover, is now such that, owing to over-production combined with reduced consumption, large accumulations of stock have taken place and prices have fallen disastrously, but, by means of bounties and subsidies, producers have everywhere been buoyed up and output has been maintained. Restrictions, e.g. the Chadbourne *quota* scheme, have been of little effect and there are no indications of a radical change taking place in the near future. These factors will have to be borne in mind when the claims of British beet-growers are set against those of the tax-payer. It is of course certain that a large drop in the area devoted to the crop would take place if no form of State assistance were forthcoming, but, since it has so abundantly proved its value and become part of the normal rotation upon certain soils and in particular localities, it is equally clear that, even in those circumstances, it would not disappear from the countryside.

In 1925 the taking of the Census of Production enabled an estimate to be made of the position then occupied by the agriculture of these Islands. It stood revealed that, as compared with 1908, the value of the gross output—exclusive of that of the Irish Free State—had, when values were adjusted, despite the depression, remained constant. There had been marked increases in the outturn of fruit and of poultry, and, not unnaturally, a slight decline in that of the staple crops and of livestock. The total production of field crops in

England and Wales was as follows—the Table being a continuation of that upon p. 502 of the previous Chapter.

	Wheat	Barley	Oats	Potatoes
	(qrs.)	(qrs.)	(qrs.)	(tons)
1922	7,664,000	5,068,000	9,289,000	4,012,000
1923	6,859,000	5,006,000	9,534,000	2,758,000
1924	6,220,000	5,297,000	10,526,000	2,696,000
1925	6,127,000	5,208,000	9,522,000	3,214,000
1926	5,893,000	4,715,000	10,317,000	2,763,000
1927	6,512,000	4,480,000	9,606,000	3,055,000
1928	5,659,000	5,185,000	9,900,000	3,518,000
1929	5,650,000	5,047,000	10,499,000	3,588,000
1930	4,913,000	3,889,000	9,502,000	2,743,000
1931	4,418,000	4,063,000	8,856,000	2,454,000
1932	5,006,000	3,985,000	8,719,000	3,308,000

	Turnips and Swedes	Mangolds	Hay (from permanent and temporary grass)
	(tons)	(tons)	(tons)
1922	10,908,000	8,560,000	5,789,000
1923	10,879,000	6,944,000	7,707,000
1924	11,538,000	7,828,000	7,999,000
1925	9,198,000	7,130,000	7,100,000
1926	10,983,000	7,120,000	7,123,000
1927	8,630,000	5,448,000	6,265,000
1928	9,953,000	5,755,000	6,418,000
1929	8,303,000	5,687,000	5,336,000
1930	7,931,000	5,438,000	7,904,000
1931	6,978,000	4,529,000	7,925,000
1932	7,542,000	4,336,000	6,835,000

On the cultivational side it appeared that, even in England and Wales, the proportion of land under the plough to that of crops and grass had also been kept up, for it stood at 41·5 per cent. as compared with 41·0 per cent. in 1911–15.

For purposes of comparison with the statistics given for pre-war years upon page 481 the values of imported human food-stuffs in 1925 (mainly derived from *The Agricultural Output of Great Britain*) were as follows: wheat and flour, £60,300,000; all forms of meat, £123,900,000; poultry and eggs, £22,400,000; cheese and butter, £63,300,000; vegetables and potatoes, £13,200,000; raw fruit, £10,800,000; fish, £9,600,000. These gave a total of £306,000,000 (exclusive of the Irish Free State) as compared with some £200,000,000 in 1913–14; of the former, 37 per cent. was derived from Imperial sources and 63 per cent. from non-Imperial. The addition of food-stuffs not normally produced at home raised the figure to £388,000,000. Of all cereals, including those destined for livestock, £113,000,000 worth was imported and of wool £69,900,000 worth. As an indication of the extraordinary drop in world values that was yet to come, the corresponding figures for 1931, derived from the Board of Trade returns, follow: all cereals, £51,500,000; wheat and flour, £30,300,000; meat, £106,400,000; cheese and butter, £55,400,000; wool, £32,700,000.

An independent analysis of the 1925 Census material, the results of which, under the title of "Our food supply before and after the war", formed the basis of Mr A. W. Flux's Presidential address to the Royal Statistical Society in 1930, indicated that, so far as "energy values" were concerned, the proportion of food derivable from home sources stood at 37·5 per cent. as compared with 41 per cent. in the pre-war period.

Numbers of Livestock in Great Britain and the Irish Free State, 1922–1932

	Cattle	Sheep	Pigs
1922	12,026,000	23,689,000	3,506,000
1923	11,979,000	24,080,000	4,179,000
1924	12,063,000	24,964,000	4,554,000
1925	12,027,000	26,391,000	3,642,000
1926	12,065,000	27,594,000	3,388,000
1927	12,230,000	28,328,000	4,302,000
1928	12,103,000	27,866,000	4,578,000
1929	12,027,000	27,692,000	3,646,000
1930	11,797,000	28,185,000	3,722,000
1931	11,983,000	29,949,000	4,408,000
1932	12,331,000	30,665,000	4,678,000

The Tabular statements appearing upon these pages will, in conjunction with their counterparts in the preceding Chapter, afford a conspectus of the position then and subsequently occupied by the crop and livestock branches of the industry. The former had already declined, the latter showed a steady expansion, especially in that typically British undertaking of sheep farming, where it was necessary to revert to the year 1910 to find as large flocks as were to appear in 1932; the pig population in that latter year was larger than it had ever been before, the numbers of cattle had only upon one or two occasions exceeded those then in evidence, and the yield of milk per cow had, according to the more accurate estimates then available, been notably augmented.

Percentage of Home Production of Cereals to Total Supply in Great Britain (1923–24 *to* 1931–32)

	Wheat	Barley	Oats	Beans	Peas	All Cereals
1923–24	20·2	52·3	81·2	76·2	41·1	39·6
1924–25	19·2	56·3	86·2	74·1	51·9	41·8
1925–26	19·9	58·8	83·2	74·7	48·7	42·1
1926–27	18·2	61·3	90·2	80·8	42·4	41·8
1927–28	20·1	56·6	85·3	78·8	36·9	40·6
1928–29	18·6	62·6	88·6	66·0	41·3	42·2
1929–30	18·7	64·1	86·0	63·8	48·5	42·6
1930–31	14·8	49·5	82·0	81·0	40·7	36·5
1931–32	13·4	58·3	85·0	70·1	39·1	35·1

The prices of feeding-stuffs and of fertilisers were by the year 1925 below the levels occupied by agricultural products themselves and by commodities in general. There had been no widespread lowering of rents, and bankruptcies amongst farmers rested at almost exactly the pre-war level. Indeed, in the grass-land areas of the country—especially in the South and West—the position, if not one of prosperity, certainly as yet showed no signs of distress. After the return to the gold standard at the pre-war parity, however, it soon became apparent that this unsheltered industry would feel the full effects of the economic and financial repercussions, which were also exaggerated by the resumption of wages control.

Cost of Production studies and other methods of approach that had, a year or two previously, been facilitated by means of grants from the Ministry of Agriculture, are henceforward available for the purpose of estimating the position in which different types of producers found themselves. This expansion in the delegated work of the Department had synchronised with the establishment, in some eleven provincial centres, of Economic Advisory Officers, who now function side by side with colleagues engaged in the spheres of mycology, entomology and chemistry. There was thus created a complete service complementary to that maintained—in the persons of County Organisers, Horticulturists and other experts—by the County Councils. The latter have been likened to the general practitioner, the former to the specialist, whose services are available in case of urgent need. The multiplication of Research Institutes and their endowment upon a generous scale went additionally to prove that the Ministry of Agriculture was thoroughly alive to the importance of scientific knowledge in every branch of the industry. Economics, although perhaps the most fundamental subject, was thus the last to be recognised, but the personnel concerned got quickly to work and utilised progressively every available method of investigating the problems that faced the industry.

For instance, concerning the Eastern Counties, than which there could be no district more representative of arable conditions, the various economic *Reports* of the Cambridge University Department of Agriculture afford illuminating material. Here, during the period under discussion, over-all returns relating to some fifteen widely dispersed holdings, covering nearly 3000 acres, were as follows: in 1924–5 the net profit, with no allowances made either for interest upon capital or for the value of unpaid or managerial work, was 12·5 per cent.; in 1925–6, 8·3 per cent. and in 1926–7 only 0·9 per cent. If the two items just referred to were included in the calculations, then the individual results for each year were converted into losses of 0·3 per cent., of 5·8 per cent. and of 8·6 per cent., respectively. The net, or social, output accruing to labour in these same years advanced concurrently with the decline in "profits", from 51 per cent. to 71 per cent. The next two seasons showed a slight improvement, for the losses averaged 5·9 per cent. in 1927–8 and 0·9 per cent. in 1928–9, the principal cause being the temporary arrest of falling prices, which the diagram between pp. 540 and 541 illustrates. Neglecting the wider ranges inherent to grouped results, it may be said, in very general terms, that the lighter soils secured better returns than did the heavy ones, and that this tendency was evidenced in the case of livestock production as well as in that of crop raising. In all years under review the fattening of cattle was shown to be unremunerative, the profits derivable from pigs fluctuated in the accustomed cycle, sheep brought in moderate, and farm poultry high, returns, while milk gave a satisfactory profit only when retailed by its producer. Cereals and root-crops range so widely in their costs of production that generalisation is unsafe, but it may be stated that individual growers secured profits in each year and that it was difficult for all to avoid doing so in the case of sugar-beet. It must be emphasised that the sample upon which these results were based was, statistically, very small and it must also be remembered that conditions elsewhere in the British Isles were as yet much less affected by the depression.

This last point is borne out by reference to such a monograph as D. Skilbeck's and M. Messer's *Incidence of Farming Prosperity and Depression*, which comprises the results of a wide-flung enquiry into the numbers of notices to quit issued, and of requests for reductions in rent occurring, in 1928, in England and Wales. Actual quotations will best illustrate the conclusions of these investigators, for, in regard to the Midlands, we read that "the clay farms are weathering the storm with less difficulty, though there is no indication of general prosperity", while in the West "depression cannot be said to exist" and is "comparatively unknown" in the South-Western Counties; the hill sheep-farmers, scattered over the North of England, Devonshire and Somerset, had suffered very little, and "nothing approaching distress" was discovered; in Derbyshire there was "no mention of any depression"; Durham reports stated that most farmers were "doing passably well, and some were willing to admit it"; from Warwickshire, Shropshire and Lancashire there were no complaints and farms were easy to let. The tale could be continued almost indefinitely, but may be summarised in the statement, "where there is good grass-land, where there are naturally protected markets, where direct retailing can be carried on...and where family labour is extensively utilised, farming is still holding its own".

In that same year Mr R. J. Thompson, in his Presidential address to the Agricultural Economics Society, attempted to assess "the nature and extent of the present agricultural depression". He, too, founded his conclusions mainly upon a geographical basis, holding that perhaps some 17 per cent. of the farmed land—that predominantly under the plough and situated in the East and South-East of England—was affected. In his corresponding address to the same Society in 1930 Sir William Dampier, under the title of "The Economics of Rural Landowning", when analysing the landlord's position in the case of some 42,000 acres of agricultural property during the years 1928 and 1929 (previously referred to upon p. 74), also differentiated between estates in the Western Counties, which yielded a return upon capital—defined as the estimated cost of equipment—of 2·9 per cent. and those in the East of England which gave only 1·9 per cent. He, too, agreed that soil was a potent influence. In yet another paper read to this Society, Mr R. R. Enfield weighed the economic causes that had brought about the situation and convincingly demonstrated that the non-monetary factors were of but minor importance and that deflation, once set in motion, had been vigorously countered by the sheltered industries whilst agriculture, in common with others exposed to outside competition, found itself in both external and internal economic maladjustment.

After 1929 the decline in agricultural commodity prices was resumed and it became apparent that some further steps would have to be taken to relieve the situation. The extent to which individual products were affected can be seen by a glance at the Table appearing on p. 534, for, by the cereal year 1930–31 wheat, oats, hay, beans, peas, hops and wool had all failed to command prices equal to those ruling in 1911–13, and the composite index-number of all commodities sold off farms stood at only 25 per cent. above that base.

Farmers themselves were restive, landlords, after reducing rents to approximately their pre-war levels, were, in the face of inflated costs of maintenance and repairs, impotent to do more; each political party had its own nostrum which was abhorrent to its rivals. Yet it cannot be denied that there were still forthcoming both prospective purchasers and tenants for any land, save the heaviest of arable, that came upon the market, nor, since 1921, had the numbers of regular workers in husbandry shown any real diminution. It is legitimate to point out, also, that, while up to the beginning of 1929 wholesale prices of general commodities had moved in very close harmony with those relating to agriculture, thenceforward, as the relevant diagram clearly indicates, the latter remained above the "Statist's" indicator—for two years, indeed, markedly above—expressive of the fact that other industries (and other countries) were suffering yet more severely.

The farmer's requirements, too, were in most instances comparatively lower in price than what he sold, for fertilisers cost less than in 1914 and all feeding-stuffs were procurable at prices only 25 to 40 per cent. above their pre-war cost. The really serious item of expenditure, viz. labour, now, however, cost on the average double what it had, and it formed one-third of arable farmers' total out-

Prices of Agricultural Products in the Cereal Years
1922–23 *to* 1931–32 (1911–13 = 100)

Commodity	1922–23	1923–24	1924–25	1925–26	1926–27	1927–28	1928–29	1929–30	1930–31	1931–32
Wheat	132	138	165	162	157	135	131	116	79	79
Barley	119	143	165	131	145	145	131	103	100	101
Oats	138	133	140	132	124	148	131	94	86	100
Fat Cattle	153	152	151	146	131	135	133	134	126	118
Fat Sheep	193	183	197	160	150	163	157	160	147	108
Bacon Pigs	171	133	152	181	161	133	150	162	121	92
Porkers	184	143	154	183	170	138	154	172	138	101
Hay	142	104	101	105	103	115	115	132	93	73
Potatoes	91	235	237	138	181	179	127	91	162	222
Milk	177	170	171	170	163	160	167	164	159	140
Butter	162	160	169	158	143	148	152	140	114	106
Cheese	161	172	154	173	137	167	172	135	119	118
Poultry	184	174	166	159	148	148	153	149	148	126
Eggs	170	174	167	163	149	146	156	148	125	109
Fruit	186	220	180	198	165	170	183	157	119	132
Hops	123	152	102	114	126	137	126	44	47	64
Wool	144	192	137	120	137	176	126	82	52	45
Beans and Peas	197	158	147	139	155	126	138	117	78	76
Vegetables	122	188	155	178	135	187	154	147	141	158
General index-number	159	160	162	153	147	147	144	139	125	114

goings. These, so far as the Eastern Counties were concerned, may be taken to have been apportioned as follows: labour 31·2 per cent.; rent and rates, 14·8 per cent.; feeding-stuffs, seeds and manures, 29·2 per cent.; livestock, 10·0 per cent.; other payments, 14·8 per cent. Having been subjected to certain slight modifications during the passage of two years, the corresponding figures diagrammatically

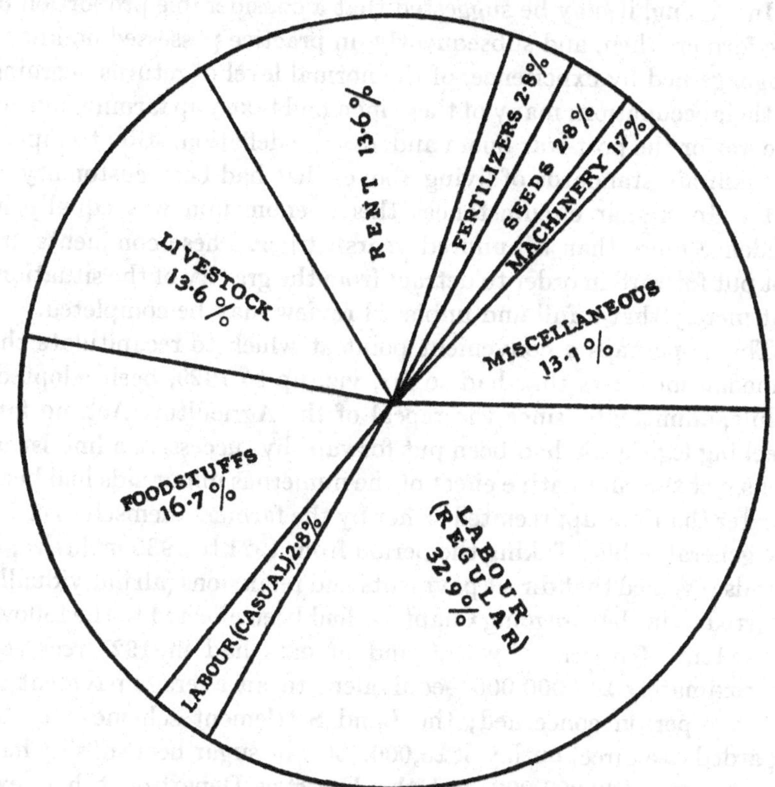

Distribution of arable farmers' outgoings, 1931
(Based on data relating to 988 Eastern Counties farms)

represented above are in this latter instance based upon the frequently referred to economic Survey of nearly one thousand farms in East Anglia. If it be sought to construct a composite (weighted) index-number based upon these individual figures the result, for what it is worth—for, statistically, the project is a hazardous one—reveals an increase of at least 50 per cent. above the level ruling in the period 1911–14. As the corresponding number for commodities sold by farmers had fallen below the figure in question during 1926, averaged 39 in 1929–30 and the next year declined to 25, the growing seriousness of the position can be appreciated, although, in the absence of data indicative of the profits ruling before the war, this disparity cannot be regarded as measuring the exact degree of loss suffered even by arable farmers.

In passing, it may be suggested that a considerable proportion of the farmers then, and subsequently, in practice possessed no knowledge, gained by experience, of the normal level of returns accruing to their occupation: many of these men had taken up farming during the war or the post-war boom and, despite deflation, still attempted to maintain standards of living above what had been customary in 1914. In similar circumstances this phenomenon was equally in evidence more than a hundred years earlier. These comments are not put forward in order to detract from the gravity of the situation, but merely that a full and unbiased review may be completed.

This is perhaps a convenient point at which to recapitulate the remedial measures that had so far, viz. up to 1929, been adopted. While, admittedly, since the repeal of the Agriculture Act, no far-reaching legislation had been put forward by successive administrations, yet the cumulative effect of the numerous minor aids had been greater than was appreciated either by the farmers themselves or by the general public. Taking the period from 1921 to 1930 inclusive, it stands revealed that direct payments and remissions (all individually referred to in the foregoing Chapters) had been effected to the following extent. Growers of wheat and of oats had in 1921 received approximately £18,000,000—equivalent to an average payment of £75 per person concerned; the Land Settlement scheme may be regarded as a direct outlay of £8,000,000; the sugar-beet subsidy had already cost £30,000,000 and the Forestry Department had expended £3,650,000. Under the head of local taxation no less a sum than £27,740,000 had been contributed by the Exchequer to the local authorities of England and Wales in order to implement the de-rating Acts of 1923 and 1925, and, as £1,320,000 had also been deflected each year under the provisions of the Act of 1896, it is apparent that £38,000,000 had, under this head, already been paid. In addition, the final Act of 1928 relinquished £4,132,000 a year, which the national tax-payer and, to a very slight extent, the non-agricultural rate-payer met. If none of this legislation had been passed farmers in England and Wales would have been contributing annually about £16,000,000 to local rates. Scotch and Irish agriculturists also benefited under a similar policy to the extent of £2,000,000 per annum. But for the two relieving Acts, tithe-payers would, upon an average, have been contributing over £1,000,000 more each year since 1918. Transport charges, to the extent of £800,000 annually, had, under the final de-rating Act, been remitted to agriculturists in respect of rail freights. The Ministry of Agriculture, the Development Commissioners and the Empire Marketing Board were together spending several millions every year upon fostering the industry in every conceivable direction. Verily, short of subsidies or protection, it seemed impossible to suggest any means by which further financial assistance could be accorded, and those engaged in struggling to uphold many other sorely pressed industries looked with envy at the primary producers in this country. British ship-builders, steel-manufacturers, textile-workers and coal miners, for example, saw their occupations placed in jeopardy from similar causes—falling prices and overseas competition—but only the last mentioned secured any State assistance, and that compared with the help accorded to farmers was both brief in duration and negligible in quantity.

Nevertheless, constructive proposals for the rehabilitation of the industry were constantly being put forward. Prominent among them were subsidies based either upon farm wages, upon the use of fertilisers or upon soil types. In regard to the first scheme, which, upon the basis of a subvention of £10 per employee per annum, had been originally discussed by the Tribunal, it was pointed out that real wages in agriculture, when compared with those ruling both in pre-war years and among farm workers in other countries as well as in other unsheltered trades at home, were now relatively high. Evidence for the existence of this increased spending power upon the part of agricultural employees could be seen in every village in the land. It would, moreover, have been a questionable policy to promise the expenditure, over a period of years, of public funds in supplementing cash wages without knowledge as to the future purchasing power of money, changes in value of agricultural commodities or relative movements in other items of expenditure incurred by farmers and landowners. At the time in question it was estimated that an average increment of only one shilling per week per man employed would have cost, for Great Britain, £1,725,000, a sum which, even if the scheme had proved administratively workable, would, from the national standpoint, have been wholly disproportionate to the small increment derived by the individuals concerned. Numerous economic and other factors had determined the varying rates of remuneration existing in the different Counties, yet, despite this historical basis, there would have been an immediate demand for a grading up of certain areas. Employers, too, would almost certainly have been antagonistic to any scheme by which they formed intermediaries between the State and their own employees. If, on the other hand, they themselves were also to derive benefit in proportion to their wages bill, then this method would have been expensive and uneconomic. Lastly, there were certain obvious political dangers inherent in such a method of procedure.

Fertilisers at the time in question presented the one commodity purchasable by the farmer at prices below those ruling in 1911–14, and, although on cultivational grounds a case could doubtless have been made out for a subvention based upon the utilisation of, say, sulphate of ammonia, the propriety of thus encouraging a monopolistic trade would have been very questionable and the additional response upon the part of users—especially those situated in the most depressed arable areas—might have been very small. The cost to the State, also, would have been uncertain and liable to fluctuate seasonally under climatic stress.

The third proposal, emanating, unlike the others, from neither official nor corporate organisations, had more serious claim to consideration, for the advantages accruing to a plan, which took as its primary basis of remuneration geological conditions, were obvious. First and foremost, the administrative problem would have been simplified for, unlike other direct grants, there would have been no need annually to check, both by reference to the Ordnance Map and by personal inspection, some hundreds of thousands of separate fields in order to issue certificates that a crop had, in fact, been both sown and harvested. It is, indeed, clear from the experience of 1921, when, after the repeal of the Agriculture Act, acreage bounties were granted on wheat and oats, that the process of payment is, in such cases, long-drawn, as, in order to avoid duplicate and fictitious claims, extremely close inspection is necessitated; nor can any of this machinery be set in motion until after the June 4 schedules have provided the basis for claims. On the other hand, a subsidy confined to heavy land or other specific types could have brought relief where it was most wanted, could have enabled that relief to be given on an adequate scale and over a considerable period of time, and, most important of all, would have been relatively easy to administer. Thus, a single inspection made, in the first instance, by a competent soil expert, would have provided the basis for a certificate holding good indefinitely—no farmer can alter the inherent nature of his land. Whilst, in most cases, whole farms would have been scheduled as falling within the requisite category, there would have been no difficulty, where Nature so dictated, in confining the grant even to particular fields or to part of a holding. No question of the adequacy of cropping would have arisen, field boundaries could have been altered at will, no arbitrary standard of husbandry would have been called for, no investigation into elusive costs of production embarked upon and no official would have had occasion to visit the land a second time; all payments to occupiers could, therefore, have been annually effected without delay upon a given day. What form of cultivation—whether grass or crop, fruit or fallow—the land, once scheduled, had subsequently assumed, would, during the life-time of the subsidy, have been immaterial. Once registered as eligible, the sole condition would have been that it remained "agricultural land" for local taxation purposes; despite changes of ownership, automatically recorded by Crop Reporters, it could have received its grant over any period of years. By such means the land most subject to depression, whether cropped or fallow, might expeditiously have received substantial aid without vexatious control.

The originator of this proposal, which appeared in the press early in 1929, estimated that there were in all some 1,200,000 acres of land subject to extreme depression. Included in this total were nearly 200,000 acres of London clay situated in Essex—typical of the worst possible conditions—and over 400,000 acres of Oxford clay, gault and lias in East Anglia and the East Midlands, together with a smaller extent of boulder clay in Essex and Suffolk. The occupiers of all these lands, as had been for long demonstrated, were suffering to a far greater extent than any other English farmers. Probably the next most affected classes were those, again on preponderatingly arable holdings, whose soil was of the lightest variety.

Prominent among the areas thus involved were the breck-lands of Norfolk and Suffolk (170,000 acres) and the light chalks stretching from thence into Wiltshire, whose ploughed area might be taken at 400,000 acres. What a help to these 600,000 acres under the plough even a pound an acre would have afforded, figures previously quoted relative to farms so situated in East Anglia demonstrate, for an average loss of 4*s.* 3*d.* an acre would thereby have been converted into a profit of 15*s.* 9*d.* Again, half this sum (10*s.* an acre) allocated to the similar area of chalk and breck-land would, in sufficing to pay its rent, have relieved the situation in the other depressed districts enumerated and classified above. A subvention amounting to less than £1,000,000 per annum would thus have brought adequate financial help to all those farmers—forming, incidentally, less than 6 per cent. of the total in England and Wales—who, from causes outside their control, were labouring under a grave economic handicap. Such persons would probably not have exceeded 20,000 in number, and, if comparison is effected between this figure and the 186,000 claimants concerned in the production of wheat and oats or the still larger number in occupation of arable land, the relative advantages of this type of subsidy, as compared with those previously recommended by the Tribunal, will be appreciated. A sum of nine or ten million pounds devoted to a "Geological" bonus would have lasted for ten years, whereas, if deflected to arable maintenance, such funds would have sufficed for less than two years. Two possible drawbacks must be set against the above-mentioned advantages. In the first place, unlike most other methods, it would, while staying a decline, not necessarily have led to any increase in production; secondly, some complementary form of rent restriction would have been required, as, failing this, landlords would in the long run have secured a proportion of the grants in the form of increased rents.

Nothing beyond academic discussions, however, upon these and more familiar proposals took place, while, in the course of the next three years, the situation deteriorated as values fell steadily, averaging only 25 per cent. above their *datum* in 1930–1, 14 per cent. a year later, and actually touching that level in October 1932: now, too, the grass-land farmer was, to a greater extent, joined with his arable brother, for the price of sheep, of cattle and of dairy products suffered reductions commensurate with those experienced in previous

THE COURSE OF WHOLESALE PRICES OF AGRICULTU

—— Ministry of Agriculture inde

---- "Statist" index-number of

Average o

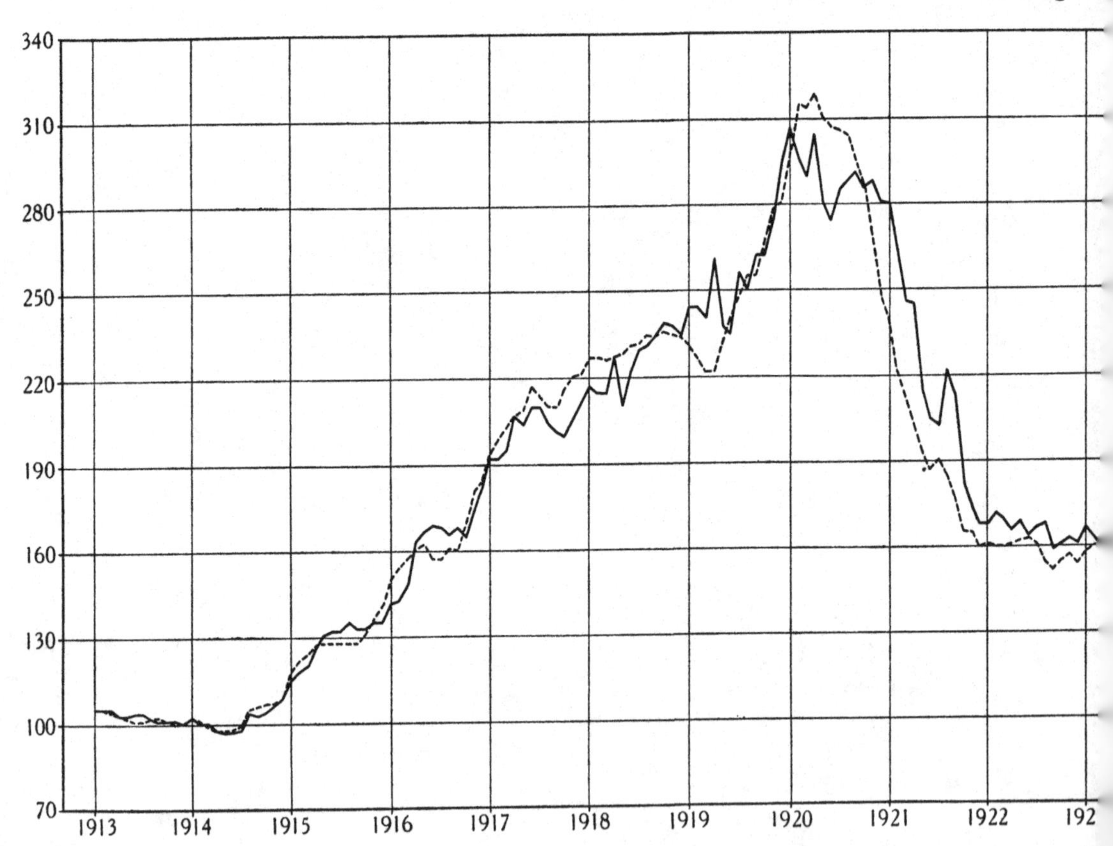

PRODUCTS AND OF GENERAL COMMODITIES, 1913–1933

ber of agricultural commodity prices

ale prices

1913=100

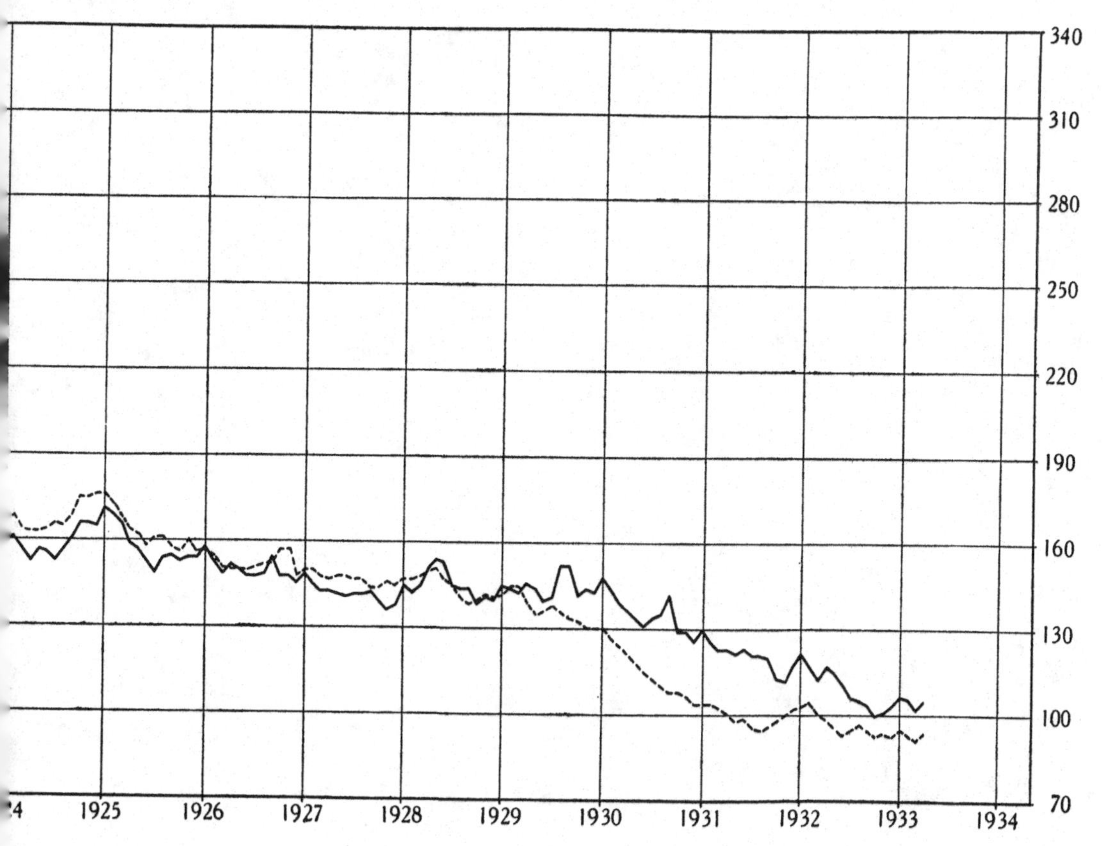

seasons by the staple crops. In this connection the best that could be said was that the general price-index applicable to all commodities had fallen faster and had plunged even lower, for it sank below its pre-war level in 1931. Meanwhile, farm outgoings had been susceptible to no appreciable reduction—weekly wages had, upon the average, fallen a few pence, fertilisers were, in 1930, further below their pre-war cost than they had yet been and the price of purchased feeding-stuffs was practically stationary.

In these circumstances the first of a series of economic Surveys to be extended to British agriculture (material from which has already been quoted in the second Chapter upon Labour and elsewhere) was particularly apposite, especially as it applied to the Eastern Counties. Conditions upon approximately one thousand farms, of all sizes above 20 acres in extent and situated upon every type of soil, were, in the autumn of 1931, investigated when outstanding data were as follows: rents averaged no more than 19*s.* 6*d.* per acre, the capital value of land, buildings and improvements was only £18 10*s.* per acre and as large a proportion as 68·5 per cent. of the gross income was, even in this area, derived, in some form or another, from livestock. Here was evidence that, within their respective spheres, both landlords and tenants had done their utmost to meet the altered circumstances of arable farming. Yet the "farm income", ranging from £44 on the smallest size of holding to *minus* £46 on those over three hundred acres in extent, averaged only £8, while, if allowance were made for interest upon the capital involved and for remuneration to the occupier for his own labour and supervision, the "loss" was represented by an average sum of £182. The compilers of this enquiry (*Report* No. 19, Farm Economics Branch, Department of Agriculture, Cambridge University) explained that it would have been necessary for prices to stand 18 per cent. higher in order to assure under these two heads a fair return to those concerned. Yet worse would have followed had not State intervention taken place, for a similar Survey, conducted exactly a year later, revealed an over-all "loss" of £37 as compared with the £8 "profit" of 1931—which only the wheat deficiency payments transformed into a credit of £31—with a final figure, after the corresponding adjustments were made, of *minus* £156.

Now, too, for the first time, bankruptcies amongst farmers began seriously to increase, for hitherto, as the diagram overleaf reveals, their numbers had not been greatly in excess of what might be regarded as normal; for example, during the ten immediate pre-war years such bankruptcies and deeds of arrangement had, in England and Wales, averaged 317 annually, while from 1921 to 1930 the corresponding number was 385. The last-mentioned figure, representing a yearly failure of no more than one farmer in eight hundred, could perhaps not be regarded as affording a true indication of the financial status of the industry. In 1931 the numbers rose to 497, a level which had not been attained since such a significant year as 1895, and in 1932 the total was 615, thereby exceeding the failures recorded in any twelve months of the previous forty

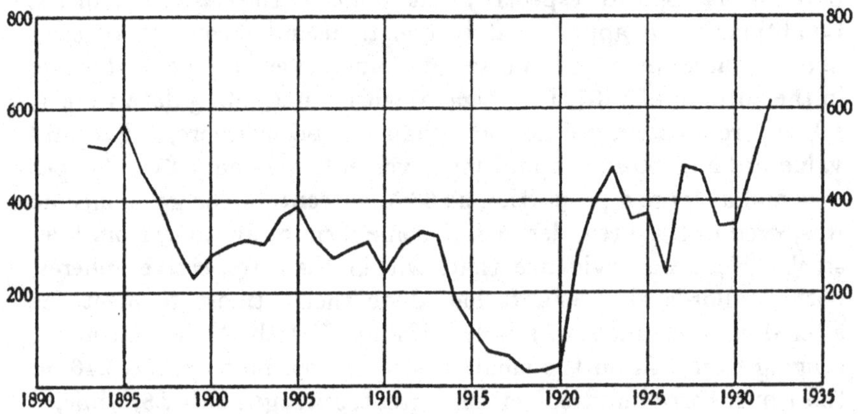

Bankruptcies and deeds of arrangement among farmers in England and Wales, 1893–1932

years, although, again, this was equivalent to merely one in about 500 practising farmers or, expressed alternatively, ten per County. The statements, alleging "widespread bankruptcies", then freely disseminated, were, therefore, not only erroneous but actually, upon psychological grounds, conducive of harm by inculcating a spirit of defeatism.

Events have been somewhat anticipated in an endeavour to show that evidence was now clear as to the critical position in which, prior to the passing of revolutionary legislation in 1932, very many farmers found themselves. The different political parties were individually impotent, and abortive "National", and other, Conferences had so far failed in their endeavours to persuade Parliament to move, when the advent of a Government pledged, with the aid of a large majority, to pursue an all-embracing policy completely altered the situation. The Agricultural Marketing Acts have already been described in detail, as has the wheat *quota* scheme, the former of which will, in the long run, doubtless be increasingly regarded as an economic weapon for internal use, while the latter has already demonstrated, not only its practicability, but also its financial efficacy; at this juncture, therefore, a few words can be said concerning the quantitative control of imports and the other measures that followed upon the Imperial Economic Conference held at Ottawa in August 1932. These mainly appertained to the livestock side of the industry and aimed at reducing imported supplies by means of friendly agreements with foreign nations and our own Dependencies. As a result, a 20 per cent. cut in mutton and lamb deliveries, to be immediately effective, was negotiated with representatives of Argentina and a gradual attainment of larger curtailments, extending, chronologically, up to 1934, was promised in the case of chilled beef. The Scandinavian groups of ham and bacon exporters also agreed to limit their consignments of these products to acceptable figures for predetermined periods of time. Australia and New Zealand came into line, by undertaking not to ship to this country during the calendar year 1933, larger supplies of mutton and lamb than they had consigned in the twelve months ending June 30th, 1932. When announcing, in the House of Commons, details of these agreements, the Minister of Agriculture stated that the Government hoped, by means that "went a long way further than any other policy that had been outlined", to secure control "over an emergency position", but he warned his hearers that the resultant oscillations in price might be greater than was anticipated.

The prices of home-produced agricultural commodities did not revert after the customary seasonal increase in the last two months of the year, but continued to rise (see diagram) and stood at 106 in February 1933; this sustained improvement was entirely attributable to the enhanced values of livestock, e.g. the index-number for fat sheep, which had stood at 87 in November 1932, reached 106 in February, that of bacon pigs rose from 85 to 98 and all store animals correspondingly appreciated in price: no similar rise had benefited the products of crop husbandry. Thus, by quantitative regulation, or, as it was euphemistically termed, a "system of contracts", the value of those products which, so far as the home producer was concerned, formed practically three-quarters of his total output, was artificially raised. Credit for this was, not unnaturally, taken by the Government, which also drew attention to the fact that neither had retail prices risen nor had the channels of trade become dislocated. It was further claimed that this policy would, by ensuring a steady flow of imports whenever scarcity appeared and prices rose, prove effective against any deleterious movement of the pendulum.

There this matter must be left for the passage of time to prove whether both human nature and economic laws can be thus forced into new moulds. Time, too, will show whether British farmers take advantage of the situation by increasing their own output which, in the case of beef, had shrunk since the war, both in quantity and quality, owing to excessive foreign competition in the cheapest varieties. The Ottawa agreements also relaxed the conditions under which Canadian cattle might be introduced into Great Britain and secured reciprocal treatment for home-bred pedigree stock. The dispute over the Land Annuities with the Irish Free State had resulted in heavy duties being imposed upon cattle—and, indeed, upon all agricultural products—crossing from thence St George's Channel. These, together with the general *ad valorem* tariff of 10 per cent.—buttressing the resolutions of the Imperial Conference—and the special charges leviable on horticultural produce, raised fiscal walls against most non-Imperial and even against some Imperial agricultural commodities. Such a combination of protective and revenue raising expedients was, however, officially regarded as nothing more than a palliative until, by concerted monetary action, it should become possible internationally to raise wholesale prices.

Matters were viewed from a wide angle by the Government, for it was hoped by the above described means to strengthen the hands of the primary producer in all parts of the Empire—if nothing more than as a counter to the cartels, bounties and similar methods employed on the Continent to make possible the overcoming of still higher tariff edifices. Private individuals and semi-official organisations, the latter not always political in character, hinted at the potential dangers that would exist if a European Customs Union *contra mundum* were successfully negotiated, while the Empire Marketing Board seized the opportunity to emphasise the advantages of increased inter-Imperial trade by stressing the growing dependence of British secondary industries upon Empire as opposed to European markets. The latter body pointed out that, whereas before the war our Dominions and Colonies had absorbed some 36 per cent. of all the British exports, the corresponding figure now stood at 42 per cent., while our share of the total world trade had declined from 13·9 per cent. in 1913 to 11·4 per cent. in 1927 (F. L. McDougall in E.M.B. Monograph No. 23). Various explanations of this shrinkage have been put forward, including, amongst others, the following: planned output from deliberately established secondary industries in certain countries—notably the Far East—which the events of 1914–18 facilitated; the return of this country to the gold standard in 1925; the inability of overseas customers to absorb our manufactures in exchange for their greatly depreciated primary products. The policy of the Empire Marketing Board itself, as was related in a previous Chapter, has been to afford every form of assistance—financial, technical and economic—to British producers, wherever situated, and to encourage each member-country of the Empire to give preference to the products of that territory. A general extension of reciprocal preferences had, admittedly, been one result of the Imperial Conference, but, it was urged, there was room for a further movement in this direction.

It is opportune to envisage the economic position in which our own Dependencies and foreign countries collectively found themselves at this juncture, for which purpose there exists a mass of unbiased material, principally derived from the very thorough investigations conducted by the League of Nations. From this it is learnt that, in the more immediate post-war years, while Europe had recovered her productivity, both her trade and her exports still flagged, as the latter of the two following Tables (derived from the League's *World Economic Survey, 1931–2*) indicates. Between 1925 and 1929, however, she had participated in a genuine trade revival which, for the world at large, is statistically recorded in the second column below.

	Percentage increase 1925 over 1913	Percentage increase 1929 over 1925
World population	5	4
Production of food-stuffs	10	5
Production of raw materials	25	20
Quantum of world trade	7	19

The disproportionate supply of raw materials, especially in the first period, will be remarked. Territorially, the League placed the *quantum* of trade for each respective period thus:

	1925 (1913 = 100)		1929 (1925 = 100)	
	Total production	*Quantum*	Total production	*Quantum*
Europe	102	91	117	122
North America	126	139	105	119
Rest of World	124	126	109	112
World	116	107	111	119

In the following two years there was the very small reduction of 3 per cent. in the world's agricultural output and one of 20 per cent. in that of raw materials for secondary industries. The events of the whole period in question were thus lucidly described in the *World Economic Survey*:

The rebuilding of the pre-war world would have been a difficult task; but the actual task of constructing a new world order in which many elements of change had to find a place, was infinitely greater. New vested interests had grown up, together with new social doctrines, and a general fear of social disorder reinforced the pleas that were insistently put forward for protection of threatened groups and industries by extraordinary public measures. In the reconstruction boom, based as it was upon large extensions of credit to countries which had never before been able to borrow upon such a considerable scale, there were inevitably some elements of wasteful expenditure, a phenomenon that was by no means confined to the borrowing countries. When the flow of credit dwindled suddenly in 1928 and 1929, this waste was revealed. The burden of debt incurred, largely for sound productive purposes, but partly also for expenditure that proved to be uneconomic, was then recognised to have created obligations that were extremely difficult of fulfilment. In order to discharge these obligations, a greatly expanded volume of world trade at a relatively high level of prices would have been necessary; but international trade, even after 1925, had barely kept pace with production, and some of the major creditor countries, so far from facilitating the payment of the obligations due to them in the only practicable way—by the receipt of goods—imposed greater restrictions upon imports. Payment might have been accepted for a time in the form of securities representing a continuing export of capital; but, in the long run, expanding exports from the debtor countries, at least sufficient to pay the growing interest and depreciation charges, was the only permanent solution. Towards the end of 1929, therefore, an unstable position had developed in the world's financial structure. The basic causes of this instability lay far back in the disorganisation produced by the war and the burdens of debt and taxation which it bequeathed to the post-war generation. The integration of world industry or, to use a pre-war phrase, the "territorial division of labour", was greatly hampered by the operation of cartels, pools, tariffs, and all the paraphernalia of the new economic nationalism, while the overhead financial obligations of nations were top-heavy and, by that very fact, created extreme nervousness. The emergence of structural maladjustments as the construction boom died away would not normally have precipitated such a severe crisis as that which developed in 1929–1932; but the circumstances were not normal. When the credit expansion of 1925–1929 collapsed, it was seen that the fundamental disequilibria of economic organisation had been, not merely postponed, but aggravated. Under the pressure of heavy financial obligations, both public and private, the debtor communities endeavoured, by pressure on the credit and price structure, to increase their active balances of external payments. Selling pressure created in this way was an important factor in causing a sharp fall in prices, but it was resisted by the imposition of further restrictions upon imports into almost all countries. The impossible situation was thus created in which virtually every country endeavoured to increase its exports at the same time as it restricted its imports, so that the selling pressure necessarily became concentrated on those few countries which endeavoured to retain a free market. The sharp downward tendency of prices thus engendered was aggravated by the disturbance of both the financial and the monetary systems of the world. As prices fell, the inevitable result was to increase the real burden of the financial obligations which were fixed in terms of the appreciating monetary units and, therefore, to accentuate the necessity for providing surpluses upon international account. Since, however, the restrictions upon imports imposed by some of the principal creditor countries made it impossible for them to receive payment in goods, resort was necessarily had to payment in gold. Debtor countries and those which endeavoured to retain a free market lost their gold reserves steadily and were therefore forced into further deflation. Many of them eventually were forced, by their reluctance to carry deflation further, either to abandon the gold standard or so to restrict foreign trade and foreign payments as to maintain the nominal stability of their currencies at the cost of a virtual paralysis of international dealings. As this vicious spiral developed, even those investments which were economically sound when they were made in the boom period were rendered much more doubtful, so that the waste of the boom was, at least temporarily, greatly increased. There had, in fact, been only one practical possibility of sound reconstruction in 1925. This was to facilitate the restoration of material production by extending the range and volume of international trade, providing outlets for the increased production, not only of the reconstructed regions of Europe, but also of the outlying areas that had been stimulated during the war, allowing the forces of competition in world markets to rearrange territorial specialisation, and making possible the payment of the vastly increased financial obligations which resulted from the war and the subsequent reconstruction, by increased export of goods, particularly to the creditor countries. Only in this way might it have been possible to carry and gradually liquidate the financial legacies of the war, as the similar legacies of the wars of 1793–1815 and 1870 were liquidated.

It is supererogatory in such a work as this to describe the experiences of individual countries during the intensification of this world-wide depression that extended from the autumn of 1931 to the American crisis of March 1933; here, it must suffice to emphasise the almost universal character of the phenomenon and its disastrous influence upon the purchasing power of rural peoples, leading in turn to the further detriment of the secondary industries. Mechanisation of agriculture proceeded apace, stocks of raw materials piled up in every part of the world, while wage rates tended to be immovable. In so far as the fall in prices of agricultural commodities and of raw materials was concerned, it appeared that they had receded most in those countries of the New World which were producing cereals and textiles—thus affording evidence of the comparatively fortunate position occupied by British farmers—and that manufactured goods everywhere retained a price level disproportionately above the products of agriculture. In its two separate volumes, entitled *The Agricultural Crisis*, the League's Economic Committee provided abundant evidence in regard to these tendencies, which was independently fortified by an excellent *Survey of World Agriculture* undertaken by the Royal Institute of International Affairs. There these questions must be left in the certain knowledge that, sooner or later, they—in common with the interwoven reparation, debt and disarmament problems—will have harmoniously to be attacked by peoples reawakened to their insistent responsibilities.

British agriculture had, and still has, two matters of paramount importance to study, viz. internally, the repeatedly referred to maladjustment of wages and, externally, the reactions of monetary policy. While the return to the gold standard in 1925 had added to its then difficulties, our abandonment of it again in 1931 did not alleviate the position since there was no resultant increase in prices. These, individually, and coincident with the cost of living, continued steadily to fall. Costs in the exporting trades also did not rise, so here, in relation to foreign countries, Great Britain automatically improved her position by reason of the depreciated exchanges. However, a measure of inflation, or, rather, of the more innocuous sounding "reflation", was shortly being demanded in place of what was termed the "official deflationary" tactics of British monetary policy. In the meantime the successive departure from the gold standard of country after country rendered idle all speculations as to the time at which, or upon what basis, Great Britain might re-anchor herself to that medium, and the increased world output of gold—which rose from 82 million gold pounds in 1926 and 1927 to 101 million gold pounds in 1932—normally suggestive of the maintenance of price levels—thereafter possessed but an academic interest, as did also the promised extension in the life of the Rand mines themselves. In 1931 and early in 1932 most authorities were discussing the possibility of reducing the gold reserves of Central Banks or otherwise of rationing internationally the metal, while advocates of other measures included those who sought to stabilise the pound upon some composite index-number based upon commodity prices.

Yet by the spring of 1933, when the preparatory Commission of the World Economic Conference was in session, Sir Robert Horne could unequivocally state that Great Britain was in so powerful a position that "more than half the world's trade was being conducted in sterling", and he commented upon the fact that even in the remaining gold standard countries trading interests were beginning to find it easier to make their bargains in sterling. All indications pointed to a more favourable outlook: the national finances had been placed upon a sound footing, a large reduction had been effected in the proportions borne by imports to exports and sterling had proved itself to be easily the most dependable of the currencies divorced from gold. In these circumstances once again monetary expansion, as opposed to contracted production, was put forward by economists as being the most obvious method of raising sterling prices—without prejudice, of course, to the partial restriction of imports already enforced by tariffs and *quotas*—especially if international agreement concerning gold prices could similarly be reached. Mr J. M. Keynes independently advocated a bold policy of loan-expenditure at home and abroad for purposes of employment, concurrently with relief in taxation and the provision of fresh reserves (based upon gold holdings) for the world's Central Banks; such measures, he held, could alone be effective in raising and maintaining prices.

The British farmer frankly did not understand these matters, but was satisfied that highly important steps had been taken to ameliorate his particular position, and he observed that in consequence there had begun a slight upward movement in the prices of agricultural commodities. Accordingly, although loath to adopt wholeheartedly any of the new measures that called for active co-operation on his own part, he looked to the future with less apprehension. What that future may bring to him no man can say, but, assuredly, a controlled monetary system, a rigid policy of import restriction, the pursuit of arable husbandry upon an extensive basis or, possibly, an abundant supply of cheap electricity will, in due course, either singly or in combination, rehabilitate him. Be that time far distant or be it near, the agriculture of these Islands will then resume prosperity—its position it has never lost—and unborn generations will look back on the present situation as affording one of those many trials from which, during countless centuries, the industry has emerged unscathed but remoulded. Let its present representatives take off their hats to the past and their coats to the future.

APPENDIX

TABLE I

Acreage under Wheat, Barley, Oats and Potatoes in the United Kingdom from 1866 to 1932

Year	Thousands of acres			
	Wheat	Barley	Oats	Potatoes
1866	3661	2398	4471	1555
1867	3641	2440	4422	1501
1868	3951	2348	4469	1584
1869	3982	2483	4480	1635
1870	3774	2624	4425	1639
1871	3831	2617	4362	1694
1872	3840	2544	4341	1564
1873	3670	2575	4198	1426
1874	3831	2507	4089	1421
1875	3514	2751	4176	1432
1876	3125	2762	4299	1392
1877	3321	2652	4239	1398
1878	3382	2723	4124	1365
1879	3056	2932	3998	1393
1880	3066	2695	4192	1381
1881	2967	2663	4306	1443
1882	3164	2452	4245	1388
1883	2713	2486	4370	1360
1884	2751	2346	4277	1374
1885	2553	2447	4283	1356
1886	2355	2436	4404	1354
1887	2384	2248	4403	1357
1888	2663	2257	4163	1394
1889	2539	2308	4128	1366
1890	2479	2294	4124	1310
1891	2388	2291	4115	1286
1892	2295	2212	4234	1265
1893	1953	2244	4420	1251
1894	1977	2261	4508	1221
1895	1454	2338	4512	1251
1896	1732	2278	4289	1269
1897	1939	2214	4226	1194
1898	2158	2069	4098	1201
1899	2055	2159	4110	1222
1900	1899	2164	4131	1215
1901	1744	2134	4096	1212
1902	1771	2077	4139	1208
1903	1619	2017	4238	1184
1904	1406	1999	4332	1188
1905	1835	1868	4118	1225
1906	1799	1928	4119	1182

Table I (*contd.*)

Year	Thousands of acres			
	Wheat	Barley	Oats	Potatoes
1907	1664	1883	4198	1139
1908	1663	1822	4169	1149
1909	1867	1827	4018	1155
1910	1856	1897	4095	1132
1911	1951	1756	4051	1163
1912	1971	1814	4075	1207
1913	1792	1932	3983	1184
1914	1906	1873	3899	1209
1915	2335	1524	4182	1214
1916	2053	1653	4171	1155
1917	2106	1797	4789	1377
1918	2796	1839	5631	1518
1919	2372	1871	5144	1230
1920	1979	2049	4635	1291
1921	2084	1782	4415	1280
1922	2073	1691	4359	1288
1923	1838	1639	4082	1158
1924	1632	1624	4014	1140
1925	1574	1618	3787	1170
1926	1681	1413	3771	1169
1927	1743	1289	3602	1179
1928	1490	1428	3597	1152
1929	1413	1340	3723	1178
1930	1431	1245	3591	1031
1931	1271	1234	3395	1055
1932	1365	1135	3365	—

Table II

Acreage under Wheat, Barley and Oats in England and Wales from 1870 *to* 1932

Year	Thousands of acres			Year	Thousands of acres		
	Wheat	Barley	Oats		Wheat	Barley	Oats
1870	3375	2128	1744	1881	2731	2172	1871
1871	3439	2134	1708	1882	2925	1993	1784
1872	3463	2064	1698	1883	2545	2046	1929
1873	3369	2090	1664	1884	2608	1938	1869
1874	3509	2042	1592	1885	2423	2020	1894
1875	3240	2245	1659	1886	2230	2023	2028
1876	2917	2263	1777	1887	2267	1879	2024
1877	3087	2148	1729	1888	2496	1860	1867
1878	3148	2211	1665	1889	2390	1898	1873
1879	2813	2389	1652	1890	2324	1895	1889
1880	2885	2203	1760	1891	2254	1890	1907

TABLE II (*contd.*)

Year	Thousands of acres			Year	Thousands of acres		
	Wheat	Barley	Oats		Wheat	Barley	Oats
1892	2158	1824	1999	1913	1702	1559	1975
1893	1853	1863	2155	1914	1807	1505	1930
1894	1883	1878	2229	1915	2170	1232	2088
1895	1384	1950	2288	1916	1912	1332	2085
1896	1656	1886	2087	1917	1918	1460	2259
1897	1839	1803	2068	1918	2557	1501	2780
1898	2046	1666	1962	1919	2221	1510	2564
1899	1954	1742	2002	1920	1875	1637	2272
1900	1796	1750	2077	1921	1976	1436	2148
1901	1665	1737	2041	1922	1967	1364	2157
1902	1679	1680	2103	1923	1740	1327	1976
1903	1540	1644	2167	1924	1545	1314	2037
1904	1338	1640	2272	1925	1499	1318	1868
1905	1748	1502	2088	1926	1592	1148	1863
1906	1706	1533	2086	1927	1636	1049	1751
1907	1577	1502	2172	1928	1396	1185	1762
1908	1583	1470	2160	1929	1330	1120	1854
1909	1774	1464	2038	1930	1346	1020	1778
1910	1756	1537	2063	1931	1197	1029	1652
1911	1843	1424	2047	1932	1287	960	1580
1912	1863	1457	2072				

TABLE III

Extent of Arable, Permanent Grass and Corn (wheat, oats, barley) in England and Wales from 1870 *to* 1932

Year	Thousands of acres			Year	Thousands of acres		
	Arable	P. grass	Corn		Arable	P. grass	Corn
1870	14,849	11,108	7246	1886	13,412	14,325	6275
1871	14,946	11,375	7280	1887	13,278	14,476	6169
1872	14,943	11,522	7225	1888	13,251	14,555	6222
1873	14,721	11,819	7123	1889	13,195	14,650	6160
1874	14,615	12,072	7143	1890	13,080	14,792	6109
1875	14,607	12,203	7144	1891	12,904	15,098	6060
1876	14,527	12,386	6957	1892	12,764	15,020	5981
1877	14,453	12,590	6964	1893	12,627	15,127	5872
1878	14,407	12,758	7019	1894	12,627	15,111	5990
1879	14,255	13,007	6854	1895	12,460	15,223	5621
1880	14,096	13,267	6798	1896	12,335	15,331	5630
1881	13,978	13,471	6773	1897	12,505	15,122	5709
1882	13,892	13,638	6702	1898	12,406	15,178	5673
1883	13,721	13,874	6520	1899	12,316	15,244	5697
1884	13,570	14,084	6416	1900	12,217	15,321	5623
1885	13,576	14,122	6337	1901	12,118	15,399	5442

Table III (*contd.*)

Year	Thousands of acres			Year	Thousands of acres		
	Arable	P. grass	Corn		Arable	P. grass	Corn
1902	12,103	15,388	5462	1918	12,399	14,589	6837
1903	11,932	15,520	5348	1919	12,309	14,439	6295
1904	11,761	15,668	5249	1920	12,020	14,487	5783
1905	11,656	15,750	5338	1921	11,618	14,526	5552
1906	11,589	15,805	5324	1922	11,311	14,715	5492
1907	11,547	15,830	5250	1923	11,181	14,762	5045
1908	11,406	15,942	5213	1924	10,929	14,948	4897
1909	11,358	15,965	5276	1925	10,682	15,073	4685
1910	11,320	15,972	5355	1926	10,548	15,128	4604
1911	11,299	15,950	5314	1927	10,310	15,280	4256
1912	11,335	15,839	5392	1928	10,108	15,397	4343
1913	11,058	16,071	5235	1929	9,948	15,490	4304
1914	10,998	16,116	5242	1930	9,833	15,547	4145
1915	10,966	16,087	5489	1931	9,582	15,701	3878
1916	11,051	16,023	5328	1932	9,366	15,839	3828
1917	11,246	15,835	5638				

Table IV

Yield in bushels per acre of Wheat, Barley and Oats in Great Britain 1885 *to* 1931

Year	Wheat	Barley	Oats	Year	Wheat	Barley	Oats
1885	31·3	35·1	36·8	1909	33·7	36·6	41·3
1886	26·9	32·2	37·8	1910	30·3	32·7	40·3
1887	32·1	31·3	34·7	1911	32·9	31·9	38·0
1888	28·0	32·8	37·2	1912	29·0	31·1	36·3
1889	29·9	31·8	39·3	1913	31·5	33·0	38·1
1890	30·7	35·0	41·4	1914	32·7	33·4	39·8
1891	31·3	34·1	38·8	1915	31·5	29·9	39·8
1892	26·4	34·6	38·8	1916	28·8	31·0	38·9
1893	25·9	28·7	35·6	1917	30·2	30·8	39·5
1894	30·7	34·5	41·6	1918	33·2	32·7	41·3
1895	26·2	31·7	37·1	1919	29·1	29·6	36·4
1896	33·7	33·6	36·8	1920	28·7	31·8	38·6
1897	29·1	32·8	38·5	1921	35·4	30·1	37·5
1898	34·7	35·7	40·8	1922	31·4	30·5	35·9
1899	32·7	34·2	38·8	1923	31·8	30·7	38·4
1900	28·5	31·3	37·9	1924	32·4	32·7	41·1
1901	30·8	31·0	36·7	1925	32·9	32·3	41·0
1902	32·8	34·8	42·6	1926	29·9	33·3	43·8
1903	30·1	32·0	39·7	1927	32·0	34·2	42·2
1904	26·8	31·1	39·2	1928	32·7	35·3	44·5
1905	32·8	33·9	38·2	1929	34·3	36·5	45·4
1906	33·7	34·6	40·6	1930	29·6	31·2	42·4
1907	34·0	35·3	43·0	1931	29·8	31·9	42·2
1908	32·3	32·8	39·8				

TABLE V

United Kingdom wheat yields, 1852 to 1932 (derived from Lawes' and Gilbert's estimates up to 1884, and thenceforward from official statistics) together with the ten-year (moving) average and annual deviations from the latter (Bushels per acre)

Year	Actual yield	Moving average	Deviation from average	Year	Actual yield	Moving average	Deviation from average
1852	22·9	—	—	1893	26·1	29·9	− 3·8
1853	20·9	—	—	1894	30·7	30·2	+ 0·5
1854	34·7	—	—	1895	26·3	30·0	− 3·7
1855	27·4	—	—	1896	33·6	29·9	+ 3·7
1856	27·0	27·1	− 0·1	1897	29·1	30·6	− 1·5
1857	33·1	27·7	+ 5·4	1898	34·7	31·0	+ 3·7
1858	31·5	29·5	+ 2·0	1899	32·7	30·7	+ 2·0
1859	26·2	29·6	− 3·4	1900	28·6	31·4	− 2·8
1860	22·1	29·9	− 7·8	1901	30·9	31·3	− 0·4
1861	25·2	29·7	− 4·5	1902	32·9	31·9	+ 1·0
1862	29·2	28·5	+ 0·7	1903	30·1	31·6	− 1·5
1863	38·7	28·7	+ 10·0	1904	27·0	31·7	− 4·7
1864	35·2	28·8	+ 6·4	1905	32·9	31·9	+ 1·0
1865	30·6	29·6	+ 1·0	1906	33·7	32·2	+ 1·5
1866	25·1	29·5	− 4·4	1907	34·0	31·7	+ 2·3
1867	21·0	29·0	− 8·0	1908	32·4	31·9	+ 0·5
1868	34·0	27·3	+ 6·7	1909	33·8	32·3	+ 1·5
1869	27·0	26·7	+ 0·3	1910	30·5	32·2	− 1·7
1870	30·0	26·0	+ 4·0	1911	33·0	31·7	+ 1·3
1871	24·0	26·0	− 2·0	1912	29·1	31·4	− 2·3
1872	24·0	26·5	− 2·5	1913	31·7	31·6	+ 0·1
1873	22·5	26·1	− 3·6	1914	32·8	31·1	+ 1·7
1874	29·2	25·0	+ 4·2	1915	31·7	31·0	+ 0·7
1875	22·9	24·4	− 1·5	1916	29·1	31·2	− 2·1
1876	25·0	24·4	+ 0·6	1917	30·6	31·4	− 0·8
1877	26·5	24·6	+ 1·9	1918	33·3	31·5	+ 1·8
1878	30·0	25·1	+ 4·9	1919	29·2	31·4	− 2·2
1879	15·5	25·2	− 9·7	1920	28·7	31·5	− 2·8
1880	24·5	26·0	− 1·5	1921	35·4	31·6	+ 3·8
1881	24·0	26·2	− 2·2	1922	31·5	31·7	− 0·2
1882	25·6	26·7	− 1·1	1923	31·8	31·7	+ 0·1
1883	28·0	26·5	+ 1·5	1924	32·4	32·2	+ 0·2
1884	29·4	28·0	+ 1·4	1925	32·9	32·3	+ 0·6
1885	31·2	28·6	+ 2·6	1926	30·1	31·8	− 1·7
1886	26·9	29·3	− 2·4	1927	32·2	31·8	+ 0·4
1887	32·0	29·4	+ 2·6	1928	32·8	—	—
1888	28·0	29·2	− 1·2	1929	34·4	—	—
1889	29·9	29·3	+ 0·6	1930	29·8	—	—
1890	30·7	28·8	+ 1·9	1931	29·9	—	—
1891	31·3	29·5	+ 1·8	1932	31·6	—	—
1892	26·5	29·2	− 2·7				

TABLE VI

Yields of Barley and Oats in the United Kingdom from 1884 to 1932, together with the ten-year (moving) average and annual deviations from the latter (Bushels per acre)

Year	Barley			Oats		
	Actual yield	Moving average	Deviation	Actual yield	Moving average	Deviation
1884	34·2	—	—	37·8	—	—
1885	35·2	—	—	37·6	—	—
1886	32·3	—	—	38·5	—	—
1887	31·1	—	—	34·2	—	—
1888	33·0	33·2	− 0·2	37·9	38·6	− 0·7
1889	32·4	33·3	− 0·9	39·7	39·0	+ 0·7
1890	35·2	33·0	+ 2·2	41·5	39·1	+ 2·4
1891	34·7	33·1	+ 1·6	40·5	39·1	+ 1·4
1892	34·8	33·3	+ 1·5	39·8	39·5	+ 0·3
1893	29·3	33·6	− 4·3	38·1	40·0	− 1·9
1894	34·8	33·5	+ 1·3	42·3	40·0	+ 2·3
1895	32·1	33·5	− 1·4	38·7	39·9	− 1·2
1896	34·2	33·2	+ 1·0	38·0	39·8	− 1·8
1897	32·9	33·3	− 0·4	38·8	40·3	− 1·5
1898	36·2	33·6	+ 2·6	42·3	40·5	+ 1·8
1899	34·6	33·3	+ 1·3	40·6	40·4	+ 0·2
1900	31·7	33·5	− 1·8	40·0	40·5	− 0·5
1901	31·7	33·6	− 1·9	39·3	41·0	− 1·7
1902	35·8	33·9	+ 1·9	44·5	41·5	+ 3·0
1903	32·4	33·6	− 1·2	40·8	41·5	− 0·7
1904	31·2	33·9	− 2·7	40·8	41·9	− 1·1
1905	34·8	34·1	+ 0·7	40·4	42·2	− 1·8
1906	35·0	34·2	+ 0·8	42·4	42·2	+ 0·2
1907	35·6	33·8	+ 1·8	43·8	41·8	+ 2·0
1908	33·8	34·0	− 0·2	42·2	41·9	+ 0·3
1909	37·7	34·4	+ 3·3	44·5	42·2	+ 2·3
1910	33·2	34·0	− 0·8	42·9	42·4	+ 0·5
1911	32·9	33·7	− 0·8	40·2	42·2	− 2·0
1912	32·1	33·6	− 1·5	40·4	42·2	− 1·8
1913	34·0	33·4	+ 0·6	41·7	42·6	− 0·9
1914	34·5	32·7	+ 1·8	42·6	42·1	+ 0·5
1915	30·8	32·5	− 1·7	42·9	41·7	+ 1·2
1916	32·0	32·3	− 0·3	41·2	41·4	− 0·2
1917	32·0	32·2	− 0·2	43·7	41·1	+ 2·6
1918	33·8	31·9	+ 1·9	44·5	40·8	+ 3·7
1919	30·9	30·7	+ 0·2	39·9	40·6	− 0·7
1920	32·1	30·9	+ 1·2	39·1	40·2	− 1·1
1921	30·4	32·2	− 1·8	37·3	41·2	− 3·9
1922	31·5	32·6	− 1·1	37·5	41·4	− 3·9
1923	31·1	32·8	− 1·7	38·7	41·7	− 3·0
1924	32·9	33·5	− 0·6	41·4	42·6	− 1·2
1925	33·1	33·5	− 0·4	43·3	43·2	+ 0·1
1926	34·5	33·8	+ 0·7	46·7	43·9	+ 2·8
1927	35·7	34·1	+ 1·6	46·1	44·9	+ 1·2
1928	36·2	—	—	47·3	—	—
1929	27·6	—	—	48·5	—	—
1930	32·5	—	—	45·7	—	—
1931	32·7	—	—	43·5	—	—
1932	34·8	—	—	48·2	—	—

Table VII

Yield of Wheat, Barley and Oats for five periods in each County of England and Wales (Bushels per acre)

	Wheat					Barley					Oats				
	1885–1894	1895–1904	1905–1914	1915–1924	1925–1932	1885–1894	1895–1904	1905–1914	1915–1924	1925–1932	1885–1894	1895–1904	1905–1914	1915–1924	1925–1932
Bedfordshire	28·82	29·66	31·19	30·05	31·55	32·10	29·62	30·89	28·27	32·12	39·42	37·53	41·02	37·04	40·92
Berkshire	28·06	28·92	29·95	30·58	29·14	31·19	28·23	29·48	28·50	30·42	41·66	38·52	36·60	38·60	40·70
Buckinghamshire	27·48	28·54	30·96	29·69	30·20	31·87	29·74	31·76	29·41	30·85	38·42	36·20	36·78	37·26	40·36
Cambridgeshire and the Isle of Ely	32·99	31·81	34·18	33·92	32·96	35·47	32·73	36·66	32·86	33·88	58·30	47·25	54·60	47·55	51·38
Cheshire	30·39	31·13	33·42	32·99	33·02	29·89	31·72	30·87	30·62	31·25	35·74	36·00	34·02	34·62	43·60
Cornwall	25·96	30·34	29·88	31·75	33·65	28·37	32·56	32·10	37·03	39·00	37·67	40·65	38·16	42·28	47·35
Cumberland	30·09	32·25	31·10	30·70	31·22	32·36	34·15	35·44	32·13	30·38	38·08	42·97	43·38	40·86	40·59
Derbyshire	29·07	30·21	34·11	31·49	30·27	32·87	32·84	34·41	30·39	31·90	37·47	36·42	36·74	34·42	41·48
Devonshire	21·18	24·40	28·27	28·74	29·88	27·03	28·21	31·36	30·31	32·79	32·85	34·75	37·75	37·87	40·51
Dorset	28·49	30·33	31·74	30·50	29·94	33·81	32·86	33·21	30·08	32·79	40·93	43·68	43·85	40·52	46·51
Durham	26·38	30·70	34·43	35·02	32·78	31·38	36·41	36·69	34·92	34·68	34·16	37·98	37·61	38·86	41·86
Essex	30·71	30·68	32·45	30·96	32·14	34·54	33·69	33·64	30·49	34·16	45·96	45·57	44·25	42·53	48·20
Gloucestershire	27·82	28·28	30·07	27·25	28·74	30·44	28·66	30·28	25·65	28·31	37·32	35·99	36·91	32·97	37·80
Hampshire	26·71	28·28	29·53	28·09	27·34	31·62	31·27	30·98	28·25	29·92	41·33	40·62	40·04	36·65	39·59
Herefordshire	26·72	29·05	31·12	29·55	28·76	28·12	30·34	32·31	27·64	28·78	33·88	35·47	36·32	36·03	40·02
Hertfordshire	28·36	29·83	31·37	29·56	29·10	32·82	31·78	31·90	29·90	33·09	40·69	38·36	37·22	38·51	42·09
Huntingdonshire	29·21	30·11	28·60	30·86	29·13	30·30	29·20	28·85	30·02	28·72	43·98	41·87	36·13	38·64	39·26
Kent	32·12	33·90	35·19	34·05	35·03	37·38	37·83	38·03	33·13	37·86	47·72	46·60	44·52	44·72	51·74
Lancashire	29·93	32·81	36·20	33·43	32·79	33·85	36·14	35·39	31·33	33·90	40·22	42·74	42·48	40·17	47·85
Leicestershire	31·00	29·43	31·59	31·67	30·44	31·79	30·48	32·65	30·91	31·65	34·48	32·62	35·42	36·26	39·95
Lincolnshire	32·46	34·04	34·93	33·95	32·78	34·95	33·75	34·41	31·05	33·56	48·22	48·92	49·32	46·39	49·12
Middlesex	30·02	31·50	35·04	31·85	32·77	34·32	29·86	31·21	26·25	32·18	45·90	38·53	43·95	37·94	48·87

TABLE VII (*contd.*)

	Wheat					Barley					Oats				
	1885–1894	1895–1904	1905–1914	1915–1924	1925–1932	1885–1894	1895–1904	1905–1914	1915–1924	1925–1932	1885–1894	1895–1904	1905–1914	1915–1924	1925–1932
Monmouthshire	24·46	24·29	27·78	29·77	28·81	25·88	25·74	27·63	27·71	28·15	30·69	30·66	31·69	35·32	37·49
Norfolk	31·36	32·57	32·87	31·09	33·59	34·52	33·59	33·00	30·65	35·06	46·51	47·62	47·05	44·00	52·72
Northamptonshire	31·16	31·65	34·09	30·81	30·14	33·38	30·99	35·12	30·27	31·61	38·68	36·37	40·05	38·31	42·53
Northumberland	29·85	33·14	36·26	32·83	33·57	35·34	35·79	35·77	32·03	34·42	36·00	37·72	36·50	35·80	41·62
Nottinghamshire	28·72	27·97	30·67	29·64	28·32	32·53	31·21	32·94	28·46	30·08	38·55	36·22	38·09	34·87	40·12
Oxfordshire	27·98	29·20	31·46	28·88	29·26	32·42	30·82	32·76	27·75	29·47	40·75	38·73	38·94	35·21	41·80
Rutland	30·50	30·60	34·20	31·30	33·25	32·16	29·03	35·04	30·25	33·16	37·39	34·51	41·64	38·60	44·17
Shropshire	29·59	30·09	30·75	30·30	30·01	31·61	31·57	31·60	28·47	31·69	35·38	35·90	34·34	33·32	44·38
Somersetshire	28·14	29·19	31·58	31·32	31·98	33·05	31·91	32·40	30·98	35·06	35·68	35·92	37·61	35·99	43·48
Staffordshire	28·08	29·96	32·45	31·76	31·91	30·53	30·80	31·25	28·99	32·85	33·57	33·42	35·50	34·33	43·99
Suffolk	29·05	29·63	31·75	30·48	32·22	32·81	32·06	32·87	29 87	33·04	40·86	43·32	46·64	41·41	45·67
Surrey	27·44	28·86	30·10	27·97	28·51	30·73	28·95	30·09	27·05	27·54	41·96	39·11	39·99	34·50	39·83
Sussex	30·58	31·92	32·47	30·27	30·59	34·50	32·82	32·54	28·61	30·47	46·25	46·33	42·69	38·10	43·32
Warwickshire	29·08	29·20	30·73	29·00	29·74	31·15	31·54	32·16	30·00	30·02	33·77	34·47	34·86	33·18	40·39
Westmorland	28·41	32·09	33·38	32·46	30·47	31·96	32·10	32·67	32·15	32·29	31·74	32·96	35·03	35·06	41·56
Wiltshire	29·13	31·17	32·23	29·45	29·47	32·80	30·06	32·03	28·53	29·57	44·53	43·97	41·59	37·81	41·29
Worcestershire	28·52	29·26	30·39	28·38	26·83	31·71	31·08	31·25	27·37	25·80	34·59	37·85	37·09	33·54	36·49
Yorkshire, E. Riding	29·88	31·07	31·13	31·89	31·97	33·56	34·14	33·14	31·38	33·17	45·86	43·64	42·12	40·65	44·44
Yorkshire, N. Riding	27·45	31·18	31·89	31·75	31·87	33·59	35·28	34·47	32·95	33·14	39·47	40·66	38·07	41·59	44·29
Yorkshire, W. Riding	27·04	28·34	30·43	31·50	32·74	32·80	33·84	33·97	30·65	33·57	42·21	40·36	39·73	36·33	45·15
Anglesey	26·84	38·11	34·02	29·35	30·15	31·77	40·46	34·11	30·46	35·04	41·02	45·54	44·62	40·93	45·42
Brecknockshire	21·29	25·49	26·42	26·26	29·90	22·55	23·87	23·40	22·49	32·00	25·87	25·31	26·27	25·11	35·76
Cardiganshire	25·81	24·72	27·69	25·57	26·29	29·27	28·61	32·49	28·34	29·52	34·25	31·33	33·05	29·07	34·38
Carmarthenshire	19·16	20·70	23·44	26·17	26·11	23·10	24·93	24·64	28·25	28·54	27·64	25·79	28·48	30·42	32·77
Carnarvonshire	23·24	23·61	29·51	29·05	27·78	29·84	28·40	28·57	26·54	27·67	32·68	31·47	35·41	31·99	34·52
Denbighshire	26·60	28·42	32·88	31·11	31·69	31·32	33·89	34·52	29·61	31·64	33·99	33·93	38·54	32·60	43·58
Flintshire	28·22	29·33	30·39	31·28	29·58	31·18	32·15	30·84	30·27	30·01	35·91	35·30	37·50	34·33	39·22
Glamorganshire	26·52	28·78	30·89	30·09	28·62	31·90	32·01	32·72	30·21	29·76	36·75	39·85	41·05	36·32	37·88
Merionethshire	26·31	26·18	30·51	26·03	25·69	35·19	32·84	30·69	27·57	25·91	44·96	38·65	38·76	33·37	32·67
Montgomeryshire	20·72	21·71	25·01	26·79	28·09	29·36	28·09	27·25	25·54	24·09	26·98	29·42	26·53	26·89	41·77
Pembrokeshire	20·68	27·51	29·03	24·83	26·64	26·50	33·23	36·00	31·34	31·93	31·64	37·27	43·93	39·77	40·96
Radnorshire	21·20	25·41	25·22	23·77	25·84	24·34	28·53	26·14	23·60	27·90	26·11	27·26	26·56	24·73	33·21

Table VIII

Comparative yields of the three principal cereals on old and new arable land in 1918 (*Bushels per acre*)

	Wheat		Oats		Barley	
	New arable	Old arable	New arable	Old arable	New arable	Old arable
Bedfordshire	27·8	30·1	31·0	39·3	20·7	30·8
Berkshire	25·6	31·0	32·0	40·0	20·0	29·5
Buckinghamshire	19·3	31·1	35·7	39·5	20·6	29·3
Cambridgeshire and the Isle of Ely	23·9	32·4	34·2	48·8	—	—
Cheshire	31·3	35·5	38·5	39·0	28·2	31·3
Cornwall	38·5	35·1	48·3	45·4	34·3	37·6
Cumberland	—	—	50·1	44·2	—	—
Derbyshire	36·4	36·0	43·3	37·2	28·7	33·4
Devonshire	29·8	32·4	41·9	41·4	23·9	32·6
Dorset	43·2	36·5	49·7	48·2	21·3	31·8
Durham	34·3	39·1	41·6	42·8	29·8	37·1
Essex	36·9	32·9	39·3	45·3	29·0	32·1
Gloucestershire	27·3	30·7	32·6	36·9	24·2	29·3
Hampshire	30·8	30·7	33·6	37·5	28·3	30·0
Herefordshire	33·6	32·7	40·5	39·3	26·6	30·9
Hertfordshire	31·4	32·3	30·0	43·5	26·2	31·6
Huntingdonshire	23·8	28·3	29·6	36·9	19·9	28·4
Kent	24·3	36·2	31·4	46·0	22·8	33·0
Lancashire	40·0	33·8	40·6	36·6	37·9	29·0
Leicestershire	26·7	35·8	29·3	43·3	25·2	33·7
Lincolnshire	31·1	35·6	43·1	50·5	26·3	33·2
Middlesex	—	—	—	—	—	—
Monmouthshire	37·9	30·2	42·6	38·7	34·0	29·7
Norfolk	28·6	33·0	38·3	48·4	23·9	31·3
Northamptonshire	28·4	32·7	30·1	37·7	28·6	33·2
Northumberland	—	—	—	—	—	—
Nottinghamshire	28·5	32·6	35·9	39·8	34·2	30·8
Oxfordshire	28·3	32·0	30·1	35·7	29·6	30·2
Rutland	31·7	32·7	31·3	36·4	23·6	32·9
Shropshire	31·7	33·1	41·3	40·3	25·3	32·6
Somersetshire	30·9	35·7	40·8	37·7	29·4	36·2
Staffordshire	35·1	36·4	48·5	40·4	32·9	31·4
Suffolk	36·0	32·2	42·6	46·2	23·3	31·7
Surrey	22·5	30·3	27·4	39·6	22·1	29·6
Sussex	18·3	31·2	36·3	40·7	28·2	29·3
Warwickshire	30.5	29·6	48·3	36·0	30·1	34·0
Westmorland	—	—	45·2	37·6	—	—
Wiltshire	35·9	32·5	43·5	41·3	27·1	30·9
Worcestershire	31·2	30·8	44·3	37·2	31·2	29·7
Yorkshire, E. Riding	29·7	33·0	38·2	42·6	39·3	32·7
Yorkshire, N. Riding	39·5	35·2	45·5	45·3	41·5	36·1
Yorkshire, W. Riding	32·2	32·0	38·0	34·8	36·3	33·1
Anglesey	—	—	—	—	—	—
Brecknockshire	29·6	28·2	44·0	29·6	28·3	24·4
Cardiganshire	33·8	28·4	25·6	30·4	29·0	30·3
Carmarthenshire	—	—	—	—	—	—
Carnarvonshire	37·4	27·9	41·8	33·6	37·2	28·3
Denbighshire	34·0	32·7	40·1	35·6	38·0	32·0
Flintshire	35·5	34·8	43·5	39·2	31·0	31·4
Glamorganshire	34·6	32·4	45·2	41·1	32·7	32·2
Merionethshire	40·0	25·9	31·4	42·5	35·8	31·9
Montgomeryshire	30·0	28·8	43·9	29·4	38·0	27·1
Pembrokeshire	25·2	29·1	57·9	50·5	38·3	37·3
Radnorshire	—	—	25·0	25·1	26·0	22·9
England and Wales	31·3	32·9	40·7	41·3	28·8	32·4

TABLE IX

Comparative yields of the three principal cereals on old and new arable land in 1919 (*Bushels per acre*)

	Wheat		Oats		Barley	
	New arable	Old arable	New arable	Old arable	New arable	Old arable
Bedfordshire	25·5	26·7	27·5	37·4	19·0	27·1
Berkshire	26·1	29·2	34·7	38·4	23·6	29·2
Buckinghamshire	21·1	26·9	29·7	33·7	16·7	28·6
Cambridgeshire and the Isle of Ely	29·1	28·5	—	—	—	—
Cheshire	35·1	30·8	42·1	37·4	22·7	31·4
Cornwall	—	—	—	—	—	—
Cumberland	—	—	48·9	41·6	6·0	33·9
Derbyshire	14·7	25·3	25·9	25·5	17·8	25·0
Devonshire	31·2	29·2	32·2	37·7	25·2	31·5
Dorset	32·5	30·3	33·4	36·0	31·4	29·5
Durham	28·8	32·8	32·7	32·5	26·8	34·1
Essex	—	—	—	—	—	—
Gloucestershire	30·1	26·9	26·5	31·7	25·5	25·6
Hampshire	26·5	28·3	29·0	34·2	27·2	26·3
Herefordshire	28·7	28·7	25·5	29·3	38·1	25·1
Hertfordshire	28·2	26·6	35·6	37·6	—	—
Huntingdonshire	—	—	—	—	—	—
Kent	21·4	29·3	24·1	38·4	18·9	27·2
Lancashire	—	—	—	—	—	—
Leicestershire	—	—	—	—	—	—
Lincolnshire	31·3	30·5	40·4	38·9	27·9	28·6
Middlesex	—	—	—	—	—	—
Monmouthshire	32·4	30·1	31·9	32·4	25·1	25·3
Norfolk	28·8	28·6	44·1	42·6	24·6	29·9
Northamptonshire	—	—	—	—	—	—
Northumberland	15·6	30·8	31·6	35·1	23·3	35·7
Nottinghamshire	32·0	26·1	26·2	28·8	22·3	25·3
Oxfordshire	—	—	—	—	—	—
Rutland	22·9	31·7	29·0	40·1	22·1	31·9
Shropshire	37·9	30·1	41·0	25·7	35·9	26·3
Somersetshire	31·7	31·7	33·9	37·3	30·5	29·9
Staffordshire	32·0	29·3	40·5	26·6	27·8	27·3
Suffolk	27·2	26·3	40·1	35·9	30·7	27·4
Surrey	27·0	26·7	34·1	30·4	21·2	24·4
Sussex	27·5	31·0	42·0	36·6	38·2	28·0
Warwickshire	29·4	28·6	27·3	23·2	21·1	27·0
Westmorland	—	—	32·2	33·4	36·0	32·2
Wiltshire	28·6	28·0	26·4	36·4	16·2	26·0
Worcestershire	27·6	27·0	29·7	26·4	20·0	25·3
Yorkshire, E. Riding	30·6	31·7	39·1	36·5	33·1	30·2
Yorkshire, N. Riding	25·4	30·1	43·1	37·4	33·1	32·2
Yorkshire, W. Riding	—	—	—	—	—	—
Anglesey	—	—	—	—	—	—
Brecknockshire	27·0	26·4	32·0	25·6	31·9	22·9
Cardiganshire	—	—	—	—	—	—
Carmarthenshire	25·1	29·8	27·6	35·1	32·0	32·6
Carnarvonshire	33·6	30·0	42·2	34·4	32·8	28·8
Denbighshire	36·5	28·5	41·8	33·9	31·9	29·0
Flintshire	31·6	30·8	34·5	34·8	38·5	31·3
Glamorganshire	32·5	30·4	32·5	30·4	31·1	33·5
Merionethshire	13·2	23·0	21·5	30·3	24·3	25·2
Montgomeryshire	16·3	26·4	40·2	25·4	—	—
Pembrokeshire	37·3	26·6	53·9	44·6	—	—
Radnorshire	47·6	23·2	22·2	21·6	21·0	23·8
England and Wales	28·4	28·7	36·6	35·6	28·0	29·0

Area and Production of certain Crops on Large and Small Holdings in Roumania (Old Kingdom)

(From official Roumanian publications)

Year	Large holdings			Small holdings		
	Area hectares	Yield hectolitres	Hecto-litres per hectare	Area hectares	Yield hectolitres	Hecto-litres per hectare
	WHEAT					
1907	924,419	8,464,001	9·2	789,898	6,420,306	8·1
1908	965,554	10,488,724	10·9	836,131	8,827,394	10·5
1909	907,338	11,752,595	12·9	781,706	8,246,284	10·5
1910	1,044,101	22,515,763	21·6	904,116	16,516,030	18·2
1911	983,827	17,340,919	17·7	946,337	15,687,176	16·6
1912	1,043,451	16,832,584	16·1	1,025,969	14,504,238	14·1
1913	758,582	14,573,290	19·2	864,523	14,758,893	17·0
1914	927,592	8,578,695	9·2	1,184,138	8,783,918	7·4
1915	852,022	15,732,206	18·4	1,052,227	15,716,086	14·9
1916	—	—	—	—	—	—
1917	—	—	—	—	—	—
1918*	672,189	2,681,522	3·99	943,858	3,838,771	4·06
1919	340,863	—	—	858,895	—	—
1920	91,550	—	—	746,986	—	—
	OATS					
1907	129,841	2,728,308	21·0	222,627	3,559,031	15·9
1908	186,197	2,579,369	13·8	304,141	3,486,058	11·4
1909	171,310	3,828,389	22·3	313,194	5,314,648	16·9
1910	150,254	3,860,545	25·7	296,506	6,587,078	22·2
1911	132,583	3,517,893	26·5	268,832	5,722,736	21·3
1912	116,483	2,704,217	23·2	265,302	4,616,813	17·4
1913	192,577	5,236,472	27·1	329,572	7,145,988	21·6
1914	131,063	3,056,344	23·3	296,443	5,758,731	19·4
1915	146,905	3,950,079	26·9	284,058	6,288,469	22·1
1916	—	—	—	—	—	—
1917	—	—	—	—	—	—
1918*	141,017	765,498	5·4	189,197	966,639	5·1
1919	39,766	—	—	201,945	—	—
1920	73,954	—	—	385,971	—	—
	BARLEY					
1907	126,626	2,098,895	16·6	383,067	4,970,963	12·9
1908	168,965	1,713,261	10·1	451,225	2,823,138	6·2
1909	152,889	2,249,931	14·7	396,297	4,782,257	12·0
1910	140,717	2,991,646	21·3	408,674	7,354,286	17·9
1911	121,928	2,404,794	19·7	385,273	6,812,933	17·7
1912	115,158	2,072,278	18·0	384,727	5,431,863	14·1
1913	146,276	2,868,273	19·7	416,263	6,765,934	16·2
1914	123,120	2,139,457	17·3	445,302	6,848,416	15·4
1915	122,121	2,390,998	19·6	432,779	7,718,754	17·8
1916	—	—	—	—	—	—
1917	—	—	—	—	—	—
1918*	81,136	313,747	3·8	165,915	465,459	2·8
1919	30,168	—	—	207,490	—	—
1920	49,388	—	—	402,387	—	—

* Excluding the Dobrudja.

Year	MAIZE					
	Large holdings			Small holdings		
	Area hectares	Yield hectolitres	Hecto-litres per hectare	Area hectares	Yield hectolitres	Hecto-litres per hectare
1907	367,839	4,865,411	13·2	1,560,753	15,424,105	9·9
1908	300,199	4,610,535	15·3	1,720,116	23,190,685	13·4
1909	308,586	4,355,353	14·1	1,814,887	20,361,128	11·2
1910	266,845	6,027,817	22·5	1,719,414	30,503,609	17·7
1911	292,135	6,562,379	22·4	1,793,116	32,452,435	18·1
1912	226,716	5,671,372	25·0	1,812,504	30,950,013	17·1
1913	264,341	5,656,065	21·4	1,882,630	34,750,803	18·4
1914	235,732	4,901,840	20·8	1,829,834	31,237,206	17·0
1915	222,188	3,731,784	16·8	1,885,101	26,719,736	14·2
1916	—	—	—	—	—	—
1917	—	—	—	—	—	—
1918*	237,981	998,481	4·2	1,479,840	7,492,088	5·0
1919	83,795	—	—	1,883,667	—	—
1920	85,704	—	—	1,869,170	—	—
	SUGAR-BEET					
	Hectares	Quintals	Quintals per hectare	Hectares	Quintals	Quintals per hectare
1907	3,875	723,287	186·6	2,764	368,274	133·2
1908	5,741	1,160,695	202·2	3,277	507,735	154·9
1909	7,402	1,398,348	188·9	4,004	680,854	169·9
1910	7,808	1,954,380	250·3	5,510	1,126,979	204·5
1911	7,614	1,661,862	218·2	5,989	968,656	161·7
1912	8,483	1,670,772	196·9	5,880	1,251,617	212·8
1913	7,764	1,726,172	222·3	5,250	1,097,474	209·0
1914	7,329	1,265,725	172·7	7,456	983,900	131·9
1915	7,708	1,043,606	135·4	6,125	810,843	132·4
1916	—	—	—	—	—	—
1917	—	—	—	—	—	—
1918*	4,057	278,116	68·5	2,080	178,810	85·9
1919	277	—	—	1,689	—	—
1920	260	—	—	2,976	—	—
	POTATOES					
1907	2,447	268,240	109·6	7,339	549,066	74·8
1908	2,406	304,073	126·4	7,482	500,963	66·9
1909	1,559	192,465	123·4	7,091	474,756	66·9
1910	2,807	348,441	124·1	7,485	698,491	93·3
1911	3,310	361,893	109·3	8,721	792,050	90·8
1912	3,244	308,537	95·1	8,753	711,483	81·3
1913	2,353	186,401	79·2	7,792	500,247	64·2
1914	2,441	174,911	71·6	8,115	547,331	67·4
1915	2,437	266,995	109·5	8,851	757,713	85·6
1916	—	—	—	—	—	—
1917	—	—	—	—	—	—
1918*	2,724	68,270	25·0	11,234	385,864	34·3
1919	1,250	—	—	11,929	—	—
1920	1,100	—	—	13,026	—	—

* Excluding the Dobrudja.

Table XI

Average size of Holdings in English and Welsh Counties, 1931

	Acres		Acres
Bedfordshire	60·1	Oxfordshire	106·7
Berkshire	101·5	Rutland	123·0
Buckinghamshire	77·4	Shropshire	64·6
Cambridgeshire	60·3	Somersetshire	60·5
Isle of Ely	47·8	Staffordshire	55·5
Cheshire	47·0	Suffolk, East	82·9
Cornwall	46·1	Suffolk, West	100·8
Cumberland	70·3	Surrey	56·3
Derbyshire	47·8	Sussex, East	58·6
Devonshire	65·9	Sussex, West	79·8
Dorset...	86·2	Warwickshire	73·3
Durham	66·1	Westmorland	76·4
Essex	85·9	Wiltshire	96·8
Gloucestershire	70·2	Worcestershire	47·1
Hampshire (and Isle of Wight)	69·2	Yorkshire (East Riding)	100·9
Herefordshire...	66·9	Yorkshire (North Riding)	75·0
Hertfordshire...	96·8	Yorkshire (West Riding)	50·0
Huntingdonshire	88·3	Anglesey	32·2
Kent	60·9	Brecknockshire	70·0
Lancashire	41·4	Cardiganshire	41·1
Leicestershire...	75·0	Carmarthenshire ...	48·6
Lincolnshire (Holland) ...	44·0	Carnarvonshire	26·8
Lincolnshire (Kesteven) ...	105·5	Denbighshire	44·4
Lincolnshire (Lindsey) ...	78·5	Flintshire	37·0
Middlesex and London ...	47·9	Glamorganshire	48·1
Norfolk	75·4	Merionethshire	47·1
Northamptonshire	113·2	Monmouthshire	51·1
Soke of Peterborough ...	84·0	Montgomeryshire ...	49·9
Northumberland	124·5	Pembrokeshire	49·8
Nottinghamshire	70·3	Radnorshire	73·9
		England and Wales ...	64·5

Table XII

Varieties of Wheat grown in certain Counties in the East of England in 1925

County	Number of variety returns received	Acreage of each variety					Total acreage of wheat in County
		Little Joss	Yeoman (including Yeoman II)	Squarehead Master	Other varieties	Total acreage covered by variety returns	
		(Acres)	(Acres)	(Acres)	(Acres)	(Acres)	(Acres)
Bedfordshire	315	839	5,372	2,639	8,256	17,106	31,790
Huntingdonshire	325	1,854	5,158	2,206	10,061	19,279	34,862
Cambridgeshire	453	6,860	4,934	9,025	7,377	28,196	48,409
Isle of Ely	359	6,994	9,262	1,695	5,392	23,343	46,886
Suffolk, East	538	4,252	6,117	5,436	7,281	23,086	53,950
Suffolk, West	513	6,182	8,981	5,065	7,137	27,365	43,742
Essex	966	5,595	21,686	5,772	17,769	50,822	96,435
Hertfordshire	506	4,980	7,471	5,593	12,177	30,221	46,040
Norfolk	1,053	6,801	7,698	15,234	21,031	50,764	102,744
Lincolnshire (Holland)	247	787	11,745	288	6,575	19,395	88,634
Lincolnshire (Kesteven)	566	6,769	7,371	3,224	12,632	29,996	52,867
Rutland	44	291	570	217	742	1,820	4,437
Northamptonshire	354	923	5,418	3,347	5,926	15,609	35,140
Soke of Peterborough	57	449	814	453	981	2,697	6,342
Total ...	6,296	53,576	102,592	60,194	123,337	339,699	642,278

Table XIII

Acreage under Wheat in the Principal Countries of the World from 1909–13 *to* 1930

(Derived from *Wheat Studies* of the Food Research Institute, Stanford University, California.)

	1909–13	1920	1922	1924	1926	1928	1930
	Million acres						
British Isles	1·89	1·98	2·07	1·63	1·68	1·49	1·43
Australia	7·60	9·07	9·76	10·82	11·69	14·84	18·15
Canada	9·94	18·23	22·42	22·06	22·90	24·12	24·90
Egypt	1·31	1·19	1·52	1·42	1·53	1·59	1·58
India	29·22	29·95	28·21	31·18	30·47	32·19	31·65
New Zealand	0·24	0·22	0·27	0·16	0·22	0·25	0·24
Union of S. Africa	0·74*	0·87	0·84	0·75	0·88	0·82	1·13
Algeria	3·52	3·45	3·74	3·53	3·74	3·66	3·98
Argentina	14·88	13·22	16·06	15·98	18·95	20·08	18·94
Belgium	0·40	0·30	0·30	0·34	0·35	0·40	0·41
Bulgaria	2·41	2·17	2·30	2·49	2·62	2·81	3·00
Chile	1·00	1·26	1·47	1·43	1·48	1·72	1·61
Czecho-Slovakia	1·72	1·57	1·53	1·51	1·80	1·92	1·98
Denmark	0·15	0·18	0·23	0·14	0·25	0·25	0·24
France	16·50	12·59	13·07	13·62	12·97	12·80	12·99
Germany	4·03	3·40	3·40	3·62	3·96	4·27	4·40
Hungary	3·71	2·66	3·52	3·50	3·71	4·14	4·19
Italy	11·79	11·38	11·40	11·28	12·14	12·26	11·90
Japan	1·75	2·18	2·12	2·03	2·04	2·10	2·05
Jugo-Slavia	3·98	3·56	3·67	4·24	4·18	4·68	5·36
Mexico	2·17†	—	2·62	1·40	1·29	1·28	1·22
Morocco	1·70	1·99	2·07	2·46	2·56	2·66	2·96
Netherlands	0·14	0·15	0·15	0·11	0·13	0·14	0·14
Poland	3·35	1·79	3·02	3·16	3·25	3·19	4·07
Portugal	1·21‡	1·10	1·16	1·04	1·06	1·12	1·10
Roumania	9·52*	5·00	6·55	7·84	8·22	7·92	7·55
Soviet Russia	74·01	—	—	52·73	73·90	71·96	83·80
Spain	9·55	10·25	10·31	10·38	10·78	10·48	11·13
Switzerland	0·10	0·11	0·11	0·11	0·13	0·13	0·12
Tunis	1·31	1·32	1·07	1·32	1·84	2·02	1·92
U.S. America	47·10	61·14	62·32	52·54	56·36	58·27	61·14
Uruguay	0·79*	0·70	0·66	0·85	1·00	1·26	0·86

* 4-year average. † 2-year average. ‡ 3-year average.

Table XIV

Production of Wheat in the Principal Countries of the World from 1909–13 *to* 1930

(Derived from *Wheat Studies* of the Food Research Institute, Stanford University, California.)

	1909–13	1920	1922	1924	1926	1928	1930	Average yield in bushels per acre 1920–30
	Million bushels							
British Isles	59·6	58·0	66·5	53·9	52·2	51·0	43·3	32·2
Australia	90·5	145·9	109·5	164·6	160·8	159·7	212·6	12·2
Canada	197·1	263·2	399·8	262·1	407·1	566·7	397·9	17·1
Egypt	33·7	31·7	36·0	34·2	37·2	37·3	41·0	25·6
India	351·8	377·9	367·0	360·6	324·7	290·9	390·8	11·1
New Zealand	6·9	6·9	8·4	5·4	8·0	8·8	6·5	31·2
Union of S. Africa	6·3*	7·6	6·3	7·1	8·3	7·2	10·2	8·9
Algeria	35·2	16·2	18·9	17·3	23·6	30·3	32·2	7·7
Argentina	147·1	156·1	195·8	191·1	230·1	349·1	236·0	13·0
Belgium	15·2	10·3	10·6	13·0	12·8	17·2	13·2	37·9
Bulgaria	37·8	29·9	32·6	24·7	36·5	49·2	57·3	14·4
Chile	20·1	28·2	25·9	24·5	23·3	29·7	21·2	17·4
Czecho-Slovakia	37·9	26·4	33·6	32·2	39·9	52·9	50·6	23·8
Denmark	6·3	7·4	9·2	5·9	8·8	12·2	10·2	42·4
France	325·6	236·9	243·3	281·2	231·8	281·3	231·1	21·1
Germany	131·3	82·6	71·9	89·2	95·4	141·6	139·2	28·0
Hungary	71·5	37·9	54·7	51·6	74·9	99·2	84·3	18·8
Italy	184·4	142·3	161·6	170·1	220·6	228·6	210·1	17·3
Japan	32·0	39·4	38·1	35·7	38·7	39·4	38·5	18·3
Jugo-Slavia	62·0	43·0	44·5	57·8	71·4	103·3	80·3	15·5
Mexico	11·5*	15·0	13·6	10·4	10·3	11·0	11·4	7·1†
Morocco	17·0	17·9	12·9	28·8	25·0	28·1	21·3	9·7
Netherlands	5·0	6·0	6·2	4·6	5·5	7·3	6·1	43·1
Poland	63·7	22·7	46·8	37·5	52·5	59·2	82·3	17·0
Portugal	11·8*	10·4	10·0	10·6	8·6	7·5	18·5	9·9
Roumania	158·7*	61·3	92·0	70·4	110·9	115·5	130·8	13·5
Soviet Russia	756·9§	—	—	472·2	913·8	795·2	1084·0	10·9‡
Spain	130·4	138·6	125·5	121·8	146·6	122·6	146·7	13·5
Switzerland	3·3	3·6	2·5	3·3	4·2	4·5	3·8	31·2
Tunis	6·2	5·2	3·7	5·1	13·0	12·1	10·4	5·7
U.S. America	690·1	833·0	867·6	864·4	831·4	914·9	858·2	14·2
Uruguay	6·5*	7·8	5·2	9·9	10·2	12·3	8·0	11·0

* 4-year average. † Average 1921–30. ‡ Average 1923–30.
§ Regarded as too low by some Soviet officials, whose estimate is 908 million bushels.

Table XV

Bankruptcies and deeds of arrangement among Farmers in England and Wales, 1893–1932

(From the *General Annual Report* of the Board of Trade.)

Year	No.	Year	No.	Year	No.	Year	No.
1893	523	1903	307	1913	326	1923	472
1894	518	1904	368	1914	189	1924	360
1895	564	1905	389	1915	132	1925	368
1896	466	1906	318	1916	78	1926	342
1897	407	1907	279	1917	65	1927	468
1898	308	1908	298	1918	30	1928	462
1899	237	1909	310	1919	33	1929	345
1900	282	1910	245	1920	44	1930	350
1901	302	1911	305	1921	285	1931	497
1902	318	1912	336	1922	403	1932	615

INDEX

CAMBRIDGE: PRINTED BY WALTER LEWIS, M.A., AT THE UNIVERSITY PRESS

Printed in the United States
By Bookmasters